Big Data

Big Data
Principles and Paradigms

Edited by

Rajkumar Buyya
The University of Melbourne and Manjrasoft Pty Ltd, Australia

Rodrigo N. Calheiros
The University of Melbourne, Australia

Amir Vahid Dastjerdi
The University of Melbourne, Australia

AMSTERDAM • BOSTON • HEIDELBERG • LONDON
NEW YORK • OXFORD • PARIS • SAN DIEGO
SAN FRANCISCO • SINGAPORE • SYDNEY • TOKYO

Morgan Kaufmann is an imprint of Elsevier

Morgan Kaufmann is an imprint of Elsevier
50 Hampshire Street, 5th Floor, Cambridge, MA 02139, USA

Library of Congress Cataloging-in-Publication Data
A catalog record for this book is available from the Library of Congress

British Library Cataloguing-in-Publication Data
A catalogue record for this book is available from the British Library

ISBN: 978-0-12-805394-2

For information on all Morgan Kaufmann publications
visit our website at https://www.elsevier.com/

www.elsevier.com • www.bookaid.org

Publisher: Todd Green
Acquisition Editor: Brian Romer
Editorial Project Manager: Amy Invernizzi
Production Project Manager: Punithavathy Govindaradjane
Designer: Victoria Pearson

Typeset by SPi Global, India

Contents

List of contributors

T. Achalakul
King Mongkut's University of Technology Thonburi, Bangkok, Thailand

P. Ameri
Karlsruhe Institute of Technology (KIT), Karlsruhe, Baden-Württemberg, Germany

A. Berry
Deontik, Brisbane, QLD, Australia

N. Bojja
Machine Zone, Palo Alto, CA, USA

R. Buyya
The University of Melbourne, Parkville, VIC, Australia; Manjrasoft Pty Ltd, Melbourne, VIC, Australia

W. Chen
University of News South Wales, Sydney, NSW, Australia

C. Deerosejanadej
King Mongkut's University of Technology Thonburi, Bangkok, Thailand

A. Diaz-Perez
Cinvestav-Tamaulipas, Tamps., Mexico

H. Ding
Xi'an Jiaotong University, Shaanxi, China

X. Dong
Huazhong University of Science and Technology, Wuhan, Hubei, China

H. Duan
The University of Melbourne, Parkville, VIC, Australia

S. Dutta
Max Planck Institute for Informatics, Saarbruecken, Saarland, Germany

A. Garcia-Robledo
Cinvestav-Tamaulipas, Tamps., Mexico

V. Gramoli
University of Sydney, Sydney, NSW, Australia

X. Gu
Huazhong University of Science and Technology, Wuhan, Hubei, China

J. Han
Xi'an Jiaotong University, Shaanxi, China

B. He
Nanyang Technological University, Singapore, Singapore

S. Ibrahim
Inria Rennes – Bretagne Atlantique, Rennes, France

Z. Jiang
Xi'an Jiaotong University, Shaanxi, China

S. Kannan
Machine Zone, Palo Alto, CA, USA

S. Karuppusamy
Machine Zone, Palo Alto, CA, USA

A. Kejariwal
Machine Zone, Palo Alto, CA, USA

B.-S. Lee
Nanyang Technological University, Singapore, Singapore

Y.C. Lee
Macquarie University, Sydney, NSW, Australia

X. Li
Tsinghua University, Beijing, China

R. Li
Huazhong University of Science and Technology, Wuhan, Hubei, China

K. Li
State University of New York–New Paltz, New Paltz, NY, USA

H. Liu
Huazhong University of Science and Technology, Wuhan, China

P. Lu
University of Sydney, Sydney, NSW, Australia

K.-T. Lu
Washington State University, Vancouver, WA, United States

Z. Milosevic
Deontik, Brisbane, QLD, Australia

G. Morales-Luna
Cinvestav-IPN, Mexico City, Mexico

A. Narang
Data Science Mobileum Inc., Gurgaon, HR, India

A. Nedunchezhian
Machine Zone, Palo Alto, CA, USA

D. Nguyen
Washington State University, Vancouver, WA, United States

L. Ou
Hunan University, Changsha, China

S. Prom-on
King Mongkut's University of Technology Thonburi, Bangkok, Thailand

Z. Qin
Hunan University, Changsha, China

F.A. Rabhi
University of News South Wales, Sydney, NSW, Australia

K. Ramamohanarao
The University of Melbourne, Parkville, VIC, Australia

T. Ryan
University of Sydney, Sydney, NSW, Australia

R.O. Sinnott
The University of Melbourne, Parkville, VIC, Australia

S. Sun
The University of Melbourne, Parkville, VIC, Australia

Y. Sun
The University of Melbourne, Parkville, VIC, Australia

S. Tang
Tianjin University, Tianjin, China

P. Venkateshan
Machine Zone, Palo Alto, CA, USA

S. Wallace
Washington State University, Vancouver, WA, United States

P. Wang
Machine Zone, Palo Alto, CA, USA

C. Wu
The University of Melbourne, Parkville, VIC, Australia

W. Xi
Xi'an Jiaotong University, Shaanxi, China

Z. Xue
Huazhong University of Science and Technology, Wuhan, Hubei, China

H. Yin
Hunan University, Changsha, China

G. Zhang
Tsinghua University, Beijing, China

M. Zhanikeev
Tokyo University of Science, Chiyoda-ku, Tokyo, Japan

X. Zhao
Washington State University, Vancouver, WA, United States

W. Zheng
Tsinghua University, Beijing, China

A.C. Zhou
Nanyang Technological University, Singapore, Singapore

A.Y. Zomaya
University of Sydney, Sydney, NSW, Australia

About the Editors

Dr. Rajkumar Buyya is a Fellow of IEEE, a professor of Computer Science and Software Engineering, a Future Fellow of the Australian Research Council, and director of the Cloud Computing and Distributed Systems (CLOUDS) Laboratory at the University of Melbourne, Australia. He is also serving as the founding CEO of Manjrasoft, a spin-off company of the University, commercializing its innovations in cloud computing. He has authored over 500 publications and four textbooks, including *Mastering Cloud Computing*, published by McGraw Hill, China Machine Press, and Morgan Kaufmann for Indian, Chinese and international markets respectively. He also edited several books including *Cloud Computing: Principles and Paradigms* (Wiley Press, USA, Feb. 2011). He is one of the most highly cited authors in computer science and software engineering worldwide (h-index=98, g-index=202, 44800+ citations). The Microsoft Academic Search Index ranked Dr. Buyya as the world's top author in distributed and parallel computing between 2007 and 2015. *A Scientometric Analysis of Cloud Computing Literature* by German scientists ranked Dr. Buyya as the World's Top-Cited (#1) Author and the World's Most-Productive (#1) Author in Cloud Computing.

Software technologies for grid and cloud computing developed under Dr. Buyya's leadership have gained rapid acceptance and are in use at several academic institutions and commercial enterprises in 40 countries around the world. Dr. Buyya has led the establishment and development of key community activities, including serving as foundation chair of the IEEE Technical Committee on Scalable Computing and five IEEE/ACM conferences. These contributions and international research leadership of Dr. Buyya are recognized through the award of 2009 IEEE TCSC Medal for Excellence in Scalable Computing from the IEEE Computer Society TCSC. Manjrasoft's Aneka Cloud technology that was developed under his leadership has received 2010 Frost & Sullivan New Product Innovation Award. Recently, Manjrasoft has been recognized as one of the Top 20 Cloud Computing Companies by the *Silicon Review Magazine*. He served as the foundation editor-in-chief of "IEEE Transactions on Cloud Computing". He is currently serving as co-editor-in-chief of *Journal of Software: Practice and Experience*, which was established 40+ years ago. For further information on Dr. Buyya, please visit his cyberhome: www.buyya.com.

Dr. Rodrigo N. Calheiros is a research fellow in the Department of Computing and Information Systems at The University of Melbourne, Australia. He has made major contributions to the fields of Big Data and cloud computing since 2009. He designed and developed CloudSim, an open source tool for the simulation of cloud platforms used at research centers, universities, and companies worldwide.

Dr. Amir Vahid Dastjerdi is a research fellow with the Cloud Computing and Distributed Systems (CLOUDS) laboratory at the University of Melbourne. He received his PhD in computer science from the University of Melbourne and his areas of interest include Internet of Things, Big Data, and cloud computing.

Preface

Rapid advances in digital sensors, networks, storage, and computation, along with their availability at low cost, are leading to the creation of huge collections of data. Initially, the drive for generation and storage of data came from scientists; telescopes and instruments such as the Large Hadron Collider (LHC) generate a huge amount of data that needed to be processed to enable scientific discovery. LHC, for example, was reported as generating as much as 1 TB of data every second. Later, with the popularity of the SMAC (social, mobile, analytics, and cloud) paradigm, enormous amount of data started to be generated, processed, and stored by enterprises. For instance, Facebook in 2012 reported that the company processed over 200 TB of data per hour. In fact, SINTEF (The Foundation for Scientific and Industrial Research) from Norway reports that 90% of the world's data generated has been generated in the last 2 years. These were the key motivators towards the Big Data paradigm.

Unlike traditional data warehouses that rely in highly structured data, this new paradigm unleashes the potential of analyzing any source of data, whether structured and stored in relational databases; semi-structured and emerging from sensors, machines, and applications; or unstructured obtained from social media and other human sources.

This data has the potential to enable new insights that can change the way business, science, and governments deliver services to their consumers and can impact society as a whole. Nevertheless, for this potential to be realized, new algorithms, methods, infrastructures, and platforms are required that can make sense of all this data and provide the insights while they are still of interest for analysts of diverse domains.

This has led to the emergence of the Big Data computing paradigm focusing on the sensing, collection, storage, management and analysis of data from variety of sources to enable new value and insights. This paradigm enhanced considerably the capacity of organizations to understand their activities and improve aspects of its business in ways never imagined before; however, at the same time, it raises new concerns of security and privacy whose implications are still not completely understood by society.

To realize the full potential of Big Data, researchers and practitioners need to address several challenges and develop suitable conceptual and technological solutions for tackling them. These include life-cycle management of data; large-scale storage; flexible processing infrastructure; data modeling; scalable machine learning and data analysis algorithms; techniques for sampling and making trade-off between data processing time and accuracy and dealing with privacy and ethical issues involved in data sensing, storage, processing, and actions.

This book addresses the above issues by presenting a broad view of each of the issues, identifying challenges faced by researchers and opportunities for practitioners embracing the Big Data paradigm.

ORGANIZATION OF THE BOOK

This book contains 18 chapters authored by several leading experts in the field of Big Data. The book is presented in a coordinated and integrated manner starting with Big Data analytics methods, going through the infrastructures and platforms supporting them, aspects of security and privacy, and finally, applications.

The content of the book is organized into four parts:

I.   Big Data Science
II.   Big Data Infrastructures and Platforms
III. Big Data Security and Privacy
IV.   Big Data Applications

PART I: BIG DATA SCIENCE

Data Science is a discipline that emerged in the last few years, as did the Big Data concept. Although there are different interpretations of what Data Science is, we adopt the view that Data Science is a discipline that merges concepts from computer science (algorithms, programming, machine learning, and data mining), mathematics (statistics and optimization), and domain knowledge (business, applications, and visualization) to extract insights from data and transform it into actions that have an impact in the particular domain of application. Data Science is already challenging when the amount of data enables traditional analysis, which thus becomes particularly challenging when traditional methods lose their effectiveness due to large volume and velocity in the data.

Part I presents fundamental concepts and algorithms in the Data Science domain that address the issues rose by Big Data. As a motivation for this part and in the same direction as what we discussed so far, Chapter 1 discusses how what is now known as Big Data is the result of efforts in two distinct areas, namely machine learning and cloud computing.

The velocity aspect of Big Data demands analytic algorithms that can operate data in motion, ie, algorithms that do not assume that all the data is available all the time for decision making, and decisions need to be made "on the go," probably with summaries of past data. In this direction, Chapter 2 discusses real-time processing systems for Big Data, including stream processing platforms that enable analysis of data in motion and a case study in finance.

The volume aspect of data demands that existing algorithms for different analytics data are adapted to take advantage of distributed systems where memory is not shared, and thus different machines have only part of data to operate. Chapter 3 discusses how it affects natural language processing, text mining, and anomaly detection in the context of social media.

A concept that emerged recently benefiting from Big Data is deep learning. The approach, derived from artificial neural networks, constructs layered structures that hold different abstractions of the same data and has application in language processing and image analysis, among others. Chapter 4 discusses algorithms that can leverage modern GPUs to speed up computation of Deep Learning models.

Another concept popularized in the last years is graph processing, a programming model where an abstraction of a graph (network) of nodes and vertices represents the computation to be carried out. Likewise the previous chapter, Chapter 5 discusses GPU-based algorithms for graph processing.

PART II: BIG DATA INFRASTRUCTURES AND PLATFORMS

Although part of the Big Data revolution is enabled by new algorithms and methods to handle large amounts of heterogeneous data in movement and at rest, all of this would be of no value if computing platforms and infrastructures did not evolve to better support Big Data. New platforms providing different abstractions for programmers arose that enable problems to be represented in different ways. Thus, instead of adapting the problem to fit a programming model, developers are now able to select the abstraction that is closer to the problem at hand, enabling faster more correct software solutions to be developed. The same revolution observed in the computing part of the analytics is also observed in the storage part; in the last years, new methods were developed and adopted to persist data that are more flexible than traditional relational databases.

Part II of this book is dedicated to such infrastructure and platforms supporting Big Data. Starting with database support, Chapter 6 discusses the different models of NOSQL database models and systems that are available for storage of large amounts of structured, semi-structured and structured data, including key-value, column-based, graph-based, and document-based stores.

As the infrastructures of choice for running Big Data analytics are shared (think of clusters and clouds), new methods were necessary to rationalize the use of resources so that all applications get their fair share of resources and can progress to a result in a reasonable amount of time. In this direction, Chapter 7 discusses the general problem of resource management techniques for Big Data frameworks and a new efficient technique for resource management implemented in Apache YARN. Chapter 8 presents a novel technique for increasing resource usage and performance of Big Data platforms by applying a "resource-shaping" technique, whereas Chapter 9 contains a survey on various techniques for optimization of many aspects of the Hadoop framework, including the job scheduler, HDFS, and Hbase.

Whereas the previous three chapters focused on distributed platforms for Big Data analytics, parallel platforms, which rely on many computing cores sharing memory, are also viable platforms for Big Data analytics. In this direction, Chapter 10 discusses an alternative solution that is optimized to take advantage of the large amount of memory and large number of cores available in current servers.

PART III: BIG DATA SECURITY AND PRIVACY

For economic reasons, physical infrastructures supporting Big Data are shared. This helps in rationalizing the huge costs involved in building such large-scale cloud infrastructures. Thus, whether the infrastructure is a public cloud or a private cloud, multitenancy is a certainty that raises security and privacy concerns. Moreover, the sources of data can reveal many things about its source; although many times sources will be applications and the data generated is in public domain, it is also possible that data generated by devices and actions of humans (eg, via posts in social networks) can be analyzed in a way that individuals can be identified and/or localized, an issue that also raises privacy issues. Part III of this book is dedicated to such security and privacy issues of Big Data.

Chapter 11 addresses the issue of spatial privacy of users of social networks and the threats to it enabled by Big Data analytics. Chapter 12 addresses the issue of the use of shared resources for Big Data computing and ways to protect queries and prevent loss of privacy on correlated data.

Chapter 13 is dedicated to methods to perform consumer analytics when shopping. It introduces methods to infer the location of mobile devices and to estimate human behavior in shopping activities.

PART IV: BIG DATA APPLICATIONS

All the advances in methods and platforms would be of no value if the capabilities offered them did not generate value (whatever definition of value we take into consideration). Thankfully, this is not the case, and a range of applications in the most diverse areas were developed to fulfill the goal of delivering value via Big Data analytics. These days, financial institutions, governments, educational institutions, and researchers, to name a few, are applying Big Data analytics on a daily basis as part of their business as usual tasks. Part IV of this book is dedicated to such applications, featuring interesting use cases of the application of Big Data analytics.

Social media arose in the last 10 years, initially as a means to connect people. Now, it has emerged as a platform for businesses purposes, advertisements, delivery of news of public interest, and for people to express their opinions and emotions. Chapter 14 introduces an application in this context, namely a Big Data framework for mining opinion from social media in Thailand. In the same direction, Chapter 15 presents an interesting case study of application of Big Data Analytics to mine social media to evaluate the effect of the weather in people's emotions.

The entertainment industry can also benefit from Big Data, as demonstrated in Chapter 16, with an application of Big Data analytics for optimization of delivery of video on demand via the Internet.

Big Data analytics is also disrupting core traditional sectors. As an example, Chapter 17 presents a case study on application of Big Data Analytics in the energy sector; the chapter shows how data generated by smart distribution lines (smart grids) can be analyzed to enable identification of faults in the transmission line.

e-Science is one of the first applications driving the Big Data paradigm in which scientific discovery are enabled by large-scale computing infrastructures. As clusters and grids became popular among research institutions, it became clear that new discoveries could be made if these infrastructures were put to work to crunch massive volumes of data collected from many scientific instruments. Acknowledging the importance of e-Science as a motivator for a substantial amount of innovation in the field leading to the establishment of Big Data, Chapter 18 concludes with various e-Science applications and key elements of their deployment in a cloud environment.

Acknowledgments

We thank all the contributing authors for their time, effort, and dedication during the preparation of this book.

Raj would like to thank his family members, especially his wife, Smrithi, and daughters, Soumya and Radha Buyya, for their love, understanding, and support during the preparation of this book. Rodrigo would like to thank his wife, Kimie, his son, Roger, and his daughter, Laura. Amir would like to thank his wife, Elly, and daughter, Diana.

Finally, we would like to thank the staff at Morgan Kauffman, particularly, Amy Invernizzi, Brian Romer, Punitha Govindaradjane, and Todd Green for managing the publication in record time.

Rajkumar Buyya
The University of Melbourne and Manjrasoft Pty Ltd, Australia

Rodrigo N. Calheiros
The University of Melbourne, Australia

Amir Vahid Dastjerdi
The University of Melbourne, Australia

BIG DATA SCIENCE

BIG DATA ANALYTICS=MACHINE LEARNING+CLOUD COMPUTING

1

C. Wu, R. Buyya, K. Ramamohanarao

1.1 INTRODUCTION

Although the term "Big Data" has become popular, there is no general consensus about what it really means. Often, many professional data analysts would imply the process of extraction, transformation, and load (ETL) for large datasets as the connotation of Big Data. A popular description of Big Data is based on three main attributes of data: volume, velocity, and variety (or 3Vs). Nevertheless, it does not capture all the aspects of Big Data accurately. In order to provide a comprehensive meaning of Big Data, we will investigate this term from a historical perspective and see how it has been evolving from yesterday's meaning to today's connotation.

Historically, the term Big Data is quite vague and ill defined. It is not a precise term and does not carry a particular meaning other than the notion of its size. The word "big" is too generic; the question how "big" is big and how "small" is small [1] is relative to time, space, and circumstance. From an evolutionary perspective, the size of "Big Data" is always evolving. If we use the current global Internet traffic capacity [2] as a measuring stick, the meaning of Big Data volume would lie between the terabyte (TB or 10^{12} or 2^{40}) and zettabyte (ZB or 10^{21} or 2^{70}) range. Based on the historical data traffic growth rate, Cisco claimed that humans have entered the ZB era in 2015 [2]. To understand the significance of the data volume's impact, let us glance at the average size of different data files shown in Table 1.

The main aim of this chapter is to provide a historical view of Big Data and to argue that it is not just 3Vs, but rather 3^2Vs or 9Vs. These additional Big Data attributes reflect the real motivation behind Big Data analytics (BDA). We believe that these expanded features clarify some basic questions about the essence of BDA: what problems Big Data can address, and what problems should not be confused as BDA. These issues are covered in the chapter through analysis of historical developments, along with associated technologies that support Big Data processing. The rest of the chapter is organized into eight sections as follows:

1) A historical review for Big Data
2) Interpretation of Big Data 3Vs, 4Vs, and 6Vs
3) Defining Big Data from 3Vs to 3^2Vs
4) Big Data and Machine Learning (ML)
5) Big Data and cloud computing

Big Data. http://dx.doi.org/10.1016/B978-0-12-805394-2.00001-5

Table 1 Typical Size of Different Data Files

Media	Average Size of Data File	Notes (2014)
Web page	1.6–2 MB	Average 100 objects
eBook	1–5 MB	200–350 pages
Song	3.5–5.8 MB	Average 1.9 MB/per minute (MP3) 256 Kbps rate (3 mins)
Movie	100–120 GB	60 frames per second (MPEG-4 format, Full High Definition, 2 hours)

6) Hadoop, Hadoop distributed file system (HDFS), MapReduce, Spark, and Flink
7) ML + CC (Cloud Computing) → BDA and guidelines
8) Conclusion

1.2 A HISTORICAL REVIEW OF BIG DATA

In order to capture the essence of Big Data, we provide the origin and history of BDA and then propose a precise definition of BDA.

1.2.1 THE ORIGIN OF BIG DATA

Several studies have been conducted on the historical views and developments in the BDA area. Gil Press [3] provided a short history of Big Data starting from 1944, which was based on Rider's work [4]. He covered 68 years of history of evolution of Big Data between 1944 and 2012 and illustrated 32 Big Data-related events in recent data science history. As Press indicated in his article, the fine line between the growth of data and Big Data has become blurred. Very often, the growth rate of data has been referred as "information explosion"; although "data" and "information" are often used interchangeably, the two terms have different connotations. Press' study is quite comprehensive and covers BDA events up to December 2013. Since then, there have been many relevant Big Data events. Nevertheless, Press' review did cover both Big Data and data science events. To this extent, the term "data science" could be considered as a complementary meaning to BDA.

In comparison with Press' review, Frank Ohlhorst [5] established the origin of Big Data back to 1880 when the 10th US census was held. The real problem during the 19th century was a statistics issue, which was how to survey and document 50 million of North American citizens. Although Big Data may contain computations of some statistics elements, these two terms have different interpretations today. Similarly, Winshuttle [6] believes the origin of Big Data was in the 19th century. Winshuttle argue if data sets are so large and complex and beyond traditional process and management capability, then these data sets can be considered as Big Data. In comparison to Press' review, Winshuttle's review emphasizes enterprise resource planning and implementation on cloud infrastructure. Moreover, the review also makes a predication for data growth to 2020. The total time span of the review was more than 220 years. Winshuttle's Big Data history included many SAP events and its data products, such as HANA.

The longest span of historical review for Big Data belongs to Bernard Marr's description [7]. He traced the origin of Big Data back to 18,000 BCE. Marr argued that we should pay attention to historical foundations of Big Data, which are different approaches for human to capture, store, analyze, and re-trieve both data and information. Furthermore, Marr believed that the first person who casted the term "Big Data" was Erik Larson [8], who presented an article for *Harper's Magazine* that was subsequently reprinted in *The Washington Post* in 1989 because there were two sentences that consisted of the words of Big Data: "The keepers of Big Data say they do it for the consumer's benefit. But data have a way of being used for purposes other than originally intended."

In contrast, Steve Lohr [9] disagrees with Marr's view. He argues that just adopting the term alone might not have the connotation of today's Big Data because "The term Big Data is so generic that the hunt for its origin was not just an effort to find an early reference to those two words being used together. Instead, the goal was the early use of the term that suggests its present interpretation — that is, not just a lot of data, but different types of data handled in new ways." This is an important point. Based on this reasoning, we consider that Cox and Ellsworth [10] as proposers of the term Big Data because they assigned a relatively accurate meaning to the existing view of Big Data, which they stated, "...data sets are generally quite large, taxing the capacities of main memory, local disk and even remote disk. We call this the problem of Big Data. When data sets do not fit in main memory (in core), or when they do not fit even on local disk..." Although today's term may have an extended meaning as opposed to Cox and Ellsworth's term, this definition reflects today's connotation with reasonable accuracy.

Another historical review was contributed by Visualizing.org [11]. It focused on the timeline of how to implement BDA. Its historical description is mainly determined by events related to the Big Data push by many Internet and IT companies, such as Google, YouTube, Yahoo, Facebook, Twitter, and Apple. It emphasized the significant impact of Hadoop in the history of BDA. It primarily highlighted the significant role of Hadoop in the BDA. Based on these studies, we show the history of Big Data, Hadoop, and its ecosystem in Fig. 1.

Undoubtedly, there will be many different views based on different interpretations of BDA. This will inevitably lead to many debates of Big Data implication or pros and cons.

1.2.2 DEBATES OF BIG DATA IMPLICATION
Pros
There have been many debates regarding Big Data's pros and cons during the past few years. Many advocates declare Big Data to be a new rock star [12] and that it will be the next frontier [13,14] for innovation, competition, and productivity because data is embedded in the modern human being's life. Data that are generated every second by both machines and humans is a byproduct of all other activi-ties. It will become the new epistemologies [15] in science. To certain degree, Mayer and Cukier [16] argued that Big Data would revolutionize our way of thinking, working, and living. They believe that a massive quantitative data accumulation will lead to qualitative advances at the core of BDA: ML, paral-lelism, metadata, and predictions: "Big Data will be a source of new economic value and innovation" [16]. Their conclusion is that data can speak for itself, and we should let the data speak.

To a certain extent, Montjoye et al. [17] echoed the above conclusion. They demonstrated that it is highly probable (over 90% reliability) to reidentify a person with as few as four spatiotemporal data points (eg, credit card transactions in a shopping mall) by leveraging BDA. Their conclusion is that "large-scale data sets of human behavior have the potential to fundamentally transform the way we fight diseases, design cities and perform research."

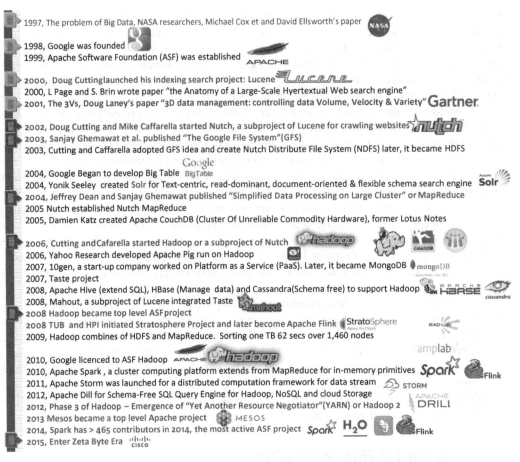

1997, The problem of Big Data, NASA researchers, Michael Cox et and David Ellsworth's paper

1998, Google was founded

1999, Apache Software Foundation (ASF) was established

2000, Doug Cuttinglaunched his indexing search project: Lucene

2000, L Page and S. Brin wrote paper "the Anatomy of a Large-Scale Hyertextual Web search engine"

2001, The 3Vs, Doug Laney's paper "3D data management: controlling data Volume, Velocity & Variety"

2002, Doug Cutting and Mike Caffarella started Nutch, a subproject of Lucene for crawling websites

2003, Sanjay Ghemawat et al. published "The Google File System"(GFS)

2003, Cutting and Caffarella adopted GFS idea and create Nutch Distribute File System (NDFS) later, it became HDFS

2004, Google Began to develop Big Table

2004, Yonik Seeley created Solr for Text-centric, read-dominant, document-oriented & flexible schema search engine

2004, Jeffrey Dean and Sanjay Ghemawat published "Simplified Data Processing on Large Cluster" or MapReduce

2005 Nutch established Nutch MapReduce

2005, Damien Katz created Apache CouchDB (Cluster Of Unreliable Commodity Hardware), former Lotus Notes

2006, Cutting andCafarella started Hadoop or a subproject of Nutch

2006, Yahoo Research developed Apache Pig run on Hadoop

2007, 10gen, a start-up company worked on Platform as a Service (PaaS). Later, it became MongoDB

2007, Taste project

2008, Apache Hive (extend SQL), HBase (Manage data) and Cassandra(Schema free) to support Hadoop

2008, Mahout, a subproject of Lucene integrated Taste

2008 Hadoop became top level ASFproject

2008 TUB and HPI initiated Stratosphere Project and later become Apache Flink

2009, Hadoop combines of HDFS and MapReduce. Sorting one TB 62 secs over 1,460 nodes

2010, Google licenced to ASF Hadoop

2010, Apache Spark , a cluster computing platform extends from MapReduce for in-memory primitives

2011, Apache Storm was launched for a distributed computation framework for data stream

2012, Apache Dill for Schema-Free SQL Query Engine for Hadoop, NoSQL and cloud Storage

2012, Phase 3 of Hadoop – Emergence of "Yet Another Resource Negotiator"(YARN) or Hadoop 2

2013 Mesos became a top level Apache project

2014, Spark has > 465 contributors in 2014, the most active ASF project

2015, Enter Zeta Byte Era

FIG. 1

A short history of big data.

Cons

In contrast, some argue that Big Data is inconclusive, overstated, exaggerated, and misinformed by the media and that data cannot speak for itself [18]. It does not matter how big the data set is. It could be just another delusion because "it is like having billions of monkeys typing, one of them will write Shakespeare" [19]. In Dobelli's term [20], we should "never judge a decision by its outcome — outcome bias." In other words, if one of the monkeys can type Shakespeare, we cannot conclude or inference that a monkey has sufficient intelligence to be Shakespeare.

Gary Drenik [21] believed that the sentiment of the overeager adoption of Big Data is more like "Extraordinary Popular Delusion and the Madness of Crowds," the description made by Charles Mackay [22] in his famous book's title. Psychologically, it is a kind of a crowd emotion that seems to have a perpetual feedback loop. Drenik quoted this "madness" with Mackay's warning: "We find that whole communities suddenly fix their minds upon one subject, and go mad in its pursuit; that millions of people become simultaneously impressed with one delusion, and run it till their attention is caught by some new folly more captivating than the first." The issue that Drenik has noticed was "the hype overtaken reality and there was little time to think about" regarding Big Data. The former Obama's campaign CTO: Harper Reed, had the real story in terms of adoption of BDA. His remarks of Big Data were "literally hard" and "expensive" [23].

Danah Boyd et al. [24] are quite skeptical in regarding big data in terms of its volume. They argued that bigger data are not always better data from a social science perspective. In responding to "The End of Theory" [25] proposition, Boyd asserted that theory or methodology is still highly relevant for today's statistical inference and "The size of data should fit the research question being asked; in some cases, small is best." Boyd et al. suggested that we should not pay a lot of attention to the volume of data. Philosophically, this argument is similar to the debate between John Stuart Mill (Mill's five classical or empirical methods) and his critics [26]. Mill's critics argued that it is impossible to bear on the intelligent question just by ingesting as much as data alone without some theory or hypothesis. This means that we cannot make Big Data do the work of theory.

Another Big Data critique comes from David Lazer et al. [27]. They demonstrated that the Google flu trends (GFT) prediction is the parable and identified two issues (Big Data hubris and algorithm dynamics) that contributed to GFT's mistakes. The issue of "Big Data hubris" is that some observers believe that BDA can replace traditional data mining completely. The issue of "algorithm dynamics" is "the changes made by [Google's] engineers to improve the commercial service and by consumers in using that service." In other words, the changing algorithms for searching will directly impact the users' behavior. This will lead to the collected data that is driven by deliberated algorithms. Lazer concluded there are many traps in BDA, especially for social media research. Their conclusion was "we are far from a place where they (BDA) can supplant more traditional methods or theories."

All these multiple views are due to different interpretations of Big Data and different implementations of BDA. This suggests that in order to resolve these issues, we should first clarify the definition of the term BDA and then discover the clash point based on the same term.

1.3 HISTORICAL INTERPRETATION OF BIG DATA
1.3.1 METHODOLOGY FOR DEFINING BIG DATA

Intuitively, neither yesterday's data volume (absolute size) nor that of today can be defined as "big." Moreover, today's "big" may become tomorrow's "small." In order to clarify the term Big Data precisely and settle the debate, we can investigate and understand the functions of a definition based on the combination of Robert Baird [28] and Irving Copi's [29] approaches (see Fig. 2).

Based on Baird or Irving's approach of definition, we will first investigate the historical definition from an evolutionary perspective (lexical meaning). Then, we extend the term from 3Vs to 9Vs or 3^2Vs based on its motivation (stipulative meaning), which is to add more attributes for the term. Finally, we will eliminate ambiguity and vagueness of the term and make the concept more precise and meaningful.

1.3.2 DIFFERENT ATTRIBUTES OF DEFINITIONS
Gartner — 3Vs definition

Since 1997, many attributes have been added to Big Data. Among these attributes, three of them are the most popular and have been widely cited and adopted. The first one is so called Gartner's interpretation or 3Vs; the root of this term can be traced back to Feb. 2001. It was casted by Douglas Laney [30] in his

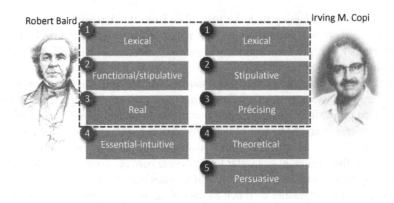

FIG. 2

Methodology of definition.

white paper published by Meta group, which Gartner subsequently acquired in 2004. Douglas noticed that due to surging of e-commerce activities, data has grown along three dimensions, namely:

1. Volume, which means the incoming data stream and cumulative volume of data
2. Velocity, which represents the pace of data used to support interaction and generated by interactions
3. Variety, which signifies the variety of incompatible and inconsistent data formats and data structures

According to the history of the Big Data timeline [30], Douglas Laney's 3Vs definition has been widely regarded as the "common" attributes of Big Data but he stopped short of assigning these attributes to the term "Big Data."

IBM — 4Vs definition
IBM added another attribute or "V" for "Veracity" on the top of Douglas Laney's 3Vs notation, which is known as the 4Vs of Big Data. It defines each "V" as following [31,32]:

1. Volume stands for the scale of data
2. Velocity denotes the analysis of streaming data
3. Variety indicates different forms of data
4. Veracity implies the uncertainty of data

Zikopoulos et al. explained the reason behind the additional "V" or veracity dimension, which is "*in response to the quality and source issues our clients began facing with their Big Data initiatives*" [33]. They are also aware of some analysts including other V-based descriptors for Big Data, such as variability and visibility.

Microsoft — 6Vs definition
For the sake of maximizing the business value, Microsoft extended Douglas Laney's 3Vs attributes to 6 Vs [34], which it added variability, veracity, and visibility:

1. Volume stands for scale of data
2. Velocity denotes the analysis of streaming data
3. Variety indicates different forms of data

4. Veracity focuses on trustworthiness of data sources
5. Variability refers to the complexity of data set. In comparison with "Variety" (or different data format), it means the number of variables in data sets
6. Visibility emphasizes that you need to have a full picture of data in order to make informative decision

More Vs for big data

A 5 Vs' Big Data definition was also proposed by Yuri Demchenko [35] in 2013. He added the value dimension along with the IBM 4Vs' definition (see Fig. 3). Since Douglas Laney published 3Vs in 2001, there have been additional "Vs," even as many as 11 [36].

All these definitions, such as 3Vs, 4Vs, 5Vs, or even 11 Vs, are primarily trying to articulate the aspect of data. Most of them are data-oriented definitions, but they fail to articulate Big Data clearly in a relationship to the essence of BDA. In order to understand the essential meaning, we have to clarify what data is.

Data is everything within the universe. This means that data is within the existing limitation of technological capacity. If the technology capacity is allowed, there is no boundary or limitation for

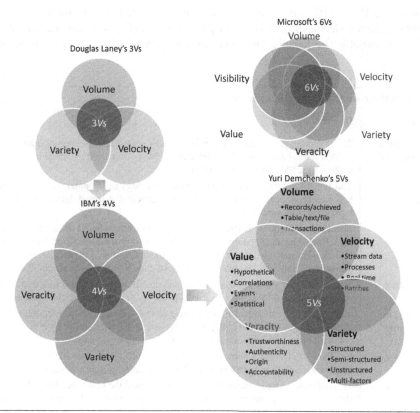

FIG. 3

From 3Vs, 4Vs, 5Vs, and 6Vs big data definition.

data. The question is why we should capture it in the first place. Clearly, the main reason of capturing data is not because we have enough capacity to capture high volume, high velocity, and high variety data rather than to find a better solution for our research or business problem, which is to search for actionable intelligence. Pure data-driven analysis may add little value for a decision maker; sometimes, it may only add the burden for the costs or resources of BDA. Perhaps this is why Harper believes Big Data is really hard [23].

1.3.3 SUMMARY OF 7 TYPES DEFINITIONS OF BIG DATA

Table 2 shows seven types of definitions, summarized by Timo Elliott [36] and based on more than 33 Big Data definitions [41].

Each of the above definitions intends to describe a particular issue from one aspect of Big Data only and is very restrictive. However, a comprehensive definition can become complex and very long. A solution for this issue is to use "rational reconstruction" offered by Karl Popper, which intends to make the reasons behind practice, decision, and process explicit and easier to understand.

1.3.4 MOTIVATIONS BEHIND THE DEFINITIONS

The purpose of Big Data or BDA is to gain hindsight (ie, metadata patterns emerging from historical data), insight (ie, deep understanding of issues or problems), and foresight (ie, accurate prediction in near future) in a cost-effective manner. However, these important and necessary attributes are often

Table 2 Seven Popular Big Data Definitions

No	Type	Description
1	The original big data (3Vs)	The original type of definition is referred to Douglas Laney's volume, velocity, and variety, or 3Vs. It has been widely cited since 2001. Many have tried to extend the number of Vs, such as 4Vs, 5Vs, 6Vs … up to 11Vs
2	Big Data as technology	This type of definition is oriented by new technology development, such as MapReduce, bulk synchronous parallel (BSP — Hama), resilient distributed datasets (RDD, Spark), and Lambda architecture (Flink)
3	Big Data as application	This kind of definition emphasizes different applications based on different types of big data. Barry Devlin [37] defined it as application of process-mediated data, human-sourced information, and machine-generated data. Shaun Connolly [38] focused on analyzing transactions, interactions, and observation of data. It looks for hindsight of data
4	Big Data as signals	This is another type of application-oriented definition, but it focuses on timing rather than the type of data. It looks for a foresight of data or new "signal" pattern in dataset
5	Big Data as opportunity	Matt Aslett [39]: "Big data as analyzing data that was previously ignored because of technology limitations." It highlights many potential opportunities by revisiting the collected or archived datasets when new technologies are variable
6	Big Data as metaphor	It defines Big Data as a human thinking process [40]. It elevates BDA to the new level, which means BDS is not a type of analytic tool rather it is an extension of human brain
7	Big Data as new term for old stuff	This definition simply means the new bottle (relabel the new term "big data") for old wine (BI, data mining, or other traditional data analytic activities). It is one of the most cynical ways to define big data

neglected by many definitions that only focus on either single-issue or data aspects. In order to reflect all aspects of Big Data, we consider all attributes from different aspects.

1.4 DEFINING BIG DATA FROM 3Vs TO 3²Vs

The real objective of BDA is actually to seek for business intelligence (BI). It enables decision makers to make the right decisions based on predictions through the analysis of available data. Therefore, we need to clarify new attributes of Big Data and establish their relationship meaning cross three aspects (or domain knowledge), namely:

- Data domain (searching for patterns)
- Business intelligence domain (making predictions)
- Statistical domain (making assumptions)

1.4.1 DATA DOMAIN

Laney's 3Vs have captured the importance of Big Data characteristics reflecting the pace and exploration phenomena of data growth during the last few years. In this, the key attribute in data aspect is volume. If we look the history of data analytics, the variation of velocity and variety is relatively small in comparison with volume. The dominated V that often exceeds our current capacity for data processing is volume. Although volume cannot determine all attributes of data, it is one of the crucial factors in BDA.

1.4.2 BUSINESS[1] INTELLIGENT (BI) DOMAIN

When we discuss BI of BDA, we mean value, visibility, and verdict within the business intelligent domain. These 3Vs are the motivations or drivers for us to implement BDA process at the first place. If we cannot achieve BI, the pure exercise of data analytics will be meaningless. From a decision maker's perspective, these 3Vs are how to leverage data's 3Vs for BI's 3Vs.

- Visibility: It does not only focus on the insight but also focuses on metadata or sometimes the wisdom of data crowds or hierarchical level of abstraction data patterns. From a BI perspective, it provides hindsight, insight, and foresight of a problem and an adequate solution associated with it.
- Value: the purpose of V for value is to answer the question of "Does the data contain any valuable information for my business needs?" In comparison with 5Vs definition, it is not just the value of data but also the value of BI for problem solving. It is the value and utility for the long-term or strategic pay off.
- Verdict: It is a potential choice or decision that should be made by a decision maker or committee based on the scope of the problem, available resources, and certain computational capacity. This

---

[1]Here, the term of business includes research activities.

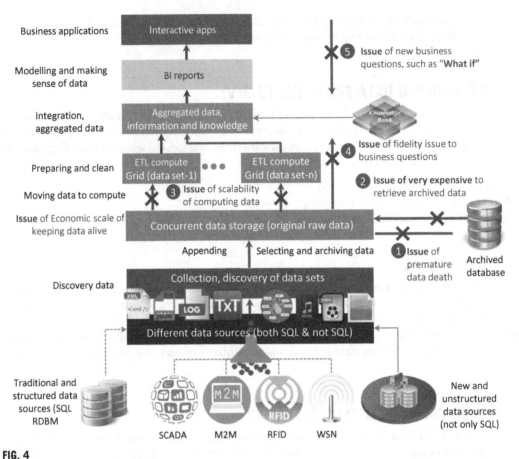

FIG. 4

Key motivations of big data analytics.

is the most challenging V to be quantified at the beginning of BDA. If there are many hypotheses or "What-ifs," the cost of collecting, retrieving data, and ETL, especially to extract archived data, will be costly (see Fig. 4).

These business motivations led to the new BDA platforms or MapReduce processing frameworks, such as Hadoop. It intends to answer the five basic questions in Big Data, as shown in Fig. 4. These questions reflect the bottom line of BI:

1. How to store massive data (such as in PB or EB scale currently) or information in the available resources
2. How to access these massive data or information quickly
3. How to work with datasets in variety formats: structured, semi-structured, and unstructured
4. How to process these datasets in a full scalable, fault tolerant, and flexible manner
5. How to extract BI interactively and cost-effectively

In this domain, the key notation of V is visibility, which is to obtain the prediction or real-time insight from BDA exercises. The relationship of these 3Vs in BI is that without visibility, other 2Vs will be impossible.

1.4.3 STATISTICS DOMAIN

Similarly, we should have another set of 3 V attributes in the statistic domain, which are veracity, validity, and variability. These 3Vs should establish the statistic models based on the right hypothesis (What if), which is the trustworthiness of the data sets and the reliability of the data sources. If the hypothesis is inadequate or the data source is contaminated or the statistics model is incorrect, the BDA might lead to a wrong conclusion. There have been many lessons regarding contaminated data samples. A famous example was the opinion poll for the 1936 US presidential election that was carried by *Literary Digest* magazine before the election [42]. Because the sample data (2.4 million survey responses) were accidentally contaminated, the result of their predication (or president winner in 1936) became a disaster for the polling company. Therefore, the statistics domain should consist of following attributes:

- Veracity: Philosophically speaking, it is the true information (or fact) is the resolution of data uncertainty. V of Veracity is searching for trustworthiness and certainty of data sets.
- Validity: It is to verify the quality of data being logically sound. The V of validity emphasizes how to correctly acquire data and avoid biases. Another essential meaning of validity is the inference process based on a statistical model.
- Variability: It is the implication of data complexity and variation. For example, Bruce Ratner [43] believed that if there are more than 50 variables or different features in one dataset, it could be considered as "Big Data." Statistically, it is how to use the logical inference process to reduce data complexity and reach desirable outcomes or predictions for business needs.

The key attribute of this aspect is veracity, which emphasizes how to build a statistical model close to the reality. The process to approach veracity can be considered an exercise of a curve fitting: If we have few constraints, the regression errors of the curve will be too large. If we adopt too many constraints, it will cause an overfitting problem.

1.4.4 3² Vs DEFINITION AND BIG DATA VENN DIAGRAM

Once all 3² Vs attributes have been defined from three different aspects, we can establish a combined Venn diagram and their relationships. This has become our definition of Big Data (see Fig. 5), which is comprehensive enough to capture all aspects of Big Data.

As shown in Fig. 5, each Venn diagram is supported by one V shape of a triangle to illustrate 3Vs' attributes in one aspect. Moreover, three key attributes from each Venn diagram can also form a single hierarchical triangle diagram. It represents the essential meaning of Big Data.

If the original 3Vs' data attributes represented a syntactic or logical meaning of Big Data, then 3²Vs (or 9Vs) represent the semantic meaning (relationship of data, BI, and statistics). For many complex problems or applications, the 3²Vs could be interpreted as a hierarchical model, for which three key attributes form a higher level 3Vs to be learnt by a machine. At the heart of BDA, there is "machine learning" because without the machine (computer), the mission of learning from Big Data would be impossible.

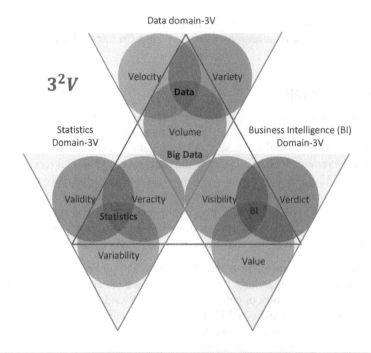

FIG. 5

3^2Vs Venn diagrams in hierarchical model.

1.5 BIG DATA ANALYTICS AND MACHINE LEARNING
1.5.1 BIG DATA ANALYTICS

If 3^2Vs represent semantic meaning of Big Data, then BDA represents pragmatic meaning of Big Data. We can view from computational viewpoint, Big Data Venn diagram with a BDA's Venn diagram in Fig. 6.

According to Arthur Samuel, the original definition of ML was "*The field of study that gives computers (or machines) that ability to learn without being explicitly programmed*" [44]. Historically, there have been many terms that intend to describe the equivalent meaning of ML, such as learning from data, pattern Recognition, data science, data mining, text mining, or even BI, etc. If we list all terms based on their different orientations, we can probably find there are more than 32 different descriptions that contain certain meanings of ML from four aspects (see Table 3):

- Data
- Information
- Knowledge
- Intelligence

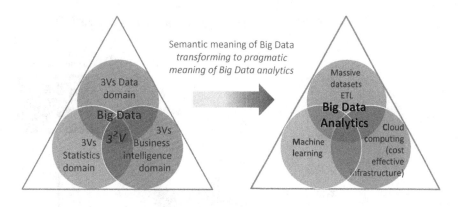

FIG. 6

Correlation of 3^2Vs to machine learning Venn diagrams.

Table 3 Popular Interpretation of ML			
Data	**Information**	**Knowledge**	**Intelligence**
Data mining	Information analytics	Real-time analytics	Business analysis
Data science	Information visualization	Predictive analytics	Business intelligence
Data warehouse	Information system management	Machine learning	Artificial intelligence
Learning from data	Text analytics	Knowledge base system	Decision support system
Data smart	Text mining	Pattern recognition	Actionable intelligence
Data analytics	Web analytics	Statistical application	Business forecasting
Making sense of data	Web semantic analysis	Knowledge discovery	Business strategy
Data ingestion	Web searching	Expert systems	Business transformation

1.5.2 MACHINE LEARNING

The essence of ML is an automatic process of pattern recognition by a learning machine. The main objective of ML is to build systems that can perform at or exceed human level competence in handling many complex tasks or problems. ML is a part of artificial intelligence (AI). During the early AI research era, the goal was to build robots and to simulate human activities. Later, the application of AI has been generalized to solve general problems by a machine. The popular solution was to feed a computer with algorithms (or a sequence of instructions) so it can transform the input data to output answers. This is often called a rule-based system or Good Old-Fashioned of Artificial Intelligence (GOFAI), such as expert systems.

However, we cannot easily find suitable algorithms for many problems; for example, the recognition of human handwriting. We do not know how to transform the input of handwriting letter to the output of the standard recognized letter; an alternative is learning from data. The principle of learning from data is similar as both trial and error and "The Wisdom of Crowds" [45]. This means that having

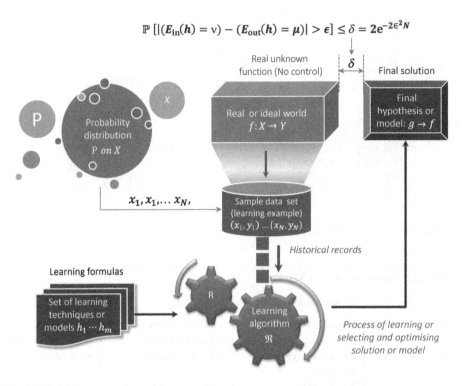

$$\mathbb{P}\left[|(E_{in}(h)=v)-(E_{out}(h)=\mu)|>\epsilon\right]\leq\delta=2e^{-2\epsilon^2 N}$$

FIG. 7

Machine learning process [46].

one trial could have a large error but if we can aggregate many trials, the error will be reduced down to an acceptable level or convergence. Fig. 7 illustrates a typical example of a ML process or learning from data.

Since the dotcom boom started in late 1990s, the volume of data has become increasingly larger. A logical question is how to deal with these large volumes of data and how to find useful or meaningful patterns from a larger volume of data. This leads to knowledge discovery in database, or KDD, which is also called data mining. In other words, we want to dig into the database and discover the meaning or knowledge for decision making. Larose et al. [47] defined the term as "the process of discovering useful patterns and trends in large datasets." In order to discover meaningful patterns from a massive data set, statistics are the vital tools to add value to data sampling, modeling, analysis, interpretation, and presentation, just as Jiawei Han et al. [48] indicated, *"Data mining has an inherent connection with statistics."* This leads to the converging of data mining and fuzzy expert system under the big umbrella of ML. From ML evolution perspective, the statistics theory or probability modeling has shifted AI discipline from rule-based expert systems or schema-on-write learning to a schema-on-read or data-driven methodology, which is to resolve the uncertainty issue with parameters' probability of a model. From this perspective, the statistics have been embedded into ML. As Witten et al. [49] indicated, *"In truth, you should not look for a dividing line between machine learning and statistics because there is a continuum — and a multidimensional one at that — of data analysis techniques."*

Since the 1950s, there have been many functional definitions of ML. Different authors would emphasize different aspects of ML, such as process, application, and utility. For example, Arthur Samuel's definition emphasized "automatically learning" of ML. Mitchell described every component of ML process [50]. Murphy [51] and Bishop [52], on the other hand, stressed the function of pattern recognition. Nisan and Schocken [53] argued that ML could turn abstract thoughts into a physical operation. In the summary of over 30 definitions, we can find some essential and common ingredients of these ML definitions:

- Train the machine to learn automatically and improve results as it gets more data
- Discover or recognize patterns and intelligence with input data
- Predicate on unknown inputs
- The machine will acquire knowledge directly from data and solve problems

According to these elements, we can find that fundamentally, ML is "*an outgrowth of the intersection of computer science and statistics, aims to automatically learn to recognize complex patterns and make intelligent decisions based on existing datasets*" [54]. Another way to say that is "*Machine learning is turning data into information*" [55]. The ultimate goal of ML is to build systems that are of at the level of human competence (see Fig. 8) in performing complex tasks.

ML underpins the BDA implementation. Without ML to mine ever-growing massive data, BDA would be impossible. In conclusion, ML is the centerpiece of any BDA. All other components within a framework of Big Data aim to support ML process. In terms of computational support to BDA, there are four major architectural models that are able to process large amounts of data in a reasonable time, according to Wadkar et al. [56]:

- Massively parallel processing database system: For example, EMC's Greenplum and IBM's Netezza
- In-memory database systems, such as Oracle Exalytics, SAP's HANA, and Spark
- MapReduce processing model and platforms such as Hadoop and Google File System (GFS)
- Bulk Synchronous Parallel (BSP) systems such as Apache HAMA and Giraph

To perform BDA in the most cost-effective way, a fifth model, cloud computing (CC), has become a preferred solution especially for small and media businesses.

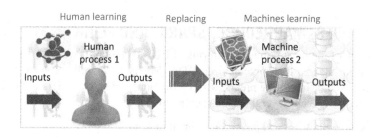

FIG. 8

Replacing humans in the learning process.

1.6 BIG DATA ANALYTICS AND CLOUD COMPUTING

CC plays a critical role in the BDA process as it offers subscription-oriented access to computing infrastructure, data, and application services [57]. The original objective of BDA was to leverage commodity hardware to build computing clusters and scale-out the computing capacity for web crawling and indexing system workloads. Due to the massive volume of dataset, searching for lower cost and fault-tolerance computational capacity is an important factor for implementing BDA. On the other hand, the implementation of CC were underpinned with three service models, four deployment models, and five characteristics [58], which is the so-called 3S-4D-5C definition.

o Service orientation or 3S Service models (SaaS, PaaS, and IaaS)
o Customized delivery or 4D Deployment models (private, public, community, and hybrid cloud)
o Shared infrastructure or 5C characteristics (on-demand, broad network access, resource pool, rapid elasticity, and measured service)

This means that the nature of cloud characteristics makes it the most accessible infrastructure for many small to medium companies to be able to implement BDA.

The cloud does not only enable us to easily scale-out, but also scale down to fit all sizes of dataset. When BDA is discussed, it is quite often that the only focus is how to scale-out. However, it is not necessarily the case. Although the overall data volume may tend to increase, the daily volume for each individual case could be moderate and fluctuating, or Big Data processing requirements needed for BI can vary from time to time. If we can leverage the elastic nature of cloud, we can save a substantial amount of the cost due to amortization benefits provided by the cloud systems. The elastic nature of cloud can reduce the overall cost of computation for different types of Big Data workloads, such as batch, micro-batch, interactive, real-time, and near real-time.

Taking Yahoo sorting one TB data as an example, it took 3.5 minutes over 910 nodes to complete the task in 2008, but it only took 62 seconds over 1460 nodes in 2009. To "scale-out" computational capacity will make a huge difference regardless of an improvement of each node due to technological advances. This implies that cloud infrastructure provides computational flexibility if Big Data workload or business requirements need it. For example, Amazon Web Service (AWS) offers spots instances at a fraction of the regular rate. If the workload only requires batch mode, we can leverage AWS's spots instances to increase computational capacity and complete the job in a much shorter time.

A popular and open platform that is widely deployed on a cloud infrastructure is Hadoop, whose implementation is inspired by Google MapReduce and GFS.

1.7 HADOOP, HDFS, MAPREDUCE, SPARK, AND FLINK

Fig. 9 highlights one of the most popular platforms of BDA, Hadoop. It was the first choice for many analysts and decision makers for implementing BDA. Michael Cafarella, one of the two Hadoop's founders once remarked, "Nutch (the predecessor of Hadoop) is The National Public Radio (NPR) of search engines" [59]. There are several reasons behind this development:

1. It is an open source platform and also programmed in Java
2. It is linearly scalable and reliable and accepts hardware failure
3. It is a fault-tolerant system

FIG. 9

Overview of Hadoop framework or technology stack and ecosystem.

4. It is a practical platform to store and process data amounts greater than tens of TB
5. It leverages a commodity-type of hardware
6. It is "schema-on-read" or has "data agility" character
7. It is best fit for diversified data sources

The basic idea to create Hadoop is driven by both ever-growing data and cost of computational hardware. The objective of Hadoop is to leverage the commodity hardware for large-scale workload processing, which used to be accomplished only by expensive mainframe computers. From an infrastructure perspective, Hadoop enables the computational capacity to be scale-out rather than scale-up. Notice that it is quite often we use both terms interchangeably [60] but based on a standard definition, "scale-up" has a quality improvement sense while "scale-out" implies adding or repeating the same unit horizontally.

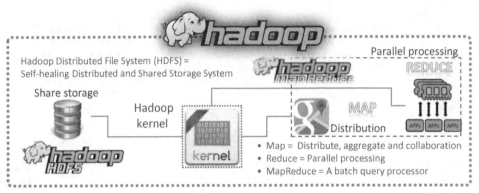

FIG. 10

Hadoop kernel.

The advantage to adopt Hadoop [60] platform is that "*Hadoop is a free and open source distributed storage and computational platform. It was created to allow storing and processing large amounts of data using clusters of commodity hardware.*" This statement also describes the basic principle of Hadoop architecture that consists of three essential components (see Fig. 10): HDFS for file storage function, Map for distribute function, and Reduce for parallel processing function.

However, Hadoop's main disadvantage is that it processes all workloads in batch mode because "*Hadoop is a generic processing framework designed to execute queries and other batch read operations on massive datasets that can scale from tens of terabytes to petabytes in size*" [61]. This means that the early version of Hadoop cannot handle streaming and interactive workloads. Table 4 summarizes main characteristics of Hadoop.

The origin of Hadoop can be traced back to Nutch project under Apache Software Foundation (ASF) in 2002 (see Fig. 11). The initial platform was built as an open source implementation of MapReduce [62] processing model and distributed file system [62] proposed by Google. In 2010, Google granted a license to Apache for incorporating the MapReduce model into Hadoop software freely and distributed it without any patent or IP rights infringement concerns.

1.7.1 GOOGLE FILE SYSTEM (GFS) AND HDFS

The Hadoop project adopted GFS architecture and developed HDFS. The original authors (Google's engineers) laid out four pillars for GFS:

- System principles
- System architecture
- System assumptions
- System interfaces

The GFS principles departed from the traditional system design dogma that a failure was not allowed and a computation system should be designed to be as reliable as possible. In contrast, GFS anticipates the certain number of system failures with specified redundancy or replicating factor

Table 4 Common Aspects of Hadoop

Attributes	Characteristics of Hadoop
Initiators	Doug Cutting and Michael J. Cafarella
Predecessor	Nutch
Subsequent version	YARN or Hadoop 2.0
Hadoop written language	Java
Philosophy of computation	Divide and conquer for large datasets
Principle of computational processing	Bring computer to data rather than bring data to computer
System	A distributed programming framework
Main characteristics	Accessible, robust, scalable, simple, and fault tolerant
Storage-Hadoop distributed file system (HDFS)	Self-healing distributed and shared storage element
Initial computational program — MapReduce	Distributed, aggregated, and collaborated parallel processing
MapReduce library written language	C++ code
Process type	Batch
Hardware type	Heterogeneous commodity hardware
Software license	Open source
Initial applications	IR and searching index and web crawler
Solution type	Software solution, not hardware solution
Scalability solution	Scale-out, not scale-up
Typical size of data set	From a few GBs to a few TBs
Capable size of data set	From tens of TBs to a few PBs
Simple coherency model	Write once and read many
Default replication factor	3
Typical size of data block for HDFS	64 MB
Permission model	Relaxing POSIX[a] model
Main application modules	Mahout, Hive, Pig, HBase, Sqoop, Flume, Chukwa, Pentaho …
Typical vendors	MapR, Cloudera, Hortonworks, IBM, Teradata, Intel, AWS, Pivotal Software, and Microsoft

[a] *POSIX is the portable operating system interface. Few POSIX rules (permissions model for supporting multiuser environment) have been relaxed in order to gain a higher throughput of data uploads.*

and automatic recovery. In comparison to the traditional file standard, GFS is capable of handling billions of objects, so I/O should be revisited. Moreover, most of files will be altered by appending rather than overwriting. Finally, the GFS flexibility is increased by balancing the benefits between GFS applications and file system API. The GFS architecture consists of three components (see Fig. 12):

- Single master server (or name node)
- Multiple chunk servers (or data nodes for Hadoop)
- Multiple clients

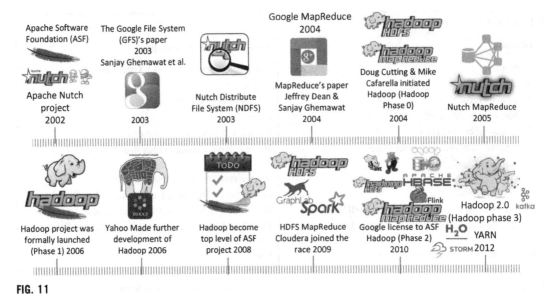

FIG. 11

Briefing history of Hadoop.

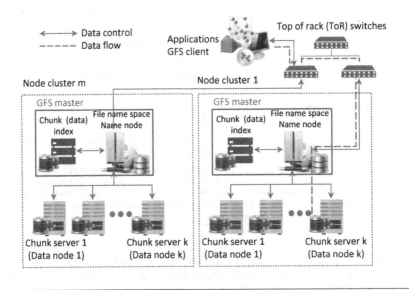

FIG. 12

GFS or HDFS architecture.

The master server maintains six types of the GFS metadata, which are: (1) namespace; (2) access control information; (3) mapping from files to chunks (data); (4) current locations of chunks or data; (5) system activities (eg, chunk lease management, garbage collection of orphaned chunks, and chunk migration between chunk servers); (6) master communication of each chunk server in heartbeat messages.

GFS was designed with five basic assumptions, [63] according to its particular application requirements:

1. GFS will anticipate any commodity hardware outages caused by both software and hardware faults. This means that an individual node may be unreliable. This assumption is similar to one of its system design principles
2. GFS accepts a modest number of large files. The quantity of "modest" is few million files. A typical file size is 100MB/per file. The system also accepts smaller files, but it will not optimize them
3. The typical workload size for stream reading would be from hundreds of KBs to 1MB, with small random reads for a few KBs in batch mode
4. GFS has its well defined sematic for multiple clients with minimal synchronization overhead
5. A constant high-file storage network bandwidth is more important than low latency

In contrast to other file systems, such as Andrew File System, Serverless File System, or Swift, GFS does not adopt a standard API POSIX permission model rather than relax its rules to support the usual operations to create, delete, open, close, and write.

According to these workload processing assumptions, GFS is actually a file storage system or framework that has two basic data structure: logs (metadata) and sorted string table (SSTable). The main object of having GFS is to implement Google's data-intensive applications; initially, it was designed to handle the issues of web crawler and a file indexing system under the pressure of accelerating data growing.

The aim for Google publishing these influential papers [63] was to show how to scale-out the file storage system for large distributed data-intensive applications. Doug Cutting and Mike Cafarella leveraged the Google's GFS idea to develop their file system, Nutch or Nutch Distribute File System (NDFS) for web crawling application, namely Apache Lucene. NDFS was the predecessor of HDFS (see Figs. 13 and 15). Although HDFS is based on a GFS concept and has many similar properties and assumptions as GFS, it is different from GFS in many ways, especially in term of scalability, data mutability, communication protocol, replication strategy, and security.

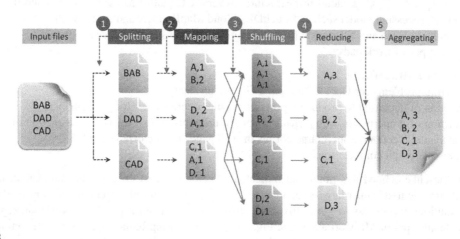

FIG. 13

Five steps MapReduce programming model. Step 1: Splitting, Step 2: Mapping (distribution), Step 3: Shuffling and sorting, Step 4: Reducing (parallelizing), and Step 5: Aggregating.

1.7.2 MAPREDUCE

MapReduce is a programming model used to process large dataset workloads. In contrast to imperative programming (describing computation as a bunch of statements to change program state), MapReduce treats computation as the evaluation of mathematic functions. In essence, functional programming can avoid state and just list in-and-out states.

The basic strategy of MapReduce is to divide and conquer. In order to perform different data-intensive applications effectively with MapReduce on the GFS framework, Dean and Ghemawat [62] presented a five-step process or programming model, as shown in Fig. 13.

Lin et al. [64] simplified this process down to three steps: mapping, shuffling, and reducing. As shown in Fig. 13, the first step involves splitting the input file into three files. The second step is to generate a process of a key/value pair by a user (or client) who specifies the function. In the above example, it is to count the number of different letters (A, B, C, and D) with a corresponding quantity within each split file. The first split file contains the letters "BAB." The letter "A" is counted as 1 and letter "B" is counted as 2. In the third step, the shuffling function is to generate an intermediate key/value pair, which is to sort the same letter (or key) and quantity (or value) from different split files into one file. The fourth step is to merge all intermediate values (3, 2, 1, and 2) associated with the same intermediate key (A, B, C, and D). The final step aggregates these key/value pairs into one output file. Here, "key" is equal to the different types of letters to be counted and "value" is equal to the quantity of each letter.

From a programming perspective, MapReduce has two other meanings; "mapping" is splitting for distribution and "reducing" is shuffling and sorting in parallel. A major advantage of MapReduce is its capability of shared-nothing data processing, which means all mappers can process its data independently.

The characteristic of shared-nothing data processing enables MapReduce to run a simple program across thousands or even millions of unreliable and homogeneous machines in parallel and to complete a task in very short time. Theoretically speaking, it allows any programmer to access an almost unlimited commodity type of computing resources instantly (theoretically) or within an acceptable time frame (practically), eg, cloud infrastructure. Several CC platforms have implemented their own MapReduce processing model such as CouchDB, Cloud MapReduce, and Aneka [57].

According to Dean and Ghemawat [62], the original Google's MapReduce is potentially capable to handle five types of workloads:

1. Large-scale ML problems
2. Clustering problems for Google News and Google products
3. Extraction of data used to produce reports of popular queries (eg, Google Zeitgeist)
4. Extraction of properties of web pages for new experiments and products (eg, extraction of geographical locations from a large corpus of web pages for localized search)
5. Large-scale graph computations

Eric Bieschke echoed this point and indicated, "Hadoop is cost efficient, but more than that, it makes it possible to do super large-scale machine learning" [65]. To this extent, the history of Hadoop is an evolutionary progress to generalize data processing task from a particular workload (eg, web crawler) to all types of ML workloads (see Fig. 14). However, MapReduce is not very efficient in performing an iterative and recursive process that is widely utilized for a simulation type of workload in ML. In order to understand the issue, it is necessary to see how the Hadoop project has been evolved.

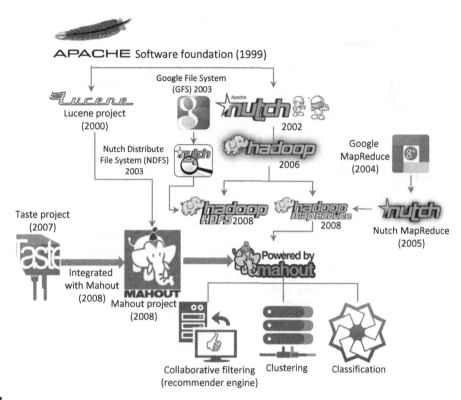

FIG. 14

Evolution of GFS, HDFS MapReduce, and Hadoop.

1.7.3 THE ORIGIN OF THE HADOOP PROJECT

Lucene

According to Hatcher and Gospodnetic [59], Lucene is a high-performance scalable information retrieval (IR) library. It lets developers add indexing and searching capabilities to their applications. Lucene was a mature, free, open source project implemented in Java. It is a member of the popular Apache Jakarta family of projects, licensed under the liberal Apache Software License (see Fig. 15). Lucene was written by Doug Cutting in 2000 in Java. In Sep. 2001, Lucene was absorbed by ASF.

However, Lucene is not an application or search engine rather it is a toolbox or searching tool kit that enables many applications to borrow or use it. It serves as a classification index. It converts any data to a textual format and enables them to be searchable. Its powerful searching capability is beneficial to many third parties. At the heart of Lucene IR library is its searching and indexing capability. In order to utilize Lucene's searching and indexing functions, another open source software, Nutch, is required, which was also built by Doug Cutting in 2002 (see Fig. 14).

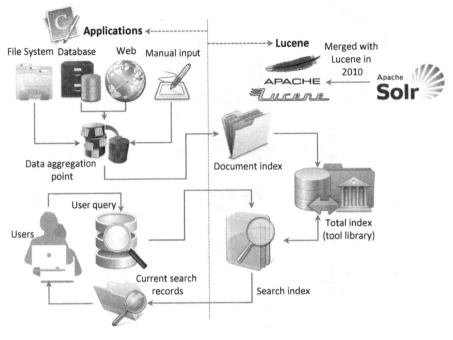

FIG. 15

Connection between Apache Lucene and other applications.

Nutch

Nutch is the predecessor of Hadoop, which is an open source and executable search engine file system. There are two main reasons to develop Nutch:

- Create a Lucene index (web crawler)
- Assist developers to make queries of their index

There are a lot of codes in Nutch program (such as HTTP fetcher and URL database). Michael J. Cafarella indicated that the text searching was the centerpiece of any search engine or web crawler, which was included in Nutch.

Based on Laliwala and Shaikh [66], another Apache project called Solr was developing with similar searching function to Nutch. It was also an open source enterprise platform for full text search, which was initiated by CNET in 2004. It became an Apache project in 2007. Since then, Solr has absorbed many tools in Apache Lucene's library to enhance and extend its full text search capability. Like Apache Lucene, Solr was not an executable search engine rather than a toolkit or IR library [67]. Therefore, Solr and Lucene had been merged into a single development project since 2010 [68]. As shown in Fig. 15, although both Lucene and Solr had adopted many different techniques for index searching, text mining, and IR algorithms, they can be generalized as classification algorithms.

In general, BDA applications need different algorithms or techniques, such as clustering, collaborative filtering (or recommender engine), and others. These requirements lead to the beginning of Mahout Project in 2008 as a subproject of Apache Lucene. Since all the algorithms of both

Lucene and Mahout are closely related to machine learning, In Apr. 2010, Mahout has risen as a top-level project in its own right.

Mahout

The original object of Mahout was to build a Java-based ML library that covers all ML algorithms or techniques in theory, but it can mainly handle three types of ML algorithms in practice:

- Collaborative filtering (recommender engines)
- Clustering
- Classification

If other learning algorithms are required, we have to check the Apache Mahout URL [69] and find out whether MapReduce can support a particular algorithm or not before this algorithm can be applied in a large scalable environment. In other words, Mahout is not a universal ML library. In addition of scalable issue, Hadoop is very slow for ML workloads. It led to the development of complimentary ecosystems, such as Hama, Storm, Spark, and Flink that addressed weakness of MapReduce-based systems.

1.7.4 SPARK AND SPARK STACK

Spark was developed by the UC Berkeley RAD Lab (now called as AMP Lab). The main contributor is Matei Zaharia et al. [70,71]. Its original objective was to extend Hadoop to a general-purpose framework that adopts resilient distributed datasets (RDDs) in memory computation (micro batch) technique. In a simple terms, it intends to replace a MapReduce model with a better solution. It emphasizes the computational efficiency of iterative and recursive algorithms and interactive queries of data mining. It claimed that it would be 10–20 times faster than MapReduce for certain type of workload, such as performing iterative algorithm.

Although it attempts to replace MapReduce, it did not abandon HDFS; instead, it leverages Hadoop's file storage system. Like many other Hadoop related projects, it is an open source project under ASF. In June 2013, it was moved to ASF as an incubator. Since 2014, it has become an Apache top-level project and supported by many Big Data vendors, such as Cloudera, Horton, SAP, and MapR, as noted in Fig. 16.

Generally, Spark is a fast- and general-purpose computation platform based on large clusters. In contrast to MapReduce that is basically designed for a web crawler, indexing system, and limited ML, Spark includes SQL, interactive query, data stream, graph, and ML analytic functions in its computation platform.

Based on the Berkeley data analytics stack architecture, Spark developed as a unified stack integrating all libraries and higher level components together (see Fig. 17). Spark consists of seven major elements: Spark core of data engine, Spark cluster manager (includes Hadoop, Apache Mesos, and built-in Standalone cluster manger), Spark SQL, Spark streaming, Spark Machine Learning Library, Spark GraphX, and Spark programming tools.

1.7.5 FLINK AND OTHER DATA PROCESS ENGINES

Apart from Spark, there are several data processing engines such as Microsoft Dryad, Storm, Tez, Flink, and CIEL (see Fig. 18) that are capable of supporting MapReduce-like processing requirements. They aim to support more computational functions, such as standard queries, stream analysis, machine learning, graphic analysis, and interactive or ad hoc queries efficiently. The effort made by these platforms is to generalize Hadoop to be able to support a wide variety of BDA workloads.

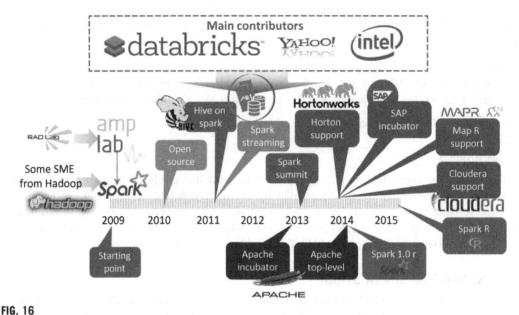

FIG. 16

Spark history.

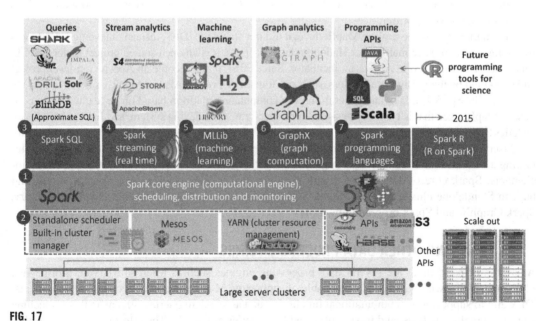

FIG. 17

SPARK analytic stack.

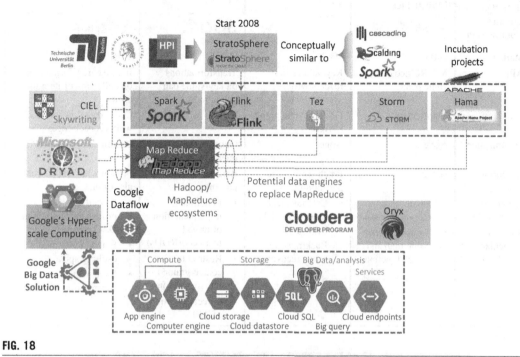

FIG. 18

Potential data processing engines to replace MapReduce.

Ewen et al. [72], Tzoumas [73], and Balassi and Fora [74] argued that Flink is the next generation or the 4th generation data processing engine in comparison with others (see Table 5 and Fig. 19), although each data processing engine has its own special feature. Flink data engine is truly a general-purpose framework for BDA. They claim that Flink is capable of outperforming Spark by 2.5 times.

A possible reason for Ewen et al. to claim that Flink is better than Spark is that it is based on Lambda architecture and able to process arbitrary Big Data workloads in real time. The basic concept of Lambda architecture is to build the data processing engine or system with the number of layers in order to deal with a subset of data with stream properties. These layers are only a few thousand line of code to implement a total of seven steps (two for the batch layer, two for the serving layer, and three for speed layers; see Figs. 20 and 21).

The purpose for establishing these three layers, according to Nathan Marz [75], is to meet the characteristic requirements of all types of Big Data workloads. They are:

- Robustness and fault tolerance
- Low-latency reads and updates
- Scalability
- Generalization
- Extensibility
- Ad hoc queries
- Minimal maintenance
- Debuggability

Table 5 Data Processing Engine Comparison

Data Process Engines Comparison	MapReduce	Tez	Spark	Flink
Start at	2004	2007	2009	2010
API	MapReduce on key/value pairs	Key/value pair readers/writers	Transformations on key/value pair collections	Iterative transformations on collection or iteration aware
Paradigm	MapReduce	Direct acyclic graph (DAG)	RDD	Cyclic data flows or dataflow with feedback edges
Optimization	None	None	Optimization of SQL queries	Optimization in all APIs
Execution	Batch	Batch sorting and partitioning	Batch with memory pinning	Stream with "out-of-core" algorithms
Enhanced features plus Specialize particular workloads	• Small recoverable tasks • Sequential code inside map and reduce functions	• Extends map/reduces model to DAG model • Backtracking-based recovery	• Functional implementation of Dryad recovery (RDDs) • Restrict to coarse-grained transformations • Direct execution of API	• Embed query processing runtime in DAG engine • Extend DAG model to cyclic graphs • Incremental construction of graphs

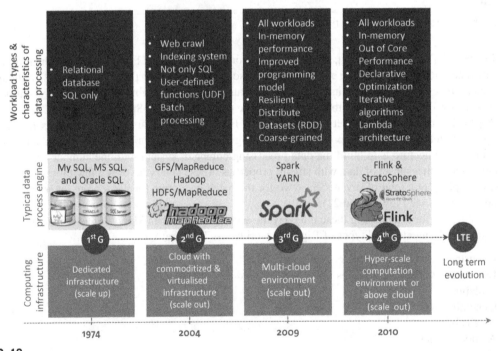

FIG. 19

Evolution of data and big data process engines.

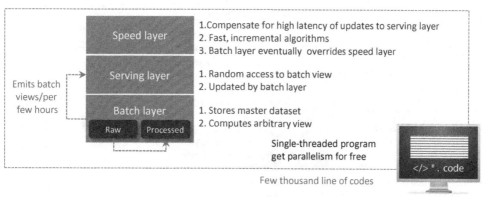

FIG. 20

The process steps of Lambda architecture.

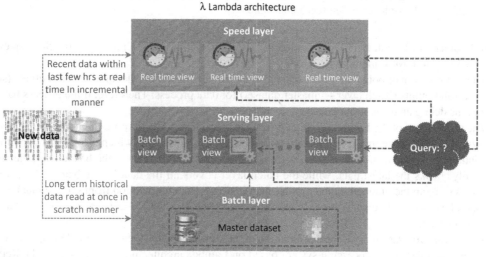

FIG. 21

The elements of Lambda architecture.

Fig. 22 shows that the batch layer as a part of Hadoop can easily meet robustness and fault tolerance requirements. Scalability is the requirement for both batch and serving layers so that both Hadoop and Elephant DB can handle it. Extensibility means the data stream adds a new function to the master dataset. The batch layer allows users to recompute another entire batch view from scratch. To some extent, this also means that a batch layer can perform ad hoc queries because the master dataset in one location. Due to the robustness nature of Hadoop minimal maintenance is acceptable. The reason for robustness is because a serving layer database only gets a batch view per few hours, which emits from the batch

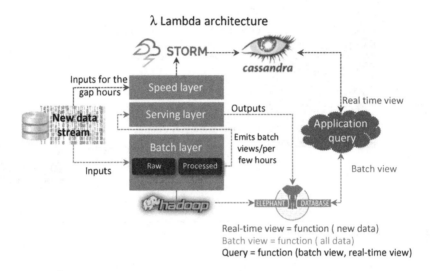

FIG. 22

An example of implementation of Lambda architecture.

layer. In other words, it doesn't write randomly very often and has so few moving parts. Subsequently, it is less likely to have something go wrong.

The combination of both batch and serving layers can record all intermediate steps of outputs (serving layer) and inputs (batch layer — master dataset) for data process. Therefore, if the process has any hiccup, the debug analysis is quite easier.

The top element of the Lambda architecture is the speed layer. The purpose of having speed layer is to perform an arbitrary computing function on arbitrary data in real time, which is to fill the gap time of new data for both batch and serving layers that have been left. In contrast to the batch layer, the speed layer only checks the latest data, while the batch layer covers all the data in one batch. Moreover, it only does so in an incremental manner rather than in doing a re-computation from scratch manner that the batch layer does. The speed layer capability meets the Big Data requirements for low-latency reads and updates.

The overall Big Data query is the combination of real-time and batch views, as noted in Fig. 22, which shows an example query processing system based on Lambda architecture. In contrast to MapReduce (batch only), the Lambda architecture can meet all requirements of Big Data query, whether it is in batch or real time.

In addition to Flink and Spark, more than 40 processing engines are available, which are capable of processing different types of BDA workloads (see Table 6).

1.7.6 SUMMARY OF HADOOP AND ITS ECOSYSTEMS

Hadoop has become the standard framework to run distributed BDA that can process massive scale of data on large clusters based on the commodity hardware or a cloud infrastructure. Along with its evolutionary journey, it has absorbed and integrated some Apache projects that have similar functionalities, such as Taste, Solr, and Mahout. Due to the demand for processing all types of BDA workloads, many

Table 6 40 Alternative Platforms for Big Data Processing

Bashreduce	Gearman	Mincemeat	R3
Ceph	GoCircuit	Mincemeat	Riak
Cloud MapReduce	GPMR	Misco	SAMOA
Cloud-crowd	HaLoop	MongoDB	Skynet
Condor	HPCC	Octopy	Spark
Data core	HTTPMR	Oryx	Sphere
DISCO	Aneka MapReduce	Plasma MapReduce	Storm
Elastic phoenix	MapRedus	Peregrine	Tachyon
Filemap	MapRejuice	QFS	TEZ
Flink (stratosphere)	MARS	Qizmt	Weka

of Hadoop's ecosystems have been developed, such as Spark, Storm, Hama, Tachyon, TEZ, S4, and Flink. These ecosystems intend to overcome MapReduce's shortcomings and specialize in a particular type of BDA workload. Consequently, some platforms have been generalized to handle all types of BDA workloads.

Hadoop key functions

When Douglas Cutting and Michael J. Cafarella created it in early 2006, their original idea was to build Apache Nutch (or a web crawler engine) on a cheaper infrastructure. It consists of five key functional components (see Fig. 5):

1. ETL tools for data integration
2. Functional element or programming model: MapReduce
3. Core units: distributed framework or storage system
4. Processing modules or libraries: machine learning
5. Administration models

In comparison to many other conventional databases, Hadoop is not a database but a distributed storage and computational framework. It is a free and open source ecosystem. It has six characteristics:

1. Scale-out with distributed computing
2. Expect failures with redundancies
3. Focus on smart software rather than dumb hardware
4. Share-nothing architecture
5. Move processors not data (taking computer to data, rather than other way around)
6. Build applications, not infrastructure

Hadoop's distinguishing features

One of Hadoop's unique features is that it is supported by so many auxiliary tools, especially administration tools such as monitoring, management, and maintenance (see Fig. 9). It also has many APIs to interface with other BDA applications. Many ASF incubation projects (such as Spark and Flink) can replace MapReduce, but it would be too costly to substitute the entire Hadoop framework.

1.8 ML + CC → BDA AND GUIDELINES

We discussed the role of ML, CC, and Hadoop-like systems. We see that ML and CC are the two most important components of BDA. If there are no advances in ML and CC, BDA could not be implemented or operated cost effectively. Of course, BDA needs a good understanding of application

Table 7 Guidelines for BDA

3 Aspects	9Vs	Fit for BDA	Not Fit for BDA
Data	Volume	• Datasets do not fit into one node (eg, PB–EB size datasets) • Bringing computing to the data	• Dataset can be fit into one node • Bringing data to the computing node
	Variety	• Not only SQL • Collection and discovery of datasets from different data sources (eg, M2M, WSN, RFID, SCADA, SQL, and NoSQL) • Schema[a] on read	• One type workload (RDBMS or SQL) • Single data source • Schema on write
	Velocity	• Data agility • Interactive and dynamic data stream	• Traditional stable environment • Static dataset
Statistics	Veracity	• Datasets are not clean • Models construction need many "What-ifs" for fidelity issues • Rely on archived data for reliability and credibility	• Dataset is relatively clean • Model construction is relatively simple • Require live data
	Variability	• Heterogeneous dataset • Dynamic or flexible schemas • Numerous variables of dataset (eg, > 50 variables)	• Homogeneous dataset • Fixed schema • Few variables of dataset
	Validity	• Require independent and transparent criteria to verify the result of BDA (eg, GFT)	• Simple and straightforward approach to verify the result of data mining
Business Intelligence	Value	• Solving strategic problems that have long-term consequences (eg, competitive advantages, integrity, excellence, sustainability, success, and cost leadership) • Leveraging business values from all data sources	• Routine issues for a short term • Exploring business value from single source
	Verdict	• Ask for an answer	• Ask for the answer
	Visibility	• Search for strategic insight	• Search for temporary solutions
Other Aspects		• Large-scale computing needing high fault tolerance • Scale-out • High percentage of parallel and distributed processing workload	• Fault tolerance may not be essential • Scale-up • Percentage of serial processing workloads is higher

[a] *"Schema-on-Read" means a table or a set of statements is not predefined. Sometime it is also named as "Schemaless" or "Schema free." In contrast, "Schema-on-Write" means that a table is predetermined. Sometime, it is also called as "fixed schema" [76–78].*

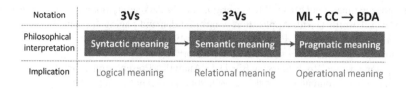

Notation	**3Vs**	**3²Vs**	**ML + CC → BDA**
Philosophical interpretation	Syntactic meaning →	Semantic meaning →	Pragmatic meaning
Implication	Logical meaning	Relational meaning	Operational meaning

FIG. 23

Comprehensive meaning of big data.

domain. Effective BDA needs an appropriate choice of ML techniques and the use of CC to handle Big Data sets for both training and extracting new meaningful data patterns. CC can provide an affordable solution for many individuals and small- to medium-scale enterprises. Therefore, we assert that ML + CC → BDA. Hadoop's history and its ecosystems with machine learning applications have demonstrated this concept adequately.

Finally, BDA is not an ideal solution for every analytics problem. For some cases, it may only add the burden to the business. Table 7 provides guidelines to decide which cases could be applied for BDA solutions and which ones would not benefit from BDA. These guidelines help in determining the case for BDA.

1.9 CONCLUSION

We have discussed many major events and debates in Big Data and introduced the original concept of Big Data and its 3Vs attributes. We proposed an extension to this view of Big Data from 3Vs to 3²Vs (9 Vs) to capture the full meaning of BDA to include additional attributes of BI and statistics aspects (see Fig. 23). We provided an overview of many popular platforms for BDA such as Hadoop, Spark, and Flink that are affordable to small- and medium-scale enterprises. We have developed the notion that ML + CC → BDA; that is, the execution of ML tasks on large data sets in CC environments that is often called BDA.

REFERENCES

[1] Smith TP. How big is big and how small is small, the size of everything and why. USA: Oxford University Press; 2013 p. 14–29.
[2] http://www.cisco.com/c/en/us/solutions/collateral/service-provider/visual-networking-index-vni/VNI_Hyperconnectivity_WP.html.
[3] Gil Press, "A Very Short History Of Big Data," Forbes Tech Magazine, May 9, 2013. URL: http://www.forbes.com/sites/gilpress/2013/05/09/a-very-short-history of-big-data/.
[4] Rider F. The scholar and the future of the research library. A problem and its solution. New York: Hadham Press; 1944.
[5] Ohlhorst F. Big data analytics, turning big data into big money. Canada: John Wiley & Sons, Inc ; 2013 p. 2. p. 171.
[6] http://www.winshuttle.com/big-data-timeline/.
[7] http://au.linkedin.com/pulse/brief-history-big-data-everyone-should-read-bernard-marr.
[8] Diebold FX. A Personal Perspective on the Origin(s) and Development of 'Big Data': The Phenomenon, the Term, and the Discipline, Second Version, SSRN, PIER working paper No 13–003, http://dx.doi.org/10.2139/ssrn.2202843.

[9] http://bits.blogs.nytimes.com/2013/02/01/the-origins-of-big-data-an-etymological-detective-story/?_r=0.

[10] Cox Michael, Ellsworth David. Application-controlled demand paging for out-of-core visualization. In: Proceedings of Visualization '97, Phoenix AZ, October 1997; 1997. p. 1–12.

[11] http://visualizing.org/visualizations/big-data-brief-history.

[12] IEEE Computer Society, Rock Stars of Big Data Analytics Presentations, October 21, 2014, San Jose, California. http://www.computer.org/web/rock-stars/big-data-analytics/presentations.

[13] National Research Council of the National Academies, Frontiers in Massive Data Analysis, the National Academy of Sciences, 2013.

[14] Manyika J, et al. Big data: the next frontier for innovation, competition, and productivity. USA: McKinsey Global Institute; 2011 p. 1–13.

[15] Kitchin R. Big data, new epistemologies and paradigm shifts, big data & society. UK: SAGE; 2014. p. 1–12.

[16] Schonberger VM, Cukier K. Big data, a revolution that will transform how we live, work and think. USA: Houghton Mifflin Harcourt Publishing Company; 2013. p. 10

[17] de Montjoy Y-A, et al. Unique in the shopping mall: on the re-identifiability of credit card metadata. Am Assoc Adv Sci Sci 2015;347(6221):536–9.

[18] Redman TC. Data doesn't speak for itself. Harvard business review; 2014 April. 29.

[19] Gomes L. Machine-learning maestro Michael Jordan on the delusions of big data and other huge engineering efforts. IEEE Spectr 2014. Oct 20. http://spectrum.ieee.org/robotics/artificial-intelligence/machinelearning-maestro-michael-jordan-on-the-delusions-of-big-data-and-other-huge-engineering-efforts.

[20] Dobelli R. The art of thinking clearly. UK: Sceptre books; 2013. p. 55.

[21] Drenik G. "Big Data and the Madness of Crowds," Forbes Tech Magazine, USA, Jun 17, 2014. http://www.forbes.com/sites/prospernow/2014/06/17/big-data-and-the-madness-of-crowds/.

[22] Mackay C. Extraordinary popular delusions and the madness of crowds. UK: Harriman House Ltd; 2003.

[23] Pearce R. "Big data is BS: Obama campaign CTO," CIO Magazine, May 28, 2013. http://www.cio.com.au/article/462961/big_data_bs_obama_campaign_cto/.

[24] Boyd D, et al. Critical questions for big data. Inf Commun Soc 2012;15(5):662–79.

[25] Anderson C. "The End of Theory: The Data Deluge Makes the Scientific Method Obsolete," Wired Magazine, June 23, 2008. http://www.wired.com/2008/06/pb-theory/.

[26] Loizides A. Mill's system of logic critical appraisals. UK: Routledge; 2014. p. 11, 192–213.

[27] Lazer D, Kennedy R, King G, Vespignani A. The parable of Google flu: traps in big data analysis. Science 2014;343(6176):1203–5.

[28] Tweed TA. Crossing and dwelling: a theory of religion. USA: Harvard University Press; 2008.

[29] Copi IM, Cohen C, McMahon K. Introduction to logic. 14th ed. USA: Pearson Education; 2014. p. 83–90.

[30] Laney D. 3D data management: controlling data volume, velocity and variety. USA: Application Delivery Strategies, Meta Group; 2001. p. 1–4.

[31] http://www-01.ibm.com/software/data/bigdata/.

[32] http://www.ibmbigdatahub.com/infographic/four-vs-big-data.

[33] Zikopoulos PC, et al. Harness the power of big data, the IBM Big data platform. US: McGraw-Hill; 2013. p. 9

[34] www.microsoft.com/bigdata.

[35] Demchenko Y. Defining architecture components of the big data ecosystem. In: IEEE Collaboration Technologies and System (CTS); 2014. p. 104–12.14501649, ieeexplore.ieee.org/xpl/login.jsp?tp=&arnumber=6867550&url=http%3A%2F%2Fieeexplore.ieee.org%2Fxpls%2Fabs_all.jsp%3Farnumber%3D6867550, US.

[36] http://timoelliott.com/blog/2013/07/7-definitions-of-big-data-you-should-know-about.html.

[37] http://books.google.com.au/books/about/Data_Warehouse.html?id=hdRQAAAAMAAJ.

[38] http://hortonworks.com/blog/implementing-the-blueprint-for-enterprise-hadoop/.

[39] https://451research.com/biography?eid=333.

[40] http://thehumanfaceofbigdata.com/.

[41] http://www.opentracker.net/article/definitions-big-data.

[42] http://www.qualtrics.com/blog/the-1936-election-a-polling-catastrophe/.

[43] Ratner B. Statistical modelling and analysis for database marketing effective techniques for mining big data. USA: CRC Press; 2003.

[44] Samuel A. Some studies in machine learning using the game of checkers. IBM J Res Dev 1959; 3(3): 211–29.

[45] Surowiecki J. The wisdom of crowds, why the many are smarter than the few and how collective wisdom shapes business, economies, societies and nations. USA: Anchor Books; 2004. p. 66–83.

[46] Abu-Mostafa YS, et al. Learning from data, a short course. AMLBook.com. 2012.

[47] Larose D, Larose C. Discovering knowledge in data: an introduction to data mining. USA: John Wiley & Sons; 2014.

[48] Han J, Kamber M, Pei J. Data mining concepts and techniques. 3rd ed. USA: Elsevier Inc; 2012. p. 23.

[49] Witten IH, Frank E. Data mining practical machine learning tools and techniques. 3rd ed. USA: Elsevier Inc; 2011.

[50] Mitchell TM. Machine learning. USA: McGraw-Hill Science; 1997. p. 2.

[51] Murphy KP. Machine learning, a probabilistic perspective. USA: The MIT Press; 2012.

[52] Bishop CM. Pattern recognition and machine learning. USA: Springer; 2006.

[53] Nisan N, Schocken S. The element of computing systems building a modern computer from first principles. USA: MIT press; 2005. p. 57–8.

[54] Liu X, et al. Computational trust models and machine learning. USA: CRC Press; 2015.

[55] Harrington P. Machine learning in action. USA: Manning Publications; 2012.

[56] Wadkar S, Siddalingaiah M. Pro Apache Hadoop. 2nd ed. USA: Apress; 2014.

[57] Buyya R, Vecchiola C, Selvi T. Mastering cloud computing. USA: Morgan Kaufmann; 2013.

[58] Wu C, Buyya R. Cloud data centers and cost modeling. USA: Morgan Kaufmann; 2015.

[59] Hatcher E, Gospodnetic O. Lucene in action, a guide to the java search engine. USA: Manning Publication Co; 2005.

[60] Zburivsky D. Hadoop cluster deployment. UK: Packt Publishing; 2013.

[61] Srinivasa KG, Muppalla AK. Guide to high performance distributed computing: case studies with hadoop, scalding and spark. Germany: Springer; 2015.

[62] Dean J, Ghemawat S. MapReduce: simplified data processing on large clusters. Commun ACM 2008;107–13.

[63] Ghemawat S., Gobioff H., and Leung S-T. "The Google File System," SOSP'03, October 19–22, 2003, p. 1–15.

[64] Lin J, Dyer C. Data-intensive text processing with map reduce. USA: Morgan & Claypool; 2010.

[65] Mone G. Beyond hadoop, the leading open source system for processing big data continues to evolve, but new approaches with added features are on the rise. Commun ACM 2013.

[66] Laliwala Z, Shaikh A. Web crawling and data mining with Apache Nutch. UK: Packt Publishing; 2013.

[67] Grainger T, Potter T. Solr in action, forward by Yonik Seeley. USA: Manning Publications Co; 2014.

[68] Serafini A. Apache Solr beginner's guide, configure your own search engine experience with real-world data with this practical guide to Apache Solr. UK: Packt Publishing; 2013.

[69] http://mahout.apache.org/.

[70] Zaharia M, et al. Resilient distributed datasets: a fault-tolerant abstraction for in-memory cluster computing. In: Proceedings of the 9th USENIX Symposium on Networked Systems Design and Implementation, April 25–27; 2012.

[71] Karau H, Konwinski A, Wendell P, Zaharia M. Learning spark. USA: O'Reilly Media Inc; 2015.

[72] Ewen S, Schelter S, Tzoumas K, Warneke D, Markl V. Iterative parallel processing with stratosphere an inside look. In: Proceedings of the 2013 ACM SIGMOD International Conference on Management of Data, SIGMOD 13; 2013. p. 1053–6.

[73] Tzoumas K. Apache Flink Next Generation Analysis, http://www.slideshare.net/FlinkForward/k-tzoumas-s-ewen-flink-forward-keynote.

[74] Balassi M, Fora G. The Flink Big Data Analytics Platform, https://apacheconeu2014.sched.org/overview/type/big+data#.Vj_-9r8nK1I.

[75] Marz N. Big data principles and best practices of scalable real-time data systems. UK: Manning Publications Co; 2015.

[76] Date CJ. SQL and relational theory how to write accurate SQL code. 3rd ed. US: O'Reilly Media, Inc; 2015. p. 523.

[77] Sullivan D. NoSQL for mere mortals. US: Pearson Education Inc; 2015.

[78] Celko J. Joe Celko's complete guide to NoSQL, what every SQL professional need to know about nonrelational databases. US: Elsevier Inc; 2014.

REAL-TIME ANALYTICS

2

Z. Milosevic, W. Chen, A. Berry, F.A. Rabhi

2.1 INTRODUCTION

This chapter focuses on real-time analytics and in particular, relevant analytics approaches, ie, *the velocity aspects of Big Data*. Real-time analytics is increasingly gaining prominence in business and social applications as a result of the need to deal with the proliferation of data and the need to act instantly in response to data triggers. A recent *Harvard Business Review* article refers to such data as "Fast Data" and states that "… large enterprises have spent heavily on managing large volumes and disparate varieties of data for analytical purposes, but they have devoted far less to managing high velocity data" [1]. This is in spite of the fact that data volumes are expected to double every 2 years, with the greatest growth coming from the vast amounts of new data being produced by intelligent devices and the Internet of Things. "That's a problem, because high velocity data provides the basis for real-time interaction and often serves as an early-warning system for potential problems and systemic malfunctions" [1].

It should be noted that many of the requirements, principles, characteristics, and solutions associated with real-time analytics have a foundation in the distributed computing infrastructure, event processing, and machine learning, as well as in real-time applications from the pre-Internet era. The key differences are in the growing audience for data insights, increasing use of cloud computing and commodity infrastructure, and the proliferation of new data sources, such as social media and mobile devices. This is in contrast to the early distributed systems applications, which were developed using high-end proprietary computing infrastructures and intended for limited audience, eg, subject matter experts, engineers, and other professionals in specific industry sectors. Further, data is increasingly arriving continuously in so-called data streams or event streams. This introduces computational and resource challenges in processing such data in a real-time fashion, and in particular when looking for new insights through applying various statistical techniques.

This chapter describes the new real-time infrastructure, tools, and analytics techniques while also positioning them in relation to current stored-data analytics and the event-driven architectures and complex event processing (CEP) technologies of the last decade.

The chapter is structured as follows. The next section introduces a hierarchy of abstractions for Big Data and analytics, which we refer to as the *analytics stack* for Big Data (see Fig. 1). This stack was developed to position real-time analytics and facilitate discussion on various analytics concepts, technologies, and principles described in this chapter; later sections of this chapter are structured according to the stack.

Big Data. http://dx.doi.org/10.1016/B978-0-12-805394-2.00002-7

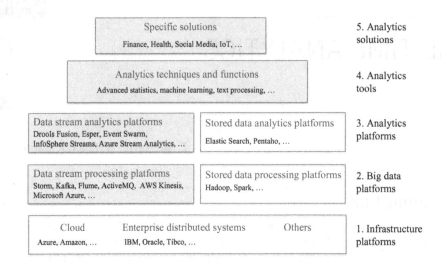

FIG. 1

Real-time analytics stack.

The subsequent section highlights key characteristics of real-time systems considered from the standpoint of Big Data, while outlining their roots in early distributed system developments and related industrial applications. This section sets a scene for the solutions and challenges to be discussed in the remaining sections. Following that, the chapter describes key concepts and platforms used when designing and implementing real-time systems and analytics solutions, with a particular focus on the event-driven technologies. This is followed by the description of real-time data processing platforms for Big Data environments (or "fast data" systems), which we refer to as *data stream processing platforms*, including a number of open source platforms and proprietary solutions. The subsequent section describes analytics solutions that can apply analytics techniques to the real-time data streams, and we refer to these as *data stream analytics platforms*. The key *analytics techniques and functions* support development of specific analytics solutions on top of these platforms, and these are described in the following section.

Finally, we describe an example application in the finance domain that is built upon one of the analytics platforms and associated techniques and tools. The chapter concludes with a list of interesting research topics we have identified based on our industrial and academic experience.

2.2 COMPUTING ABSTRACTIONS FOR REAL-TIME ANALYTICS

This section introduces a hierarchy of abstractions for building analytics solutions, including real-time analytics solutions. These abstractions were developed to facilitate the description of different capabilities and features of analytics solutions, as well as to position real-time analytics in the broader spectrum of analytics platforms and solutions. We refer to these layers informally as the *analytics stack*. Fig. 1 depicts these abstractions.

Note that the real-time analytics topics in the stack are distinguished in the figure as grayed boxes. The other topics are included for completeness and positioning, but are not discussed in any more detail beyond this section.

The bottom layer reflects infrastructure platforms needed to provide computing resources over which analytics systems are built. These include traditional enterprise distributed system components provided by vendors such as IBM, Oracle, and Tibco, cloud PaaS offerings of these companies, as well as other companies such as Amazon and Microsoft Azure. There are also other infrastructure platforms for building real-time systems, such as for industrial applications in utility, mining, and transportation industries.

The second layer identifies Big Data platforms developed for processing huge amounts of data, including both data at rest and data in motion (ie, "fast data"). These are software platforms that are built using the underlying resources provided by infrastructure platforms. We distinguish the *stored data processing platforms* such as Hadoop, Spark, distributed file systems, and NoSQL databases [2] from the *data stream processing platforms*, which provide a basis for real-time analytics and will be described in the later sections of this chapter.

One special kind of Big Data processing is in support of analytics applications. A number of analytics platforms were developed in recent times to support such applications. These are software platforms that make use of the components and functions provided by Big Data platforms. As with the Big Data platforms, we distinguish them based on their ability to process "data at rest" versus "data in motion," namely *stored data analytics platforms,* such as ElasticSearch [3] and Pentaho [4], and *data stream analytics platforms*. The data stream analytics platforms are described in more detail later in this chapter.

The next layer is termed *analytics techniques and tools. This layer can be regarded as a library* of methods for developing analytics solutions for specific business problems. Examples include various advanced statistics, machine learning, and text processing algorithms and models. Note that the implementation of these methods is left to the specific requirements of the layer below, ie, whether it is real-time data or stored data layers.

It should be noted that many technologies and solutions can be difficult to position at one layer only. For example, Microsoft Azure and Amazon provide components in most of these layers.

2.3 CHARACTERISTICS OF REAL-TIME SYSTEMS

The term *real-time system* signifies the requirement for IT systems to process events as they occur and within a specified time interval. This time interval is typically in order of milli-, micro-, or even nano-seconds, depending on the system in question. Real-time systems are often said to be the systems in which timeliness is essential to correctness [5]. While this statement is true for safety critical systems, in the context of Big Data analytics, this requirement is somewhat relaxed and *real time* refers to the ability to process data as it arrives, rather than storing the data and retrieving it at some point in the future. In this chapter, the terms *real time* and *real-time analytics* imply this more relaxed requirement, which some refer to as *near real time.*

In either case, this real-time property requires the collection of data associated with various data sources and processing them as they arrive. It often involves generating notifications to humans about significant occurrences in the environment, invoking functions of the system's components to perform some tasks, or sometimes both.

In the pre-Internet era, many real-time IT systems were developed for monitoring and controlling industrial plants. They include real-time operating systems, embedded systems that control operations of a specific component within a larger electrical/mechanical system, and programmable logical controllers that control operations of electromechanical processes, eg, factory assembly lines. They also included large supervisory control and data acquisition systems [6] that typically collect real-time data from an industrial plant, present information to operators, and react to significant events, including generating alerts or performing some automatic control functions in response to events. There have been also many other real-time systems specifically developed for time-sensitive applications in industries such as finance, telecommunication, aviation, transportation, space exploration, and so on.

Many of these early real-time systems have required the development of a foundational distributed computing infrastructure, leveraging the power of the telecommunication network capabilities at the time. The distributed computing systems, although providing many benefits, required solutions to many difficult problems such as true concurrency (vs. interleaved), partial state, unreliable communication media, prolonged and variable transmission delays, possibility of independent partial system failures, and so on. These difficulties in turn led to many innovations in the field of distributed computing, including the development of key distributed systems principles, techniques, and algorithms. Examples include various solutions for dealing with different types of failure models, unreliable communications, synchrony in the presence of unreliable computer clocks, etc. Many of these distributed solutions provide foundations for the understanding of requirements in the new generation of real-time systems of the Internet era and in particular for Big Data and analytics.

Some key requirements are discussed in the following subsections, based on an excellent overview provided in [7].

2.3.1 LOW LATENCY

In general, latency can be defined as the time delay between the cause and the effect of some physical change in the system being observed.

In a real-time system, latency refers to the time between an event occurring in an environment of the system and the start of its processing in the system. This latency typically involves network latency and computer processing latency.

Real-time systems require low latency in order to respond to the events within specified time bounds. A number of strategies can be adopted to support these requirements in analytics. These include:

- In-memory processing — needed to minimize processing delay associated with the use of disks and I/O; this is increasingly viable due to the decreasing cost of memory
- Use of flash technology to store all data that does not need to be in main memory; this approach increase access speed to data
- Incremental evaluation, that is, updating calculations and query results for each new data item without reevaluating the entire data set
- Parallel processing with high bandwidth connection between processors
- Anticipatory fetching and processing, enabling faster access to data from multiple data streams

2.3.2 HIGH AVAILABILITY

Availability means the ability of a system to perform its function when required.

Real-time systems require high availability; otherwise the events arriving from the outside world are not immediately processed and are difficult to store or buffer for subsequent processing, especially with high volume/high velocity data streams.

In order to support this requirement, a number of strategies can be adopted to support enable effective analytics. These include:

- Distribute processing to multiple nodes so that if one machine fails, another can take over
- Replication of data to several servers, so that of one machine fails, the data can still exist on another machine
- Redundant processing of data; that is, having more than one node calculating a result for a data set (which implies both of the above)

2.3.3 HORIZONTAL SCALABILITY

This characteristic refers to the ability to add servers to an existing pool to improve performance or increase capacity. The ability to dynamically add new servers as data volume or processing workload requires is of high importance for real-time systems to ensure that data is processed within specified time intervals.

Horizontal scalability is especially important if one cannot control the rate of data ingress. If a system is consuming a known, fixed-volume feed, then it can be sized to ensure that real-time requirements are met.

Note that horizontal scalability is to be contrasted to vertical scalability, which refers to the ability to add resources to a single server to improve performance and capacity [7].

2.4 REAL-TIME PROCESSING FOR BIG DATA — CONCEPTS AND PLATFORMS

This section provides an outline of concepts and techniques for architecting and designing real-time systems in a Big Data environment, as well as for building analytics applications on top of it. It begins by describing the concept of event, event processing, and streams, which are central concepts to many real-time analytics applications today. These concepts will be used in describing key features of several Big Data processing platforms and analytics approaches.

2.4.1 EVENT

Many recent modeling and implementation approaches for developing real-time applications are centered around the concept of an *event*. An event signifies some occurrence in the system's environment. This naturally reflects the nature of many real-time applications, where event-driven computing can provide a more timely response and better throughput while leveraging availability and scalability properties of the underlying distributed infrastructure. For example, many real-time applications involve (often distributed) sensors that detect and report events, which in turn need to be analyzed in real time to detect patterns that signify some opportunity or threat. Other real-time applications need to monitor events capturing actions of users and detect patterns of interest associated with their activities and subsequently record this information or generate alerts. Some other applications need to distribute the data associated with external events for processing on multiple computers to allow computations to be performed in parallel and thus improve the performance of the applications.

2.4.2 EVENT PROCESSING

Event processing is computing that performs operations on events as they are reported in a system that observes or listens to the events from the environment. Common information processing operations include reading, creating, transforming, and processing events [8].

Event processing has its origins in active database systems [9], distributed event-based systems [10], and simulation work, such as the Stanford Rapide project. Luckham [11] and Bacon et al. [12] pioneered research into event processing in the 1990s. The former mainly focused on simulation and pattern matching, whereas the latter focused on the construction of distributed applications using event-driven approaches.

Many event processing applications are built to react to events from the environment, and the design of such applications follows the principles of event-driven architecture. Note that these applications might not need to deal with temporal properties of events, whether of single events or between multiple events, even if data associated with an event carries a timestamp. In fact, many event-driven applications merely need to perform some computation or action in response to an event. In this case, we are talking about event-based programming or event-driven architectures [8].

2.4.3 EVENT STREAM PROCESSING AND DATA STREAM PROCESSING

Many real-time applications involve a continuous flow of information that is transferred from one location to another over an extended period of time [13]. This type of interaction is called a *stream* and it implies the transfer of a sequence of related information; for example, video and audio data. It is also used frequently to describe a sequence of data associated with real-world events, eg, as emitted by sensors, devices, or other applications, such as a stock ticker.

Processing these kinds of events is thus referred to as *event stream processing* or *data stream processing*. The latter is taken to mean processing over data carried in the stream of events, essentially with the same meaning as event stream processing. Note also that some earlier references, mainly coming from database applications and data stream applications focus on filtering and aggregation of a stream data using SQL queries.

Note that in principle, one can model any discrete data flow (ie, where individual data elements are distinguished in time and space) using events, and that all digital data streams are, in essence, discrete. Note also that event stream processing typically refers to processing of a single stream, which is a simplified form of CEP, as described in the following section.

2.4.4 COMPLEX EVENT PROCESSING

Some more CEP applications need to perform complex computations over multiple events coming from the same or different sources in the environment. This is required when the combination of events and their relationships have some meaning beyond the discrete events alone. These relationships can be of any type, including causal relationships, data relationships, or temporal dependences (ie, before or after relationship). This kind of event processing is often referred to as CEP [14]. In practice, the terms event stream processing and CEP are often used interchangeably [15], and considering that the same is often the case between event stream and data stream processing, we will use these concepts interchangeably, with the same meaning apply to all three concepts.

CEP provides abstractions (event processing logic) for operations on events that are separated from the application logic (event producers and event consumers). This can reduce the cost of development and maintenance. Event processing logic is often expressed in domain specific languages that we refer to as *event processing languages* (EPLs).

Large enterprise vendors (IBM, Tibco, and Oracle in particular) have developed or acquired several enterprise scale CEP systems, eg, InfoSphere Streams [16], Tibco Stream Base [17], and Oracle Stream Explorer [18]. These systems have influenced the development of a number of recent data stream processing and analytics platforms, which will be described in the next two sections.

2.4.5 EVENT TYPE

An event processing system (EPS) thus needs a definition of an *event type*, which describes properties of events occurring in the environment for the purpose of the processing of data associated with events arriving from the environment. Typical attributes of an event type are the timestamp when it has occurred and various data types associated with event payload, such as data format of a message emitted by a physical sensor or data format associated with a messaging system, such as HL7 messages, SWIFT messages, and so on.

2.4.6 EVENT PATTERN

An *event pattern* is one of the key concepts used in many advanced real-time analytics approaches, particularly CEP systems. It captures relationships between events in the real world. There are many examples of event patterns that can signify some opportunity or threat, eg, unusual money deposits by one person in a number of banks, of interest to antimoney laundering applications; unusual pathology orders in eHealth systems, or some causal relationships between rise or falls of trades of one stock on the market, preceded or followed by social media postings about the stock.

As with an event type, an EPS needs a description of an *event pattern type* so that the system can detect the occurrence of event patterns in the environment.

2.5 DATA STREAM PROCESSING PLATFORMS

This section describes the most recent and prominent data stream processing platforms. Many of these are open source solutions. These platforms facilitate the construction of real-time applications, in particular message-oriented or event-driven applications which support ingress of messages or events at a very high rate, transfer to subsequent processing, and generation of alerts. These platforms are mostly focused on supporting event-driven data flow through nodes in a distributed system or within a cloud infrastructure platform. They provide a basis for building an analytics layer on top, such as many abstractions typical to CEP.

The section first provides a brief description of stored data processing platforms to facilitate positioning of several specific data stream processing platforms, which will be described in subsequent sections.

The *Hadoop* ecosystem covers a family of projects that fall under the umbrella of infrastructure for distributed computing and large data processing [19,20]. It is developed to support processing large sets of structured, unstructured, and semi-structured data, but it was designed as a batch processing system. Consequently, it doesn't support fast data analytics performance requirements. In order to support real-time processing, it can be linked with the Storm environment described in the next section.

Hadoop includes a number of components, and below is the list of components of relevance for this chapter [19]:

- MapReduce, a distributed data processing model and execution environment that runs on large clusters of commodity machines
- Hadoop Distributed File System (HDFS), a distributed file system that runs on large clusters of commodity machines
- ZooKeeper, a distributed, highly available coordination service, providing primitives such as distributed locks that can be used for building distributed applications
- Pig, a dataflow language and execution environment for exploring very large datasets. Pigs runs on HDFS and MapReduce clusters
- Hive, a distributed data warehouse

The MapReduce component supports parallel processing of computation through breaking up work into small tasks, all while dealing with task failures and without compromising the job to which they belong. This supports near linear scalability — as the data size increases, it is possible to add more computers and see jobs complete in the same amount of time. Note that a new version of MapReduce, referred to as YARN (Yet Another Resource Negotiator) addresses some of the scalability shortcomings of the "classic" MapReduce [21], but the details of this are beyond the scope of this chapter.

2.5.1 SPARK

Apache *Spark* is more recent framework that combines an engine for distributing programs across clusters of machines with a model for writing programs on top of it. It is aimed at addressing the needs of the data scientist community, in particular in support of Read-Evaluate-Print Loop (REPL) approach for playing with data interactively.

Spark maintains MapReduce's linear scalability and fault tolerance, but extends it in three important ways [22]. First, rather than relying on a rigid map-then-reduce format, its engine can execute a more general directed acyclic graph (DAG) of operators. This means that in situations where MapReduce must write out intermediate results to the distributed file system, Spark can pass directly to the next step in the pipeline. Second, it complements this capability with a rich set of transformations that enable users to express computation more naturally. Third, Spark supports in-memory processing across a cluster of machines, thus not relying on the use of storage for recording intermediate data, as in MapReduce.

Spark supports integration with the variety of tools in the Hadoop ecosystem. It can read and write data in all of the data formats supported by MapReduce. It can read from and write to NoSQL databases like HBase and Cassandra.

Finally, its stream processing library, Spark Streaming, is an extension of the Spark core framework and is well suited for real-time processing and analysis, supporting scalable, high throughput, and fault-tolerant processing of live data streams. Spark Streaming generates a discretized stream (DStream) as a continuous stream of data. Internally, a DStream is represented as a sequence of resilient distributed datasets (RDD), which is Spark's abstraction of an immutable distributed dataset. RDDs are distributed collections that can be operated in parallel by arbitrary functions and by transformations over a sliding window of data (sliding window computations). DStreams can be emitted either straight from input data streams sources, such as Apache Kafka or Flume (see later); HDFS; and databases; or by passing the RDDs from other DStreams output. Regarding input stream, Spark Streaming receives live input data streams through a receiver and divides data into micro batches, which are then processed by the Spark engine to generate the final stream of results in batches. The processing components, similar to Storm bolt (see later), are referred to as window transformation operators. Spark Streaming utilizes a small-interval (in seconds) deterministic batch to dissect stream into processable units. The size of the interval dictates throughput and latency, so the larger the interval, the higher the throughput and the latency. Since Spark core framework exploits main memory (as opposed to Storm, which is using Zookeeper) its mini batch processing can appear as fast as "one at a time processing" adopted in Storm, despite of the fact that the RDD units are larger than Storm tuples. The benefit from the mini batch is to enhance the throughput in internal engine by reducing data shipping overhead, such as lower overhead for the ISO/OSI transport layer header, which will allow the threads to concentrate on computation.

Spark was written in Scala [23], but it comes with libraries and wrappers that allow the use of R or Python.

2.5.2 STORM

Storm is a distributed real-time computation system for processing large volumes of high-velocity data. It makes it easy to reliably process unbounded streams of data and has a relatively simple processing model owing to the use of powerful abstractions:

- A *spout* is a source of streams in a computation. Typically, a spout reads from a queuing broker, such as RabbitMQ, or Kafka, but a spout can also generate its own stream or read from somewhere like the Twitter streaming API. Spout implementations already exist for most queuing systems.
- A *bolt* processes any number of input streams and produces any number of new output streams. They are event-driven components, and cannot be used to read data. This is what spouts are designed for. Most of the logic of a computation goes into bolts, such as functions, filters, streaming joins, streaming aggregations, talking to databases, and so on.
- A *topology* is a DAG of spouts and bolts, with each edge in the DAG representing a bolt subscribing to the output stream of some other spout or bolt. A topology is an arbitrarily complex multistage stream computation; topologies run indefinitely when deployed.

Trident provides a set of high-level abstractions in Storm that were developed to facilitate programming of real-time applications on top of Storm infrastructure. It supports joins, aggregations, grouping, functions, and filters. In addition to these, Trident adds primitives for doing stateful incremental processing on top of any database or persistence store.

2.5.3 KAFKA

Kafka is an open source message broker project developed by the Apache Software Foundation and written in Scala [23]. The project aims to provide a unified, high-throughput, low-latency platform for handling real-time data feeds. A single Kafka broker can handle hundreds of megabytes of reads and writes per second from thousands of clients. In order to support high availability and horizontal scalability, data streams are partitioned and spread over a cluster of machines [23]. Kafka depends on Zookeeper from the Hadoop ecosystem for coordination of processing nodes.

The main uses of Kafka are in situations when applications need a very high throughput for message processing, while meeting low latency, high availability, and high scalability requirements.

2.5.4 FLUME

Flume is a distributed, reliable, and available service for efficiently collecting, aggregating, and moving large amounts of log data. It has a simple and flexible architecture based on streaming data flows [24]. It is robust and fault tolerant with tunable reliability mechanisms and many failover and recovery mechanisms. It uses a simple extensible data model that allows for online analytic application.

While Flume and Kafka both can act as the event backbone for real-time event processing, they have different characteristics. Kafka is well suited for high throughput publish-subscribe messaging applications that require scalability and availability. Flume is better suited in cases when one needs to support data ingestion and simple event processing, but is not suitable for CEP applications. One of the benefits of Flume is that it supports many sources and sinks out of the box.

Note that several real-time applications have combined Flume and Kafka to leverage their individual features, as reported in [25].

2.5.5 AMAZON KINESIS

Amazon Kinesis is a cloud-based service for real-time data processing over large, distributed data streams. Amazon Kinesis can continuously capture and store terabytes of data per hour from hundreds of thousands of sources such as website clickstreams, financial transactions, social media feeds, IT logs, and location-tracking events [26].

Kinesis allows integration with Storm, as it provides a Kinesis Storm Spout that fetches data from a Kinesis stream and emits it as tuples. The inclusion of this Kinesis component into a Storm topology provides a reliable and scalable stream capture, storage, and replay service.

2.6 DATA STREAM ANALYTICS PLATFORMS

The data stream processing platforms introduced above provide a basis for additional functionality needed to support real-time analytics solutions. This additional functionality incorporates a number of key constructs implemented in various EPS. We refer to this software layer as *data stream analytics platforms*.

There are broadly three types EPS: query-based approaches, rule-based approaches, and programmatic approaches. These three types of EPSs are discussed next.

2.6.1 QUERY-BASED EPSs

Query-based EPSs typically support an EPL extended from the relational database language SQL to query event data. The queries expressed in a query-based EPL are often referred to as continuous/continual queries [27]. In contrast to traditional non-persisting queries that work on persistent data, continuous queries are stored persistently in the database and applied to event streams. The processing paradigm in such systems is:

- Define queries in an SQL-like language
- Process queries
- Results of the processing step are only selectively stored in the database

In order to handle unbounded input streams, a common feature among these query-based languages is "the extensive operations on sliding windows" [28]. Sliding windows are used to divide the event stream into segments so that these segments can then be manipulated and analyzed without the system running into unlimited wait time and memory usage. There are different types of sliding windows [29]:

- Time-driven model: The window is reevaluated only at the end of each time step. CQL [30] adopts this model.
- Tuple-driven model: The window is reevaluated every time a new tuple arrives. StreamSQL [31] adopts this model.

Since CQL and StreamSQL adopt different sliding window models, not all queries that can be expressed in CQL can also be expressed in StreamSQL, and vice versa [29]. In any one particular query-based language, it is important to stick to the consistent semantics so that all implementations using this EPL work in a consistent manner and generate expected results.

Query-based EPLs are considered as good at defining patterns of "low-level aggregation views according to event types defined as nested queries" [32]. However, any of these languages have shortcomings when expressing event pattern types. For example, CQL does not have the ability of expressing windows with a variable slide parameter [29]. Additionally, when detecting occurrences of the same event pattern type, different query-based EPLs may generate different results, but the user does not have the power to control which result should be generated [33].

A more recent solution is Azure Stream Analytics from Microsoft, which supports CEP over streaming data in the cloud [34]. CEP processing is realized through an SQL-like language to specify streaming analytics tasks, such as correlation, aggregation, sliding windows and calculations over those windows, comparing current conditions to historical values, and so on [34].

2.6.2 **RULE-ORIENTED EPSs**

Compared with query-based EPSs and general purpose EPSs, rule-oriented EPSs work best on describing higher-level conditional business event pattern types.

Production rules

Production rules techniques originated in the area of expert systems (or knowledge-based systems) in the 1980s. Since then they have been investigated comprehensively and have become very popular; they also have been successfully applied commercially in various domains such as medicine, telecommunications networks, and computer configuration systems [32].

Most production rule systems, as well as their database implementations, adopt forward-chaining operational or execution semantics [32]. The rules have the form of "if Condition then assert Conclusion/ Action." Whenever the rule base manager needs to modify the condition, the conclusion/action needs to be updated accordingly.

While production rules in nature "react to condition state changes and have no connections to event data" [32], recent work has attempted to extend production rule systems with new features like object models and a fact base to make CEP possible. Specifically, in the declarations of production rules, event types are defined. Incoming events are initialized as instances of the declared event types and are dynamically added to the fact base. In the rule condition, some operations such as filters and event pattern detection may be applied to the instances of events. If the condition is fulfilled, the action is triggered. Representative tools include Drools [35] and Business Events [17].

However, contemporary production rule systems still lack expressiveness as "they do not have a clear declarative semantics, suffer from termination and confluence problems of their execution sequences, and typically do not support expressive nonmonotonic features, such as classical or negation-as-finite failure or preferences" [32]. Therefore, certain event pattern types can be difficult to express. Some research in this area focuses on extending the core production systems to enhance their expressiveness [36], but this results in more complication of the usage of the system.

Event-condition-action rules

The event-condition-action (ECA) rules [37] approach was developed to support the need to react to different kinds of events occurring in active databases [38]. There are three components in an ECA rule:

- Event: Specifies the event that triggers the invocation of the rule. The event itself can be a composition of different event types, in which case it is called a composite event.
- Condition: Consists of the conditions that need to be satisfied in order to carry out the specified action. The condition is only checked upon occurrence of the specified event.
- Action: Specifies the actions to be taken on the data.

Examples of active database systems using ECA rules include ACCOOD [39] and Chimera [40]. Expert system techniques are sometimes integrated to allow rule triggering to be automatic. Apart from active databases, ECA rules have also been applied in conventional databases, where the condition is a traditional query to the local database, and in memory-based rule engines, where the condition is a test on the local data.

EPSs applying ECA rules in the corresponding EPL include Amit [41] and InfoSphere Streams [16]. These systems support event algebra operators analogous to those provided by active database event algebras, eg, Snoop [9], where complex expressions can be created using operators like And, Or, Sequence, etc. to describe event pattern types that can be applied over the event streams in real time.

Two typical usages of ECA rules in event data analysis include detecting and reacting to occurrences of particular event pattern types in the database that may undermine the data integrity in real time, and executing some business logic on incoming event streams.

2.6.3 PROGRAMMATIC EPSs

As mentioned above, programmatic EPSs provide a wide range of functionality for processing complex (or composite) events. They mostly follow the high-level architecture such as EventSwarm software framework. Its conceptual model is shown in Fig. 2. As many CEP engines, EventSwarm can process any type of event streams, such as trading event from stock market; eHealth messages, such as HL7 V2 messages and Twitter streams and generate alerts; or invoke a service, when a specific event pattern type occurs. The event patterns are specified using predefined constructs that define processing rules, such as length of sliding time windows, type of events to be monitored and their relationships. These event pattern types can, for example, specify monitoring rules for trading events (see our finance case study), for business contracts and also alerting rules.

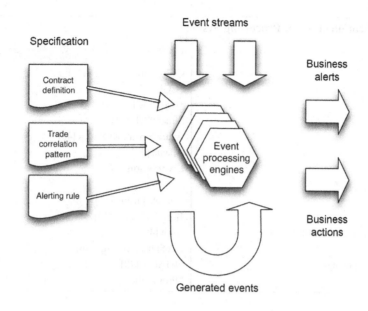

FIG. 2

EventSwarm architecture.

EventSwarm provides a programming framework based on Java and offers "a range of pre-defined abstractions and pattern components implemented in the Java programming language" [42]. There are two typical styles of applications built using this framework, namely applications built for specific, predefined patterns or abstractions, and domain-specific applications that allow end users to define new patterns. For the latter, a graphical interface can be developed and provided for the user. It also has the following outstanding features [42]:

- "the ability to filter on any computed abstraction that matches a single event, including statistical analysis"
- the capability of "using causal precedence in sequence patterns"
- the ability to manage time and ordering issues through, buffering, flexible relationships between events, time skew allowance, and causal ordering
- the ability to incrementally update statistics on sliding windows

It is to be noted that one of the production rules based systems, Drools [35], has adopted similar semantics, and this product is referred to as Drools Fusion.

Table 1 lists different types of EPSs. There are some common event operations (key features) in these products:

- Event expressions — the fundamental building block of an EPS, allowing the specification of matching criteria for a single event [42].
- Filter — the component for reducing the set of events to be processed by an EPS to a subset of events relevant for the given processing task, eg, removing erroneous or incomplete data. The complexity of filtering mechanism in EPSs can vary depending on the expressiveness of the

Table 1 Classification of Event Processing Systems

Type	Product
Query-based	CCL/Aleri [43]
	*CQL [44]
	*Esper [45]
	StreamSQL [31]
	Azure Stream Analytics [43]
Programmatic	Apama [46]
	EventSwarm [47]
Rule-oriented	
Production rules	*Drools Fusion [35]
	BusinessEvents [17]
Event-condition-action rules (ECA rules)	Amit [48]
	InfoSphere Streams [16]
Other (logic programming)	*ETALIS [49]
	*Prova [50]

system, from basic static inspection of event attributes to comparisons against complex computed abstractions.

- Transformation — changing event data from one form to another, including translation, splitting, aggregation, composition, etc.
  - Translation takes each incoming event and operates on it independently of preceding or subsequent events. It performs a "single event in, single event out" operation.
  - Splitting takes a single incoming event and emits a stream of multiple events, performing a "single event in, multiple events out" operation.
  - Aggregation takes a stream of incoming events and produces one output event that is a function of the incoming events. It performs a "multiple events in, one event out" operation.
  - Composition takes two streams of incoming events and operates on them to produce a stream of output events. This is akin to the join operator in relational algebra, except that it joins streams of events rather than tables of data.
- Event pattern detection — component for detecting high-level patterns by examining a collection of events (using correlation, aggregation, abstraction, etc.). This operation can be further broken down into three steps:
  - Predetection: Event pattern types are validated (eg, syntax and grammar errors), then compiled into executable EPL code by the EPL Compiler.
  - Detection: The EPL executes the EPL code of the selected event pattern type generated from the previous step. Input event data is generated by a particular source and pushed to the EPL. The EPL then monitors the incoming event stream, matches the selected event pattern type in data, and produces an output of detected occurrences of this event pattern type.
  - Post-detection: The EPL stores all occurrences of the selected event pattern type into the Event Database, and notify relevant targets to perform corresponding actions.

2.7 DATA ANALYSIS AND ANALYTIC TECHNIQUES

2.7.1 DATA ANALYSIS IN GENERAL

The purpose of data analysis is to answer questions, to suggest conclusions, and to support decision making for data analysts. It is a process of converting raw data into useful information by systematically applying statistical and/or logical techniques. The following phases are normally included in data analysis [51]:

- Data collection — the process of gathering data of interest from certain data sources that are required to answering research questions.
- Data cleansing — the process of detecting and correcting (or removing) corrupt or inaccurate records from a record set, table, or database [52].
- Data transformation — denotes preparing data for further analysis via standardization or normalization. It is needed since in many applications of data analysis, the raw data or cleansed data cannot be used directly due to formatting issues. The formatting of values into consistent layouts is performed based on various elements, including industry standards, local standards, business rules, and domain knowledge bases.
- Statistical analysis — the goal of this phase is to find interesting patterns so as to identify trends. This phase involves various algorithms and can be broken down into five discrete steps, namely data nature description, data relation exploration, data modeling on how the data relates to the underlying population, validation of the model, and predictive analytics. Statistical analysis is often accompanied with or followed by data visualization to interpret the results of the analysis.

Note that these phases are akin to the phases in knowledge discovery in databases, which focuses on data analysis in databases.

There are different types of data processing tools, reflecting different stages of the data analysis activities as introduced above. Examples of such tools are:

- Pre-processing tools, such as OpenRefine [53,54] and Data Wrangler [55]
- Database management systems, making of use of SQL (eg, MySQL [56] and PostgreSQL [57]), as well as NoSQL queries to search for data-satisfying specific parameters; the NoSQL are more amenable to real-time applications, with some examples of being Cassandra [58] and MongoDB [59]
- Statistical data analysis tools, such as R, SAS, Stata, and SPSS

2.7.2 DATA ANALYSIS FOR STREAM APPLICATIONS

Data stream analytics requires a special set of techniques for processing data that may be quite different to the analytics applied for historic data.

One reason for this is that the computation over streams, whether mathematical or statistical, needs to take into account that the data sets over which computations are performed are not fixed. These data sets are typically included as part of the sliding window abstraction, supported by most EPSs. Rather, such data sets change over time, such as when new events arrive and old events need to be removed.

The effect of this is that continuous updates of computations must occur over the sliding time window. Some of these such as stream related computations are relatively simple, such as calculation of minima, maxima, mean, or averages, and even simpler statistical calculations such as standard deviation. They can be computed with one update at a time, triggered by either event arrival or removal.

Other computations may be more involved, either due to the complexity of an algorithm, such as in multivariable regressions or when some sort of sampling over streams needs to be applied. The latter may be required when it is too costly or time consuming to perform calculations over the large population of data in the stream or when there is an infinite stream of data. Examples of techniques for sampling from a streaming population are sliding window reservoir sampling and biased reservoir sampling.

This property of streams will also have an impact on some other statistical techniques that are used in the context of predictive modeling. When, for example, one needs to perform a sampling of data over streams to apply forecasting techniques such as regression modeling, one needs to apply appropriate sampling algorithms as well.

Another complication of data stream analytics is that the computation needs to support processing out of order events. This is because in some cases, due to network delay or failures, the earlier event (ie, the one with earlier timestamp) can arrive later than the events currently being processed. There are various mechanisms that can be used to address these issues, including buffering for a defined period before processing, recalculation when an out-of-order event is received, or the use of calculation methods that are correct in the face of out-of-order events.

It may be noted that in general, a significant class of real-time analysis has the character of time series analysis, and many time series analysis techniques can be applied, although they need to be modified to reflect the specifics of stream analytics requirements, as illustrated by the several examples introduced above.

2.8 FINANCE DOMAIN REQUIREMENTS AND A CASE STUDY

This section will illustrate how some of the concepts, technologies, and techniques described in previous sections can be used to address a class of real-time analytics solutions in finance domain. The section begins by outlining some of the requirements when analyzing real-time financial market data, describes two example problems, and shows how one specific type of a CEP solution can be used to address these problems.

2.8.1 REAL-TIME ANALYTICS IN FINANCE DOMAIN

The area of financial markets has witnessed significant changes in recent years due to a dramatic reduction in trading latency resulting from the use of high-speed computers and networks. High-frequency algorithmic trading, in which market and news data must be analyzed and trading decisions must be made, now occurs within a window of few microseconds. This results in huge volumes of "real-time tick data" or "tick-by-tick data" being generated. High-frequency datasets of typically hundreds of megabytes to many gigabytes in size are being used by finance researchers to study market behavior [60]. Studies have used high-frequency data to analyze many aspects of market microstructure, including volatility and price jumps [61,62]. There are many empirical works related to financial markets research that use such datasets.

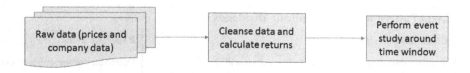

FIG. 3

Example of data pre-processing (for event studies).

Financial market data is a source of knowledge about trading behavior, strategies and patterns, market design, operations and efficiency, products being traded, and financial news. For this reason, there are many financial market data providers that sell either real-time data or historical data. Examples of financial market data providers or portals include Thomson Reuters [63], Bloomberg [64], and WRDS [65].

An example of real-time analytics in the finance domain is the data quality control. For instance, there are many data quality issues associated with data that is obtained from on-line feeds. Another example is determining the potential impact of a new event that requires an event study [66,67] to be carried out within a time window surrounding the event. Real-time price data needs to be preprocessed to accurately determine the returns timeseries (see Fig. 3). If the data preprocessing is not done properly, the data analysis will end up with errors or unreliable results.

In this case study, we will simulate a real-time feed using historical data downloaded from Thomson Reuters Tick History (TRTH) [63] provided by Sirca [68].

2.8.2 SELECTED SCENARIOS

We used two scenarios that are both representative in financial market data quality control and involve CEP rules. The purpose of the data analysis involved in these two scenarios is to detect occurrences of particular event pattern types related to the data preprocessing.

The first scenario involves dealing with duplicate dividend announcement events, which require six rules, as shown in Table 2.

The second scenario involves calculating and comparing the price-earnings ratios (P/E) of different companies in the same industry to indicate whether investors of a particular company are expecting a higher earnings growth in the future than other companies. To calculate the P/E ratio, we need both price data that provides price information and corporate action data that provides earnings information. There are totally six rules (business logic) for earnings calculation (see Table 3).

2.8.3 CEP APPLICATION AS A CASE STUDY

This section introduces a CEP application that deals with the selected scenarios for financial market data processing. The application consists of two major components, namely financial user front-end system and a back-end CEP engine (see Fig. 4).

The role of the Financial User Front-End is to permit financial data analysts to select the rules they want to process on financial market data streams. The CEP engine serves to detect event pattern occurrences for each rule defined in the two selected scenarios.

A prototype was developed using the EventSwarm software framework for matching patterns against data sets. Communication with between the front end and the back end took place via a RESTful interface. Upon completion of processing, the CEP passes the result back to the calling application using an

Table 2 Event Pattern Rules for Duplicate Dividends

Rule	Condition Description	Expected Action
1	Simple duplicate dividend records: Two events with Type "Dividend" have the same timestamp, the same "Div Amt." and the same "Div Ex Date"	Delete the former dividend event
2	No "End Of Day" event exists with "Div Ex Date" of a Dividend event as the timestamp	Report it: missing data
3	An event with the type "Dividend" has null or empty value in the field "Div Amt." or "Div Ex Date"	Discard this Div event and report missing value
4	A pair of duplicate dividends (pattern type No. 4) have different "Div Mkt Lvl ID." Although these two dividends are issued at the same time (Date), the Div IDs are different which indicates they are two different dividends rather than a duplicate	This cannot be counted as a "duplicate dividends" case
5	A "Dividend" event has a value other than "APPD" in the field "Payment Status." This dividend event is not approved (a value other than APPD) so it should be considered as an out-dated record	This dividend event cannot be counted in any "duplicate dividends" case
6	A "Dividend" event has "1" in the field "Div Delete Marker." This dividend event is virtually deleted by the data provider, so this is not a valid entry	This dividend event cannot be counted in any "duplicate dividends" case

Table 3 Event Pattern Rules for Earnings Calculation

Rule	Condition Description	Expected Action
1	An event with type "Earning" (E) happens before an event with type "End Of Day" (EOD)	Calculate the earnings of the EOD event using the following formula: $EOD.earnings = E.epsAmount * 10^{EPS\_scaling\_factor}$
2	Two events $E_{6(1)}$ and $E_{6(2)}$ with type "Earning" ($E_{6(2)}$ before $E_{6(1)}$) happen before an event with type "End Of Day" (EOD)	Calculate the earnings of the EOD event using the following formula: $EOD.earnings = (E_{6(1)}.epsAmount + E_{6(2)}.epsAmount) * 10^{EPS\_scaling\_factor}$
3	Three events with type "Earning" ($E_{3(2)}$ before $E_{3(1)}$ before E_6) happen before an event with type "End Of Day" (EOD)	Calculate the earnings of the EOD event using the following formula: $EOD.earnings = (E_6.epsAmount + E_{3(1)}.epsAmount + E_{3(2)}.epsAmount) * 10^{EPS\_scaling\_factor}$
4	One 3-month earning E_3 and one 9-month earning E_9 occur before End Of Day	Calculate the earnings of the EOD event using the following formula: $EOD.earnings = E_9.epsAmount + E_3.epsAmount$
5	Four 3-month earnings events ($E_{3(1)}$, $E_{3(2)}$, $E_{3(3)}$, $E_{3(4)}$) before End Of Day	Calculate the earnings of the EOD event using the following formula: $EOD.earnings = (E_{3(1)}.epsAmount + E_{3(2)}.epsAmount + E_{3(3)}.epsAmount + E_{3(4)}.epsAmount) * 10^{EPS\_scaling\_factor}$
6	One 9-month earning event E_9 and one 3-month earning event E_3 occur before End Of Day	Calculate the earnings of the EOD event using the following formula: $EOD.earnings = (E_3.epsAmount + E_9.epsAmount) * 10^{EPS\_scaling\_factor}$

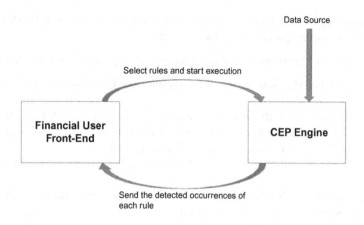

Select rules and start execution

**Financial User
Front-End**

CEP Engine

Send the detected occurrences of
each rule

FIG. 4

Example CEP application.

HTTP POST request containing matches encoded using the wire format, which is implemented using JSON [8] for simple and efficient cross-platform processing.

The EventSwarm service is implemented using Ruby on Rails on the JRuby platform. The specified patterns were coded in Ruby and are called in response to requests from a user or external application. The Ruby "patterns" are primarily constructors that build a CEP graph using EventSwarm core constructs. These constructs are provided through the EventSwarm core Java library with convenient Ruby wrappers to facilitate rapid development. Pattern matching execution primarily occurs in Java for maximum performance, although some elements of the earnings patterns are implemented in Ruby. Encoding of results into the wire format and sending is also implemented in Ruby.

Patterns are matched inside EventSwarm by feeding events through one or more processing graphs that select matching events or sets of events. Processing graph nodes can include sliding windows, filters, splitters (powersets), and abstractions. Abstractions are values or data structures calculated or constructed from the stream of events; for example, the EventSwarm statistics abstractions maintains sum, mean, variance, and standard deviation over numeric data extracted from events in a stream. Events can be added to and removed from the stream by a node, although downstream nodes can choose to ignore removals. For example, a sliding window works by instructing downstream nodes to remove events that have "fallen out" of the window.

The following steps were applied in deploying and testing the finance event pattern types [69]:

- A financial data analyst specifies a set of interesting event pattern rules. The specifications of the event pattern types are described in a natural language conveyed in writing or verbally to an IT expert.
- The IT expert implements the event pattern types in the event pattern detection service and makes them available for invocation by the Front-End application.
- The researcher selects the rules to be executed via the Front-End. The Front-End then passes these parameters to EventSwarm using an HTTP GET request to a configurable URL. Alternatively, the researcher can conduct event pattern detection tasks via the EventSwarm pattern detection service GUI.

- The EventSwarm engine then returns detected event pattern occurrences in JSON format. Finally, the occurrences are further processed by the front end.

As reported in [69], this application provides a number of implementation benefits, including:

- Simple and easy-to-use API; developers can easily integrate EventSwarm into their own applications.
- Very fast and efficient CEP, with the average speed of processing of more than 10,000 events per second on TRTH daily data provided by Sirca. This is almost as fast as a bespoke program dedicated to a fixed event processing process and executed locally.
- Very fast deployment of a new event pattern; it normally takes less than a day to implement five event pattern types.
- Well-structured output; JSON as the output format is well structured and it is convenient for developers to parse and further analyze the results.

Some limitations of the implementation prototype are:

- No user-friendly way of defining event pattern types via the GUI or an API; thus, the development cycle largely depends on the availability of the IT experts.
- The communication between the researcher and the IT expert can be very involving to help the IT expert in properly understanding the semantics of event pattern types described by the researcher. Any failure in the communication may cause issues that will be hard to diagnose in the future.

Overall, the implementation of the patterns using EventSwarm was mostly straightforward and required only minimal programmer effort, and most work required was on pattern specification and implementation.

2.9 FUTURE RESEARCH CHALLENGES

There are a number of research challenges in the area of real-time analytics. A major challenge is related to how to best apply and refine existing analytics techniques and functions, such as statistics or machine learning methods to streaming data. This is needed for applications such as more precise monitoring of the system under question, including detection of business, quality or security and privacy issues, more up-to-date data insights development, and predictive analytics outcomes.

Another problem is the lack of standard formats for facilitating interoperation of systems across the different layers of the real-time analytics stack. For example, there is no standard for representing event abstractions, such as events and event patterns. This issue should be addressed by proposing new models and standards that can accurately represent streaming data abstractions and can be used to facilitate interoperability between solutions across streaming and stored data platforms.

The final challenge is in developing user friendly solutions that reflect existing analysis methods and practices in specific application domains. For example, our financial study suggests that while data analysts are empowered to manage the event processing rules, they are unable to define suitable analytics abstractions (ie, event pattern types) by themselves. Ideally, there should be some domain-specific analysis models that drive the analytics infrastructure in a "model-driven" way. Whether such models should be based on a Domain-Specific Language approach or Semantic Technologies is still an open question.

REFERENCES

[1] Bean R. Your data should be faster, not just bigger. Harvard Business Review. https://hbr.org/2015/02/your-data-should-be-faster-not-just-bigger.

[2] NoSQL, https://en.wikipedia.org/wiki/NoSQL.

[3] https://en.wikipedia.org/wiki/Elasticsearch.

[4] Pentaho, http://www.pentaho.com/.

[5] Douglass Bruce Powel. Real-time UML: developing efficient objects for embedded system. Essex: Addison-Wesley; 2004.

[6] SCADA, https://en.wikipedia.org/wiki/SCADA.

[7] Ellis B. Real-time analytics: techniques to analyze and visualize streaming data. Indianapolis, IN: Wiley; 2014.

[8] Etzion O, Niblett P. Event processing in action. Stamford, CT: Manning Publications Co.; 2011.

[9] Chakravarthy S, Mishra D. Snoop: an expressive event specification language for active databases. Data Knowl Eng 1994;14:1–26.

[10] Gero M, Ludger F, Peter P. Distributed event-based systems. Springer-Verlag, 2006.

[11] Luckham D. The power of events: an introduction to complex event processing in distributed enterprise systems. Boston, MA: Addison Wesley; 2002.

[12] Bacon J, Moody K, Bates J, Hayton R, Ma C, McNeil A, et al. Generic support for distributed applications. IEEE Computer 2000;33:68–76.

[13] Linington P, Milosevic Z, Tanaka A, Vallesillo A. Building enterprise systems with ODP. Chapman Hall: CRC Press; 2012.

[14] Luckham D. Event processing for business: organizing the real-time enterprise. Hoboken, NJ: John Wiley & Sons, Inc.; 2012.

[15] SAP. Continuous Computation Language. http://help.sap.com/saphelp_esp51sp08gsg/helpdata/en/e7/931cee6f0f101486068ade550250ad/content.htm?frameset=/en/e7/74cec06f0f1014bd1e98b8d524e830/frameset.htm&current_toc=/en/e7/74cec06f0f1014bd1e98b8d524e830/plain.htm&node_id=45&show_children=false; 2015.

[16] IBM. InfoSphere Streams. http://www-03.ibm.com/software/products/en/infosphere-streams/; 2015.

[17] TIBCO. TIBCO BusinessEvents. http://www.tibco.com/products/event-processing/complex-event-processing/businessevents/default.jsp; 2015.

[18] Oracle, http://www.oracle.com/technetwork/middleware/complex-event-wprocessing/overview/complex-event-processing-088095.html.

[19] White T. Hadoop: the definitive guide. 3rd ed. Sebastopol, CA: O'Reilly; 2012.

[20] Apache. Hadoop. http://hadoop.apache.org/; 2014.

[21] Dean J, Ghemawat S. MapReduce: simplified data processing on large clusters. Comm ACM 2008;51:107–13.

[22] Ryza S, Laserson U, Owen S, Wills J. Advanced Analytics with Spark. Sebastopol, CA: O'Reilly Media Inc.; 2015.

[23] Kafka, https://kafka.apache.org/.

[24] Apache, https://flume.apache.org/.

[25] Shapira G, Holoman J. Flafka: Apache Flume Meets Apache Kafka for Event Processing. http://blog.cloudera.com/blog/2014/11/flafka-apache-flume-meets-apache-kafka-for-event-processing/; 2014.

[26] Amazon, https://aws.amazon.com/kinesis/.

[27] Chen J, DeWitt DJ, Tian F, Wang Y. NiagaraCQ: a scalable continuous query system for Internet databases. In: Presented at the Proceedings of the 2000 ACM SIGMOD International Conference on Management of Data, Dallas, Texas, USA; 2000.

[28] Liu L, Pu C, Tang W. Continual queries for Internet scale event-driven information delivery. IEEE Trans Knowl Data Eng 1999;11:610–28.

[29] Robert K. Evaluation of the Stream Query Language CQL. Sweden: The European Library; 2010.

[30] Arasu A, Babu S, Widom J. The CQL continuous query language: semantic foundations and query execution. VLDB J 2006;15:121–42.

[31] TIBCO. StreamSQL guide. http://www.streambase.com/developers/docs/latest/streamsql/; 2014.

[32] Paschke A, Kozlenkov A. Rule-based event processing and reaction rules. In: Governatori G, Hall J, Paschke A, editors. Rule interchange and applications, vol. 5858. Berlin, Heidelberg: Springer; 2009. p. 53–66.

[33] Jain N, Mishra S, Srinivasan A, Gehrke J, Widom J, Balakrishnan H, et al. Towards a streaming SQL standard. Proc VLDB Endow 2008;1:1379–90.

[34] Azure, https://azure.microsoft.com/en-us/documentation/articles/stream-analytics-introduction/.

[35] RedHat. Drools Fusion. http://drools.jboss.org/drools-fusion.html; 2015.

[36] Phan Minh D, Mancarella P. Production systems with negation as failure. IEEE Trans Knowl Data Eng 2002;14:336–52.

[37] Dittrich K, Gatziu S, Geppert A. The active database management system manifesto: a rulebase of ADBMS features. In: Sellis T, editor. Rules in database systems, vol. 985. Berlin, Heidelberg: Springer; 1995. p. 1–17.

[38] Paton NW, Díaz O. Active database systems. ACM Comput Surv 1999;31:63–103.

[39] Erikson J. CEDE: composite event detector in an active database. University of Skode, 1993.

[40] Meo R, Psaila G, Ceri S. Composite events in Chimera. In: Apers P, Bouzeghoub M, Gardarin G, editors. Advances in database technology — EDBT '96, vol. 1057. Berlin, Heidelberg: Springer; 1996. p. 56–76.

[41] IBM. Amit. http://www.research.ibm.com/haifa/projects/software/extreme_blue/papers/eXB_AMIT.pdf; 2015.

[42] Berry A, Milosevic Z. Real-time analytics for legacy data streams in health: monitoring health data quality. In: Presented at the 17th IEEE International Enterprise Distributed Object Computing Conference (EDOC), 2013, Vancouver, BC; 2013.

[43] Sybase. Sybase Aleri Event Stream Processor. http://infocenter.sybase.com/help/topic/com.sybase.infocenter. dc01286.0311/pdf/ProductOverview.pdf?noframes=true; 2014.

[44] Oracle. CQL. http://docs.oracle.com/cd/E17904_01/apirefs.1111/e12048/intro.htm; 2014.

[45] Esper (2013). http://esper.codehaus.org/.

[46] SoftwareAG. Apama. http://www.softwareag.com/corporate/products/apama_webmethods/analytics/overview/default.asp; 2015.

[47] Deontik. EventSwarm. http://deontik.com/Products/EventSwarm.html; 2013.

[48] Adi A, Botzer D, Etzion O. The situation manager component of amit — active middleware technology. In: Halevy A, Gal A, editors. Next generation information technologies and systems, vol. 2382. Berlin, Heidelberg: Springer; 2002. p. 158–68.

[49] Google (2014). https://code.google.com/p/etalis/.

[50] Prova (2011). https://prova.ws/confluence/display/EP/Event+processing.

[51] Chen W. Enabling user-driven rule management in event data analysis. Doctor of Philosophy, School of Computer Science and Engineering, University of New South Wales, 2015.

[52] wikipedia, https://en.wikipedia.org/wiki/Data_cleansing.

[53] datos.gob.es. Data Processing and Visualisation Tools, European PSI Platform 2013.

[54] GitHub. Documentation for users. https://github.com/OpenRefine/OpenRefine/wiki/Documentation-For-Users; 2014.

[55] DataWrangler (2013). http://vis.stanford.edu/wrangler/.

[56] Oracle. MySQL. http://www.mysql.com/; 2015.

[57] PostgreSQL (2015). http://www.postgresql.org/.

[58] Apache. Cassandra. http://cassandra.apache.org/; 2009.

[59] MangoDB (2015). http://www.mongodb.org/.

[60] Goodhart CAE, O'Hara M. High frequency data in financial markets: issues and applications. J Empir Finance 1997;4(2–3):73–114.

[61] Andersen TG. Some reflections on analysis of high-frequency data. J Bus Econ Stat 2000;18(2):146–53.

[62] Bollersleva T, Lawb TH, Tauchena G. Risk, jumps, and diversification. J Econ 2008;144(1):234–56.

[63] Thomson-Reuters (2014). http://www.thomsonreuters.com.au/.

[64] Bloomberg (2015). http://www.bloomberg.com/.

[65] WRDS. Wharton Research Data Services. http://wrds-web.wharton.upenn.edu/wrds/; 2015.

[66] Binder J. The event study methodology since 1969. Rev Quant Finance Account 1998;11:111–37.

[67] Eventus (2012). http://www.eventstudy.com/.

[68] Sirca (2015). http://www.sirca.org.au/.

[69] Milosevic Z, Chen W, Berry A, Rabhi FA. An event-based model to support distributed real-time analytics: finance case study. In: Presented at the EDOC; 2015.

BIG DATA ANALYTICS FOR SOCIAL MEDIA

3

S. Kannan, S. Karuppusamy, A. Nedunchezhian, P. Venkateshan, P. Wang, N. Bojja, A. Kejariwal

3.1 INTRODUCTION

Big Data analytics has become pervasive in every sphere of life. The most common formats of Big Data include video, image, audio, numeric, and text [1]. Typically, numeric data is more commonly used than text data for analytics purposes. Over the last decade, analysis of text data has been a key component of a large set of widely used industry applications. A web search is an example of such an application, which has a very large daily audience around the globe.

State-of-the-art machine learning models can effectively model numeric attributes but do not fare well in presence of text attributes. Examples of text attributes include words, their frequencies, underlying grammar structure, or entire sequences of words. These text attributes (or features) are generated from a given corpus of text. Often, corpora are large and the resultant text features can be sparse; therefore, they require special data modeling. Furthermore, the dimensionality of text data is typically much higher than that of numeric data. Text features are built on words or combination of words in a particular sequence. Given the large variation that languages offer, the feature space encompassing an entire grammar and vocabulary is large.

In this chapter, we present how analysis of text results in applications that have a significant influence on our online presence. We discuss how *natural language processing (NLP)* techniques [2] have been used to analyze text and understand nuances in text data. Furthermore, we discuss how *text mining* applications have improved latent mining and parsing of text originating from social media outlets and e-commerce portals. Finally, we present approaches to detect anomalies in social media data, which can in turn provide interesting insights.

3.2 NLP AND ITS APPLICATIONS

Language is a fundamental medium through which all of us can communicate. Languages have independently evolved over the years in every corner of the world along with corresponding cultures and have given a sense of identity to entire populations. In today's Big Data age, language is being used as a critical medium of communication. Hence, it is imperative to study language, its underlying grammar (i.e., the rules of which give structure to a language), and the vocabulary, which forms the content of a given language.

Traditional linguistics have focused on understanding the syntax of a given language [2,3]. As more and more languages were studied, linguistic resources, such as lexicon and grammar notations, multiplied along with the number of languages under study. As a consequence, the field of computational

Big Data. http://dx.doi.org/10.1016/B978-0-12-805394-2.00003-9

linguistics emerged to address the limitation and help study languages with technology, as opposed to traditional handwritten rules. Eventually, the field evolved into being called natural language processing (NLP), with increased emphasis on using computers to analyze language.

In recent years, a large volume of text data is being generated at high velocity on a routine basis. The infographic created by DOMO [1] shows that there are 200 million emails, 30,000 new blog posts (Tumblr), and over 300,000 new tweets generated on the Internet *every minute*. NLP methods are routinely being used to parse this avalanche of text and extract the most useful information. Traditional methods of text analysis have been centered around syntactic methods; however, there has been a systematic shift in the NLP community towards the use of statistical methods for text and language processing in recent years. The statistical NLP methods that are being used to parse text are central to building everyday applications such as, but not limited to, search engines, recommender systems, spell checkers, machine translation systems, and question answering machines.

It can be hard to imagine how statistics can simulate and replicate the finer nuances of complicated language grammars. In the following sections, we shall walk through how traditional NLP problems, such as language detection (LD) and named entity recognition (NER), have been addressed using statistical methods. Further, we highlight how NLP tasks can use machine learning methods to achieve higher accuracy and to overcome the need for dedicated linguistic resources. Moreover, we focus specifically on social media text (e.g., *microblogs, texts,* and *instant messaging*). Social media text constitutes a majority of text that is being generated online everyday; therefore, applying NLP on this data can have potentially wide ranging implications.

3.2.1 LANGUAGE DETECTION

LD, or Language identification, is to detect language(s) of a given text. Most of the NLP applications are language specific, as they are usually trained on data in limited languages. Thus, given a text, accurate LD is key to subsequent analysis. This is particularly important for NLP applications in a multilingual context.

A large amount of research has been done on LD over the years [4,5]. Many of these methods are covered in literature and are fairly accurate [6,7]. However, researchers have shown that LD on short texts is very difficult. For example, in Ref. [8], Baldwin and Lui showed that LD became increasingly difficult when reducing the length of texts or increasing the number of languages. In a similar vein, other researchers noticed the LD of microblogs was challenging for state-of-the-art LD methods [9].

One of the most widely used methods is the character n-gram-based approach proposed by Cavnar and Trenkle [10]. The method computes and compares profiles of n-gram frequencies via "Out Of Place" (OOP) distance, a ranking-based distance. An n-gram is an n-unit slice of a given string. N-gram when used in the context of words is a sequence of n words in a given string. A character n-gram is an n-character slice of a given string. The first step is to compute a profile for each language in a multilingual training set. Given a test document, the computed profile was then compared to each language profile obtained from the training set. The document was detected as a language that had the smallest distance to the document's profile. This approach achieved 99.8% accuracy on Usenet newsgroup articles. One of the disadvantages of Cavnar and Trenkle's approach is that it requires the input to be character tokenized. Another similar approach used byte n-grams instead of character n-grams, avoiding the tokenization problem [4]. This approach achieved 99.9% accuracy on documents longer than 500 bytes.

In recent research, the difficulty in LD for short texts has been highlighted. For instance, in Ref. [8], Baldwin and Lui presented a detailed investigation of various approaches to carry LD and evaluated their performance. They also show that LD became increasingly difficult when we increased the number of languages, reduced the size of training data, and reduced the length of texts. In Ref. [11], Vatanen et al. investigated a LD task where the test samples had only 5–21 characters. The authors compared two approaches: a naive Bayes classifier based on character n-gram models, and the OOP method [10]. To improve LD on short and ill-written texts, Tromp and Pechenizkiy proposed a graph-based n-gram approach (LIGA) [12] that performed better than the character n-gram approach [10] on Twitter messages. Based on LIGA, Vogel and Tresner-Kirsch proposed linguistically motivated changes to LIGA, achieving 99.8% accuracy on Twitter messages in six European languages, while the accuracy of LIGA was 97.9% on the same test set [13]. In Ref. [14], Bergsma et al. addressed LD for short, informal texts in resource-poor languages (languages with limited training data), annotating and releasing a large collection of Twitter messages in nine languages using three scripts: Cyrillic, Arabic, and Devanagari. The authors also presented two LD systems that achieved accuracy close to 98% on Twitter messages.

The aforementioned techniques focused on LD using only text-based features. In contrast, Carter et al. used nontext features to improve the LD of Twitter messages [9]. The authors used text-dependent features together with several text-independent features, such as the language profile of a blogger, the content of an attached hyperlink, the language profile of a tag, and the language of the original post. Wang et al. used a technique based on text-based features and user language profile, i.e., language distribution of messages sent by a user, to further improve LD for very short messages in mobile games [15].

Next, some of the typical methods for LD are discussed and followed by a discussion on how to combine LD methods together to take advantage from the individual methods.

Alphabet-based LD

A straightforward way to carry out LD is to count the number of characters of each language in a given message and then select the language with the highest count of characters. This method is referred to as alphabet-based LD. A sample algorithm for this method is shown in Fig. 1.

This method is effective when distinguishing languages written in different scripts, for example, Chinese and English. However, it does not perform well when distinguishing languages using similar scripts, for example, languages using the Latin script. Thus, this method should be used together with other methods, for example, one could use this method to detect languages using almost separate scripts (e.g., Thai, Chinese, Japanese, Korean, etc.) and then use other methods, such as the character n-gram

---

INPUT: a raw message **M** whose length is **N**
RETURN: the detected language for **M**
1: initialize a map **char2langList** which maps a character to a list of languages;
2: initialize a map **lang2count** which maps a language to the count of characters of the language in **M**;
3: **for** $i \leftarrow 0$ **to N-1 do**
4:     **for each** *lang* **in char2langList[M[**i**]] do**
5:         **lang2count[***lang***]** $\leftarrow$ **lang2count[***lang***]** + 1;
6:   **return** the language in **lang2count** with the highest count;

FIG. 1

Alphabet-based language detection.

based approach proposed by Cavnar and Trenkle [10] and the graph-based *n*-gram approach (LIGA) [12] to detect remaining languages. Note that here "almost separate scripts" depends on the target language to be detected. For example, if the set contains Russian and Ukrainian — both use the Cyrillic script — then the alphabet-based LD method should not be used to detect Russian or Ukrainian; in contrast, if the language set only contains Russian, then the alphabet-based LD method can be used. Having said that, multiple languages may have the same highest count. To address this, a priority list of languages could be set according to the language frequencies in the context and language-specific knowledge.

Dictionary-based LD

Assuming words in an input message are space delimited, one could count the number of words in each language, then select the language with the highest count of words as the detected language. This method is referred to as dictionary-based LD. A sample algorithm is shown in Fig. 2. A language priority list can be used to address the problem of multiple languages have the same highest count of words.

The advantage of this method is that it works well on short messages, even if the input message is only one word. On the other hand, the disadvantage of this method stems from its assumption that the words in the input message should be space delimited, which limits the applicability of this method. For example, without knowing that an input message is in Chinese, the input message cannot be tokenized into words properly.[1] Furthermore, it might be difficult to get suitable word lists for languages, because many word lists available on the Internet are usually noisy and also for different contexts, one might want adapted word lists, for example, players tend to use slang words in mobile games, so one may want word lists containing slang words in such context.

Byte n-gram-based LD

A byte *n*-gram-based LD approach was proposed by Lui and Baldwin [16]. This approach was shown to fare better than many other methods. Examples include, TextCat, an implementation of the technique proposed by Cavnar and Trenkle [10] and CLD[2] that is the embedded LD system and is used in Google's Chromium Browser.

INPUT: a raw message **M**
RETURN: the detected language for **M**

1: tokenize **M** into a sequence of words **WORDS** whose length is **N**,
    ignoring punctuation;
2: initialize a map **word2langList** which maps a word to a list of languages;
3: initialize a map **lang2count** which maps a language to the count of words of the language in **WORDS**;
4: **for** $i \leftarrow 0$ **to** N-1 **do**
5:     **for each** *lang* **in word2langList[WORDS[i]] do**
6:         **lang2count[***lang***]** $\leftarrow$ **lang2count[***lang***]** + 1;
7: **return** the language in **lang2count** with the highest count;

FIG. 2

Dictionary-based language detection.

---

[1]This gives rise to a circular problem, as determining the language of the input message is the objective of LD.
[2]https://github.com/CLD2Owners/cld2

This approach uses a naive Bayes classifier with byte n-gram features. Lui and Baldwin released an off-the-shelf LD tool as an implementation of the approach [16]. The tool also contains a pretrained model that was used on a large number of multilingual texts from various domains in 97 languages [17]. One major advantage of this approach is that it can avoid encoding issues. One language could be encoded using different character encodings,[3] for example, Chinese could be encoded in Unicode, GBK, etc. Prior to this approach, one would have had to convert the input texts to required encodings, then feed the input texts to LD systems. This approach could be trained on data comprising of many different encodings, as the elementary unit for its features is byte.

User language profile

As mentioned earlier, LD methods that rely on only text-based features often perform poorly on very short texts. In light of this, we overview methods based on nontext features (i.e., user language profiles) [9,15].

A language profile for a user is a vector of real numbers, which are the probabilities of sending a message in a particular language. The size of the vector is the same for all the users, i.e., the number of supported languages. In order to build the language profiles, ideally, human editors would annotate all the messages sent by a user. However, this is impractical. Therefore, an automatic LD system is needed to detect the language of each message sent by a user and obtain a vector of counts of messages written in each language. Then, the counts are normalized to compute probabilities and obtain a vector of probabilities as the language profile for the user. For example, the byte n-gram-based LD system could be used to build language profiles. Of course, the byte n-gram-based LD might make errors, especially on short messages. In Ref. [15], Wang et al. demonstrated that this way of building language profiles is effective. For a new user, the probabilities in the language profile are all 0, meaning that the language the new user will use is not known.

Combined system

As discussed earlier, different LD methods have different advantages and limitations. The approach proposed by Wang et al. combines different LD methods together to take advantages from all the methods [15]. Their approach has two phases:

- Phase 1 uses the alphabet-based LD to detect languages using "separate" scripts.
- Phase 2 uses a linear model from LibLinear [18] to combine the dictionary-based method, the byte n-gram-based method, and the user language profile to detect the remaining languages. The workflow of the approach is presented in Fig. 3.

For example, if the target language set is *{Chinese, English, French, Thai}* in Phase 1, the alphabet-based LD method detects the four languages. If the result is in *{Chinese, Thai}*, we return the result. Otherwise, English and French are detected in Phase 2. The input feature vector of LibLinear [18] is a concatenation of the normalized output vectors from the three methods. Each output vector has two numbers indicating the probability of English or French. Note that the output vector of some methods could be less than two numbers. This may happen, for instance, when the dictionary-based method is not applicable to some languages due to a lack of dictionaries or words that are not space delimited.

---

[3]https://en.wikipedia.org/wiki/Character_encoding

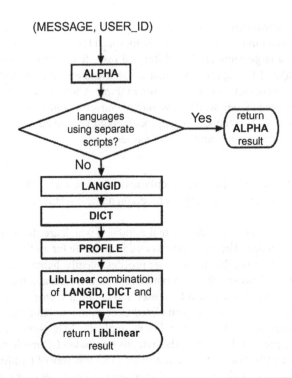

FIG. 3

Work flow of the combination approach.

Going forward, research on LD could explore how to use social media text normalization [19,20] to assist LD of social media texts, as social media texts usually contain many informal words, which pose difficulties for LD systems trained on formal data. Another potential avenue of further research is to use deep learning methods for LD [21].

3.2.2 NAMED ENTITY RECOGNITION

NER delves with identification and classification of named entities (NEs) in a given sentence, such as person, organization, place, time, quantities, and monetary values. For example, consider the sentence in Fig. 4.

An NER system should be able to identify *Australia*, *Chris Rogers,* and *Edgbaston* as NEs in the sentence. NER plays a key role in larger information extraction (IE) from natural language texts. NER finds practical use in a wide range of applications such as machine translation, speech recognition, chat bots, and search engines.

Australia opener Chris Rogers has come through
a nets session against the tourists' pace attack
with no visible ill-effects at Edgbaston

FIG. 4

Named entities highlighted.

Traditional approaches to NER include matching a list of names with documents to identify NEs and other simple rule-based approaches. The *Conference on Natural Language Learning (CoNLL)* conducted a shared task in 2003, which saw a lot of significant contributions to NER. Many statistical NLP approaches were presented here that achieved success in NER with groundbreaking results. Some of these approaches are discussed in the following sections.

NER pipeline

A typical NER system pipeline includes preprocessing the data such as tokenization, sentence splitting, feature extraction, applying ML models on the data for tagging, and then post-processing to remove some tagging inconsistencies. Fig. 5 illustrates this pipeline.

Statistical NLP methods

NER can be treated as a standard classification problem, for example, identifying if a token is an entity or not. Statistical machine learning algorithms can be applied to solve this problem. Supervised classifiers yielded better NER systems compared to rule-based ones, as they are easier to maintain and adapt to different domains. Hidden Markov models (HMMs) [22] and support vector machine (SVM)-based models [23] were used in NER tasks with varying degree of success.

Maximum entropy (ME) models were highly successful [24]. These models use posterior probability of a tag given a word within a limited window $w_{n+i}^{n-i} = w_{n-i...} \cdot w_{n+i}$ around nth word w_n with a window size of $2i + 1$ [8]. The models comprised of set of binary features such as lexical, word based, transition, prior, compound, and dictionary features. Chieu and Ng added other features to the system such as useful word suffixes, class suffixes, and initial capital letters [25].

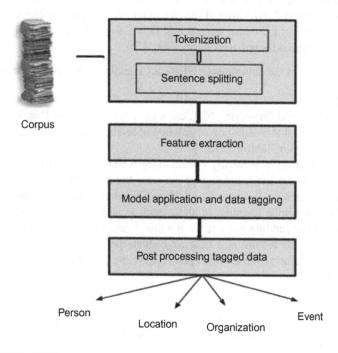

FIG. 5

NER pipeline.

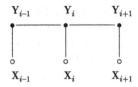

FIG. 6

Graphical structure of CRFs. *Unfilled circle* indicates variables that are not generated by models [26].

In recent years, conditional random field (CRF) [26] replaced ME model as a popular choice for sequence labeling task such as part-of-speech (POS) tagging and NER. A typical CRF structure is illustrated in Fig. 6. CRF provides many advantages over ME or HMMs.

Why CRF?

- It overcomes the problems of generative models as the problem is modeled as a conditional probability of the label sequence, given an observation sequence rather than a joint probability.
- The conditional probability of label sequences can depend on arbitrary nonindependent features[4] of the observation sequence.
- The probability of transition between labels depends on past and future observations rather than strict independent assumptions in generative models.
- *Label bias problem*: In maximum entropy Markov models and other discriminative Markov models, the transitions leaving the current state compete only with each other, not with all the transitions in the model. By virtue of the fact that CRF has a single exponential model for the joint probability of the entire sequence of labels given the observation sequence, the aforementioned problem does not arise when using CRF.

Stanford's NER is one of the cutting-edge NER tool available that uses CRF based classifier [27].

Features for NER

Most of the systems employed for solving NER use a large set of features. Domain adaptation of NER entails feature engineering, that is, addition or deletion of features for that particular data. Some of the important features are listed in Table 1 [23,27].

Feature engineering involves manually constructing features for a particular domain, which involves understanding of the domain and also of the classifier used. The effect of each feature can be manually measured by simple inclusion and exclusion of features. There are a number of feature selection algorithms used in machine learning. Methods such as adding features based on domain knowledge, forward selection (i.e., adding one feature at a time to evaluate performance [28]), and backward selection (i.e., removing one feature at a time to evaluate performance [28]), can be used initially. Models based on simple Information Gain [29] and chi-square [29,30] help improve the feature selection process drastically.

---

[4]Nonindependent features can be variables not directly associated with inputs but have a tertiary effect on the outcome. CRFs are a good way to factor in such variables. Some examples could be length of the string, number of characters per word, etc.

Table 1 Table With Sample Features

Features	Examples
Initial capital letter	Australia
All capital letter	US
4-digit string	1996
Words within a window of *n* characters around a word	"Australia," "Opener," "Chris," "Rogers," and "has" around the word "Chris"
Prefix for money and person	"$", "Mr."
Suffix for time	"a.m.," "o'clock"
Gazette-based features	"Chris" is in a list of names

Tags and evaluation

Traditionally, *Begin, Inside, Outside (BIO)* prefixes are used along with individual NE tags, with manually curated training data. For example, the sentence in Fig. 4 will be tagged as follows:

Australia/B-LOC opener/O Chris/B-PER Rogers/I-PER has/O come/O through/O a/O nets/O session/O against/O the/O tourist/O 's/O pace/O attack/O with/O no/O visible/O ill-effects/O at/O Edgbaston/B-LOC.

Since the number of NEs in a sentence is much smaller compared to other words, NER is measured using *F*-score. *F*-Score is a harmonic mean between precision and recall.

Applications

NER is used in a wide variety of application domains. For instance:

- *Biomedical data:* NER is used extensively in biomedical data for gene identification, DNA identification, and also the identification of drug names and disease names. These experiments use CRFs with features engineered for their domain data [31].
- *Search queries:* NER combined with topic identification is used in optimizing search queries and for better ranking the search results [32].
- *Translation:* NER is used in machine translation, as certain NEs should be translated and others need not be.

Recent trends in NER

With the advent of social media like online chat, Facebook and Twitter status updates, and instant messaging, there has been vast proliferation of social media data [1]. Traditional NER methods do not fare well with this type of data. This can primarily be attributed to the nature of the data (e.g., free speech form, abbreviations, introduction of emojis and emoticons, and typing errors). Lack of good annotated data, tagged by qualified linguists, have been extant problems in NLP as a whole and specifically for social media data. The impact of social media is very pronounced in today's world, literally being the "word-of-mouth" information, making IE from social media very important. Twitter updates have become popular for IE tasks due to their high volume and free availability of data. Twitter data introduces its own categories of NEs, such as *FACILITY, PRODUCT, MOVIE, SPORTSTEAM*, along with original *PERSON, PLACE, and ORGANIZATION.*

One of the early works focused on building NER on Twitter data was done by Ritter et al. [33]. For instance, a whole IE pipeline was retrained specifically for Twitter data encapsulating POS tagging and NER identification, segmentation, and classification [33]. The system also uses labeled-Latent Dirichlet Allocation as additional features for unlabeled data. *PERSON* names had *F*-score above 85 due to availability of large number training data for the *PERSON* category. Since then, a lot of research has been done using Twitter data.

TwitIE [34], a complete NLP pipeline for Twitter data modeled after ANNIE, an IE pipeline for formal data [35], was developed by Bontcheva et al. TwitIE includes a tokenizer, sentence splitter, POS tagger, chunker,[5] lemmatizer,[6] Gazetteer for NER [36], and features that were adapted to better suit Twitter data. Twitter-specific User IDs can be easily identified with simple regular expression with almost 100% accuracy [34].

3.3 TEXT MINING

Social media platforms have changed the nature of text data on the web. This, in part, can be ascribed to the unstructured nature of the text and the presence of slang text. Millions of blogs, microblogs, and short messages are generated each day on the web and on mobile devices [1]. Understanding and parsing these massive amounts of real-time text data streams is very valuable. For instance, text mining text helps in learning users' interests and usage patterns so as to build products with which users can better engage. Such personalization also has applications in advertising, search, and discovery. The systems also need to be tuned for speed and accuracy. Consequently, different machine learning models need to be employed depending on the problem at hand.

Recent advances in machine learning have been in the area of deep learning [37–40] — primarily geared towards classification and recognition tasks on image and audio data. These methods have also found applications in text analysis in the form of recurrent neural networks (RNNs) [41]. Word2vec [42] is a tool built using these methods for learning text association. The tool is being increasingly used to convert text data into numeric feature vectors. These feature vectors are then used in machine learning models for prediction, classification, and clustering.

In the following sections, applications of text mining such as sentiment analysis, recommender systems, and trending analysis are presented with a focus on social text streams.

3.3.1 SENTIMENT ANALYSIS

In this techno-social world, events such as a revolution in Egypt, a national election in the United States, or an entertaining movie have people flocking to social media platforms to express their thoughts and opinions. Sentiment analysis delves with automatically detecting sentiments in any text media. Analyzing sentiments from text, like any NLP problem, is hard because of the recursive and ambiguous nature of natural language. With new words and symbols being regularly coined in today's digital

---

[5]Chunker is a shallow parser that identifies different phrases in a sentence like noun phrase, verb phrase, etc.
[6]Lemmatizer returns the base or dictionary form of a sentence.

world (e.g., selfie, #yolo, ☺, and tl;dr), language evolution poses serious challenges to the task of sentiment analysis. Sarcasm is another problem, which affects the performance of sentiment analysis systems. Although heuristics such as pronunciation lapses[7] and other vocal cues [43] have been proposed for sarcasm detection in speech content, sarcasm detection in text is still one of the more challenging NLP tasks [44].

One of the most important applications of sentiment analysis is the rating system of online stores where each product is rated and reviewed by the buyers. Depending on the kind of rating given by the buyers, the online stores suggest a list of recommended items for buyers so that they can increase the sales and revenue of the company. Knowing the sentiment of users towards a company's new products or services and that of their competitors guides better decision making. Forecasting stock market trends and predicting election results are some other applications. Concepts related to this topic will be explained using different kinds of review datasets, including a major chunk of opinionated data on the web.

Lexicon-based approach

The Lexicon-based approach uses pre-prepared sentiment lexicon to score a document by aggregating the sentiment scores of all the words in the document [45–47]. The pre-prepared sentiment lexicon should contain a word and corresponding sentiment score to it. The negation form of vocabulary words should be added to the lexicon as individual entries, and they should be given higher precedence over the corresponding nonnegation terms. Simple rules can also be used to handle negation terms. There are several issues with this approach. For instance, most of the time, in online reviews or any other online text source, the presence of more positive words does not necessarily make the review to be positive or vice versa. In most cases, it is impossible to use the same lexicon for scoring documents of different domains. To address this, a new set of sentiment lexicons should be prepared based on the nature of the target domain. There has been some research work done to build domain-specific sentiment lexicons for specific target domains by bootstrapping from an initial smaller lexicon [48].

Rule-based approaches

Rule-based approaches, along with the sentiment lexicon, use lists of emoticons, emojis, bias words, and certain idioms. Rule-based approaches usually have a set of rules which ascribe importance to terms in sentiment lexicon, emoticon lists, emoji lists, bias word lists, and idiom lists; these approaches score a document based on these lists and the importance associated with each list. A classic example of this method computes the sentiment of reviews by averaging semantic orientation of phrases that have an adjective or adverb in it [49]. This approach has limitations similar to that of a lexicon-based approach. The main advantage with lexicon-based and rule-based approaches is that manual labor is needed only for building a sentiment dictionary.

Statistical methods

Machine learning algorithms can be applied on opinionated documents or reviews to learn the latent patterns and other aspects that capture the sentiment of a given document. The learned model can be applied on real-time social media data to assess the opinions of people on any particular entity. Sentiment analysis has mainly been modeled as a supervised learning problem; hence, it needs (manually) labeled training data to build the initial model. The difficulty in obtaining training data depends on the domain

---

[7]Pronunciation lapse: time gap between utterances.

where the sentiment model is going to be applied. Some of the most common statistical techniques are discussed next.

Bag of words: The most common statistical approach for sentiment analysis is to treat the text content in an input document as a bag of n-grams without taking into account the grammar and the n-grams order. The frequency of each term (n-gram) occurring in the input is usually considered as a feature vector for the machine learning model. Sentiment, emoticon, and emoji dictionary-based features can be effectively combined with n-gram features and a hybrid machine learning model can be built to learn underlying sentiment patterns. Since 2003, the majority of the research work in sentiment analysis using statistical approaches mainly employs the bag of words approach with notable work being done by Pang et al. [50].

Aspect-based sentiment analysis: In online rating systems, the overall rating of an entity does not necessarily explain the quality of the different dimensions of an entity. Consider, for example, the restaurant dining domain. The objective of a sentiment analysis system in this domain is to analyze the opinions of people on different aspects of a restaurant (e.g., ambience, food quality, service and price range). A typical restaurant review looks like the following (Fig. **7**):

> "What a nice restaurant – perfect atmosphere. The steak of course was great and the drinks were made nice and strong. Service was just as good. I would definitely suggest have dinner one night if you are in the area. Bit pricy though"

FIG. 7

Example review for aspect-based sentiment analysis.

On analysis, one should be able to categorize the review into multiple categories (Fig. 8):

Ambience — Positive

Food Quality — Positive

Service — Positive

Price Range — Negative

FIG. 8

Example aspects and their corresponding sentiments.

The challenge is to train a model to do this type of an interpretation. The simplest solution is to associate each sentence or a phrase in a review to some aspect and the sentiment value of those aspects could be then summed up to find the overall sentiment of the review. For this kind of an approach the list of aspects to be analyzed is usually predetermined. There has been some research done to treat sentence labeling as a separate topic modeling task [51]. Applying the modified form of latent Dirichlet allocation (LDA) called *local LDA*, which treats each sentence as a document, sentences in an input document are labeled to be associated with some topic. Sentiment models can then be applied to learn sentiments from those sentences. In Ref. [51], a sentence is assumed to have a single aspect. In Ref. [52], Pavlopoulos and Androutsopoulos proposed a method to aggregate sentiments for different aspects at multiple granularities. Their method also handles cases where the same aspect is represented using different terms.

Compositional models: The techniques discussed so far do not take into account the way a sentiment progresses across individual components of a sentence, say, phrases and even words. Recent work by Socher et al. explored the importance of compositionality in sentiment analysis task [53]. In particular, a tree-bank was built from a movie review dataset, where individual words, phrases, and sentences were tagged with the sentiment conveyed. The input sentence/phrase is represented as a parse tree as shown in Fig. 9.

Their main focus was to compute compositional vector representation for phrases and feed those vectors into a classifier to make the classifier learn propagation of sentiments from granular word levels to phrase and sentence levels. Socher et al. [53] employed recursive neural networks [41,54–57] to compute compositional vector representation of phrases.

A compositional function takes the vector representation of child nodes at each level and computes the vector representation of a current node in a bottom-up fashion. The function uses the vector representation of a node as a feature of a sentiment classifier to compute the sentiment value at the node level. Socher et al. [53] compute sentiment values with the softmax classifier [58,59], as shown in Fig. 10.

Recursive neural nets, matrix vector recursive neural nets [60], and a new model proposed by Socher et al. [53] called recursive neural tensor networks (RNTN) were evaluated for this task. From their experiments, they show that RNTN perform better than the other compositional models mentioned above.

The main advantage of the system of Socher et al. [53] is that it is able to capture negation words more effectively than any other methods. However, one limitation of this system is that if a new model

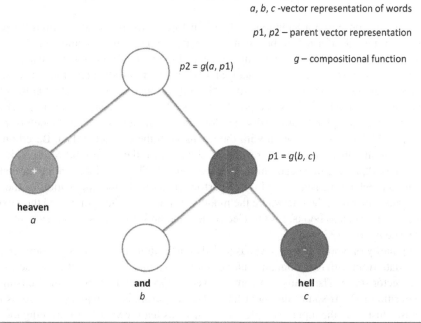

a, b, c -vector representation of words

*p*1, *p*2 – parent vector representation

g – compositional function

$p2 = g(a, p1)$

$p1 = g(b, c)$

heaven
a

and
b

hell
c

FIG. 9

Recursive vector computation using compositionality function [53].

$$y^{\mathbf{a}} = \text{softmax}(W_s . \mathbf{a})$$

where $W_s = R^{n*d}$ —— sentiment classification matrix

n —— number of sentiment classes

d —— dimensions of word vector

$\mathbf{a}$ —— d-dimensional word vector representation

$y^{\mathbf{a}}$ —— sentiment vector at that node $\mathbf{a}$ containing posterior probability of sentiment labels

FIG. 10

Sentiment value computation at each node [53].

needs to be trained for another domain, a new sentiment tree-bank needs to be manually prepared for that target domain, which can be time consuming.

Domain adaptation

The statistical methods discussed so far need a large amount of training data to achieve a good performance. It is very time consuming to generate such a tagged dataset. For ratings-related domains, such as online stores or app stores, there is a way to approximate user ratings to corresponding sentiment scores and prepare a training dataset; however, for any other domain, it is impractical to prepare a large-scale training dataset. The approximation enables the use of both supervised and unsupervised methods.

Blitzer et al. [61] proposed a technique called structural correspondence learning to select pivot features based on mutual information between source and target domain features in an unsupervised setting, thereby making the built sentiment model adaptable to target domains. For example, consider two domains: "*cell phones*" as a target domain and "*computers*" as a source domain. A sample cell phone reviews often read as "Awful battery life," "Excellent touch response," etc. On the other hand, computer reviews often read as "Awesome processing speed," "Awful design," etc. The technique proposed by Blitzer et al. completely aligns distinct domain specific terms such as "touch response" and "processing speed" based on correlation with their context in the unlabeled data. Based on this, they were able to relate that the terms "touch response" should have the same kind of effect in the target domain as the term "processing speed" in the source domain. They used an evaluation metric called *transfer error rate*, which measures the loss of performance due to the application of the sentiment model on domains other than the one where the model is trained on. They conducted their experiments on different domains, such as books, DVDs, electronics, and online reviews, and they could reduce the transfer error rate up to 4.9% on average.

Recent popularity of word2vectors [42] has added another dimension to this problem. In particular, the unlabeled data from different domains can be trained together to represent terms across domains in a common vector space. The terms in a common vector space can then be clustered using K-means clustering algorithm [62]. If some sentiment labeled data is available, frequency of words belonging to each of those clusters in the input examples can be used as feature vectors for training the sentiment classifier (a.k.a., bag of centroids approach). Similarly, the average of the vector representations of input words in the input examples can also be treated as feature vectors for training a sentiment classifier. Specifically, the idea is that the pivot features across domains will be represented closely in the semantic vector space. The trained sentiment classifier can then be effectively used to analyze sentiments on any of the domains whose data were used in building a word2vector model.

Recent research in sentiment analysis has improved the sentence level accuracy to over 85% [53]. But aggregating the sentence-level sentiments to document-level values is still another problem that has to be handled appropriately. Subtle changes to the aggregation techniques of sentiment analysis, based on the problem for which the sentiment system is designed, would result in better performance of these systems.

NLP resources for languages other than English are sparse, which makes building sentiment systems for other languages challenging. There has been some early work in this regard, wherein researchers have used machine translation-based sentiment analysis for Latin/Scandinavian family of languages [63]. Others have tried to address sentiment analysis in their respective languages by manually creating training data, such as sentiment lexicon and rules, then modeling sentiment analysis systems based on the handcrafted data.

Financial news stories are commonly analyzed in real-time to assess the market sentiment for a given stock. In recent times, sentiment analysis systems have been employed to automate this process. But critical applications such as stock market sentiment analysis require systems to be nearly perfect before making any decisions. For this, rather than using a limited set of manually labeled training examples, it is possible to exploit unsupervised learning techniques to model the underlying sentiment patterns. Another important aspect of stock market sentiment analysis is time sensitivity. Sentiments of people for a given stock might fluctuate in matter of few seconds. Thus, an ideal system for this problem should be scalable, reliable, and fast.

As we mentioned earlier, sarcasm, word sense ambiguities, etc. are few other problems that affect the performance of sentiment analysis system. To address these, recently, a few approaches have been proposed [53,64,65].

3.3.2 TRENDING TOPICS

People discuss a variety of topics on online social media. Sifting through the noise and identifying the popular topics being talked about can be a challenge. Further, some topics can go viral in a small period of time and begin "trending." Topics that are trending among users change over time. Extracting these trending topics can help us understand what users are talking about in social media. An existing example is the Twitter home page, which shows top trending topics at any given point of time, as shown in Fig. 11.

It would be useful to build a similar system with more custom features that are useful for any stream of text. This could help us discover any new hacks, events, and news within the text stream compared to having a person manually read through all the text.

Given a system to identify trends from a stream of text, one can extend the underlying algorithm to custom time intervals, such as hour of the day, day of the week, etc. The same system can be used to build a user profile based on the topics he/she talks most about. Lastly, topics can be grouped by different locations.

Trend detection on data streams is done using two major methods: document pivot method and feature pivot method. Both methods have advantages and disadvantages depending on the target application.

Worldwide Trends · Change

#SoundsGoodFeelsGood

Gisele

#الهلال_النصر

Hisashi Iwakuma

#DeChiquitoCreia

Rex Ryan

#ShawnsNewCover

Tom Brady

Cuenca

Tony Blair

FIG. 11

Worldwide trending topics on Twitter — Aug. 12, 2015.

The document pivot method clusters the documents using a similarity metric. Similarity is computed between the existing clusters and an incoming document/message, which is assigned to the nearest cluster. Topics are then extracted from each of the clusters. This method is used for applications like breaking news detection [66], first story detection [67], etc. A document that has a low similarity score with all the existing clusters implies that the document represents a new topic. In that case, a new cluster is created for that topic.

The feature pivot method is related to using topic modeling algorithms [68] to extract a set of terms that represent the topics in a document collection. Another variation of the feature pivot method is a graph-based approach [69] that builds a term co-occurrence graph and related topics are connected based on textual similarity. Unfortunately, graph-based approaches are hard to compute and have poor recall[8] [69].

Document pivot methods are more suited for a large stream of data with novelty detection as its primary focus. Locality sensitive hashing (LSH) is the traditional method for online clustering of documents [70]. LSH creates a k-bit signature for each document and assigns them to a bucket. LSH involves having k hashing vectors. Cosine similarity is computed between a document and each hashing vector. Based on the k cosine similarity values, a k-bit signature is created where each bit represents similarity score of the document with each hashing vector. Once the documents are clustered, topic keywords are extracted from clusters.

Twitter uses chi-square metric between the observed frequency and the expected frequency and if it is greater than a threshold, it is considered to be a trending topic [71]. A distribution is created on the words from past history of tweets. This is referred to as the *expected distribution*. Another distribution is computed over current tweets for a given time interval and is referred to as the *observed distribution*. Words with chi-square scores greater than a threshold are considered as trending topics.

---

[8]Recall is the ratio of the total number of topics detected and the total number of topics present in the data.

The social sensor algorithm introduces a new feature selection method by using a new metric *df-idft*, where the score is computed for each *n*-gram of the current time slot based on document frequency for this slot and penalized by the log of the average document frequencies in previous *t* time slots [72]. This score creates a ranking of *n*-grams. These *n*-grams are clustered based on a similarity measure where the score between two *n*-grams is the fraction of posts that contain both of them. Then, hierarchical clustering is used to iteratively merge clusters till the scores fall below a threshold. Finally, clusters are ranked based on the highest *df-idft* in each cluster.

Trending topic detection

A trending topic detection system can have four stages to extract trends from a user generated text stream:

- Online clustering
- Extracting *n*-grams
- Removing duplicate clusters
- Ranking clusters

The algorithm can be done in batch [72] or streaming [73,74] mode. For batch mode, the data is pulled for a given time interval (e.g., 24 hours) and provided as input to the system. Messages are clustered based on similarity and on *n*-grams extracted from clusters. Topics are then ranked based on certain metrics. Top *k* topics are returned as trends. In the streaming mode, trending topics are extracted by detecting bursty keywords. Bursty keywords are grouped by co-occurrences in tweets.

Online clustering

LSH [70] is used to cluster the input text messages. The major advantage of LSH clustering is that it can be done online. Also, the number of clusters need not be specified a priori. LSH needs three parameters to be defined:

- N: number of hash tables
- b: number of hash functions
- V: size of hash vector/vocabulary

After one iteration of n chat messages, the size of the vocabulary is identified as V (~20,000). The vocabulary can be optimized using some feature selection methods. Next, approximately 8–12 random vectors of size V are created. These vectors are hash functions that are used to hash the incoming messages. Hash vectors are represented as $h_{r1} \ldots h_{rb}$. The hash tables are replicated N (~2) times to improve recall as randomly generated hash vectors are used. Therefore, there are $b*N$ hash vectors in total.

Let s be the vector space model representation of an incoming message with the term frequency-inverse document frequency (tf-idf) scores for each word based on the input dataset. A dot product of s with each of the b hash vectors is computed to get b scalar values. The hash signature for s is computed by taking the sign of the scalar values. Positive values are represented as 1 and negative values are represented as 0. Thus, b scalar values are converted to b-bit hash signature. This hash signature is the bucket id of the hash table where the input message will be added.

Extract n-grams

Once clusters are formed, for every message in each cluster, *n*-grams (1, 2, 3) are extracted. Relevant *n*-grams are filtered, as there can potentially be too many *n*-grams associated with each cluster. POS tagging is done on the messages to identify *n*-grams that have nouns in it. NER [75] is done to extract entities and give higher importance to n-grams that are entities. N-grams whose frequency in a cluster is below a threshold are dropped. Then, each cluster is represented by a list of n-grams instead of raw text. This implies that topics dominant in that cluster can be identified from the set of n-grams extracted.

Let **Observed** (x) term frequency of a word x in that cluster.
Users (x) count of distinct users who have used word x in their messages in that cluster.

Let $expected_t(x)$ be the expected frequency of the same word to occur in the time interval t under consideration. This expected value is computed offline from historic data. Older messages are collected from a database for some longer interval (e.g., 24 hours) and processed to compute the frequency of n-grams in that dataset. This value is divided by 24 to yield the expected frequency of that word to occur in 1 hour. Therefore, $expected_t(x)$ is computed as follows:

$$expected_1(x) = expected_{24}(x) / 24$$

where $expected_1(x)$, is the expected frequency of the word in 1 hour:

$$expected_t(x) = expected_1(x) * t$$

where t is the time interval under consideration in hours.

After extracting n-grams, some metrics such as frequency ratios or chi-square ratios can be used for ranking each n-gram. From this point, a cluster is represented by set of keywords instead of raw messages.

Jaccard similarity
The clusters containing raw messages are reduced to a set of keywords. However, often some clusters are repeated, as there are multiple hash tables storing the same data. To remove duplicates, "Jaccard similarity"[9] for a set of keywords associated with each cluster is computed. Then, if the similarity score is greater than a threshold, those clusters are removed as duplicates.

Computing jaccard similarity on all pairs of clusters is an $O(n^2)$ algorithm and the number of n-grams in each cluster may be large at times (e.g., 20,000). This can potentially be a prohibitively computationally expensive step if an exact Jaccard similarity is computed. There are approximate algorithms for computing set similarity which employ Minhashing algorithm [76].

Given a set of hash functions (e.g., 50), a hash over each element in the set is computed and a minimum hash value for a given set is selected. This process is repeated for all hash functions (e.g., 50) to obtain multiple minhash values. These values represent an approximation of the original set that had around 20,000 elements. This reduces the cardinality of a given set significantly (from 20,000 to 50) and therefore reduces the computation time for Jaccard similarity. Clusters can be formed over the reduced sets that are similar based on their hashed values. This obviates comparing all the n^2 pairs of the set for Jaccard similarity; instead, pairs are compared only if they belong to the same cluster. This step improves the runtime significantly even when executed in a distributed fashion.

Ranking clusters
Post-removal of the duplicates from clusters, each n-gram is ranked and clustered. Recall that metrics such as frequency ratio or chi-square ratio of observed and expected frequencies are computed during the n-gram extraction phase. Metrics are aggregated using a machine learning model to get a single

---

[9]https://en.wikipedia.org/wiki/Jaccard_index

score per n-gram. Then, each cluster is ranked with the highest score of n-grams associated with that cluster. Clusters are then sorted and the top-N clusters and their keywords are output as a result. The highest scoring n-gram will be the topic of that cluster, and the other n-grams following it can be considered as related subtopics.

3.3.3 RECOMMENDER SYSTEMS

Recommender systems are software tools and techniques that provide suggestions for items to a user [77]. They personalize a user's experience by recommending items (e.g., products to purchase, movies/videos to watch [78], news to read [79], people to follow) that are best suited to their interests [80]. Likewise, related search query systems also employ recommender systems to assist a user [81].

One of the first automated recommender systems was from the GroupLens lab in the University of Minnesota [82]. They created the "GroupLens" recommender, a Usenet article recommendation engine, as well as MovieLens, a popular movie recommendation site.[10] In 2003, Amazon published its paper on using collaborative filtering (CF) for product recommendations [83].

From 2006 to 2009, Netflix announced a Netflix Prize for collaborative systems that performed better than its own movie recommender system, CineMatch.[11] It attracted around 44,014 submissions made by 5169 teams and led to an increased interest in recommender systems and CF. Since then, the use of recommender systems has become more widespread, with every e-commerce and media website having one to help their users find content that they like. Social media platforms also use recommender systems to suggest contacts, content, and activities [84,85]. The advertising industry widely uses recommender systems to improve targeting of ads to users.

Types of recommender systems

There are several types of recommender systems [80] based on the features and methods used to compute what content would be most likeable for an end user. They can be classified as follows:

Content-based recommender systems: Content-based systems use ratings, item descriptions, or other information to create a user/item profile [86]. These profiles are then used to recommend items that are similar to those a user has rated highly in the past, or to recommend items that have been rated highly by other users with a similar profile. In order to find similar users or items, content-based systems make use of several similarity measures, such as Jaccard similarity and cosine similarity. Algorithms such as k-nearest neighbors are used to find similar items and users.

CF-based systems: CF is the most widely used method to implement recommender systems [87]. CF uses opinions of similar users in order to recommend items to the active users. This is based on two assumptions:

- User preferences stay stable over a period of time.
- If two users had similar preferences in the past, they will have similar preferences in the future.

There are two types of CF systems:

- *Model-based systems:* Model-based systems use machine learning models to learn and predict ratings. Ratings can be binary, or a real valued number. Hence, given a user and a product, the

---

[10] http://grouplens.org/datasets/movielens/
[11] http://www.netflixprize.com

system predicts the rating the user would give the product. Different algorithms can be used to perform these predictions, such as logistic regression, neural networks, SVMs, or Bayesian networks. The most successful method for model-based recommender systems, however, has been matrix factorization methods [88,89].

- *Memory-based systems:* Memory-based systems use user rating data to compute the similarity between users or items and make recommendations. This was an early approach used in many commercial systems; it is effective and easy to implement. Typical examples of this approach are neighborhood-based CF [90] and item-based/user-based top-N recommendations [77,91].

For example, in user-based approaches, the value of ratings user u gives to item i is calculated as an aggregation of some similar users' ratings of the item:

$$r_{u,i} = aggr_{u' \in U} \, r_{u',i}$$

where U denotes the set of top-N users that are most similar to user u who rated item i. Some examples of the aggregation function include:

$$r_{u,i} = \frac{1}{N} \sum_{u' \in U} r_{u',i}$$

$$r_{u,i} = \underline{r_u} + k \sum_{u' \in U} Simil(u,u') \left(r_{u,i} - \underline{r_{u'}} \right)$$

where k is a normalizing factor defined as:

$$k = 1 / \sum_{u' \in U} Simil(u,u')$$

and $\underline{r_u}$ is the average rating of user u for all the items rated by u.

The neighborhood-based algorithm calculates the similarity between two users or items, making a prediction for the user by taking the weighted average of all the ratings. Similarity computation between items or users is an important part of this approach. Multiple measures, such as the Pearson correlation and vector cosine-based similarity are used for the similarity computation. The cosine-based approach defines the cosine similarity between vectors of associated with two users x and y as follows:

$$Simil(x,y) = \cos(\underline{x}, \underline{y}) = \frac{x.y}{\|x\| \times \|y\|} = \frac{\sum_{i \in I_{xy}} (r_{x,i} - \underline{r})(r_{y,i} - \underline{r})}{\sqrt{\sum_{i \in I_x} r^2_{x,i}} \sqrt{\sum_{i \in I_y} r^2_{y,i}}}$$

The user-based top-N recommendation algorithm uses a similarity-based vector model to identify the k most similar users to an active user. After the k most similar users are found, their corresponding user-item matrices are aggregated to identify the set of items to be recommended.

A popular method for finding the similar users is the LSH, which implements the nearest neighbor mechanism in linear time.

Social recommender systems

The techniques discussed earlier assume that all the users and items are i.i.d.; that is, independent and identically distributed. However, when users within a system interact with each other, it is well known that users who are friends with each other have similar tastes and influence each other's choices. Additionally, people are more likely to choose items that they know their friends have chosen. Social recommender systems take into account the social aspect of users' preferences [92,93]. Based on how the social network is inferred, there are three types of social recommender systems:

- *Explicit social links:* These methods can be used when the users are explicitly connected, like "friends" on Facebook, and "followers" on Twitter or Instagram. Most social recommender systems utilize CF methods. As in CF systems, there are two types:
- *Model-based systems:* Model-based systems represent the users and items as a latent-space vector, and they make sure that users' vectors are close to that of their friends.
- *Memory-based systems:* These systems are the same as the memory-based systems discussed earlier, except that they use the explicit social network to compute similarities.

Trust- and influence-based links: Trust relationships are different from social relationships. A trust relationship between users A and B is defined such that A's recommendation of an item influences B to increase their preference to the item. It takes into account the "word-of-mouth" effect, where a user is more likely to prefer a product that is endorsed by he/she trusts. Trust relationships are directional (i.e., if A influences B, it does not imply that B influences A). In explicit trust networks, users provide the system with trust statements for their peers, be it ratings on a continuous scale, lists of trusted and nontrusted people, or lists of allies. Then, for a recommendation to a specific user u, trust is estimated between u and the relevant users. The trust is used to weight the recommendation computation. The weighting is done either via a trust-based weighted mean (rating from user u for item i is an ordinary weighted mean of the ratings of users which have evaluated i, where the weights are the trust estimates for these users) or trust-based CF (as in classical CF methods, replacing similarity-based weights by trust-based weights obtained via propagation and aggregation strategies as described above).

Implicit social links: Some social recommender systems rely upon networks that can be derived from users. Users will be implicitly connected if, for example, they take pictures at the same location(s) and they attend the same events or click on the same ads. The implicit users' social networks can then be used to build recommendations.

Recommender systems datasets

There are several standard, publicly available datasets to train and test algorithms for recommender systems.

- Last.fm dataset[12]: This dataset contains 92,834 listening information counts of 17,632 artists by 1892 users of the website Last.fm. There is an explicit friends' network with 25,434 links.
- Movielens dataset[13]: This dataset contains 1,000,209 ratings of approximately 3900 movies made by 6040 users who joined MovieLens in 2000.
- Million song dataset: This was part of a Kaggle[14] challenge. It contains 48M listening counts of 380,000 songs by 1.2M users.
- Flixster dataset[15]: This dataset contains 8.2M ratings of about 49,000 movies by about 1M users. There is an explicit friends' network with 26.7M links.

---

[12] http://files.grouplens.org/datasets/hetrec2011/hetrec2011-lastfm-2k.zip
[13] http://files.grouplens.org/datasets/movielens/ml-1m.zip
[14] http://www.kaggle.com
[15] http://www.cs.ubc.ca/~jamalim/datasets/

Evaluation metrics for recommender systems

Given a choice between two or more different recommender systems, how does one select the best system? How does one compare and contrast the strengths and weaknesses of a variety of systems? One can potentially use one or more criteria that are generally used for systems deployed in production, such as memory and CPU footprint, as well as the type, quality and availability of the data that is fed as input into the system. For example, let us consider a movie recommender system that considers only the ratings a user has provided over the past month versus a movie recommender system that considers all ratings the user has ever made. When the user base is small, (<1M users), there probably isn't much of a difference in the time taken to retrieve 1 month's worth of data versus the time taken to retrieve all the ratings for a particular user. However, if the user base is sufficiently large, this difference increases. In this case, it would be more prudent to choose the system that relies on a smaller quantum of data to make its predictions.

However, recommender systems are primarily gauged by their prediction accuracy. There are three categories of metrics, depending on the kind of prediction [77]:

- *Rating prediction accuracy*: Netflix rating predictions exemplifies this. The ratings can be binary (thumbs up/thumbs down) or on a scale (1 star to 5 stars).
  - *Root mean squared error (RMSE)*: This is perhaps the most popular metric used in evaluating accuracy of predicted ratings. The system generates predicted ratings r_{ui} for a test set T of user-item pairs $\langle u,i \rangle$ for which the true ratings r_{ui} are known. Typically, r_{ui} are known because they are hidden in an offline experiment, or because they were obtained through a user study or online experiment. The RMSE between the predicted and actual ratings is given by:

$$RMSE = \sqrt{\frac{1}{\tau} \sum_{(u,i) \in \tau} \left(r'_{ui} - r_{ui} \right)^2}$$

  - *Mean absolute error (MAE)* is a popular alternative, given by

$$MAE = \sqrt{\frac{1}{\tau} \sum_{(u,i) \in \tau} \left| r'_{ui} - r_{ui} \right|}$$

  Compared to MAE, RMSE disproportionately penalizes large errors. For instance, given a test set with four hidden items, RMSE would prefer a system that makes an error of 2 on three ratings and 0 on the fourth over a system that makes an error of 3 on one rating and 0 on all three others. MAE would prefer the second system.

- *Usage prediction accuracy:* Several applications do not require predictions of the user's preferences in the form of ratings, but they utilize lists of items that the user may choose from. For example, on a shopping website, based on a user's purchase history, the website might want to recommend a list of items the user might be interested in purchasing. Here, the number of items from the list the user actually bought measures the success of the recommendations. Thus, *precision* would be a good measure of usage prediction.

$$\text{precision} = \# \text{True Positives} / \left(\# \text{True Positives} + \# \text{False Positives} \right)$$

  A more useful metric is *precision at n* (or *P@n*), which is defined as the value of precision considering only the top-n results. A broader picture of the system can be obtained by measuring precision at n for several values of n.

Ranking accuracy

In several applications, a recommender system is required to output an ordered list of recommendations, the order being how much the user would prefer an item. The system's ordering is measured against a correct ordering of items from the same superset of items. One popular measure is *normalized discounted cumulative gain (NDCG)*, whereby the positions are discounted logarithmically. Assuming each user u has a "gain" g_{ui} from being recommended an item i, the average *discounted cumulative gain (DCG)* for a list of J items is defined as:

$$DCG = \frac{1}{N}\sum_{u=1}^{N}\sum_{j=1}^{J}\frac{g_{ui_j}}{\max(1,\log_b j)}$$

where, the logarithm base is a free parameter, typically between 2 and 10. A logarithm with base 2 is commonly used to ensure all positions are discounted. NDCG is the normalized version of DCG given by

$$NDCG = \frac{DCG}{DCG*}$$

where DCG* is the ideal DCG, calculated on the "correct" ranking.

NLP in recommender systems

As ratings in recommender systems are an expression of users' preference, sentiment analysis is widely used in order to supplement user ratings [94]. User ratings may be unreliable as user experiences are complex and are often imperfectly condensed into a rating on a scale of 1–5 or 1–10. Hence, sentiment analysis performed on user reviews can be used to garner more accurate ratings on products and movies.

In the absence of sufficient number of ratings, these ratings extracted from user reviews can serve as proxy ratings to reduce sparsity in the user ratings dataset [95]. Emotions extracted from the lines of a movie plot have also been successfully used as additional features in order to address the cold start problem for movies with few or no ratings [96].

There are several new directions in recommender systems as their use becomes more widespread. One prominent area of research is privacy-sensitive recommender systems, where the user's data is protected from inference attacks while providing the best possible recommendations [97,98]. There is also a push towards giving users greater control over systems and algorithms used to recommend items to them. As different approaches might benefit different users, giving a user the choice to use the algorithm that fits them best provides better results [99]. This also helps in solving the "cold start" problem [100], as well as adapting to changing user preferences [101].

3.4 ANOMALY DETECTION

A lot of anomaly detection research has been done in various domains such as, but not limited to: statistics, signal processing, finance, econometrics, manufacturing, e-commerce, and networking. For a detailed coverage of the same, the reader is referred to books and survey papers [102–105]. As mentioned in a recent survey [106], anomaly detection is highly contextual in nature (an excerpt from the survey [106] is given below):

> A data instance might be a contextual anomaly in a given context, but an identical data instance (in terms of behavioral attributes) could be considered normal in a different context. This property is key in identifying contextual and behavioral attributes for a contextual anomaly detection technique.

Detection of anomalies in the presence of seasonality and an underlying trend, both of which are characteristic of the time series data of social networks, is nontrivial.

The roots of early work in anomaly detection can be traced to manufacturing processes. Anomaly detection manifests itself in manufacturing in the form of determining if a particular process is in a state of normal and stable behavior. To this end, statistical process control (SPC) was proposed in the early 1920s to monitor and control the reliability of a manufacturing process [107,108]. *Control charts* are one of the key tools used in SPC.

In essence, the premise of SPC is that a certain amount of variation can occur at any one point of a production chain. The variation is "common" if it is controlled and within normal or expected limits. However, the variation is "assignable" if it is not present in the causal system of the process at all times (i.e., falls outside of the normal limits). Identifying and removing the assignable sources which have impact on the manufacturing process is thus crucial to ensure the expected operation and quality of the manufacturing process.

A traditional control chart includes points representing a statistical measurement (such as the mean) of a quality characteristic in samples taken over a period of time. The mean of this characteristic is calculated over all samples, and plotted as the centerline. The standard deviation is calculated over all samples, and the upper control limit and lower control limit (LCL) defined as the threshold at which the process is considered statistically unlikely to occur (typically set at three standard deviations, denoted by 3σ, about the mean/centerline). When the process is "in control," 99.73% of all points are within the upper and LCLs. A signal may be generated when observations fall outside of these control limits, signifying the introduction of some other source of variation outside of the normal expected behavior.

Methodologies for improving the performance of control charts have been investigated since Shewhart's early work [107,108]. Roberts proposed the geometrical moving average control chart — also known as the EWMA (exponentially weighted moving average) control chart — which weights the most recent samples more highly than older samples [109]. The EWMA chart tends to detect small shifts ($1–2\sigma$) in the sample mean more efficiently; however, the Shewhart chart tends to detect larger shift (3σ) more efficiently. In case the quality characteristic follows a Poisson distribution, alternatives to the EWMA chart have been proposed [110]. Other types of control charts, such as the CUSUM (cumulative sum) chart [111], have been proposed.

Grubbs test [112,133], one of the most widely used statistical tests, was developed for detecting the largest anomaly within a univariate sample set. The test assumes that the underlying data distribution is normal. Grubbs test is defined for the hypothesis:

H_0: There are no outliers in the dataset
H_1: There is at least one outlier in the dataset

The Grubbs test statistic is defined as follows:

$$C = \frac{\max_t |x_t - \bar{x}|}{s}$$

For the two-sided test, the hypothesis of no outliers is rejected at significance level α if:

$$C > \frac{(N-1)}{\sqrt{N}} \sqrt{\frac{\left(t_{\alpha/(2N),N-2}\right)^2}{N-2+\left(t_{\alpha/(2N),N-2}\right)^2}}$$

where $t_{\alpha/(2N),N-2}$ denotes the upper critical values of the t-distribution with $N-2$ degrees of freedom and a significance level of $\alpha/(2N)$. For one-sided tests, $\alpha/(2N)$ becomes α/N. The largest data point in the time series that is greater than the test statistics labeled as an anomaly.

In practice, we observe that there is more than one anomaly in the time series data obtained from production. Conceivably, one can iteratively apply Grubbs' z-test to detect multiple anomalies. Removal of the largest anomaly in each iteration reduces the value of N; however, Grubbs' test does not update the value obtained from the t-distribution tables. Consequently, Grubbs' test is not suited for detecting multiple outliers in a given time series data. Several other approaches, such as the Tietjen-Moore test[16] [113], and the extreme studentized deviate (ESD) test [114,115] have been proposed to address the aforementioned issue.

The ESD test [114] (and its generalized version [115]) can also be used to detect multiple anomalies in the given time series. Unlike the Tietjen-Moore test, it only requires an upper bound on the number of anomalies (k) to be specified. In the worst case, the number of anomalies can be at most 49.9% of the total number of data points in the given time series. In practice, our observation, based on production data, has been that the number of anomalies is typically less than 1% in the context of application metrics and less than 5% in the context of system metrics. ESD computes the following test statistic for the k most extreme values in the dataset:

$$C_k = \frac{\max_k |x_k - \bar{x}|}{s}$$

where s is the standard deviation. The test statistic is then compared with a critical value, computed using the equation given below, to determine whether a value is anomalous. If the value is indeed anomalous, it is removed from the dataset, and the critical value is recalculated from the remaining data.

$$\lambda_k = \frac{(n-k)t_{p,n-k-1}}{\sqrt{\left(n-k-1+t_{p,n-k-1}^2\right)(n-k+1)}}$$

where n is the number of elements in the dataset. ESD repeats this process k times, with the number of anomalies equal to the largest k such that $C_k > \lambda_k$. In practice, C_k may swing above and below λ_k multiple times before permanently becoming less then λ_k. In the case of Grubbs' test, the above would cause the test to prematurely exit; however, ESD will continue until the test has run for k outliers.

Techniques from signal processing such as, but not limited to, spectral analysis, have been adopted for anomaly detection. For instance, in Ref. [116], Cheng et al. employed spectral analysis to complement existing DoS defense mechanisms that focus on identifying attack traffic, by ruling out normal TCP traffic, thereby reducing false positives. Similarly, wavelet packets and wavelet decomposition have been used for detecting anomalies in network traffic [117–121]. Benefits of wavelet-based techniques include the ability to accurately detect anomalies at various frequencies with relatively fast computation due to the inherent time-frequency property of decomposing signals into different components at several frequencies. In Ref. [122], Gao et al. proposed a speed optimization for real-time use using sliding windows. Recently, Lu and Ghorbani proposed an approach consisting of three components: (1) feature analysis, (2) normal daily traffic modeling based on wavelet approximation, ARX

---

[16] Although the Tietjen-Moore test can be used to detect multiple anomalies, it requires the number of anomalies to detect to be prespecified. This is not practical in the current context.

(AutoRegressive with eXogenous), and intrusion decision [123]. An overview of signal-processing techniques for network anomaly detection, including PSD (power spectral density) and wavelet-based approaches, is presented in Ref. [124].

Additionally, Kalman filtering and principle component analysis (PCA) based approaches have been proposed in the signal-processing domain for anomaly detection. In Ref. [125], Ndong and Salamatian reported that PCA-based approaches exhibit improved performance when coupled with Karuhen-Loeve (KL) expansion; on the other hand, Kalman filtering approaches outperformed the PCA-KL method when combined with statistical methods, such as Gaussian mixture and HMMs.

Applications to text streams

Several applications have been developed atop of text data streams. For example, detecting trending terms, potentially across languages, has proven useful in determining early signs of flu outbreak. In a similar vein, detecting patterns/anomalies in chat messages in multiplayer games can potentially guide the development of new features and can potentially help players to develop better strategies. Detecting change/anomalies in sentiment (derived via mining of text data streams) has direct applications in, for example, financial markets. Detecting anomalies in time series of terms, obtained from mining of text data streams, is nontrivial owing to, but not limited to, for example, the presence of an underlying trend, seasonality, and other data characteristics (which are mostly not accounted for by the existing techniques). Further, there is a tradeoff between accuracy and time to detect (TTD). A high TTD can potentially result in revenue loss and impact the brand of a company.

In general, detecting anomalies in social media based on conventional term frequency-based approaches may not be appropriate, as the information exchanged is not only text but also images, URLs, and videos. To this end, in Ref. [126], Takahashi et al. proposed to exploit the links between users that are generated dynamically whether intentionally or unintentionally through replies, mentions, and retweets. Specifically, the authors proposed a probabilistic model of the mentioning behavior of a social network user and detected the emergence of a new topic from the anomaly measured through the model. The authors combined the proposed mention anomaly score with a change-point detection technique based on the sequentially discounting normalized maximum likelihood [127], or with Kleinberg's burst model [128]. A variety of other probabilistic models such as probabilistic latent semantic indexing and LDA [68,129,130] have been proposed for anomaly text in social media text. In Ref. [131], Yu et al. proposed a proposed a hierarchical Bayes model — the Group Latent Anomaly Detection model — to automatically infer groups and detects group anomalies simultaneously.

As mentioned earlier, anomaly detection has been studied in a large set of domains for over five decades. Going forward, anomaly detection techniques from neural networks and signal processing can potentially be leveraged and adapted to social media text. For instance, the use of autoencoders with nonlinear dimensionality reduction can help discover subtle anomalies (as demonstrated by Sakurada and Yairi on spacecrafts' telemetry data [132]).

Acknowledgments

We would like to acknowledge Francois Orsini (CTO @ Machine Zone) for his support and the editors for this opportunity.

REFERENCES

[1] James J. Data never sleeps 2.0, https://www.domo.com/blog/2014/04/data-never-sleeps-2-0/ [accessed 01.07.15].

[2] Jurafsky D, Martin JH. Speech and language processing: an introduction of natural language processing, speech processing, and computational linguistics. 2nd ed. Upper Saddle River, NJ: Prentice-Hall; 2009.

[3] Fox BA, Jurafsky D, Michaelis LA, editors. Cognition and function in language. Stanford, CA: CSLI Publications; 1999.

[4] Dunning T. Statistical identification of language. New Mexico State University: Computing Research Laboratory; 1994.

[5] Grothe L, Luca EWD, Nürnberger A. A comparative study on language identification methods. In: Proceedings of LREC; 2008.

[6] Ahmed B, Cha S, Tappert C. Language identification from text using n-gram based cumulative frequency addition. In: Proceedings of student/faculty research day, CSIS, Pace University; 2004.

[7] Hughes B, Baldwin T, Bird S, Nicholson J, MacKinlay A. Reconsidering language identification for written language resources. In: Proceedings of LREC; 2006.

[8] Baldwin T, Lui M. Language identification: the long and the short of the matter. In: Proceedings of NAACL-HLT; 2010.

[9] Carter S, Weerkamp W, Tsagkias M. Microblog language identification: overcoming the limitations of short, unedited and idiomatic text. Lang Resour Eval 2013;47(1):195–215.

[10] Cavnar WB, Trenkle JM. Ngram-based text categorization. In: Proceedings of the third symposium on document analysis and information retrieval; 1994.

[11] Vatanen T, Väyrynen JJ, Virpioja S. Language identification of short text segments with n-gram models. In: Proceedings of LREC; 2010.

[12] Tromp E, Pechenizkiy M. Graph-based n-gram language identification on short texts. In: Proceedings of the 20th machine learning conference of Belgium and The Netherlands; 2011.

[13] Vogel J, Tresner-Kirsch D. Robust language identification in short, noisy texts: improvements to LIGA. In: Proceedings of the third international workshop on mining ubiquitous and social environments; 2012.

[14] Bergsma S, McNamee P, Bagdouri M, Fink C, Wilson T. Language identification for creating language-specific Twitter collections. In: Proceedings of the second workshop on language in social media; 2012.

[15] Wang P, Bojja N, Kannan S. A language detection system for short chats in mobile games. In: Proceedings of the third international workshop on natural language processing for social media (SocialNLP), Denver, US, June; 2015.

[16] Lui M, Baldwin T. langid.py: an off-the-shelf language identification tool. In: Proceedings of ACL system demonstrations; 2012.

[17] Lui M, Baldwin T. Cross-domain feature selection for language identification. In: Proceedings of IJCNLP; 2011.

[18] Fan R, Chang K, Hsieh C, Wang X, Lin C. LIBLINEAR: A library for large linear classification. J Mach Learn Res 2008;9:1871–4.

[19] Wang P, Ng HT. A beam-search decoder for normalization of social media text with application to machine translation. In: Proceedings of the 2013 conference of the North American chapter of the Association for Computational Linguistics: Human Language Technologies (NAACL-HLT), Atlanta, Georgia, June; 2013.

[20] Liu F, Weng F, Jiang X. A broad-coverage normalization system for social media language. In: Proceedings of the 50th annual meeting of the Association for Computational Linguistics (ACL), Jeju Island, Korea, July; 2012.

[21] Socher R, Bengio Y, Manning C. Deep learning for NLP. In: Tutorial at the 50th annual meeting of the Association for Computational Linguistics, Jeju Island, Korea, July; 2012.

[22] Zhou G, Su J. Named entity recognition using an HMM-based chunk tagger. In: Proceedings ACL '02, proceedings of the 40th annual meeting on Association for Computational Linguistics (ACL); 2002. p. 473–80.

[23] Isozaki H, Kazawa H. Efficient support vector classifiers for named entity recognition. In: Proceedings COLING '02, proceedings of the 19th international conference on computational linguistics — vol. 1; 2002. p. 1–7.

[24] Bender O, Och FJ, Ney H. Maximum entropy models for named entity recognition. In: Proceedings of CoNLL-2003; 2003.

[25] Chieu HL, Ng HT. Named entity recognition with a maximum entropy approach. In: Proceedings of CoNLL-2003; 2003.

[26] Lafferty JD, McCallum A, Pereira FCN. Conditional random fields: probabilistic models for segmenting and labeling sequence data. In: Proceedings ICML '01, proceedings of the eighteenth international conference on machine learning; 2001. p. 282–9.

[27] Finkel JR, Grenager T, Manning C. Incorporating non-local information into information extraction systems by Gibbs sampling. In: Proceedings of the 43nd annual meeting of the Association for Computational Linguistics (ACL 2005); 2005. p. 363–70.

[28] Guyon I, Elisseeff A. An introduction to variable and feature selection. J Mach Learn Res 2003;3:1157–82.

[29] Klinger R, Friedrich CM. Feature subset selection in conditional random fields for named entity recognition. In: International conference RANLP 2009, Borovets, Bulgaria; 2009. p. 185–91.

[30] Liu H, Setiono R. Chi2: feature selection and discretization of numeric attributes. In: Proceedings of the IEEE 7th international conference on tools with artificial intelligence; 1995.

[31] Settles B. Biomedical named entity recognition using conditional random fields and rich feature sets. In: Proceedings JNLPBA '04, proceedings of the international joint workshop on natural language processing in biomedicine and its applications; 2004. p. 104–7.

[32] Guo J, Xu G, Cheng X, Li H. Named entity recognition in query. In: Proceedings SIGIR '09, proceedings of the 32nd international ACM SIGIR conference on research and development in information retrieval; 2009. p. 267–74.

[33] Ritter A, Clark S, Mausam, Etzioni O. Named entity recognition in tweets: an experimental study. In: Proceedings of empirical methods for natural language processing (EMNLP), Edinburgh, UK; 2011.

[34] Bontcheva K, Derczynski L, Funk A, Greenwood MA, Maynard D, Aswani N. TwitIE: an open-source information extraction pipeline for microblog text. In: Proceedings of the international conference on recent advances in natural language processing. ACL; 2013.

[35] Cunningham H, Maynard D, Bontcheva K, Tablan V. Gate: an architecture for development of robust HLT applications. In: Proceedings of the 40th annual meeting on Association for Computational Linguistics; 2002. p. 168–75.

[36] Tkachenko M, Simanovsky A. Named entity recognition: exploring features. In: Proceedings of KONVENS 2012; 2012.

[37] Bengio Y. Learning deep architectures for AI. Found Trends Mach Learn 2009;1(2):1–127.

[38] Schmidhuber J. Deep learning in neural networks: an overview. Neural Netw 2015;61(January):85–117.

[39] Deng L, Yu D. Deep learning: methods and applications. Found Trends Signal Process 2013;7(3–4):197–387.

[40] LeCun Y, Bengio Y, Hinton G. Deep learning. Nature 2015;521(7553):436–44.

[41] Graves A. Supervised sequence labeling with recurrent neural networks, vol. 385. New York: Springer; 2012.

[42] Mikolov T, Chen K, Corrado G, Dean J. Efficient estimation of word representations in vector space. In: Proceedings of workshop at ICLR; 2013.

[43] Rockwell P. Lower, slower, louder: vocal cues of sarcasm. J Psycholinguist Res 2000;29(5).

[44] González-Ibáñez R, Muresan S, Wacholder N. Identifying sarcasm in Twitter: a closer look. In: Proceedings of the 49th annual meeting of the Association for Computational Linguistics (ACL '11), Portland, Oregon, June 19–24; 2011. p. 581–6.

[45] Whissell CM. Emotion theory, research and experience. The dictionary of affect in language, vol. 4. Cambridge: Academic Press, Inc; 1989.

[46] Hatzivassiloglou V, McKeown KR. Predicting the semantic orientation of adjectives. In: Proceedings of the 35th annual meeting of the Association for Computational Linguistics and eighth conference of the European chapter of the Association for Computational Linguistics; 1998.

[47] Turney PD, Littman ML. Measuring praise and criticism: inference of semantic orientation from association. ACM Trans Inf Syst 2003;21(4).

[48] Kanayama H, Nasukawa T. Fully automatic lexicon expansion for domain-oriented sentiment analysis. In: Proceedings of the 2006 conference on empirical methods in natural language processing (EMNLP 2006), Sydney, July; 2006. p. 355–63.

[49] Turney PD. Thumbs up or thumbs down? Semantic orientation applied to unsupervised classification of reviews. In: Proceedings of the 40th annual meeting of the Association for Computational Linguistics (ACL), Philadelphia, July; 2002.

[50] Pang B, Lee L, Vaithiyanathan S. Thumbs up? Sentiment classification using machine learning techniques. In: Proceedings of the conference on empirical methods in natural language processing (EMNLP), Philadelphia, USA, July; 2002.

[51] Lu B, Ott M, Cardie C, Tsou B. Multi-aspect sentiment analysis with topic models. In: Proceedings of the 2011 IEEE 11th international conference on data mining workshops, Washington, DC, USA; 2011.

[52] Pavlopoulos J, Androutsopoulos I. Multi-granular aspect aggregation in aspect-based sentiment analysis. In: Proceedings of the 14th conference of the European chapter of the Association for Computational Linguistics, Gothenburg, Sweden, April 26–30; 2014. p. 78–87.

[53] Socher R, Perelygin A, Wu JY, Chuang J, Manning CD, Ng AY, et al. Recursive deep models for semantic compositionality over a sentiment treebank. In: Proceedings of the 2013 conference on empirical methods in natural language processing (EMNLP), Seattle, Washington, USA, October; 2013. p. 18–21.

[54] Bishop CM. Neural networks for pattern recognition. Oxford, UK: Clarendon; 1995.

[55] Giles CL, Kuhn GM, Williams RJ. Dynamic recurrent neural networks: theory and applications. IEEE Trans Neural Netw 1994;5(April):153.

[56] Pollack JB. Recursive distributed representations. Artif Intell 1990;46(1–2):77–106.

[57] Collobert R, Weston J. A unified architecture for natural language processing: deep neural networks with multitask learning. In: Proceedings of the 25th international conference on machine learning (ICML), New York, NY, USA; 2008.

[58] Duan K, Keerthi SS, Chu W, Shevade SK, Poo AN. Multi-category classification by soft-max combination of binary classifiers. In: Proceedings of 4th international workshop — multiple classifier systems, Guildford, UK, June 11–13; 2003.

[59] Duan K, Keerthi SS. Which is the best multiclass SVM method? An empirical study. In: Proceedings of 6th international workshop — multiple classifier systems, Seaside, CA, USA, June 13–15; 2005.

[60] Socher R, Huval B, Manning CD, Ng AY. Semantic compositionality through recursive matrix–vector spaces. In: Proceedings of joint conference on empirical methods in natural language processing and computational natural language learning; 2012.

[61] Blitzer J, McDonald R, Pereira F. Domain adaptation with structural correspondence learning. In: Proceedings of the 2006 conference on empirical methods in natural language processing (EMNLP 2006), Sydney, July; 2006.

[62] Macqueen J. Some methods for classification and analysis of multivariate observations. In: Proceedings of the fifth Berkeley symposium on Maths statistics and probability, vol. 1. Berkeley, CA: University of California Press; 1967.

[63] Balahur A, Turchi M. Multilingual sentiment analysis using machine translation? In: Proceedings of the 3rd workshop on computational approaches to subjectivity and sentiment analysis, Jeju, Republic of Korea, July 12; 2012.

[64] Cambria E, Fu J, Bisio F, Poria S. ActiveSpace 2: enabling active intuition for concept-level sentiment analysis. In: Proceedings of twenty-ninth AAAI conference on artificial intelligence; 2015.

[65] Kranjca J, Smailovića J, Podpečana V, Grčara M, Žnidaršiča M, Lavrača N. Active learning for sentiment analysis on data streams: methodology and workflow implementation in the ClowdFlows platform. Inform Process Manage 2015;51(2).

[66] Phuvipadawat S, Murata T. Breaking news detection and tracking in Twitter, Web Intelligence and Intelligent Agent Technology. In: International conference on IEEE/WIC/ACM, vol. 3; 2010. p. 120–3.

[67] Petrovic S, Osborne M, Lavrenko V. Streaming first story detection with application to Twitter. In: Proceedings of HLT, annual conference of the North American chapter of the Association for Computational Linguistics. Stroudsburg, PA: Association for Computational Linguistics. 2010. p. 181–9.

[68] Blei DM, Ng AY, Jordan MI. Latent Dirichlet allocation. J Mach Learn Res 2003;3(March):993–1022.

[69] Sayyadi H, Hurst M, Maykov A. Event detection and tracking in social streams. In: Proceedings of the international conference on Weblogs and Social Media (ICWSM 2009). AAAI; 2009.

[70] Andoni A, Indyk P. Near-optimal hashing algorithms for approximate nearest neighbor in high dimensions. Commun ACM 2008;117–21.

[71] Tsioutsiouliklis K. Trend and event detection in social streams. Analyzing Big Data with Twitter. UC Berkeley iSchool course; 2012.

[72] Aiello LM, Petkos G, Martin C, Corney D, Papadopoulos S, Skarba R, et al. Sensing trending topics in Twitter. IEEE Trans Multimedia 2013.

[73] Mathioudakis M, Koudas N. TwitterMonitor: trend detection over the twitter stream. In: Proceedings of the 2010 ACM SIGMOD international conference on management of data, SIGMOD; 2010. p. 1155–8.

[74] Kim D, Kim D, Rho S, Hwang E. Detecting trend and bursty keywords using characteristics of Twitter stream data. Int J Smart Home 2013;7(1):209–20.

[75] Rifer A, Clark S, Etzioni M, Etzioni O. Named entity recognition in tweets: an experimental study. In: Proceedings of the conference on empirical methods in natural language processing (EMNLP); 2011. p. 1524–34.

[76] Broder AZ. On the resemblance and containment of documents. In: Compression and complexity of sequences proceedings, June; 1997. p. 21–9.

[77] Ricci F, Rokach L, Shapira B, Kantor PB. Recommender systems handbook. 1st ed. New York, NY: Springer-Verlag; 2011.

[78] Davidson J, Liebald B, Liu J, Nandy P, Van Vleet T, Gargi U, et al. The YouTube video recommendation system. In: Proceedings of the fourth ACM conference on recommender systems (RecSys '10); New York, NY: ACM; 2010. p. 293–6.

[79] Das AS, Datar M, Garg A, Rajaram S. Google news personalization: scalable online collaborative filtering. In: Proceedings of the 16th international conference on World Wide Web (WWW '07) New York, NY: ACM; 2007. p. 271–80.

[80] Bernardes D, Diaby M, Fournier R, FogelmanSoulié F, Viennet E, Social A. Formalism and survey for recommender systems. SIGKDD Explor Newsl 2015;16(2):20–37.

[81] Reda A, Park Y, Tiwari M, Posse C, Shah S. Metaphor: a system for related search recommendations. In: Proceedings of the 21st ACM international conference on information and knowledge management (CIKM '12); New York, NY: ACM; 2012. p. 664–73.

[82] Sarwar B, Karypis G, Konstan J, Riedl J. Item-based collaborative filtering recommendation algorithms. In: Proceedings of the 10th international conference on World Wide Web (WWW '01). New York, NY: ACM; 2001. p. 285–95.

[83] Linden G, Smith B, York J. Amazon.com recommendations: item-to-item collaborative filtering. IEEE Internet Comput 2003;7(1):76–80.

[84] Wu L, Shah S, Choi S, Tiwari M, Posse C. The Browsemaps: collaborative filtering at LinkedIn. RSWeb@ RecSys 2014.

[85] Gupta P, Goel A, Lin J, Sharma A, Wang D, Zadeh R. WTF: the who to follow service at Twitter. In: Proceedings of the 22nd international conference on World Wide Web (WWW '13), international World Wide Web Conferences Steering Committee, Republic and Canton of Geneva, Switzerland; 2013. p. 505–14.

[86] Pazzani MJ, Billsus D. Content-based recommendation systems. In: Brusilovsky P, Kobsa A, Nejdl W, editors. The adaptive web. Lecture notes in computer science, vol. 4321. Berlin, Heidelberg: Springer-Verlag; 2007. p. 325–41.

[87] Su X, Khoshgoftaar TM. A survey of collaborative filtering techniques. Adv Artif Intell 2009. 1 p. Article 4.

[88] Salakhutdinov R, Mnih A. Probabilistic matrix factorization. In: Proceedings of the 20th conference in advances in neural information processing systems; 2007.

[89] Yehuda Koren. Factorization meets the neighborhood: a multifaceted collaborative filtering model. In: Proceedings of the 14th ACM SIGKDD international conference on knowledge discovery and data mining (KDD '08); New York, NY: ACM; 2008. p. 426–34.

[90] Adomavicius G, Tuzhilin A. Toward the next generation of recommender systems: a survey of the state-of-the-art and possible extensions. IEEE Trans Knowl Data Eng 2005;17(6):734–49.

[91] Deshpande M, Karypis G. Item-based top-N recommendation algorithms. ACM Trans Inf Syst 2004;22(1):143–77.

[92] He J. A social network-based recommender system. PhD dissertation, Los Angeles, CA, USA: University of California at Los Angeles; 2010. Advisor(s) Wesley W. Chu.

[93] Su X, Khoshgoftaar TM. A survey of collaborative filtering techniques. Adv Artif Intell 2009;(January): 1. Article 4.

[94] Kasper W, Vela M. Sentiment analysis for hotel reviews. In: Jassem K, Fuglewicz P, Piasecki M, Przepiorkowski A, editors. Proceedings of the computational linguistics-applications conference (CLA-2011), Jachranka, October; 2011. p. 45–52.

[95] Leung CWK, Chan SCF, Chung F. Integrating collaborative filtering and sentiment analysis: a rating inference approach. In: Proceedings of the ECAI 2006 workshop on recommender systems; 2006. p. 62–6.

[96] Moshfeghi Y, Piwowarski B, Jose JM. Handling data sparsity in collaborative filtering using emotion and semantic based features. In: Proceedings of the 34th international ACM SIGIR conference on research and development in information retrieval (SIGIR '11). New York, NY: ACM; 2011. p. 625–34.

[97] Aimeur E, Brassard G, Fernandez JM, Onana FSM. Alambic: a privacy-preserving recommender system for electronic commerce. Int J Inf Secur 2008;7(5):307–34.

[98] Nikolaenko V, Ioannidis S, Weinsberg U, Joye M, Taft N, Boneh D. Privacy-preserving matrix factorization. In: Proceedings of the 2013 ACM SIGSAC conference on computer & communications security (CCS '13). New York, NY: ACM; 2013. p. 801–12.

[99] Ekstrand MD, Kluver D, Harper FM, Konstan JA. Letting users choose recommender algorithms: an experimental study. In: Proceedings of the ninth ACM conference on recommender systems (RecSys '15). New York, NY: ACM; 2015.

[100] Kapoor VK, Terveen L, Konstan JA, Schrater P. 'I like to explore sometimes' — adapting to dynamic user novelty preferences. In: Proceedings of the ninth ACM conference on recommender systems (RecSys '15). New York, NY: ACM; 2015. in press.

[101] Drachsler-Cohen D, Somekh O, Aharon M, Golan S, Avigdor-Elgrabli N, Anava O. ExcUseMe: asking users to help in item cold-start recommendations. In: Proceedings of the ninth ACM conference on recommender systems (RecSys '15). New York, NY: ACM; 2015. in press.

[102] Hawkins DM. Identification of outliers, vol. 11. London: Chapman and Hall; 1980.

[103] Barnett V, Lewis T. Outliers in statistical data, vol. 3. New York: Wiley; 1994.

[104] Hodge VJ, Austin J. A survey of outlier detection methodologies. Artif Intell Rev 2004;22(2):85126.

[105] Aggarwal CC. Outlier analysis. New York: Springer; 2013.

[106] Chandola V, Banerjee A, Kumar V. Anomaly detection: a survey. ACM Comput Surv 2009;41(3):15:1–15:58.

[107] Shewhart WA. Quality control charts. Bell Syst Tech J 1926;5(4):593–603.

[108] Shewhart WA. Economic control of quality of manufactured product. New York, NY: Van Nostrand Reinhold Co.; 1931.

[109] Roberts SW. Control chart tests based on geometric moving averages. Technometrics 1959;1(3):239–50.

[110] Montgomery DC. Introduction to statistical quality control. New York: Wiley; 2007.

[111] Page ES. Continuous inspection schemes. Biometrika 1954;41(1/2):100–15.

[112] Grubbs FE. Procedures for detecting outlying observations in samples. Technometrics 1969;11(1):121.

[113] Tietjen GL, Moore RH. Some Grubbs-type statistics for the detection of several outliers. Technometrics 1972;14(3):583–97.

[114] Rosner B. On the detection of many outliers. Technometrics 1975;17(2):221–7.

[115] Rosner B. Percentage points for a generalized ESD many-outlier procedure. Technometrics 1983;25(2):165–72.

[116] Cheng C-M, Kung HT, Tan K-S. Use of spectral analysis in defense against DoS attacks. In: Global telecommunications conference, vol. 3; 2002. p. 2143–8.

[117] Barford P, Kline J, Plonka D, Ron A. A signal analysis of network traffic anomalies. In: Proceedings of the 2nd ACM SIGCOMM workshop on internet measurement; 2002. p. 71–82.

[118] Alarcon-Aquino V, Barria JA. Anomaly detection in communication networks using wavelets. IEEE Proc Commun 2001;148(6):355–62.

[119] Li L, Lee G. DDoS attack detection and wavelets. Telecommun Syst 2005;28(3–4):435–51.

[120] Detecting traffic anomalies through aggregate analysis of packet header data. In: NETWORKING 2004. Networking technologies, services, and protocols; performance of computer and communication networks; mobile and wireless communications. New York: Springer; 2004. p. 1047–59.

[121] Ramanathan A. WADeS: a tool for distributed denial of service attack detection. PhD thesis, Texas: Texas A&M University; 2002.

[122] Gao J, Hu G, Yao X, Chang RKC. Anomaly detection of network traffic based on wavelet packet. In: Asia-Pacific conference on communications; 2006. p. 15.

[123] Lu W, Ghorbani AA. Network anomaly detection based on wavelet analysis. EURASIP J Adv Signal Process 2009;4:2009.

[124] Zhang L. Signal processing methods for network anomaly detection; 2005. http://www.cs.unc.edu/~jeffay/courses/nidsS05/slides/8-Signal-Processing2.pdf.

[125] Ndong J, Salamatian K. Signal processing-based anomaly detection techniques: a comparative analysis. In: INTERNET 2011, the third international conference on evolving Internet; 2011. p. 32–9.

[126] Takahashi T, Tomioka R, Yamanishi K. Discovering emerging topics in social streams via link anomaly detection. In: Proceedings of the 11th IEEE international conference on data mining; 2011. p. 1230–5.

[127] Kleinberg J. Bursty and hierarchical structure in streams. Data Min Knowl Discov 2003;7(4):373–97.

[128] Urabe Y, Yamanishi K, Tomioka R, Iwai H. Real-time change-point detection using sequentially discounting normalized maximum likelihood coding. In: Proceedings of the 15th PAKDD; 2011.

[129] Hoffman T. Probabilistic latent semantic indexing. In: ACM SIGIR conference; 1999.

[130] Blei DM, Lafferty J. Dynamic topic models. In: Proceedings of international conference on machine learning; 2006.

[131] Yu Q, He X, Liu Y. Group anomaly detection in social media analysis — extended abstract. http://arxiv.org/abs/1410.1940.

[132] Sakurada M, Yairi T. Anomaly detection using autoencoders with nonlinear dimensionality reduction. In: Proceedings of the MLSDA 2014 2Nd workshop on machine learning for sensory data analysis; 2014. p. 4:4–4:11.

[133] Grubbs FE. Sample criteria for testing outlying observations. Ann Math Statistics 1950;21:27–58.

DEEP LEARNING AND ITS PARALLELIZATION

4

X. Li, G. Zhang, K. Li, W. Zheng

4.1 INTRODUCTION

Big Data has become more and more important because many institutes and companies need to collect useful information from massive amounts of data. Traditional machine learning algorithms were designed to make machines cognize and understand the real world, which means that computers can learn a new knowledge and experience by themselves in a limited dataset with some special customized methods of machine learning. However, it is difficult to learn and analyze in Big Data environment for traditional machine learning algorithms because Big Data has amount of data samples, complicated structures and wide range of varieties. Fortunately, deep learning is a very promising method for solving analytic problems in Big Data. A significant feature of deep learning, which is also the core of Big Data analytics, is to learn high-level representations and complicated structures automatically from massive amounts of raw input data to obtain meaningful information. At the same time, Big Data can provide a large amount of training datasets for deep learning networks, which can help in extracting more meaningful patterns and improve the state of the art performance. Training on large-scale deep learning networks with billions or even more of parameters can dramatically improve the accuracy of the deep networks. But training on those large deep networks involves a large number of forward and backward propagations, which is time-consuming and needs massive amount of computing resources. Therefore, it is necessary to accelerate those large deep networks in high performance computing resources (eg, GPUs, super computers, and distributed clusters).

4.1.1 APPLICATION BACKGROUND

Deep learning is able to find out complicated structures in high-dimensional data, which eventually reaps benefits in many areas of society.

In visual field, the records of image classification have been broken in the ImageNet Challenge 2012 by using deep convolutional neural network (CNN) [1]. Additionally, deep learning has a significant impact on other visual problems, such as face detection, image segmentation, general object detection, and optical character recognition.

Deep learning can also be used for speech recognition, natural language understanding, and many other domains, such as recommendation systems, web content filtering, disease prediction, drug discovery, and genomics [2]. With the improvement of the deep network architectures, training samples and high performance computing, deep learning will be applied successfully in more applications in the near future.

Big Data. http://dx.doi.org/10.1016/B978-0-12-805394-2.00004-0

4.1.2 PERFORMANCE DEMANDS FOR DEEP LEARNING

Deep learning networks are good at discovering the intricate structures of a multidimensional training data set and are well suited to tackle large-scale learning problems, such as image, audio, and speech recognition. Training on large dataset and large-scale deep networks, which has more layers and huge number of parameters, can result in the state of the art performances. But it also means that training on those large models becomes much more time consuming and we have to wait for a very long time (several months or even years) to get a model well trained. With the rapid development of modern computing device and parallel techniques, it's possible to train these large-scale models with high performance computing techniques, such as distributed systems with thousands of Central Processing Unit (CPU) cores, Graphic Processing Units (GPUs) with thousands of computing threads and other parallel computing devices.

4.1.3 EXISTING PARALLEL FRAMEWORKS OF DEEP LEARNING

Many research institutes and companies have explored the ability of accelerating deep learning models in parallel. Dean et al. presented that training large deep learning models with billions of parameters using 16,000 CPU cores can dramatically improve training performance [3]. Krizhevsky et al. [1] showed that training a large deep convolutional network with 60 million parameters and 650,000 neurons on 1.2 million high-resolution images can obtain a great performance based on GPU processors. From then on, a lot of frameworks, which are aimed to facilitate researchers experimenting on deep networks, were constantly emerging, including Theano [5], Torch [6], cuda-convnet and cuda-convnet2 [31], Decaf [10], Overfeat [8], and Caffe [7]. Most of these frameworks are open source and optimized by NVIDIA GPUs using Compute Unified Device Architecture (CUDA) programming interface. Moreover, some GPU-based libraries were developed to enhance many of those frameworks, such as the NVIDIA CUDA Deep Neural Network library (cuDNN) [9] and Facebook FFT (fbfft) [11].

The rest of this chapter is organized as follows. In Section 4.2, we will introduce concepts of deep learning, including two fundamental deep learning models, as well as a popular one. In Section 4.3, we will present three popular frameworks of parallel deep learning based on GPU and distributed systems. In the last section, we will discuss challenges and future directions.

4.2 CONCEPTS AND CATEGORIES OF DEEP LEARNING

In this section, we will introduce the concepts of deep learning, including neural networks. And then we will introduce several foundational and popular deep learning models.

4.2.1 DEEP LEARNING

Artificial neural networks

The basic theory of deep learning is from the artificial neural network (ANN) that was a quite popular method of machine learning in the 1980s and 1990s. The idea behind ANN was to develop a novel way for machines to explain and understand data, such as image, speech, and text [4]. The ANN, inspired by the natural neurons, is composed of massive amounts of interconnected computational elements called neurons with numeric weights that can be tuned and be adaptive to inputs.

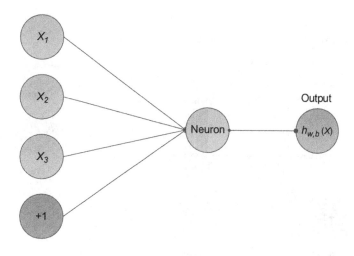

FIG. 1

A simple neuron network.

A simple neural network is shown in Fig. 1. There are four input units and one output. Each input unit (x_1, x_2, x_3, and bias +1) is multiplied by a weight value W_i and then summed (Eq. 1). The summed value will be taken as the input of the activation function: $f(z)$.

$$h_{w,b}(x) = f(W^T x) = f\left(\sum_{i=1}^{3} W_i x_i + b\right)$$ (1)

We can choose sigmoid function (one of the activation functions that commonly used in deep learning models) to act as activation function (Eq. 2):

$$f(z) = \frac{1}{1+e^{-z}}$$ (2)

The single neuron was explained exactly according to the mapping relationship between input and output by logistic regression [5].

A neural network consists of many simple neurons and more layers (Fig. 2).

As shown in Fig. 2, the neural network is composed of three layers, four inputs, and one output. The leftmost layer is input layer that consists of three inputs (x_1, x_2, x_3) and one bias unit. The rightmost layer is called an output layer with a single output unit. In the middle of the network, layer L2 is called the hidden layer.

One can extend the neural network by adding input and a hidden layer to train a large problem. Researchers have created many kinds of ANN models and those models have been applied in the field of artificial intelligence, such as pattern recognition, time series prediction, signal processing, control, soft sensors, anomaly detection, and so on. However, when learning from more complicated problems, ANN mainly has several restrictions [6]:

- It requires a huge amount of training data to train the network for a decent model.
- A neural network is prone to overfitting.
- The parameter of a neural network is difficult to be tuned.
- A neural network has limited ability to identify complicated relationships.

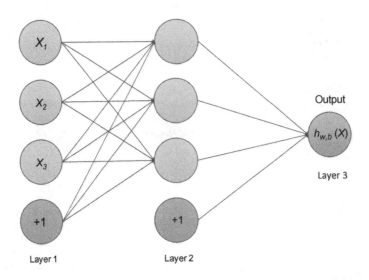

FIG. 2

Neuron network with three layers.

- The configuration of a neural network is empirical and many methodologies have not yet been figured out.
- A neural network is time consuming.

Because of the above restrictions, ANN was not applied extensively. Deep learning has the same network structure as ANN's, but deep learning has totally different training methods.

Concept of deep learning

The idea of deep learning was based on ANNs, but deep learning methods can automatically extract a complex data representation and identify more complicated relationships between input and output.

In a conventional machine learning model, the engineer and researcher were required to design a feature extractor manually from raw input data before classifying an object (Fig. 3). In comparison to a deep learning model, the key limitation of machine learning is that it cannot efficiently generate complicated and nonlinear patterns automatically from raw input data.

From 2006, a new research area of machine learning named deep structured learning or deep learning was introduced to the world. In comparison to conventional machine learning, the engineer and researcher

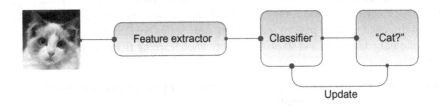

FIG. 3

Classification process in traditional machine learning.

do not need to extract features manually. Instead, these features can be generated automatically by using deep learning. We can refer to the following definition of deep learning: "Deep learning is a new area of machine learning research, which has been introduced with the objective of moving machine learning closer to one of its original goals: artificial intelligence. Deep learning is about learning multiple levels of representation and abstraction that help to make sense of data such as images, sound, and text" [13].

In recent years, compared to deep structured model, research in machine learning and signal process has explored shallow structured models that usually contain one or two layers of nonlinear feature transformations, such as Gaussian mixture models, support vector machines, extreme learning machines, and so on. Many shallow models are a good choice to solve simple or well-constrained problems, but they are inefficient in handling more complicated applications such image recognition, speech recognition, and natural languages understanding.

The mainstream models in deep learning are mainly divided into three classes: supervised learning, unsupervised learning, and hybrid learning model. The model of unsupervised learning can be used to cluster the input based on their statistic properties without being provided with the correct answer during the training. Main unsupervised learning models include:

- Auto-encoders
- Stacked denoising auto-encoders
- Restricted Boltzmann machines
- Deep belief networks

In contrast, the training dataset of a supervised learning model includes both the input data and the desired output (correct answer) data during the training process. Supervised learning models include:

- Logistic regression
- Multilayer perceptron
- Backpropagation (BP)
- Deep convolutional network

In addition, practitioners usually complement hybrid models that are combined with the use of unsupervised model and supervised model. In the hybrid models, in order to initialize the preset training parameters to sensible values, unsupervised learning is used as a pretraining method and extracts more useful features for the supervised model.

4.2.2 MAINSTREAM DEEP LEARNING MODELS

Autoencoders

An autoencoder was first designed in the 1980s by Hinton to address unsupervised learning problems. It has two or three layers of a neural network and applies BP to learn nonlinear codes to reconstruct the input data. It aims at learning an identity equation, which makes the output approximately equal to input (Eq. 3). In fact, some interesting structures of the input data can be found by making some constraints on the hidden layer of the network (like limiting the number of hidden units) [12]. If given a set of unlabeled training dataset $(x_0, x_1, x_2, \ldots)$, x_i is N dimensional. Fig. 3 shows how autoencoder model works:

$$h\left(x_i \, ; \, w, \, b\right) = x_i \tag{3}$$

$$\text{minimize}_{w,b} \sum_{i=0}^{m} \| h\left(x_i \, ; \, w, \, b\right) - x_i \| \tag{4}$$

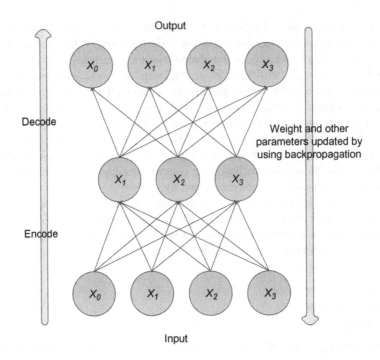

FIG. 4

A simple model of the autoencoder.

There are three layers in an autoencoder model (Fig. 4): input layer, hidden layer, and output layer. The hidden layer is forced to compress the input data into a high-level representation, which is called "encode the input data." After encoding, the network minimizes the objective function by BP that adjusts weight values and other parameters according to output (Eq. 4).

Backpropagation

BP was introduced in the 1970s and has become the workhorse of learning in neural networks. You can see a simple three-layer BP network model in Fig. 5.

BP algorithm mainly consists of two computing processes: feedforward and back propagation. When in feedforward pass, the BP model computes the outputs to each hidden layer and then squashes the outputs using activation functions (such as sigmoid function). It then repeats the process with the output layer. If the actual output ($h_{w,b}(x)$) is different with the expected output (label (y)), the back propagation begins. In a BP pass, the model will apply the BP equation repeatedly to propagate gradients through all the layers, from the output layer all the way to the input layer [2]. During BP, the weights of each layer will be updated according to these gradients in order to minimize the cost function: $J(w, b; x, y)$ (Eq. 5). Given a set of training samples:

$$\left\{ \left(x^1, y^1 \right), \left(x^2, y^2 \right), \dots \left(x^m, y^m \right) \right\}$$

For a single training sample: (x^i, y^i), we can define the cost function as follows (Eq. 5):

$$J\left(w, b;\ x,\ y \right) = \frac{1}{2} \| h_{w,b}\left(x \right) - y^2 \| \tag{5}$$

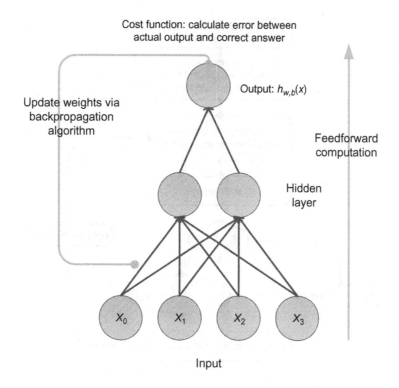

Cost function: calculate error between actual output and correct answer

Update weights via backpropagation algorithm

Output: $h_{w,b}(x)$

Feedforward computation

Hidden layer

X_0 X_1 X_2 X_3

Input

FIG. 5

A simple model of the backpropagation algorithm.

When the difference between the actual output and expected output has become small enough, or the network reaches a preset number of stop iterations (Epoch$_{max}$), the algorithm will stop the training. You can see the detailed mathematical equation and derivation in [14–16]. The whole BP algorithm flow shows in Fig. 6. The summary of the BP algorithm is as follows:

Step 1: Initialize the training net: Construct a new BP network and its parameters, set some necessary parameters (eg, the learning rate), and randomly initialize the weights and bias to small values between −1 and +1.
Step 2: Randomly choose an input from training samples and conduct the feed-forward computation.
Step 3: Calculate the errors (E) between the actual output and expected output.
Step 4: Check against the stopping criteria.
Step 5: If it does not meet the stop condition, it conduct the back propagation (computes the gradients and update weights). After Step 5 is finished, return to Step 2.

Convolutional neural network

The most popular deep learning models used to train image data are known as convolutional neural networks (CNNs). The inspiration of CNNs is from Hubel and Wiesel's early research on cat's visual cortex [16]. It was designed to handle multiple array problems, such as signal and sequences, images,

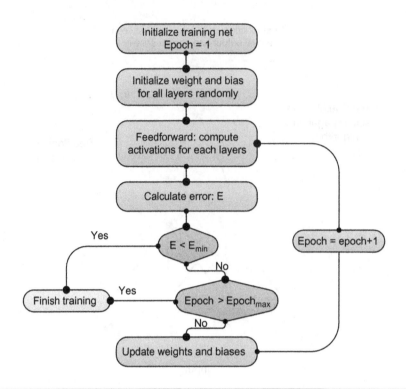

FIG. 6

BP training flowchart.

speech, videos, etc. [2]. CNNs have achieved great success in image recognition, speech recognition, and natural language understanding.

Architecture overview of CNNs

Essentially, deep CNNs are typical feedforward neural networks, which are applied BP algorithms to adjust the parameters (weights and biases) of the network to reduce the value of the cost function. However, it is very different from the traditional BP networks in four new conceptions: local receptive fields, shared weights, pooling, and combination of different layers. A typical structure of CNNs is shown in Fig. 7 (LeNet-5) [21].

The network consists of one or more convolutional layers (often followed by a subsampling layer), and then ends with one or more fully connected layers.

Input layer

The input layer can be images, sounds, or one or more real numbers. In the example of LeNet-5, the input data is two-dimensional (2D) arrays of pixels. Generally, each input image will be an $M \times N \times K$ real array. M and N are the height and width of the image and K is the number of channels per pixel (eg, an RGB image has $K=3$). For example, the input image is a $28 \times 28 \times 3$ real array in LeNet-5.

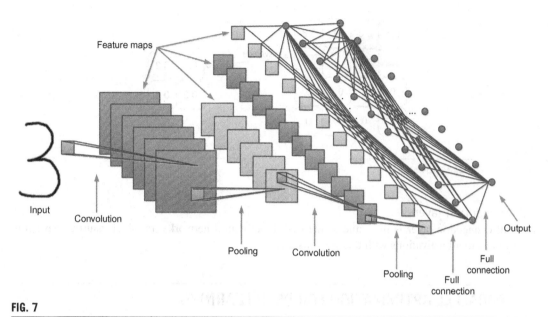

Feature maps

Input

Convolution

Pooling

Convolution

Pooling

Full
connection

Full
connection

Output

FIG. 7

The simple architecture of CNN (LeNet-5).

Convolutional layer

After the input layer received the input images, these images will be convolved by the convolution layer, which consists of a set of different learnable filter banks of size $m \times n \times r$. Each filter is smaller than the input size, but it extends through the full depth of the input volume. During the convolution, each filter bank will be slid across the height and width of the input images, generating a 2D feature map of that filter. When we slide the filter across the input image, we compute the dot production between the values of the filter and the input and then pass the result of the dot production into a non-linearity activation function (such as a ReLU, Sigmoid, and Tanh). For each filter bank, we repeat the above convolution operations and then a set of 2D feature maps will be generated as the output of convolutional layers. The number feature maps are the same as the number filter banks, and all neurons in the same feature map share the same weights (filter bank).

Local connectivity. Unlike the traditional fully connected neural networks, each neuron of the feature map in CNNs is only connected to a local region of the input. This spatial extent of connectivity is named a local receptive field. With these local receptive fields, elementary features like oriented edges, endpoints, and corners can be extracted and then combined to detect higher-level features by the subsequent layers.

Pooling layer

After each convolutional layer, it is commonly to insert a pooling layer. Pooling layers can reduce the resolution of feature maps, and thus reduce the amount of parameters and computation in CNNs. Pooling layers are also can be used to control the over-fitting problems [19]. There are two methods of pooling: max pooling and average pooling, and that means each pooling unit calculates the maximum or average of a local patch in one feature map. A simple example of average pooling is shown in Fig. 8.

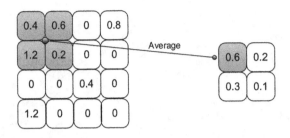

FIG. 8

Example of average pooling.

Full connection layer

The full connection layer is the same as the traditional neural networks, in which neurons have full connections to all activations with the previous layer.

4.3 PARALLEL OPTIMIZATION FOR DEEP LEARNING

It has been found that the accuracy of deep learning models will be greatly improved by increasing the scale and the number of parameters in the deep model. But it also means we have to spend more time to train these large-scale deep learning models. The traditional serial algorithms are hard to handle these large deep models in a fast speed. Therefore, parallelizing the deep learning model is necessary. The parallel of deep learning has been explored for many years and the main development is shown in Table 1.

In this section, we will introduce two popular parallel frameworks and discuss a general parallel method of the large deep learning model.

4.3.1 CONVOLUTIONAL ARCHITECTURE FOR FAST FEATURE EMBEDDING

Convolutional architecture for fast feature embedding (Caffe) was aimed to provide a clean, quick start and a modular deep learning framework for scientists in research area and industry. It was developed and maintained by Berkeley Vision and Learning Center (BVLC) and community contributors.

Table 1 The Development of Deep Learning Model in Parallel	
Solution	**Contribution**
CPU to multicore CPUs	Train the model in parallel by using different cores
Multicore CPUs to GPU	Train the model in parallel by GPU by using huge numbers of threads in a GPU device with zero schedule overhead and powerful float computing ability
GPU to multi-CPUs	Train large-scale deep neural network by using CPU clusters for the sake of the limitation of single GPU memory
Multi-CPUs to multi-GPUs	The problem of limited memory of a single GPU does not exist when using multi-GPUs to train the large-scale deep networks

Caffe is one of the most popular deep learning frameworks due to five good points: expressive architecture, extensible code, fast training speed, open source, and active community. The users don't have to rewrite the code of Caffe to set up new deep neural networks. Instead, they just need to modify several lines of configuration files to start a new network. Computation mode between CPU and GPU can be easily switched by changing a single line flag [20].

CUDA programming

GPU is extensively used as a computational device, thanks to its excellent computational power and parallel hardware architecture with thousands of arithmetic logic unit (ALU) cores. We can see the difference in computational power between GPUs and CPUs in Fig. 9.

The large gap of the performance lies in the different design philosophy between GPUs and CPUs. The design of CPU is that more transistors on the chip are used for control and cache units, while most of the transistors on GPU are used for computational units and few for control and cache, which makes GPU handle multiple tasks more efficiently [18].

The architecture of GPU

GPU is connected to the host device through the PCI Express (PCIe) and it has its own device memory that is up to several gigabytes in modern devices. GPU hardware mainly consists of memory, streaming multiprocessors (SMs), and streaming processors (SPs).

GPU is an array of SMs that consist of SPs and memory (Fig. 10). Each SM can execute in parallel with the others. NVIDIA Kepler k40 has 15 multiprocessors and 2880 cores and each core can execute a sequential thread in SIMT (single instruction, multiple thread). Each SM is associated with a private

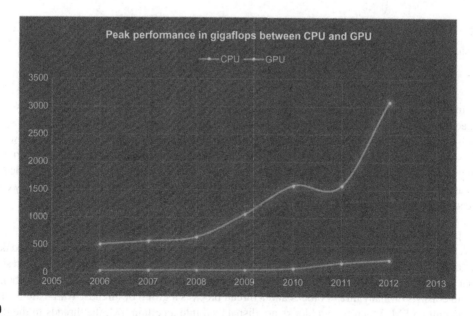

FIG. 9

Performance between CPU and GPU.

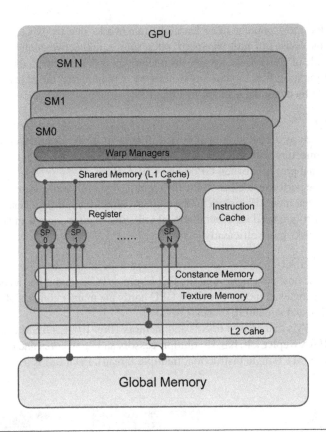

FIG. 10

A simplified architecture of GPU hardware.

shared memory (L1 cache), read-only texture memory, registers, L2 cache, etc. Each core has a fully pipelined integer ALU, a floating point unit, a move and compare unit, and a branch unit [17,18].

Each thread can access register and shared memory at a very high speed in parallel, and we also refer to shared memory as on-chip memory. Registers are private to individual threads, and each thread can only access its own registers. Thirty-two threads are grouped into a warp, which is scheduled by a warp manager, and the threads in a warp are executed in SIMT mode. The computational ability can be enhanced by extending more SMs and memory resources.

CUDA programming framework

In 2007, the CUDA was introduced to the world. This easy-to-use program framework pushed the development of GPGPU and allows the programmer to write codes without having to learn complicated shader languages. CUDA supports high-level programming languages such as C/C++, Fortran, and Python.

A grid consists of many thread blocks and a thread block is a group of threads. Warps are the basic execution unit on SM. When thread blocks are dispatched into a certain SM, the threads in the thread block are grouped into warps (32 consecutive threads) (Fig. 11).

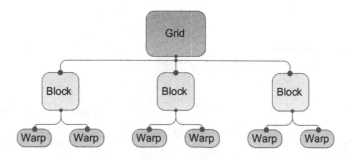

FIG. 11

Thread organization of CUDA.

Thread. A thread runs on the individual core of SM and executes an instance of the kernel. Each thread has a thread ID within in its thread block, program counter, register, per-thread private, inputs, and output results.

Block. Each block is a logical unit that contains a number of threads. A block is an array of concurrent threads that cooperate to compute a result. The threads of a block can be indexed by using 1D, 2D, or 3D indexes.

Grid. A grid is an array of blocks that are all running on the same kernel. Each grid reads from global memory, writes results to global memory, and synchronizes between dependent kernel calls.

Warp. The warp is the basic execution element on GPU and CUDA codes actually run as warp. The size of a warp depends on GPU hardware. Each CUDA core executes 32 threads simultaneously on K40c. At runtime, a block is divided into a number of warps.

A GPU can execute one or more kernel grids and an SM can execute one or more thread blocks. If you want to run program on GPU, you should define kernel functions that N different CUDA threads execute in parallel.

In CUDA program framework, GPU works as a coprocessor of the CPU. The program is switched to GPU when kernel function is called for by the CPU. CPU is optimized for low-latency access to cached data sets and control logic; therefore, it is well suited for those serial codes with complicated logic control. Instead, GPU is optimized for data-parallel and throughput computation, so it is good for the computational intensive work (Fig. 12).

Architecture of Caffe
Data storage in Caffe

All the data (such as images, weights, biases, and derivatives) in Caffe is stored in a 4D array which is called a blob. For example, the batches of images data in 4D blobs are stored like this: Number × Channel × Height × Width.

For each layer, the input data are stored in the bottom blob and the output data are in the top blob (Fig. 13), while the next layer will take the top blob from the previous layer as its input data (bottom blob).

Layer topology in Caffe

The essence of different networks is the different combination of functional layers. Caffe supports a complete set of functional layers like convolution, pooling, inner products, nonlinearities, and losses [20].

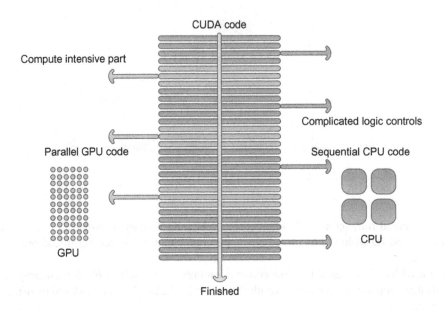

FIG. 12

The execution mode of CUDA code.

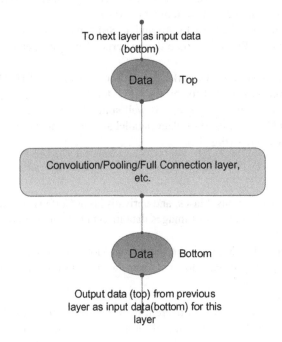

FIG. 13

Layer communication in Caffe.

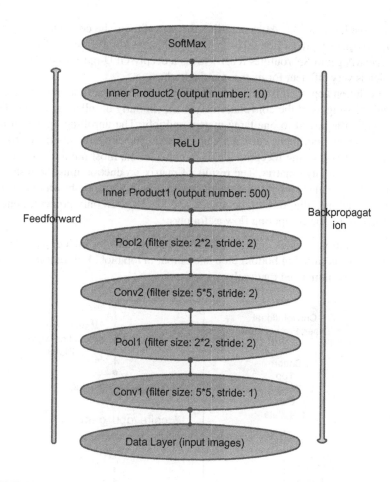

FIG. 14

A simple example of LeNet topology in Caffe.

A simple example of LeNet architecture in Caffe is shown in Fig. 14. The operations of these layers are convolution, pooling, full connection, and SoftMax. In the forward phase, the computation of the input data starts from the data layer at the bottom all the way to the output layer at the top. The BP algorithm is applied to compute the gradients in the backward phase and update parameters for each layer.

Parallel implementation of convolution in Caffe

In all of the deep CNNs, convolution operations are computationally expensive and dominant most of the runtime. Therefore, an important way to improve performance of the whole network is to reduce the runtime of convolution.

There are three approaches to implement convolution operations. The first common way is to compute the convolution directly. This will be efficient when batch sizes are large enough and inefficient when the batch size is below 64 [9]. The second approach is to employ the fast Fourier transform to compute the convolution, which can lower the complexity of the convolutions [11]. This way has turned out to be the fastest convolution, but it is limited by memory consumption. The third way is to unroll the convolution into a large matrix. After unrolling the convolution, the computation of each convolution turns to a matrix-matrix production by using highly efficient libraries (eg, cuBLAS). The NVIDIA CUDA Basic Linear Algebra Subroutines (cuBLAS) is a deeply GPU-optimized version of the BLAS library [22], which is very efficient for matrix-matrix production.

The third convolution approach is used in Caffe: The local regions of the input image are unrolled into columns and the weights of the convolution layer are similarly unrolled into rows. Therefore, the result of a convolution is turned to one large matrix multiply. The unrolling operation in Caffe is in a function called im2col_gpu; then, cuBLAS can be used efficiently for matrix-matrix production. Because there is an overlap of the receptive fields in convolution, most numbers in the input may be duplicated in the unrolled large matrix. The results of matrix production must be reshaped to proper output dimension. The detailed computing flow of convolution in Caffe is shown in Fig. 15.

Fixed steps are used in Caffe to train the model, and the program only processes one images of a batch during an iteration. The computing flow as follows:

Step 1: Data preparation, such as input, output, weights, and bias for im2col_gpu. The input data of convolution layer is stored in bottom blob and output in top blob. Before training, the weight and biases need to be initialized randomly.

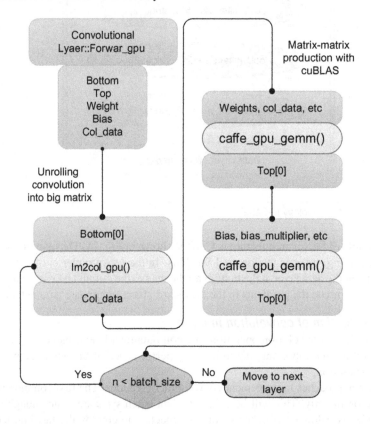

FIG. 15

Computing the flow of the convolution layer in Caffe.

Step 2: Unroll the convolution data into large matrix. The image is transformed into a big matrix in parallel by using im2col_gpu. The result of unrolling is stored in col_data.

Step 3: The funtion caffe_gpu_gemm is called to conduct matrix multiplication between unrolled input and weights on GPU by using cuBLAS.

Step 4: The function caffe_gpu_gemm is called to conduct matrix multiplication between unrolled input and bias on GPU by using cuBLAS.

Step 5: Check stop criteria. If all images in a batch are processed, the program moves to next layer. Otherwise, go to Step 2.

4.3.2 DISTBELIEF

Introduction of DistBelief

It was reported by the *New York Times* in 2012 that Google DistBelief [3] could identify the key features of a cat from millions of You Tube videos. The key technique behind DistBelief is deep learning. Moreover, DistBelief is a very complicated and large distributed system composed by 1000 machines, including a total of 16,000 cores and 1 billion network parameters. This parallel deep learning framework supports model parallelism both within a machine by multithreading and across machines by message passing. Meanwhile, it also supports data parallelism to train different replicas of a model. The main algorithms in DistBelief are Downpour stochastic gradient descent (SGD) and L-BFGS. It has been applied in image classification and speech recognition fields [23].

A significant advance has been brought by using GPU to train deep learning networks. But the bottleneck using GPU to train large deep networks with billions of training examples and parameters is the limitation of a single GPU memory. DistBelief was designed to address this problem, and it provides an alternative method to train a large deep network by using large-scale clusters in distributed way [24].

Downpour SGD

Many researchers have accelerated machine learning algorithms by distribution methods before DistBelief [25–27]. SGD is extensively applied in deep learning algorithms to reduce output error. The designer of DistBelief provides us with Downpour SGD, a new method suitable for distributed systems. The key advantages of Downpour SGD are asynchronous stochastic gradient, adaptive learning rates and numerous model replicas. Compared to traditional SGD, the convergence rate of Downpour SGD has been improved significantly.

The basic idea of Downpour SGD is as follows: The training samples are divided into different small parts and each model replica computes gradients for each small part. Before each model replica starts to train its small part, the model replica sends a request to parameter server to ask for the latest parameter (Fig. 16). When the model replica receives the latest parameter from parameter server, it begins to compute parameter gradients for its own small part and sends the gradients result back to the parameter server. The parameter server will be updated with the latest gradients. In this way, the parameter can hold the latest state of parameters for the model. The parameter server consists of different machines, and the total workload is averaged by each machine in parameter server [24].

Sandblaster L-BFGS

Training deep networks on batch can get good performances in small deep networks [26,27], but it is not well suited for large deep networks. The Sandblaster batch optimization framework (L-BFGS) was introduced to address this problem.

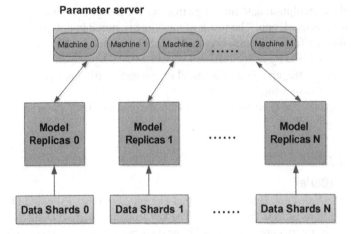

FIG. 16

The basic idea of Downpour SGD.

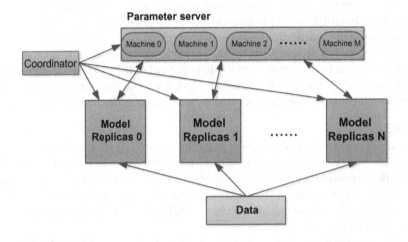

FIG. 17

The basic idea of Sandblaster L-BGGS.

In Sandblaster L-BGGS algorithm, each model replica runs on the whole training sample. The key idea of the algorithm resides in the coordinator (Fig. 17), which sends a set of commands to store and manipulate model parameters distributively [24].

4.3.3 DEEP LEARNING BASED ON MULTI-GPUs

The data in deep learning can be divided into two types of data: parameters and input/output data. Parameters in CNNs include the learning rate, convolutional parameters (eg, filter numbers, kernel size, and stride), pooling parameters (kernel size, stride), bias, etc. Input data includes the raw data (eg, images and speeches) received from the input layer, and output data keep the intermediate output of each layer, such as the convolutional and pooling layers. The key to train large scale CNN models with multiple GPUs is how to divide tasks between different GPUs. We have three ways to train these large models with multiple GPUs: data parallelism, model parallelism, and data-model parallelism.

Data parallelism

Data parallelism can be easily implemented and it is thus the most widely used implementation strategy on multi-GPUs.

Data parallelism means that each GPU uses the same model to trains on different data subset. In data parallel, there is no synchronization between GPUs in forward computing, because each GPU has a fully copy of the model, including the deep net structure and parameters. But the parameter gradients computed from different GPUs must be synchronized in BP (Fig. 18).

Model parallelism

Model parallelism means that each computational node is responsible for parts of the model by training the same data samples.

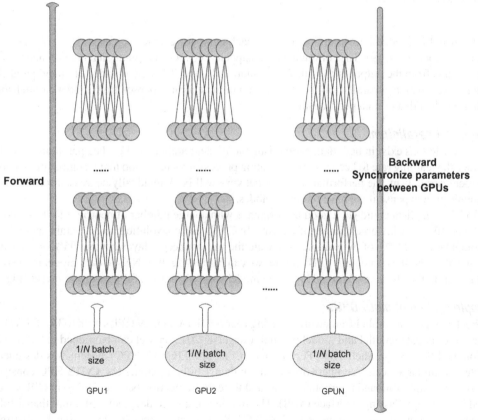

FIG. 18

The illustration of data parallelism mode.

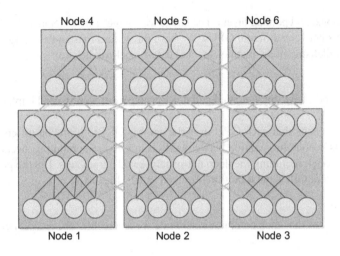

FIG. 19

The illustration of model parallelism mode.

The model is divided into several pieces and each computing node such as GPU is responsible for one piece of them (Fig. 19). The communication happens between computational nodes when the input of a neuron is from the output of the other computational node. The performance of model parallelism is often worse than data parallelism, because the communication expenses from model parallelism are much more than that of data parallelism.

Data-model parallelism

Several restrictions exist in both data parallelism and model parallelism. For data parallelism, we have to reduce the learning rate to keep a smooth training process if there are too many computational nodes. For model parallelism, the performance of the network will be dramatically decreased for the sake of communication expense if we have too many nodes.

Model parallelism could get a good performance with a large number of neuron activities, and data parallel is efficient with large number of weights. In CNNs, the convolution layer contain about 90% of the computation and 5% of the parameters, while the full connected layer contain 95% of the parameters and 5%-10% the computation. Therefore, we can parallelize the CNNs in data-model mode by using data parallelism for convolutional layer and model parallelism for a fully connected layer (Fig. 20).

Example system of multi-GPUs

Facebook designed a parallel framework by using four NVIDIA TITAN GPUs with 6 GB of RAM on a single server in data parallel and model parallel. ImageNet 2012 dataset can be trained in 5 days [28].

Commodity Off-The-Shelf High Performance Computing (COTS HPC) system was designed by Google to train large-scale deep networks on more than 1 billion parameters. COTS HPC consists of GPU servers with Infiniband interconnections, and the communication between different GPUs is controlled by Message Passing Interface (MPI). The training of a large deep net with more than 1 billion parameters was completed in 3 days on COTS HPC [29]. The same experiment was done by DistBelief, but COTS HPC provides us with a much cheaper and faster way of doing it.

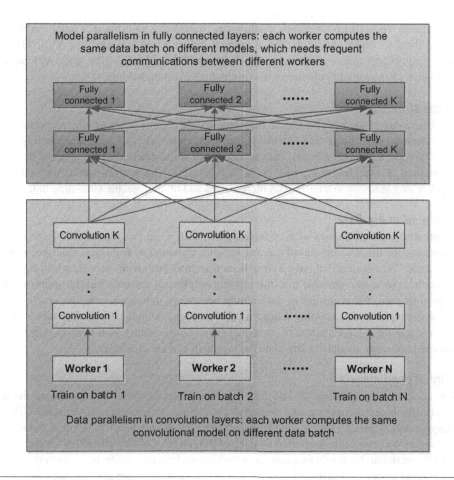

FIG. 20

The illustration of data-model parallelism mode.

4.4 DISCUSSIONS

4.4.1 GRAND CHALLENGES OF DEEP LEARNING IN BIG DATA

With the development of powerful computing devices (eg, GPUs), the potentially valuable datasets provided by Big Data and the advanced CNN architecture, deep learning models are promising to fully make use of huge amounts of data to mine and extract meaningful representations for classification and regression. However, deep learning poses some specific challenges in Big Data, including processing massive amounts of training data, learning from incremental streaming data, the scalability of deep model, and learning speed.

Massive amounts of training sample

Generally, learning from a large number of training samples provided by Big Data can obtain complex data representations (features) at high levels of abstraction which can be used to improve the accuracy of classification of the deep model. An obvious challenge of deep learning in Big Data is the various formats of datasets. Including high dimensionality data, massive unsupervised or unlabeled data, noisy and poor quality data, highly distributed input sources imbalanced input data, etc. [30]. The existing deep learning algorithms cannot adapt to train such various kinds of training samples, and thus dealing with data diversity is a really big challenge to current deep learning models.

Incremental streaming data
Streaming data is one of the key features of Big Data, which is large, fast moving, dispersed, unstructured, and unmanageable. Such data extensively exist in many areas of society, including websites, blogs, news, videos, telephone records, data transfer, and fraud detection [30]. One of the big challenges of learning meaningful information with deep learning models from streaming data is how to adapt deep learning methods to handle such incremental and unmanageable streaming data.

Learning speed in Big Data
The big challenge in training speed of deep learning is mainly from two aspects: the large scale of the deep network and the massive amount of training samples provided by Big Data. It has been turned out that a large-scale CNN models that have a complicated architecture (with more than billions of parameters and much more layers) are able to extract more complicated features and thus improve the state of the art performance, and accordingly, the training become prohibitively computationally expensive and time-consuming. Besides, training a deep model on a huge amount of training data is also time-consuming and requires a large amount of compute cycles. Consequently, how to accelerate the training speed of those large-scale models in Big Data environment is a big challenge.

Scalability of deep models
To train large-scale deep learning models faster, an important method is to accelerate the training process with distributed computing and powerful computing devices (eg, clusters and GPUs). The existing approaches of parallel training includes data parallel, model parallel, and data-model parallel. But when training on large-scale deep models, each of them will be of low efficiency for the sake of parameter synchronization that needs frequent communications between different computing nodes (such as different server nodes in distributed system, and heterogeneous computing systems between CPU and GPUs). Additional, the memory limitation of modern GPUs can also lead to scalability of deep networks. The big challenge is how to optimize and balance workload computation and communication in large-scale deep learning networks.

4.4.2 FUTURE DIRECTIONS

Big data provides us with a very important chance to improve the existing deep learning models and to propose novel algorithms to address specific problems in Big Data. The future work will focus on algorithms, applications, and parallel computing.

In the perspective of algorithms, we have to research how to optimize the existing deep learning algorithms or explore novel approaches of deep learning to train massive amounts of data samples and streaming samples from Big Data. Moreover, we also need to create novel methods to support Big Data analytics, such as data sampling for extracting more complex features from Big Data, incremental deep learning methods for dealing with streaming data, unsupervised algorithms for learning from massive amounts of unlabeled data, semi-supervised learning, and active learning.

Application is one of the most researched areas in deep learning. Many traditional research areas have benefited from deep learning, such as speech recognition, visual object recognition, and object detection, as well as many other domains, such as drug discovery and genomic. The application of deep learning in Big Data also needs to be explored, such as generating complicated patterns from Big Data, semantic indexing, data tagging, fast information retrieval, and simplifying discriminative tasks.

The last important point of future work is parallel computing in deep learning. We could research existing parallel algorithms or open source parallel frameworks and optimize them to speedup training process. We could also propose novel distributed and parallel deep learning computing algorithms and frameworks to support quick training of large-scale deep learning models. However, to train a larger deep model, we have to figure out the scalability problem of large-scale deep models.

REFERENCES

[1] Krizhevsky A, Sutskever I, Hinton G. ImageNet classification with deep convolutional neural networks. In: Proc. Advances in Neural Information Processing Systems 25; 2012. p. 1090–8.
[2] LeCun Y, Bengio Y, Hinton G. Review: Deep learning. Nature 2015;521:436–44.
[3] Dean J, Corrado G, Monga R, Chen K, Devin M, Mao M, et al. Large scale distributed deep networks. Adv Neural Inf Process Syst 2012;25:1232–40.
[4] Schmidhuber J. Deep learning in neural networks: an overview. arXiv: 1404.7828, 2014.
[5] http://deeplearning.stanford.edu/wiki/index.php/Neural_Networks.
[6] Tu JV. Advantages and disadvantages of using artificial neural networks versus logistic regression for predicting medical outcomes. J Clin Epidemiol 1996;49(11):1225–31.
[7] Jia Y, Shelhamer E, Donahue J, Karayev S, Long J, Girshick R, et al. Caffe: convolutional architecture for fast feature embedding. arXiv. preprint arXiv:1408.5093, 2014.
[8] Sermanet P, Eigen D, Zhang X, Mathieu M, Fergus R, LeCun Y. Overfeat: integrated recognition, localization and detection using convolutional networks. In: ICLR; 2014.
[9] Chetlur S, Woolley C, Vandermersch P, Cohen J, Tran J, Catanzaro B, et al. cudnn: efficient primitives for deep learning. *CoRR*, abs/1410.0759, 2014. http://arxiv.org/abs/1410.0759.
[10] Donahue J, Jia Y, Vinyals O, Hoffman J, Zhang N, Tzeng E, et al. Decaf: a deep convolutional activation feature for generic visual recognition. *CoRR*, abs/1310.1531, 2013.
[11] Vasilache N, Johnson J, Mathieu M, Chintala S, Piantino S, LeCun Y. Fast convolutional nets with fbfft: a GPU performance evaluation. arXiv: 1412.7580, 2015.
[12] http://deeplearning.stanford.edu/wiki/index.php/Autoencoders_and_Sparsity.
[13] https://github.com/lisa-lab/DeepLearningTutorials.
[14] http://deeplearning.stanford.edu/wiki/index.php/Backpropagation_Algorithm.
[15] LeCun Y, Bottou L, Orr G, Muller K. Efficient BackProp. In: Orr G, Muller K, editors. Neural networks: tricks of the trade. Heidelberg: Springer; 1998.
[16] Hubel D, Wiesel T. Receptive fields and functional architecture of monkey striate cortex. J Physiol (London) 1968;195:215–43.
[17] http://www.nvidia.com/object/what-is-gpu-computing.html.
[18] NVIDIA, Tesla K40 GPU Active Accelerator. BD-06949-001_V03, 2013.
[19] He K, Zhang X, Ren S, Sun J. Spatial pyramid pooling in deep convolutional networks for visual recognition. In: ECCV; 2014.
[20] http://caffe.berkeleyvision.org/.
[21] Tompson J, Jain A, LeCun Y, Bregler C. Joint training of a convolutional network and a graphical model for human pose estimation. *CoRR*, abs/1406.2984, 2014.

[22] https://developer.nvidia.com/cublas.

[23] Zinkevich M, Weimer M, Smola A, Li L. Parallelized stochastic gradient descent. In: NIPS; 2010.

[24] Le QV, Ngiam J, Coates A, Lahiri A, Prochnow B, Ng AY. On optimization methods for deep learning. In: ICML. 2011.

[25] Agarwal A, Duchi J. Distributed delayed stochastic optimization. In: NIPS; 2011.

[26] Niu F, Retcht B, Re C, Wright SJ. Hogwild. A lock-free approach to parallelizing stochastic gradient descent. In: NIPS; 2011.

[27] Dean J, Corrado GS, Monga R, Ng AY, et al. Large scale distributed deep networks. In: Advances in Neural Information Processing 25 (NIPS 2012). Cambridge, MA: MIT Press; 2012.

[28] Yadan O, Adams K, Taigman Y, Ranzato MA. Multi-GPU training of ConvNets. arXiv: 1312.5853v4 [cs.LG] (February 2014).

[29] Coates A, Huval B, Wang T, Wu DJ, Ng AY, Catanzaro B. Deep learning with COTS HPC systems. In: Proc. International Conference on Machine Learning (ICML'13); 2013.

[30] Najafabadi MM, Villanustre F, Khoshgoftaar TM, Seliya N, Wald R, Muharemagic E. Deep learning applications and challenges in Big Data analytics. J Big Data 2015;2:1. http://dx.doi.org/10.1186/s40537-014-0007-7; Cs. 2015.

[31] https://code.google.com/p/cuda-convnet2/.

CHARACTERIZATION AND TRAVERSAL OF LARGE REAL-WORLD NETWORKS

5

A. Garcia-Robledo, A. Diaz-Perez, G. Morales-Luna

5.1 INTRODUCTION

Big Data analytics and current high-performance computing (HPC) platforms are facing the challenge of supporting a new set of graph processing applications, such as centrality calculation and community detection, in order to process large volumes of connected data in an efficient manner.

Recent years have witnessed the rise of *network science*, defined as:

the study of network representations of physical, biological, and social phenomena leading to predictive models of these phenomena.

[1].

The rise of network science has been possible thanks to ever-increasing computing resources, open databases that enable the analysis of large volumes of data, and the growing interest in holistic approaches that explain the behavior of complex systems as a whole.

Complex networks, the main study object in network science, have proved to be extremely useful to abstract and model the massive amount of interrelated data corresponding to a variety of real-world phenomena [2]: the worldwide Facebook network, the Internet topology at the autonomous system level, thematic networks of Wikipedia, protein-protein interaction networks (PPI) of various bacteria, and scientific collaboration maps (to name but a few examples).

Complex networks model real-world phenomena integrated by thousands of millions of entities. For example, as of the first quarter of 2015, GenBank reported 171 million sequences stored in its biological database [3], Facebook reported 1.44 billion registered users [4], and as of Aug. 2015, Google indexed more than 46 billion web pages [5].

Big Data and complex networks share interesting properties: They are large scale (volume), they are complex (variety), and they are dynamic (velocity). As stated in [6]:

The combination of Big Data and network science offers a vast number of potential applications for the design of data-driven analysis and regulation tools, covering many parts of the society and academia.

The study of complex networks is gaining more attention in the analysis of Big Data. It is argued, for example, that the combination of Big Data with social science techniques would be useful for the prediction of social and economic crises [6].

Big Data. http://dx.doi.org/10.1016/B978-0-12-805394-2.00005-2

There are many efforts in network science that are dedicated to the definition of metrics that provide the means for characterizing different aspects of the topology of complex networks [7]. The measurement of metrics, such as average shortest-path length, clustering coefficient, and degree distribution, is the first step for the analysis of the structure of a national airport [8], the analysis of a subway train system [9], and the measurement of properties such as redundancy and connectivity of a water distribution system [10].

The emerging network science has also motivated a renewed interest in classical graph problems, such as breadth-first search (BFS) and the k-core decomposition of graphs. These algorithms are the main building blocks for a new set of applications related to the analysis of the centrality and the hierarchy of entities of massive real-world phenomena. However, the size and dynamics of complex networks introduce large amounts of processing times that can be only tackled by modern and pervasive parallel hardware architectures, such as graphics processing units (GPUs).

In this two-part chapter, the authors present the synergy between network science, HPC, and Big Data by studying: (1) techniques to accelerate the traversal of the structure of massive real-world networks, and (2) a graph partitioning strategy based on the coreness of complex networks for load distribution on heterogeneous computing platforms. This chapter follows a practical computer science approach that focuses on presenting algorithms for the efficient processing of large real-world graphs.

5.2 BACKGROUND

Networks and graphs are becoming increasingly important in representing multirelational Big Data and in modeling complicated data structures and their interactions. The storage and analysis capabilities needed for big graph analytics have motivated the development of a new wave of HPC software technologies including: MapReduce/Hadoop-like distributed graph analytics, NoSQL graph data storage and querying, and new heterogeneous computig platforms for graph processing.

An HPC initiative for network analytics are NoSQL graph databases, which address the challenge of "leveraging complex and dynamic relationships in highly connected data to generate insight and competitive advantage." [11]. Graph databases, such as Neo4j [12], OrientDB [13], and InfiniteGraph [14], are able to store networks with up to billions of nodes and provide network-oriented query languages, a flexible data model, pattern-matching queries, traversal-optimized storage, path retrieval, and in some cases distributed storage capabilities.

There are implementations of MapReduce-like graph processing platforms in distributed computing environments. Prominent examples include Google Pregel [15] and Apache Giraph [16]. Pregel and Giraph are inspired in MapReduce in that they organize graph computation in sets of supersteps and global synchronization points. In each superstep, a user-defined function is executed in parallel in every vertex and the platforms are in charge of managing the data integration tasks.

Many algorithms in Big Data analytics can be accelerated by exploiting the power of low-cost but massively parallel architectures, such as multicores and GPUs. These kinds of parallel commodities are playing a significant role in large-scale modeling [17]. However, existing results reveal a gap between complex network algorithms (e.g., distance-based centrality metrics) and architectures like GPUs, stressing the need for further research [18]. Nonetheless, GPUs already show impressive speedups in other tasks, such as network visualization [19].

The combination of existing general-purpose multicore processors and hardware accelerators, such as GPUs, accelerated processing units (APUs), and many integrated cores (MICs), has the potential to overcome the limitations of single-architecture implementations, and lead to an improvement of the performance of complex network applications to process large volumes of interconnected data.

In the first part of the chapter, the authors review widely used complex network metrics. We then introduce a recurrent algorithm in a complex network measurement: all-sources BFS (AS-BFS). We present the visitor and the algebraic approaches for AS-BFS, and then we describe and compare a series of kernels for accelerating graph traversals on GPU.

In the second part of the chapter, we introduce the need for heterogeneous computing platforms for large graph processing. We also focus on the use of the k-core decomposition for the design of a unbalanced graph bisection algorithm, which is an important first step towards obtaining a heterogeneous computing platform that leverages the potential of different parallel architectures.

5.3 CHARACTERIZATION AND MEASUREMENT

A complex network $G = (V, E)$ is a non-empty set V of nodes or vertices and a set E of links or edges, such that there is a mapping between the elements of E and the set of pairs $\{i,j\}$, $i, j \in V$. Let $n = |V|$ be the number of vertices and $m = |E|$ be the number of edges of G. The degree k_i of a vertex $i \in V$ is the number of neighbors of i. Let n_k be the number of vertices of degree k in G, such that $\sum_k n_k = n$. Let $P(k) = n_k / n$ be the degree distribution of G.

Complex networks, random graphs, and graphs arising in scientific computing (e.g., meshes and lattices) are all sparse. However, unlike these kinds of graphs, complex networks present the combined properties of random but highly clustered graphs with a few vertices having the largest number of connections.

Complex networks from a variety of application domains share characteristics that differentiate them from random and regular networks: scale-freeness, small-worldliness, and community structure:

- *Scale-free* (SF) *degree distribution*. Barabási and Albert found that the degree distributions $P(k)$ of many real-world networks obey a power law, in which the number of vertices of degree k is proportional to $k^{-\alpha}$, with $\alpha \in [2,3]$. This is in contrast to classical Erdös-Rényi random graphs that show a Poisson degree distribution. A power-law distribution implies the existence of only a few vertices with very high degree, called hubs, and that the majority of vertices have a very low degree.
- *Small-world phenomenon*. Let d_{ij} be the length of the shortest (geodesic) path between two vertices $i, j \in V$. The average shortest-path length $\langle L \rangle$ is the average of all shortest path lengths d_{ij} in G. The clustering coefficient of a vertex i $\langle CC_i \rangle$ is the ratio of the number of edges between the neighbors of i to the maximum possible number of edges among them. Strogatz and Watts [20] found that the six degrees of separation phenomenon can be observed in many real-world networks: the majority of the vertex pairs in complex networks are a few steps away, in spite of their elevated number of vertices. This property can be characterized by $\langle L \rangle$, which grows logarithmically with n in a variety of real-world graphs. Networks that show both a small average path length $\langle L \rangle$ and a high clustering coefficient $\langle CC_i \rangle$ are known as *small-world networks*.

- *Community structure.* Girvan and Newman found that a variety of complex networks show groups of tightly interconnected nodes called clusters or communities. The members of a community are loosely connected to the members of other communities. The presence of communities reveals important information on the functional role of nodes in the same community.

Complex network metrics help us to determine if a given graph shows the topology and characteristics of a complex network. Complex network metrics can be roughly classified into clustering, distance, centrality, and scaling metrics, as shown in Table 1:

- *Degree metrics.* Directly derived from the degree of vertices k_i and the degree distribution $P(k)$. An example is the graph density d.

Table 1 Examples of Degree, Clustering, Distance, Centrality, and Scaling Complex Network Metrics [7]

Metric	Symbol	Type	Equations
Density	d	Degree	$2m / n(n-1)$
Clustering coefficient	CC_i	Clustering	$\dfrac{2\left|\{e_{jk}\}\right|}{k_i(k_i-1)} : j,k \in N_i, e_{jk} \in E$
Avg. path length	$\langle L \rangle$	Distance	$\dfrac{1}{n(n-1)}\sum_{i,j \in V: i \neq j} d_{ij}$
Diameter	D	Distance	$\max_{i,j \in V: i \neq j}\{d_{ij}\}$
Betweenness centrality	nBc_u	Centrality	$\sum_{i,j \in V: i \neq j}\dfrac{\sigma(i,u,j)}{\sigma(i,j)}$
Central point dominance	CPD	Centrality	$\dfrac{1}{n-1}\sum_{i \in V}(nBc_{max} - nBc_i)$
Closeness centrality	Cc_i	Centrality	$\dfrac{1}{\sum_{j \in V} d_{ij}}$
Avg. neighbor degree	$\langle k_n \rangle$	Centrality	$\dfrac{k_u}{k_i} : u \in N_i$
Scaling of the degree distribution	$\langle P(k) \rangle_k$	Scaling	$COR\left(\log(K), \log\left((P(k)\mid k \in K)\right)\right)$

$i,j,k,u \in V$ *represent vertices, n, number of nodes; m, number of edges; k_i, degree of i; N_i is the neighbors of vertex i; e_{jk}, edges connecting the neighbors j, k of i; d_{ij}, length of the shortest path between i, j; $\sigma(i,u,j)$, number of shortest paths between i and j that pass through u; $\sigma(i,j)$, total number of shortest paths between i and j; nBc_{max}, maximum vertex betweenness; COR(X, Y), Pearson correlation coefficient between tuples X and Y; K, tuple of different vertex degrees in G; log(S), function that returns a set with the logarithm of each element in the set S.*

- *Clustering metrics.* The clustering coefficient CC_i is an example of a clustering metric that measures the cohesiveness of the neighbors of a node.
- *Distance metrics.* The average path length $\langle L \rangle$ is a well known distance metric. The diameter D of a graph, another well known distance metric, is defined as the length of the longest shortest path in G.
- *Centrality metrics.* Centrality metrics try to quantify the intuitive idea that some vertices and edges are more "important" than others. A popular example is the vertex betweenness centrality nBc_u that measures the proportion of shortest paths in which a vertex participates. The central point dominance CPD evaluates the importance of the most influential node in terms of the maximum betweenness centrality. The closeness centrality of a vertex i, Cc_i is inversely proportional to the sum of the distances of i to every other vertex in the graph.
- *Scaling metrics.* The presence of high-level properties of complex networks, such as the scale-freeness or the presence of a hierarchy of clusters, can be determined by observing the log-log plot of the scaling of local metrics with the degree of vertices. For example, the scaling of the degree distribution with the degree k, $\langle P(k) \rangle_k$ can reveal the power-law nature of a graph.

Table 2 shows evidence that many of the metrics used for the study of complex networks could be redundant [7,22–25]. Metrics correlation patterns are dataset-specific and are affected by topological aspects such as the graph size, degree distribution, and density. The reader can refer to the mentioned works to find metrics correlations on graphs from different application domains.

The algorithms to calculate most of the distance and centrality metrics listed in Table 1, such as the betweenness centrality, the closeness centrality, the average path length, and the central point dominance, are all based on BFS searches.

These distance/centrality metrics are computing intensive. Their calculation in large sparse graphs involves many full BFS traversals, resulting in hours to months of processing in modern CPU architectures if parallelism is not exploited, or if repeated measurements are needed.

The computational cost of BFS-based complex network metrics and the size of real-world networks stress the necessity for parallel approaches that exploit modern hardware architectures. The following section is devoted to this issue.

Table 2 Works on Correlation Patterns on Complex Network Metrics

References	Complex Networks	Observations
[7,21,22]	Random, technological, social, biological, and linguistic.	Sets of highly correlated metrics are presented. Do not consider that some of the studied metrics are size-dependent.
[7]	Erdös-Rényi, Barabási-Albert, geographic networks.	Correlations patterns for individual network datasets do not agree with the correlations when the datasets are combined.
[23,24]	Erdös-Rényi, Barabási-Albert, autonomous system networks.	Metric correlations are affected by the degree distribution. Correlation patterns change with the size and density of graphs.
[25]	Erdös-Rényi, random modular, random hierarchies, US airlines, Wikipedia networks.	Warn against mixing network ensembles from different domains to extract global metric correlation patterns. Size-dependent metrics distort the correlations between metrics.

5.4 EFFICIENT COMPLEX NETWORK TRAVERSAL

BFS is an intuitive search strategy that discovers the vertices of a graph by levels. Starting from a given vertex, BFS visits all the vertices at distance 1 from that vertex, then all the vertices at distance 2, and so on.

BFS represents an important core in a variety of complex network applications. BFS-based centrality metrics, such as the betweenness centrality, have been used, for example, to identify key proteins in protein interaction networks [26], and to identify the most relevant agents (leaders and gateways) in terrorist social networks [27]. Additionally, the betweenness centrality appears as a kernel of the HPC scalable graph analysis benchmark. Likewise, both the Graph500 and GreenGraph500 benchmarks include a kernel that consists of the repetition of BFS on huge networks.

However, even when a single BFS takes only $O(n+m)$ time, the mentioned applications need to perform an elevated number of BFSs (i.e., as many as the number of vertices in the graph). This is called AS-BFS. AS-BFS needs $O(n^2 + nm)$ time, where n can range from thousands to billions of nodes. The computational cost a variety of BFS applications on complex networks reveal the need for parallel strategies that exploit the features of modern HPC hardware architectures, in order to speed up the analysis of large and evolving networks.

5.4.1 HPC TRAVERSAL OF LARGE NETWORKS

Multicore processors have few yet complex processing units or cores with an on-chip hierarchy of large caches for general purpose and HPC processing. HPC clusters, a type of distributed memory architecture, is a group of workstations or dedicated machines connected via high-speed switched networks optimized for computing intensive large-scale calculations.

There is a list of publicly available libraries that exploit homogeneous parallel processing, (i.e., the use of a single HPC parallel architecture, such as a multicore server or a HPC cluster). Examples of such libraries include the Small-World Network Analysis and Partitioning (SNAP) library [28], The MultiThreaded Graph Library (MTGL) [29], the Parallel Boost Graph Library (PBGL) [30], the ParallelX Graph Library (PXGL) [31], and the Combinatorial BLAS library [32].

A GPU is a special-purpose HPC processor composed of many multithread cores. GPUs were initially designed as graphics accelerators for the PC and video game industry. Nowadays, GPUs are being used to accelerate a wide variety of scientific algorithms. Its popularity has increased since GPUs offer massive parallelism, huge memory bandwidth, and a general-purpose instruction set.

Most of the current GPU-accelerated BFS algorithms (e.g., [33–38]) are visitor/level-synchronous; each level is visited in parallel, preserving the sequential ordering of BFS frontiers [36]. Some works change the queue data structure to either increase locality or decrease intralevel synchronization overhead [35,36]. Other works avoid using a queue frontier structure by exhaustively examining nodes [34] or edges [38] in the current frontier, or by a warp-centric programming method [39]. Finally, there are works that try to reduce the number of traversed edges [33] and to reduce the interlevel synchronization overhead [35,40].

However, current results show that it has been difficult to leverage the massive parallelism of GPUs to accelerate the visitor approach on real-world graphs [34–36]. Speedups heavily depends on the graph instances, and there are real-world instances where the GPU implementation is slower than its CPU counterpart [34,35]. The performance of level-synchronous strategies is strongly influenced by topological properties, such as the diameter [36,39] or the degree distribution (due to load imbalance on SF graphs).

Sparse matrix operations provide a rich set of data-level parallelism, which suggest that algebraic formulations of BFS, based on sparse matrix-vector multiplications (SpMVs), might be more appropriate for the GPU data-parallel architecture [37,41]. Even when SpMV is considered a challenging problem due to the insufficient data locality and the lack of memory access predictability on real-world sparse matrices [37,42], it still offers higher arithmetic loads and clearer data access patterns than the classical visitor approach. In the following sections, we further discuss the use of GPUs for accelerating AS-BFS by describing and comparing two algorithmic approaches: visitor and algebraic (SpMV) AS-BFS.

5.4.2 ALGORITHMS FOR ACCELERATING AS-BFS ON GPU

There are two levels of parallelism that may be appropriate for GPUs: (1) medium-grain: for each BFS frontier, the exploration of all vertices in the frontier can proceed totally in parallel; and (2) fine-grain: for each BFS frontier, the exploration of the edges that go from the current frontier to the next one can be traversed in parallel. In this section, we describe two level-synchronous algorithmic approaches for AS-BFS that exploit these two different levels of parallelism on GPU: (1) visitor AS-BFS and (2) SpMV AS-BFS.

Algorithm 1 GPU-visitor algorithm (host)

    Input: G, number of nodes n
    Output: none
    $l[i] \leftarrow -1$ **for** $i = 0...n$
    for each node s **in** G **do**
            frontier $\leftarrow 0$
            while *continue* **do**
                    continue $\leftarrow$ *false*
                    run in GPU: *continue*, $l \leftarrow$ visitor kernel (G, l, *continue*, *frontier*)
                    frontier $\leftarrow$ *frontier* $+1$
            end while
    end for

For the visitor BFS, we describe the GPU strategy reported in [38], which exploits both fine- and medium-grain parallelism. This efficient dual parallelism strategy leads to load balance even on SF graphs [38]. For the SpMV AS-BFS, we describe a two-phase strategy: SpMV and then zero-counting. The SpMV approach is also efficient on SF graphs. Both strategies perform frontier-wise synchronization with kernel relaunching, in such a way that each kernel launch triggers the exploration of the next BFS frontier.

Algorithm 2 Visitor kernel (GPU)

    Input: G, l, *continue*, *frontier*
    Output: updated *continue* and l
    for each thread i **do in parallel**
            $u,v \leftarrow i^{th}$ edge in G
            if $l[u] = $ *frontier* **then**
                    if $l[v] = -1$ **then**

$$continue \leftarrow true$$
$$l[v] \leftarrow frontier + 1$$
    end if
   end if
  end for
  return *continue*, *l*

Algorithms 1 and 2 show the pseudocode of the visitor AS-BFS strategy on GPU, first proposed in [38]. The vector *l* stores the distance between the source vertex and every other vertex by using the number of the current BFS *frontier*. Starting from every vertex $s \in V$, Algorithm 1 invokes the visitor kernel on GPU as many times as the number of BFS frontiers.

Algorithm 2 shows the pseudocode of the GPU kernel for the concurrent examination of all edges in the current BFS frontier. In each kernel invocation, all the edges of *G* are distributed among the GPU threads. Each GPU thread then examines if its edge connects the current BFS frontier to the following frontier. If so, it raises a flag (*continue*) to indicate that there is a new BFS frontier that must be explored in the following kernel invocation.

Algorithm 3 GPU-SpMV algorithm (host)
Input: *G*, number of nodes *n*
Output: none
 $A \leftarrow$ adjacency matrix of *G*
 $A' \leftarrow A + I_n$, where I_n is the identity matrix of order *n*
 for each node *s* **in** *G* **do**
   $x[k] \leftarrow 0$ **for** $k = 0...n-1$
   $x[s] \leftarrow 1$
   $zeros \leftarrow \infty$
   while $zeros > 0$ **do**
     run in GPU: $y \leftarrow A'x$
     run in GPU: $zeros \leftarrow$ number of zeros in *y*
     swap pointers x, y **in GPU**
   end while
 end for

Algorithm 3 shows a pseudocode for the medium-grain SpMV AS-BFS on GPU. As the reader may notice, the strategy is very similar to the visitor algorithm for GPU: We perform a full BFS from each vertex $s \in V$, sequentially. However, in this case we accelerate the SpMVs and the zero-counting on GPU.

Then, we simply interchange the device pointers of the *x* and *y* vectors, so that we can reuse the allocated space and intermediated data produced in the device during the whole AS-BFS calculation. Algorithms 1 and 3 have no output, as they only show how to traverse the graph.

5.4.3 PERFORMANCE STUDY OF AS-BFS ON GPU's

We study the performance of the described GPU AS-BFS algorithms by comparing them to multi-threaded (MT) CPU implementations. To make a comprehensive study, we experimented by varying the topology (degree distribution $P(k)$ and density *d*) of synthetic regular and non-regular complex network-like networks.

To simulate different graph loads, we made use of the classical Gilbert and the Barabási-Albert random graph models, which allowed the creation of random graphs with exponential decay (Exp) and SF degree distributions, respectively. For the regular graphs, we experimented with the r-regular graph model (graphs where every vertex is connected to r other vertices).

For each degree distribution (Exp, SF and regular), we generated a dataset of very sparse ($d \in [0.0006, 0.003]$) and sparse ($d \in (0.003, 0.006]$) graphs with 40,000 vertices; and a dataset of dense ($d \in [0.01, 0.5]$) and very dense ($d \in (0.5, 1]$) graphs with 3,000 vertices. In spite of the difference in the number of vertices between the two datasets, the number of edges is comparable (up to around 4 M edges).

We implemented the MT visitor and the SpMV AS-BFS algorithms in a straightforward fashion, by uniformly distributing the single-source BFSs at random among the available cores. Both the MT and the GPU implementations were compared to a baseline sequential CPU visitor AS-BFS implementation.

The GPU visitor/SpMV experiments ran on a NVIDIA C2070 (Fermi) GPU with 448 CUDA cores at 1.15 GHz and 6GB GDDR5 of DRAM. The multicore visitor/SpMV experiments ran on AMD Opteron 6274 (Interlagos) processors at 2.2 GHz and 64 GB of RAM, by using 16 cores. The sequential CPU visitor experiments ran on the same CPU architecture, but by using only a single core.

Fig. 1 summarizes the best speedups among the MT and GPU implementations over the sequential visitor approach, averaged over very-sparse, sparse, dense, and very-dense nonregular (Exp and SF) and regular graphs.

Fig. 1 shows that the visitor approach is better suited for CPU multicore, whereas the SpMV approach is better suited for GPUs. On the other hand, it can be seen that GPUs are not suitable for regular sparse graphs: both SpMV and visitor approaches performed poorly on GPU (sequential CPU was 25 times (very sparse) and 7 times (sparse) faster than GPU visitor).

	MT		GPU	
Density	Regular	Non-regular	Regular	Non-regular
Very sparse $d = [0.0006, 0.003]$	Visitor (1.97x)	Visitor (Exp.) (3.99x)	Visitor (0.04x)	SpMV (Exp.) (8.1x)
Sparse $d = [0.003, 0.006]$	Visitor (4.28x)	Visitor (Exp.) (6.88x)	Visitor (0.14x)	SpMV (SF) (11.83x)
Dense $d = [0.01, 0.5]$	Visitor (5.85x)	Visitor (Exp.) (6.9x)	SpMV (4.87x)	SpMV (Exp.) (9.57x)
Very dense $d = [0.5, 1.0]$	Visitor (7.27x)	Visitor (Exp.) (8.07x)	SpMV (12.83x)	SpMV (Exp.) (13.97x)

FIG. 1

Comparison of speedups between the multicore and GPU AS-BFS implementations over a single-core CPU visitor implementation, on graphs with different densities and degree distributions. In the non-regular column, "Exp." stands for "exponential" and "SF" stands for "scale-free" degree distribution.

Gain of GPU over sequential CPU increased with the graph density. With larger amounts of edges comes larger workloads that can exploit the massive multithreading capabilities of this architecture for performing parallel SpMVs. Overall, the best speedup over sequential CPU was obtained with the SpMV GPU implementation on very dense graphs.

We observed that structural properties present in complex networks influence the performance of level-synchronous AS-BFS strategies in the following (decreasing) order of importance: (1) whether the graph is regular or nonregular, (2) the graph density and (3) whether the graph is SF or not. Note that CPUs and GPUs are suitable for complementary kinds of graphs. GPUs performed notably better on sparse graphs. This is in contrast to multicore CPUs, which performed better than GPUs on regular graphs.

These results suggest that the processing of BFS on large real-world graphs could benefit from a topology-driven heterogeneous computing strategy, that combines CPUs and GPUs in a single heterogeneous platform by considering the presented empirical evidence of the suitability of a variety graph loads to different parallel architectures.

5.5 *K*-CORE-BASED PARTITIONING FOR HETEROGENEOUS GRAPH PROCESSING

Heterogeneous computing seeks to divide a compute intensive task into parts that can be processed separately by different parallel architectures in a synchronized manner. The ultimate goal of heterogeneous computing is to maximize the data processing throughput of an application by executing computing intensive part of an algorithm in accelerators, usually in a GPU [43].

Two major strategies for graph heterogeneous computing processing are [44]: (1) heterogeneous switching and (2) heterogeneous partitioning. In heterogeneous switching, the computation switches among different architectures according to a scheduler policy. The scheduler determines if the data can be better processed by another device. In heterogeneous partitioning, the computation proceeds in parallel on two or more parallel architectures at the same time.

Table 3 shows heterogeneous computing works for a variety graph problems (e.g., BFS, PageRank, connected components) that present different combinations of parallel architectures, including: CPU+GPU, CPU+APUs, and CPU+MICs.

The first problem faced by any heterogeneous computing platform is to decide the best way to partition the load for later distribution among the available processors. Most existing graph partitioning algorithms produce equivalent partitions of the graph nodes [53], i.e., the produced partitions have a balanced number of nodes and the crossing links are minimized. In heterogeneous computing, however, the computing capabilities of the available processors varies, as do the size and properties of the scheduled tasks.

According to [45,46], a good graph partitioning strategy for heterogeneous computing should have: (1) low space and time complexity, (2) the ability to handle SF graphs, (3) the ability to handle large graphs, and (4) focus on the reduction of computation time.

In this section, we tackle the problem of graph partition for graph heterogeneous computing as an important step towards the efficient traversal of large graphs on heterogeneous HPC platforms.

Table 3 Works on Heterogeneous Computing of Graphs

References	Architectures	Architectures	Algorithm(s)	Partitioning
[45–47]	CPU+GPU	Heterogeneous partition	BFS, PageRank	Node degree
[48]	CPU+GPU	Heterogeneous switching	BFS	Frontier size
[44]	CPU+APU	Heterogeneous partition and heterogeneous switching	BFS, PageRank	Node degree
[49]	CPU+GPU	Heterogeneous partition and heterogeneous switching	BFS	Architecture memory bandwidth
[50]	CPU+GPU	Heterogeneous partition	BFS, connected components, all pairs shortest paths	Not specified
[51]	CPU+MIC	Heterogeneous switching	BFS	Frontier size
[52]	CPU+GPU	Heterogeneous switching	BFS	Frontier size

The last column lists the graph topological aspects used as criteria for partitioning the complex networks.

5.5.1 GRAPH PARTITIONING FOR HETEROGENEOUS COMPUTING

It is possible to render communication overhead negligible in kernels like BFS and PageRank on SF graphs by exploiting aggregation techniques and a BSP parallel model [45,46]. As a consequence, the graph partitioner does not need to minimize the communication time, and it should instead focus on producing partitions that minimize computing time [45,46].

Partitions should offer two levels of parallelism: (1) a heterogeneous level to maximize the utilization of the processors, (2) and a homogeneous level to balance the workload across the vertices of a partition [45,46]. A simple criteria for distributing the vertices among the parallel processors is the vertex degree. Placing high-degree vertices in the CPU and low-degree vertices in the GPU [45,46] provides homogeneity of the nodes placed in the GPU, and minimizes GPU thread divergence as well [44]. This intuitive strategy also leads to partitions that are cache-friendly, an important property for memory-bounded algorithms like BFS [44–46]. Finding a bisection that splits the graph into two partitions with very different vertex degrees helps to leverage the computing power of CPUs and GPUs when combined into a single heterogeneous platform [44,45,47].

In Section 5.4.3, we showed that graph density is an important factor that affects the suitability of graphs to parallel architectures. Density, in addition to homogeneity, needs to be considered when partitioning a graph. There is evidence that complex networks are integrated of: (1) a dense partition of well-connected vertices and (2) a comparatively larger, sparse and homogeneous partition of low-degree vertices [54]. How can we exploit this property to identify the vertices that belong to the dense area of a complex network?

5.5.2 *K*-CORE-BASED COMPLEX-NETWORK UNBALANCED BISECTION

The k-core of a graph is its largest subgraph whose vertices have degree at least k [55] and can be calculated efficiently by recursively pruning the vertices with degree smaller than k in $O(m)$ time. The concept of coreness is a natural notion of the importance of a node. For example, it has been reported that autonomous system networks show a "core" [54], integrated of highly connected hubs that represent the backbone of the Internet. The k-core decomposition defines a hierarchy of nodes that allow us to differentiate between core and noncore components of a network.

Algorithm 4 KCMax graph bisection

> **Input**: G, k
> **Output**: V_{dense}, V_{sparse}
> $V_{dense}, V_{sparse} \leftarrow \{\}$
> $V_{crust} \leftarrow$ get nodes at the k-crust
> $V_{sparse} \leftarrow V_{crust}$
> $G \leftarrow$ remove nodes in V_{crust} from G
> **while** there are nodes in G **do**
>> $V_{kmax} \leftarrow$ get nodes at the k_{max}-shell of G
>> $V_{dense} \leftarrow V_{dense} \cup V_{kmax}$
>> $G \leftarrow$ remove nodes in V_{kmax} from G
>> $V_{sparse} \leftarrow V_{sparse} \cup$ nodes of G not in the giant component of G
>> $G \leftarrow$ get the giant component of G
> **return** V_{sparse}, V_{dense}

Vertices at the highest k-cores are located in the network's densest area, the area that maintains the clustering structure of the graph. Thus, the k-core decomposition represents a useful yet easy to calculate heuristic for deciding which vertices belong to the dense partition and which vertices belong to the sparse one.

The authors propose the KCMax heuristic [56], listed in Algorithm 4, to produce a graph bisection algorithm that exploits the notion of k-core decomposition. The main idea behind the KCMax approach is: by repeatedly extracting the core of the network, we can separate the dense area of the network from the sparse one.

This separation would produce an unbalanced bisection of the graph that can be exploited for load distribution on heterogeneous platforms.

Formally, a k-core of a graph $G = (V, E)$ is a subgraph $H = (C, L|C)$, induced by the set $C \subseteq V$, if and only if $\forall v \in C : k_v \geq k$ and H is a maximum subgraph with this property. The k-cores are nested, i.e., $i < j \rightarrow H_j \subseteq H_i$, like Russian nested dolls [57]. The k-crust is the graph G with the k-core removed. A node $v \in V$ is said to belong to the k-shell if and only if it belongs to the k-core but not to the $(k+1)$-core. We say that if v is in the k-shell then v has a shell index of k.

The KCMax algorithm starts by appending to the sparse partition, V_{sparse}, the nodes located at the k-crust of the graph. Then, it removes the k-crust from G. This preprocessing step is motivated by the fact that the k-crust nodes are unlikely to belong to the dense partition of the graph as they are very likely to hold a low clustering degree (Fig. 2). In practice, a large percentage of nodes in complex networks can be readily assigned to the sparse partition and removed from the graph to speed up the algorithm.

The search for the dense area begins by identifying the nodes at the highest nonempty k-shell, the k_{max}-shell. Then, it appends the vertices at k_{max}-shell to the list of nodes in the dense partition, V_{dense}. The nodes at k_{max}-shell are removed from G, and only the giant component of G is retained for the next iteration. The nodes that are not in the giant component are assigned to the sparse partition, V_{sparse}. The algorithm repeats this procedure until the graph is depleted and all the nodes have been assigned to either the sparse or the dense partition.

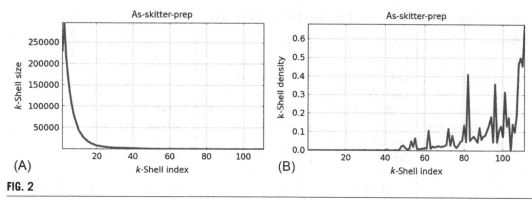

FIG. 2

Decomposition of the AS-Skitter graph. Horizontal axis shows the *k*-sell index. The vertical axis shows: (A) the number of nodes inside each *k*-shell and (B) the density of the subgraph induced by each *k*-shell. Note how most of the nodes belong to the least-dense *k*-shells. These nodes can be readily assigned to the sparse partition in a preprocessing stage to accelerate the KCMax heuristic.

The objectives of keeping the giant component after removing the k_{max}-shell are: (1) to help the heuristic to focus on the connected component that is more likely to contain clusters of nodes, and (2) to help the heuristic to reduce the number of iterations by discarding small components that result from the removal of the highest shell.

Table 4 lists large complex networks from a variety of application domains partitioned by exploiting the KCMax heuristic. Most of the graphs are real-world complex networks, with the exception of the R-MAT Graph500 synthetic graph. roadNet-PA, a road network of Pennsylvania, is unique in its large diameter and very low clustering (the small-world property is not present).

Tables 5 and 6 present the properties of the produced sparse and dense partitions, respectively. Note that, in general, the sparse partition concentrates more than the 50% of the vertices. In the AS-Skitter, soc-LiveJournal1, and cit-Patents graphs, the sparse partition accounts for more than the 90% of vertices.

Table 4 Complex Network Dataset					
Graph	**Type**	*n*	*m*	$\langle CC \rangle$	*D*
AS-Skitter	Internet	1,696,415	11,095,298	0.2581	25
soc-LiveJournal1	Social	4,847,571	68,993,773	0.2742	16
cit-Patents	Citation	3,774,768	16,518,948	0.0757	22
com-orkut-ungraph	Social	3,072,441	117,185,083	0.1666	9
soc-pokec-relationships	Social	1,632,803	30,622,564	0.1094	11
R-MAT	Synthetic	388,317	16,777,184	0.1996	ND
roadNet-PA	Road	1,088,092	1,541,898	0.0465	786
Wiki-Vote	Vote	7115	103,689	0.1409	7
Email-Enron	Email	36,692	183,831	0.4970	11
Cit-HepPh	Citation	27,770	352,807	0.3120	13
n, number of nodes; m, number of edges; $\langle CC \rangle$, avg. clustering coefficient; D, diameter; and ND, no data.					

Table 5 Properties of the Sparse Partition Produced by KCMax

Graph	n	$\sum k_i$	d	c	Avg. deg.
AS-Skitter	1,565,489 (92.38%)	11,041,869 (49.76%)	2.17×10^{-6}	242,272	7.05
soc-LiveJournal1	4,687,387 (96.77%)	59,300,536 (69.20%)	2.35×10^{-6}	182,963	12.65
cit-Patents	3,641,824 (96.75%)	28,351,467 (85.85%)	2×10^{-6}	18,396	7.78
com-orkut-ungraph	2,365,979 (77.01%)	94,072,948 (40.14%)	1.13×10^{-5}	68,191	39.76
soc-pokec-relationships	909,797 (55.72%)	5,999,391 (13.45%)	1.76×10^{-6}	360,457	6.59
R-MAT	286,526 (73.80%)	2,278,227 (7.67%)	1.46×10^{-6}	226,227	7.95
roadNet-PA	214,395 (19.71%)	260,233 (8.44%)	1.99×10^{-6}	168,628	1.21
Wiki-Vote	4595 (65.03%)	18,246 (9.06%)	5.09×10^{-5}	4062	3.97
Email-Enron	26,011 (77.19%)	92,145 (25.48%)	4.36×10^{-5}	16,375	3.54
Cit-HepPh	11,060 (32.15%)	82,111 (9.76%)	7.02×10^{-5}	7051	7.42

n, nodes; $\sum k_i$, sum of the degrees of the vertices in the partition; d, density of the graph induced by the partition; c, number of components in the graph induced by the partition; and avg. deg., average degree of the vertices in the partition.

Table 6 Properties of the Dense Partition Produced by KCMax

Graph	n	$\sum k_i$	d	c	Avg. deg.
AS-Skitter	129,127 (7.62%)	11,146,549 (50.24%)	3.2×10^{-4}	2	86.32
soc-LiveJournal1	156,566 (3.23%)	26,390,832 (30.80%)	7.6×10^{-4}	12	168.56
cit-Patents	122,293 (3.25%)	4,672,013 (14.15%)	1.9×10^{-4}	12	38.20
com-orkut-ungraph	706,462 (22.99%)	140,297,218 (59.86%)	2.2×10^{-4}	1	198.59
soc-pokec-relationships	723,006 (44.28%)	38,604,537 (86.55%)	6.51×10^{-5}	1	53.39
R-MAT	101,711 (26.20%)	27,413,457 (92.33%)	2.4×10^{-3}	1	269.52
roadNet-PA	873,167 (80.29%)	2,822,795 (91.56%)	3.48×10^{-6}	3	3.23
Wiki-Vote	2471 (34.97%)	183,226 (90.94%)	2.72×10^{-2}	1	74.15
Email-Enron	7685 (22.81%)	269,477 (74.52%)	3.5×10^{-3}	5	35.06
Cit-HepPh	23,341 (67.85%)	759,457 (90.24%)	1.25×10^{-3}	2	32.53

n, nodes; $\sum k_i$, sum of the degrees of the vertices in the partition; d, density of the graph induced by the partition; c, number of components in the graph induced by the partition; and avg. deg., average degree of the vertices in the partition.

Likewise, note that in complex networks, a small proportion of vertices in the dense partitions concentrates a high number of edges. Take as examples the Email-Enron network, where 22.81% of the vertices are connected by 74.52% of the links; the R-MAT network, where the 26% of the vertices are connected by 92% of the links; and the Wiki-Vote network, where the 34% of the vertices are connected by 90% of the links.

In some complex networks, a degree of balance between the sparse and the dense partitions arises, either in the number of nodes or in the number of links. For example, in the soc-pokec-relationships and Wiki-Vote networks the 55% and the 65% of the vertices are assigned to the sparse partition, respectively; whereas in the AS-Skitter and com-orkut-ungraph networks the 49% and 40% of the links are assigned to the sparse partition, respectively.

The dense partition of most of the experimented graphs is several orders of magnitude denser than the sparse partition. An exception was the roadNet-PA, whose partitions showed the same order of density. In all graphs, however, the density of both the sparse and the dense partitions was relatively low.

Finally, note that the dense partitions are generally composed of at most a dozen of connected components, while the sparse partitions are composed of thousands of connected components. Additionally, the average degree of the vertices in the dense partition is one order of magnitude larger than in the sparse partition in virtually all graphs (with the exception of roadNet-PA, where it is two orders of magnitude higher). The remarkable difference in the number of components, the density and the average degree in the partitions suggest that KCMax was able to locate those vertices that integrate the densest part of the graphs in all cases.

5.6 FUTURE DIRECTIONS

The processing of AS-BFS-related algorithms on large real-world graphs can exploit a topology-driven heterogeneous computing strategy, that combines CPUs and GPUs by considering the presented empirical evidence shown in Section 5.4.3 of the suitability of a variety graph loads and algorithms to different parallel architectures and different BFS algorithms approaches.

The authors have observed that Totem [45–47], a graph computation framework that exploits single-node multicore + GPU heterogeneous systems, can benefit from the KCMax partitioning heuristic [56]. Other projects that follow a BSP-like parallel computational model and that focus on minimizing the computation time of partitions could take advantage of the partitions produced by the KCMax algorithm as well.

Future work include: (1) the extension of the KCMax algorithm to calculate an arbitrary number of partitions by recursively applying the KCMax heuristic to the bisection, in order to provide support, for example, to multi-GPU architectures; and (2) producing a graph library that exploits a variety of BFS kernels accelerated by different hardware architectures, while hiding the heterogeneous computing workload distribution details from the user for the acceleration of traversal-based complex network applications.

5.7 CONCLUSIONS

Network science and complex network are becoming increasingly relevant for representing and analyzing multi-relational Big Data and in modeling complicated data structures and their interactions. The main idea behind a complex network is to model high-order interactions among the individual components of large systems by means of graphs, to increase our understanding of not only immediate but also high-order interactions, as well as the implications of these interactions on the mechanisms that govern the underlying phenomenon.

We presented algorithms for performing HPC traversals on large sparse graphs by exploiting CPU multicores and GPUs. By comparing the visitor and algebraic BFS approaches, we showed that structural properties present in complex networks influence the performance of AS-BFS strategies in the following (decreasing) order of importance: (1) whether the graph is regular or non-regular (2) whether the graph is dense or not, and (3) whether the graph is SF or not. In addition, we showed that CPU's and GPU's are suitable for complementary kinds of graphs.

Finally, we described the KCMax graph bisection heuristic, that capitalizes on the notion of k-core decomposition to identify and separate the dense area of a complex network from the sparse one. This separation would produce a bisection of the graph where each partition is suitable for different parallel architectures, that can be exploited for load distribution on parallel heterogeneous platforms. We partitioned a collection of large real-world graphs and showed the properties of the partitions induced by the bisection.

Ongoing work includes the adaption of the unbalanced graph partitioning algorithm KCMax to BSP-like heterogeneous platforms, to minimize computation time instead of communications, and accelerate the traversal and calculation of BFS-based metrics on big real-world networks, with the objective of overcoming the limitations of homogeneous platforms.

ACKNOWLEDGMENTS

The authors acknowledge the General Coordination of Information and Communications Technologies (CGSTIC) at Cinvestav for providing HPC resources on the Hybrid Cluster Supercomputer "Xiuhcoatl" that have contributed to the research results reported within this chapter.

REFERENCES

[1] Committee on Network Science for Future Army Applications. Network science. Washington, DC: National Academies Press; 2005.

[2] Lima M. Visual complexity, 2015. http://www.visualcomplexity.com/vc/ [accessed 01.07.15].

[3] National Center for Biotechnology Information. Growth of GenBank and WGS, 2015. http://www.ncbi.nlm.nih.gov/genbank/statistics [accessed 25.10.15].

[4] Facebook. Facebook reports first quarter 2015 results. Menlo Park, CA: Facebook; 2015. http://investor.fb.com/releasedetail.cfm?ReleaseID=908022; [accessed 25.10.15].

[5] WorldWideWebSize.com. The size of the world wide web (the internet), 2015. http://www.worldwidewebsize.com [accessed 25.10.15].

[6] Joseph I, Vodenska E, Stanley E, Chen G. Netconomics: novel forecasting techniques from the combination of Big Data. Netw Scie Econ 2014. arXiv:1403.0848.

[7] Costa LF, Rodrigues FA, Travieso G, Boas PRV. Characterization of complex networks: a survey of measurements. Adv Phys 2007;56(1):167–242.

[8] Guida M, Maria F. Topology of the Italian airport network: a scale-free small-world network with a fractal structure? Chaos Solitons Fract 2007;31(3):527–36.

[9] Angeloudis P, Fisk D. Large subway systems as complex networks. Phys A Stat Mech Appl 2006;367(15):553–8.

[10] Yazdani A, Jeffrey P. Complex network analysis of water distribution systems. Chaos 2011;21(1):016111.

[11] Robinson I, Webber J, Eifrem E. Graph databases. Boston, MA: O'Reilly Media; 2013.

[12] Neo4j. The world's leading graph database, 2015. http://www.neo4j.org [accessed 01.07.15].

[13] OrientDB, OrientDB graph-document NoSQL DMBS, 2015. http://www.orientdb.org [accessed 01.07.15].

[14] Objectivity. InfiniteGraph, 2015. http://www.objectivity.com/products/infinitegraph/ [accessed 01.07.15].

[15] Malewicz G, Austern MH, Bik AJC, Dehnert JC, Horn I, Leiser N, et al. Pregel: a system for large-scale graph processing. In: Proceedings of the 16th international conference on management of data (COMAD'2010), Indianapolis, USA, June 6–11; 2010.

[16] Giraph. Welcome to Apache Giraph! http://giraph.apache.org [accessed 01.07.15].

[17] Hassibi K, Dean J. High performance data mining and Big Data analytics. New York: Wiley; 2012.

[18] Lumsdaine A. Challenges in parallel graph processing. Parallel Process Lett 2007;17(1):5–20.

[19] Sharma P, Khurana U, Shneiderman B, Scharrenbroich M, Locke J. Speeding up network layout and centrality measures for social computing goals. In: Proceedings of the 2011 international conference on social computing, behavioral-cultural modeling and prediction; 2011.

[20] Strogatz SH, Watts DJ. Collective dynamics of 'small-world' networks. Nature 1998;393(6684):440–2.

[21] Filkov V, Saul ZM, Roy S, D'Souza RM, Devanbu PT. Modeling and verifying a broad array of network properties. Europhys Lett 2009;86(2):28003.

[22] Jamakovic A, Uhlig S. On the relationships between topological measures in real-world networks. Netw Heterogen Media 2008;3(2):345–59.

[23] Garcia-Robledo A, Diaz-Perez A, Morales-Luna G. Correlation analysis of complex network metrics on the topology of the internet. In: Proceedings of the 10th international conference and expo on emerging technologies for a smarter world, Melville, USA, October 21–22; 2013.

[24] Li HW, de Haan W, Stam CJ, Van Mieghem P. The correlation of metrics in complex networks with applications in functional brain networks. J Stat Mech Theory Exper 2011;2011(11):P11018.

[25] Bounova G, de Weck O. Overview of metrics and their correlation patterns for multiple-metric topology analysis on heterogeneous graph ensembles. Phys Rev E 2012;85(1):016117.

[26] Koschützki D, Schreiber F. Centrality analysis methods for biological networks and their application to gene regulatory networks. Gene Regul Syst Biol 2008;2(1):193–201.

[27] Yang CC. Knowledge discovery and information visualization for terrorist social networks. In: Chen H, Yang CC, editors. Intelligence and security informatics: techniques and applications. Philadelphia, PA: Springer; 2008.

[28] Madduri K. A high-performance framework for analyzing massive complex networks. PhD thesis, Atlanta, GA: Georgia Institute of Technology; 2008.

[29] Berry JW, Hendrickson B, Kahan S, Konecny P. Software and algorithms for graph queries on multithreaded architectures. In: Proceedings of the 21st IEEE international symposium on parallel and distributed processing (IPDPS'2007), Long Beach, USA, March 30; 2007.

[30] Gregor D, Lumsdaine A. The parallel BGL: a generic library for distributed graph computations. In: Proceedings of the 5th workshop on parallel/high-performance object-oriented scientific computing, Glasgow, UK, July 25; 2005.

[31] Stark D. Advanced semantics for accelerated graph processing. PhD thesis, Baton Rouge, LA: Louisiana State University; 2011.

[32] Buluç A. Linear algebraic primitives for parallel computing on large graphs. PhD thesis, Santa Barbara, CA: University of California; 2010.

[33] Beamer S, Asanovic K, Patterson D. Direction-optimizing breadth-first search. In: Proceedings of the 2012 ACM/IEEE international conference for high performance computing, networking, storage and analysis, Salt Lake City, USA, November 10–16; 2012.

[34] Harish P, Narayanan PJ. Accelerating large graph algorithms on the GPU using CUDA. In: Proceedings of the 14th international conference on high performance computing, Goa, India, December 18–21; 2007.

[35] Luo L, Wong M, Wen-Mei H. An effective GPU implementation of breadth-first search. In: Proceedings of the 47th design automation conference, Anaheim, USA, June 13–18; 2010.

[36] Merrill D, Garland M, Grimshaw A. Scalable GPU graph traversal. In: Proceedings of the 17th ACM SIGPLAN symposium on principles and practice of parallel programming, LA, USA, February 25–29; 2012.

[37] Qian H, Deng Y, Wang B, Mu S. Towards accelerating irregular EDA applications with GPU's. Integr VLSI J 2012;45(1):46–60.

[38] Shi Z, Zhang B. Fast network centrality analysis using GPU's. BMC Bioinform 2011;12(149):1–7.

[39] Hong S, Kim SK, Oguntebi T, Olukotun K. Accelerating CUDA graph algorithms at maximum warp. In: Proceedings of the 16th ACM symposium on principles and practice of parallel programming, San Antonio, TX, February 12–16; 2011.

[40] Liu G, An H, Han W, Li X, Sun T, Zhou W. FlexBFS: a parallelism-aware implementation of breadth-first search on GPU. In: Proceedings of the 17th ACM symposium on principles and practice of parallel programming, New Orleans, USA, February 25–29; 2012.

[41] Kepner J, Gilbert J. Graph algorithms in the language of linear algebra. Philadelphia, PA: Society for Industrial and Applied Mathematics; 2011.

[42] Goumas GI, Kourtis K, Anastopoulos N, Karakasis V, Koziris N. Performance evaluation of the sparse matrix-vector multiplication on modern architectures. J Supercomput 2009;50(1):36–77.

[43] Gelado I, Stone JE, Cabezas J, Patel S, Navarro N, Hwu WW. An asymmetric distributed shared memory model for heterogeneous parallel systems. In: Proceedings of the 15th edition of architectural support for programming languages and operating systems (ASPLOS'2010), New York, USA, March 13; 2010.

[44] Nilakant K, Yoneki E. On the efficacy of APUs for heterogeneous graph computation. In: Proceedings of the 4th workshop on systems for future multicore architecture, University of Cambridge, UK; 2014.

[45] Gharaibeh A, Santos-Neto E. Efficient large-scale graph processing on hybrid CPU and GPU systems. J Supercomput 2013;71(4):1563–86.

[46] Gharaibeh A, Costa LB, Santos-Neto E, Ripeanu M. On graphs, GPU's, and blind dating: a workload to processor matchmaking quest. In: Proceeding of the 2013th international parallel and distributed processing symposium, Boston, USA, May 20–24; 2013.

[47] Gharaibeh A, Costa LB, Santos-Neto E, Ripeanu M. A yoke of oxen and a thousand chickens for heavy lifting graph processing. In: Proceedings of the 21st international conference on parallel architectures and compilation techniques, Minneapolis, MN, USA, September 19–23; 2012.

[48] Hong S, Oguntebi T, Olukotun K. Efficient parallel graph exploration on multi-core CPU and GPU. In: Proceedings of the 2011 international conference on parallel architectures and compilation techniques, Washington, DC, USA, October 10–14; 2011.

[49] Zou D, Dou Y, Wang Q, Xu J, Li B. Direction-optimizing breadth-first search on CPU-GPU heterogeneous platforms. In: Proceedings of the 10th IEEE international conference on high performance computing and communications and 2013 IEEE international conference on embedded and ubiquitous computing, Zhangjiajie, November 13–15; 2013.

[50] Banerjee DS, Sharma S, Kothapalli K. Work efficient parallel algorithms for large graph exploration. In: Proceeding of the 20th annual international conference on high performance computing, Bangalore, India, December; 2013.

[51] Gao T, Lu Y, Zhang B, Suo G. Using the Intel many integrated core to accelerate graph traversal. Int J High Perform Comput Appl 2014;28(3):255–66.

[52] Munguia LM, Bader DA, Ayguade E. Task-based parallel breadth-first search in heterogeneous environments. In: Proceedings of the 19th international conference on high performance computing, Pune, December 18–22; 2012.

[53] Chamberlain BL. Graph partitioning algorithms for distributing workloads of parallel computations. Seattle, WA: University of Washington; 1998. Technical report.

[54] Carmi S, Havlin S, Kirkpatrick S, Shavitt Y, Shir E. A model of internet topology using k-shell decomposition. Proc Nat Acad Sci USA May 2007;104(27):11150–4.

[55] Dorogovtsev SN, Goltsev AV, Mendes JFF. K-core organization of complex networks. Phys Rev Lett 2006;96:040601.

[56] Garcia-Robledo A, Diaz-Perez A, Morales-Luna G. Exploring the feasibility of heterogeneous computing of complex networks for Big Data analysis. In: Proceedings of the 12th international conference and expo on emerging technologies for a smarter world, Melville, USA, October 19–20; 2015.

[57] Batagelj V, Zaversnik M. An O(m) algorithm for cores decomposition of networks. Adv Data Anal Classi 2003;5(2):129–45.

BIG DATA INFRASTRUCTURES AND PLATFORMS

DATABASE TECHNIQUES FOR BIG DATA

6

P. Ameri

6.1 INTRODUCTION

For a long time, most of data management functionalities used to be provided only by relational database management systems. However, in the last decades, new applications emerged and new requirements were raised that could hardly be met by relational databases. It made database designers question some of the fundamental properties of relational databases. This new approach resulted in appearance of NoSQL databases.

In this chapter, we start by looking into fundamentals of databases. We will gain insight into different data models, from navigational to relational and then to NoSQL data models. The advantages of each model will be obvious, demonstrated by their specific use cases. The most important challenges and solutions, raised by the emergence of Big Data, will be presented. This information enables you to decide which database model is more appropriate for an application based on its requirements.

6.2 BACKGROUND

A *database* is a collection of related data that is organized to ease and speed up access to data in a standardized format. The interface between the database, users, and other applications is integrated into a software system known as *Database Management System* (DBMS) [1]. Each DBMS not only provides numerous functionalities to create and query data, but also offers management and administrative functionalities.

DBMSs are classified based on various aspects, such as the data model they apply, the query language they provide, their use of hardware, and their internal design, which affects their performance and scalability. However, DBMSs are primarily categorized according to their data model. Since both a database and its DBMS conform to a particular data model, the data model defines the logical structure of the database, that is, a data model standardizes how the data elements relate to each other. Based on this classification, database technology can be studied through three historical generations: navigational, relational, and post-relational (NoSQL).

6.2.1 NAVIGATIONAL DATA MODELS

When data could only be stored on magnetic tape, *navigational databases* were common. Navigational systems rely on references to navigate through data. Each basic data structure contains a reference to the location on tape where referenced objects are stored. Thus, relevant information can be retrieved without sequential reading of tapes.

Big Data. http://dx.doi.org/10.1016/B978-0-12-805394-2.00006-4

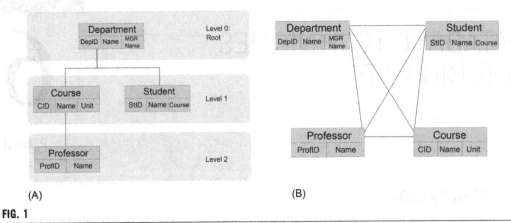

FIG. 1

Most important navigational models are hierarchical and network models. (A) Hierarchical model has a tree-like structure. (B) Network model has a graph-like structure.

Two major navigational database models are the hierarchical model and the network model [1]. The hierarchical model arranges data as a tree. Trees are nonlinear directional data structures consisting of *nodes*. Each node consists of data elements with values. Each node can have one or more nodes that directly follow it as *children*. A tree has a root node and subtrees of *children* and their *parents*. In the hierarchical model, data retrieval is possible by traversing through the tree starting from the root node. In contrast, the network model applies a graph-like structure. Graphs allow cycles of connections between their nodes. A tree is a special graph structure that allows no cycles. Both of these structures are shown in Fig. 1.

When tapes were the only medium available to store data, one of the problems with the navigational models was related to the difficulty of adding data to or removing data from tapes. It requires rewriting the entire underlying indexes that were stored with the data on the same tape. Although navigational models displaced by relational ones for a long time, the hierarchical and the network data model both resurfaced by the emergence of technologies like XML and graph databases respectively (more details in Section 6.3).

6.2.2 RELATIONAL DATA MODELS

In 1956, IBM [2] introduced *hard disk drives*. Thereby *random access* to data became feasible and affordable. Around 1961, the price and capacity of disks got to the level that they could be widely used [3]. It enabled more efficient data models. Among all of the models, the relational data model proposed by Codd [4] became the adopted solution by the most popular database systems from 1980s to about 2010. Codd's work is a mathematical description of a *set-theory* branch called *relational algebra*, which is the foundation of *Relational Database Management Systems* (RDBMSs). (For further study on relational algebra see Ref. [5].)

The well-known standard declarative *Structured Query Language* (SQL) is widely used to interact with relational databases. A *query language* is the language allowing users to access and manipulate databases. SQL has a direct relationship to relational algebra — a combination of projection, selections, Cartesian products, and more operations that can be performed on tables [6].

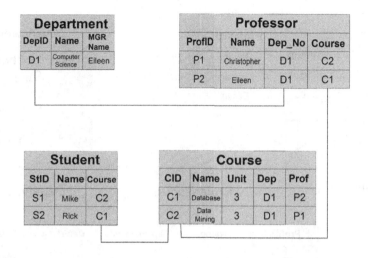

FIG. 2

Tabular organization of relational data model.

Rather than asking the system *how* to navigate the data, the relational model using SQL language emphasizes *what* to fetch. Relational databases organize data into *relations* (ie, tables) consisting of sets of *tuples* (ie, rows), which map *attributes* to atomic values with limited length. This tabular organization of data is illustrated in Fig. 2.

The data modeling process in relational databases typically starts by defining a *schema*. The schema formalizes the data in form of *tables* that include *rows (records)* and *columns (attributes)*. There are several well-defined methods in relational database theory regarding how to transfer data into tabular format. These are known as *normal forms*. The normal forms provide a set of rules for designing records with concentration on attributes and dependencies. The general goal of normalization is to remove data redundancy and to prevent inconsistent state after any update, insert, or delete operation.

Schema normalization generally begins with putting the application data into the *First Normal Form* (1NF). The first normal form deals with the shape of a record in each table. All records in a table under 1NF must have the same number of fields. It means that data must be designed in tabular format composed of rows and columns. In addition, each intersection of a row and column, known as a *cell*, must contain exactly one value. The data in Fig. 2 is in first normal form. For further information on normal forms, refer to Ref. [7].

The issue with the normalization rises when the data is queried. The performance of a well-normalized data model is challenged by the number of *join* operations required to execute queries. A join is a SQL operation in relational databases that combines records of two or more database tables based on their matching column values and is shown with ⋈ symbol. Complicated operations in relational databases include several join operations. Fig. 3 shows the result of joining two relations, *Professor* and *Department*, where they have equal values in two of their specific columns. The join operation includes many seek processes to find the proper requested data in each table and then many sequential accesses to read the found data. On a spinning disk, seeking to the location of the data takes much longer than the actual sequential reading of the data. On a distributed system, where each of these tables or part of them

Input tables

Professor		
ProfID	Name	Dep_member
P1	Christopher	D1
P2	Eileen	D3

Department	
DepID	DName
D1	Physics
D2	Mathematics
D3	Computer Science

Output table

Professor $\bowtie_{Dep\_member = DepID}$ Department

ProfID	Name	Dep_member	DepID	DName
P1	Christopher	D1	D1	Physics
P2	Eileen	D3	D3	Computer Science

FIG. 3

Results of join operation on Professor and Department relations where the Dep_member of the Professor relation is equal to the DepID of the Department relation.

might be on different physical servers, having this join operation means data from one of these servers should be transferred to the other one so that the output table can be build and the query can be answered. Therefore, the cost of processing the join operation on distributed systems gets even higher.

Transactions also play an important rule in most traditional relational databases. A transaction is a unit of one or more *create*, *read*, *update*, and *delete* (*CRUD*) operations that complete a single task. Database transactions normally all have particular characteristics known as ACID. It is an acronym standing for the following properties:

- *Atomicity*: "all or nothing" — If the transaction fails to complete any of its single operations, the database will be rolled back to its original state.
- *Consistency*: "valid data" — The database is taken from one consistent state into another consistent state. Intermediate states are not necessarily consistent.
- *Isolation*: "separation ensured" — Concurrent transactions do not affect each other.
- *Durability*: "no loss" — After any transaction commits successfully, the changes committed by the transaction are stored persistently, even if there is a subsequent system crash.

Ensuring transaction's ACID properties on distributed systems has implications in terms of atomicity and consistency. Regardless of the physical location of distributed components towards each other, the decision to commit or roll back transactions should be managed by the database. The common management solution for handling transactions on distributed systems is the *two-phase commit*. A *two-phase* commit consists of two phases: *request* and *commit*. At the request phase, a *coordinator* process sends a query to all *participants* processes to prepare for necessary actions. It expects to receive

YES messages from all of them. If any participant sends *NO* as an answer, the transaction is *aborted*. If everyone is ready, the coordinator sends the message to complete their commit. Again, if any process fails to do so, all processes will roll back.[1]

Difficulty of handling join operations and ACID transactions on distributed systems and emergence of Big Data motivated new movements in database design. In the following, the NoSQL movement is discussed.

6.3 NoSQL MOVEMENT

Mass usage of interactive web applications resulted in new demands from databases that could not easily be met by conventional database designs. Emergence of interactive web not only impacted the size of produced data, but also demanded support for various formats of web applications (eg, social networking websites, Internet of Things, and document integration) that could conveniently fit to other formats than a tabular design. In addition to web applications, the e-science communities (eg, physics, astronomy, earth science, biology, humanities, etc.) also produced a large volume of data and required fast processing ability from database systems. As it turns out, Big Data's *volume, velocity,* and *variety* are all causes for new movements in database research field [8]. Moreover, a shift in hardware and computing architecture played a role in encouraging NoSQL movement.

Defining NoSQL is challenging for two reasons: First, because the term is not representing the core concept of the movement; rather, it is even misleading. Second, because this term is an umbrella term for many features that might not all be present in one particular database at the same time. The term NoSQL was first used in late 1990s as a name for a lightweight relational database product [9] that did not use SQL as its query language. The product itself had nothing to do with the so-called NoSQL movement. The term NoSQL or "not only SQL" was then used in 2009 for a series of meetups and discussions over common issues of open source distributed databases. It stuck as a general name for all databases that are differentiating from traditional relational databases. We define NoSQL as the following:

> NoSQL refers to a series of database management concepts that process data in a performant and reliable manner.

This is intentionally a broad definition. It even can still include relational database management systems that use SQL as their query language. Therefore, we subsequently identify the core concepts that NoSQL databases focus on.

NoSQL databases have mostly the following common characteristics:

- *No requirement for fixed rows in a table schema.* There are many data models that are used by NoSQL databases including the key-value, column-based, graph-based, and document-based models. (These models are discussed in Section 6.5.)
- *Horizontal scaling.* Most of NoSQL systems enable partitioning of data and processing over multiple nodes.
- *Multiprocessor support.* NoSQL systems are designed to work on multiprocessor machines in a way that by adding more processors, a linear scaling in performance is feasible.

---

[1]Oracle developed a three-phase commit process, which is still known as two-phase commit.

- *Elimination of join operations*. NoSQL databases offer simple interfaces that are free from join operations.
- *Support weaker concurrency models than the standard ACID transaction model*. Not all applications require ACID transactions. Therefore, many NoSQL database management systems relax some aspects of ACID transactions.
- *Be schemaless*. For the purpose of agility and to gain performance, NoSQL systems also store data without any fixed schema. It allows for dynamically adding new fields to arbitrary data records.
- *Utilize shared-nothing architecture*. Many NoSQL databases (with exception of graph-based databases) are designed to be functional on a cluster of commodity hardware that does not share any RAM or disk with each other.

It should not be implied that NoSQL databases are better database management systems than relational ones. The functionality and criteria to use each one is different. The proper database management type should be chosen dependent on the application requirements. The challenges that the emergence of Big Data brought for databases and NoSQL solutions are discussed in more depth in the following.

6.4 NoSQL SOLUTIONS FOR BIG DATA MANAGEMENT

The emergence of *Big Data* is very demanding for databases. This era is concurring with business models based on web and cloud applications. By expansion of mass usage of web applications, some of their requirements exceeded the capabilities of traditional relational databases capabilities. These applications not only have a massive amount of data, but they usually offer services across the globe; therefore, they must be highly distributed and always available so that their customers access them 24/7. Therefore, they are highly concerned with accessibility, availability, and load balancing on several geographically distributed servers. But there are some barriers in achieving availability and consistency for such applications at the same time.

At the beginning of 21st century, Brewer made a conjecture [10] known as CAP theorem stating that on any distributed database system, it is impossible to have the following three properties guaranteed all at the same time on a distributed data system (though two of them can), as depicted in Fig. 4. This theorem was then proved by Gilbert and Lynch [11]. CAP stands for:

- *Consistency*: Propagation of the same and most recent updated version of the data to all nodes of a distributed system. This property ensures consistency of data on replicated partitions of the database. It is different from ACID consistency. Consistency in ACID transactions ensures data integrity for all database connections using two-phase commit. Consistency in CAP theorem is related to how fast data changes appear in a distributed system.
- *Availability*: Possibility of client interaction with the distributed database system. This property is concerned with the availability of the system to users, even if a failure in communication within replicated parts of database happens.
- *Partition tolerance*: Ability of two segments of the system (*partitions*) to proceed in the presence of a temporary communication failure in their network. With more partition tolerance, the database is more available to clients, but the accessible data is less consistent and vice versa.

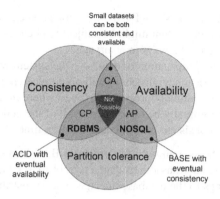

FIG. 4

CAP theorem describes database model's behavior on distribute systems.

The CAP theorem suggests that we analyze distributed systems in cases when there is an interruption of communication. Distributed databases should be tunable upon having more safety on data consistency and more availability to the clients. The balance of tuning these properties is dependent on the requirements of each application. Therefore, every Big Data application that is usually maintained on a distributed database system has to make a tradeoff between its availability and consistency.

For most web applications, availability is crucial. Being unavailable or slow for web applications means losing customers. Performance of web applications is dependent on handling many database factors, such as handling ACID transactions and join operations. But web applications are often not transactional applications. Instead, they are mostly able and willing to cope with inconsistency in their data rather than their service availability. As an example, an online retail store that shows how many items are still available. Imagine they lock a part of the database system every time a customer enters a purchasing process, so that other customers will see the actual number of available items to avoid purchasing more items than they have in their storehouse. This model might ensure the consistency of the item count shown to customers, but it will certainly not scale for huge web services with thousands of clients. The more clients the application has, the longer the lock time will be, because more clients may enter in purchasing mode. Slow processes in a web application might cause the business to lose its clients to its better-performing rivals.

Not only do web applications business models prefer inconsistency over unavailability, but they also are often willing to mess with *isolation* of ACID transactions. They often can tolerate the probability of simultaneous actions interference, but not losing clients. For example, in the case of an online retail store, imagine two customers simultaneously purchase the last item in the inventory. The business can deal with the consequences of such events (eg, compensating a gift card to one of them) rather than blocking the whole system and disturbing all customers by the slow processes of their site.

Therefore, in order to propose a solution, many NoSQL databases apply BASE (basic availability, soft state, and eventual consistency) instead of ACID transactions [12]. ACID enforces consistency at the end of each operation. However, BASE is considered to be optimistic. It accepts that the system might be in a soft state at each point in time and get to its consistent state eventually. In the following, the key features of BASE are explained:

- *Basic availability*: "availability ensured" — All requests are guaranteed to receive a response, but the response data is not guaranteed to be in a consistent state.

- *Soft state*: "continues changing states" — Even during times when there is no input to the database system, the state of the system might be subject to changes to get an eventual state per operation. Therefore the system is always in a *soft* state.
- *Eventual consistency*: "ensure propagation of data" — The system will not stop at the end of each operation to enforce consistency; instead it will go on receiving input, and ensures that the received changes will be eventually propagate to everywhere in the system. It ensures that changes to the system will eventually be distributed to all of the nodes, but does not ensure that all of the nodes will be in a consistent mode at each point in time [13].

In practice, implementing the system with fault-tolerant BASE states requires more complicated analysis of operations within logical transactions than a typical ACID implementation. But the amount of gained flexibility that it brings to the database management on distributed systems might be worth the effort for certain applications.

Additionally, with regard to the ever-increasing size of data and the increasing popularity of *cloud computing* [14] that empowers access to computational clusters, *linear scalability* of distributed systems becomes very import. A linear scalable architecture provides a constant performance increase when incrementing resources such as storage and processing power to the system. Whereas often in distributed systems, due to the additional necessary communication load between system's components, the system is subject to some barriers that prevents its linear scalability. In such systems, the performance might exceed a given limit by steps, but the real problem is the cost to achieve such performance. Nonlinear scalable systems require much hardware to exceed a given performance level, which at some point would not be cost-efficient anymore, as shown in Fig. 5.

However, the demand for scaling-out (adding more nodes) outshines the need for scaling-up (adding more resources to a server like disks, CPU, and RAM memory). As the system scales out, there are several logical models that multiprocessor systems use to share their resources such as shared-disk, shared-memory, and shared-nothing architecture that are depicted respectively in Figs. 6A–C. The more resources the system shares, the more overhead resulting from synchronization messages

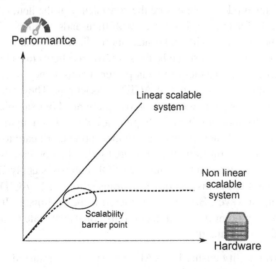

FIG. 5

Comparison of performance of linear and nonlinear scalable systems by adding more hardware to the system.

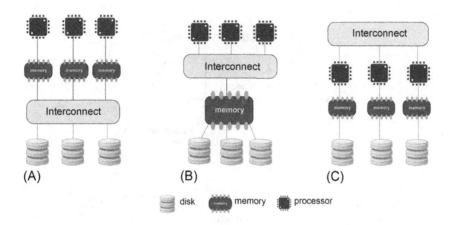

FIG. 6

Logics of multiprocessor system design. (A) Fibre channel architecture is an example of shared-disk design. (B) Classical multiprocessor design is an example of shared-memory architecture. (C) NUMA architecture and Infiniband connected nodes are examples of shared-nothing design.

would be generated. Thus, the scalability of the system is compromised. Therefore, shared-nothing architecture gets more popular. It not only provides a more scalable solution, but it also empowers the use of commodity hardware that is generally more cost-effective.

As a result, the so-called *horizontal scalability* of database systems became an important factor. *Horizontal scalability* is the ability to increase performance by connecting more nodes together so that they can work as a single unit. It is related to the strategy of the NoSQL database systems for growing with data partitioning tolerance. This partition tolerance solution for horizontal scaling is also known as *sharding* [15]. Each individual partition of data is known as a *shard*. Fig. 7 shows an example of applying sharding to a dataset.

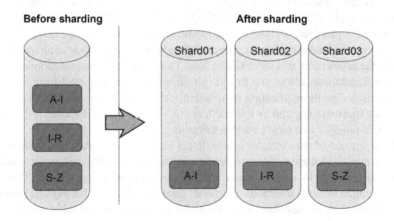

FIG. 7

Sharding based on first letter of names as splitter (shard-key). Shard-key should be picked very carefully, because it might cause lots of data be written to one shard, whereas the others do not have that much work load.

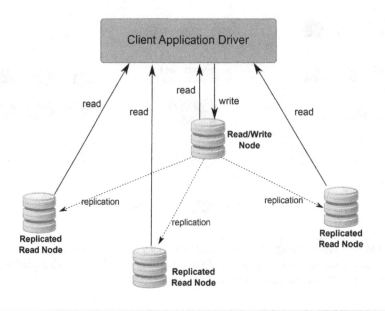

FIG. 8

Replication improves read scalability.

Although sharding helps to distributed data over many nodes, by adding more shards to the system, the possibility of failure of each sharded node remains the same. Therefore, there should be a strategy how to proceed in case of failure. This strategy will define level of adjustment between availability and consistency based on application requirement.

This strategy can also affect where to read data from: from the write node or from a *replicating* node. *Replicating* data nodes can be used to achieve read scalability. Each replication node keeps a backup copy of the data that is written to a specific node and is shown as read/write node in Fig. 8. It is common in many applications to read the data right after writing it with little or no delay. Normally this does not cause any problem, because an immediate read after write can be done on the same node. But if a user attempts to read data from a replicating node before this node receives the update from read/write node, the answer contains inconsistent data. This problem should be addressed at application level. Most NoSQL databases allow you to add rules implying where to read from to each session in application level. Based on the application requirements, the strategy can be either read from the replicating node if data inconsistency can be tolerated, or read from a read/write node if the latency caused by directing certain requests to a single node is tolerable.

Moreover, the amount of data transfer affects linear scalability of a database system. Therefore, it is crucial for distributed database systems to send the issued query to the dataset for processing and to avoid moving a large dataset to a central place to be processed to fulfill the request. This rather simple idea is not implemented in many traditional relational databases. In order for SQL queries to work even on a database where tables are distributed on two nodes, the data from one table must be moved to the other one, be reassembled, and then compared in order to answer the query.

Another issue with using traditional relational databases on distributed systems is their need for join operations between tables, as mentioned in Section 6.2. Join operations can be very costly if they involve tables residing on distinct nodes. Having several joins on tables that are stored on different nodes means that a large amount of data needs to be transferred between these two nodes to execute the query. Therefore, having many joins is equivalent to slow down the performance of the system especially over multiple nodes. After normalization of the data contained in the database, we often have to *denormalize* tables again in order to eliminate the number of join operations and gain performance. Nowadays, many NoSQL data models (such as *document-based*) not only eliminate join operations, but also prefer to denormalize and store duplicated data to gain performance.

Many NoSQL databases also adopted the idea of *MapReduce* [16] to allow transformation of Big Data over locally distributed nodes instead of transferring large amount of data between nodes. MapReduce core functions are *map* and *reduce*. As shown in Fig. 9, the *map* operation is applied to data on each node. It processes the data independently from and in parallel to *map* operations on the other nodes. The result of each *map* operation is a collection of lightweight key-value pairs. The *shuffle* operation is a complementary step that was added on to the proprietary MapReduce algorithm later in continued development process of the MapReduce algorithm. It optimizes the communication cost on each working node by redistributing outputs of map operations based on their key. The *reduce* operation takes these results as input and processes them based on keys in parallel. The final values are returned to the user. MapReduce allows more data locality and minimizes volume and frequency of data transfer. Therefore, it is a core component for many Big Data solutions to ensure system scalability.

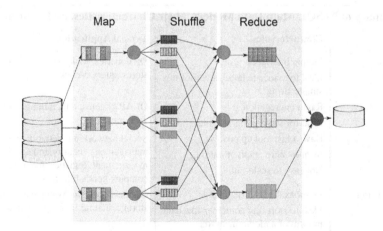

FIG. 9

MapReduce is a parallel, distributed algorithm for processing large datasets on distributed systems. Map, shuffle, and reduce empower data locality.

6.5 NoSQL DATA MODELS

NoSQL databases can be categorized based on their data storage model to four important database concepts: *key-value* stores, *column-based* stores, *graph-based* stores, and *document-based* stores.[2] A summary of these data models descriptions and their typical applications are listed in Table 1. In the following, each of these data models is described in more depth.

6.5.1 KEY-VALUE STORES

The *key-value* stores are simplistic, though nontrivial and efficient database management systems. These systems store data in a data type of a programming language or an object.

The data consist of two parts: a *key* and a *value*. The *key* is a string defined by the programmer that is used as an index to find its value. The keys are distinct and used to index the database. *Secondary indices* or keys are not offered in these databases. The *value* is the actual data that can be any arbitrary large data like *Binary Large Objects* (BLOB). But in key-value stores do not allow to search or sort directly by value. These functionalities can be provided by external software. Together they create a *key-value* pair. Both key and value are flexible and can be in any machine readable format. The key-value stores are ideal for applications associating large data files with an indexable string, such as dictionaries, catalogs, or image stores.

Key-value stores do not generically introduce a query language. They usually provide just a simple *application programming interface* (API) with standard web service requests such as *put*, *get*, *delete*, and *alter*. These operations provide a way to modify key-value pairs in the database system.

Modern key-value stores are designed to be scalable. Omitting ad hoc queries and analytic features like joins and aggregations makes it possible to keep the interface simple. The simpler the interface is,

Table 1 Summary of NoSQL Main Data Models, Their Characteristics, and Typical Usages

Data Model	Characteristics	Typical Applications
Key-value stores	Simple interfaces Ideal to associate large data files to a simple string	Dictionaries, lookup tables, image and video stores, query caches
Column-based stores	Rapid aggregation Ideal for storing sparse tables	OLAP systems, data mining, data analytics, web crawling
Graph-based store	Have a fast lookup process Ideal to store graph of data Not easy to scale-out	Social networking, network and cloud management, security and access control management, logistics, manufacturing of complex goods like cars
Document-based store	Be indexable and searchable Ideal to store any container-like data in form of a hierarchical tree	Online streaming, Web pages, image and video storage, natural language processing

[2]There are also multimodel databases that provide support for several of these models against an integrated backend, such as OrientDB [28].

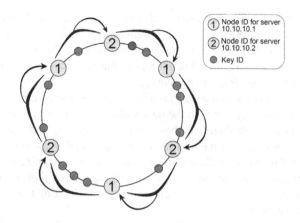

FIG. 10

Consistent hash rings is a scalable method to distribute data based on their key identifiers to servers.

the more scalable the system can be. Simple interfaces also enable nonexperts as well as experienced data model designers to easily utilize the system. In addition, simple APIs result in more portable systems and therefore reduce the system deployment costs. The key-value stores simplicity also helps database modelers to focus on service level precision. Amazon DynamoDB [17] and Memcached [18] are two pioneers in proving the concept. Redis[3] [19] and Riak [20] are two scalable key-value store databases that are used for Big Data projects.

Having a scalable method for distributing keys across a cluster of servers is an important issue in distributed systems. The common method used by key-value stores — and especially those utilizing MapReduce — is *consistent hashing*. The main idea is to map keys and nodes (servers) to the same name space formed around a ring, as shown in Fig. 10. The identifiers are produced by applying a hash function to an address scheme of the node, such as IP address and the key-value's key. One way to map keys to a specific node is to assign all of key IDs in range of two node IDs clockwise to the next node id. Since node IDs are produced by hashing IPs, we might have two node identifiers close to each other. This can cause an odd geographical distribution of load. To address this problem, we map multiple points instead of mapping just one point for each node ID. Consistent hashing allows implementing a mechanism to coping with node failures, network partitions, and to add or remove nodes to the server cluster. (For further study on consistent hashing see Ref. [21].)

6.5.2 COLUMN-BASED STORES

The *column-based* store family has a more sophisticated data model than key-value stores. The column-based stores differ from relational *column-store* databases. The relational column-stores keep their data in tables similar to traditional row-based relational databases, but instead of keeping rows together, they keep columns together. Although column-based stores utilize roughly also this concept, they allow schema flexibility. Not all of the attributes have to have a value for each row of data, and each cell can

---

[3]At the time of writing this book, Redis is ranked as the most popular key-value store engine according to DB-Engines Ranking [24].

include more than one value of data in column-based stores. In addition, unlike relational column-stores where the lookup key is a combination of just the column and row identifier, the key in column-stores can have arbitrary number of attributes combined. Storing data in column-based structure allows for rapid aggregation of the data with less I/O. Therefore, column-stores are more suitable for applications like in online analytical processing (OLAP) systems [22].

The basic data model of column-based stores is a hybrid of row and column models. Similar to key-value stores, a general-purpose key can help the data search process. In column-based stores, the key is a combination of one or more attributes, as shown in Fig. 11. Adding timestamps to the attributes of a key enables version controlling over data. In such cases, each cell keeps several values of data over time. The timestamps in Fig. 11 are indicated by t_n. The data in column-based stores can be sorted based on part of the key, usually the *column-family*. Specifying *column-family* for columns is a way to identify which columns are best to be stored together in case any splitting is needed. Adding new data is very easy based on this data structure.

The column-based stores provide scalability to manage large volumes of data. Their high scalability makes them a strong data model in NoSQL databases family. Their scalability model is based on splitting both rows (horizontal scalability through sharding the primary key) and columns (vertical scalability thorough distributing *column-families* over multiple nodes).

The column-based stores are especially helpful in data mining and data analytics applications. However, using them for small datasets might not be appropriate, because their true advantage is their design for working on cluster of computers.

The Google's BigTable [23] is the pioneer in column-based NoSQL movement. BigTable is a high-performance database built on the Google File System and is used in many high scalable services. The other column-based stores are still massively influenced by BigTable design. Cassandra and HBase are two most popular column-based stores (according to DB-Engines Ranking [24]) that are used in many active organizations with large datasets. Inspired by BigTable high performance and parallelization with help of MapReduce, the column-based stores are usually closely tied with MapReduce systems. The column-based stores often have their specific high-level query language (such as Cassandra's CQL [25]), used to generate batch MapReduce jobs.

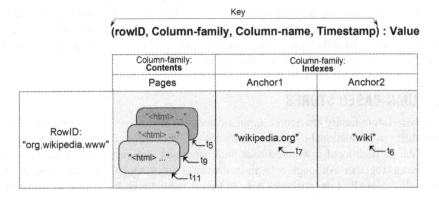

FIG. 11

The key in the column-based stores is a combination of one or many attributes. Unlike RDBMS, not all the attributes should have values for each row. Additionally, each cell can keep multiple values of data over time.

6.5.3 GRAPH-BASED STORES

Graph-based stores are databases that store sequences of vertices and relationships that form a graph. Their main focus is on the relationship between data elements. So far in both key-value stores and column-based stores, there were two building blocks in data structure: keys and values. But in graph-based stores, the data structure consists of three main building blocks: *vertices, relationships (or edges),* and *properties (or colors).*

Each *vertice* is an entity which can contain several attributes (key-value pairs). It can be considered as a real-world representative object such as a person, a telephone number, or a web page. Vertices are usually shown with circles in diagrams, as shown in Fig. 12. The edges that link vertices together and show their connection to each other are *relationships*. Each relationship always has a type and a direction from start vertices to end vertices. The graph also consists of *properties* related to both vertices and relationships. Properties are shown as labels in Fig. 12. Properties of vertices can be used to represent their role in a domain or attach metadata (such as indexes) to those vertices, whereas properties of relationships are mostly quantitative such as time intervals, distances or costs.

By these means, graph-based stores provide schemaless structure and very efficient storage solution for semi-structured data. They also provide a valuable graph processing technique named *index-free*

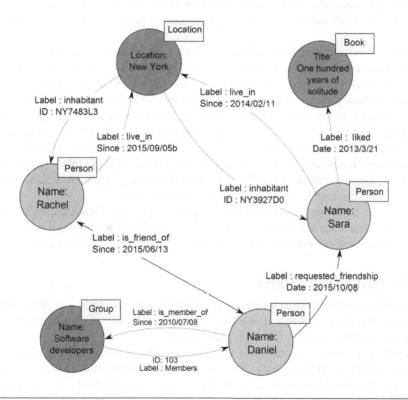

FIG. 12

Graph store databases consist of vertices, relationships and their properties. Vertices are aware of their adjacent vertices.

adjacency. This technique is based on having vertices consisting of pointers to their adjacent vertices. Therefore, vertices know the location of their immediate neighbors without the need to perform an index lookup. It is based on a navigational model that we discussed in Section 6.2. This technique enables traversing graphs more efficiently than processing based on heavy graph indexes: because the cost of lookup using a binary tree index with size of n, is $O(\log n)$, whereas the cost of lookup using an index-free adjacency is $O(1)$, which is constant and independent of the size of the dataset. Therefore, for a network of m vertices, instead of traversing an index with cost of $O(m \log n)$, the cost is minimized to $O(m)$ using index-free adjacency technique [26]. Thereby, in order to traverse a particular relationship in graph-based stores, an index is used only once to find the starting point of the traverse. Then the database should only chase pointers around a data structure and compute cheap vertices identifiers.

Interacting with graph databases is mostly similar to querying in other databases. We can do all CRUD operations with their query language. But the type of query that we use is different. Graph queries help traversing vertices of the graph. The results of these queries are usually sets of connected vertices that show the relationship between the data. For example, these queries can help with finding the nearest neighbors as well as finding patterns in our data.

Furthermore, graph-based stores assign internal identifiers to vertices. They use these internal identifiers to understand that two vertices with the same identifier are actually the same. These identifiers are also used to join networks. Therefore, graph-based stores can eliminate expensive join operation as they appear in RDBMS and use this lightweight algorithm to emulate join operations in networks instead.

With their emphasis on relations between data, graph-based stores are most helpful in applications that need to analyze relationships or the ones that should quickly find a structure of a complex network or find a pattern within such structures. Examples of such applications are social network applications, network and cloud management, security and access control, and rule-based engines applications.

On the other hand, unlike other NoSQL databases that we discussed so far, scaling-out is challenging for graph-based stores. Close connection of vertices and their relationships makes the task of distributing graphs over cluster of computing nodes for sharding very difficult. Completely replicating data from one computing node to another one is possible to scale read operation, but writing to several nodes to scale writing operations is troublesome. Therefore use of commodity hardware for graph-based stores with large amounts of data might not be easily possible.

Neo4j [27] is the most popular and among few open source graph databases. There are also powerful multi-model databases that usually combine graph databases with other data models, such as OrientDB [28], that combines the document, key-value, and graph data models together.

6.5.4 DOCUMENT-BASED STORES

Document-based stores store data in form of *documents*. *Documents* can be any object without references. These documents are usually in simple markup standard formats like *JavaScript Object Notation* (JSON) [29], or *Extensible Markup Language* (XML) [30].

Each document consists of several *fields* with their associated values (similar to key-value structure). *Fields* are simply any arbitrary name. Documents are grouped together in directories that in most document-based stores are known as *collections*. Usually, the logically similar documents are grouped in the same collection. Documents are almost equivalent to records in relational term, and collections are more similar to tables, whereas fields are similar to attributes (columns) in each relation.

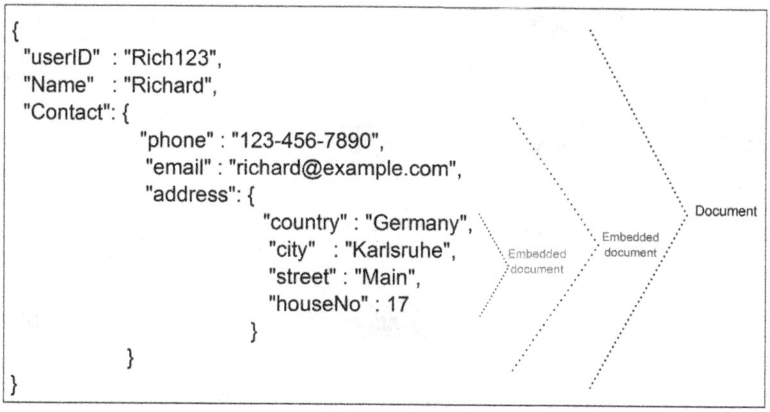

```
{
  "userID"  : "Rich123",
  "Name"    : "Richard",
  "Contact": {
            "phone" : "123-456-7890",
            "email" : "richard@example.com",
            "address": {
                        "country" : "Germany",
                        "city"    : "Karlsruhe",
                        "street"  : "Main",
                        "houseNo" : 17
                      }
            }
}
```

Document
Embedded document
Embedded document

FIG. 13

A document can have many types of value such as scalar, lists, and nested documents.

The difference is that records in the same database table contain a fixed number of attributes and have to store empty values of an attribute as well. But fields in documents are not predefined and can be similar or different from one document to another in each collection. Therefore, document-stores are providing support for schemaless data structures.

On the other hand, each cell in a relational database's record should contain a scalar value, such as a number or a string. In document-based stores, fields can not only contain scalar values, but they also can include another document or a list as their values, as shown in Fig. 13. Nesting one document as a field inside another is known as *embedding* the documents. In addition, document-based stores often support transactions per document, but not in multidocument level. Therefore, in order to increase data locality, atomicity and isolation in document level, we can use documents embedding [31].

The value in a document-based store can be a whole document or a list, similar to key-value stores. But unlike key-value stores, document-based stores provide means to efficiently query, search, and extract subsections of documents with specific values from within large number of documents.

The document-based stores are indexable and searchable. Indexes are defined explicitly per collection level. Documents can be addressed by a unique key that is used as a representative ID of each document. This ID is automatically added to each new document that is stored in the database and can help find the content of that document.

Documents content can be considered as tree structures, as shown in Fig. 14. The documents then can be searched using the document path as the key. Document-based stores can be complex, but the search API remains simple. Their query languages provide possibility to search and retrieve for any item with specific field value or content.

Document-based stores offer great performance and are usually designed to have good horizontal scalability. These databases should not be used for applications that are highly normalized, and their data can fit into tables. After all, they are denormalizing in order to gain performance, and a perfectly normalized set of data can fit in relational databases. Document-based databases should be used for applications with document-like data with a need for high scalability. Document-based stores can serve best the applications with, for example, image, video, and web content such as online steaming

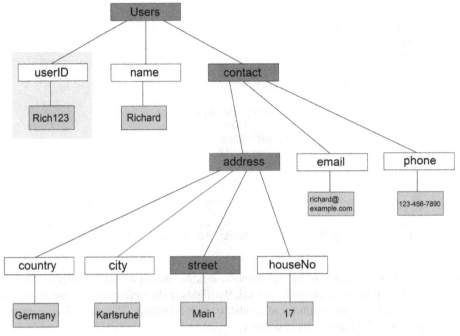

FIG. 14

To access data, document-based stores traverse a path. The dark-colored nodes show the path of a query to find street address of user with userID="Rich123."

applications. Two of very well-known document-base stores are MongoDB [32] and CouchDB [33]. MongoDB supports a full-index support and high availability, and CouchDB supports ACID semantics using multiversion concurrency control and structuring stored data using views.

6.6 FUTURE DIRECTIONS

The challenges of Big Data still have an influence on database research. The increasing volume of data and the continuous hardware evolution provide many research opportunities, that is, the emergence of *Solid State Drives* (SSD) and the reduction in memory price have already affected database architecture designs. It resulted in more in-memory and SSD database developments and researches [34,35]. Availability of commodity hardware is also a motivation for scaling-out to several nodes. Therefore, all aspect of scalability of a system with regard to storage [36], processing power and network architecture are of research interest [37].

In order to satisfy velocity, research on parallel processing [38], as well as stream processing is pursued [39,40]. Moreover, data locality and elastic services without moving data are also studied [41]. These all show the demand for databases with empowered hardware-software utilization.

There are several studies on different concurrency and consistency models for NoSQL databases [42,43]. As some of those models are hard to implement and the demand for ACID transaction for many applications exists, there is a trend to include transactions on distributed new databases [27,44]. However, relational databases are also evolving and improving scalability of relational databases [45].

NoSQL databases also tend to include higher-level query languages. Providing a unified query language that can properly support all data store models is a challenge [46] and not yet solved. In addition, developing a cost-aware query optimizer for a system with several nodes requires careful research and design [47].

Databases should also address the diversity of data sources and cover Big Data variety demands. Due to the popularity of cloud computing, its related database issues such as data sharing, security, and privacy need to be investigated.

The Beckman 2014 report on database research recommended significant attention to five research areas:

- Scalable big/fast data infrastructures
- Coping with diversity in the data management landscape
- End-to-end processing and understanding of data
- Cloud services
- Managing the diverse roles of people in the data life cycle [48]

As discussed in this section, the database research community offers lots of challenges yet to be solved!

6.7 CONCLUSIONS

Database models and research were always affected by the evolution of hardware and new rising applications requirements. The emergence of the Web 2.0 and subsequently Big Data motivated NoSQL movement. Cheaper hardware and increasing size of data caused the need for systems to scale-out and increased the importance of horizontal scalability. However, the handling of transactions in distributed systems resulted in weaker concurrency models. In addition, popularity of new applications that could be handled more easily with other data models than relational ones motivated different types of NoSQL data models.

Relational databases show undeniable and great abilities. However, some requirements can only be covered by the selection of the proper NoSQL database type. We don't expect that further development of NoSQL databases and their increasing popularity will result in relational databases dying out. Not only are relational databases mature, well-established solutions, but they are also under constant development to meet new requirements of applications, such as relaxed ACID transactions or possibility to manage documents. Determining which database is a proper choice among relational and different types of NoSQL is merely dependent on the requirements of the application.

REFERENCES

[1] Blazewicz J, Kubiak W, Morzy T, Rusinkiewicz M. Handbook on data management in information systems. Berlin, Heidelberg, New York: Springer; 2003.
[2] IBM, IBM, 11 Apr 2015 [Online]. Available from: http://www.ibm.com/en-us/homepage-d.html [accessed 27.07.15].
[3] Goddard W, Lynott J. Direct access magnetic disc storage device. US Patent Patent 3,503,060; Mar 1970.

[4] Codd EF. A relational model of data for large shared data banks. Commun ACM 1970;(June):377–87.

[5] Date CJ. Database in depth: relational theory for practitioners. Sebastopol, CA: O'Reilly Media, Inc.; 2005.

[6] Date C, Darwen H. A guide to the SQL standard (4th Ed.): a user's guide to the standard database language SQL. Boston, MA: Addison-Wesley Longman Publishing Co., Inc.; 1997.

[7] Kent W. A simple guide to five normal forms in relational database theory. Commun ACM 1983;120–5.

[8] Agrawal R, Ailamaki A, et al. The Claremont report on database research. SIGMOD Rec 2008;37(3):9–19.

[9] Strozzi C. NoSQL: a non-SQL RDBMS. NOSQL [Online]. Available from: http://www.strozzi.it/cgi-bin/CSA/tw7/I/en_US/nosql/Home%20Page [accessed 27.07.15].

[10] Eric AB. Towards robust distributed systems. In: Proceedings of the nineteenth annual ACM symposium on principles of distributed computing. Portland, OR: ACM; 2000. p. 7.

[11] Gilbert S, Lynch N. Brewer's conjecture and the feasibility of consistent, available, partition-tolerant web services. SIGACT News 2002;51–9.

[12] Pritchett D. BASE: an acid alternative. Queue 2008;(May):48–55.

[13] Bailis P, Ghodsi A. Eventual consistency today: limitations, extensions, and beyond. Commun ACM 2013;(May):55–63.

[14] Armbrust M, Fox A, Griffith R, Joseph AD, Katz R, Konwinski A, et al. A view of cloud computing. Commun ACM 2010;(April):50–8.

[15] McCreary D, Kelly A. Achieving horizontal scalability with database sharding. In: Making sense of NoSQL. Greenwich, CT: Manning; 2013. p. 28–9.

[16] Dean J, Ghemawat S. MapReduce: simplified data processing on large clusters. Commun ACM 2008;(January):107–13.

[17] Amazon DynamoDB. Amazon, 2012 [Online]. Available from: http://docs.aws.amazon.com/amazondynamodb/latest/developerguide/Introduction.html [accessed 24.07.15].

[18] Memcached. Memcached [Online]. Available from: http://memcached.org/ [accessed 24.07.15].

[19] Redis. Redis [Online]. Available from: http://redis.io/ [accessed 27.07.15].

[20] Basho. Big Data products | Riak for Big Data application products | Basho [Online]. Available from: http://basho.com/products/#riak [accessed 27.07.15].

[21] Karger D, Lehman E, Leighton T, Levine M, Lewin D, Panigrahy R. Consistent hashing and random trees: distributed caching protocols for relieving hot spots on the World Wide Web. In: Proc. 29th ACM symposium on theory of computing (STOC); 1997.

[22] Codd E, Codd S, Salley C. Providing OLAP (On-line Analytical Processing) to user-analysts: an IT mandate. Codd & Associates; 1993.

[23] Chang F, Dean J, Ghemawat S, Hsieh WC, Wallach DA, Burrows M, et al. BigTable: a distributed storage system for structured data. In: Proceedings of the 7th USENIX symposium on operating systems design and implementation, vol. 7; 2006. p. 15.

[24] DB-Engines Ranking. DB-Engines Ranking — popularity ranking of database management systems [Online]. Available from: http://db-engines.com/en/ranking [accessed 27.07.15].

[25] CQL for Cassandra 2.1/DataStax CQL 3.1.x Documentation. Cassandra, 23 Jul 2015 [Online]. Available from: http://docs.datastax.com/en/cql/3.1/cql/cql_intro_c.html [accessed on 27.07.15].

[26] Robinson I, Webber J, Eifrem E. Graph database internals. In: Graph databases. Sebastopol, CA: O'Reilly Media, Inc.; 2013. p. 141–50.

[27] Neo4j Graph Database. Neo4j [Online]. Available from: http://neo4j.com/ [accessed on Jul 2015].

[28] OrientDB. OrientDB — OrientDB multi-model NoSQL database. OrientDB [Online]. Available from: http://orientdb.com/orientdb/ [accessed on Jul 2015].

[29] JSON [Online]. Available from: http://json.org/ [accessed on Jul 2015].

[30] XML 22 Jul 2004 [Online]. Available from: http://www.xml.com/ [accessed 27.07.15].

[31] Copeland R. Embbeding for locality. In: MongoDB applied design patterns. Sebastopol, CA: O'Reilly Media, Inc.; 2013. p. 9.

[32] MongoDB. MongoDB for GIANT ideas [Online]. Available from: https://www.mongodb.org/ [accessed 27.07.15].

[33] Apache CouchDB [Online]. Available from: http://couchdb.apache.org/ [accessed 27.07.15].

[34] Kang W-H, Lee S-W, et al. Durable write cache in flash memory SSD for relational and NoSQL databases. In: Proceedings of the 2014 ACM SIGMOD international conference on management of data (SIGMOD '14); Snowbird, UT: ACM; 2014. p. 529–40.

[35] Polychroniou O, Raghavan A, Ross K. Rethinking SIMD vectorization for in-memory databases. In: Proceedings of the 2015 ACM SIGMOD international conference on management of data (SIGMOD '15); Melbourne, VIC: ACM; 2015. p. 1493–508.

[36] Aapo K, Carlos G. GraphChi-DB: simple design for a scalable graph database system — PC. CoRR 2014;.

[37] Witten D, Klein I. Method and systems for flexible and scalable databases. US Patent App., Google Patents Patent 14/680,178; 2015.

[38] Ahn J, Hong S, et al. A scalable processing-in-memory accelerator for parallel graph processing. In: Proceedings of the 42nd annual international symposium on computer architecture. Portland, OR: ACM; 2015. p. 105–17.

[39] Mahmood K, Truong T, Risch T. NoSQL approach to large scale analysis. In: Data science (30th British international conference on databases). New York: Springer International Publishing; 2015. p. 152–6.

[40] Falt Z, Krulis M, et al. Locality aware task scheduling in parallel. In: Intelligent distributed computing VIII. New York: Springer International Publishing; 2015. p. 331–42.

[41] Zamanian E, Binnig C, Salama A. Locality-aware partitioning in parallel database systems. In: Proceedings of the 2015 ACM SIGMOD international conference on management of data (SIGMOD '15); New York, NY: ACM; 2015. p. 17–30.

[42] Padhye V, Tripathi A. Scalable transaction management with snapshot isolation on cloud data management systems. In: Proc. of IEEE 5th intl. conference on cloud computing; 2012.

[43] Lin N, Dongming L, Yongqi H. Optimization method of concurrency scheduling of graphical database transaction. In: 2014 international conference on computer science and electronic technology (ICCSET 2014); 2014. p. 22–6.

[44] Oracle Berkeley DB., Oracle, 11.2.2015 [Online]. Available from: http://www.oracle.com/technetwork/database/database-technologies/berkeleydb/overview/index.html [accessed 27.07.15].

[45] Serafini M, Mansour E, et al. Accordion: elastic scalability for database systems supporting distributed transactions. In: Proc. VLDB Endow; 2014. p. 1035–46.

[46] Alomari E, Barnawi A, Sakr S. CDPort: a portability framework for NoSQL datastores. Arab J Sci Eng 2015;2531–53.

[47] Soliman M, Antova L, et al. Orca: a modular query optimizer architecture for Big Data. In: Proceedings of the 2014 ACM SIGMOD international conference on management of data. New York: ACM; 2014. p. 337–48.

[48] Abadi D, Agrawal R, et al. The Beckman report on database research. SIGMOD Rec 2014;(December):61–70.

RESOURCE MANAGEMENT IN BIG DATA PROCESSING SYSTEMS

7

S. Tang, B. He, H. Liu, B.-S. Lee

7.1 INTRODUCTION

In many application domains such as social networks and bioinformatics, data is being gathered at unprecedented scale. Efficient processing for Big Data analysis poses new challenges for almost all aspects of state-of-the-art data processing and management systems. For example, there are a few challenges as follows: (i) the data can be arbitrarily complex structures (eg, graph data) and cannot be efficiently stored in relational database; (ii) the data access of large-scale data processing are frequent and complex, resulting in inefficient disk I/O accesses or network communications; and (iii) last but not least, a variety of unpredictable failure problems must be tackled in the distributed environment, so the data processing system must have a fault tolerance mechanism to recovery the task computation automatically.

Cloud computing has emerged as an appealing paradigm for Big Data processing over the Internet due to its cost effectiveness and powerful computational capacity. Current infrastructure-as-a-service (IaaS) clouds allow tenants to acquire and release resources in the form of virtual machines (VMs) on a pay-as-you-use basis. Most IaaS cloud providers such as Amazon EC2 offer a number of VM types (such as *small*, *medium*, *large*, and *extra-large*) with fixed amount of CPU, main memory, and disk. Tenants can only purchase fixed-size VMs and increase/decrease the number of VMs when the resource demands change. This is known as *T-shirt and scale-out model* [1]. However, the T-shirt model leads to inefficient allocation of cloud resources, which translates to higher capital expenses and operating costs for cloud providers, as well as an increase of monetary cost for tenants. First, the granularity of resource acquisition/release is coarse in the sense that the fix-sized VMs are not tailored for cloud applications with dynamic demands delicately. As a result, tenants need to overprovision resource (costly), or risk performance penalty and service level agreement (SLA) violations. Second, elastic resource scaling in clouds [2], also known as a scale-out model, is also costly due to the latencies involved in VM instantiating [3] and software runtime overhead [4]. These costs are ultimately borne by tenants in terms of monetary cost or performance penalty.

Resource sharing is a classic and effective approach to resource efficiency. As more and more Big Data applications with diversifying and heterogeneous resource requirements tend to deploy in the cloud [5,6], there are vast opportunities for resource sharing [1,7]. Recent work has shown that fine-grained and dynamic resource allocation techniques (eg, resource multiplexing or overcommitting [1,8–11]) can significantly improve the resource utilization compared to T-shirt model [1]. As adding/removing resources is directly performed on the existing VMs, a fine-grained resource allocation is also known as a scale-up model, and the cost tends to much smaller compared to the scale-out model. Unfortunately, current IaaS clouds do not offer resource sharing among VMs, even if those VMs belong

Big Data. http://dx.doi.org/10.1016/B978-0-12-805394-2.00007-6

to the same tenant. Resource sharing models are needed for better cost efficiency of tenants and higher resource utilization of cloud providers.

Researchers have been actively proposing many innovative solutions to address the new challenges of large-scale data processing and resource management. In particular, a notable number of large-scale data processing and resource management systems have recently been proposed. The aims of this chapter are (i) to introduce canonical examples of large data processing, (ii) to make an overview of existing data processing and resource management systems/platforms, and more importantly, (iii) to make a study on the economic fairness for large-scale resource management on the cloud, which bridges large-scale resource management and cloud-based platforms. In particular, we present some desirable properties including sharing incentive, truthfulness, resource-as-you-pay fairness, and pareto efficiency to guide the design of fair policy for the cloud environment.

The chapter is organized as follows: We first present several types of resource management for Big Data processing in Section 7.2. In Section 7.3, we list some representative Big Data processing platforms. Section 7.4 presents the single resource management in the cloud, following by Section 7.5 that introduces multiresource management in the cloud. For the completeness of discussions, Section 7.6 gives an introduction to existing work on resource management. A discussion of open problems is provided in Section 7.7. We conclude the chapter in Section 7.8.

7.2 TYPES OF RESOURCE MANAGEMENT

Resource management is a general and fundamental issue in computing systems. In this section, we present the resource management for typical resources including CPU, memory, storage, and network.

7.2.1 CPU AND MEMORY RESOURCE MANAGEMENT

Current supercomputers and data centers (eg, Amazon EC2) generally consist of thousands of computing machines. At any time, there are tens of thousands of users running their high-performance computing applications (eg, MapReduce [12], Message Passing Interface (MPI), Spark [13]) on it. The efficient resource management of the computing resources such as CPU, memory is nontrivial for high performance and fairness. Typically, the resource management includes resource discovery, resource scheduling, resource allocation, and resource monitoring. Resource discovery identifies the suitable computing resources in which machines that match the user's request. Resource scheduling selects the best resource from the matched computing resources. It actually identifies the physical resource where the machines are to be created to provision the resources. Resource allocation allocates the selected resource to the job or task of the user's request; it means the job submission to the selected cloud resource. After the submission of the job, the resource is monitored.

There are a number of resource management tools available for supercomputing. For example, Simple Linux Utility for Resource Management (SLURM) is a highly scalable resource manager widely used in supercomputers [14]. It allocates exclusive and/or nonexclusive access to resources (computer nodes) to users for some duration of time so they can perform work. Second, it provides a framework for starting, executing, and monitoring work (typically a parallel job) on a set of allocated nodes. Finally, it arbitrates contention for resources by managing a queue of pending work. For data-intensive computing in data center, YARN [15] and Mesos [16] are two popular resource management systems.

7.2.2 STORAGE RESOURCE MANAGEMENT

Storage resource management (SRM) is a proactive approach to optimizing the efficiency and speed with which available drive space is utilized in a storage area network, which is a dedicated high-speed network (or subnetwork) that interconnects and presents shared pools of storage devices to multiple servers [17]. The SRM software can help a storage administrator automate data backup, data recovery, and Storage Area Network (SAN) performance analysis. It can also help the administrator with configuration management and performance monitoring, forecast future storage needs more accurately, and understand where and how to use tiered storage, storage pools, and thin provisioning.

7.2.3 NETWORK RESOURCE MANAGEMENT

Managing and allocating the network flows to different applications/users is nontrivial work. Particularly, software-defined networking [18] is a popular approach that allows network administrators to manage network services through the abstraction of lower-level functionality. This is done by decoupling the system that makes decisions about where traffic is sent (the control plane) from the underlying systems that forward traffic to the selected destination (the data plane).

7.3 BIG DATA PROCESSING SYSTEMS AND PLATFORMS

In the era of Big Data, characterized by the unprecedented volume of data, the velocity of data generation, and the variety of the structure of data, support for large-scale data analytics constitutes a particularly challenging task. To address the scalability requirements of today's data analytics, parallel shared-nothing architectures of commodity machines (often consisting of thousands of nodes) have been lately established as the de facto solution. Various systems have been developed mainly by the industry to support Big Data analysis, including MapReduce [12], Pregel [19], Spark [13], etc. In this section, we give a brief survey of some representative solutions.

7.3.1 HADOOP

Hadoop [20] is an open source Java implementation of MapReduce [12], which is a popular programming model for large-scale data processing proposed by Google. It runs on top of a distributed file system called HDFS, which splits input data into multiple blocks of fixed size (typically 64 MB) and replicates each data block several times across computing nodes. Users can submit MapReduce jobs to the Hadoop cluster. The Hadoop system breaks each job into multiple map tasks and reduce tasks, with its map tasks computed before its reduce tasks. Each map task processes (ie, scans and records) a data block and produces intermediate results in the form of key-value pairs.

Moreover, Hadoop has evolved to the next generation of Hadoop (ie, Hadoop MRv2) called YARN [15], as a large-scale data operating platform and cluster resource management system. There is a new architecture for YARN, which separates the resource management from the computation model. Such a separation enables YARN to support a number of diverse data-intensive computing frameworks including Dryad [21], Giraph [22], Spark [13], Storm [23], and Tez [24]. In YARNs architecture, there is a global master named ResourceManager (RM) and a set of per-node slaves called NodeManagers (NM), which forms a generic system for managing applications in a distributed manner. The RM is responsible for tracking and arbitrating resources among applications. In contrast, the NM has responsibility for launching tasks and monitoring the resource usage per slave node. Moreover, there is another component called ApplicationMaster, which is a framework-specific entity. It is responsible for negotiating resources from the RM and working with the NM to execute and monitor the progress of tasks. Particularly, all resources of YARN are requested in the form of container, which is a logical bundle of resources (eg, 1 CPUs, 2G memory). As a multitenant platform, YARN organizes user submitted applications into queues and share resources between these queues. Users can set their own queues in a configuration file provided by YARN.

7.3.2 DRYAD

Dryad [21] is a distributed execution engine that simplifies the process of implementing data-parallel applications to run on a cluster. The original motivation for Dryad was to execute data mining operations efficiently, which has also lead to technologies such as MapReduce or Hadoop. Dryad is a general-purpose execution engine and can also be used to implement a wide range of other application types, including time series analysis, image processing, and a variety of scientific computations. The computation is structured as a directed graph: Programs are graph vertices, while the channels are graph edges. A Dryad job is a graph generator, which can synthesize any directed acyclic graph. These graphs can even change during execution in response to important events in the computation. Dryad handles job creation and management, resource management, job monitoring and visualization, fault tolerance, reexecution, scheduling, and accounting.

7.3.3 PREGEL

Pregel [19] is a specialized model for iterative graph applications. In Pregel, a program runs as a series of coordinated supersteps. With each superstep, each vertex in the graph runs a user function that can update state associated with the vertex, change the graph topology, and send messages to other vertices for use in the next superstep. This model can express many graph algorithms, including shortest paths, bipartite matching, and PageRank.

7.3.4 STORM

Storm [23] is a distributed real-time computation system. In a similar way to how Hadoop provides a set of general primitives for doing batch processing, Storm provides a set of general primitives for doing real-time computation, which greatly eases the writing of parallel real-time computation. It can be used for processing messages and updating databases (stream processing), performing a continuous query on data streams and streaming the results into clients (continuous computation), parallelizing an intense query like a search query on the fly (distributed Remote Procedure Calls (RPC)), and more. Storm's small set of primitives satisfies a stunning number of user needs. For example, Storm scales to massive numbers of messages per second. To scale a topology, all you have to do is add machines and increase the parallelism settings of the topology. As an example of Storm's scale, one of Storm's initial applications processed 1,000,000 messages per second on a 10-node cluster, including hundreds of database calls per second as part of the topology.

7.3.5 SPARK

Spark [13] is a fast in-memory data processing system that achieves high performance for applications through caching data in memory (or disk) for data sharing across computation stages. It is achieved with the *resilient distributed dataset* (RDD) in-memory storage abstraction for computing data, which is a read-only, partitioned collection of records [25]. Each RDD is generated from data in stable storage or other RDDs through *transformation* operations such as *map, filter*, and *reduceByKey*. Notably, the *transformation* is a *lazy* operation that only defines a new RDD without immediately computing it. To launch RDD computation, Spark provides another set of *action* operations such as *count, collect*, and *save*, which return a value to the application or export data to a storage system. For RDD caching, Spark offers five storage levels, ie, *memory only, memory and disk, memory only ser, memory and disk ser*, and *disk only*. For a Spark application in execution, the Spark system will spawn a master called *driver*, which is responsible for defining and managing RDDs, and a set of slavers called *executors*, which perform the computations dynamically. The Spark applications can run on either YARN, Mesos, local, or standalone cluster modes. In this paper, we focus on the standalone cluster mode.

7.3.6 SUMMARY

In this section, we summarize some representative Big Data processing systems elaborated in the previous section in terms of computation model, in-memory computation, resource management type (ie, CPU, memory, storage, and network), and fairness in Table 1.

There are some other high-level as well as application-specific systems that are built on top of previous data computing systems to form an ecosystem for a variety of applications. For example, for Hadoop, Apache Pig [26], and Hive [27] are both Structured Query Language (SQL)-like systems that are running on it to support analytical data querying processing. HBase [28] is a NoSql database system built on top of Hadoop system. Apache Giraph [22] is an iterative graph processing system running on Hadoop. Similarly, for Spark, Shark [29], and Spark SQL [30] are two analytical data query systems built on Spark, while Graphx [31] is a graph processing system for graph applications. We have also witnessed some other data processing systems/platforms that are running on currently emerging computing devices, such as GPUs. For example, as an extension of Pregel for GPU platform, a general-purpose programming framework called Medusa [32] has been developed for graph applications.

Table 1 Comparison of Representative Big Data Processing Systems

Systems	Computation Model	In-Memory Computation	Resource Management Type				Resource Fairness	
			CPU	Memory	Storage	Network	Single	Multiple
Hadoop	MapReduce	No	Yes	Yes	No	No	Yes	Yes
Dryad	Dryad	No	Yes	No	No	No	Yes	No
Pregel	Pregel	No	Yes	No	No	No	Yes	No
Storm	Storm	No	Yes	No	No	No	Yes	No
Spark	RDD	Yes	Yes	Yes	No	No	Yes	Yes

7.4 SINGLE-RESOURCE MANAGEMENT IN THE CLOUD

Single-resource management refers to the management of single-resource type. This is the basic form of resource management. For example, Hadoop manages CPU resources of a computing cluster in the form of slots.

Cloud computing has emerged as a popular platform for users to compute their large-scale data applications, attracting from its merits such as flexibility, elasticity, and cost efficiency. At any time, there can be tens of thousands of users concurrently running their large-scale, data-intensive applications on the cloud. Users pay money on the basis of their resource usage. To meet different users' needs, cloud providers generally offer several options of price plans (eg, on-demand price, reserved price). When users have a short-term computation requirement (eg, 1 week), they can choose an on-demand price plan that charges compute resources by each time unit (eg, an hour) with a fixed price. In contrast, if users have long-term computation requests (eg, 1 year), choosing a reserved price plan can enable them to have a significant discount on the hourly charge for the resources in comparison to the on-demand one, thereby saving money.

To improve the resource utilization and in turn the cost efficiency, resource sharing is an effective approach [7]. Consider the reserved resources for example: With a reservation plan, users need to pay a one-time fee for a long time (eg, 1 or 3 years), and in turn get a significant discount on the hourly usage charge. However, to achieve the full cost savings, users must commit to having a high utilization. In practice, the resource demand of a user can fluctuate over time, and the resources cannot be fully utilized all the time from the perspective of an individual user. With resource sharing, users can complement each other in the resource usage in a shared cluster and the resource utilization problem can be thereby solved. To make resource sharing possible among users, the resource allocation fairness is a key issue.

As shown in Table 1, there are single- and multiple-resource fairness, both of which are supported by some of computing systems. In this section, we mainly focus on the fairness of single-resource management and defer the fairness for multiple resource management to Section 7.5. Notably, we observe that the fair policies implemented in these systems are all memoryless (ie, allocating resources fairly at instant time without considering history information). We refer to those schedulers as *memoryless resource fairness* (MLRF). In the following subsections, we first present several desirable resource allocation properties for cloud computing. Next, we show the problems for MLRF. Finally, we explore a new policy to address it.

7.4.1 DESIRED RESOURCE ALLOCATION PROPERTIES

This section presents a set of desirable properties that we believe any cloud-oriented resource allocation policy in a shared pay-as-you-use system should meet

- *Sharing incentive*: Each client should be better off sharing the resources via group-buying with others, than exclusively buying and using the resources individually. Consider a shared pay-as-you-use computing system with n clients over t period time. Then a client should not be able to get more than t/n resources in a system partition consisting of $1/n$ of all resources.
- *Nontrivial workload incentive*: Clients should reap benefits by submitting nontrivial workloads and yielding unused resources to others when not needed. Otherwise, they may unnecessarily hold unneeded resources under their share by running trivial tasks in a shared computing environment.

- *Resource-as-you-pay fairness*: The resource that clients gain should be proportional to their payment. This property is important, as it is a resource guarantee to clients.
- *Strategy-proofness*: Clients should not be able to get benefits by lying about their resource demands. This property is compatible with sharing incentive and resource-as-you-pay fairness, since no client can obtain more resources by lying.
- *Pareto efficiency*: In a shared resource environment, it is impossible for a client to get more resources without decreasing the resource of at least one client. This property can ensure the system resource utilization to be maximized.

7.4.2 PROBLEMS FOR EXISTING FAIRNESS POLICIES

One of the most popular fair allocation policies is (*weighted*) *max-min fairness* [7], which maximizes the minimum resource allocation obtained by a user in a shared computing system. It has been widely used in many popular large-scale data processing frameworks such as Hadoop [20], YARN [15], Mesos [16], and Dryad [21]. Unfortunately, we observe that the fair polices implemented in these systems are all *memoryless* (ie, allocating resources fairly at instant time without considering history information). We refer those schedulers as MLRF. MLRF is *not* suitable for a cloud computing system due to the following reasons.

Trivial workload problem

In a pay-as-you-use computing system, we should have a policy to incentivize group members to submit *nontrivial* workloads that they really need (see *Nontrivial workload incentive* property in Section 7.4.1). For MLRF, there is an implicit assumption that all users are unselfish and honest towards their requested resource demands, which, however, is often not true in real world. It can cause trivial workload problems with MLRF. Consider two users A and B sharing a system. Let D_A and D_B be the *true* workload demand for A and B at time t_0, respectively. Assume that D_A is less than its share,[1] while D_B is larger than its share. In that case, it is possible that A is selfish and will try to possess all of his/her share by running some trivial tasks (eg, running some duplicated tasks of the experimental workloads for double checking) so that his/her extra unused share will not be preempted by B, causing the inefficiency problem of running nontrivial workloads and also breaking the sharing incentive property (see the definition in Section 7.4.1).

Strategy-proofness problem

It is important for a shared system to have a policy to ensure that no group member can get any benefits by lying (see Strategy-proofness in Section 7.4.1). We argue that MLRF cannot satisfy this property. Consider a system consisting of three users A, B, and C. Assume A and C are honest whereas B is not. It could happen at a time that the *true* demands of both A and B are fewer than their own shares, while C's *true* demands exceed his/her share. In that case, A yields his/her unused resources to others honestly. But B will provide *false* information about his/her demand (eg, far larger than his/her share) and compete with C for unused resources from A. Lying benefits B, hence violating strategy-proofness. Moreover, it will break the sharing incentive property if all other users also lie.

---

[1]By default, we refer to the *current* share at the designated time (eg, t_0), rather than the *total* share accumulated over time.

Resource-as-you-pay unfairness problem

For group-buying resources, we should ensure that the total resource received by each member is proportional to his/her monetary cost (see *Resources-as-you-pay fairness* in Section 7.4.1). Due to the varied resource demands (eg, workflows) for a user at different time, MLRF cannot achieve this property. Consider two users A and B: At time t_0, it could happen that the demand D_A is less than its share; hence, its extra unused resource will be possessed by B (ie, lent to B) according to the work-conserving property of MLRF. Next at time t_1, assume that A's demand D_A becomes larger than its share. With MLRF, user A can only use her current share (ie, cannot get lent resources at t_0 back from B), if D_B is larger than its share, due to *memoryless*. If this scenario often occurs, it will be unfair for A to get the amount of resources that she should have obtained from a long-term view.

7.4.3 LONG-TERM RESOURCE ALLOCATION POLICY

In this section, we first give a motivation example to show that MLRF is *not* a suitable cloud computing system. Then we propose long-term resource fairness (LTRF), a cloud-oriented allocation policy to address the limitations of MLRF and meet the desired properties described in Section 7.4.1.

Motivation example

Consider a shared computing system consisting of 100 resources (eg, 100 GB RAM) and two users A and B with equal share of 50 GB each. As illustrated in Table 2, assume that the new requested demands at time t_1, t_2, t_3 and t_4 for client A are 20, 40, 80 and 60, and for client B are 100, 60, 50 and 50, respectively. With MLRF, we see in Table 2A that, at t_1, the total demand and allocation for A are both 20. It lends 30 unused resources to B and thus 80 allocations for B. The scenario is similar at t_2. Next at t_3 and t_4, the total demand for A becomes 80 and 90, bigger than its share of 50. However, it can only get 50 allocations based on MLRF, being *unfair* for A, since the total allocations for A and B become 160(=20+40+50+50) and 240(−80+60+50+50) at time t_4, respectively. Instead, if we adopt LTRF, as shown in Table 2B, the total allocations for A and B at t_4 will finally be the same (eg, 200), being *fair* for A and B.

LTRF scheduling algorithm

Algorithm 1 shows pseudocode for LTRF scheduling. It considers the fairness of total allocated resources consumed by each client instead of currently allocated resources. The core idea is based on the "loan (lending) agreement" [33] with free interest. That is, a client will yield unused resources to others as a *lend* manner at a time. When the client needs resources at a later time, he/she should get the resources back from others that were yielded before (ie, *return* manner). In our previous two-client example with LTRF in Table 2B, client A first lends his/her unused resources of 30 and 10 to client B at time t_1 and t_2, respectively. However, at t_3 and t_4, the client has a large demand and then collects all 40 extra resources back from B that were lent before, making *fair* between A and B.

Due to the *lending agreement* of LTRF, in practice, when A yields the unused resources at t_1 and t_2, B might not want to possess extra unused resources from A immediately. In that case, the total allocations for A and B will be 160(=20+40+50+50) and 200(=50+50+50+50) at time t_4, causing the inefficiency problem for the system utilization. To solve this problem, we propose a discount-based approach. The idea is that, anybody possessing extra unused resources from others will have a discount

Table 2 A Comparison Example of *MemoryLess Resource Fairness* (MLRF) and *Long-Term Resource Fairness* (LTRF in a Shared Computing System Consisting of 100 Computing Resources for Two Users A and B)

	Client A					Client B				
	Demand		Allocation			Demand		Allocation		
	New	Total	Current	Total	Preempt	New	Total	Current	Total	Preempt
(A) Allocation results based on *MLRF*. *Total Demand* refers to the sum of the new demand and accumulated remaining demand in previous time										
t_1	20	20	20	20	-30	100	100	80	80	+30
t_2	40	40	40	60	-10	60	80	60	140	+10
t_3	80	80	50	10	0	50	70	0	190	0
t_4	60	90	50	*160*	0	50	70	50	*240*	0
(B) Allocation results based on *LTRF*										
t_1	20	20	20	20	-30	100	100	80	0	+30
t_2	40	40	40	60	-10	60	80	60	140	+10
t_3	80	80	80	140	+30	50	70	20	160	-30
t_4	60	60	60	*200*	+10	50	100	40	*200*	-10
(C) Counted allocation results under *discount*-based approach of *LTRF*. There is a discount (eg, 50%) for the extra unused resources to incentivize clients to preempt resources actively for system utilization maximization. In this example, although the *counted* allocations for A and B are 180, their real allocations are both 200, which is the same as Table 2B										
t_1	20	20	20	20	-30	100	100	65	65	+30
t_2	40	40	40	60	-10	60	80	55	120	+10
t_3	80	80	65	125	+30	50	70	20	140	-30
t_4	60	60	55	*180*	+10	50	100	40	*180*	-10

(eg, 50%) on resource counting. It will incentivize B to preempt extra unused resources from A, since it is cheaper than his/her own share of resources. From a perspective from A, it also does not get resource lost, as it can get the same discount on future resource use later.

Table 2C demonstrates this point. It shows the discounted resource allocation for each client over time by discounting the possessed extra unused resource. At time t_1, A yields his/her 30 unused resources to B, and B's discounted resources are $65(=50+30*50\%)$ instead of $80(=50+30)$. Similarly at t_3, it preempts 30 resources from B and its discounted resources are $65(50+30*50\%)$. Still, both of them are *fair* at time t_4.

ALGORITHM 1 LTRF PSEUDOCODE

1: R: total resources available in the system.
2: $\ddot{R} = (\ddot{R}, \ldots, \ddot{R}_n)$: current allocated resources. $\ddot{R}_i$ denotes the current allocated resources for client i.

3: $U = (u_1, \ldots, u_n)$: total used resources, initially 0. u_i denotes the total resource consumed by client i.
4: $W = (w_1, \ldots, w_n)$: weighted share. w_i denotes the weight for client i.
5: **while** there are pending tasks **do**
6:    **Choose** client i with the smallest total weighted resources of u_i/w_i.
7:    $d_i \leftarrow$ the next task resource demand for client i.
8:    **if** $\ddot{R} + d_i \leq R$ **then**
9:      $\ddot{R}_i \rightarrow \ddot{R}_i + d_i$. /*Update current allocated resources.*/
10:     Update the total resource usage u_i for client i.
11:     Allocate resource to client i.
12:   **else**
13:     /*The system is fully utilized.*/
14:     **Wait** until there is a released resource r_i from client i.
15:     $\ddot{R}_i \leftarrow \ddot{R}_i - r_i$. /*Update current allocated resources */

7.4.4 EXPERIMENTAL EVALUATION

We ran our experiments in a cluster consisting of 10 compute nodes, each with 2 Intel X5675 CPUs (6 CPU cores per CPU with 3.07 GHz), 24 GB DDR3 memory, and 56 GB hard disks. The latest version of YARN-2.2.0 is chosen in our experiment, used with a two-level hierarchy. The first level denotes the root queue (containing one master node and nine slave nodes). For each slave node, we configure its total memory resources with 24 GB. The second level denotes the applications (ie, workloads). We ran a macrobenchmark consisting of four different workloads. Thus, four different queues are configured in YARN/LTYARN, namely, *Facebook*, *Purdue*, *Spark*, *HIVE/TPC-H*, corresponding to the following workloads, respectively. (1) A MapReduce instance with a mix of small and large jobs based on the workload at Facebook. (2) A MapReduce instance running a set of large-sized batch jobs generated with Purdue MapReduce Benchmarks Suite [34]. (3) Hive running a series of TPC-H queries. (4) Spark running a series of machine learning applications.

A good sharing policy should be able to first minimize the sharing loss, then maximize the sharing benefit as much as possible (ie, sharing incentive). We make a comparison between MLRF and LTRF for four workloads over time in Fig. 1. All results are relative to the static partition case (without sharing) with sharing benefit/loss degrees of zero. ig. 1A and B present the sharing benefit/loss degrees, respectively, for MLRF and LTRF. The following observations can be obtained: first, the sharing policies of both MLRF and LTRF can bring sharing benefits for queues (workloads). This is due to the sharing incentive property, ie, each queue has an opportunity to consume more resources than her share at a time, which is better than running at most all of her shared partition in a nonshared partition system. Second, LTRF has a much better result than MLRF. Specifically, Fig. 1A indicates that the sharing loss problem for MLRF is constantly available until all the workloads complete (eg, about −0.5 on average), In contrast, there is no more sharing loss problem after 650 s for LTRF (ie, all workloads get sharing benefits after that). The major reason is that MLRF does not consider historical resource allocation. In contrast, LTRF is a history-based fairness resource allocation policy. It can dynamically adjust the allocation of resources to each queue in terms of historical consumption and lending agreement so that each queue can obtain the required amount of total resources over time. Finally, regarding the sharing loss problem at the early stage (eg, 0~650 s) of LTRF in Fig. 1B, it is mainly due to the unavoidable waiting allocation problem at the starting stage (ie, the first workload possess all resources, leading late arriving workloads to wait until some tasks complete and release resources).

The problem exists in both MLRF and LTRF. Still, LTRF can smooth this problem until it disappears over time via a lending agreement, while MLRF cannot.

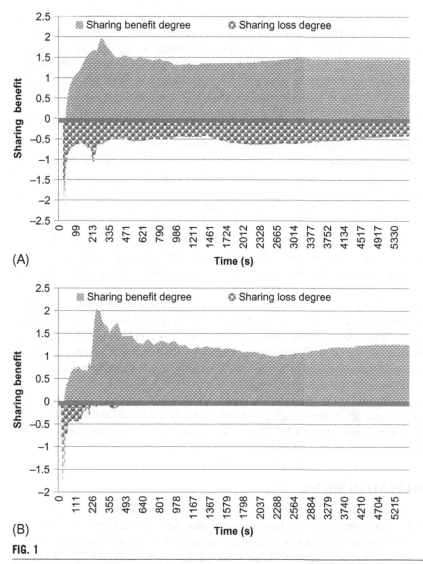

FIG. 1

Comparison of fairness results over time for workloads under MLRF and LTRF in YARN. All results are relative to the static partition scenario (ie, nonshared case) whose sharing benefit/loss is zero. (A) and (B) show the overall benefit/loss relative to the nonsharing scenario.

7.5 MULTIRESOURCE MANAGEMENT IN THE CLOUD

Despite the resource sharing opportunities in the cloud, resource sharing, especially for *multiple resource types* (ie, multiresource), poses several important and challenging problems in pay-as-you-use commercial clouds. (1) *Sharing incentive*. In a shared cloud, a tenant may have concerns about the gain/loss of her asset in terms of resource. (2) *Free riding*. Tenants may deliberately buy fewer resources than their demand and always expect to benefit from others' contribution (ie, unused resource). However, free riders would seriously hurt other tenants' sharing incentive. (3) *Lying*. When there exists resource contention, a tenant may lie about resource demands for greater benefit. Lying also hurts tenants' sharing incentive. (4) *Gain-as-you-contribute fairness*. It is important to guarantee that the allocations obey the rule "more contribution, more gain." In summary, those problems are eventually attributed to economic fairness of resource sharing in IaaS clouds. Unfortunately, the popular allocation policies such as (weighted) max-min fairness (WMMF) [35] and dominant resource fairness (DRF) [7] cannot address all the problems of resource sharing in IaaS.

This section introduces F2C, a cooperative resource management system for IaaS clouds. F2C exploits statistical resource complementarity to group tenants together in order to realize the resource sharing opportunities, and it adopts a novel resource allocation policy to guarantee fairness of resource sharing. Particularly, we describe *reciprocal resource fairness* (RRF), a generalization of max-min fairness to multiple resource types [36]. The intuition behind RRF is that tenant should preserve their assets while maximizing the resource usage in a cooperative environment. Different types of resource are advocated to trade among different tenants and to share among different VMs belonging to the same tenant. For example, a tenant can trade his/her unused CPU share for another tenant's overprovisioned memory share. In this section, we consider two major kinds of resources, including CPU and main memory. Resource trading (RT) can maximize tenants' benefit from resource sharing.

RRF decomposes the multiresource fair sharing problem into a combination of two complementary mechanisms: intertenant resource trading (IRT) and intratenant weight adjustment (IWA). These mechanisms guarantee that tenants only allocate minimum shares to their nondominant demands and maximize the share allocations on the contended resource. Moreover, RRF is able to achieve some desirable properties of resource sharing, including sharing incentive, gain-as-you-contribute fairness, and strategy-proofness (guarding against free riding and lying).

In the following, we first introduce the resource allocation model in F2C. Second, we analyze the problems of two popular resource allocation policies including WMMF [35] and DRF [7]. Third, we present RRF, the resource allocation model in F2C. Finally, we evaluate F2C and show how RRF can address resource fair allocation problems in IaaS clouds.

7.5.1 RESOURCE ALLOCATION MODEL

We consider the resource-sharing model in multitenant cloud environments, where tenants may rent several VMs to host their applications and VMs have multiresource demands. By *multiresource*, we mean resources of *different resource types*, instead of multiple units of the same resource type. In this paper, we mainly consider two resource types: CPU and main memory. Tenants can have different *weights* (or *shares*) to the resource. The *share* of a tenant reflects the tenant's priority relative to other tenants. A number of tenants can form a resource pool based on the opportunities of resource sharing. The VMs of these tenants then share the same resource pool with negotiated resource *shares*, which are determined by tenants' payments.

In our resource allocation model, each unit of resource is represented by a number of shares. To simplify multiresource allocation, we assume each unit of resource (such as 1 compute unit[2] or 1 GB

---

[2]One EC2 compute unit provides equivalent CPU capacity of a 1.0–1.2 GHz 2007 Opteron or 2007 Xeon processor, according to Amazon EC2.

RAM) has its fixed share according to its market price. A study on Amazon EC2 pricing data [37] had indicated that the hourly unit cost for 1 GB memory is twice as expensive as 1 EC2 compute unit. A tenant's *asset* is then defined as the aggregate shares that he/she pays for.

In the following, we use an example to demonstrate our resource allocation model. Fig. 2 shows three tenants colocated on two physical hosts. Each tenant has two VMs. The shares of different resources (eg, CPU, memory) are uniformly normalized based on their market prices [37]. To some extent, a tenant actually purchases resource shares instead of fix-sized resource capacity. A share of a VM reflects the VM's priority relative to other VMs, cloud providers can directly use shares as billing and resource allocation policies. The concrete design of those policies is beyond the scope of this paper. Thus, we simply define a function f_1 to translate tenants' payments into shares $payment \xrightarrow{f_1} share$, and another function f_2 to translate shares into the resource capacity $share \xrightarrow{f_2} resource$. For example, in Fig. 2, 1 compute unit and 1 GB memory are priced at 100 and 200 shares, respectively. If VM1 is initialized with 3 compute units and 2 GB of memory, VM1 is allocated with total $100 \times 3 + 200 \times 2 = 700$ shares.

This model enables fine-grained resource allocation based on shares, and thus provides the opportunities for dynamic resource sharing. Now, the fairness has become a major concern in such a shared system. Informally, we define a kind of *economic fairness*: tenants should try to maximize their aggregate multiresource shares if there are unsatisfied resource demands.

We find that RT between different tenants can reinforce the economic fairness of resource sharing. Normalizing multiple resources with uniform shares provides advantages to facilitate RT. For example, a tenant can trade overprovisioned CPU shares for other tenants' underutilized memory shares. In Fig. 2, VM1 may trade its 200 CPU shares for VM3's 100 memory shares. RT can prevent tenants from

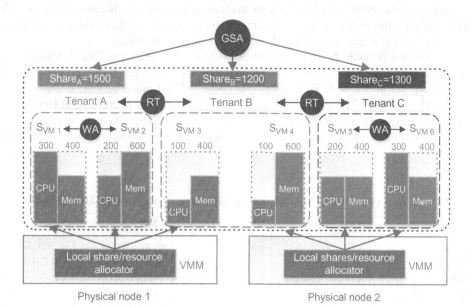

FIG. 2

Hierarchical resource allocation based on resource trading and weight adjustment.

losing underutilized resource. Moreover, tenants can dynamically adjust share allocation of VMs based on actual demands. For example, in Fig. 2, tenant A may deprive 200 memory shares from VM2 and reallocate them to VM1. In this paper, we propose RT between different tenants and dynamic weight adjustment (WA) among multiple VMs belonging to the same tenant. Fig. 2 shows the hierarchical resource allocation based on these two mechanisms. The global share allocator first reserves capacity in bulk based on tenants' aggregate resource demands, then allocates shares to tenants according to their payment. The local share/resource allocator in each node is responsible for RT between tenants, and WA among multiple VMs belonging to the same tenant.

7.5.2 MULTIRESOURCE FAIR SHARING ISSUES

In the following, we demonstrate the deficiency of WMMF and DRF for multiresource sharing in clouds.

Example 1: Assume there are three tenants, each of which has one VM. All VMs share a resource pool consisting of total 20 GHz CPU and 10 GB RAM. Each VM has initial shares for different types of resource when it is created. For example, VM1 initially has CPU and RAM shares of 500 each, simply denoted by a vector x500, 500y. The VMs may have dynamic resource demands. At a time, VM1 runs jobs with demands of 6 GHz CPU and 3 GB RAM, simply denoted by a vector x6*GHz*, 3*GB*y. The VMs' initial shares and demand vectors are illustrated in Table 3. We examine whether the T-shirt model, WMMF, and DRF can achieve resource efficiency and economic fairness.

With the T-shirt model, we allocate the total resources to tenants in proportion to their share values of CPU and memory separately. The T-shirt model guarantees that each tenant precisely receives the resource shares that the tenant pays for. However, it wastes scarce resource because it may overallocate resource to VMs that has high shares but low demand, even as other VMs have unsatisfied demand. As shown in Table 3, VM2 wastes 1.5 GB RAM and VM3 wastes 2 GHz CPU.

We now apply the WMMF algorithm on each resource type. As shown in Table 3, VM1, VM2, and VM3 initially owns 25%, 25%, 50% of total resource shares, respectively. However, VM1 is allocated with 30% of total resources, with 5% "stolen" from other VMs. Ironically, VM2 contributes 1.5 GB RAM and VM3 contributes 2 GHz CPU to other tenants. However, they do not benefit more than VM1 from resource sharing because CPU and memory resources are allocated separately. In this case, if VM1 deliberately provisions fewer resources than its demand and always counts on others' contributions,

Table 3 Comparison of Resource Allocation Polices Between T-shirt, WMMF, and DRF

VMs	VM1	VM2	VM3	Total
Initial shares	<500, 500>	<500, 500>	<1000, 1000>	<2000, 2000>
Demands	<GHz, 3 GB>	<8 GHz, 1 GB>	<8 GHz, 8 GB>	<22 GHz, 12 GB>
T-shirt allocation	<5 GHz, 2.5 GB>	<5 GHz, 2.5 GB>	<10 GHz, 5 GB>	<18 GHz, 8.5 GB>
WMMF allocation	<6 GHz, 3 GB>	<6 GHz, 1 GB>	<8 GHz, 6 GB>	<20 GHz, 10 GB>
WDRF dominant share	6/20 = 3/10	8/20 CPU	8/(10*2) RAM	100%
WDRF allocation	<6 GHz, 3 GB>	<7 GHz, 1 GB>	<7 GHz, 6 GB>	<20 GHz, 10 GB>

then VM1 becomes a free rider. Although WMMF can guarantee resource efficiency, it cannot fully preserve tenant resource shares, and it eventually results in economic unfairness.

We also apply weighted DRF (WDRF) [7] to this example. Both CPU and RAM shares of VM1, VM2, and VM3 correspond to a ratio of 1:1:2. VM1's dominant share can be CPU or memory, both equal to 6/20. VM2's dominant share is CPU share as $max(8/20, 1/10) = 8/20$. For VM3, its unweighted dominant share is memory share 8/10. Its weight is twice that of VM1 and VM2, so its weighted dominant share is $8/(10*2) = 8/20$. Thus, the ascending order of three VM's dominant shares is VM1 < VM2 = VM3. According to WDRF, VM1's demand is first satisfied, then the remanding resources are allocated to VM2 and VM3 based on max-min fairness. We find that VM1 is again a free rider.

In summary, the T-shirt model is not resource efficient, and WMMF and DRF are not economically fair for multiresource allocation. Intuitively, in a cooperative environment, the more one contributes, the more one should gain. Otherwise, tenants would lose their sharing incentives. This is especially important for resource sharing among multiple tenants in pay-as-you-use clouds. Thereby, a new mechanism is needed to reinforce the fairness of multiresource sharing in IaaS clouds.

7.5.3 RECIPROCAL RESOURCE FAIRNESS

In the following, we consider the fair sharing model in a shared system with p types of resource and m tenants. The total system capacity bought by the m tenants is denoted by a vector Ω (ie, $<\Omega_{CPU}, \Omega_{RAM}>$), denoting the amount of CPU and memory resource, respectively. Each tenant i may have n VMs. Each VM j is initially allocated with a share vector $s(j)$ that reflects its priority relative to other VMs. The amount of resource shares required by VM j is characterized by a demand vector $d(j)$. Correspondingly, the resource share lent to other tenants becomes $s(j) - d(j)$, and we call it a contribution vector $c(j)$. At last, let $s'(j)$ denote the current share vector when resources are reallocated. For simplicity, we assume that resource allocation is oblivious, meaning that the current allocation is not affected by previous allocations. Thus, a VM's priority is always determined by its initial share vector $s(j)$ in each time of resource allocation.

Intertenant resource trading

For multiresource allocation, it is hard to guarantee that the demands of all resource types are nicely satisfied without waste. For example, a tenant's aggregate CPU demand may be less than the initial CPU share, but memory demand exceeds the current allocation. In this case, the tenant may expect to trade CPU resources with other tenants' memory resources. Thus, the question is how to trade resources of different types among tenants while guaranteeing economic fairness. RRF embraces an IRT mechanism with the core idea that tenants' gains from other tenants should be proportional to their contribution. The only basis for underutilized resource allocation is the tenant's contribution, rather than the initial resource share or unsatisfied demand. As shown in Fig. 3, the memory resource contributed by tenant A is twice more than that of tenant B, and tenant A should receive twice more the unused CPU resource (contributed by tenant C) than tenant B at first. Then, we need to check whether the CPU resource of tenant A is overprovisioned. If so, the unused portion should be redistributed to other tenants. This process should be *iteratively* performed by all tenants because each round of resource distribution may affect other tenants' allocations. While this naive approach works, it can cause unacceptable computation overhead. We further propose a work backward strategy to speed up the unused resource distribution.

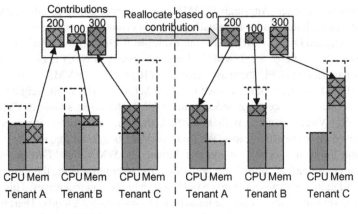

FIG. 3

Sketch of intertenant resource trading.

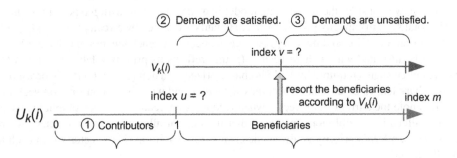

FIG. 4

Sketch of the IRT algorithm.

For each type of resource, we divide the tenants into three categories: contributors, beneficiaries whose demands are satisfied, and beneficiaries whose demands are unsatisfied, as shown in Fig. 4. Tenants in the first two categories are *directly* allocated with their demands exactly, and tenants in the third category are allocated with their initial shares, plus a portion of contributions from the first category. However, a challenging problem is how to divide the tenants into these three categories efficiently. Algorithm 2 describes the sorting process by using some heuristics.

Let vectors $D(i)$, $S(i)$, $C(i)$, and $S'(i)$ denote the total demand, initial share, contribution, and current share of the tenant i, respectively. Correspondingly, let $D_k(i)$, $S_k(i)$, $C_k(i)$, and $S'(i)$ denote the total demand, initial share, contribution, and current share of resource type k, respectively. We consider a scenario where m tenants share a resource pool with capacity Ω, with resource contentions (ie, $\sum_{i=1}^{m} D_i(i) \geq \Omega$). Our algorithm first divide the total capacity on the basis of each tenant's initial share, and then caps each tenant's allocation at the total demand. Actually, each tenant will receive an initial total share $Spiq$, and then the total contribution becomes $C(i) = S(i) - D(i)$ (if $S(i) > D(i)$). For resource type $k(1 \leq k \leq p)$, the unused resource $C_k(i)$ is redistributed to other unsatisfied tenants in the ratio of their total contributions.

Algorithm 2 shows the pseudocode for IRT. We first calculate each tenant's total contribution $\Lambda(i)$ (lines 6–8). To reduce the complexity of resource allocation, for each resource type k, we define the normalized demand of tenant i as $U_k(i) = D_k(i)/S_k(i)$, and reindex the tenants so that the $U_k(i)$ are in ascending order, as shown in Fig. 4. Then, we can easily find the index u so that $U_k(u) < 1$ and $U_k(u+1) \geq 1$. The tenants with index $[1,\ldots, u]$ are contributors and the remaining are beneficiaries. For tenants with index $[u+1,\ldots, m]$ $(U_k(i) \geq 1)$, we define the ratio of unsatisfied demand of resource type k to her total contribution as $Vk(i) = (Dk(i) - Sk(i))/\sum_{k=1}^{p} C_k(i)$ (lines 12–13), and reindex these tenants according to the ascending order of $V_k(i)$, as shown in Fig. 4. Thus, tenants with index $[1,\ldots, u]$ are ordered by $U_k(i)$ while tenants with index $[u+1,\ldots, m]$ are ordered by $V_k(i)$. The demand of tenants with the largest index will be satisfied at last. We need to find a pair of successive indexes $v, v+1, (v \geq u)$, so that the share allocations of tenants with index $[1,\ldots, v]$ are capped at their demands, and the remaining contribution $\sum_{i=v+1}^{m} \Psi_k(i) = \Omega_k - \sum_{i=1}^{m} D_k(i) - \sum_{i=v+1}^{m} S_k(i)$ is distributed to tenants with index $[v+1,\ldots, m]$ in proportion to their total contributions. Some heuristics can be employed to speed up the index searching. First, searching should start from index $u+1$ because tenants with index $[1,\ldots, u]$ are contributors. Second, we can use a binary search strategy to find two successive indices $v, v+1$ that cannot be satisfied. Namely, the following inequality (1) and (2) must be satisfied:

$$S_k(v) + \frac{\sum_{i=v}^{m} \Psi_k(i) \times \Lambda(v)}{\sum_{i=v}^{m} \Lambda(i)} \geq D_k(v) \tag{1}$$

$$S_k(v+1) + \frac{\sum_{i=v+1}^{m} \Psi_k(i) \times \Lambda(v+1)}{\sum_{i=v+1}^{m} \Lambda(i)} < D_k(v+1) \tag{2}$$

where $\sum_{i=v}^{m} \Psi_k(i)$ and $\sum_{i=v+1}^{m} \Psi_k(i+1)$ represent the remaining contributions that will be redistributed to tenants with unsatisfied demands. Once the index v is determined, we can calculate the remaining contribution. The tenants with index $[1,\ldots, v]$ receive shares capped at their demands (lines 16–17), and the tenants with index $[v+1,\ldots, m]$ receive their initial shares plus the remaining resource in proportion to their contributions (lines 19–20).

ALGORITHM 2 INTERTENANT RESOURCE TRADING (IRT)

Input: $D = \{D(1), \ldots, D(m)\}, S = \{S(1),\ldots,S(m)\}, \Omega$
Output: $S' = \{S'(1),\ldots,S'(m)\}$
Variables: $[i, C(i), \Lambda(i), U(i), V(i), \Psi(i)] \leftarrow 0$

```
 1: for resource–type k = 1 to p do
 2:    for Tenant i = 1 to m do
 3:        /*Allocate each tenant (i) her initial share S(i) */
 4:        S'_k(i) ← S_k(i)
 5:        U_k(i) ← D_k(i) / S_k(i)
 6:        if S_k(i) ≥ D_k(i) then
 7:            C_k(i) ← S_k(i) − D_k(i)
```

/*Calculate tenant(i)'s total contribution $\Lambda(i)$ on all type of resource */

8: 　　$\Lambda(i) \leftarrow \Lambda(i) + C_k(i)$

9: **for** *resource-type* $k = 1$ **to** p **do**

10: 　Sort $U_k(i)$ in ascending order;

11: 　Find the index u so that $U_k(k) < 1 \le U_k(u+1)$

12: 　**for** *Tenant* $i = u + 1$ **to** m **do**

13: 　　$V_k(i) \leftarrow (D_k(i) - S_k(i))/\Lambda(i)$

14: 　Sort $V_k(i)$ in ascending order;

15: 　Find the index v using binary search algorithm so that Equation (1) and (2) are satisfied;

16: 　**for** *Tenant* $i = 1$ **to** v **do**

17: 　　$S_k'(i) \leftarrow D_k(i)$ /*share is capped by demand*/

　　　/*Calculate the remaining contributions for re-allocation*/

18: 　$\sum_{i=v+1}^{m} \Psi_k(i) \leftarrow \Omega_k - \sum_{i=1}^{v} D_k(i) - \sum_{i=v+1}^{m} S_k(i)$

19: 　**for** *Tenant* $i = v + 1$ **to** m **do**

20: 　　$S_k'(i) \leftarrow S_k(i) + \dfrac{\sum_{i=v+1}^{m} \Psi_k(i) \times \Lambda(v+1)}{\sum_{i=v+1}^{m} \Lambda(i)}$

Intratenant weight adjustment

A tenant usually needs more than one VM to host her applications. Workloads in different VMs may have dynamic and heterogeneous resource requirements. Thus, dynamic resource flows among VMs belonging to the same tenant can prevent loss of tenant's asset. In F2C, we use IWA to adjust the resource among VMs belonging to the same tenant. We allocate *share* (or weight) for each VM using a policy similar to WMMF. For each type of resource, we first reset each VM's current weight to its initial share. However, if the allocation made to a VM is more than its demand, its allocation should be capped at its real demand, and the unused share should be reallocated to its sibling VMs with unsatisfied demands. In contrast to WMMF that reallocates the unused resource in proportion to VMs' share values, we reallocate the excessive resource share to the VMs in the ratio of their unsatisfied demands.

Note that once a VM's resource share is determined, the resource allocation made to the VM is simply determined by the function $share \xrightarrow{f_2} resource$.

ALGORITHM 3 INTERTENANT WEIGHT ADJUSTMENT (IWA)

Input: $d = \{d(1),\dots,d(n)\}, s = \{s(1),\dots,s(n)\}, S$

Output: $s' = \{s'(1),\dots,s'(n)\}$

Variables: $[j,\Gamma,\Phi] \leftarrow 0$

/* Allocate initial share $s(j)$ to each VM(j) */

1: 　$\Phi \leftarrow S - \sum_{j=1}^{n} s(j)$ /*Calculate the difference of initial total share and new allocated capacity */

2: **for** *VM* $j = 1$ **to** n **do**

3: 　**if** $d(j) \ge s(j)$ **then**

4: 　　$\Gamma \leftarrow \Gamma + (d(j) - s(j))$ /*total unsatisfied demand*/

5: 　**else**

6: 　　$\Phi \leftarrow \Phi + (s(j) - d(j))$ /*total remaining capacity */

　　/* distribute remaining capacity to VMs with unsatisfied demand */

7: **for** *VM* $j = 1$ **to** n **do**

8: 　**if** $d(j) \ge s(j)$ **then**

9: 　　$s'(j) \leftarrow s(j) + \dfrac{d(j) - s(j)}{\Gamma} \times \Phi$

10: 　**else**

11: 　　$s'(j) \leftarrow d(j)$

Algorithm 3 shows the pseudocode for IWA. A tenant with n VMs is allocated with total resource share S. Note that S is a global allocation vector, which corresponds to the output of Algorithm 2. Thus, Algorithm 3 is performed by accompanying Algorithm 2. For each tenant, we first calculate the total unsatisfied demand and total remaining capacity for reallocation, respectively (lines 2–6), then distribute the remaining capacity to unsatisfied VMs in a ratio of their unsatisfied demands (lines 7–11). As VM provisioning is constrained to physical hosts' capacity, it is desirable to adjust weights of VMs on the same physical node, rather than across multiple nodes. In practice, we execute the IWA algorithm only on each single node.

7.5.4 EXPERIMENTAL EVALUATION

RRF is implemented on top of Xen 4.1. The prototype F2C is deployed in a cluster with 10 nodes. The following workloads with diversifying and variable resource requirements are used to evaluate resource allocation fairness and application performance.

TPC-C: We use a public benchmark DBT-2 as clients to simulate a complete computing environment where a number of users execute transactions against a database. The clients and MySQL database server run in two VMs separately. We assume these two VM belong to the same tenant. We configure 600 terminal threads and 300 database connections. We evaluate its application performance by throughput (transactions per minute).

RUBBoS (Rice University Bulletin Board System) [38]: it is a typical multitier web benchmark. RUBBoS simulates an online news forum like https://slashdot.org. We deploy the benchmark in a three-tier architecture using Apache 2.2, Tomcat 7.0, and MySQL 5.5.

Kernel-build: We compile Linux 2.6.31 kernel in a single VM. It generates a moderate and balanced load of CPU and memory.

Hadoop: We use Hadoop WordCount microbenchmark to setup a virtual cluster consisting of 10 worker VMs and 1 master VM. The 10 worker VMs are evenly distributed in the 10 physical machines and co-run with other three workloads.

On our testbed, we consider multiple tenants sharing the cluster. Each tenant only runs one kind of the above workloads. All workloads are running in VMs whose initial share values are set according to the workloads' average demands. In addition, we can configure the initial share of tenant (i) based on a provisioning coefficient:

$$\alpha = S(i) / \overline{D(I)}$$

which reflects the ratio of initial resource share to the average demand. We continuously launch the tenants' applications to the cluster one by one until there is no room to accommodate any more applications.

We evaluate F2C by comparing the following alternative approaches for IaaS clouds:

- *T-shirt (static)*: Workloads are running in VMs with static resource provision. It is the current resource model adopted by most IaaS clouds [1].
- *WMMF*: WMMF [35] is used to allocate CPU and memory resources to each VM separately.
- *DRF*: DRF [7] is used to allocate multiple resources to each VM.
- *IWA*: We conduct only weight adjustment for VMs belonging to the same tenant, without considering IRT. This is to assess the individual impact of IRT.
- *RRF (IRT + IWA)*: We conduct hierarchical resource allocation using both IRT and IWA.

Results on fairness

In general, in a shared computing system with resource contention, tenants want to receive more resources or at least the same amount of resource than they buy. We call it *fair* if a tenant can achieve this goal (ie, sharing benefit). In contrast, it is also possible that the total resources tenants receives is fewer than that without sharing, which we call *unfair* (ie, sharing loss). Thus, we define the economic fairness degree $\beta(i)$ for tenant i in a time window T as follows:

$$\beta(i) = \sum_{i=1}^{T} S_i'(i) / (T \times S(i))$$

It represents the ratio of average resource shares received to the tenant's initial shares in the time window T; more exactly speaking, it denotes the ratio of resource value to tenants payments. $\beta(i)=1$ implies absolute economic fairness. $\beta(i)>1$ implies the tenant benefits from resource sharing, while $\beta(i)<1$ implies the tenant loses her asset.

We evaluate the economic fairness of different schemes for the four workloads in a long period of time. All VMs' capacities are provisioned based on their average demands (ie, $\alpha=1$). Fig. 5 shows the comparison of economic fairness of different resource allocation schemes. Each bar shows the average result of the same workload run by multiple tenants. Overall, RRF achieves much better economic fairness than other approaches. Specifically, RRF leads to smaller difference of β between different applications, indicating 95% economic fairness (geometric mean) for multiresource sharing among multitenants.

We make the following observations:

First, the T-shirt (static) model achieves 100% economic fairness, as VMs share nothing with each other. However, it results in the worst application performance for all workloads, as shown in Fig. 6.

Second, both WMMF and DRF show significant differences on β for different workloads. As all WMMF-based algorithms always try to satisfy the demand of smallest applications first, both kernel-build and TPC-C gain more resources than their initial shares. This effect is more significant for DRF if the application shows a tiny skewness of multiresource demands (such as kernel-build). DRF always completely satisfies the demand of these applications first. Thus, DRF and WMMF are susceptible to application's

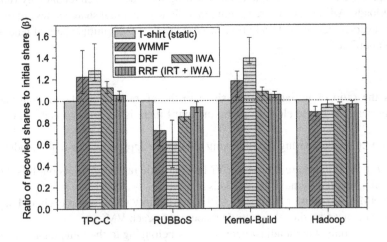

FIG. 5

Comparison of the economic fairness of several resource allocation schemes.

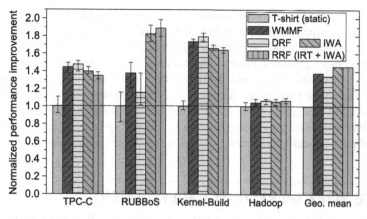

FIG. 6

Comparison of the application performance improvement of several resource allocation schemes.

load patterns. Applications with large skewness of multiresource demands usually lose their asset. Even for a single-resource type, a large deviation of resource demand also lead to distinct economic unfairness.

Third, workloads with different resource demand patterns show different behaviors in resource sharing. RUBBoS has a cyclical workload pattern, its resource demand shows the largest temporal fluctuations. When the load is below its average demand, it contributes resource to other VMs and thus loses its asset. However, when it shows a large value of $D_t piq\{Spiq$, its demand always cannot be fully satisfied if there exists resource contention.

Thus, RUBBoS has smaller value of β than other applications. For TPC-C and kernel-build, although they show comparable demand deviation and skewness with RUBBoS, they have much more opportunities to benefit from RUBBoS because their absolute demands are much smaller. For Hadoop, although it requires a large amount of resources, it demonstrates only a slight deviation of resource demands, and there are few opportunities to contribute resources to other VMs (except in its *reduce* stage).

Fourth, IWA allows tenants to properly distribute VMs' spare resources to their sibling VMs in proportion to their unsatisfied demands. It guarantees that tenants can effectively utilize their own resource. IRT can further preserve tenants' assets as each tenant tries to maximize the value of spare resource. In addition, RRF is immune to free riding.

We also studied the impact of different α values. For space limitation, we omit the figures and briefly discuss the results. When we decrease the provisioning coefficient α (ie, reduce the resource provisioned for applications), the β of all applications approaches to one. In contrast, a larger α leads to a decrease of β. That means, applications tend to preserve their resources when there exist intensive resource contention. Nevertheless, a larger value of α implies better application performance.

Improvement of application performance

Fig. 6 shows the normalized application performance for different resource allocation schemes. All schemes provision resources according to the applications' average demand ($\alpha = 1$). In the T-shirt model, all applications show the worst performance and we refer it as a baseline. In other models, all applications show performance improvement due to resource sharing. For RUBBoS, RRF leads to much more improved application performance than other schemes. This is because RRF provides two mechanisms (IRT + IWA) to preserve tenants' assets, and thus RRF allow RUBBoS receive more resources than other schemes, as shown in Fig. 5. For other workloads, RRF is also comparable to the other resource-sharing schemes. In summary, RRF achieves 45% performance improvement for all workloads on average (geometric mean). DRF achieves the best performance for kernel-build and TPC-C, but achieves very bad performance for RUBBoS. It shows the largest performance differentiation for different workloads. DRF always tends to satisfy the demand of the application with the smallest dominant share, and thus applications that have resource demands of small sizes or small skewness always benefit more from resource sharing. In contrast, the performance of Hadoop shows slight variations between different allocation schemes due to its rather stable resource demands.

7.6 RELATED WORK ON RESOURCE MANAGEMENT

In this section, we review the related work of resource management from the aspects of performance, fairness, energy, and power cost, as well as monetary cost. For more related work on resource management, we refer readers to three comprehensive surveys [39–41].

7.6.1 RESOURCE UTILIZATION OPTIMIZATION

For resource management, different resource allocation strategies can lead to significantly varied resource utilization [42]. Various resource allocation approaches have therefore been proposed for different workloads and systems/platforms [43–46]. For MapReduce workloads, Tang et al. [45] observed that different job submission order can have a significant impact on the resource utilization, and therefore improved the resource utilization for MapReduce cluster by reordering the job submission order of arriving MapReduce jobs. Grandl et al. [44] proposed a dynamic multiresource packing system called Tetris that improves the resource utilization by packing tasks to machines based on their requirements along multiple resources. Moreover, resource sharing is another approach to improve the resource utilization in a multitenant system by allowing overloaded users to possess unused resources from underloaded users [47]. In addition, task/VM migration and consolidation [48–50], widely used in cloud computing, is also an efficient method to improve resource utilization of a single machine.

7.6.2 POWER AND ENERGY COST SAVING OPTIMIZATION

Power and energy are a big concern in current data centers and supercomputers, which consists of hundreds of servers. Efficient resource management is nontrivial for power and energy cost saving. There are a number of techniques proposed to alleviate it. One intuitive approach is shutting down some low-utilized servers [51,52]. Moreover, VM migration and consolidation is an effective approach to reduce the number of running machines and, in turn, save the power and energy cost [53,54]. Finally, we refer readers to a survey [55] for more solutions.

7.6.3 MONETARY COST OPTIMIZATION

Monetary cost optimization has become a hot topic in recent years, especially for cloud computing. A lot of job scheduling and resource provisioning algorithms have been proposed by leveraging market-based techniques [56], rule-based techniques [57], and model-based approaches [58]. Many relevant cost optimization approaches can be found in databases [59], Internet [60], distributed systems [61], grid [17], and cloud [56].

7.6.4 FAIRNESS OPTIMIZATION

Fairness is an important issue in a multiuser computing environment. There are various kinds of fair policies in the traditional HPC and grid computing, including round-robin [62], proportional resource sharing [63], weighted fair queuing [64], and max-min fairness [65]. In comparison, max-min fairness is the most popular and widely used policy in many existing parallel and distributed systems, such as Hadoop [66], YARN [15], Mesos [16], Choosy [67], and Quincy [68]. Hadoop [66] partitions resources into slots and allocates them fairly across pools and jobs. In contrast, YARN [15] divides resources into containers (ie, a set of various resources like memory and CPU) and tries to guarantee fairness between queues. Mesos [16] enables multiple diverse computing frameworks such as Hadoop and Spark sharing a single system. It proposes a distributed two-level scheduling mechanism called resource offers, which decides how many resources to offer. Each framework decides which resources to accept or which computation to run on them. Choosy [67] extends the max-min fairness by considering placement constraints. Quincy [68] is a fair scheduler for Dryad that achieves a fair scheduling of multiple jobs by formulating it as a min-cost flow problem. In addition to the single-resource fairness, there are some work focusing on multiresource fairness, including DRF [7] and its extensions [69–72].

7.7 OPEN PROBLEMS

Despite many recent efforts on resource management, there are a number of open problems remained to be explored in future. We briefly elaborate on them from the following aspects.

7.7.1 SLA GUARANTEE FOR APPLICATIONS

In practice, users' applications are often with different performance (eg, latency, throughput) and resource requirements. For example, latency-sensitive applications in memcached require a high response time, whereas batch jobs in Hadoop are often require high throughput [73]. When these applications run together in a shared computing system, it becomes challenging work to provide the quality of services for each application. Despite the many research efforts that have been made [74,75], there is a lack of systematic approach that takes into account different types of resources and application requirements integrally. Most of them either focus on a specific resource type (eg, network flow) [73,74] or a kind of application [76]. Existing works do not address how to systematically ensure SLA guarantee for different applications.

7.7.2 VARIOUS COMPUTATION MODELS AND SYSTEMS

As listed in Section 7.3, there are a number of computation models, as well as computing systems proposed for different applications in recent years. From a user's perspective, it becomes a headache and a time-consuming problem for the user to choose and learn those computation models and corresponding computing systems. Designing a general computing and resource management system like an operation system becomes a challenging issue.

7.7.3 EXPLOITING EMERGING HARDWARE

Emerging hardware is available at different layers. For example, in the storage layer, we now have solid-state disk and nonvolatile RAM, which are much faster than Hard Disk (HD). In the computation layer, there are a set of accelerators such as GPU, AMD Accelerated Processing Unit (APU), and Field Programmable Gate Array (FPGA). Moreover, in the network layer, remote direct memory access is an efficient hardware tool for speeding network transfer. For a computing system, it is important to adopt this emerging hardware to improve the performance of applications. Currently, the study on this aspect is still at early stage. More research efforts are required to efficiently utilize this emerging hardware at different layers for existing computing systems.

7.8 SUMMARY

In this chapter, we have discussed the importance of resource management for Big Data processing and surveyed a number of existing representative large-scale data processing systems. One of the classic issues for resource management is fairness. The chapter reviewed the memory less fair resource allocation policies for existing systems and showed their unsuitability for cloud computing by presenting three problems. A new LTRF policy was then proposed to address these problems, and we formally and experimentally validate the merits of the proposed policy. This chapter next focused on the resource management for VMs on the cloud, considering VM migration and consolidation in the cloud environment. Finally, there are many open problems that need more research efforts in this field.

REFERENCES

[1] Gmach D, Rolia J, Cherkasova L. Selling t-shirts and time shares in the cloud. In: Proceedings of the 2012 12th IEEE/ACM international symposium on cluster, cloud and grid computing (CCGRID 2012), CCGRID'12. Washington, DC: IEEE Computer Society; 2012. p. 539–46.
[2] AutoScaling. http://aws.amazon.com/autoscaling.
[3] Mao M, Humphrey M. A performance study on the VM startup time in the cloud. In: IEEE 5th international conference on cloud computing (CLOUD). Washington, DC: IEEE Computer Society; 2012. p. 423–30.
[4] Nguyen H, Shen Z, Gu X, Subbiah S, Wilkes J. Agile: elastic distributed resource scaling for infrastructure-as-a-service. In: USENIX ICAC; San Jose, CA: USENIX Association; 2013, pp. 69–82.
[5] Amazon. http://aws.amazon.com/solutions/case-studies/.
[6] Google. https://cloud.google.com/customers/.
[7] Ghodsi A, Zaharia M, Hindman B, Konwinski A, Shenker S, Stoica I. Dominant resource fairness: fair allocation of multiple resource types. In: Proceedings of the 8th USENIX conference on networked systems design and implementation, NSDI'11. Berkeley, CA: USENIX Association; 2011. p. 24.
[8] Barham P, Dragovic B, Fraser K, Hand S, Harris T, Ho A, et al. Xen and the art of virtualization. In: Proceedings of the nineteenth ACM symposium on operating systems principles, SOSP'03. New York, NY: ACM; 2003. p. 164–77.

[9] Cherkasova L, Gupta D, Vahdat A. Comparison of the three CPU schedulers in Xen. ACM SIGMETRICS Perform Eval Rev 2007;35(2):42–51.

[10] Gulati A, Merchant A, Varman PJ. mclock: handling throughput variability for hypervisor io scheduling. In: Proceedings of the 9th USENIX conference on operating systems design and implementation, OSDI'10. Berkeley, CA: USENIX Association; 2010. p. 1–7.

[11] Waldspurger CA. Memory resource management in VMware ESX server. In: Proceedings of the 5th symposium on operating systems design and implementation — copyright restrictions prevent ACM from being able to make the PDFs for this conference available for downloading, OSDI'02; New York, NY: ACM; 2002. p. 181–94.

[12] Dean J, Ghemawat S. MapReduce: simplified data processing on large clusters. Commun ACM 2008;51(1):107–13.

[13] Zaharia M, Chowdhury M, Franklin MJ, Shenker S, Stoica I. Spark: cluster computing with working sets. In: Proceedings of the 2nd USENIX conference on hot topics in cloud computing, HotCloud'10. Berkeley, CA: USENIX Association; 2010. p. 10.

[14] Yoo AB, Jette MA, Grondona M. SLURM: simple Linux utility for resource management. In: Job scheduling strategies for parallel processing. Seattle, WA: Springer; 2003. p. 44–60.

[15] Vavilapalli VK, Murthy AC, Douglas C, Agarwal S, Konar M, Evans R, et al. Apache Hadoop YARN: yet another resource negotiator. In: Proceedings of the 4th annual symposium on cloud computing, SOCC'13. New York, NY: ACM; 2013. p. 15–6.

[16] Hindman B, Konwinski A, Zaharia M, Ghodsi A, Joseph AD, Katz R, et al. Mesos: a platform for fine-grained resource sharing in the data center. In: Proceedings of the 8th USENIX conference on networked systems design and implementation, NSDI'11. Berkeley, CA: USENIX Association; 2011. p. 22.

[17] Storage resource management. https://en.wikipedia.org/wiki/Storage_Resource_Management.

[18] Software-defined networking. https://en.wikipedia.org/wiki/Software-defined-networking.

[19] Malewicz G, Austern MH, Bik AJ, Dehnert JC, Horn I, Leiser N, et al. Pregel: a system for large-scale graph processing. In: Proceedings of the 2010 ACM SIGMOD international conference on management of data, SIGMOD'10. New York, NY: ACM; 2010. p. 135–46.

[20] Hadoop. http://hadoop.apache.org/.

[21] Isard M, Budiu M, Yu Y, Birrell A, Fetterly D. Dryad: distributed data-parallel programs from sequential building blocks. In: Proceedings of the 2nd ACM SIGOPS/EuroSys European conference on computer systems 2007, EuroSys'07. New York, NY: ACM; 2007. p. 59–72.

[22] Giraph. http://giraph.apache.org/.

[23] Storm. http://storm-project.net/.

[24] Tez. https://tez.apache.org/.

[25] Zaharia M, Chowdhury M, Das T, Dave A, Ma J, McCauley M, et al. Resilient distributed datasets: a fault-tolerant abstraction for in-memory cluster computing. In: Proceedings of the 9th USENIX conference on networked systems design and implementation, NSDI'12. Berkeley, CA: USENIX Association; 2012. p. 2.

[26] Olston C, Reed B, Srivastava U, Kumar R, Tomkins A. Pig latin: a not-so-foreign language for data processing. In: Proceedings of the 2008 ACM SIGMOD international conference on management of data. New York, NY: ACM; 2008. p. 1099–110.

[27] Thusoo A, Sarma JS, Jain N, Shao Z, Chakka P, Anthony S, et al. Hive: a warehousing solution over a map-reduce framework. Proc VLDB Endowment 2009;2(2):1626–9.

[28] George L. HBase: the definitive guide. Newton, MA: O'Reilly Media; 2011.

[29] Xin RS, Rosen J, Zaharia M, Franklin MJ, Shenker S, Stoica I. Shark: SQL and rich analytics at scale. In: Proceedings of the 2013 ACM SIGMOD international conference on management of data. New York, NY: ACM; 2013. p. 13–24.

[30] Armbrust M, Xin RS, Lian C, Huai Y, Liu D, Bradley JK, et al. Spark SQL: relational data processing in spark. In: Proceedings of the 2015 ACM SIGMOD international conference on management of data. New York, NY: ACM; 2015. p. 1383–94.

[31] Gonzalez JE, Xin RS, Dave A, Crankshaw D, Franklin MJ, Stoica I. Graphx: Graph processing in a distributed dataflow framework. In: Proceedings of OSDI; Broomfield, CO: USENIX Association 2014. p. 599–613.

[32] Zhong J, He B. Medusa: simplified graph processing on gpus. IEEE Trans Parallel Distrib Syst 2014;25(6):1543–52.

[33] Loan agreement. http://en.wikipedia.org/wiki/Loan_agreement.

[34] Faraz A, Seyong L, Mithuna T, Puma VTN. Purdue MapReduce benchmarks suite. Technical report EECS-2012, October, West Lafayette, IN: School of Electrical and Computer Engineering, Purdue University; 2012.

[35] Keshav S. An engineering approach to computer networking: atm networks, the internet, and the telephone network. Boston, MA: Addison-Wesley; 1997.

[36] Liu H, He B. Reciprocal resource fairness: towards cooperative multiple-resource fair sharing in IaaS clouds. In: International conference for high performance computing, networking, storage and analysis, SC14, November; New Orleans, LA: IEEE; 2014. p. 970–81.

[37] Williams D, Jamjoom H, Liu Y-H, Weatherspoon H. Overdriver: handling memory overload in an oversubscribed cloud. In: Proceedings of the 7th ACM SIG-PLAN/SIGOPS international conference on virtual execution environments, VEE'11. New York, NY: ACM; 2011. p. 205–16.

[38] RUBBoS. http://jmob.ow2.org/rubbos.html.

[39] Jennings B, Stadler R. Resource management in clouds: survey and research challenges. J Netw Syst Manag 2014;23(3):1–53.

[40] Krauter K, Buyya R, Maheswaran M. A taxonomy and survey of grid resource management systems for distributed computing. Softw Pract Exper 2002;32(2):135–64.

[41] Weingrtner R, Brscher GB, Westphall CB. Cloud resource management: a survey on forecasting and profiling models. J Netw Comput Appl 2015;47:99–106.

[42] Anuradha V, Sumathi D. A survey on resource allocation strategies in cloud computing. In: International conference on IEEE information communication and embedded systems (ICICES) Chennai, TN: IEEE; 2014. p. 1–7.

[43] Delimitrou C, Kozyrakis C. Quasar: resource-efficient and QoS-aware cluster management. ACM SIGPLAN Not 2014;49(4):127–44.

[44] Grandl R, Ananthanarayanan G, Kandula S, Rao S, Akella A. Multi-resource packing for cluster schedulers. In: Proceedings of the 2014 ACM conference on SIGCOMM, SIGCOMM'14. New York, NY: ACM; 2014. p. 455–66.

[45] Tang S, Lee B-S, He B. MROrder: flexible job ordering optimization for online MapReduce workloads. In: Wolf F, Mohr B, Mey D, editors. Euro-Par 2013 parallel processing. Lecture notes in computer science, vol. 8097. Berlin, Heidelberg: Springer; 2013. p. 291–304.

[46] Verma A, Pedrosa L, Korupolu M, Oppenheimer D, Tune E, Wilkes J. Large-scale cluster management at Google with borg. In: Proceedings of the tenth European conference on computer systems. New York, NY: ACM; 2015. p. 18.

[47] Tang S, Lee B-s, He B, Liu H. Long-term resource fairness: towards economic fairness on pay-as-you-use computing systems. In: Proceedings of the 28th ACM international conference on supercomputing, ICS'14. New York, NY: ACM; 2014. p. 251–60.

[48] Beloglazov A, Buyya R. Managing overloaded hosts for dynamic consolidation of virtual machines in cloud data centers under quality of service constraints. IEEE Trans Parallel Distrib Syst 2013;24(7):1366–79.

[49] Corradi A, Fanelli M, Foschini L. VM consolidation: a real case based on openstack cloud. Futur Gener Comput Syst 2014;32:118–27.

[50] Hsu C-H, Chen S-C, Lee C-C, Chang H-Y, Lai K-C, Li K-C, et al. Energy-aware task consolidation technique for cloud computing. In: IEEE third international conference on cloud computing technology and science (CloudCom). Washington, DC: IEEE; 2011. p. 115–21.

[51] Lang W, Patel JM. Energy management for MapReduce clusters. Proc VLDB Endowment 2010;3(1-2):129–39.

[52] Rajamani K, Lefurgy C. On evaluating request-distribution schemes for saving energy in server clusters. In: IEEE international symposium on performance analysis of systems and software, ISPASS, 2003. Washington, DC: IEEE; 2003. p. 111–22.

[53] Clark C, Fraser K, Hand S, Hansen JG, Jul E, Limpach C, et al. Live migration of virtual machines. In: Proceedings of the 2nd conference on symposium on networked systems design & implementation. vol. 2. Berkeley, CA: USENIX Association; 2005. p. 273–86.

[54] Ranganathan P, Leech P, Irwin D, Chase J. Ensemble-level power management for dense blade servers. ACM SIGARCH Computer Architecture News 2006;34:66–77.

[55] Beloglazov A, Buyya R, Lee YC, Zomaya A, et al. A taxonomy and survey of energy-efficient data centers and cloud computing systems. Adv Comput 2011;82(2):47–111.

[56] Fard HM, Prodan R, Fahringer T. A truthful dynamic workflow scheduling mechanism for commercial multicloud environments. IEEE Trans Parallel Distrib Syst 2013;24(6):1203–12.

[57] Malawski M, Juve G, Deelman E, Nabrzyski J. Cost-and deadline-constrained provisioning for scientific workflow ensembles in IaaS clouds. In: Proceedings of the international conference on high performance computing, networking, storage and analysis. Los Alamitos, CA: IEEE Computer Society Press; 2012. p. 22.

[58] Byun E-K, Kee Y-S, Kim J-S, Maeng S. Cost optimized provisioning of elastic resources for application workflows. Future Generation Computer Systems 2011;27(8):1011–26.

[59] Gray J, Graefe G. The five-minute rule ten years later, and other computer storage rules of thumb. ACM SIGMOD Record. New York, NY: ACM. 1997;26(4):63–68.

[60] Ma RT, Chiu DM, Lui J, Misra V, Rubenstein D. Internet economics: the use of Shapley value for ISP settlement. IEEE/ACM Trans Networking 2010;18(3):775–87.

[61] Gray J. Distributed computing economics. Queue 2008;6(3):63–8.

[62] Drozdowski M. Scheduling for parallel processing. 1st ed. New York, NY: Springer; 2009.

[63] Waldspurger CA, Weihl WE. Lottery scheduling: flexible proportional-share resource management. In: Proceedings of the 1st USENIX conference on operating systems design and implementation, OSDI'94. Berkeley, CA: USENIX Association; 1994.

[64] Demers A, Keshav S, Shenker S. Analysis and simulation of a fair queueing algorithm. In: Symposium proceedings on communications architectures & protocols, SIGCOMM'89. New York, NY: ACM; 1989. p. 1–12.

[65] Max-min fairness (wikipedia). http://en.wikipedia.org/wiki/Max-min_fairness.

[66] White T. Hadoop: the definitive guide. 1st ed. Sebastopol, CA: O'Reilly; 2009. June.

[67] Ghodsi A, Zaharia M, Shenker S, Stoica I. Choosy: max-min fair sharing for datacenter jobs with constraints. In: Proceedings of the 8th ACM European conference on computer systems, EuroSys'13; New York, NY: ACM; 2013. p. 365–78.

[68] Isard M, Prabhakaran V, Currey J, Wieder U, Talwar K, Goldberg A. Quincy: fair scheduling for distributed computing clusters. In: Proceedings of the ACM SIGOPS 22nd symposium on operating systems principles, SOSP'09. New York, NY: ACM; 2009. p. 261–76.

[69] Bhattacharya AA, Culler D, Friedman E, Ghodsi A, Shenker S, Stoica I. Hierarchical scheduling for diverse datacenter workloads. In: Proceedings of the 4th annual symposium on cloud computing, SOCC'13. New York, NY: ACM; 2013. p. 14–5.

[70] Kash I, Procaccia AD, Shah N. No agent left behind: Dynamic fair division of multiple resources. In: Proceedings of the 2013 international conference on autonomous agents and multi-agent systems, AAMAS'13. Richland, SC: International Foundation for Autonomous Agents and Multiagent Systems; 2013. p. 351–8.

[71] Parkes DC, Procaccia AD, Shah N. Beyond dominant resource fairness: extensions, limitations, and indivisibilities. In: Proceedings of the 13th ACM conference on electronic commerce, EC'12. New York, NY: ACM; 2012. p. 808–25.

[72] Wang W, Li B, Liang B. Dominant resource fairness in cloud computing systems with heterogeneous servers. In: Proceedings IEEE INFOCOM, April 2014. Toronto, ON: IEEE; 2014. p. 583–91.

[73] Grosvenor MP, Schwarzkopf M, Gog I, Watson RN, Moore AW, Hand S, et al. Queues dont matter when you can jump them!. In: NSDI'15 proceedings of the 12th USENIX conference on networked systems design and implementation. Berkeley, CA: USENIX Association; 2015. p. 1–14.

[74] Chowdhury M, Stoica I. Coflow: an application layer abstraction for cluster networking. Proceedings of the 11th ACM Workshop on Hot Topics in Networks. New York, NY: ACM Hotnets; 2012. pp. 31–36. ACM.

[75] Mace J., Bodik P., Fonseca R., Musuvathi M.. Retro: targeted resource management in multi-tenant distributed systems. In: Proceedings of the 12th USENIX Conference on Networked Systems Design and Implementation (NSDI'15). Berkeley, CA: USENIX Association; 2015. p. 589–603.

[76] Lim N, Majumdar S, Ashwood-Smith P. A constraint programming-based resource management technique for processing MapReduce jobs with SLAS on clouds. In: 43rd international conference on IEEE parallel processing (ICPP). Minneapolis, MN: IEEE; 2014. p. 411–21.

LOCAL RESOURCE CONSUMPTION SHAPING: A CASE FOR MAPREDUCE

8

P. Lu, Y.C. Lee, T. Ryan, V. Gramoli, A.Y. Zomaya

8.1 INTRODUCTION

A major concern in today's distributed computing systems, including cloud data centers, is unacceptably low resource utilization (ie, lower than 10%) [1]. Maximizing resource utilization is often sought by intensifying workload consolidation rate, and this tends to cause high resource contention and, in turn, performance interference/degradation. While minimizing resource contention and improving performance seem rather mutually inclusive and they simultaneously can be achieved with exclusive resource usage (eg, space sharing), performance may suffer in terms of throughput unless resource capacity is abundant (ie, little or no waiting time). Performance improvement even with abundant resource capacity is limited when data locality is a major performance parameter (ie, MapReduce [2] in particular).

Although there have been many proposals for new resource management and scheduling approaches for distributed systems [3–8], these previous approaches are concrete and reactive in that workloads are placed taking into account their resource usage pattern, and their resource usage is often explicitly controlled by virtual machine (VM) migration, for example. The challenge lies in the nature of its multiobjective optimization combining maximization of resource utilization, minimization of resource contention, and improvement of performance.

Our solution to this problem of workload consolidation with minimal resource contention is the local resource shaper (LRS). The LRS solution is well suited for distributed systems (such as MapReduce) in which a job consists of many similar tasks, and the fairness in resource sharing at the task level within the same job is not a major concern. Our work is inspired by the idea of "resource consumption shaping" at a data center level, proposed by James Hamilton and Dave Treadwell [1,9]. This data center-level resource consumption shaping strives for smoothing workload peaks by deferring nontime-critical workloads to low utilization periods or valleys. At the internet scale, this shaping is explained by the time of day that sweeps around the world.

LRS is a novel resource management strategy in the following ways: LRS differs from global resource consumption shaping. As our goal does not encompass reducing node-local resources, it is not necessary to knock off peaks. By contrast, it makes sense to lower peaks at the Internet scale to reduce, for example, the power consumption of a data center. LRS speeds up the execution of tasks within a single job whereas others [5–8,10] target fair resource sharing. As opposed to reactive solutions [4,11,12] that react to resource contention a posteriori by migrating the load, LRS takes a preventive approach by minimizing resource contention.

Big Data. http://dx.doi.org/10.1016/B978-0-12-805394-2.00008-8

In this chapter, we illustrate LRS by implementing it in the Hadoop framework both in the classic Hadoop 1.x and the recent Hadoop 2.x (YARN) [13]. While resource consumption shaping originally aimed at the data center level, the resource consumption shaping we consider focuses instead on local, individual nodes and cores. Motivated by the fact that individual jobs may also incur load peaks and valleys on individual resources, like CPU (Central Processing Unit) or I/O (Input/Output) we propose to smooth resource consumption by automatically tuning the execution of concurrent tasks to increase performance without overprovisioning. The main challenge is twofold, as it consists of characterizing concurrent local tasks and of scheduling them appropriately to maximize resource utilization while minimizing resource contention.

Our focus lies on MapReduce applications, where each task processes a chunk of data using the same predefined (map/reduce) function. In operating systems, processes are usually fairly treated in that each receives an identical CPU time slice (quantum) without the explicit consideration of its resource usage pattern. We argue that this fair resource sharing is detrimental to MapReduce applications. In particular, the inherent synchronous nature of map/reduce rounds forces these tasks with similar resource utilization patterns to occur simultaneously, thus increasing contention. Typically, I/O-bound tasks incur significant contention at similar periods of time when trying to access the same disk, translating into idle time of the CPU resources. By filling valleys where one resource is underutilized, one can reduce contention and overall job duration.

LRS leverages resource consumption shaping at the local node/core level by layering two priority tiers on each processor core using cgroups.[1] In particular, Splitter in LRS manages two slot/container tiers: Active and Passive, with the latter being able to use resources only when the former is not using them. Splitter is a generic resource management component for Hadoop that can be incorporated with other Hadoop schedulers. We demonstrate the capability and applicability of Splitter by integrating it with three well-known Hadoop schedulers: FIFO, Fair, and Capacity.

Also, we show the further potential of LRS by developing an LRS-aware MapReduce scheduler, namely Interleave. This scheduler adopts a dual-purpose "task slot" that is capable of accommodating either type of MapReduce task. Interleave implements two components, a resource monitor and a task scheduler, in order to take full advantage of LRS. The resource monitor is in charge of dynamic configuration of Passive slots when it detects spare resource capacity, while the task scheduler implements an LRS-aware scheduling algorithm with the explicit consideration of the task slot.

We have conducted an extensive analysis of MapReduce to evaluate LRS. Our platform consists of a Hadoop cluster of 11 nodes in Amazon EC2 [14]. We have compared LRS against existing Hadoop alternatives on the six MapReduce benchmarks depicted in Table 1. These benchmarks are specialized in text retrieval, decryption, sorting, scientific computation, etc. and are all taken from the MapReduce literature [7,15–17]. Additionally, we have also compared LRS to a recently proposed Hadoop scheduler called Delay [8] in treating a Facebook workload. Our results indicate that LRS improves these Hadoop-based alternatives in three main ways:

1. *Increasing CPU usage.* LRS allows us to achieve CPU utilization of up to 89% when considering both system and user CPU times. Even without Interleave, LRS (with the default Hadoop FIFO scheduler) still achieves an average CPU utilization of 85%, which remains higher than the peak CPU utilization that one could obtain without LRS with any of the three Hadoop schedulers.

---

[1]cgroups (control groups) is a Linux kernel feature that enables the limiting, accounting, and isolating of resource usage between groups of processes; hence, the name "control groups."

Table 1 A Summary of MapReduce Benchmarks

Name	Type	Description
Grep	CPU bound	Search text matching regular expression
PiEst	CPU bound	Estimate Pi using Monte-Carlo method
WordCount (WC)	Moderate CPU	Count words in the input file
Crypto (Crpt)	Moderate CPU	Decrypt cipher text in the input file
Sort	I/O bound	Sort the input data
TeraSort (TS)	I/O bound	Sort the input data

2. *Lowering I/O contention.* Our MapReduce scheduler, Interleave, exploits the Active/Passive slots differentiation to reduce I/O contention by filling the valleys where I/O do not occur. This reduces the time each task spends waiting on I/O. Specifically, LRS benefits from Interleave by halving the I/O wait time of Hadoop.

3. *Reducing job duration.* We have experimentally tested LRS against Delay [8], which was shown to perform well under a Facebook workload. We thus have evaluated the job completion time using LRS against Hadoop using Delay and observed that LRS reduces the job duration by up to 20% under the Facebook workload.

An interesting conclusion of our work is that the constraints of Hadoop slot configuration seemingly impact performance. We have tested all possible static configurations of map/reduce slots, as recommended by Yahoo! [18], and have observed a performance variation of 22% based on the configuration the user could choose, therefore motivating the search for the best configuration. LRS relieves the programmer from the burden of finding such a best configuration. We have also observed that LRS, with the adoption of a task slot, always outperforms the best static slot configuration both in terms of resource utilization and performance. In that respect, our work tends to support the attempt of developers to trade map/reduce slots for containers [13].

Lastly, we implement the two-tier LRS model in Hadoop YARN in order to investigate its effectiveness as a general-purpose resource management technique. However, Hadoop YARN has also moved to multipurpose resource containers, resulting in much higher baseline resource utilization than Classic Hadoop (Hadoop 1.x). During evaluation, we have found that in a Hadoop YARN environment, the two-tier resource allocation strategy provides slight benefits in terms of resource utilization and resource contention, with significant improvements only in I/O-bound applications.

8.2 MOTIVATION

In this section, we give our analysis of resource usage patterns and resource contention sourced from the current practice of fair resource sharing. This analysis is carried out using Hadoop and the benchmarks of Table 1. The Hadoop framework, an open source implementation of MapReduce, harnesses hundreds of workers and dispatches the tasks across those workers to utilize resources within the cluster. Its architecture follows the master/slave paradigm: a master machine (JobTracker) is responsible for scheduling tasks, while a set of worker machines (TaskTracker) are in charge of managing resources and performing tasks dispatched by the master. As the capacity of each worker grows, more tasks can be executed simultaneously in order to maximize resource utilization. Hence, Hadoop uses slots as the finest granularity to manage resources and execute a task. The number of slots across the cluster represents the cluster's capacity, and the number of slots per TaskTracker determines the maximum number of concurrent tasks that are allowed to run in a worker. Moreover, the number of slots needs to be statically configured before launching TaskTracker and takes effect during the lifetime of the TaskTracker. Such slot-based resources allocation is widely applied to most of distributed systems (eg, Message Passing Interface or MPI [19], Condor [20]).

8.2.1 PITFALLS OF FAIR RESOURCE SHARING

Current operating systems allow multiple jobs (even more than there are CPUs) to run at a time. This is generally done via time sharing (ie, each job is given an equally short CPU time in turn). Although some cost is involved when switching jobs, it is very useful for these interactive applications, making them have a quick response. It is also a good approach for running multiple jobs that share resources on a machine. However, we argue that such fair resource sharing is detrimental to many distributed systems, Hadoop in particular; we believe that there is much need for resource-sharing approaches that remove/relieve that detrimental impact. To motivate this need, we have run several experiments with Hadoop on a single 4-core machine.

Ideally, resource utilization and performance can be improved if there is unused resource capacity that is exploited for running another task. This ideal case has been shown in Fig. 1. We run a Grep job with varying slot configurations from four map slots and four reduce slots (4m4r) to eight map slots and eight reduce slots (8m8r) as suggested in Ref. [18]. As the number of slots increases, idle CPU time decreases (ie, higher resource utilization) and so does the job execution time.

However, the case with WordCount (nonnegligible I/O activity) in Fig. 2 shows the adverse effect on performance when the concurrency level is 2 (8m8r). This poorer performance is due to the fact that the time spent by CPU on the I/O wait dramatically increases as the number of slots increases. This effect even counterbalances the decrease of idle CPU time as in the Grep case, as depicted in Fig. 2C. The main reason for a poor performance is that the current approach based on fair resource sharing tends to improve in resource utilization at the cost of exacerbating resource contention. CPU utilization for the other four benchmarks is shown in the Appendix. The actual execution times for all six benchmarks are shown in Fig. 8.

Now we show a microscopic view of the case with WordCount in Fig. 3A and B for 4m4r and 8m8r, respectively. We plot the CPU utilization and the task's writing rate.[2] In both configurations, we run the

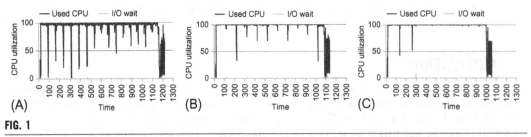

FIG. 1

CPU utilization for Grep with different slot configurations: (A) 4m4r, (B) 6m6r, and (C) 8m8r.

---

[2]The number of kilobytes the task has caused or shall cause to be written to disk per second.

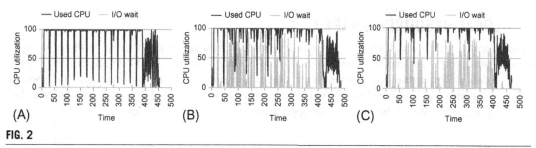

FIG. 2

CPU utilization for WordCount with different slot configurations: (A) 4m4r, (B) 6m6r, and (C) 8m8r.

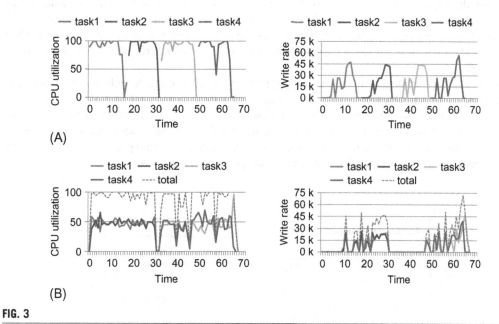

FIG. 3

Resource usage patterns (CPU utilization and writing rate) of WordCount with different concurrency levels on a single core: (A) tasks running sequentially and (B) 2 concurrent tasks.

job in the way that each core executes four tasks (a total of 16 tasks). While tasks with the 4m4r slot configuration run sequentially with minimal resource contention, tasks with the 8m8r slot configuration run in tandem with substantial resource contention. As shown in Fig. 3B Task 1 and Task 2 have a similar CPU resource usage pattern and start to intensively use I/O resources at the same time because of sorting and merging. This contention in I/O resources is also indicated by the high and bulky I/O wait in Fig. 2C. Although the CPU utilization is increased with 8m8r, I/O resource contention is much worse. Specifically, CPU I/O wait time accounts for 9.01% compared to 0.11% in the case of 4m4r. To conclude, while using fair resource sharing to improve resource utilization, we have to face the risks of resource contention and performance degradation (ie, decrease in the overall system throughput).

8.3 LOCAL RESOURCE SHAPER

In this section, we present LRS as a new resource management technique with its two main components, Splitter and Interleave, for MapReduce (Fig. 4). Splitter is at the core of LRS and defines Active/Passive slots to shape resource consumption. Interleave encompasses the slot manager (SM), which adapts the number of Passive slots dynamically in order to maximize CPU usage, and the task dispatcher (TD), which dispatches tasks to the appropriate Active and Passive slots.

8.3.1 DESIGN PHILOSOPHY

The notion of local resource consumption shaping is novel in this work in that the tasks are colocated, with their access to resources in consideration of each other (ie, autonomously shaping use of resources), to deal with the dynamicity of resource usage/sharing. While fair resource sharing is still meaningful for some purposes, such as responsiveness and multitenancy, it causes resource contention as colocated tasks often compete for the same resource (eg, a hard disk drive) that cannot be perfectly multiplexed.

LRS best suits distributed systems, such as MapReduce and MPI, in which a job consists of multiple tasks and the fairness in resource sharing at the task level within the same job is not a major concern. Unless system capacity is sufficient for a given job, some of its tasks have to either wait for resources (space sharing) or (fairly) share resources (time sharing). On the other hand, abundant resource capacity leads to poor resource utilization; and this excessive resource provisioning is a main issue leading to inefficiency in energy consumption and capital and operating expenditures.

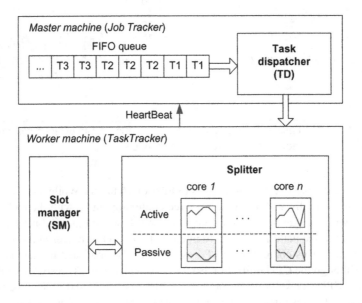

FIG. 4

The architecture of LRS.

8.3.2 SPLITTER

A major issue with the slot configuration[3] is that the best choice is subject to job characteristics; thus, there is no rule of thumb. Moreover, resource utilization is essentially limited by the underlying fair resource-sharing strategy, even with the "best" slot configuration. To tackle the problem of slot configuration, LRS uses Splitter as a "pluggable" resource manager. Splitter pairs up slots in two priority modes: the Active and Passive slot. A task in an Active slot takes up as many resources as possible to keep its original usage. A task in a Passive slot makes use of any unused resources, while the task in the Active slot is either waiting I/O operations to be completed or has completed its execution. Active and Passive slots are realized using cgroups and their resource-sharing ratio (for CPU and I/O resources) is 100:1.

Splitter works with TaskTracker to allocate resources to slots. Before a TaskTracker is launched, Splitter collects the CPU information of the current worker machine using the lscpu Linux command to determine the numbers of Active and Passive slots, respectively. In our implementation, we have configured two slots per core and layered them in Active and Passive priority modes. We adopt this two-slot priority approach as most MapReduce tasks consume more than 50% of available CPU resources [5].

Splitter is triggered by a change in the status of a running task. When receiving new tasks from JobTracker, Splitter follows a FIFO policy to first fill Active slots and then Passive slots. The transition of a task from a Passive slot to an Active slot takes place when a task running in the Active slot finishes. The early-assigned task in Passive is switched to the idle Active slot and that Passive slot is allocated to a new task. This transition takes place repeatedly.

The focus of this paper is on CPU and disk I/O. Other resources, like memory or network bandwidth, are not considered, but LRS can easily incorporate previous work, including Capacity scheduler [21], Mantri [15], and Sailfish [22]. The Capacity scheduler enforces a limit on the percentage of memory allocated to a user/job. The Delay scheduler delays a task to favor high data locality and reduce network usage. Mantri and Sailfish avoid network hotspots by decreasing intermediate data transmission.

8.3.3 THE INTERLEAVE MAPREDUCE SCHEDULER

The Interleave scheduler implements a SM and a TD on top of Splitter (Fig. 4), with the adoption of a "task slot." As the coexistence of map and reduce slots leads to resource contention when both map and reduce tasks are running concurrently on a core, we merge the map slot and reduce slot into an undifferentiated and dual-purpose task slot. The incorporation of task slots with LRS helps eliminate such resource contention. A task slot takes any task at a time, regardless of task type (map or reduce); we refer to task slot when we use the term "slot" in the context of Interleave.

Before a TaskTracker starts to work, its corresponding Splitter configures the number of slots (two by default). SM keeps track of the overall resource usage. Once it detects spare resources (ie, the CPU is underutilized) in its worker machine, it notifies TaskTracker to increase the maximum number of Passive slots to obtain more tasks from TD in JobTracker. TD dispatches tasks accounting for the existence of dual-purpose task slots.

---

[3]The issue with finding the optimal slot configuration is specific to Hadoop 1.x, as Hadoop 2.x has abandoned the concept of slot, with the introduction of containers. However, the latter container-based model still faces the issue of resource utilization with fair resource sharing.

Task slot

Managing resources based on LRS eliminates the inefficient resource utilization caused by static slot configuration with fair resource sharing. However, the coexistence of map and reduce slots still results in an inappropriate representation of the capacity of resources when processing multiple jobs. Therefore, we merge the map slot and reduce slot in Hadoop into a dual-purpose "task slot" for more effective resource management. A task slot[4] takes any task at a time, regardless of task type (map or reduce).

We illustrate the problem we have found with separate map and reduce slots in Fig. 5. A two-core worker node is configured with two map slots and two reduce slots. The assumption is that this configuration best represents the resource capacity expecting all four slots (map and reduce slots) to be constantly occupied. Consider the submission of two jobs, WordCount and TeraSort in order, each of which includes two map tasks and two reduce tasks. In this case, resources in region B are only adequately used, while resources in regions A and C are underutilized. Increasing the numbers of slots here is a partial solution resulting in overloading in region B. The adoption of a task slot resolves this issue of inefficient resource use, although the resource contention between map tasks and reduce tasks illustrated in Fig. 5 is not a critical issue, as they tend to have different characteristics.

Slot manager

The SM seeks to further increase resource utilization by dynamically configuring (expanding and shrinking) the maximum number of Passive slots. As the resource usage for Active slots is guaranteed and the resource contention between Passive slots is a lesser concern, an increase in the maximum number of Passive slots on a particular worker node helps make use of every spare resource (particularly with I/O intensive jobs).

SM uses 3 seconds as a monitoring cycle, the same interval as the cycle of heartbeat. For each cycle, we calculate the (average) effective CPU utilization (ie, CPU^{eff} = user mode + system mode) and average I/O wait (IO^{wait}). The actual usage of CPU (CPU^{used}) is then defined as the summation of CPU^{eff} and IO^{wait}. If all slots are occupied but there is some spare resource, SM calculates the number of additional Passive slots as follows:

$$N = \begin{cases} \lfloor 1 - CPU^{used} / (CPU^{used*} \# cores / Slot^{MAX}) \rfloor & \text{if } CPU^{eff} < 0.9 \wedge IO^{wait} \leq T \\ 1 & \text{if } IO^{wait} > T \end{cases}$$

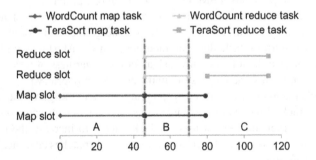

FIG. 5

Slot usage with two jobs.

---

[4]We refer to task slot when we use the term "slot" in the context of Interleave.

where Slot^{MAX} is the maximum number of allocated slots. T is a threshold configured by the user to determine the characteristic of running tasks. The empirical value for T that we have obtained from our experiments is 30%. Note that if this threshold is too high, there is no performance impact on a single node, but the problem of stragglers would occur for a cluster [2,23].

Task dispatcher

The LRS-aware TD resides in JobTracker and is triggered by heartbeats sent from TaskTrackers. For each worker, TD dispatches tasks to either Active or Passive slots, but not both at any given scheduling event. Tasks of all submitted jobs are organized in a FIFO queue. The dispatcher processes tasks in order and is data-locality aware. The dispatcher consists of two phases: reduce task scheduling and map task scheduling.

The behavior of TD is presented in Algorithm 1. The first part is the reduce task scheduling. Since slots in Interleave are able to run either map tasks or reduce tasks, reduce tasks need to be first dispatched in case map tasks of the latest jobs keep occupying all slots and earliest jobs hang due to insufficient slots to run reduce tasks. Only one reduce task is dispatched per heartbeat, as in the original design of Hadoop.

The second part is map task scheduling, which has two stages. Stage 1 assigns tasks to run on Active slots in a FIFO manner. Stage 2 assigns tasks to run on Passive slots, but data-local tasks from all submitted jobs take priority in order to improve data locality. Note that we never dispatch map tasks to both Active and Passive slots in the same scheduling cycle, which enables tasks to be evenly distributed across all workers when the number of tasks is less than the number of slots in the cluster.

Algorithm 1. LRS-Aware Task Dispatcher
When a heartbeat is received from worker n:
/* Reduce task scheduling */
if n has free Active/Passive slots **then**
  for j in jobs **do**
    if j has unassigned reduce tasks t **then**
      assign t to n
    end if
  end for
end if

/* Map task scheduling */
/* Stage 1: assigning map tasks to Active slots */
for $\forall$ slot $\in$ *Active* slots of n **do**
  for j in jobs **do**
    if j has unassigned map task t **then**
      assign t to n
    end if
  end for
end for

/* Stage 2: assigning map tasks to Active slots */
if no map tasks are assigned to Active slots in the current scheduling cycle **then**
  for $\forall$ slot $\in$ *Passive* slots of n **do**

```
        for j in jobs do
            if j has unassigned map task t with data on n then
                assign t to n
            end if
        end for
    end for
    for ∀ slot ∈ Passive slots of n do
      for j in jobs do
        if j has unassigned map task t then
            assign t to n
        end if
      end for
    end for
end if
```

8.4 EVALUATION

In this section, we evaluate LRS extensively with five different schedulers (three Hadoop built-in schedulers, Delay [8], and our own Interleave scheduler) under seven different benchmarks. Each of the first six benchmarks has been previously used to evaluate MapReduce [7,15–17]. The last benchmark is based on a workload from Facebook [8].

In the following, we present our results obtained from experiments with Hadoop 1 and Hadoop 2 (YARN), respectively. In particular, we show results with Hadoop 1 as follows: (1) we show that Splitter (the core component of LRS), even without our Interleave scheduler,[5] addresses our motivating problem by shaping resource consumption to a certain extent; (2) we observe that this resource shaping translates into performance improvements, regardless of the underlying scheduler used; (3) we measure how our LRS (with Interleave scheduler) further reduces the I/O utilization; (4) we show that LRS effectively alleviates the need for manual slot configuration; and (5) we compare LRS to a solution that proved efficient in handling Facebook workloads [8]. We then show our evaluation of LRS implemented in YARN.

8.4.1 EXPERIMENTS WITH HADOOP 1.X

We performed all our experiments on a Hadoop cluster consisting of n11 EC2 m1.xlarge instances. Each instance has four cores, 15 GB RAM, and is running Hadoop-1.0.0 with a block size of 64 MB. The cluster was configured such that one node is dedicated to run JobTracker and NameNode, and each of the remaining 10 nodes hosts a TaskTracker and a DataNode. Based on the empirical rule provided in [18], we varied the slot configuration from four map slots and four reduce slots (4m4r) to eight map slots and eight reduce slots (8m8r) in our experiments. This makes the capacity of our tested cluster equal to 80–160 slots.

---

[5]We use the notation LRS^{FIFO} to denote LRS when it uses the Hadoop FIFO scheduler (without Interleave).

Results: shaping resources using splitter

To observe the effect of local resource consumption shaping, we reproduce the same motivating experiments of Figs. 1 and 2, but with our LRS solution. As Splitter essentially enables such shaping, we simply integrate Splitter with the default FIFO scheduler in Hadoop, ie, LRS^{FIFO}. In the rest of this section, we refer to LRS as LRS^{FIFO}.

The results are depicted in Figs. 6 and 7. All results for the single-node experiment with concrete values are presented in Fig. 8. These results show that Splitter alone substantially improves resource utilization.

An immediate observation is that LRS maximizes CPU resource utilization (Fig. 6); that is, effective CPU utilization is 95.71% for Grep and 89.15% for WordCount (Fig. 8). In particular, LRS utilizes CPU resources similarly to the 8m8r configuration for a CPU-bound application (8m8r has 94.42% effective CPU utilization for Grep). By contrast, LRS always exploits two different slots per core (Active and Passive), and thus ensures maximum CPU resource utilization in the general case. Note that more than two slots per core would not bring much CPU utilization improvement, as it is known that a MapReduce task generally exploits more than half of the CPU resource [5].

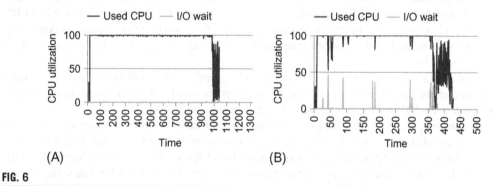

FIG. 6

CPU utilization using LRS^{FIFO}: (A) Grep (exec: 1090) and (B) WordCount (exec: 435).

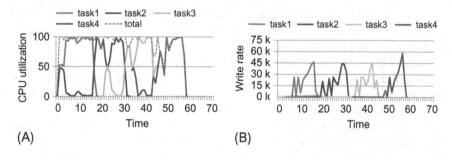

FIG. 7

Resource usage pattern of WordCount when running two tasks concurrently on a single core using LRS^{FIFO}. In comparison with resource usage patterns based on fair resource sharing (Fig. 3B), resource consumption using LRS^{FIFO} is well shaped, resulting in performance improvement (job execution times: 69 vs. 60): (A) CPU utilization and (B) write rate.

	PiEst				Grep				Wordcount				Crypto				Sort				TeraSort			
	4m4r	6m6r	8m8r	LRS^{FIFO}	4m4r	6m6r	8m8r	LRS^{FIFO}	4m4r	6m6r	8m8r	LRS^{FIFO}	4m4r	6m6r	8m8r	LRS^{FIFO}	4m4r	6m6r	8m8r	LRS^{FIFO}	4m4r	6m6r	8m8r	LRS^{FIFO}
■ exec	177	192	177	164	1279	1198	1118	1090	464	496	479	435	412	425	439	393	349	330	308	292	461	426	472	384
■ idle	22.8	22.4	22.5	14.9	9.23	6.66	5.53	4.26	16.4	14.6	11.6	9.99	10.6	12.7	11.5	11.2	24.2	20.4	13.9	12.6	17.8	15.0	15.6	11.0
■ iowait	0.05	0.03	0.03	0.01	0.04	0.02	0.02	0.01	0.11	9.07	9.01	0.86	8.45	6.95	10.4	5.88	12.8	9.22	10.1	8.30	12.3	11.6	15.7	7.27
■ system	5.10	4.81	5.47	5.60	2.44	2.78	3.12	3.01	4.64	4.16	4.51	4.95	18.3	21.1	19.5	18.6	15.6	18.0	20.2	19.8	15.1	15.6	15.4	16.9
■ user	72.0	66.7	73.9	79.4	88.2	90.5	91.3	92.7	78.8	72.1	74.8	84.2	62.5	59.1	58.4	64.2	47.2	52.2	55.6	59.2	54.6	57.6	53.2	64.7

FIG. 8

CPU utilization for six jobs running on a single node. Comparisons are made between plain FIFO (with three static configurations) and LRS^{FIFO}. While "exec" in the figure indicates execution times in seconds, the rest are CPU usage for idle, IO wait, system and user times, respectively.

On nonCPU-bound applications, LRS tends to obtain higher CPU resource utilization than the 8m8r slot configuration. More precisely, on WordCount, the 8m8r configuration only achieves 79.31% effective CPU utilization, while LRS achieves 89.15%. The reason for this disparity is that when LRS is not used, the adequate number of slots to use while ensuring fair resource sharing changes depending on various parameters, such as the type of running tasks and the size of input data, thus creating valleys in CPU utilization (Fig. 2).

By contrast, LRS achieves high CPU utilization while incurring a low amount of resource contention. In particular, we can see in Fig. 6 that the I/O wait duration with LRS remains lower in both experiments than in the Section 8.2, regardless of the chosen slot configuration.

To better illustrate that CPU utilization valleys may arise from I/O resource contention, Fig. 7 depicts the CPU and disk resource utilization of a single-core-running WordCount (cf. Fig. 3 for comparison). By distinguishing between Active and Passive slots, LRS lets the task in the Active slot fully exploit the CPU resource. The other task in the Passive slot keeps waiting until the Active task shows usage valleys due to, for example, I/O wait. Once the Active task's CPU consumption decreases as it terminates, LRS switches the Passive task to active mode to keep leveraging the CPU resource. This behavior is reproduced cyclically (a third incoming task would become Passive until the Active task finishes, and so on). Local resource shaping is illustrated by the complementary variations in CPU utilization of the four tasks in Fig. 7A as expected, this harmonious shape contrasts significantly with the disharmony present without LRS (Fig. 3B).

LRS also shapes I/O resource consumption in the same way as CPU consumption. In fact, this I/O resource shaping allows LRS to decrease the portion of CPU time spent waiting for I/O from 9.07% with a 6m6r configuration, to 0.86%. Thus, LRS helps minimize the contention of simultaneous disk writes as depicted in Fig. 7B which would otherwise significantly limit performance.

To conclude, the combination of low I/O resource contention with increased CPU resource utilization translates directly into performance improvement. We observe that LRS can decrease by 10 times the I/O waiting time and can achieve 13% higher CPU utilization over a seemingly appropriate slot configuration (6m6r) on the same nonCPU-bound application (WordCount). As a result, LRS outperforms by 12% the execution time of WordCount running with 6m6r (ie, 435 vs. 496 seconds, see Fig. 8).

For the complete set of comparative results on all six benchmarks, refer to Fig. 8 and the optional Appendix.

Results: incorporating splitter into existing MAPREDUCE schedulers

In this section, we show that the core component of the LRS (Splitter) is complementary to its scheduler. To this end, we incorporate three state-of-the-art Hadoop schedulers into LRS: the FIFO scheduler, the Fair scheduler, and the Capacity scheduler. Since these schedulers still use separate map and reduce slots, their incorporation with LRS is realized by configuring 4m4r for Active and 4m4r for Passive. The schedulers were run on our 11-node cluster with the six jobs in Table 1. We compare job execution time using Splitter to manage resource with three optimal configurations based on the number of cores. Results (Fig. 9) are normalized based on job execution time with LRS. Even though we did not modify these schedulers, Splitter improves the overall performance by managing resources more effectively. The FIFO scheduler achieves performance improvement of 8% on average for the six jobs compared with three different configurations. The Fair scheduler and Capacity scheduler achieve, on average, performance improvements of 7% and 5%, respectively.

Results: performance of interleave

For Crypto and the I/O-bound jobs in Table 1, part of the unused CPU resources caused by resource contention still exist when using LRS's core resource shaping component, Splitter (please refer to Appendix for details). The Interleave scheduler is used to alleviate this by supplementing LRS with its SM and TD (Fig. 10). Interleave further improves resource utilization by 4% on average for effective CPU utilization for Crypto and the I/O-bound jobs (Sort and TeraSort), further decreasing I/O wait by half for Crypto, 23% for Sort, and 29% for TeraSort, compared to the case when the FIFO scheduler (LRS^{FIFO}) is used. Due to small amounts of unused CPU resources, results for PiEst, Grep, and WordCount using LRS (with Interleave) are similar to that using LRS without Interleave (see LRS^{FIFO} results in Appendix), and thus are not presented.

In Figure 10C we use Sort with the Interleave scheduler as an example to show the variation in resource usage and the change in the maximum number of slots. In the first 80 seconds, the maximum number of slots is eight and the number of concurrently running tasks varies. Although unused CPU resources appear around 70 seconds, the maximum number of slots is still eight because the number of currently running tasks is less than the maximum number of slots. However, the number of concurrently running tasks reaches 10 and 9 from 70 to 120 seconds because unused CPU resources still exist when the number of concurrently running tasks reaches the maximum number of slots. All map

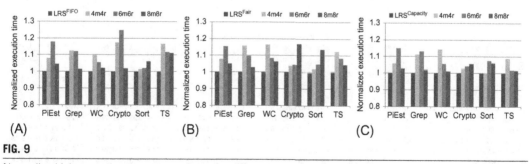

FIG. 9

Normalized job execution time comparisons for different schedulers. Job execution times are normalized due to their large differences between different benchmarks. The actual execution times can be found in the data table in Fig. 8.

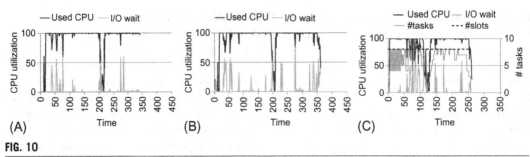

FIG. 10

CPU utilization using LRS (with Interleave). The adaptive Passive slot allocation of SM is shown in Fig. 10C. The maximum values on *x*-axes are intentionally set to 450, 450, and 350 for effective comparisons with other figures in Appendix: (A) Crypto, (B) TeraSort, and (C) Sort.

tasks finish at 120 seconds and, after that, the number of concurrently running reduce tasks gradually increases, as only one reduce task is assigned in a scheduling cycle.

Results: improving the performance of slot configurations

In another experiment, we validate LRS with the Interleave scheduler (simply LRS) on our 11-node cluster with the same six benchmarks used in earlier experiments, except that we increased the input data to 20 GB and the number of tasks for each job to 320 map tasks and 160 reduce tasks. Additional test cases for multiple jobs combinations were added to make this experiment more comprehensive. Results are shown in Figs. 11–13. We compare LRS against the default FIFO scheduler. We observe that the job execution time with LRS remains lower than with the FIFO scheduler with the optimal slot configuration (ie, by 9% on average and by up to 17%). We also observe that the effective CPU utilization increases by 11% on average and by up to a 22% (for the combination of Crypto and WordCount). Finally, the I/O wait for moderate CPU jobs and I/O-bound jobs is reduced by a factor of two on average and by up to a factor of five (for the combination of Sort and WordCount).

As the capability of Splitter to improve resource utilization and performance has been shown in Figs. 6 and 7 and the Interleave scheduler achieves yet more improvement, we only present the performance of LRS in the following sections.

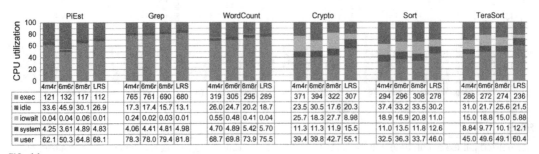

	PiEst				Grep				WordCount				Crypto				Sort				TeraSort			
	4m4r	6m6r	8m8r	LRS	4m4r	6m6r	8m8r	LRS	4m4r	6m6r	8m8r	LRS	4m4r	6m6r	8m8r	LRS	4m4r	6m6r	8m8r	LRS	4m4r	6m6r	8m8r	LRS
exec	121	132	117	112	765	761	690	680	319	305	295	289	371	394	322	307	294	296	308	278	286	272	274	236
idle	33.6	45.9	30.1	26.9	17.3	17.4	15.7	13.1	26.0	24.7	20.2	18.7	23.5	30.5	17.6	20.3	37.4	33.2	33.5	30.2	31.0	21.7	25.6	21.5
iowait	0.04	0.04	0.06	0.01	0.24	0.02	0.03	0.01	0.55	0.48	0.41	0.04	25.7	18.3	27.7	8.98	18.9	16.9	20.8	11.0	15.0	18.8	15.0	5.88
system	4.25	3.61	4.89	4.83	4.06	4.41	4.81	4.98	4.70	4.89	5.42	5.70	11.3	11.3	11.9	15.5	11.0	13.5	11.8	12.6	8.84	9.77	10.1	12.1
user	62.1	50.3	64.8	68.1	78.3	78.0	79.4	81.8	68.7	69.8	73.9	75.5	39.4	39.8	42.7	55.1	32.5	36.3	33.7	46.0	45.0	49.6	49.1	60.4

FIG. 11

CPU utilization for six jobs running on a cluster.

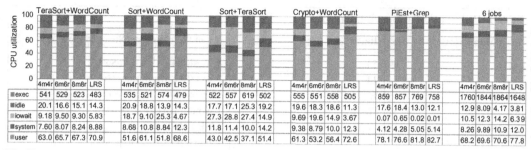

	TeraSort+WordCount				Sort+WordCount				Sort+TeraSort				Crypto+WordCount				PiEst+Grep				6 jobs			
	4m4r	6m6r	8m8r	LRS	4m4r	6m6r	8m8r	LRS	4m4r	6m6r	8m8r	LRS	4m4r	6m6r	8m8r	LRS	4m4r	6m6r	8m8r	LRS	4m4r	6m6r	8m8r	LRS
exec	541	529	523	483	535	521	574	479	522	557	619	502	555	551	558	505	859	857	769	758	1760	1844	1864	1648
idle	20.1	16.6	15.1	14.3	20.9	18.8	13.9	14.3	17.7	17.1	25.3	19.2	19.6	18.3	18.6	11.3	17.6	18.4	13.0	12.1	12.9	8.09	4.17	3.81
iowait	9.18	9.50	9.30	5.83	18.7	9.10	25.3	4.67	27.3	28.8	27.4	14.9	9.69	19.6	14.9	3.67	0.07	0.65	0.02	0.01	10.5	12.3	14.2	6.39
system	7.60	8.07	8.24	8.88	8.68	10.8	8.84	12.3	11.8	11.4	10.0	14.2	9.38	8.79	10.0	12.3	4.12	4.28	5.05	5.14	8.26	9.89	10.9	12.0
user	63.0	65.7	67.3	70.9	51.6	61.1	51.8	68.6	43.0	42.5	37.1	51.4	61.3	53.2	56.4	72.6	78.1	76.6	81.8	82.7	68.2	69.6	70.6	77.8

FIG. 12

CPU utilization for job combinations running on a cluster.

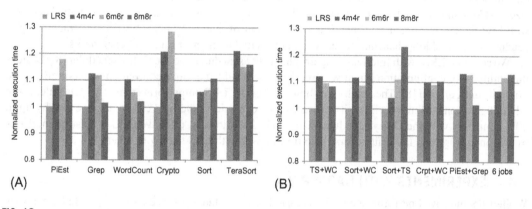

(A)   (B)

FIG. 13

Normalized execution time comparisons for jobs running on a cluster. The actual execution times can be found in the data tables in Figs. 11 and 12, respectively: (A) single job and (B) combination.

We observe for all experiments that each configuration is best suited to execute a certain job. For example, in our 11-node cluster, 8m8r is the best configuration for Grep, 6m6r is the best for the combination of Sort and WordCount, and 4m4r is the best for Sort. As workloads change over time in real systems, any one of these static configurations will cause performance degradation. Even if we try to profile a job to get a best configuration before we ran it on a production system, the best configuration still could be wrong. For example, 8m8r is the best for Sort with small input data size on a single node, but it performs the worst with large input data on our cluster. Moreover, job combinations will make the problem more complex. In our experiments, we observed an average slowdown of 9% (up to 22%) caused by different configurations. LRS allows us to overcome this problem.

Results: when running facebook workload model

In this experiment, we evaluate LRS through a set of benchmarks based on the workload trace from Facebook, which was reported in Ref. [8]. We scaled down the total number of jobs based on our cluster's scale and generated a job submission scheduler of 25 jobs. According to the Facebook trace, the

Table 2 Distribution of Benchmark Jobs

No. of Map Tasks	Rate (%)	No. of Benchmarks (No. of Maps Tasks)
1–2	54	8 WordCount (1) 6 TeraSort (2)
3–20	14	2 Sort (8) 2 WordCount (16)
21–150	15	1 Crypto (80) 2 TeraSort (120)
151–300	6	1 WordCount (240)
301–500	4	1 PiEst (400)
>500	7	1 TeraSort (520) 1 Grep (640)

distribution of job interarrival times was roughly exponential with a mean of 14 seconds. This makes our submission schedule 373 seconds long. The six benchmark jobs are mixed with different job input sizes (64 MB input block for a map task) and the job input sizes were generated based on the Facebook workload model. In particular, Table 2 lists the number of map tasks per job workload trace, the percentage of the total jobs, benchmark name, and the actual number of running benchmarks.

We compare LRS (with Interleave) against the FIFO scheduler and the Delay scheduler [8]. Besides the optimal slot configuration range we used before, we added a 4m2r configuration according to the original configuration [8]. The results are shown in Fig. 14. LRS outperforms these two schedulers with all configurations. More precisely, it decreases jobs execution time by 12% on average and by up to 20% compared with the Delay scheduler with 4m4r. Additionally, effective CPU utilization increases by 9% on average and I/O wait is about two times lower with LRS than with others.

8.4.2 EXPERIMENTS WITH HADOOP 2.X

While LRS improved performance in the Classic Hadoop (Hadoop 1.x) environment, Hadoop YARN has introduced several changes to the resource allocation model. These changes make it unclear whether the tiered approach presented in LRS will be effective in the Hadoop YARN environment. In this experiment, we implement LRS in Hadoop YARN to validate its effectiveness in YARN.

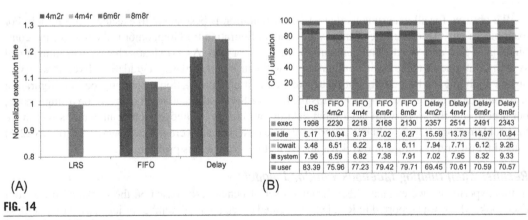

(A)   (B)

FIG. 14

Facebook workload results.

The performance of our implementation of a two-tier resource allocation model (ie, Splitter in LRS) in Hadoop YARN was tested over a range of MapReduce benchmarks (Table 1, excluding Crypto). Input data sets for the benchmarks were generated using the utilities RandomWriter (for Sort), RandomTextWriter (for Grep and WordCount), and TeraGen (for TeraSort). Input datasets of 30 GB were used for each benchmark, with the exception of PiEst and TeraSort. PiEst uses 1500 maps with 1,000,000 samples per map and TeraSort uses 10 GB of input data. These input sizes were chosen so as to be sufficiently large to utilize the whole test cluster, made up of 11 m3.2xlarge EC2 instances.

Implementation in Hadoop YARN

Following from the original LRS work, we implement a two-tiered resource allocation system with one Active and one Passive task per CPU core. A setting of two containers per CPU core also follows the rule of thumb configuration presented in several Hadoop YARN configuration guides for maximizing resource utilization [12]. The Hadoop YARN interface for managing resource containers with Linux cgroups was extended to allow for management of both CPU and I/O resources, and a mechanism for adjusting the relative resource shares was added to the interface. CPU and disk resources were shared between Active and Passive tasks in a ratio of 100:1.

To manage tier allocations, the Hadoop YARN container model was extended to include the notion of a container tier. By default, the Hadoop YARN Container Manager interface monitors resource usage within each Node Manager (worker node) in a cluster. The Container Manager was modified to update container tier allocations. A simple algorithm for managing container tiers was implemented, which assigns incoming tasks to a tier based on the amount of tasks currently executing. We always allocate the maximum amount of Active tasks before assigning a task to the Passive tier. Finally, as an Active task finishes, the longest-running Passive task is moved into the Active tier (ie, it is allocated a larger resource share). This management algorithm runs periodically within the Container Manager thread on each node. The internal container management mechanisms were optimized where possible since the management function runs frequently. These changes are only visible within the Node Manager itself; the Resource Manager (master node) and Scheduler are unaffected by the changes, maintaining the property of scheduler-independence.

Results

We compare performance to Hadoop YARN configured with one resource container per CPU core (denoted as YARN-1) and Hadoop YARN configured with two resource containers per CPU core (denoted as YARN-2). We denote the modified Hadoop YARN with two-tier resource allocation as YARN-LRS. The results for these experiments are presented in Fig. 15. To understand the results for the two-tier resource management technique, we analyse a breakdown of resource usage for the individual benchmarks. This resource breakdown, as well as absolute execution times for each benchmark, is shown in Fig. 16.

On average across the two-scheduler configurations, YARN-LRS decreases performance compared to YARN-1, which is the best YARN configuration, by a slight margin. While there is a 4% reduction in execution time across the MapReduce benchmarks compared to YARN-1 when using the Capacity scheduler, YARN-1 outperforms YARN-LRS by 6% on average when using the FIFO scheduler. YARN-LRS performs the best in the CPU-bound PiEst benchmark and the I/O-bound Sort benchmark when using the Capacity Scheduler, with average performance improvements of 5% and 14%, respectively. This suggests that the two-tier resource management technique is functioning as intended to both

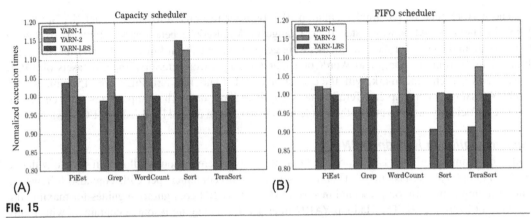

FIG. 15

Performance comparison for MapReduce benchmarks.

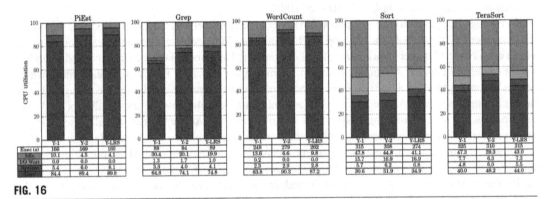

FIG. 16

Breakdown of CPU usage for MapReduce benchmarks when using the capacity scheduler.

increase CPU utilization and reduce I/O contention in some cases. We note that relative performance of the various configurations is similar for PiEst, Grep, and WordCount benchmarks across both Capacity and FIFO schedulers, and that the most significant differences between the two schedulers are for the I/O-bound Sort and TeraSort applications. Finally, we note that YARN-LRS improves performance compared to YARN-2 in almost all cases. This suggests that the tiered resource management approach is working as intended to reduce resource contention, since these two configurations have the same amount of tasks executing concurrently (two per CPU core). However, we focus our analysis on comparison between YARN-LRS and YARN-1, since it is the best performing YARN configuration.

For the PiEst benchmark, the resource breakdown confirms that the two-tier resource allocation strategy has worked as intended to increase CPU utilization. The PiEst application is CPU-bound, so we do not expect a considerable increase in performance by increasing task concurrency, as one task is enough to completely utilize a CPU core. However, analysis of CPU usage over time, as shown in Fig. 17, shows that YARN-LRS prevents the drops in utilization seen in YARN-1 (the previous best performing configuration) as each task finishes. While YARN-2 increases resource utilization

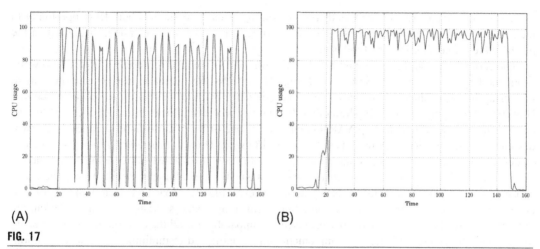

FIG. 17

CPU utilization on the PiEst benchmark.

compared to YARN-1 and also maintains more even CPU utilization (similar to the YARN-LRS utilization shown in Fig. 17), it does not result in a performance improvement due to increased resource contention between the two tasks per core.

While Grep is also CPU bound, YARN-1 performs slightly better to YARN-LRS. Analysis of task distribution, presented in Fig. 18, shows that this is because the Grep job uses significantly less parallel tasks than PiEst during the second half of its execution time. When there are a small number of tasks, no tasks are allocated to the Passive tier, meaning that the two-tier approach in YARN-LRS is effectively not used. As a result, there is a slight decrease in performance due to the additional overhead introduced by the two-tier resource allocation strategy. Significantly, this result shows that in the Hadoop YARN environment, whenever there are not enough tasks in the cluster to utilize all resource containers, there is less resource contention that can be reduced and resource utilization cannot be

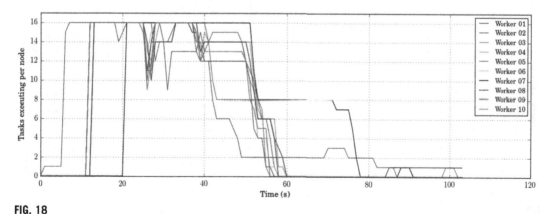

FIG. 18

Task distribution for the Grep MapReduce application.

increased, since there are so few tasks that are executing. Therefore, there is both less opportunity to increase resource utilization and less opportunity to decrease resource contention, meaning that the tier-based resource allocation method is not effective.

The performance on the I/O-bound benchmark Sort follows the results presented in Ref. [24] when using the Capacity scheduler. As shown in Fig. 16, YARN-LRS increases user execution without increasing I/O wait; that is, it increases resource utilization without increasing resource contention. However, we do note that Fig. 16 shows that the two-tier resource allocation model does not significantly affect I/O wait in a Hadoop YARN environment; one of the significant advantages of the two-tier model in the original LRS work is reduction in I/O wait. This confirms our hypothesis that since Hadoop YARN reduces resource contention by using the container-based resource allocation model, the two-tier resource management approach has less of an advantage. Initially, similar results were also expected for the I/O-bound TeraSort benchmark; however, Fig. 16 shows that there is no significant change in performance between the resource management approaches. Analysis of task distribution, presented in Fig. 19, shows why the performance is comparable for all the configurations when using the Capacity scheduler. The TeraSort implementation is optimized to minimize resource contention; as such, it never launches more three parallel tasks on each node. Therefore, for the same reasons discussed with the Grep benchmark above, we see comparable results across all configurations, as the two-tier system only uses a single tier, which does not improve performance.

Fig. 16 shows that there is a significant difference between the performance of the configurations for Grep and the I/O-bound benchmarks when using the FIFO Scheduler compared to the Capacity Scheduler. This is due to the small amount of tasks launched by the Grep, Sort, and TeraSort tasks. Since the simple FIFO scheduler does not account for data locality in the same way as the Capacity scheduler, it creates uneven task allocation across the cluster, with many tasks allocated to some nodes and no tasks allocated to others. This is a problem because some tasks on heavily utilized nodes are allocated to the Passive tier, while there are unused containers on other nodes. This causes the difference in performance between FIFO and Capacity Schedulers, since Capacity Scheduler distributes the tasks evenly (due to data locality), which allows the system to work more effectively. For this reason, YARN-LRS causes decreased performance compared to YARN-1 for applications with a small amount of tasks when using the FIFO Scheduler.

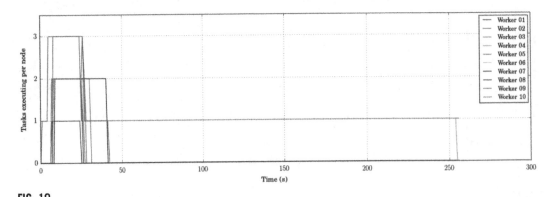

FIG. 19

Task distribution for the TeraSort MapReduce application.

This analysis of the Sort and TeraSort benchmarks when using the FIFO scheduler shows that applications with small amounts of tasks can show decreased performance when using the two-tier resource allocation strategy in a Hadoop YARN environment compared to the existing YARN configurations. However, we do not expect this to be a significant problem in real-world applications for two reasons. First, Hadoop YARN exposes an interface for applications to request task locations; any application can be easily extended to take advantage of this, resulting in evenly distributed tasks across the cluster. Second, real-world cluster environments are typically shared between multiple users and have multiple jobs running concurrently; since we have shown that two-tier resource strategy functions as intended when resource containers are saturated with tasks, we expect the two-tier strategy to result in increased throughput in that scenario.

Fig. 15 shows that for the WordCount benchmark in both schedulers, YARN-1 outperforms YARNLRS, increasing execution time by 5% on average. Analysis of the WordCount application itself shows that the overall WordCount execution time is dominated by the execution time of the reduce task. This can be seen by analysis of resource usage for individual processes. In our experimental setup, the WordCount application takes around 250 seconds to complete. The reduce task, as shown in Fig. 20, runs for around 200 seconds, and after around 130–150 seconds of total job execution time, the reduce task is the only task using CPU resources.

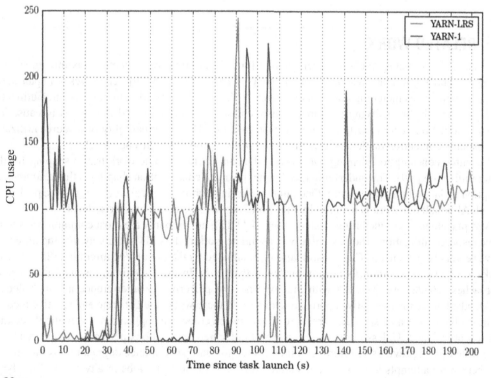

FIG. 20

Comparison of reduce task CPU usage in YARN-1 and YARN-LRS.

Fig. 20 shows that after around 130 and 150 seconds, respectively, both YARN-1 and YARN-LRS reduce tasks have very similar resource usage profiles, with the exception of YARN-LRS being 10–15 seconds behind YARN-1. This 10–15 seconds delay corresponds to the 10-15 seconds slowdown we see in YARN-LRS compared to YARN-1. This confirms that the reduce tasks are the bounding factor in the execution time of the WordCount job. Fig. 20 also shows a significant difference in CPU utilization between the two tasks at the beginning of their execution. The YARN-1 Reduce task uses 100–150% CPU over the first 15 seconds, while in this time the YARN-LRS reduce task uses very little CPU at all. Since the resource usages are otherwise comparable, we conclude that this reduced resource usage at the beginning of the execution results in the overall job execution time increase. Finally, we know that each task is first allocated to a Passive container; it follows that the reduced resource usage is because the YARN-LRS task is Passive during this time. Therefore, analysis of the WordCount benchmark shows that jobs for which execution time is bound by a single task have decreased performance when using a two-tier resource allocation strategy, since the bounding task will begin execution in the Passive tier.

This is a significant problem for the generality of the two-tier resource management technique. WordCount is a common MapReduce benchmark, and applications in other frameworks are often bounded by individual tasks as well (eg, Apache Tez). As such, this result shows that the two-tier resource management technique is not appropriate for all applications.

8.5 RELATED WORK

Efficient resource management has been studied for different purposes, such as maximizing resource utilization and minimizing resource contention [1,4,7,9,11,12,16,25–29]. These results span across various granularities including data center, server, VM, and job level. Maximizing resource utilization is often sought by intensifying workload consolidation (concurrency), and thus tends to cause high resource contention and, in turn, performance degradation. The incompatibility of resource utilization and resource contention hinders the identification of the optimal concurrency level.

Resource consumption shaping was proposed as an extension to network-traffic shaping for data center utilization [1,9]. The underlying idea behind resource consumption shaping is that resource consumption in data centers can be smoothed out by deferring nontime critical workloads in the peak usage period. Although our work is inspired by this work, our focus is at the finer node level.

VM placement and scheduling strategies (eg [4,11,12]) are probably the most common ways to improve resource utilization. They essentially consolidate workloads/VMs in the way that the number of active servers is minimized. This consolidation is facilitated by the use of VM migration [25]. Previous works are still coarser grain (VM monitor level) than ours. In the meantime, resource management approaches [26–28] are designed with the awareness of performance interference among colocated workloads. Unlike the preventive approach in our work, these works are concrete and reactive focusing on the exclusiveness and isolation of resource use between colocated applications by explicitly controlling resource usage. Unless the resource usage of colocated applications perfectly complement each other, when using previous solutions, resource contention and performance degradation is inevitable.

There were attempts to maximize resource utilization by profiling jobs in advance to find the resources bottleneck [7], and Cake [29] uses a two-level scheduling scheme to dynamically adjust the level of concurrency based on measured resource contention (device latency). In order to fully utilize one type of resource, they tend to face the underutilization of other resources. The WCO scheduler [16] combines workloads with different characteristics to reduce resource contention, whereas Choosy [30] aims at satisfying job placement constraints. These previous results are all limited in their resource management capacity by fair resource sharing. By contrast, LRS enables multiple workloads to harmoniously share resources by nonuniformly interlacing their resource usage. This is markedly distinct from fair resource sharing.

Hadoop is very popular for large-scale distributed computing particularly to process ever-increasing data volumes; hence, managing resources within Hadoop has been a challenge of practical importance. There is a large body of work on resource management [5,8,15,21,22,31], especially at the scheduling level. In contrast to these solutions, our Interleave scheduler exploits the fact that LRS trades map/reduce slots off for Active/Passive slots. The developers of Hadoop have recently decided to get rid of map/reduce slots [13]. The beta version of Hadoop 2.x does not aim at shaping local resources, but it instead relies on the user to leverage "containers" appropriately. Map/reduce slots will most likely not be part of the next stable release of Hadoop in part because of the constraints they impose on schedulers.

The Capacity scheduler [21] supports job memory resource requirement. Jobs are able to be dispatched in a way to reduce memory interference between running tasks. The Delay scheduler [8] takes into account data locality of map tasks. It replaces the relatively slow-speed network I/O with local disk I/O to achieve efficient resource utilization for performance improvement. More recently, Mantri [15] and Sailfish [22] achieve performance improvement by decreasing intermediate data transmission between map and reduce tasks to avoid network hotspots. Even automatic solutions [31] that tune Hadoop parameters to improve performance cannot disable fair resource sharing and existing resource allocation techniques, like DRF [5], share various resources but always in a fair manner. We thus believe that these solutions could also benefit from LRS to reduce their job duration by shaping their resource consumption instead of fairly consuming them.

8.6 CONCLUSIONS

Local resource consumption shaping is a novel technique to ensure that resources are leveraged at the granularity of a single node (or core) of a distributed system, despite unpredictable workload usage. We have designed LRS to be an independent and pluggable resource management component for system-wide schedulers to optimize system efficiency. LRS contrasts with existing solutions that either compensate predictable load variations ahead of time, or instead compensate unpredictable variations a posteriori (eg, after identifying resource contention). By relieving the burden of finding an appropriate slot configuration in Hadoop 1.x and by overcoming the inefficiency inherent in fair resource sharing, LRS improves the performance of MapReduce and similar applications.

We conducted an extensive analysis of LRS on a cluster of machines using 6 MapReduce benchmarks and Facebook workload model, and we evaluated the performance of four different MapReduce schedulers. We draw a number of interesting conclusions:

- The homogeneous nature of map tasks and reduce tasks make them prone to resource contention. LRS starts improving performance by limiting fairness, whereas fair resource sharing forces homogeneous tasks to acquire similar resources in overlapping periods of time, leading to contention peaks.

- The problem of local resource consumption shaping is orthogonal to the scheduling problem in that simply differentiating Active from Passive slots leads to performance improvements regardless of the scheduler. A scheduler, like ours, can leverage this differentiation to reduce I/O contention substantially.
- Letting tasks run on any slot gives room for optimization: in our experiments, LRS always outperformed the most efficient static slot configuration both in terms of performance and resource utilization.
- As YARN replaces the slot implementation/configuration of Hadoop by the introduction of containers with its creation based on resource capacity, the effectiveness of LRS, when implemented in YARN, is less universal compared to LRS in Hadoop 1.x. We conclude that the original two-tier model in LRS needs further work for use in Hadoop YARN environments.

APPENDIX CPU UTILIZATION WITH DIFFERENT SLOT CONFIGURATIONS AND LRS

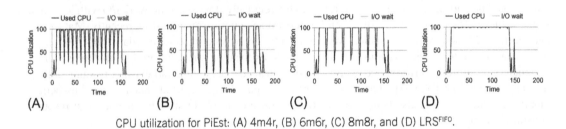

CPU utilization for PiEst: (A) 4m4r, (B) 6m6r, (C) 8m8r, and (D) LRS^{FIFO}.

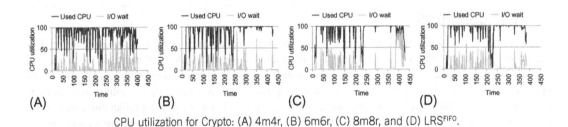

CPU utilization for Crypto: (A) 4m4r, (B) 6m6r, (C) 8m8r, and (D) LRS^{FIFO}.

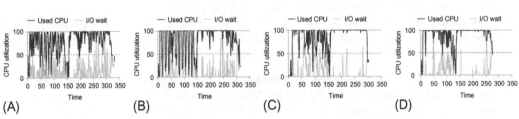

CPU utilization for Sort: (A) 4m4r, (B) 6m6r, (C) 8m8r, and (D) LRS^{FIFO}.

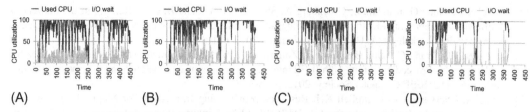

CPU utilization for TeraSort: (A) 4m4r, (B) 6m6r, (C) 8m8r, and (D) LRS^{FIFO}.

REFERENCES

[1] Greenberg A, Hamilton J, Maltz DA, Patel P. The cost of a cloud: research problems in data center networks. ACM SIGCOMM Comput Commun Rev 2008;39(1):68–73.

[2] Dean J, Ghemawat S. MapReduce: simplified data processing on large clusters. In: Proceedings of USENIX conference on Operating systems design and implementation, Berkeley, CA: USENIX Association; 2004. p. 10.

[3] Padala P, Shin KG, Zhu X, Uysal M, Wang Z, Singhal S, et al. Adaptive control of virtualized resources in utility computing environments. ACM SIGOPS Oper Syst Rev 2007;41(3):289–302.

[4] Verma A, Ahuja P, Neogi A. pMapper: power and migration cost aware application placement in virtualized systems. In: Proceedings of the 9th ACM/IFIP/USENIX international conference on Middleware. New York, NY: Springer-Verlag; 2008. p. 243–64.

[5] Ghodsi A, Zaharia M, Hindman B, Konwinski A, Shenker S, Stoica I. Dominant resource fairness: fair allocation of multiple resource types. In: Proceedings of USENIX conference on Networked systems design and implementation, Berkeley, CA: USENIX Association; 2011. p. 323–36.

[6] Hindman B, Konwinski A, Zaharia M, Ghodsi A, Joseph AD, Katz R, et al. Mesos: a platform for fine-grained resource sharing in the data center. In: Proceedings of the 8th USENIX conference on networked systems design and implementation. Berkeley, CA: USENIX Association; 2011. p. 22.

[7] Polo J, Castillo C, Carrera D, Becerra Y, Whalley I, Steinder M, et al. Resource-aware adaptive scheduling for MapReduce clusters. In: Proceedings of the 12th ACM/IFIP/USENIX international conference on Middleware. Berlin, Heidelberg: Springer-Verlag; 2011. p. 187–207.

[8] Zaharia M, Borthakur D, Sen Sarma J, Elmeleegy K, Shenker S, Stoica I. Delay scheduling: a simple technique for achieving locality and fairness in cluster scheduling. In: Proceedings of the 5th European conference on computer systems. New York, NY: ACM; 2010. p. 265–78.

[9] Resource Consumption Shaping. http://perspectives.mvdirona.com/2008/12/17/ResourceConsumption Shaping.aspx.

[10] Lu P, Lee YC, Zomaya AY. Non-intrusive slot layering in Hadoop. In: Proceedings of the 13th IEEE/ACM international symposium on cluster, cloud and the grid computing. Washington, DC: IEEE; 2013. p. 253–60.

[11] Bobroff N, Kochut A, Beaty K. Dynamic placement of virtual machines for managing SLA violations. In: Proceedings of the 10th IFIP/IEEE international symposium on integrated network management (IM). Washington, DC: IEEE; 2007. p. 119–28.

[12] Hermenier F, Lorca X, Menaud J-M, Muller G, Lawall J. Entropy: a consolidation manager for clusters. In: Proceedings of the 2009 ACM SIGPLAN/SIGOPS international conference on virtual execution environments. New York, NY: ACM; 2009. p. 41–50.

[13] Vavilapalli VK, Murthy AC, Douglas C, Agarwal S, Konar M, Graves T, et al. Apache Hadoop YARN: yet another resource negotiator. In: Proceedings of the ACM Symposium on Cloud Computing (SoCC). New York, NY: ACM; 2013.

[14] Amazon EC2 instances. http://aws.amazon.com/ec2/instance-types.

[15] Ananthanarayanan G, Kandula S, Greenberg A, Stoica I, Lu Y, Saha B, et al. Reining in the outliers in MapReduce clusters using Mantri. In: Proceedings of USENIX conference on Operating systems design and implementation. Berkeley, CA: USENIX Association; 2010. p. 1–16.

[16] Lu P, Lee YC, Wang C, Zhou BB, Chen J, Zomaya AY. Workload characteristic oriented scheduler for MapReduce. In: Proceedings of the 18th IEEE international conference on parallel and distributed systems. Washington, DC: IEEE Computer Society; 2012. p. 156–63.

[17] Verma A, Cherkasova L, Campbell RH. Resource provisioning framework for MapReduce jobs with performance goals. In: Proceedings of ACM/IFIP/USENIX international conference on Middleware. Laxenburg, Austria: International Federation for Information Processing; vol. 7049. 2011. p. 165–86.

[18] Managing a Hadoop Cluster. http://developer.yahoo.com/hadoop/tutorial/module7.html.

[19] Open MPI. http://www.open-mpi.org.

[20] Htcondor. http://research.cs.wisc.edu/htcondor/manual/v7.8/3_5Policy_Configuration.html.

[21] Capacity Scheduler Guide. http://hadoop.apache.org/docs/stable/capacityscheduler.html.

[22] Rao S, Ramakrishnan R, Silberstein A, Ovsiannikov M, Reeves D. Sailfish: a framework for large scale data processing. In: Proceedings of the ACM Symposium on Cloud Computing (SoCC). New York, NY: ACM; 2012. p. 4.

[23] Zaharia M, Konwinski A, Joseph AD, Katz R, Stoica I. Improving MapReduce performance in heterogeneous environments. In: Proceedings of USENIX conference on Operating systems design and implementation. Berkeley, CA: USENIX Association; 2008. p. 29–42.

[24] Lu P, Lee YC, Gramoli V, Leslie LM, Zomaya AY. Local resource shaper for MapReduce. In: Proceedings of the 6th international conference on cloud computing technology and science (CloudCom). Washington, DC: IEEE Computer Society; December 15–18; 2014.

[25] Clark C, Fraser K, Hand S, Hansen JG, Jul E, Limpach C, et al. Live migration of virtual machines. In: Proceedings of USENIX conference on Networked systems design and implementation. Berkeley, CA: USENIX Association; 2005. p. 273–86.

[26] Lim S-H, Huh J-S, Kim Y, Das CR. Migration, assignment, and scheduling of jobs in virtualized environment. In: Proceedings of the 3rd USENIX conference on hot topics in cloud computing. Berkeley, CA: USENIX Association; 2011. p. 2.

[27] Nathuji R, Kansal A, Ghaffarkhah A. Q-clouds: managing performance interference effects for qos-aware clouds. In: Proceedings of the 5th European conference on Computer systems. New York, NY: ACM; 2010. p. 237–50.

[28] Verma A, Ahuja P, Neogi A. Power-aware dynamic placement of HPC applications. In: Proceedings of the 22nd annual international conference on Supercomputing, ACM, New York, USA; 2008. p. 175–84.

[29] Wang A, Venkataraman S, Alspaugh S, Katz R, Stoica I. Cake: enabling high-level SLOs on shared storage systems. In: Proceedings of the ACM Symposium on Cloud Computing (SoCC). New York, NY: ACM; 2012.

[30] Ghodsi A, Zaharia M, Shenker S, Stoica I. Choosy: max-min fair sharing for datacenter jobs with constraints. In: Proceedings of the 8th European conference on Computer systems. New York, NY: ACM; 2013. p. 365–78.

[31] Babu S. Towards automatic optimization of MapReduce programs. In: Proceedings of the ACM Symposium on Cloud Computing (SoCC). New York, NY: ACM; 2010. p. 137–42.

SYSTEM OPTIMIZATION FOR BIG DATA PROCESSING

9

R. Li, X. Dong, X. Gu, Z. Xue, K. Li

9.1 INTRODUCTION

With the accelerated growth of digital information, a large amount of data is generated every day, from industrial productions to electronic commerce in life; from enterprise information management systems to e-government affairs of government departments; from social media to online video image data. According to incomplete statistics, new daily transactions of Taobao could reach 10 TB; the analysis processing data of eBay platform could go up to 100 PB; 10 million active users of Facebook [1], generate photos that can stack up at 80 Tour Eiffel daily; YouTube users upload 60 h video data every minute. According to the IDC forecasts, the amount of data stored in electronic form could reach 32 ZB globally by 2020. If one burned it to DVD discs, one could stack up dozens of back and forth from the earth to the moon base.

In recent years, Big Data [2] has become a sweeping global phenomenon and a hot topic in international academic circles. The application industries set off an unprecedented upsurge of research in this field. The data scientists, research institutes, and related companies all have proposed the concept of Big Data. However, they have not formed a unified definition of Big Data so far. The "4 V" features of Big Data implied the large quantity (volume), multimode (variety), speed (velocity), and low-density value (value). They increase the difficulty and complexity of data management and information extraction and lead that the conventional data processing is unable to meet the needs of the urgent change of data processing mode. Accordingly, the storage and management of Big Data have become a hot topic.

There are various types of real-world Big Data applications. The main processing mode can be divided into batch processing and stream processing. Batch processing is store then process, and the stream processing is straight-through processing. The processing mode of the stream processing treats the data as a stream. The data stream is composed of a constant stream of data. When new data arrive, it will be processed and returned immediately. The MapReduce programming model proposed by Google in 2004 is the most representative of the batch processing. Whether it is a stream processing or batch processing model, it is a feasible way to deal with Big Data. In the practice of Big Data processing, the combination of the two models will be used.

The data sources of Big Data are extensive. The application requirements and data types are not the same; however, the most basic processing procedure is the same. The whole Big Data processing flow can be defined as follows: With the aid of suitable tools, the data source is extracted and integrated, and the results are stored in a certain standard. Using appropriate data analysis technology to analyze the

Big Data. http://dx.doi.org/10.1016/B978-0-12-805394-2.00009-X

data stored, extract useful knowledge and use the appropriate way to show the results to the end user. Specifically, the process can be divided into data extraction and integration, data analysis, and data interpretation.

In the era of Big Data, data management, analysis, and other diverse needs to make the traditional relational database in many scenarios no longer apply. Therefore, a variety of Big Data processing tools came into being. Some of these tools are complete processing platforms, some of which are specifically tailored to the specific Big Data processing applications. Table 1 summarizes some of the mainstream processing platform and tools; most of them are based on the Hadoop function expansion or provide data interface with Hadoop. Hadoop is the most popular Big Data processing platform. Hadoop has developed into a complete ecosystem, including the file system (HDFS), database (HBase), data processing (MapReduce), and other functional modules. To some extent, Hadoop has become the de facto standard of Big Data processing tools.

Hadoop [3] has high-reliability, high-scalability, high-efficiency, and high-fault tolerance. While Hadoop has been adopted by many companies, it has some shortcomings, such as handling small files and the performance of data processing. For these problems, the study of Hadoop system performance optimization and enhancements could improve enterprise massive data processing capacity and real-time data processing, change data for the purpose of the assets, and provide references for the relevant technical personnel. In this chapter, we introduce the relevant technology of Hadoop and the system optimization of Hadoop-based Big Data processing technology, including the basic framework of Hadoop, parallel computation framework MapReduce, job scheduling of Hadoop, performance optimization of HDFS, performance optimization of HBase, and feature enhancements of Hadoop system.

In this chapter, we first compare the differences of several MapReduce-like frameworks and describe the load balancing of MapReduce and job scheduling of Hadoop. Second, we summarize performance optimization methods of HDFS and HBase. Third, we analyze and discuss a performance enhancement of Hadoop system and some directions of future optimization.

The rest of the chapter is organized as follows: Section 9.2 describes the basic framework of Hadoop system, Sections 9.3–9.7 introduce MapReduce parallel computing, framework optimized job

Table 1 List of Big Data Tools

Category		Examples
Platform	Local	Hadoop, MapR, Cloudera, Hortonworks, InfoSphere BigInsights
	Cloud	AWS, Google Compute Engine, Azure
Database	SQL	Greenplum, Aster data, Vertica
	NoSQL	HBase, Cassandra, MongoDB, Redis
	NewSQL	Spanner, Megastore, F1
Data processing	Batch	MapReduce, Dryad
	Stream	Storm, S4, Kafka
Data warehouse		Hive, HadoopDB, Hadapt
Query language		HiveQL, Pig Latin, DryadLINQ, MRQL, SCOPE
Statistic and machine learning		Mahout, Weka, R

scheduling optimization, HDFS [4] performance optimization, HBase [5], and Hadoop performance optimization enhancements individually, and finally, the summary and further research is given.

9.2 BASIC FRAMEWORK OF THE HADOOP ECOSYSTEM

Hadoop has evolved into an ecosystem from open source implementation of Google's four components, GFS [6], MapReduce, Bigtable [7], and Chubby. The basic framework of Hadoop ecosystem is shown in Fig. 1.

Fig. 1 describes each layer in the ecosystem, in addition to the core of the Hadoop distributed file system (HDFS) and MapReduce programming framework, including the closely linked HBase database cluster and ZooKeeper [8] cluster. HDFS is a master/slave architecture, which can perform a CRUD (create, read, update, and delete) operation on file by the directory entry. HDFS provides high reliability of the underlying storage support for the entire ecosystem. MapReduce adopts the "divide-and-conquer" ideas, which distributes operations of large data sets to each sub node, then merges the intermediate results of each node to get the final result. MapReduce can provide high-performance computing capacity for the system. HBase is located in a structured storage layer, and the Zookeeper cluster provides a stable service and failover mechanism for HBase.

Hadoop was originally used by applications like retrieval. However, with the advent of the era of Big Data, Hadoop was required to adapt to more extensive applications. For different types of applications, MapReduce parallel computing framework is inadequate and needs to be optimized. In order to make MapReduce process more tasks at the same time, we also need to consider the optimization of job scheduling. HBase is the open source database based on Hadoop. HBase has the problem of slow response speed and a single point of failure. In order to provide high performance, high reliability, and real-time reading and writing, we also need to optimize the performance of the HBase. HDFS is the underlying storage of Hadoop, which needs access to various sizes of files quickly in order to enhance its security performance. From the perspective of the overall balance of performance, efficiency, and availability, we can also further enhance Hadoop's features.

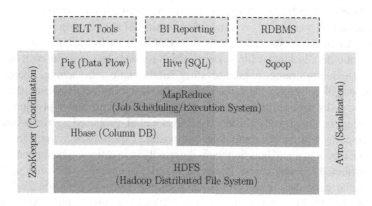

FIG. 1

The basic framework of the Hadoop ecosystem.

9.3 PARALLEL COMPUTATION FRAMEWORK: MAPREDUCE

MapReduce is a distributed programming framework proposed by Google in 2004 for massive-scale parallel data analysis. It is applicable widely, which can reduce the difficulty of parallel programming. MapReduce is designed to deal with the massive data in the field of information retrieval based on the idea of divide and conquer. With the deepening of the research, the application arrangement of MapReduce is more and more extensive. At the same time, the shortage of MapReduce in handling other types of data processing is appearing progressively, such as in iterative or recursive type of applications. With a focus on this problem, researchers have proposed a lot of improvements and optimization for MapReduce.

9.3.1 IMPROVEMENTS OF MAPREDUCE FRAMEWORK

Focusing on the deficiency of MapReduce on handling various types of applications, academicians and technicians did the following research: Yahoo! joined with the University of California, Los Angeles, and developed an improved model of MapReduce: Map-Reduce-Merge [9], which was used to handle multiple related heterogeneous data sets. The Map-Reduce-Merge adds a merge operation to combine the processing results of heterogeneous data sets. In order to solve the problem that MapReduce cannot adapt small-scale clusters well, the University of Oslo in Norway puts forward a parallel programming model named KPNs (Kahn process networks) [10]. KPNs are based on message-passing and shared-nothing models, which provide a simple and flexible tool for modeling parallel applications and could execute iterative computations automatically. However, their performance and scalability need to be verified.

The MapReduce framework itself still has some drawbacks, but some improvements have been proposed. The University of Illinois designed a parallel programming model named Barrierless MapReduce [11]. Focusing on the deficiency that the reduce operation needs to combine and sort the output key-value pairs of map tasks before processing, the model changes the features of reduce operations so that it can process the intermediate key-value pairs directly without sorting. However, it imposes new burdens on developers, who need to modify their custom reduce functions.

Limited by the design philosophy, iterative applications do not perform very well on the MapReduce framework. It is also a hot issue for researchers. The University of Tromso in Norway has improved the aforementioned Map-Reduce-Merge function and proposed Oivos [12]. It can manage and execute multiple MapReduce or Map-Reduce-Merge functions automatically so as to be more applicable for iterative applications. HaLoop [13,14] is a modified version of the Hadoop for iterative applications. The core idea of HaLoop is to improve the performance of iteration by caching static data locally. Each node caches the static data in a local file system, which remains the same in each iteration. HaLoop modifies the task scheduling strategy to take advantage of the static data caching. The tasks that process the same data input will be sent to the same node as the last iteration. However, the fixed task load allocation of reduce tasks between iterations might exist the load imbalance problem. Therefore, it is too inflexible to adapt heterogeneous clusters. Ekanayake et al. proposed a stream-based MapReduce framework that supports iterative programs, such as Twister [15]. In Twister, mappers and reducers are long running in a task pool to avoid building them repeatedly in iterations. The input and output of tasks are held in the distributed memory cache. However, in order to guarantee the same node in each iteration process, the same static data is cached in local memory; Twister uses a static scheduling strategy similar to HaLoop. Twister lacks the support of a distributed file system, and it still needs to improve its fault tolerance. Furthermore, based on the idea of asynchronous scheduling iterations, iMapReduce [16], PrIter [17], i²MapReduce [18], and iHadoop [19] were emerged in succession. They improve the

Table 2 Comparison of MapReduce-Like Frameworks

Framework	Usability	Iterative Support	Main Features
MapReduce	Easy	No	Simple and valid, based on the thought of divide-and-conquer
Barrierless MapReduce	Complex	No	Modify the Reduce function to avoid combine-and-sort intermediate results
Map-Reduce-Merge	Easy	No	Add merge operation to process heterogeneous data sets
Oivos	Easy	Yes	Can execute multiple MapReduce or Map-Reduce-Merge automatically
KPNs	Easy	Yes	Can execute iterative computations automatically
HaLoop	Complex	Yes	Extend MapReduce API; Static data caching; Based on Hadoop
Twister	Easy	Yes	Import Task Pool mechanism to avoid rebuilding of tasks; lack support of DFS

execution efficiency of iterative applications. However, these achievements are still in an exploratory stage and have limitations that hinder their utilization in production.

Table 2 shows the comparison of several MapReduce-like frameworks we mentioned earlier. In conclusion, researchers make significant efforts to try to address the imperfection of MapReduce programming model. However, all these improvements are limited to one particular aspect that has not achieved a high level of abstraction. Their performance and scalability still need to be further verified; in fact, the original MapReduce model that was proposed by Google is still the most popular framework in the industry.

9.3.2 OPTIMIZATION FOR TASK SCHEDULING AND LOAD BALANCING OF MAPREDUCE

The primitive task scheduling strategy of MapReduce only considered the distribution of data storage in map phase that MapReduce tries to assign map tasks to a node where their input data stored on. While in the reduce phase, MapReduce partitions the intermediate data output by map tasks following the principle that the key-value pairs with the same key will be sent to the same reduce task. By default, MapReduce adopts hash partitioning to partition intermediate data, that is, it takes the hash code of each key modulo the number of reduce tasks.

The hash partitioning is based on an assumption that all nodes in the cluster are homogencous (ie, the computing capability of each node is exactly the same). In fact, this assumption can hardly be set up. Experiments show that there are always some map or reduce tasks that execute much more slowly than others, therefore increasing the execution time of the whole job.

A mechanism called speculative execution is embedded into Hadoop to mitigate slow tasks. The JobTracker distinguishes slow tasks, which are called stragglers. When a tasktracker is applied for new tasks but all available tasks have already been assigned, the JobTracker would find out a straggler to launch a duplicate on the tasktracker. This mechanism tries to prevent some slow tasks or downed nodes to affect the performance of the whole job. However, in the real-world application, the mechanism is recognized as inefficient, especially in a dynamic environment.

Considering the heterogeneity and dynamics of the runtime environment, a self-adaptive scheduling policy may adapt better. Chen et al. proposed a scheduler called self-adaptive MapReduce (SAMR) [20]. By recording and analyzing the historical execution information of each node, SAMR looks up the slowest tasks dynamically. Kwon et al. at the University of Washington concentrated on the uneven distribution of input data and designed a runtime load balancing mechanism, SkewTune [21]. In a way that is similar to the speculative execution of Hadoop, when a tasktracker is idle, JobTracker will find a task with a heavy load and try to share its remaining processing with the idle tasktracker. However, in a different way from the speculative execution, SkewTune proposed a method to repartition the unprocessed input data of a task and to mitigate the subtask transparently instead of launching a duplicate of the whole task. Li et al. in National University of Defense Technology in China found the problem of an uneven data partition of hash partitioning in shuffle phase and put forward a skew-aware task scheduling iterative applications to mitigate the problem [22].

From another aspect, the spatial locality and temporal locality of the storage of input data and intermediate data would help to do a more balanced scheduling. Guo et al. proposed a scheduling policy based on the known data distribution [23]. The policy takes full account of the data distribution in the cluster and schedules tasks to proper nodes based on the priority of the tasks and nodes. Recognized that the longest approximate time to end (LATE) [24] scheduler, which is proposed and widely adopted before, did not take data locality into account, Li et al. put forward an improved version [25]. Fu et al. studied the load balancing mechanism of MapReduce framework in the environment of periodic applications [26]. Considering the similarity of its data distribution with history, they designed a load balancing strategy that partitioned intermediate data according to historical execution information in shuffle phase instead of hash partitioning to make the load more balanced. Heintz et al. at the University of Minnesota specialized in adopting MapReduce upon the geographically widely separated cluster and proposed a cross-phase optimization for MapReduce scheduling [27]. It built a feedback mechanism between the map and push phase and the shuffle and reduce phase, as well as adjusted the task scheduling scheme according to the feedback.

Generally speaking, researchers have made for fruitful discussion of the improvement of the MapReduce framework. However, for the applications that do not adopt a divide-and-conquer approach, the performance of MapReduce still needs to be promoted. In addition, there is still some room to further improve the performance of MapReduce, such as data transmission. More effective strategies for task scheduling, data caching, and load balancing are still hot topics for academics.

9.4 JOB SCHEDULING OF HADOOP

Hadoop job scheduling is the process in which JobTracker assigns tasks of submitted jobs to TaskTracker. Hadoop has a master-slave structure. This means that the master node, called JobTracker, controls the job scheduling of the whole cluster, while the rest of the slave nodes, called TaskTracker, request new tasks from the JobTracker if there are enough spare resources. In this section, we will discuss the job scheduling mechanism of Hadoop.

9.4.1 BUILT-IN SCHEDULING ALGORITHMS OF HADOOP

Many scheduling algorithms were proposed for Hadoop. Hadoop uses a first-in-first-out (FIFO) scheduling algorithm as default. The execution sequence of jobs depends on their submission time. FIFO uses a Job Queue to maintain jobs, and it is JobTracker's responsibility to assign tasks. The thought of the FIFO algorithm is very simple. However, it does not make any distinction between submitted jobs. Hadoop Fair Scheduling (HFS) [28,29] is a method that tries to allocate resources fairly, which makes each job share all resources equally. The purpose of the algorithm is to make Hadoop handle the requirements of different types of applications better. HFS adopts the thought of a hierarchical structure to assign tasks. It organizes jobs into several job pools and allocates resources fairly between pools. HFS will ensure that short jobs are completed within a reasonable amount of time and will not cause long jobs to starve to death. Capacity Scheduling [30] has a similar function to HFS, but it has obvious a difference in design and implementation. Capacity Scheduling uses multiple Job Queues to maintain jobs that are submitted by users. Each Job Queue can obtain a certain number of TaskTrackers to execute tasks according to the configuration.

Above are three common scheduling algorithms of the Hadoop platform. Generally speaking, each algorithm has its own advantages and disadvantages. The FIFO scheduling algorithm is still the most common one due to its simplicity, which is suitable for massive data processing. However, it ignores the different requirements of different type of applications. For real-time applications or interaction types of jobs, the FIFO scheduling algorithm always performs poorly. Because of this issue, HFS does better; nevertheless, it does not consider the capacity and current load of each node, which would lead to unbalanced load in a real environment. Compared with the FIFO algorithm, Capacity Scheduling algorithm supports multiuser and multijob scenarios, and it can adjust the allocation of cluster resources dynamically. However, it cannot configure and select a Job Queue automatically. If the users need to know the detailed information of a cluster, it will cause a bottleneck in the overall system performance in large-scale clusters.

Multiuser sharing and the diversification of job types put forward new requirements and ordeals for the scheduling strategy of a Hadoop cluster. Presently applied Hadoop job scheduling algorithms still have various problems, and these problems are mainly embodied in the following two aspects: (1) Job scheduling algorithms. Existing Hadoop scheduling algorithms still have some shortcomings. Considering the work characteristics, resource characteristics, and user requirements, improving fairness and efficiency of the scheduling algorithm is a key issue in the research of job scheduling. (2) Job scheduling architecture. Hadoop uses master-slave architecture to manage the resource of cluster, a master node named JobTracker is responsible for the entire cluster of job scheduling, and the rest of the nodes named TaskTrackers apply for tasks from the JobTracker when they are idle. There are two main problems with this architecture. First, one JobTracker takes charge of submitting, dispatching, and monitoring all jobs of the Hadoop cluster, as well as maintaining communication with huge numbers of TaskTrackers and monitoring the state information and statistics of all nodes in cluster. The JobTracker will be overwhelmed by the heavy load. In addition, all work of the job scheduling in the Hadoop cluster is concentrated on one JobTracker node, which increases the probability of a single-point failure (SPF). Once the JobTracker is down, the whole Hadoop platform will stop working altogether. As a result, many schemes have been proposed to improve the availability of Hadoop, many of which advise adding multiple JobTrackers to work together as backup nodes. Correspondingly, the distributed job scheduling method is also a hot area of research.

9.4.2 IMPROVEMENT OF THE HADOOP JOB SCHEDULING ALGORITHM

Focusing on the deficiency of the present Hadoop job scheduling algorithms, academia has conducted various studies. In order to make the job scheduling matchup to the expected performance requirement, some scholars proposed performance-driven schedulers to allocate resources properly in a limited-resource cluster so as to try their best to meet the performance requirement. The University of Northern California designed a job scheduling method based on job deadlines [31]. This method schedules jobs depending on the deadlines that are set by the users, but not on the number of jobs running in the cluster. According to job deadlines, they built an activity-based cost model to guide the scheduling. Polo et al. came up with a performance-driven job scheduler [32]. The scheduler could evaluate the completion time of jobs under a different resource allocation. According to the evaluated completion time, it schedules jobs with the goal of making each job meet the deadline requirements. Tang et al. oriented to the jobs with a deadline requirement upon the Hadoop platform and proposed a new job scheduler named MTSD [33]. MTSD considered the environment of heterogeneous clusters and the features of different map and reduce tasks. They classified the nodes according to the characteristics of resources and proposed different methods to evaluate the execution speed of tasks for different types of jobs. Then they built a model to predict the completion time of tasks based on the methods, scheduled jobs in the guarantee of completing before their deadline, and maximized the throughput of the cluster at the same time. Verma et al. in the University of Illinois invented a heuristic algorithm BalancedPool [34] with the goal of minimizing the execution time of the whole job set. They learned from the idea of an optimal two-stage job scheduling algorithm (Johnson) proposed in 1953. The BalancedPool can find the optimal scheduling scheme automatically based on the performance attributes of jobs in specific clusters.

In order to adapt the heterogeneity and dynamic of the runtime environment, some scholars explored self-adaptive scheduling policies. Tian et al. proposed a dynamic scheduling method for heterogeneous clusters [35]. This method classifies applications into compute-intensive and I/O-intensive; similarly, computing nodes are classified according to the CPU and I/O utilization. The classification will be determined and changed dynamically on the basis of the state information of the nodes. The research designed a policy to balance the execution of different types of applications upon different types of nodes so as to improve resource utilization efficiency. Yu et al. improved the job scheduling of Hadoop through the method of machine learning [36]. They adopted a Naive Bayes Classifier based on a feature weighting technique to classify the jobs. The research used the historical execution information as training samples and treated the usage of resources of all jobs and the state and quality of computing resources of all nodes as feature attributes.

Focusing on some specific problems, researchers have conducted representative research. Sandholm et al. came up with a scheduler based on the dynamic priority of a user-oriented cloud platform provider of acomputing service [37]. The allocation of the computing capacity was represented by the number of map or reduce task slots. This scheduler allocated task slots in proportion to the bidding of users. The more prices offered, the more capacity you get. Guyu et al. improved the scheduling model based on priority [38]. The improved model imported task priority and node priority by two parameters on the basis of the original job priority. The task priority is used to guide the scheduling of tasks inside the execution of a job. The node priority is determined by its load and historical success rate. Li et al. have put forward a fair scheduler based on the idea of data flow [39]. The scheduler organizes jobs into several data flows, and each data flow is represented by a directed acyclic graph so that each node in the graph expresses a job and each edge expresses the dependency between the two jobs. The scheduling among data flows basically adapted the idea of HFS. Ghodsi et al. proposed dominant resource fairness (DRF) [40] with the goal of a fair allocation scheme of multiple resources for multiusers in large-scale clusters. The research defined the resource with the highest usage percentage of the amount of cluster as its dominant resource. DRF achieved fairness scheduling by balancing the dominant resource of all users. Although this method pursued fairness so much that it did not meet the practical demand, its core idea of resource management was accepted and improved by Mesos and YARN.

9.4.3 IMPROVEMENT OF THE HADOOP JOB MANAGEMENT FRAMEWORK

Considering the problem of SPF in Hadoop job management framework, experts and scholars have done much research. One of the most mainstreamed ideas is to share the work of JobTracker to several nodes so as to reduce the probability through lightening the burden on the nodes.

Industry invested massive experiments in this research field. In Apache's project of the next generation of MapReduce (MRv2 or YARN) [41,42], engineers advocated to divide the responsibility of JobTracker into two parts (ie, task monitoring and resource management) and to distribute them into the cluster. YARN will launch an ApplicationMaster (AM) for each application to schedule and monitor tasks of its own, as well as to apply resources for execution from a global ResourceManager (RM). The global RM's responsibility is to manage and assign the resource of the whole cluster. In this way, the JobTracker in original Hadoop is divided into AM and RM two modules, and the AMs are distributed into the cluster. Facebook had made an open source code of its next generation of distributed computing platform Corona [43]. Its design motive and implementation strategy are almost the same with YARN. A Corona Manager is in charge of the management and assignment of cluster resource like RM in YARN. Corona JobTracker is similar to AM in that it undertakes the monitoring and fault-tolerance of applications. As with YARN, each Corona JobTracker is responsible for one application.

Academia also launched research for many years on such an issue. To optimize the performance of JobTracker, the IBM Almaden research center came up with a more flexible scheduler policy on the basis of HFS [44]. The scheduler has the traits of HFS. Moreover, it allows users to choose and optimize various parameters. Xu et al. drew lessons from YARN that decompose the work of JobTracker [45], which leads to the separation of task monitoring and resource management. They added a new ResManageNode to manage the resource of the cluster, while the function of task monitoring was reserved to the JobTracker. The JobTracker would synchronize dynamically a message necessary for task scheduling to the ResManageNode by a heartbeat mechanism. The ResManageNode would allocate resources to tasks and report the allocating results to the JobTracker. This scheme used two nodes to share the work of the original JobTracker; while it lightened the burden of the master node, it did not solve the problem of SPF completely.

The job scheduling algorithm has become pluggable components of the Hadoop platform, which benefits researchers as they carry out further exploration and helps to raise creative suggestions. Fairer and more efficient scheduling algorithms are still a hot issue for scholars and engineers; moreover, the master-slave scheduling framework will be another bone of contention. On the one hand, the load is too heavy for one master node to control all of the management of the whole system, which will certainly become a bottleneck in large-scale clusters. On the other hand, once the master node goes down, the whole system will be paralyzed. Thus, the resource management and scheduling will be conducted through the collaboration of multiple nodes, so that those nodes can back each other up.

9.5 PERFORMANCE OPTIMIZATION OF HDFS

The distributed file system is one of the core technologies in a cloud computing platform, and it is also the current research focus. There has emerged many distributed file systems in the industry, such as the GFS [6], HDFS [4], Haystack [46], and TFS [47], wherein HDFS is an open source version of GFS. It has been researched extensively, and it has been widely used in commercial enterprises such as Yahoo!, Cloudera, and Mapr. HDFS has good expansion capability, and it can store and process massive amounts of data reliably. It can also be used for low-cost business machines and for reducing development costs. Data can be processed in parallel to improve the efficiency of the system. It can automatically maintain the data copy, and after a failure, it can automatically rearrange computing tasks. Therefore, many large enterprises use HDFS to handle massive amounts of data. However, there are still many problems seriously restricting the further development of HDFS. HDFS is optimized through many ways in academia, including modifying the underlying traditional file system of HDFS. Its modification and some improvement in high-level optimization top on HDFS. We analyze the small file performance optimization and security performance optimization in the following.

9.5.1 SMALL FILE PERFORMANCE OPTIMIZATION

HDFS is designed for the efficient storage of and access to massive big files. It cuts large user files into a number of data blocks (such as 64 M). Metadata is stored in a metadata server while the data blocks are stored in the data servers. When dealing with small files, the number of data blocks in the file system increased dramatically. It also raises two issues: The first is the problem of a limited total number of files. A sharp increase of metadata results in the number of files and data blocks has limitations by the metadata server memory. The second is the performance problem. Traditional file systems have low performance when processing small files. As a consequence, there is a sharp performance decline in processing small files of data servers. Improving the ability of a distributed file system to handle a huge number of small files has become an urgent problem.

In recent years, Hadoop provides three solutions for the handle of small files, namely archive technology, sequence file technology, and merging file technology. These methods require users to write their own programs, which is why they are not widely adopted.

In view of the discrete random evenly distributed small file access, Fu et al. [48] proposed optimizing access efficiency of local blocks in data servers to optimize the performance of the distributed file system. They presented a flat lightweight file system called FlatLFS, in which the user data are managed flat in disks. FlatLFS is supposed to substitute the traditional file system when accessing user data for upper DFSs. With the improvement of the performance of small data block processing on the data servers by FlatLFS, the performance of the whole DFSs is greatly improved. But it is at the expense of flexibility in exchange for high efficiency and it is only fit for the data block management for a background data server, not for the general-purpose file directly to the user data management. Zhao et al. [49] proposed performance-optimized small file storage system access (SFSA) strategies, which not only enhance the access performance of small files, but also improve the utilization of disk space. According to the principle of locality, SFSA uses the policy of "sending high-frequency access bulk files in advance," which is also possible to optimize the performance of file transformation. Ma et al. [50] proposed a distributed file system based on distributed indexing and cataloging Polymerization—Ultra Virtual File System (HVFS) to manage billions of small files to support high-concurrency, high throughput, and low-latency access. As for the storage and retrieval of large amounts of small files, Yu et al. [51] designed and implemented a scalable, flexible distributed file system called MSFSS. It builds on the basis of the existing traditional file system. MSFSS automatically puts the file to the most appropriate file system based on the file access patterns and optimizes metadata size, separates the metadata operations from the file data transformation, and implements batch metadata operations to avoid the central bottleneck. At the same time, the system provides data migration, hot file caching, and replication to provide high scalability and throughput operation services. Mackey et al. [52] proposed a mechanism for effective storage of small files that improves metadata space utilization on HDFS—Har filing system, which has better metadata operations and more effectively HDFS usage. However, the mechanism is based on a quota of the file system's allocating space for each client and the number of files. It optimized Hadoop compression methods to better utilize HDFS, and provided new job functions to allow jobs directory and file archiving to run MapReduce program that can be completed and not terminated by JobTracker because of the quota policy. It supports random access for internal files. However, handling Har small files remains inefficient.

These optimizations are all made on HDFS. Additionally, merging the small files into large files and then storing them on HDFS to reduce the I/O access are also much mentioned as an optimization method in academia. According to the characteristics of the WebGIS system, Liu et al. [53] presented a method to optimize the I/O performance of small files on HDFS. Small files are combined to form large files to reduce the number of files and create index for each file. At the same time, according to features of WebGIS access patterns, the files are nearly grouped and some of the latest version of the data is retained; as a result, the WebGIS system performance has greatly improved. According to the features of Bluesky System (China e-learning sharing system), Dong et al. [54] proposed solutions of small file storage options on HDFS. One is merging the files that belong to the same courseware into a large file to improve storage efficiency of small files. The other is the proposed two prefetching mechanism, namely, the index file and data file, prefetching to improve the reading efficiency of small files. Liu et al. [55] stored a large number of small files into one block and stored metadata information about these small files in the Datanode memory in order to optimize the I/O performance of small files on HDFS. Zhang et al. [56] proposed a method based on a small file merging HIFM (hierarchy index file merging), which considers the directory structure of small files and correlations between small files to merge the small files into large files and generate a stratification index. Index files are managed by the combination of centralized storage and distributed storage and realize the index file preloaded. Meanwhile, it uses a data prefetching mechanism to improve the efficiency of the sequential access of small files. HIFM can effectively improve the storage and reading efficiency of small files and significantly reduce the memory overhead of DataNode and NameNode. However, it does not support deletion and update operations on small files, and it is only suitable for the application scenarios, which have standardized directory structure and bulk data storage. Li et al. [57] proposed a new efficient approach named SmartFS. By analyzing the file access log to obtain the access behavior of users, SmartFS established a probability model of file associations. The model was the reference of a merging algorithm to merge the relevant small files into large files to be stored on HDFS. When a file was accessed, the related files were prefetched according to the prefetching algorithm to accelerate the access speed. At the same time, they put forward a cache replacement algorithm. It saved the metadata space of NameNode in HDFS and interaction between users and HDFS, as well as improved the storing and accessing efficiency of small files on HDFS. Zhang et al. [58] presented a small file based on a relational database consolidation strategy. It firstly creates a file for each user and then uploads the file's metadata information to a relational database. The file is then written to the user's file when the user uploads small files. Finally, the user reads small files via a streaming mode according to the metadata information. When the user reads a file whose size is smaller than the file block, DataNode takes a load balancing strategy and stores data transfers directly so as to reduce the pressure on the master server and improve the efficiency of file transfer. Yan et al. [59] proposed a middleware HMFS to improve the efficiency of storing and accessing small files on HDFS. It is made up of three layers: (a) file operation interfaces to make it easier for software developers to submit different file requests, (b) file management tasks to merge small files into big ones or extract small files from big ones in the background, and (c) file buffers to improve the I/O performance. HMFS boosts the file upload speed by using an asynchronous write mechanism and the file download speed by adopting prefetching and caching strategy.

This approach based on merging could theoretically increase the storage and reading speed of small files, reduce the write number of small files on data nodes, and reduce the frequently block allocation problem of the master server. However, the master server needs to open up an additional cache to integrate small files, and it needs to create index structure of small files, which brings the same master server bottlenecks. The client firstly needs to send small files to the master server to cache. When a problem arises with the master server, it will result in data loss security problems. In addition, the client needs to find the appropriate file block in the index structure based on the file name, and this process may need to read the corresponding index files on disk. The speed is very slow.

Due to increasing small file applications, the HBase based on HDFS is one of the small files problems solutions. However, as a structured data storage solution, it is not a good solution. Many NameNodes structures are a solution that is researched much now. However, if a particular NameNode caches excessive metadata and receives many clients' requests, it will also cause single NameNode bottlenecks. Simultaneously, when the number of NameNode changes and a NameNode fails, it needs to move large amounts of metadata, which is a very complex process. During the migration process of metadata, it will seriously affect system performance.

9.5.2 HDFS SECURITY OPTIMIZATION

Cloud computing security and Big Data security are important topics; HDFS security has also become a research hotspot. The security and reliability of HDFS primarily lie in the following three areas: (1) In terms of certification, when a user logs in, as long as the user name and group name are consistent with the user information logged in the HDFS process, the authentication is successful. The attackers only set the user name and the group information with a legitimate user's information unanimously. They could access the user's data on HDFS. While DataNode logs on to a specific HDFS cluster, NameNode has no certification to DataNode. (2) In terms of user authorization, when client interacts with NameNode, NameNode conducted nine bits permission judgment, the information is set by the file owner, and adopted by discretionary access control. This mechanism lacks high-level security. At the same time, users receive the file address information returned by NameNode so that they can directly access to Datanode, which has no permission judgment. (3) In terms of data disaster recovery, HDFS's solution is mainly based on copying or mirroring backup. In order to prevent temporary disaster, more than doubled equipment and data resources are idle, which results in a great waste of resources and money. Many academic researchers conducted in-depth study of these issues.

O'Malley et al. [60] proposed a secure architecture of HDFS, which used the Kerberos protocol over SSL to ensure strong mutual authentication and access control. Cordova et al. [61] proposed the usc of SSL and encrypted the distributed file system prototype. However, its write speed is slower than the general HDFS 10 times. Based on the study of Kerberos and RBAC model, Cai et al. [62] proposed token-based authentication mechanisms. The access control mechanism based on a token and access control model based on the domain and role is used to solve the problem of authentication and authorization on HDFS. There are four objectives, namely, (a) unauthenticated users cannot access the HDFS, (b) users can access a file if and only if they have permission to access the file, (c) Datanode needs to authenticate the user, and (d) refinement client access control grain to DataNode. In terms of the problems that the data cannot be completely destroyed and lead to data leakage in HDFS, Qin et al. [63] designed a multilevel secure data destruction mechanism on HDFS. On the one hand, the mechanism overwrites the original data by the overwritten algorithm before deleting them. This can effectively prevent malicious data recovery and data leakage in the cloud, so as to achieve the complete elimination of data. On the other hand, the mechanism utilizes a multiple security level definite to take a variety of overwriting data by destruction algorithms. Thus, it balances the security needs and performance requirements. In facing the environment of a private cloud expanding to a public cloud, Shen et al. [64] proposed architecture with implementation of security services, including data isolation service, secure cloud data migration in cloud services, and secure data migration services between cloud services. They implemented a prototype with three security policies based on HDFS systems. Majors et al. [65] proposed application-level encryption of MapReduce, which provides support to a secure file system. Lin et al. [66] proposed a hybrid encryption HDFS of HDFS-RSA and HDFS-Pairing. However, its read performance and write performance are lower than the general HDFS. Hadoop does not support encrypted storage for HDFS block. To tackle this problem, Park et al. [67] proposed Hadoop security architecture that adds encryption and decryption capabilities in HDFS. AES encryption and decryption compression codec in Hadoop to make HDFS even more secure, and the computational overhead that MapReduce jobs generated in the encryption HDFS is affordable.

Nguyen et al. [68] proposed a novel method to encrypt files while being uploaded. Data read from a file is transferred to HDFS across a buffer. The encryption, which is transparent to the user, is applied to the buffer's data before being sent to an out stream to write to HDFS. The time needed for the whole process is much less than what is needed for the conventional method. Qian et al. [69] proposed a novel model of cloud-secure storage, which combined the HDFS with symmetric and public-key cryptography. The model used the HDFS as the storage platform and the XML format as the logical storage structure. It not only solves the problem of storing massive data, but it also provides data access control mechanisms to ensure sharing data files with confidentiality and integrity among users in cloud environment. Shen et al. [70] proposed an architectural design for enforcing data security services on the layer of HDFS in the PSC, including secure data isolation service, secure intracloud data migration service, and secure intercloud data migration service. The prototype implemented as pluggable security modules in accordance with our custom security policies through AOP (aspect-oriented programming) method was given. Cohen et al. [71] described the threat against Hadoop in a sensitive environment, and how and why an advanced persistent threat (APT) could target Hadoop, as well as how standard-based trusted computing could be an effective approach to a layered threat mitigation. Later, they created a trusted Apache Hadoop Distributed File System and evaluated a threat model for HDFS [72]. They addressed a set of common security concerns within HDFS through infrastructure and software involving data-at-rest encryption and integrity validation.

As to the problems of low storage space utilization efficiency and low data recovery efficiency brought by HDFS' multiple-copy disaster design, many scholars combined erasure codes, introduced coding and decoding modules, and designed file systems REPERA [73] and Noah [74]. They are both based on HDFS, which can ensure the cluster data security, improve data recovery speed, and reduce the cost of space and overall storage.

At present, most of the Hadoop clusters set up by major commercial companies are in private cloud architecture and are generally built for internal use. However, the cost of building private clouds is really high and would result in a waste of IT facilities. In order to enhance data security and increase user privacy protection in HDFS, they need to balance the premise of data security and high system efficiency, including the system memory space utilization and postdisaster data recovery efficiency.

From the above discussion, we can see that many researchers have conducted fruitful research on small file performance optimization and security enhancements in HDFS. While enhancing the HDFS security and privacy, we also need to optimize the performance of HDFS efficiency. Meanwhile, we need further research on low latency access, as well as maintain cache coherency and multiuser write and arbitrary modification in HDFS.

9.6 PERFORMANCE OPTIMIZATION OF HBASE

HBase [5] is a top Apache open source project, which is separated from Hadoop [3]. HBase is the database system, which possesses the characteristic of high-reliability, high-performance, column storage, scalable, and real-time read and write. It can directly use the local file system and HDFS file storage system. However, there are some problems in the applications. Carstoiu et al. [75] evaluated the performances of the HBase, including the random writing and reading of rows, sequential writing and sequential reading, and how are they affected by increasing the number of column families and using MapReduce functions. Rahman et al. [76] analyzed the performance of HBase, conducted comprehensive experiments, and identified different factors contributing to the overall latency of get and put operations. The experimental results showed that the HBase communication stack and associated operations need to be redesigned for high-performance networks like InfiniBand. In order to efficiently insert and read the massive data in business, HBase needs to be further optimized. We will discuss the optimization of HBase in three major aspects: framework, storage, and application optimization; load balancing; and configuration optimization.

9.6.1 HBASE FRAMEWORK, STORAGE, AND APPLICATION OPTIMIZATION

The current HBase is implemented by using the Java Sockets interface. Due to the overhead of the cross platform, HBase is difficult to provide high-performance services for data intensive applications. Huang et al. [77] presented a novel design of HBase for remote direct memory access (RDMA) capable networks via Java native nterface. Then they extended the existing open source HBase software and make it RDMA capable. The performance evaluation reveals that the latency of HBase get operations can be reduced. The existing interface of HBase for MapReduce to access speed is too low, so Tian et al. [78] offered an improved method. It splits the table that is not based on its logical storage element called "Region," but on its physical storage element called "block" and uses a property scheduling policy, makes data reading and computing executes in the same node. Huang et al. [79] showed how to implement the set data structure and its operations in a scalable manner on top of Hadoop HBase, and then discussed the limitations of implementing this data structure in the Hadoop ecosystem.

Their primary conclusion provided an excellent framework to implement scalable data structures for the Hadoop ecosystem.

The compression technology is commonly used to optimize HBase storage. Based on the existing compression system and the fact that column-oriented database stores information by column and the column property values are in high similarity, Luo et al. [80] proposed some lightweight introducing stored database of compression algorithm, which takes column property values as a coding units for data compression. In addition, based on the situation that different data matches different compression algorithm, they presented a method that is based on the dynamic selection strategy of a Bayesian classifier compression algorithm. According to the Bayesian formula, different data sections choose different compression algorithms, which make it possible to compress the data to reach the best compression effect. Cheng et al. [81] designed an inverted index table that includes a keyword, document ID, and position list; the table can save a lot of storage space. On the basis of the table, they provide key as dictionary compression with high compression ratio and high decompression rate for the data block.

In the aspect of HBase application, Karana [82] built a search engine, whose index is on Hadoop and HBase, to deploy in a cluster environment. Retrieval applications by nature involve read-intensive operations, which optimize the Hadoop and HBase. Ma et al. [83] proposed ST-HBase (spatiotextual HBase) that can deal with large-scale geotagged objects. ST-HBase can support high-insert throughput while providing efficient spatial keyword queries. In ST-HBase, they leverage an index module layered over a key-value store. The underlying key-value store enables the system to sustain high-insert throughput and deal with large-scale data. The index layer can provide efficient spatial keyword query processing. Awasthit et al. [84] explored the feasibility of introducing flash SSDs for HBase. They perform a qualitative and supporting quantitative assessment of the implications of storing the system components of HBase in flash SSDs. The proposed system performs 1.5–2.0 times better than a complete disk-based system. Zhang et al. [85] presented HBaseMQ, the first distributed message queuing system based on the bare-bones HBase. HBaseMQ directly inherits HBase's properties such as scalability and fault tolerance, enabling HBase users to rapidly instantiate a message queuing system with no extra program deployment or modification to HBase. HBaseMQ effectively enhances the data processing capability of an existing HBase installation. These optimization methods can significantly improve the performance of the specific system; however, it is only optimized for specific applications, and the popularity is not high.

9.6.2 LOAD BALANCING OF HBASE

The load balancing of HBase can be considered from two aspects of hardware and software. In terms of hardware, Facebook [1] built excellent physical architecture for Big Data services, such as the message service of an HBase cluster, which is divided into multiple clusters according to the user. Each cluster has 100 servers, including one NameNode and five racks, and each rack has a ZooKeeper [8] server. At the same time, the Facebook team adds a Bloom filter in HBase LSM Tree and optimizes the local read of DataNode and cache NameNode metadata, which achieve better disk-reading efficiency [86]. As for Taobao, which uses public HDFS [4] to minimize the impact of Compact, and each HDFS cluster is not more than 100 units in size. In HDFS cluster, multiple HBase clusters are built, and each HBase cluster has a master and a backup master. In addition, the Taobao team uses the ZooKeeper cluster to guarantee the independence of the HBase cluster. For the design of the software, in order to reduce the overload of the original database, a mirror database system is created for load balance. Researchers [87] designed HBase snapshot, and the proposed archive-on-delete function at the file level. That is to say, when a snapshot is created, the system only records all data files in a table without performing any copies of data. When the data file is to be deleted, and the system backups the data to ensure the normal access to the snapshot data. Therefore, the load balancing of HBase should be performed according to a specific application, a reasonable arrangement of cluster architecture, optimization software design, and avoidance of single database heavy load.

9.6.3 OPTIMIZATION OF HBASE CONFIGURATION

According to the read-and-write optimization of HBase table, we usually do three types of settings: (1) A concurrent read/write of multiple HTable, in which we create multiple HTable clients to read/write, which improve the throughput of reading data. (2) A batch read/write, in which we can access/write multiple rows to reduce the I/O overhead of network. (3) A concurrent read/write using multiple threads, a method that not only ensures that a small amount of written data can be flushed in a relatively short period of time, but also ensures the large amount of written data to be flushed when the buffer is full.

According to the optimization of HBase table's design, the common method is to precreate some empty regions in order to accelerate the batch write speed. Because the HBase data model is sorted by row-key storage, all of the continuous data will be loaded to the cache at the same time. Therefore, good row-key design can make batch read easily. In practical applications, a major compact can be used manually to form a large StoreFile with a row-key modification. At the same time, StoreFile can be set to reduce the incidence of split.

For the HBase block cache, there is a BlockCache and N Memstores in a RegionServer, and the size of the cache is not greater than the default value of HBase. The optimization of HBase block cache needs to consider the specific applications.

In summary, HBase is widely employed in many commercial production systems. The basic approach is to upgrade the business module on the foundation of original HBase. Then they develop the optimized patches of HBase. For the ordinary operators, they can adjust the configuration to achieve better performance of HBase. In recent years, the researchers focus on the optimization of framework, storage, applications, and load balance scheme of HBase.

9.7 PERFORMANCE ENHANCEMENT OF HADOOP SYSTEM

In recent years, Hadoop is widely used as a Big Data processing platform in various applications. Many works have been proposed to enhance the performance of the Hadoop system, including the high efficiency of query processing, index construction and usage, construction of data warehouse, and applying Hadoop to database management, data mining, and recommendation systems. Xu et al. [73] present five kinds of research directions of Hadoop optimization, including enhancing the performance, increasing the utilization rate, improving the efficiency, improving the availability, and various problems of consistency constraints. In the following sections, we will discuss the most focused issues in this area.

9.7.1 EFFICIENCY OPTIMIZATION OF HADOOP

To store and process large-scale data, the database management system (DBMS) and Hadoop have different merits. DBMS has outstanding performance in processing structured data, while it is relatively difficult for processing extremely large-scale data. Hadoop is suitable for processing large-scale data with a significant improvement of performance. The researchers believe that the combination of DBMS and Hadoop can effectively improve the performance of Hadoop.

Pavlo et al. [88] conclude that MapReduce is the most important model to process and analyze large-scale data. They compare DBMS and MapReduce computation models and propose that DBMS has significantly better executive performance, although data loading and parallel proposing of DBMS requires more time than MapReduce system.

Du et al. [89] present that when facing Big Data challenges, the traditional DBMS cannot accomplish the task of Big Data analysis, while MapReduce technology has the advantage of large-scale parallel processing. However, there are still a series of performance bottlenecks in the MapReduce processing model. Integrating DBMS and MapReduce technologies and designing technical framework of containing both advantages are the trends of Big Data analysis technology. Wang et al. [90] discuss the integration of DBMS and MapReduce technologies and propose a hybrid framework to solve the Big Data problem.

Some researchers use the locality characteristics of Big Data to optimize Hadoop. Hadoop cannot coordinately adjust the relevant data on the same configuration node, which is a main bottleneck for Hadoop system. Eltabakh et al. [91] present CoHadoop, a lightweight extension of Hadoop, which allows the application program to control the storage location of data and keeps the flexibility of Hadoop. The users do not need to convert the data format. It performs better than the algorithms based on redistribution and map-only algorithms. He et al. [92] proposed a new MapReduce scheduling strategy, Matchmaking, to enhance the data locality of Map tasks. It needs no complex adjustment of parameters compared to the similar algorithms. Meanwhile, it has better data locality and less response time. Xie et al. [93] introduce a prefetch mechanism in the MapReduce model while maintaining the compatibility with traditional Hadoop. When running data intensive applications on Hadoop clusters, a certain amount of data are automatically loaded into memory before being assigned to computing nodes to ease the data transmission overload problem through estimating the execution time of each task.

In order to support the applications that are not programmed by Java, a flow mechanism is introduced in Hadoop. It allows for communicating with external programs through pipeline. Due to the additional costs of pipeline communication and context switching, the performance of the Hadoop flow is significantly worse than the traditional Hadoop. Lai et al. [94] propose ShmStreaming to solve this problem, which can achieve a 20–30% performance improvement of Hadoop flow through sharing the memory.

Fault tolerance is one of the primary concerns of a cloud computing platform. When many clients require services to a server concurrently, the server may be overloaded and result in errors. The dynamic load balancing can be used to avoid this problem. Roy et al. [95] study how to enhance the efficiency of cloud computing through dynamic load balancing technology. They propose an algorithm based on the CPU utilization rate. When the rate is less than the given value, the client requests will be served. Otherwise, the requests will be transferred to other servers through the load balancer.

Chen et al. [96] propose a prediction-execution strategy to improve the task execution time and the cluster throughput of MapReduce. Premchaiswadi et al. [97] improve the performance of large-scale data processing by adjusting and optimizing the MapReduce operations. Adjusting the Hadoop configuration parameters can directly affect the performance of MapReduce workflow.

Rao et al. [98] study the improved scheduling strategies of Hadoop/MapReduce in cloud environments and present the optimization directions of Hadoop scheduling. Cherniak et al. [99] present a series of optimization methods for MapReduce. Based on data dependency, query optimization, and Hadoop workload, they can allocate the appropriate amount of resources to parallel Hive tasks.

In a traditional cloud system, the energy efficiency is not very good for the typical CPU-intensive, I/O-intensive, and interactive tasks. Song et al. [100] propose an energy efficiency model and the measurement methods in the cloud environments. They discuss the mathematical expressions, measurement methods, calculation methods, energy-efficient models, and the energy-efficient characteristics of typical operations in cloud computing. Kim et al. [101] study the evaluation of Hadoop optimization and discuss the upper and lower bounds of optimization effect by identifying the related factors.

9.7.2 AVAILABILITY OPTIMIZATION OF HADOOP

He et al. [102] propose a distributed Hadoop/MapReduce platform named HOG (Hadoop on the Grid). To relive the unreliability of a grid in Hadoop, HOG can provide a flexible, dynamic MapReduce environment. Through transplanting the modified Hadoop components to the existing MapReduce applications in order to conduct the assessment, HOG can be successfully extended to 1100 nodes on the grid and achieve the same reliability as the special Hadoop cluster.

In default, the computing nodes in the Hadoop cluster are isomorphic. However, Hadoop may meet problems in heterogeneous environments. Zaharia et al. [24] study the task of scheduling optimization for MapReduce in the heterogeneous environments and design a LATE algorithm. This algorithm has high robustness and can reduce the response time. Xie et al. [103] improve the data placement strategy under the heterogeneous Hadoop cluster so that each node had a relatively balanced load of data processing. It uses the locality characteristic of data to improve the performance of MapReduce. Ahmad et al. [104] study the poor performance problem of MapReduce under the heterogeneous cluster and present Tarazu to optimize MapReduce in the heterogeneous cluster. Hansen et al. [105] optimize the Hadoop cluster through adjusting the parameter configuration and verify the performance improvement in the actual Hadoop clusters. In the Hadoop family, in order to solve the problem of the heavy load of jobtracker, the basic design idea of Yarn is to split the JobTracker into two separate services: a global resource manager ResourceManager and each application specific ApplicationMaster. In order to further improve the real time of large data processing, Spark is a fast and general engine for large-scale data processing.

In summary, Hadoop becomes an essential platform for Big Data processing. Optimizing the Hadoop system is a meaningful work. The current work focuses on combining Hadoop with DBMS to improve the performance by optimizing the scheduling efficiency of Hadoop with load balancing, predictive execution, and parameter adjustment, as well as improving the performance of heterogeneous Hadoop system.

9.8 CONCLUSIONS AND FUTURE DIRECTIONS

Hadoop becomes the most important platform for Big Data processing, while MapReduce on top of Hadoop is a popular parallel programming model. This chapter discusses the optimization technologies of Hadoop and MapReduce, including the MapReduce parallel computing framework optimization, task scheduling optimization, HDFS optimization, HBase optimization, and feature enhancement of Hadoop. Based on the analysis of the advantages and disadvantages of the current schemes and methods, we present the future research directions for the system optimization of Big Data processing as follows:

1. Implementation and optimization of a new generation of the MapReduce programming model that is more general. The improvement of the MapReduce programming model is generally confined to a particular aspect, thus the shared memory platform was needed. The implementation and optimization of the MapReduce model in a distributed mobile platform will be an important research direction.
2. A task-scheduling algorithm that is based on efficiency and equity. The existing Hadoop scheduling algorithms consider much on equity. However, the computation in real applications often requires higher efficiency. Combining the system resources and the current state of the workload, fairer and more efficient scheduling algorithms are still an important research direction.
3. Data access platform optimization. At present, HDFS and HBase can support structure and unstructured data. However, the rapid generation of Big Data produces more real-time requirements on the underlying access platform. Hence, the design of the access platform with high-efficiency, low-delay, complex data-type support becomes more challenging.
4. Hadoop optimization based on multicore and high-speed storage devices. Future research should consider the characteristics of the Big Data system, integrating multicore technologies, multi-GPU models, and new storage devices into Hadoop for further performance enhancement of the system.

REFERENCES

[1] Borthakur D, Gray J, Sarma JS, et al. Aiyer: Apache Hadoop goes realtime at Facebook. In: Proceedings of the ACM SIGMOD international conference on management of data, Athens, Greece, Jun. 12–16; 2011.
[2] Suchanek F, Weikum G. Knowledge harvesting in the big-data era. In: Proceedings of the 2013 ACM SIGMOD international conference on management of data, New York, USA, Jun. 22–27; 2013.
[3] Apache, Hadoop, http://Hadoop.apache.org/index.html; [2015-05-19].
[4] Apache, HDFS Architecture, http://hadoop.apache.org/docs/r1.2.1/hdfs_design.html; [2015-05-19].
[5] Apache, HBase, http://HBase.apache.org/; [2015-05-19].
[6] Ghemawat S, Gobioff H, Leung S. The Google file system. In: Proceedings of the 19th ACM symposium on operating systems principles (SOSP'03), Bolton Landing, NY, USA, Oct. 19–22; 2003.
[7] Chang F, Dean J, Ghemawat S, et al. Bigtable: a distributed storage system for structured data. In: Proceedings of the 7th symposium on operating system design and implementation Seattle (OSDI'06), Seattle, WA, USA, Nov. 6–8; 2006.

[8] Apache, ZooKeeper, http://zookeeper.apache.org/; [2015-05-19].

[9] Yang H, Dasdan A, Hsiao RL, et al. Map-reduce-merge: simplified relational data processing on large clusters. In: Proceedings of the 2007 ACM SIGMOD international conference on management of data (SIGMOD'07), Beijing, China, Jun. 12–14; 2007.

[10] Vrba Z, Halvorsen P, Griwodz C, et al. Kahn process networks are a flexible alternative to MapReduce. In: Proceedings of the 11th IEEE international conference on high performance computing and communications (HPCC'09), Seoul, Korea, Jun. 25–27; 2009.

[11] Verma A, Zea N, Cho B, et al. Breaking the MapReduce stage barrier. In: Proceedings of the 2010 IEEE international conference on cluster computing (CLUSTER'10), Heraklion, Crete, Greece, Sep. 20–24; 2010.

[12] Valvag SV, Johansen D. Oivos: simple and efficient distributed data processing. In: Proceedings of the 10th IEEE international conference on high performance computing and communications (HPCC'08), Dalian, China, Sep. 25–27; 2008.

[13] Bu Y, Howe B, Balazinska M, et al. HaLoop: Efficient iterative data processing on large clusters. Proc VLDB Endowment 2010;3(1–2):285–96.

[14] Bu Y, Howe B, Balazinska M, et al. The HaLoop approach to large-scale iterative data analysis. VLDB J 2012;21(2):169–90.

[15] Ekanayake J, Li H, Zhang B, et al. Twister: a runtime for iterative MapReduce. In: Proceedings of the 19th ACM international symposium on high performance distributed computing (HPDC'10), Chicago, Illinois, USA, Jun. 21–25; 2010.

[16] Zhang Y, Gao Q, Gao L, et al. iMapReduce: a distributed computing framework for iterative computation. J Grid Comput 2012;10(1):47–68.

[17] Zhang Y, Gao Q, Gao L, et al. PrIter: a distributed framework for prioritized iterative computations. In: Proceedings of the 2nd ACM symposium on cloud computing (SoCC'11), Cascais, Portugal, Oct. 26–28; 2011.

[18] Zhang Y, Chen S. i2MapReduce: incremental iterative MapReduce. In: Proceedings of the 2nd international workshop on cloud intelligence (Cloud-I'13), Cascais, Portugal, Oct. 26–28; 2011.

[19] Elnikety E, Elsayed T, Ramadan HE. iHadoop: asynchronous iterations for MapReduce. In: Proceedings of the IEEE 3rd international conference on cloud computing technology and science (CloudCom'11), Athens, Greece, Nov. 29–Dec. 1; 2011.

[20] Chen Q, Zhang D, Guo M, et al. Samr: a self-adaptive MapReduce scheduling algorithm in heterogeneous environment. In: Proceedings of the 10th IEEE international conference on computer and information technology (CIT'10), Bradford, West Yorkshire, UK, Jun. 29–Jul. 1; 2010.

[21] Kwon YC, Balazinska M, Howe B, et al. Skewtune: mitigating skew in mapreduce applications. In: Proceedings of the 2012 ACM SIGMOD international conference on management of data (SIGMOD'12), Scottsdale, AZ, USA, May 20–24; 2012.

[22] Li D, Chen Y, Hai RH. Skew-aware task scheduling in clouds. In: Proceedings of the 7th international symposium on service oriented system engineering (SOSE'13), San Francisco, CA, USA, Mar. 25–28; 2013.

[23] Guo L, Sun H, Luo Z. A data distribution aware task scheduling strategy for MapReduce system. In: Proceedings of the first international conference on cloud computing, Beijing, China, Dec. 1–4; 2009.

[24] Zaharia M, Konwinski A, Joseph AD, et al. Improving MapReduce performance in heterogeneous environments. In: Proceedings of the 8th USENIX symposium on operating systems design and implementation (OSDI'08), San Diego, California, USA, Dec. 8–10; 2008.

[25] Li L, Tang Z, Li R. New improvement of the Hadoop relevant data locality scheduling algorithm based on LATE. Comput Sci 2011;38(11):67–70.

[26] Fu J, Du Z. Load balancing strategy on periodical MapReduce job. Comput Sci 2013;40(3):38–40.

[27] Heintz B, Wang C, Chandra A, et al. Cross-phase optimization in MapReduce. In: Proceedings of the IEEE international conference on cloud engineering (IC2E'13), San Francisco, CA, USA, Mar. 25–27; 2013.

[28] Apache, Fair Scheduler Guide, http://archive.cloudera.com/cdh/3/hadoop/fair_scheduler.html; [2015-05-19].

[29] Zaharia M, Borthakur D, Sen Sarma J, et al. Delay scheduling: a simple technique for achieving locality and fairness in cluster scheduling. In: Proceedings of the 5th European conference on computer systems (EuroSys'10), Paris, France, Apr. 13–16; 2010.

[30] Apache, Capacity Scheduler Guide, http://hadoop.apache.org/docs/r1.2.1/capacity_scheduler.html; [2015-05-19].

[31] Kc K, Anyanwu K. Scheduling Hadoop jobs to meet deadlines. In: Proceedings of the second international conference on cloud computing technology and science (CloudCom'10), Indianapolis, Indiana, USA, Nov. 30–Dec. 3; 2010.

[32] Polo J, Carrera D, Becerra Y, et al. Performance-driven task co-scheduling for MapReduce environments. In: Proceedings of the network operations and management symposium (NOMS'10), Osaka, Japan, Apr. 19–23; 2010.

[33] Tang Z, Zhou J, Li K, et al. A MapReduce task scheduling algorithm for deadline constraints. Cluster Comput 2013;16(4):1–12.

[34] Verma A, Cherkasova L, Campbell RH. Two sides of a coin: optimizing the schedule of MapReduce jobs to minimize their makespan and improve cluster performance. In: Proceedings of the 20th international symposium on modeling, analysis & simulation of computer and telecommunication systems (MASCOTS'12), Washington, DC, USA, Aug. 7–9; 2012.

[35] Tian C, Zhou H, He Y, et al. A dynamic MapReduce scheduler for heterogeneous workloads. In: Proceedings of the 8th international conference on grid and cooperative computing (GCC'09), Lanzhou, Gansu, China, Aug. 27–29; 2009.

[36] Yu Z. Research on improving Hadoop job scheduling based on learning approach. Comput Sci 2012;39(S1):220–2. 256.

[37] Sandholm T, Lai K. Dynamic proportional share scheduling in Hadoop. In: Proceedings of the job scheduling strategies for parallel processing (JSSPP'10), Atlanta, GA, USA, Apr. 23; 2010.

[38] Gu Y, Zhou L, Ding Q. Research of three-queue scheduling algorithms based on priority. Comput Sci 2011;38(10):253–6.

[39] Li Q, Liu J, Ye D, et al. FlowS: a fair scheduling method for MapReduce dataflow. Comput Sci 2012;39(09):157–61.

[40] Ghodsi A, Zaharia M, Hindman B, et al. Dominant resource fairness: fair allocation of multiple resource types. In: Proceedings of the 8th USENIX symposium on networked systems design and implementation (NSDI'11), Boston, MA, USA, Mar. 30–Apr. 1; 2011.

[41] Apache, Apache Hadoop NextGen MapReduce (YARN), http://hadoop.apache.org/docs/current2/hadoop–yarn/hadoop-yarn-site/YARN.html; [2015-05-19].

[42] Murthy AC, Douglas C, Konar M, et al. Architecture of next generation Apache Hadoop MapReduce framework, Research report, Apache Hadoop; 2011.

[43] Apache, Corona, https://github.com/facebook/Hadoop-20/tree/master/src/contrib/corona; [2015-05-19].

[44] Wolf J, Rajan D, Hildrum K, et al. Flex: a slot allocation scheduling optimizer for MapReduce workloads. In: Proceedings of the 11th international middleware conference, Bangalore, India, Nov. 29–Dec. 3; 2010.

[45] Xu C, Liu H, Tan L. New mechanism of monitoring on Hadoop cloud platform. Comput Sci 2013;40(01):112–7.

[46] Beaver D, Kumar S, Li H, et al. Finding a needle in haystack: Facebook's photo storage. In: Proceedings of the 9th USENIX conference on operating systems design and implementation, Vancouver, Canada, Oct. 4–6; 2010.

[47] Alibaba, TFS (Taobao FileSystem), http://code.taobao.org//tfs/src/; [2015-05-19].

[48] Fu S, Liao X, Huang C, et al. FlatLFS: a lightweight file system for optimizing the performance of accessing massive small files. J Nat Univ Defense Technol 2013;35(2):120–6.

[49] Zhao Y, Xie X, Cai Y, et al. A strategy of small file storage access with performance optimization. J Comput Res Dev 2012;49(7):1579–86.

[50] Ma C, Meng D, Xiong J. Research on enormous storage for small files based on distributed indexing and directory aggregation. Chin High Technol Lett 2012;22(10):1035–40.

[51] Yu L, Chen G, Wang W, et al. MSFSS: a storage system for mass small files. In: Proceedings of the 2007 11th international conference on computer supported cooperative work in design, Melbourne, Australia, Apr. 26–28; 2007.

[52] Mackey G, Sehrish S, Wang J. Improving metadata management for small files in HDFS. In: Proceedings of the 2009 IEEE international conference on cluster computing, New Orleans, USA, Aug. 31–Sep. 4; 2009.

[53] Liu X, Han J, Zhong Y. Implementing WebGIS on Hadoop: a case study of improving small file I/O performance on HDFS. In: Proceedings of the 2009 IEEE international conference on cluster computing, New Orleans, USA, Aug. 31–Sep. 4; 2009.

[54] Dong B, Qiu J, Zheng Q, et al. A novel approach to improving the efficiency of storing and accessing small files on Hadoop: a case study by PowerPoint files. In: Proceedings of the 2010 IEEE international conference on services computing, Miami, USA, Jul. 5–10; 2010.

[55] Jiang L, Li B, Song M. The optimization of HDFS based on small files. In: Proceedings of the 3rd IEEE international conference on broadband network & multimedia technology, Beijing, China, Oct. 26–28; 2010.

[56] Zhang C, Rui J, He T. An approach for storing and accessing small files on Hadoop. Comput Appl Software 2012;29(11):95–100.

[57] Li T, Yan C, Huang Y, et al. Optimization of small files storage and accessing on Hadoop distributed file system. J Comput Appl 2014;34(11):3091–5. 3099.

[58] Zhang H, Ma J. Optimizational strategy of small files stored and readed on HDFS. Comput Syst Appl 2014;23(5):167–71.

[59] Yan C, Li T, Huang Y, et al. Hmfs: efficient support of small files processing over HDFS. In: Proceedings of 14th international conference on algorithms and architectures for parallel, Dalian, China, Aug. 24–27; 2014.

[60] O'Malley O, Zhang K, Radia S, et al. Hadoop security design[R]. Yahoo Inc.; 2009.

[61] Cordova A. MapReduce over Tahoe: a least-authority encrypted distributed file system, http://blog.cloudera.com/resource/hw09_mapreduce_over_tahoe/; [2015-05-19].

[62] Huang-qi C, Cheng SU. Design of security mechanism based on HDFS. Netw Comput Security 2010;012:22–5.

[63] Qin J, Deng Q, Zhang J. Design of multi-grade safety data destruction mechanism of HDFS. Comput Technol Dev 2013;23(3):129–33.

[64] Shen Q, Yang Y, Wu Z, et al. SAPSC: security architecture of private storage cloud based on HDFS. In: Proceedings of the 26th international conference on advanced information networking and applications workshops, Fukuoka, Japan, Mar. 26–29; 2012.

[65] Majors JH. Secdoop: a confidentiality service on Hadoop clusters [D]. Auburn: Auburn University; 2011.

[66] Lin HY, Shen ST, Tzeng WG, et al. Toward data confidentiality via integrating hybrid encryption schemes and Hadoop distributed file system. In: Proceedings of the 26th IEEE international conference on advanced information networking and applications, Fukuoka, Japan, Mar. 26–29; 2012.

[67] Park S, Lee Y. Secure Hadoop with encrypted HDFS. In: Proceedings of the 8th international conference on grid and pervasive computing, Seoul, Korea, May 9–11; 2013.

[68] Nguyen TC, Shen W, Jiang J, et al. A novel data encryption in HDFS. In: Proceedings of the 2013 IEEE international conference on green computing and communications (GreenCom) and IEEE Internet of Things (iThings) and IEEE cyber, physical and social computing, Beijing, China, Aug. 20–23; 2013.

[69] Quan Q, Tian-hong W, Rui Z, et al. A model of cloud data secure storage based on HDFS. In: Proceedings of the 12th international conference on computer and information science, Niigata, Japan, Jun. 16–20; 2013.

[70] Shen Q, Yang Y, Wu Z, et al. Securing data services: a security architecture design for private storage cloud based on HDFS. Int J Grid Utility Comput 2013;4(4):242–54.

[71] Cohen J, Acharya S. Towards a more secure Apache Hadoop HDFS infrastructure[M]//network and system security. Berlin, Heidelberg: Springer; 2013. p. 735–41.

[72] Cohen JC, Acharya S. Towards a trusted HDFS storage platform: mitigating threats to Hadoop infrastructures using hardware-accelerated encryption with TPM-rooted key protection. J Inform Security Appl 2014;19(3):224–44.

[73] Xu W, Lai L, Cheng Z, et al. Research on the architecture and mechanisms of Hadoop distributed file system. In: Proceedings of the 17th national conference on networking and data communications, Hebei, China, Sep. 16; 2010.

[74] Li X, Dai X, Li W, et al. Improved HDFS scheme based on erasure code and dynamical-replication system. J Comput Appl 2012;32(8):2150–3. 2158.

[75] Carstoiu D, Lepadatu E, Gaspar M. HBase—non SQL database, performances evaluation. Int J Adv Comput Technol 2010;2(5):42–52.

[76] Wasi-ur-Rahman M, Huang J, Jose J, et al. Understanding the communication characteristics in HBase: what are the fundamental bottlenecks? In: Proceedings of the IEEE international symposium on performance analysis of systems & software (ISPASS'12), New Brunswick, NJ, USA, Apr. 1–3; 2012.

[77] Huang J, Ouyang X, Jose J, et al. High-performance design of HBase with RDMA over InfiniBand. In: Proceedings of the 26th IEEE international parallel and distributed processing symposium (IPDPS'12), Shanghai, China, May 21–25; 2012.

[78] Tian S, Xu X, Yang S, et al. Optimization for the access interface of MapReduce in HBase. In: Proceedings of the 9th China institute of communications conference, Beijing, China, Aug. 17; 2012.

[79] Konishetty VK, Kumar KA, Voruganti K, et al. Implementation and evaluation of scalable data structure over HBase. In: Proceedings of the international conference on advances in computing, communications and informatics (ICACCI'12), Chennai, India, Aug. 3–5; 2012.

[80] Luo Y. Research and implementation on HBASE based column-oriented compression algorithms [D]. Guangzhou: South China University of Technology; 2011.

[81] Cheng P, An J. The key as dictionary compression method of inverted index table under the Hbase database. J Software 2013;8(5):1086–93.

[82] Abinasha Karana, Hadoop and HBase optimization for read intensive search applications, https://software.intel.com/en-us/articles/hadoop-and-hbase-optimization-for-read-intensive-search-applications/; [2015-05-19].

[83] Ma Y, Zhang Y, Meng X. ST-HBase: a scalable data management system for massive geo-tagged objects. In: Proceedings of the 14th international conference web-age information management (WAIM'13), Beidaihe, China, Jun. 14–16; 2013.

[84] Awasthi A, Nandini A, Bhattacharya A, et al. Hybrid HBase: leveraging flash SSDs to improve cost per throughput of HBase. In: Proceedings of the 18th international conference on management of data (COMAD'12), Pune, India; 2012. p. 68–79.

[85] Zhang C, Liu X. HBaseMQ: a distributed message queuing system on clouds with HBase. In: Proceedings of the IEEE INFOCOM 2013 (INFOCOM'13), Turin, Italy, Apr. 14–19; 2013.

[86] Borthakur D, Gray J, Sen Sarma J, et al. Apache Hadoop goes realtime at Facebook. In: Proceedings of the ACM SIGMOD international conference on management of data (SIGMOD'11), Athens, Greece, Jun. 12–16; 2011.

[87] Chongxin L. Design and implementation of snapshot for distributed database HBase [D]. Hang Zhou: Zhejiang University; 2011.

[88] Pavlo A, Paulson E, Rasin A, et al. A comparison of approaches to large-scale data analysis. In: Proceedings of the 29th international conference on management of data, Providence, Jun. 29–Jul. 2, USA; 2009.

[89] Qin XP, Wang HJ, Du XY, et al. Big data analysis—competition between RDBMS and MapReduce, their inter-fusing and symbiosis. J Software 2012;23(1):32–45.

[90] Wang S, Wang HJ, Qin XP, et al. Architecting Big Data: challenges, studies and forecasts. Chin J Comput 2011;34(10):1741–52.

[91] Eltabakh MY, Tian Y, Özcan F, et al. CoHadoop: flexible data placement and its exploitation in Hadoop. Proc VLDB Endowment 2011;4(9):575–85.

[92] He C, Lu Y, Swanson D. Matchmaking: a new MapReduce scheduling technique. In: Proceedings of the 3rd international conference on cloud computing technology and science, Athens, Greece, Nov. 29–Dec. 1; 2011.

[93] Xie J, Meng FJ, Wang HL, et al. Research on scheduling scheme for Hadoop clusters. Proc Comput Sci 2013;18:2468–71.

[94] Lai L, Zhou J, Zheng L, et al. ShmStreaming: a shared memory approach for improving Hadoop streaming performance. In: Proceedings of the 27th international conference on advanced information networking and applications, Barcelona, Spain, Mar. 25–28; 2013.

[95] Roy A, Dutta D. Dynamic load balancing: improve efficiency in cloud computing. Int J Emerging Res Manage Technol 2013;2(4):78–82.

[96] Chen Q, Liu C, Xiao Z. Improving MapReduce performance using smart speculative execution strategy. IEEE Trans Comput 2014;63(4):954–67.

[97] Premchaiswadi W, Romsaiyud W. Optimizing and tuning MapReduce jobs to improve the large-scale data analysis process. Int J Intell Syst 2013;28(2):185–200.

[98] Rao BT, Reddy LSS. Survey on improved scheduling in Hadoop MapReduce in cloud environments. Int J Comput Appl 2011;34(9):29–33.

[99] Cherniak A, Zaidi H, Zadorozhny V. Optimization strategies for A/B testing on HADOOP. In: Proceedings of 39th international conference on very large data bases. Riva del Garda, Italy, Aug. 26–30; 2013.

[100] Song J, Li TT, Yan ZX, et al. Energy-efficiency model and measuring approach for cloud computing. J Software 2012;23(2):200–14.

[101] Kim WC, Baek C, Lee D. Measuring the optimality of Hadoop optimization, arXiv, preprint arXiv:1307.2915; Jul. 2013.

[102] He C, Weitzel D, Swanson D, et al. HOG: distributed Hadoop MapReduce on the grid. In: Proceedings of 25th international conference on high performance computing, networking, storage and analysis, Nov. 10–16, Salt Lake, USA; 2012.

[103] Xie J, Yin S, Ruan X, et al. Improving MapReduce performance through data placement in heterogeneous Hadoop clusters. In: Proceedings of 24th international conference on parallel & distributed processing, workshops and Phd forum, Apr. 19–23, Atlanta, USA; 2010.

[104] Ahmad F, Chakradhar ST, Raghunathan A, et al. Tarazu: optimizing MapReduce on heterogeneous clusters. In: Proceedings of 17th international conference on architectural support for programming languages and operating systems, Mar. 3–7, London, UK; 2012.

[105] Hansen CA. Optimizing Hadoop for the cluster, http://citeseerx.ist.psu.edu/viewdoc/download?doi=10.1.1. 486.1265&rep=rep1&type=pdf; [2015-05-19].

PACKING ALGORITHMS FOR BIG DATA REPLAY ON MULTICORE

10

M. Zhanikeev

10.1 INTRODUCTION

This chapter discusses the *Big Data Replay* approach to processing Big Data. Given that Hadoop [1] coupled with MapReduce are the current de facto standards in this area, the replay method reviewed in this chapter is the direct rival and alternative to the current de facto standard.

The core replay method was first introduced in Ref. [2] where the architecture of Hadoop [1] is discussed in detail and compared with the new, replay-based architecture. It presented only a crude idea of relay, while this chapter goes in depth and focuses on the various ways in which the replay method can be optimized in relay. As the title of this chapter says, the replay environment is assumed to be *multicore* — in fact, this chapter introduces the new concept of *massively multicore* — which creates many interesting challenges when trying to optimize the entire environment. In fact, Hadoop/MapReduce also attempts to optimize its resources, as well as access to them, but does it in a distributed manner, while the replay method in this chapter offers a diametrically opposing viewpoint by performing all the activities on a single, massively multicore machine.

This chapter is not the first to discuss Hadoop/MapReduce alternatives. Based on the clearly recognized performance limits of Hadoop [3] — this article is, in fact, written by one of the current developers of Hadoop — there are calls for alternative technologies (see Ref. [4]) with bold titles that yet send a clear message.

For clarity a, let us simplify the terminology. In reality, Hadoop — or the Hadoop Distributed File System (HDFS) — is an independent technology from MapReduce. The latter is, in fact, an algorithm that can be implemented by Big Data processing engines to run jobs on Hadoop. Recent software packages implement several engines other than MapReduce, which means that Hadoop/MapReduce logic is no longer true. HDFS itself is challenged by several new distributed file systems — see Ref. [3] for a short overview. However, for simplicity, let us use the term *Hadoop* to refer to both a distributed file system and an engine that runs jobs on it. By far, the current de facto technology is Hadoop/MapReduce, but this could change in the future. Given the drastic difference between any *Hadoop* technology and the *one-machine* environment discussed in this chapter, it is likely that the difference in performance shown in this chapter can be applied to newer distributed engines. From this point on, the term *Hadoop* will always mean *any distributed file system and job execution engine*.

Hadoop performance has already been modeled [5] and analyzed statistically [6] — such research has shown that there are solid limitations to the throughput, both in terms of the file system changes and job execution performance. Several parts of Hadoop have also been improved, creating a different tool. For example, there is an attempt to exploit *multicore hardware* on shards (a storage node on a Hadoop

Big Data. http://dx.doi.org/10.1016/B978-0-12-805394-2.00010-6

cluster is referred to as a *shard*). More traditional research would try to optimize the job schedule in order to maximize the overall utility of the system. There are more peculiar studies that add a structured metadata layer to the otherwise unstructured Hadoop shards, using R in Ref. [7] and Lucene indexing in Ref. [8].

The biggest improvement, however, is only possible via a drastic change of the research scenery. This change is discussed in the form of the *distributed versus one-machine* argument in Ref. [4]. In fact, the related argument is that *the distribution is a curse*, which has been admitted by the creators of Hadoop [3], but this discussion normally does not lead to a solid conclusion. Instead, even the paper that presents the *one machine is better* argument says that the one-machine environment is only for relatively small data bulks, while Hadoop remains the only choice for true Big Data.

There is a large body of literature on the various optimizations of the traditional Hadoop. Name nodes are recognized as *single points of failure* (SPOF), but a system that allows for multiple name nodes has to tackle new challenges related to the need for synchronization across the nodes and the increased overhead between the now multiple name nodes and shards.

A great deal of research work is entirely dedicated to optimizing job execution shards. For example, the Tiled MapReduce method [9] is a standard partitioning approach from parallel programming applied to the jobs competing for resources at the same shard. However, such research does not optimize the entire Hadoop system because each job is run on multiple shards, and optimizing each shard separately does not necessarily result in optimal performance for the entire system.

Returning to the *one-machine* theme, while it has been mentioned in Ref. [4], the context is very different from the technology discussed in this chapter. The context in Ref. [4] is that the bulk is lower than 10–15 GB, in which case it can be handled on the commodity hardware of a single machine. However, no assumptions are made on the multiple jobs, multicore architecture, and various other components discussed in this chapter.

The correct *one-machine* theme is the *Big Data replay method* itself [2]. The immediate difference from the idea in Ref. [4] is that the engine can easily scale up to any bulk size. But the more important difference is that the machine is assumed to be multicore — even massively multicore, if possible — which allows for the variable scale in terms of the jobs running in parallel. Although the logic of the replay method is different from the traditional Hadoop, it is expected that the scale of 10k parallel jobs can be reached on each replay node — multiple nodes can also be used without any major increase in overhead. However, the correct method for evaluating the replay method is to measure the *job throughput* as the number of jobs per unit of time, in which case, depending on the unit of time, the overall throughput of the system can easily exceed the 10k level of the current Hadoop.

This chapter uses the core replay method, but focuses specifically on the packing algorithms applied to multiple parallel jobs. The new focus requires several new components, some of which can be found in recent literature, some of which come from this author. Efficient parallelization in the *lockfree shared memory* design is discussed in Ref. [10] in a traffic-specific version which can be easily generalized and applied to Big Data. *Data streaming* [11] is offered as the main framework for jobs and, as such, replaces the *key-value* datatype used by MapReduce [12]. Data streaming can support any kind of a complex datatype, for example many-to-many structures are discussed in Ref. [13] and one-to-many (referred to as superspreaders) in Ref. [14]. There are the various algorithms and efficiency tricks in data streaming [15], but the most important feature is that data streaming algorithms are normally implemented along the timeline and require that a time window be input into the data [16]. Finally, this chapter will discuss the recently introduced *circuit emulation* technology which is used for bulk data transfer [17] — this research area is known as *Big Data networking*. The core idea of Big Data Replay was presented in Ref. [2] and early prototypes and demos in Ref. [18].

The actual contributions of this chapter are as follows: on top of the basic replay method in Ref. [2], this chapter assumes *massively multicore* hardware. There is a clear distinction between *massively multicore* and *manycore*, explained in detail further into this chapter. With the high number of cores, this chapter focuses on *packing algorithms*. The jobs are packed into *batches*, each having its own time window. The main job of the runtime optimization engine is to optimize the batches. The two specific models formulated and analyzed in this chapter are *Drag* and *Drop*, each referring to an approach to dealing with the gradual scattering of time cursors of individual jobs in each batch. The various parameters of the replay environments, however, offer a rich space which can support several other models, as well as several versions of the two main models.

10.2 PERFORMANCE BOTTLENECKS

A very good overview of the various HDFS/MapReduce bottlenecks can be found in Ref. [3]. Some are reviewed and repeated in this chapter, but the scope in this chapter is considerably larger and includes separate consideration of storage (Hard Disk Drive (HDD)/Solid State Drive (SSD)) and shared memory (shmap) performance bottlenecks. Shared memory in this chapter is shortened to *shmap*, which is the name of the most efficient/popular library used in multi- and manycore systems today. This section presents experimental data for these two components which become datasets in analysis later in this chapter.

10.2.1 HADOOP/MAPREDUCE PERFORMANCE BOTTLENECKS

Fig. 1 shows the primitive viewpoint at performance bottlenecks, which will be upgraded twice throughout this chapter. The bottlenecks are divided into *network*, *storage* and *shared memory* types, each with its own relative width — the pipe analogy here assumes that wide pipes have bigger bottlenecks and therefore offer better performance.

Network is the narrowest bottleneck and indicates strong and well-recognized performance problems. The base parameters are *delay, throughput*, and *variation* of both [13]. These parameters are very hard to predict and/or control, and become increasingly more so as multiple traffic flows compete for resources. Traditional Hadoop is a good example of a networking environment where very many small and large traffic flows complete for bandwidth.

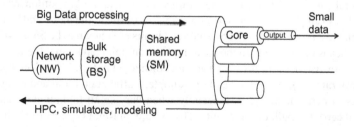

FIG. 1

The three main bottlenecks in context of Big Data processing and HPC.

Bulk storage is represented by HDD/SSD disk. They make shards in traditional Hadoop. In replay, storage can be used for temporary on-disk caching of bulks brought in from remote storage nodes. This bottleneck is actively discussed in the research. For example, one of the issues is the *HDD versus SSD* problem, where it is a widely spread myth that SSD is better than HDD, but there is also research that shows that a *hybrid* optimization engine can outperform either of the two technologies [19].

Shared memory bottlenecks depend on the capacity offered by *shmap* libraries among several offered in modern kernels [20]. Capacity can be improved by drastically reducing the overhead from locking and message passing when using the *lockfree* design [10]. Shared memory is a hot discussion topic in multi- and manycore parallel programming. Technical advice on code generation can be found in Ref. [21]. Advanced research in this area makes a clear distinction between hardware and software support, as well as between multi- and manycore systems [22]. Message passing interface (MPI) technology has recently been shown to perform the best when implemented after the lockfree design (one-side communication), based on shared memory [23].

Jobs on cores themselves are also bottlenecks. This time, the capacity is mostly affected by the computing load itself. For example, as Fig. 1 shows, the processing job is supposed to convert Big Data to Small Data, which requires complex processing logic, state, etc. This chapter will reveal an interesting revelation by showing that the overhead in jobs is the biggest contributor to overall performance degradation. Still, the batch management methods and packing algorithms presented further in this chapter can help elevate this problem, up to a given degree. The problem cannot be eliminated completely since processing data is the fundamental necessity of both Hadoop and Replay engines.

Note that Fig. 1 shows the fundamental difference between Big Data processing and high performance computing (HPC). Here, the shift from multi- to manycore systems advertised in Ref. [22] is applicable only to the HPC part as such research needs to build more and more powerful supercomputers. However, it is unlikely that the Big Data part of the research will move in the same direction. For example, manycore systems are not good for moving large bulks of data quickly — in fact, the main purpose of HPC is to *generate data* using modeling, simulation, etc. Since the process in Big Data processing is the inverse of that, the networking bottleneck is extremely important — it is like having a very small entrance into a very large stadium. Using the same analogy, HPC tries to build larger stadiums because it focuses on what is happening inside the stadium and pays little attention to what gets in and out of it — thus not paying much attention to the networking bottleneck. This is changing, however, in recent literature, which has finally come to terms with intercluster networking in manycore clusters and started to look for technologies that can improve the situation. *Circuit emulation*, discussed later in this chapter, is applicable here as well.

There are several smaller bottlenecks. The various software and logic bottlenecks are discussed in Refs. [3] and [4]. For example, it is shown that only 75% of traffic to the name node can be dedicated to job traffic, while the rest is overhead. HDFS write/read limits are known to be 55/45 MB/s, respectively. Various other overheads can cause bottlenecks in replication, job management, etc.

However, there are also bottlenecks which are not considered in Ref. [3] and are generally left without attention in programming-related areas. For example, traffic contention and congestion can cause drastic differences in performance [10], especially when very small lookup/metadata flows compete with the flows that carry the bulk of job results. The circuits in Ref. [17] cover just that fact. This general discussion is revisited several times in this chapter, and specifically when discussing the *hotspot distribution* (bulk flows in traffic can be classified as *hotspots*).

Even smaller bottlenecks are created by *unfair* competition across jobs, especially when the load is heterogeneous [5,6]. This is a recognized problem, and several ways to resolve the problem are being looked into — for example, the tool in Ref. [24] is a scheduler of heterogeneous jobs. The *key-value* output datatype for MapReduce jobs is too restrictive and creates a bottleneck for jobs. This problem is addressed in Ref. [4], where it is mentioned that the only way to counter this issue is *to run multiple Hadoop rounds*. The true resolution is discussed in this chapter, which advocates for the general *data streaming* framework for processing jobs, which offers the complete freedom of datatypes [12]. The same bottleneck is created by the lack of time awareness on Hadoop [4]. This is also countered by running multiple rounds of jobs, but can be fundamentally resolved via the data streaming approach. Note that using a free datatype is difficult on Hadoop, but is trivial on the one-machine environments such as those discussed in this chapter.

10.2.2 PERFORMANCE BOTTLENECKS UNDER PARALLEL LOADS

Fig. 2 adds more dimensions to the problem. In fact, the simple bottlenecks presented in the previous subsection should be examined from the viewpoint of

- ability to isolate a user of a resource from other parallel users
- the number of parallel users for a given resource

both applied to each separate bottleneck discussed herein.

Both of the two new parameters affect the performance (width) of the bottleneck. For example, an initially large bottleneck can be reduced if it cannot be properly isolated, and is subjected to many parallel clients, where both metrics are found at work at the same time. This, in fact, refers to the *shmap* experiment found later in this section.

The network is the hardest technology to isolate. See the argument against *network virtualization* in Ref. [25]. The good news is that not much parallel access to network resources is happening in the one-machine environment under the replay method. However, by extension, this is also the weak point of

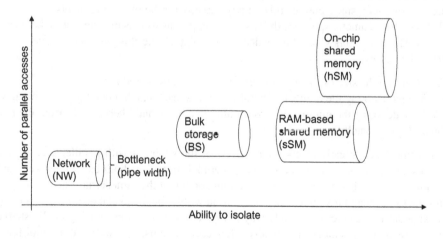

FIG. 2

The main bottlenecks plotted on isolation and parallel access scales.

the traditional Hadoop, which subjects this initially weak/narrow bottleneck to very high-count parallel loads. Recently, the same problem has been recognized in manycore systems as well [22], and recent research has started to look for ways to optimize the load for minimizing traffic between clusters. Even further, the same problem, although to a lesser extent, occurs inside the manycore clusters. The replay method offers another advantage — the replay node can use circuits to transfer the bulk from a remote node for local replay [17].

Disk and traditional *shmap* are found somewhere in the midrange of the two axes in Fig. 2. The traditional view in terms of storage is that SSD is better than HDD, but this viewpoint is wrong. First, the difference depends on the type of use. Second, when a generic use is intended, recent literature has shown that hybrid optimization — hybrid meaning that the storage has both HDD and SSD in it — performs better than either of the two technologies separately [19].

Comparing storage and shared memory, one has to keep in mind that there are far fewer parallel accesses to the storage than to *shmap*. Taking the job batches later in this chapter as an example, the difference is obvious — parallel access to storage relates to the number of batches, while parallel access to shared memory is much higher because all the jobs in batches also have to access the *shmap* library in parallel. The experiment and dataset later in this chapter reveal the practical outcome of such a difference.

The *on-chip shmap* version in Fig. 2 requires special attention. This is the special case in manycore systems which implement L1 and L2 caches on the chips themselves and supports them by hardware and software. A good description of the advantages of such an upgrade is offered in Ref. [22]. Modern manycore systems offer many efficiency tricks which drastically improve performance, and therefore, increase the size of the bottleneck. Yet, congestion from parallel access can affect performance even in such advanced systems [23].

10.2.3 PARAMETER SPACES FOR STORAGE AND SHARED MEMORY

The two further subsections in this section offer the actual experimental data and datasets related to storage (SSD) and shared memory (shmap) performance. This subsection serves as the introduction by presenting the parameter space and the related terminology for the two experiments.

Fig. 3 shows the parameter space for the two technologies as well as the connection between the two (dotted lines). The rest of this subsection is dedicated to explaining this parameter space.

Shmap is defined by

- *size*, denoting the size of the RAM memory dedicated to shared memory
- *batchcount* denoting the number of parallel batches, each batch having its own shmap space
- *batchsize* denoting the number of jobs running in a batch and, therefore, sharing the individual shmap for that batch

Note that this space already offers a clear view of the situation with parallel access. One might be tempted to think that only batches compete in parallel. In reality, both batch managers and all the individual jobs in all batches are the processes running on top of the same kernel and, as such, are competitors for the same shared resource. The competition within the batch can be minimized by using the *lockfree* design discussed herein. The only way to avoid the competition for the globally shared *kernel attention* is to separate the batches physically. Manycore systems, in a way, are the tool for physical separation between cores and core clusters. The framework discussed in this section assumes that the

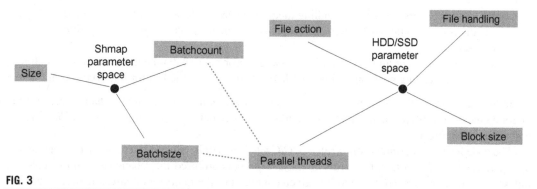

FIG. 3

Parameter spaces for SSD/HDD versus shmap. The dotted lines show that the term parallel threads in storage traces is related to batchsize and batchcount.

same will be attempted in future generations of multicore hardware, hopefully leading to *massively multicore* hardware architectures.

Storage performance is defined by

- *file action*, referring to what you do with a file, specifically read, write or append, etc.
- *file handling*, which refers to how the file is handled in the long run — where the two obvious alternatives in massively parallel systems are to keep file handles open continuously or *reopen* files for each batch; later experiments will also use the *seek* parameter for denoting whether or not the reading position in the file has to change for each new/next time window
- *blocksize*, denoting the size of the chunk in each read/write operation within each session
- finally, *parallel threads* denotes how many threads/processes are using the storage in parallel

The connection between the two parameter spaces is obvious and relates to the parallel aspects of the two technologies. The term *parallel threads* in storage relates to *batchcount*, and *batchsize* is shmap. The relationship is a bit subtle, however, since only the *batchcount* equals the number of parallel accesses to storage, while *batchsize* further contributes to the overall competition in the shmap domain.

The two remaining subsections in this section run experiments and construct datasets for these two parts.

10.2.4 MAIN STORAGE PERFORMANCE

This subsection presents the first of the two experiments — those that target the storage performance. The HDD versus SSD argument was discussed in the previous section, but for simplicity, the experiment is run only on the SSD storage. In fact, the shmap experiment described later in this chapter will show that the storage bottleneck is minor by comparison, which means that the *HDD versus SSD* argument, as well as the hybrid optimization with the combination of the two, will not offer a tangible increase in the overall performance of a Big Data Replay engine.

The following experimental design is used: only *read* operations are used — the multiGB files from which the reading is done are created in advance. Otherwise, the file handling methods are complex, and include the combination of

- the *openeach* versus *keep* file handling method, where the former refers to a method in which the file is closed after each batch and reopened for the next, and *keep*, naturally, refers to the opposite method
- *seekeach* versus *continue*, which refers to whether or not to call on a the *seek()* system call to change the reading position within the file or continue from the last (or initial) position

In the aftermath of the experiments, there was a realization that the parameters had relatively little effect on the overall performance. Instead, the *blocksize* parameter and the number of *parallel threads* had the greatest effect.

The code for the experiment was written in C/C++. The parallel threads were, in fact, implemented as separate *processes*. In fact, the terms *thread* and *process* are used interchangeably in this chapter, unless a distinction is clearly denoted in a given context. For the majority of cases, modern operating systems do not make a tangible distinction between the two. The experiment was run on a commodity 8-core (Intel i7) hardware platform.

Each experimental round was conducted as follows: first, all the threads/processes are spawned, but are designed to start at a future time — each thread monitors the global time and starts at roughly the same time as all the others. Once started, each thread/process opens the file once and then makes 10 iterations of the reading operation with the preceding parameters. For each iteration, the file can be closed and reopened, *seek()* can be used to change the reading position, but the *blocksize* of bytes is read in all iterations, resulting in the total bulk of 10 times the blocksize.

Since the experiment is conducted with the idea of creating a practical dataset, detailed measurements are taken by each thread. Each one records the time for each stage of reading in each iteration, resulting in *open*, *seek*, and *read* values for each iteration. In addition, each thread outputs the final *took in total* value that measures the time it took the thread to complete all 10 iterations. As the figures later in this subsection show, the final figure is not always the sum of the figures from individual iterations.

Fig. 4 shows the raw JSON [26] output of one of the experimental runs. The two blocks are for *light* (above) versus *heavy* (below) setups. The header has all the parameters, while the bottom part has the curtailed version of the data for each thread in the parallel pool. The first line is the legend, while all the other lines show the values for individual threads.

The following observations can be made from the raw output. In the light version (above) there are many 0 values in individual threads. This is to be expected and has to do with clock resolution. Since reading a very small block of data can be really fast, the kernel might have had no time to update the clock during the operation. Another way to put it is to say that no context switching was performed during that simple operation — this explanation is not strictly true, but is adequate for most practical cases. The total time (last number) for each thread still reflects the adequate time — this value is used when creating the dataset based on the raw data.

The heavy use at the bottom of Fig. 4 shows that the time increases by a factor of about 3. Values for individual iterations are also now adequate because it takes a much longer time to read 100 kB from the file. Same as before, the final number (total time) is used to put together the dataset.

Fig. 5 illustrates the entire dataset constructed for many experiments covering the entire parameter space, with two or more states for each parameter. Specifically, up to 512 threads (processes) and blocks from 100 bytes to 100 kB were used. The visualization method in Fig. 5 is a 2D representation of the multidimensional data. The image is cast into 2D by presenting the results in a flat sequence of all the combinations of parameter values. The most important factor in such visualizations is the *order* of parameters — depending on the order, the resulting visualizations can range from those that are

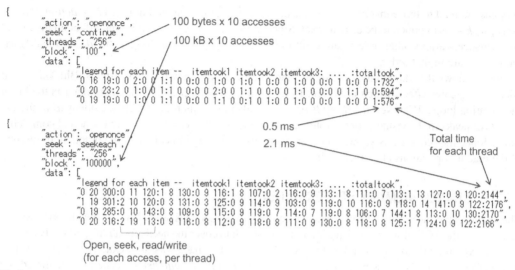

FIG. 4

Raw JSON output for low- versus high-intensity sessions in file operations.

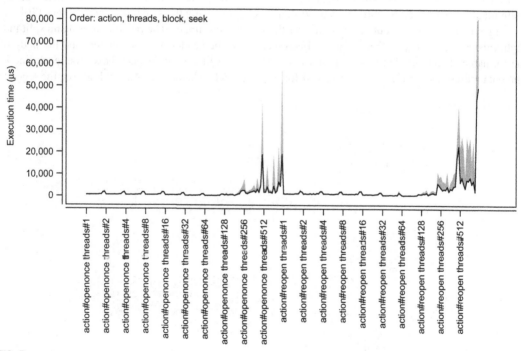

FIG. 5

SSD performance presented over the sequence of parameters in the order of action, threads, block, seek.

very easy to read to those that make no sense entirely. The order selected in Fig. 13 — *action, threads, block, seek* — is assumed to be easy to read. Since *action* and *seek* have a minimal effect on the overall performance, various other orders can result in the same rough view as long as the *threads* and *blocks* parameters are in that order.

Fig. 5 shows that the number of *threads* and *blocksize* are the two largest effects. Blocksize arguably has a greater effect, which is evident from rapidly growing peaks — this parameter is the last in the iteration loops. However, the *threads* parameter also plays its role, which is evident from the two islands of peaks in the visualization. Note that the values on the vertical scale are the actual completion times. Since the *blocksize* is known, one can easily use the image to calculate the practical throughput of the reading operations at a given setting.

10.2.5 SHARED MEMORY PERFORMANCE

The second experiment is for *shmap*. The same commodity hardware is used; this time the important system parameter is the 4 GB of RAM, which is more than enough to cover the needs for all the parallel batches.

The experiment was conducted as follows: the parameter space was used exactly as was presented in an earlier subsection — the parameters are *size, batchcount,* and *batchsize*. As before, the threads are orchestrated by defining a starting time in the future. This time, the logic is a little bit more complex because separate starting times have to be defined for managers of batches versus processing jobs. It was found that it was sufficient to start managers at 2 s in the future, which is enough time for them to write the shmap before individual jobs starting at 5 s can start reading each of their own batch's shmap individually. As before, the software was written in C/C++, using the standard *shmap* library [20].

Fig. 6 is the raw JSON output, this time for the shmap experiment. The raw output is again split into light (above) versus heavy (below) parts. Each record has the header with parameters and the body of performance data (curtailed to several lines) where the first line is the legend. This time, each line in the data represents performance aggregated for a given batch. The design of each line (see the legend)

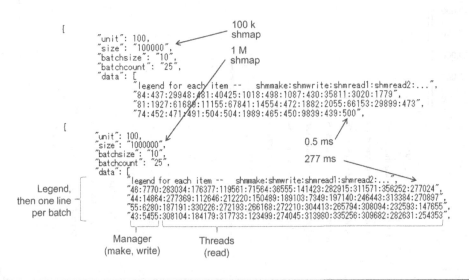

FIG. 6

Raw JSON output for low- versus high-intensity storage sessions.

accounts for that by showing the time it took for the manager thread to create and populate the shmap and then add all the reading times for individual job threads. The practical use of this data is also slightly different. The *completion time* of the batch is defined as *open* plus *write* plus the largest of the *read* times among the jobs. Simply put, this means that the batch ends only when the slowest job has finished reading and processing the content of its shmap. This feature is revisited later when the topic of *heterogeneous loads* is discussed, resulting in job packing logics which take the related problems into account.

Let us see what stands out in the raw data. The only difference between the light and the heavy runs is the size of the shmap — it changes from 100k to 1 M. The scale — defined as *batchcount times batchsize* — is the same for both experiments. However, we see a *huge* difference in raw numbers between the upper and lower parts. This effect was confirmed from raw data and the software was tested extensively to make sure that the effect was there.

Let us judge the difference in performance. In the light version, the majority of reading times are in 3 digits, some are 4, and only a few are 5 digits long. The heavy data, however, is mostly populated by 6-digit numbers, representing a decrease in performance by a magnitude of 3

The following conclusions can be drawn from raw performance. The ability to isolate RAM appears to be lower than that of storage. Obviously, both the parallel access and size of shmap have an effect on performance, but, judging from the raw data in Fig. 6, increasing the size of shmap can have a major effect by itself.

Fig. 7 offers a 2D visualization of the entire dataset. Since the size has the largest effect, the order is *size, batchcount, batchsize*. The following simple interpretation of the visualization can be offered.

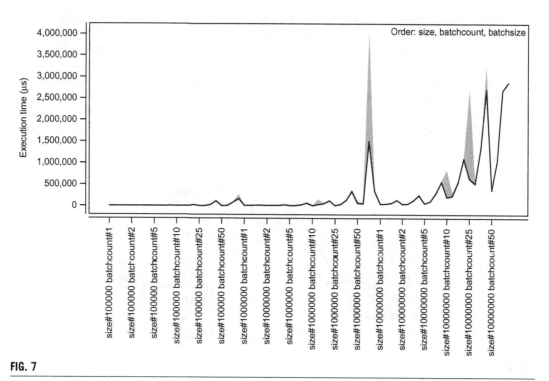

FIG. 7

Shmap performance plotted over the sequence of parameters taken in the order of size, batchcount, batchsize.

When the size is small, the other two parameters have little effect. However, when the size of shmap is large, both *batchcount* and *batchsize* start to have a major effect on performance, starting at the mid-range of the values.

This chapter will use the dataset in its current form while future research will focus on finding more details on the aforementioned drastic difference in performance.

10.3 THE BIG DATA REPLAY METHOD

This section explains the basics of the *replay method* and discusses the connection between time-aware processing of Big Data [16], specifically the *data streaming* approach [11], and the traditional Hadoop. This section also discusses recent advances in Big Data-related technology such as, for example, circuit emulation for bulk transfer. The section is concluded by a discussion of the various other performance bottlenecks which can happen in the new system.

10.3.1 THE REPLAY METHOD

This section focuses on explaining the design of the architecture powered by the replay method. For comparison with Hadoop architecture see Ref. [2].

Fig. 8 shows the architecture of the basic replay method. The following major changes are introduced:

- Shards are *dumb storage* while Hadoop assumes that jobs are executed on shards; note that the storage in shards is *time-aware* because shards can be replayed along the timeline.
- The name node is replayed by the *replay manager* — although the two are functionally very different. The name node represent the most important node in a cluster; however, in the replay method there is no name service, instead the shards are replayed in accordance with their time logic (sync operation in the figure).
- Clients and users are not the same node anymore, instead, the user can be a remote machine used to schedule jobs on clients, which can be internal to the cluster (located inside DCs) — note the

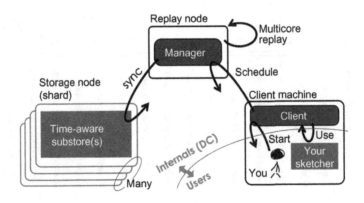

FIG. 8

The basic idea behind the Big Data replay on multicore method.

distinction of external versus internal traffic to the name node, as well as the contention between the two, which is a major problem in Hadoop.

The client/user part of the new design is an interesting element in itself. In data streaming, statistical digests of data are referred to as *sketches* [11]. The design in Fig. 8 borrows the term and shows that jobs can be implemented as *sketches*. Since sketches are statistically rigid (scientifically provable and mathematically defined), it is also likely that users would not come up with their own sketches, but would instead use a library provided at the client. This is another element where users and clients represent not only different roles, but also different physical machines.

Note that the intensive (meaning high-frequency) traffic exchange disappears both between clients and replay nodes as well as users and clients. Basically, only two exchanges are necessary — one to upload a sketcher and the other to download the results. Also note that the replay node does not strictly need to be *multicore*, but the presence of a multicore architecture greatly enhances the performance and flexibility of replay nodes. In fact, this entire chapter is dedicated to showcasing how efficient packing algorithms can help maximize both the capacity and flexibility of replay nodes.

The replay node is obviously a SPOF, just like the name node in Hadoop. However, this SPOF can be easily fixed by running multiple replay nodes and balancing between them. The difference between eplay node and name node is also fundamentally of a different nature — in the case of Hadoop the bottleneck is in the network part, where the high-rate and high-frequency traffic has to complete for the entrance into the name node. By comparison, the traffic contention in relay node is extremely rare, while jobs mostly compete for the multicore resource. In other words, upgrading the replay nodes can help with performance bottlenecks in replay, while the performance bottlenecks in Hadoop are mostly physical in nature.

10.3.2 JOBS AS SKETCHES ON A TIMELINE

Fig. 9 shows a more detailed representation of the replay method, this time naming the components of the new environment:

- *Time-awareness* is assumed for shards — it makes it possible to know which shard comes after which other shard, and, otherwise, facilitates the core replay process.

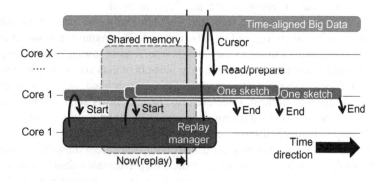

FIG. 9

The basic design of jobs implemented as data streaming sketches on a timeline.

- A *manager* is necessary to manage each of the multiple batches, where each batch is based on a *shared memory* (shmap) region.
- Shared memory is shared between managers and multiple sketches, where the communication is assumed to be designed in a *lockfree* manner and should not require any locking or message passing.
- There is a global *cursor* allowing the manager to denote the *now, here* position in shared memory, as well as individual cursors for each sketcher/job; both are necessary and are used for one-sided communication (lockfree) where jobs can detect the change in data and the manager can detect completion of batches by individual jobs.
- Finally, jobs have a clearly defined *lifespan*, which is a major improvement from the traditional Hadoop.

The obvious advantages of the new design are as follows: there is a clear parallel between *time window* and *shared memory*, where the shmap region can be, literally, treated by each sketch/job as a time-aligned window into the data. While jobs used to run in isolation, but using the same shards, in the new design, jobs are grouped in batches, where all jobs in the same batch process the same time window into data. Both these features are, in fact, on the list of requirements for the new generation of Hadoop-like systems [4]. In traditional Hadoop, such logic can only be implemented as multiple rounds of Hadoop jobs [4], each round covering the entire bulk of data. Communication between rounds may require that some kind of *state* be kept across rounds — another feature not supported by traditional Hadoop.

10.3.3 PERFORMANCE BOTTLENECKS UNDER REPLAY

"Circuits for bulk transfer" refers to the circuit emulation technology in Ref. [17]. It works both in Ethernet and optical networks, and relies on the *cut-through mode* available in any modern switching equipment, even the cheapest models [27]. A side note here is due on *circuits versus multisource aggregation* — the circuits are assumed to offer a much higher efficiency, while multisource aggregation is the technology for maximizing throughput in extremely unreliable networking — clouds and Peer-to-Peer (P2P) networks are used as examples in Ref. [28]. Another way to put it is to refer to circuits as the technology for achieving *nominal physical throughput* while multisource aggregation is the technology for squeezing out the *maximum possible performance* given the circumstances.

Fig. 10 returns to the bottleneck representation, but this time discusses new technologies which help improve performance with the aforementioned replay logic in mind.

Circuits assume that there is only one flow, and therefore, only one receiver thread/process. This explains why parallel access for *storage* in Fig. 10 is also at 1. This requires a minor change of design. Instead of requiring each manager to get its own shards from remote storage nodes, one process/thread can be given the schedule and put in charge of fetching the bulk of data and writing it into the respective *shmap*s. This is not difficult to implement in practice. On the other hand, one has to remember that the advantage of such a design is significant since even two parallel flows achieve worse network performance than two flows scheduled to be transmitted in sequence, without a time overlap.

Note that the *shmap* bottleneck discovered and discussed in the previous section is retained in the upgraded Fig. 10. This is bad news, because the dataset discussed herein shows that *shmap* is the worst performance bottleneck as it is hard to isolate, and since its performance degrades drastically with an increased parallel load. However, good news is possible here, as well, if batches are isolated physically using the experience from modern manycore clusters.

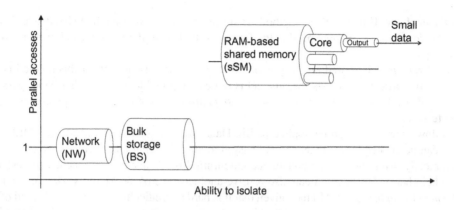

FIG. 10

How bottlenecks can be affected simply when using latest performance tricks — specifically the circuits for networking.

10.4 PACKING ALGORITHMS

This chapter expands on the basic replay method explained in the previous section and explains the various efficiency tricks which exploit the newly acquired flexibility in the new system. Specifically, the system has grown in scale, up to the level of a *massively multicore* architecture, reaching the area where the various *packing algorithms* discussed in this section finally find sufficient room for performance improvement.

10.4.1 SHARED MEMORY PERFORMANCE TRICKS

Essentially there are two ways to use shared memory, specifically, the *shmap* library referred to in this chapter — *memory map* versus *pointer exchange*. This subsection explains the two methods in detail.

The Memory Map method does exactly what the name says — all the data exchanged between the multiple users of shmap is supposed to be stored in shared memory. This is the conventional method, and it is used by the majority of shmap-based software today. Obviously the biggest problem with the method is the static structure itself. Dynamic changes and some level of variability can still be supported, however, they come at the price of having to increase the size of shmap and reduce efficiency by leaving some areas of the memory unused. This problem grows in proportion to the amount of variability/variety found in the data. Conversely, this problem is nonexistent if all data has a fixed and standard size — in fact, memory maps are the preferred format for fixed-size data structures.

Let us translate the Memory Map method into Big Data processing. Each time window is a time-aligned collection of data items. Variable-size items are standard for Big Data, with a few exceptions, such as Twitter, where one can safely assume that the message size cannot exceed 140 bytes (just as an example). There are two ways to convert such data into a memory map. First, one can find the largest size among all items in the window and then record the number globally, using it as the fixed size of all items in the shared memory. This makes *walking the data* a very simple endeavor. Alternatively, one can develop a protocol for writing variable-size records, which will drastically improve space efficiency, but will hinder *walking*, as each item will have to be parsed lightly before the system can jump to the next one. Either of these methods is sufficient, but the first method (fixed size) is always the best choice when processing speed is the first priority, hence, the fundamental problem with the memory maps.

Pointer Exchange via shared memory is possible. The proof of concept for this method is shown in Ref. [10]. It works with C/C++ threads and is not easily portable. On the other hand, passing the pointers — also referred to as *passing complex structures by reference* across processes is a very tempting feature.

The following example can be applied to Big Data processing. Double linked lists (DLLs), as in Ref. [10], can be created by the manager and passed to all processing jobs. Each job would then *walk* the DLL, mostly using the *next* pointer in each item, until the *now* cursor is reached (timestamps in items can help here). This method can also resolve another issue of the Memory Map method — the issue of *where to put the results?* In fact, given that it is hard to predict how many records (and of which size) are created by each job, one would find it very difficult to find a practical solution. In traditional multicore programming, the outcome is stringified and recorded somewhere outside of the shmap. The outcome can be put back into shmap only if its size and count are known in advance, but even in this case, communication in the opposite direction would require some form of locking or message passing. This is another reason for storing the outcome outside of *shmap* even if its size and count are known in advance.

The *lockfree* trick has already been mentioned, but requires special attention [10]. The basic description of the method is to say that the specific *design* makes it possible to minimize or completely remove locks in shared memory. The next step after design is *automatic code generation* in compilers.

A good example of a lockfree design is the aforementioned DLL. This example can also help the manager thread to process the outcome of the multiple processing threads in each batch. Let us assume that the output of each job is also put in the form of a DLL. This means that all the current items are also found in it — some outcome items may be the result of processing multiple raw items in the data stream. Let us also make a conscious decision to move an output item to the head of the DLL on each update — this is a simple operation in DLL that involves reassigning points and does not require any copy, delete, and other time-consuming operations. When this process is executed over time, one can easily visualize that old items would gradually sink to the bottom (tail) of the DLL since all update items are immediately moved to the head. This opens up the obvious hole for the *lockfree* trick — the manager can simply look at the tail of the DLL (via the direct pointer) and remove the time-outed output items without any communication with the job responsible for populating the DLL.

There is some literature on code generation for multicore parallel processing [29–32], but all such literature always uses locks and message passage as a part of its automatically generated code. In other words, the code generated with such compilers definitely performs much better than a single-core code, but much worse than the code crafted using the *lockfree* features. Note here that not all algorithms can be lockfree, by nature. For example, graph-based calculations [33] need coordination across threads, which is difficult to make *lockfree*. The good news is that Big Data processing jobs have zero need for interjob coordination, and are therefore the perfect subject for massive multicore environments.

There is a small body of literature that focuses on shared memory performance and discusses the various forms of lock optimization. Direct shmap access with kernel support is discussed in Ref. [34]. Shmap-based MPI implemented as a true one-side communication is proposed in Ref. [23].

10.4.2 BIG DATA REPLAY AT SCALE

Fig. 11 is an upgrade of the basic concept of replay presented earlier to a *massively multicore* environment. The new feature is the concept of job management within each time window. Each time window is dedicated to a given batch of jobs, where multiple batches can run on each replay node at any given point in time.

The *physical versus virtual* separation in the figure helps enhance the understanding of the nature of batches. The physical reality is that batches are shared memory regions and depend on *lockfree designs* [10], *one-sided* communication in MPI terminology [23], and the manager having to maintain the cursors for both the global position in the data and individual positions of processing jobs. However, the *virtual* representation allows for a simple abstraction which only keeps the elements required for the large-scale optimization of job packing. Which is why the simplified/virtual view only has batches and jobs allocated for each batch.

The virtual representation in Fig. 11 provides examples of the following problems. One problem involves packing a given number of jobs into a fixed number of batches — the traditional *bin packing* problem. Another problem involves transferring data too slow or too fast jobs between batches. Yet another problem can show how batches can be allocated in such a way that they would cover the largest possible span of time, in aggregate. The next subsection formulates the two most obvious packing algorithms. Future research will most likely reveal an expanded list of practical algorithms.

One main aspect to keep in mind when optimizing a scaled environment with many batches and many jobs is that *jobs are heterogeneous*. This means that one cannot know in advance whether or not a job can meet its expected timeline. The majority of attention focused on packing algorithms is spent on

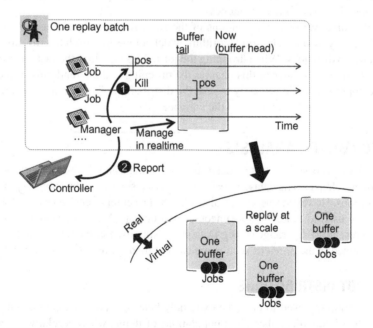

FIG. 11

The concept of job batches and their virtual representation (below) convenient for performance optimization.

countering this very aspect. Heterogeneity of jobs is also covered in recent literature on multicore code generation [32], which contributes to the foundation for the generation of lockfree code in the future.

10.4.3 PRACTICAL PACKING MODELS

Analysis described in the next section is performed based on the two practical packing algorithms. This subsection formulates each algorithm in detail.

The Drop algorithm represents the tough approach toward jobs management, hence its name. A batch is assumed to have a given fixed width (of the time window into data). The Drop algorithm would drop any job that goes beyond this width. The only alternative to dropping the job is to accommodate a larger window, which this algorithm avoids at all costs. Ideally, dropping a job does not result in that job's destruction — it can be easily mapped to another batch or a newly created batch. In fact, the replay environment in this section is assumed to be extremely fluid and such dynamics are intended to be part of its normal operation. Likewise, a new job can be mapped to the current batch to replace the removed job, thus allowing for efficient use of batches and, ultimately, resources on replay nodes.

The Drag algorithm is the opposing strategy (to the Drop algorithm). It allows the time window of the batch to grow, thus accommodating all the initially assigned jobs without having to remove or reassign them. The good part of this strategy is that it saves the overhead from removing and reassigning jobs. However, the downside of this strategy is that the increasing time window means that batches take longer to complete or, in other words, the operational grain of the system increases. Also, in cases when only a single job is very slow compared to its neighbors in the batch, this strategy can lead to the overall inefficiency of the replay node. All in all, this strategy is intuitively inefficient, but is still used in analysis covered later in this chapter in order to provide the comparison with the Drop model, as well as to study the bounds of variability in batches.

There are, of course, various combinations of the two primitive algorithms described herein. For example, one can easily assume a hybrid algorithm, which allows the batch to grow up to a given point, after which it starts to drop jobs. When dropping the jobs, does one drop the fastest or the slowest job? In fact, in analysis described later in this chapter the dropping is done randomly at the head and tail, but a more rigid approach would probably look at the distribution of cursor times and remove the node (head or tail) which contributes the most to the variance.

10.5 PERFORMANCE ANALYSIS

Analysis in this section is based on the two datasets — for storage and shared memory — created and explained earlier in this chapter. The datasets enable trace-based simulation by supplying the real data for a given set of conditions. However, this section also adds the last components necessary for analysis — the *hotspot distribution* used to model heterogeneous environments. With this added component, simulations can now represent the full range of Big Data processing used in the replay method. The Drag and Drop models explained in the previous section are used as management routines for individual batches.

10.5.1 HOTSPOT DISTRIBUTIONS

Hotspots [35] are normally used to describe extremely heterogeneous loads in a generic way. In numeric form, the distribution describes large populations of items, where a relatively small number of items contribute the overwhelming majority of the load.

The hotspots model was recently presented as a model for packet traffic [36]. The paper presents the mathematics behind the model, and the generation which can be applied both at packet and flow levels. A simplified version of the same method removes time dynamics and only uses sets of numbers [37].

The *hotspot model* is based on four sets of numbers referred to as *normal*, *population*, *hot*, and *flash*. In reality, there are only three sets, as *hot* and *flash* describe the same items at two different stages in their lifespans. The sets can be used to describe a wide range of heterogeneous phenomena occurring in nature. However, let us consider an example involving a content delivery network (CDN). In any CDN, the total number of hosted items is very large, but most of the items are rarely requested/watched — those are *normal*. The ratio of *normal* items can reach 80% in some cases; and higher with an increasing scale. A portion of the remaining items is watched more, but is not at the level of becoming hits — those are the *popular* items. The popular items rarely change during their lifespan — another way to describe it is a slow but steady demand for a given type of content (in CDN terminology).

The remaining *hot/flash* items are the core of the distribution. There are relatively few items, but they consume the majority of traffic to and from CDN. This happens because of two features hidden in the two sets. First, the level of *hot* popularity of an item can be sufficiently large and account for a major portion of traffic when the aggregate traffic with all the other *hot* items is considered. But, more importantly, *hot* items sometimes experience *flash crowds* — this is when the demand rapidly peaks for a given item — the value for this popularity comes from the *flash* set. The peak traffic can be sufficiently high to constitute the majority of CDN traffic on a given day.

In complex modeling, the process is modeled in time, allowing items to grow from *hot* to *flash* gradually. However, for the purposes of modeling in this chapter, the simplified version from Ref. [37] is applied, meaning that only the static sets are used without any time dynamics between them.

Yet, even in the simplified *sets-only* form, distributions are difficult to judge. It is helpful to classify distributions based on their curvature. The following classification method is applied in this chapter for the first time. First, imagine the log values of the sets plotted in decreasing order of value. Given the nature of the distribution, *hotspots* — there are normally only a few of them — would be plotted at the head of the distribution and then the curve would drop for the rest of the values. Note that the drop would be experienced even on the log scale. Here, the only way to classify such a distribution is to judge the size of its *head*.

So, classification in this chapter uses the following ranges for classification, all in log scale:

- if values at 80% and further into the list are 0.15 or above, then *Class A* is assigned
- if values at 60% and further into the list are 0.6 or above, then *Class B* is assigned
- if values at 40% and further into the list are 1.3 or above, then *Class C* is assigned
- if values at 30% and further into the list are 1.8 or above, then *Class D* is assigned
- if no class is assigned by this point, then *Class E* is assigned

The class preceding assignment is fine-tuned to the distributions used for analysis further in this chapter. The tuning was done in such a way that each class would get a roughly equal share of distributions, which were otherwise distributed for a reasonably large-parameter space. As another simplification, each hotspot distribution is converted into two separate curves by combining *popular+hot* and *popular+flash* sets, each classified and used separately. Only 100 values were generated for each distribution, but this is sufficient, as values during simulation are selected randomly from the list, which means that relatively low values are selected much more frequently than the large items. Otherwise, the same process is used as in Refs. [36] and [37], where there are 2–3 other parameters such as variance, number of hot items, variance across hot items, etc.

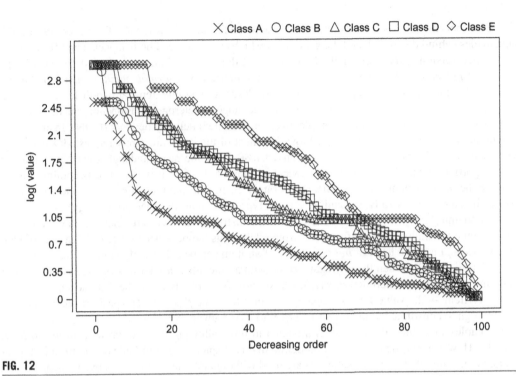

FIG. 12

Example distribution each attributed to a class from A to E. Vertical scale is in log.

Fig. 12 shows several curves from the dataset, each marked in accordance with its calculated class. We can see that the classification is successful by assigning a higher letter to a curve with a relatively higher number of hotspots. Note that the generation process has no maximum value, but, in order to avoid extremely long processing sessions, all values exceeding 1000 are brought back to 1000. The values (not logs, but the original number behind) are translated into per-item processing time, expressed in microseconds (μs). To add more flexibility to the otherwise fixed pool of hotspot distributions, the *scale parameter* was added to scale per-item overhead within 1–3 orders of magnitude down from the value found in the hotspot dataset.

10.5.2 MODELING METHODOLOGY

Fig. 13 shows the overall simulation process, which puts the two real (storage and shmap) and one synthetic (hotpost) datasets into a single simulation.

Simulation parameters come mostly from the two real datasets — one needs to set *size*, *batchcount*, *batchsize* for shmap, and *threads*, *blocksize* and others for storage. However, some simplifications are made at this stage. *Blocksize* is fixed to 100k, in which 10 iterations makes for 1 MB, shmap is *sized* to 1 MB, and *file handling* is ignored as having little effect on performance. On the other hand, *batchcount* and *batchsize* are selected randomly from the values found in the dataset. Given that the two datasets are related, *threadcount* is not selected randomly but is set after the *batchcount*, based on the logical assumption that parallel storage handling is happening for all batches currently in operation.

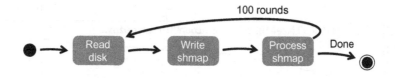

FIG. 13

Sequence of actions in each simulation run.

The only new parameter added in this section is the *class*. The base hotspot classes were explained in the previous subsection. The parameter *class* can have values *A*, *AB*, *ABC*, *ABCD*, and *ABCDE*, randomly selected for each application. The values specify the range for classes during selection — for example, when set to *ABC*, hotspot distributions for each job in a given batch can be selected from any A, B, or C classes. In practical terms, this parameter controls the heterogeneity of jobs, where *A* class is the most and *E* class is the least heterogeneous.

Each simulation run is conducted in the order described in Fig. 13. Since the target is to emulate a real replay process on a massively multicore hardware, the simulation is built to closely mirror a real process. So, as Fig. 13 shows, first, the real dataset is used to emulate the storage operations — the stage at which, in reality, managers of shmaps read data from storage and use it to populate shmaps. Shmap population incurs additional overhead and is therefore isolated into a separate stage in the sequence. Finally, the contents of shmap are processed by all jobs in all batches, at which time the hotspot dataset (only the synthetic one) is used to model the additional overhead for each item on top of the baseline value spent by each job simply on reading the contents.

The *scale* parameter in simulation specifically targets this borderline between the baseline shmap reading and item-by-item processing. The baseline shmap reading time is used as the starting value for each job. However, the job is also expected to spend some time for each item found in shmap. For simplicity, items are considered to be 100-bytes long (10,000 items in the 1 MB shmap). To define the per-item overhead, each job selects a hotspot distribution (using the preceding class range) and selects values from it randomly, as processing time is in microseconds (µs), but also multiplying each value with the scale. The scale of 0.001 would basically mean that the largest (hotspot=rare) overhead is 10 µs, since the largest value in the hotspot datasets is 1000 µs. A scale of 1 would, therefore, describe cases where per-item overhead is extremely high.

The rest of this section will be dedicated to discussing the results of the simulation conducted using the preceding methodology.

10.5.3 PROCESSING OVERHEAD VERSUS BOTTLENECKS

One major element of this chapter is the *bottleneck analysis*, since removing or improving bottlenecks is the fastest way to improve the overall performance of the system. This subsection discusses a snapshot of aggregate simulation outcomes which clearly indicate where the performance bottlenecks are given the limitations of the system.

Fig. 14 aggregates all the outcomes for the simulations running with the setup of *blocksize*=100 k (this is fixed for all), *shmap size* =1 M (also fixed), *batchcount*=10, and *batchsize*=2 — this is a relatively light setting given that only 2 jobs are running in each batch. Note that *scale*, *hotspot classes* and other parameters are not part of the aggregation conditions, which means that the distribution curve

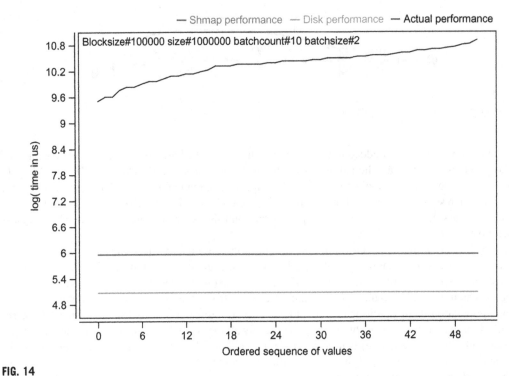

FIG. 14

Distribution of processing overhead (log values) compared with the SSD and Shmap bottlenecks taken from the datasets.

contains all the outcomes from all the values in these and other parameters, which are not indicated in the selection rule (also plotted on the figure).

Before using this particular aggregation, the various selection rules were tested. Fig. 14 was found to be objectively better than all the other selection rules — this means that the lower end of the curve shows the best possible performance, that is, the one when the scale is set to 0.001, classes selected are the widest possible, etc.

So, Fig. 14 clearly shows that the per-item processing is, in fact, the biggest bottleneck in the system. By comparison, the *shmap* and *disk/storage* bottleneck are plotted as well — these values are the same for the selection rule. The term "bottleneck" can be confusing here because the horizontal lines represent *completion time*, that is, the reverse value to the width of the bottleneck. However, conceptually, the visualization concept still stands.

The simple take-home lesson from Fig. 14 is that, even given the shmap and storage performance bottlenecks, their effect can be neglected as long as the per-item processing performance remains at the shown level. Note that physical separation of batches as is done in manycore systems is not an option here. Also note that the 0.001 scale (between 0.001 and $10\,\mu s$ per item overhead) might be too high for a realistic system, in which case the natural performance curve in some systems might be lower. Measurement of real loads as a subject is left for further study.

10.5.4 CONTROL GRAIN FOR DROP VERSUS DRAG MODELS

Fig. 15 presents several diagonal plots that compare performance between the *Drop* versus *Drag* packing algorithms. Note that performance metrics for the two methods are completely different. The Drop method is evaluated by the count of drops per unit of time. The Drag method does not allow for drops

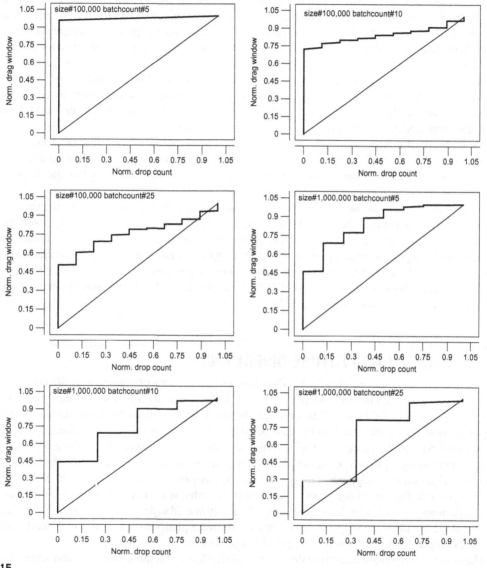

FIG. 15

Diagonal plots for normalized distributions of drop versus drag performance metrics (count and window, respectively). Each plot represents the aggregates for a given set of analysis parameters, the values for which are shown.

and can therefore be evaluated by the width of the time window after some running time. However, if the values are normalized, they can be compared in a diagonal plot. Here, the main target of the analysis is not to see the real values (10–20 drops versus 60–100 s windows were found in raw data), but to compare the distributions of values, where distribution curves can offer some insight into performance dynamics.

The 6 plots in Fig. 15 are, as before, aggregates based on specific selection rules. Each rule is shown in each plot as the values of parameters applied to the selection. In left-to-right and top-down sequences, the values in the selection rules gradually increase, thus, representing aggregates for relatively light dataset/simulation conditions at first, but gradually moving toward heavier and busier systems.

In Fig. 15, the Drag model shows far worse dynamics than the Drop model — the curve would simply jump from the minimum to the maximum value and stay there. In other words, outcomes for the Drag model are mostly around the upper margin, which explains the shape of the curve. On the other hand, the Drop model has values spread smoothly across the range.

As the aggregates move from lighter to heavier conditions, performance of the Drag model grows less extreme, with gradually more and more values in between the lower and higher extremes. In the bottom-right plot, the curve has moved very close to the diagonal line, indicating that the dynamics of the two packing algorithms are somewhat similar.

There is another way to interpret Fig. 15. Since each curve represents outcomes for the various values for parameters outside of the selector, the curve also offers some insight into whether or not the two packing algorithms can be controlled by changing the operating parameter at runtime. Smoother curves would normally represent a smooth response to changing the parameter, while extreme changes — as those in the top-left plot in Fig. 15, are examples of extreme responses.

This also links back to the discussion of hybrid packing methods which control both the drop rate and window size as part of the same algorithm.

10.6 SUMMARY AND FUTURE DIRECTIONS

This chapter extends the core idea of Big Data Replay into the area of massively multicore hardware environments. The term *massively multicore* in this chapter is distinct from the well-recognized *manycore*, both in terms of hardware — the cores on the massively multicore hardware do not need to be supported by special hardware, as is the case of GPU-based or other manycore systems, and in terms of the complexity of the processing logic running on top of such architecture. In the manycore field, cores are built at rigid physical units only loosely attached to the hardware of the host machine — for example, as hardware boards plugs into free slots on the otherwise commodity hardware. Such a design makes it possible for a good degree of isolation between what is running on the manycore board and what is running on the OS back on the host's own hardware. Manycore systems make extensive use of L1 and L2 hardware caching and have intricate software platforms which use both hardware and software components to offer the highest possible performance.

The massively multicore hardware does not need that level of intense hardware and software support. Given that Big Data processing jobs do not require coordination among each other, a simple hardware with hundreds of cores simply stacked on top of each other should work, in theory. In reality, industry today is mostly invested into manycore systems, which is why there is no hardware that fits the aforementioned description of a massively multicore system. However, based on the advantages of the replay method described in this chapter, there is hope that *massively multicore* hardware will gather more attention, even if its main applications will be limited to Big Data processing.

The replay method is a drastic change from the traditional Hadoop/MapReduce architecture. While the latter is based on the extreme level of network distribution of its various functions, the former avoids networking and favors one-machine operation. This chapter points to literature by other authors which have already raised the *one-machine* case, promising, like this chapter, a major improvement in performance.

One reason why one-machine operations may be preferred comes from the fact that network distribution is plagued with various performance bottlenecks. Some of them are discussed by the creators in a paper which denotes clear limits to the throughput of Hadoop/MapReduce clusters. Others — for example, network congestion — are not recognized in traditional Hadoop literature but are discussed in detail in this paper.

Discussing and classifying the various performance bottlenecks takes up a large portion of this chapter. The bottlenecks are first formulated simply by their width (throughput, capacity), but then are expended into a 2D space of *ability to isolate* versus *parallel access*, and finally optimized using recent advances in technology, specifically by improving the networking part of the system. As a side note, the replay method depends on one-machine operation, but the cluster is still distributed and depends on networking across the multiple nodes in the clusters. The main difference, however, is that the nodes are supposed to be passive in the replay method, while Hadoop/MapReduce supports a complex environment in which jobs are sent to run on storage nodes, referred to as shards.

An interesting revelation was made in the first two (real) datasets. As a general rule, it is assumed that shared memory can handle much more throughput than storage, even when the latter is based on SSD. However, the experiments reveal that shared memory (shmap library) on commodity hardware performs poorly under a heavy parallel load. In fact, by the definition of the batch-based replay in the chapter, parallel access to shared memory is supposed to be many times heavier than access to storage, which means that the dataset indicates a problem which can be considered *normal* in such environments.

Performance analysis in this chapter was based on three datasets. The first two came from real-life experiments in the area of parallel access to storage and shared memory, with each experiment run separately. The third dataset was completely synthetic and was used to generate heterogeneous loads based on hotspots. Given the nature of hotspot distribution, the load was extremely heterogeneous. Note that the heterogeneity of jobs is a major concern in recent literature, both in the area of Big Data processing and in multicore parallel programming.

Simulation results show that, even considering performance bottlenecks found in storage and shared memory, the bottleneck of per-item overhead is the narrowest of all, even when distribution of per-item overhead is designed using the hotspot model and the largest hotspots are only allowed to incur, at most, $10\,\mu s$ overheads. It is unlikely that a real load can offer milder distributions, which means that the throughput restricted by the per-item bottleneck is probably the maximum achievable throughput in objective reality. However, given that many batches and many jobs can run in parallel, the scale of the replay process can alleviate the negative effect of this hard performance bottleneck.

Note that this last revelation calls for comparisons with Hadoop. On one hand, Hadoop is also limited by the per-item bottleneck, which it improves by using network distribution. However, the key difference here is network distribution itself, as the key difference between the two systems. The simple statement offered by this chapter is that scaling inside a single machine is more efficient than scaling over the network. This performance margin is the key difference between Hadoop and the Replay environments.

This research opens up several topics for discussion, many of which were addressed in this chapter. The immediately obvious place for improvement is the weakness of shmap in the face of heavy parallel loads. Note that shmap in this chapter was used in the *lockfree* manner, ie, without locks and with messages that are passive across processes. This means that the overhead found in experiments is solely due to the in-kernel handling of shared memory. There is obviously room for improvement here, without resorting to hardware assistance.

Other venues include the various packing algorithms on top of the two simple ones presented and analyzed in this chapter. Simulation results show that the methods offer some level of flexibility when responding to simulation parameters. This means that a hybrid method which would regulate the drop rate together with window size at runtime could result in better performance than either of the algorithms discussed in this chapter. Moreover, there is a wide range of other parameters that can support alternative methods without resorting to the *drop* and *drag* functions. For example, algorithms which remap jobs to other batches rather than drop them entirely might result in a better overall performance of a Replay engine.

Finally, since the single replay node in a cluster is the obvious SPOF, research into running multiple replay nodes in parallel is expected. The main difference with Hadoop here is that replay nodes allow for independent operation and do not depend on syncing across the multiple nodes. Running multiple name nodes in Hadoop, on the other hand, suffers from just that problem, which puts the upper limit on the number of name nodes a Hadoop cluster can handle.

REFERENCES

[1] Apache Hadoop. Available at: http://hadoop.apache.org/(current).
[2] Zhanikeev M. Streaming algorithms for Big Data processing on multicore. In: Li K-C, Jiang H, Yang LT, Cuzzocrea A, editors. Big Data: algorithms, analytics, and applications. Boca Raton, FL: CRC; 2015, ISBN 978-1-4822-4055-9.
[3] Shvachko K. HDFS scalability: the limits to growth. Mag USENIX 2012;35(2):6–16.
[4] Rowstron A, Narayanan S, Donnelly A, O'Shea G, Douglas A. Nobody ever got fired for using Hadoop on a cluster. In: 1st ACM international workshop on hot topics in cloud data processing, April 2012. Bern, Switzerland: ACM; 2012.
[5] Chen Y, Ganapathi A, Griffith R, Katz R. The case for evaluating MapReduce performance using workload suites. In: 19th IEEE international symposium on modeling, analysis and simulation of computer and telecommunication systems (MASCOTS), July 2011. Singapore: IEEE; 2011. p. 390–9.
[6] Ren Z, Xu X, Wan J, Shi W, Zhou M. Workload characterization on a production Hadoop cluster: a case study on taobao. In: IEEE international symposium on workload characterization; San Diego, CA: IEEE; 2012. p. 3–13.
[7] Das S, Sismanis Y, Beyer K, Gemulla R, Haas P, McPherson J. Ricardo: integrating R and Hadoop. In: ACM International Conference on Management of data (SIGMOD). Indianapolis, IN: ACM; June 2010. pp. 987–99.
[8] Gao X, Nachankar V, Qiu J. Experimenting with Lucene index on HBase in an HPC environment. In: 1st annual workshop on high performance computing meets databases (HPCDB); Salt Lake City, UT: co-published by IEEE and ACM; 2012. p. 25–8.

[9] Chen R, Chen H, Zang B. Tiled-MapReduce: optimizing resource usages of data-parallel applications on multicore with tiling. In: 19th international conference on parallel architectures and compilation techniques (PACT), September 2010; Haifa, Israel: co-published by IEEE and ACM; 2010. p. 523–34.

[10] Zhanikeev M. A lock-free shared memory design for high-throughput multicore packet traffic capture. Int J Netw Manag 2014;24:304–17.

[11] Muthukrishnan S. Data streams: algorithms and applications. Found Trends Theor Comput Sci 2005;1(2):117–236.

[12] Zhanikeev M. Methods and algorithms for fast hashing in data streaming. In: Azad S, Pathan A-SK, editors. Cryptography: algorithms and implementations using C++. Boca Raton, FL: CRC; 2014.

[13] Zhanikeev M. A holistic community-based architecture for measuring end-to-end QoS at data centres. Int J Comput Sci Eng 2013;10(3):315–24.

[14] Venkataraman S, Song D, Gibbons P, Blum A. New streaming algorithms for fast detection of superspreaders. In: Distributed system security symposium (NDSS). San Diego, CA: Internet Society; 2005.

[15] Sung M, Kumar A, Li L, Wang J, Xu J. Scalable and efficient data streaming algorithms for detecting common content in internet traffic. In: ICDE workshop. Atlanta, GA: IEEE; 2006.

[16] Datar M, Gionis A, Indyk P, Motwani R. Maintaining stream statistics over sliding windows. SIAM J Comput 2002;31(6):1794–813.

[17] Zhanikeev M. Circuit emulation for big data transfers in clouds. In: Yu S, Lin X, Misic J, Shen X, editors. Networking for Big Data. Boca Raton, FL: CRC; 2015 (in print).

[18] Zhanikeev M. Replayable big data for multicore processing and statistically rigid sketching. In: Internet conference. Hiroshima, Japan; 2014. Paper no.7.

[19] Zhanikeev M. Can we benefit from solid state drives in rich multimedia content processing, storage and streaming? ITE/IEICE technical report on multimedia storage (ITE-MMS), October. vol.113, Fukuoka, Japan: IEICE; 2013. paper no.1.

[20] Kerrisk M. The Linux programming interface. San Francisco, CA: No Starch Press; 2010.

[21] Leveraging multi-core processors through parallel programming. Cognizant White Paper. Cognizant; August 2011. www.cognizant.com

[22] Jarp S, Lazzaro A, Nowak A. The future of commodity computing and many-core versus the interests of HEP software. J Phys Conf Ser 2012;396(5). paper no.052058 (online series).

[23] Potluri S, Wang H, Dhanraj V, Sur S, Panda D. Optimizing MPI one sided communication on multi-core InfiniBand clusters using shared memory backed windows. In: 18th European MPI users' group meeting (EuroMPI). LNCS, vol. 6960. Santorini, Greece: Springer; 2011. p. 99–109.

[24] Rasooli A, Down D. COSHH: a classification and optimization based scheduler for heterogeneous Hadoop systems. Technical report of McMaster University, Canada; 2013.

[25] Zhanikeev M. Experiences from measuring per-packet cost of software defined networking. IEICE technical report on service computing (SC), vol. 113(86). Tokyo, Japan: IEICE; 2013. p. 31–4. June.

[26] JSON format. Available at: www.json.org (current).

[27] Zhanikeev M. Cut-through network designs for high-throughput E2E networking. IPSJ technical meeting on high performance computing (HPC), vol.148(36). Tokyo, Japan: IEICE; 2015. p. 1–4. March.

[28] Zhanikeev M. Multi-source stream aggregation in the cloud. Pathan M, Sitaraman RK, Robinson D, editors. Advanced content delivery, streaming, and cloud services. New York, NY: Wiley; 2014, ISBN: 978-1-118-57521-5.

[29] Stoichev S, Marinova S. Parallel algorithm for integer sorting with multi-core processors. Inf Technol Control 2009;3:246–60.

[30] Madruga F, Freitas H, Navaux P. Parallel shared-memory workloads performance on asymmetric multi-core architectures. In: 18th IEEE Euromicro conference on parallel, distributed and network-based processing (PDP), February 2010. Pisa, Italy: IEEE; 2010. p. 163–9.

[31] Liu L, Feng J, Li G, Qian Q, Li J. Parallel structural join algorithm on shared-memory multi-core systems. In: 9th international conference on web-age information management (WAIM), July 2008. Zhangjiajie, China: IEEE; 2008. p. 70–7.

[32] Schneider S. Shared memory abstractions for heterogeneous multicore processors. Doctor dissertation. Virginia Polytechnic Institute; 2010.

[33] Sui X, Nguyen D, Burtscher M, Pingali K. Parallel graph partitioning on multicore architectures. In: 23rd international conference on languages and compilers for parallel computing (LCPC). Houston, TX: Springer; 2010. p. 246–60.

[34] Brightwell R. Lightweight kernel support for direct shared memory access on a multi-core processor. In: Workshop on managed many-core systems, June 2008. Boston, MA; 2008.

[35] Bodík P, Fox A, Franklin M, Jordan M, Patterson D. Characterizing, modeling, and generating workload spikes for stateful services. In: 1st ACM symposium on cloud computing (SoCC); 2010. p. 241–52.

[36] Zhanikeev M, Tanaka Y. Popularity-based modeling of flash events in synthetic packet traces. IEICE technical report on communication quality, vol. 112(288). Nagahama, Japan; 2012. p. 1–6.

[37] Zhanikeev M. The next generation of networks is all about hotspot distributions and cut-through circuits. IEICE technical report on communication quality (CQ), vol. 115(11). Fukuoka, Japan; 2015. p. 1–4.

BIG DATA
SECURITY AND
PRIVACY

PART

III

BIG DATA
SECURITY AND
PRIVACY

SPATIAL PRIVACY CHALLENGES IN SOCIAL NETWORKS

11

R.O. Sinnott, S. Sun

11.1 INTRODUCTION

New technology supporting large-scale (big) data collection and associated data analytics is challenging personal privacy in unprecedented and unforeseen ways. Big Data is typically high volume, high velocity, heterogeneous, and distributed with varying degrees of veracity [1]. Big Data can be created and collected by individuals, organisations, or external agencies, often with the aim of applying data analytics to improve services, products, or decision-making functions that can potentially add competitive advantages [2]. The tools and infrastructure for supporting the capture and analysis of Big Data are widespread, for example, MapReduce and ElasticSearch are algorithms now taught at the undergraduate level that allow processing of extensive and heterogeneous data. Data analytics is increasingly being used to derive meaningful patterns from such data. However, such approaches have a potential downside with regard to privacy. Social media is one example of Big Data that raises many challenges in terms of privacy. Many consider that the privacy issues for data that is randomly posted by individuals in tweets, blogs, and through images onto the Internet are less important; however, many social media data sets contain extensive data that can reveal information that users may be unaware of, including their geospatial location. In this chapter we explore these issues, focusing especially on the challenges of privacy, with a specific focus on location privacy.

11.2 BACKGROUND

Social media data differs from other Big Data applications such as astrophysics since, by its very nature, it operates on personal/organizational information, and hence there are often significant privacy concerns [3]. The availability of information in social networks is commonplace and users are often unaware of just how much information they reveal when they use resources such as Twitter. A single 140-character tweet can contain 9 kb of metadata about the user, including their followers, their background, and potentially their location. To make matters worse, it is easy to find patterns in these data sets through data mining and exploitation of Big Data infrastructures. This can be done directly through the content of data, or indirectly from the metadata and geospatial information that is often associated with data. This is in an increasingly common phenomenon due to the ubiquity of mobile devices with location-based services that are now available. To illustrate this issue, consider the unforeseen use of Twitter data in Fig. 1 where individuals can be tracked through the day moving around Melbourne. Here, colour codes are used to represent the daily movements of individual tweeters and the height of the lines represents the time of day of the tweet. The contents of a given tweet are also displayed.

Big Data. http://dx.doi.org/10.1016/B978-0-12-805394-2.00011-8

FIG. 1

Tracking Twitter Users around Melbourne via Tweets.

It could be argued that location-based information itself should be removed at the source, for example, by Twitter; however, there is an increasing demand to localise the aggregated analysis of such data. This can be true for real-time information on a variety of issues: congested transport routes around cities [4], using Twitter data as the basis for early warning health outbreaks (eg, avian flu, ebola virus outbreaks) [5], natural hazards (bushfires, earthquakes, floods) [6] amongst many other scenarios.

Despite the obvious privacy issues, Big Data and data analytics can provide significant benefits to society. A key element of this is increasing public understanding of the enormous growth in data collection and retention, borne in part by mobile technologies and the Internet-of-Things [7]. Society is becoming increasingly aware and suspicious of data collection techniques that exploit individuals' own data for often undisclosed and/or unforeseen purposes. Some individuals may view the loss of privacy as giving away a few personal demographics; however, the aggregation of these resources can be used to profile individuals and society as a whole [8,9]. Furthermore, data analytics and visualization, and the use of large-scale computational infrastructures and algorithms now allow for probing far more deeply into personal privacy than ever before [10,11].

An investigation of social network users' privacy management regarding their awareness of privacy issues and configurations of associated social media systems was carried out by Ref. [12] through a survey involving over 2000 randomly selected adults. The research revealed the complexity of different social network privacy settings, as half of users expressed difficulties in configuring the information access rules when using their social network privacy settings. It identified that the settings of some social networking solutions were "overly complex, ever-changing, and even obscure."

It is now widely recognized that privacy issues are exacerbated in the Big Data era. A user's privacy can be lost if he or she is tagged in an uploaded photo without his or her knowledge or permission. There are no privacy rules for dealing with such issues. Apart from the lack of awareness of losing privacy, [13] stated the (worrying!) ease of finding meaningful patterns in Big Data to predict one's future behavior given the ubiquitous amount of analytic tools and the extreme richness of such information.

Rather than focusing on the social network itself, there are a number of researchers investigating the privacy of location-based services since increasing numbers of social networks have integrated geospatial content. Metrics accessing the location privacy issues, including the precision of positioning users, were suggested by Kang et al. [14]. In addition, Tang et al. [15] explored a number of means of privacy attacks and provided corresponding protection methods. The worryingly high number of location-based services and the threat to privacy was revealed by De Montjoye's research [16]. They showed how it was possible to identify a person using just four spatiotemporal data points.

All of the aforementioned research presumes that the victim of information leakage is the end user—either an individual or organizational user of social networks using location-based services. Given the increasing capability for mining sensitive social network content and its associated location information, it is directly possible to draw patterns between the sets of information and reveal privacy information of certain locations and, hence, of individuals. One example of location privacy information is the usage of a certain building, for example, for scientific research, entertainment activity, or indeed to know what individuals in a specific household are doing. Losing the location privacy of a building obviously raises many issues, especially when linked with the users and/or usage of that building. Therefore, not only users but also locations need privacy protection, and there is a clear need for assessing the privacy issues regarding locations as well as the privacy of users and organizations. This is a different philosophy compared with the work on privacy thus far that has largely considered the individual whose rights might be violated; however, with the technologies and Big Data processing platforms now, it is actually the privacy that can arise out of a given location that is of concern. Thus, knowing what a given person tweets about is one thing, but knowing who has ever sent a tweet from a given building or indeed any specific location, for example, outside the Houses of Parliament in London, is another thing.

The chapter seeks to answer the following questions: in which form does location privacy occur when using social networks, including location-based services, and what is the consequence of this? As such, we first examine the feasibility of extracting social media content based on locations instead of users and then analyze how the extracted content may reveal the location identity, such as the name of the location, the general purpose of the location, or the events that might have happened in that location. The severity of spatial privacy issues will be assessed in terms of how critical the extracted information is and how losing spatial privacy can lead to privacy issues to users themselves.

11.3 SPATIAL ASPECTS OF SOCIAL NETWORKS

Exploring spatial privacy demands of social media through Big Data approaches implies that the social media content can be geolocated at a degree of accuracy and that large-scale data is available. Manually collecting such data is impractical, for example, by scraping web sites for data, hence open APIs to collect information (data) from the social network are essential. Let us consider an analysis of the APIs of different social networks. There are many potential social media software systems; however, here we focus on those that are mainstream and have known APIs. Specifically, we consider Google Plus, Facebook, Twitter, Instagram, and Flickr as representative of the wider social networking software systems for text, tweets, and images that are shared in vast quantities online.

Google Plus provides a representational state transfer (REST)-based API interface to perform basic create-read-update-delete (CRUD) operations on a given user's personal information, comments, and activities [17]. There are limits imposed on the amount of daily API calls that can be made to the Google Plus API. Furthermore, the location-based query capabilities available through this API are limited to the scale of a city instead of an exact location, for example, down to the precise location of a building block. As such, Google Plus does not support disaggregated data harvesting that can be used to explore fine-grained location privacy issues.

Facebook offers a graph-based API that can be used to extract user information, including a users' profile and his/her timeline/posts with location filters available [18]. However, the privacy policy of Facebook places constraints on use of this API such that the detailed information can only be extracted if the owner of the information is a friend of the API holder. For exploring location privacy issues for arbitrary individuals, this model does not satisfy the demand for large amounts of geospatially coded information.

Twitter provides a Streaming and a Search API that can be used to collect (harvest) tweets [19]. Importantly, users and developers can filter tweets based on a range of coordinate properties—typically through a bounding box, for example, tweets inside of a given set of coordinates, or a point/radius, for example, tweets within a circle of radius of 100 m from a given point. Tweets themselves can include an exact latitude/longitude (point) when the location-based service of the device is activated. If the location-based service is not activated, then the location is typically aggregated to the user's profile information, for example, the user is from Melbourne, and therefore the tweet is identified as being sent from Melbourne. Twitter imposes a limit on the data rates and will blacklist accounts streaming tweets faster than approximately 120 tweets per minute. Nevertheless, through use of multiple Twitter developer accounts and the Cloud, it is possible to parallelize the harvesting of Twitter data to get Big Data.

Instagram provides a RESTful API that can be used to retrieve uploaded photos including their description, comments, and metadata such as tagged users [20]. Like Twitter, photos can be filtered according to their coordinate properties. All photos created within a 3-km radius from a given user-defined point can be retrieved. As such, Instagram does not provide the disaggregated level of data necessary for exploration of location privacy.

Flickr also offers a RESTful API, with limited features for location-based querying supported by the API [21]. The spatial aspects of social media networking software are summarized in Table 1.

As seen, Twitter is the only social networking software that supports truly disaggregated spatial data that can lead to location privacy issues arising. This can be to a very specific latitude/longitude to within a few centimeters' degree of accuracy [22]. This chapter thus focuses on the privacy challenges of social media data from Twitter.

Table 1 API Features of Different Social Networking Software

SNS	API Type	Location Filters	Limitations
Google+	REST	Location name with the scale of city (eg, New York)	Numbers of daily requests are capped. Location filter is not precise
Facebook	REST & SDKs supporting different languages	Location name precise to the scale of a building block	Only detailed information available to Facebook friends
Twitter	REST	Location name and coordinate filters available	Stream speed is capped; however location data can be very disaggregated
Instagram	REST	Location name and coordinate filters available	Location is only down to 3 km, which is not sufficient for many privacy aspects
Flickr	REST	Not available	No geolocation information retrievable

11.4 CLOUD-BASED BIG DATA INFRASTRUCTURE

To support Big Data processing and data privacy analytics on a global scale, large-scale and scalable infrastructure is required. Clouds provide an ideal environment for data processing and storage demands through their flexibility and scalability. However, the outsourcing nature of Clouds has its own privacy issues that can impact many domains [23]. Furthermore, there are many Cloud flavors [24], including Infrastructure-as-a-Service (IaaS), Platform-as-a-Service, and Software-as-a-Service offered by a multitude of providers such as Amazon, Microsoft, and others. Across Australia, the National eResearch Collaboration Tools and Resources (NeCTAR—www.nectar.org.au) project offers an IaaS platform based on OpenStack Cloud technology (www.openstack.org). Many researchers use the NeCTAR Research Cloud for a variety of data processing tasks, from climate research [25], humanities research [26], genomics research [27], through targeted clinical data collection and processing [28].

In the NeCTAR IaaS model, researchers can request computing resources, including processors and Cloud storage, on demand. There are approximately 30,000 physical servers that are currently available through NeCTAR. These resources are distributed across eight sites throughout Australia. These are offered as availability zones to researchers who are to select the site/resources that best fits their needs. A variety of Cloud resource types are available from large-scale virtual machines with 64 Gb memory through small VMs with 4 Gb memory. Data storage is available from projects such as the Research Data Services project (RDS—www.rds.edu.au), which makes available multipetabytes of data storage to Australian researchers. The NeCTAR project itself is led by the University of Melbourne.

In collecting social media data for location privacy exploration, it is essential that extensive amounts of tweets are collected. Twitter offers APIs that allow access to streamed tweets or for targeted searches, for example, tweets from a particular user. Importantly, Twitter supports ongoing connections from Twitter clients (harvesters) and the API. This model supports continued harvesting of data. A range of existing libraries in Python and Java are freely available for accessing and using data from Twitter. At present, over 65 million tweets have been harvested on the NeCTAR Cloud for the cities of Australia and are used for a range of scenarios in a variety of projects at the University of Melbourne. This resource continues to grow—a key element of the scalability and flexibility offered by the Cloud.

The tweets themselves (and their metadata) are stored as JSON documents in a noSQL database. There are many noSQL solutions that are now available. CouchDB and CouchBase are two leading noSQL solutions [29]. CouchDB is an open source, non-SQL database dedicated to crossplatform, efficient data processing. All documents are stored in JSON format and RESTful APIs are provided to CouchDB as a consistent interface in performing CRUD operations on documents. CouchDB utilizes MapReduce in generating views of the data. All views are embedded in a B-tree structure for the sake of fast retrieval of data. Such features make CouchDB an ideal solution for storing and processing large amounts of semistructured documents such as tweets on the Cloud.

Twitter APIs cap the streaming rate and can make it challenging for harvesting large amounts of Twitter data through a single developer account to a single machine. To tackle this, multiple harvesters running on the Cloud can be used—each associated with their own Twitter developer account and with their own IP address. It is important to note that there can be many harvesters running continually and in parallel. To support the continuous data collection and indexing for rapid searches, ElasticSearch can be used.

It is also the case that visualization of data is an essential component of Big Data analytics. The ability to visualize data can help shed insight and, indeed, highlight issues with privacy as illustrated in Fig. 1. To accommodate this, PouchDB [30] and a range of Javascript libraries have been adopted.

PouchDB is an open source in-browser database with a JavaScript interface. PouchDB offers features for synchronizing data with remote CouchDB servers. As such, PouchDB can be utilized as a JavaScript library for dynamically creating data views according to user requests. This functionality overcomes a limitation of CouchDB and its realization of MapReduce, since the mapping function does not take parameters as inputs.

Other libraries that are used for data visualization include the High Chart API, which makes use of a distributed object model and supports JQuery capabilities to generate graphical results of analyses. This API is useful when analysis such as comparing and contrasting the number of tweets generated in different time periods is required.

Given that geospatial privacy is of concern here, the ability to collect, analyze, and visualize data based on its geospatial location is essential. The system utilizes the GoogleMaps API for this purpose, but we note that a range of other solutions are available, for example, OpenStreetMap [31].

The architecture for the Twitter harvesting, processing, and visualization is shown in Fig. 2. As noted, there can be multiple harvesters that are used for continually harvesting Twitter data on the Cloud. These harvesters can be pointed to certain locations, for example, Melbourne, or as identified in Table 1, by selecting a much more disaggregated region, for example, the tweets from a specific location.

It should be noted that the web application provides the interface to the system and supports the majority of the functionality offered by the system. The primary function of the web interface is to allow users to draw a bounding box on a map and retrieve tweet contents inside the region by creating views on the CouchDB according to the coordinates of the vertexes of the bounding box as shown in Fig. 3. For experimental purposes, the web application should also have the following features in addition to bounding-box based tweet retrieval:

- Being able to filter tweets containing certain keywords;
- Being able to perform accumulative analyses, for example, the amount of tweets created over certain time periods;
- Finding tokens beginning with "#" and "@" in the content of tweets to identify the frequent topics and active users inside a region based on the term frequencies.

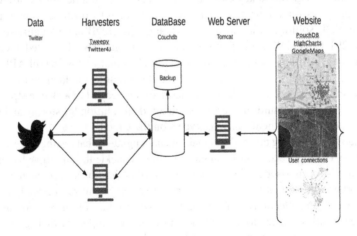

FIG. 2

Architecture for Cloud-based Big Data collection, analysis, and visualization.

FIG. 3

Bounding box tweet retrieval.

The server side of the web application uses CouchDB and makes use of the MapReduce architecture for parallel dataprocessing and hence is significantly faster in terms of computation power compared with browsers on the client side. Hence, the web application follows the "thin client" paradigm to allocate most of the computation, including splitting tweet contents into tokens, and preprocessing the tokens by removing non-ASCII characters, to name but a few activities in the MapReduce task of CouchDB. This avoids long-running scripts affecting the functionality of the browser. However, jobs such as sorting the term frequencies cannot be done through MapReduce and have to be executed on the client side since MapReduce produces key-value pairs in random order. Fortunately, the execution time of sorting the list of term frequencies is insignificant compared with the time taken for retrieving and processing large amounts of tweets on the server side.

11.5 SPATIAL PRIVACY CASE STUDIES

As described previously, we wish to explore a range of questions related to location privacy:

- How can a location lose privacy?
- How easily can we reveal location privacy?
- What are the potential consequences of a loss of location privacy?

It is obvious that location privacy can be easily given away as shown in Fig. 1. If location-based services are used, then the privacy of an individual's exact location is immediately available. Users (tweeters) may be fully conscious of this and happy to release such data; however, other users may simply be unaware of exactly how much data they are releasing. The question arises, how are those users actually identified in the first place? Location privacy is one common route to discovering such individuals.

Given the general definition of privacy as the right of both being free from secret surveillance and regulating rules of accessing personal/organizational identity [32], a possible definition of a location losing privacy might be "actively revealing a location's identity." The obvious identity of a particular location includes the location name, the location's usage, for example, is the location used for business activities or recreational activities, and the events that may have happened or be happening inside the location. Answers to the first two bullet points can be addressed by checking the feasibility and measuring and/or inferring the use of a certain location through the events that happen inside that location (based on the content of tweets generated inside the region). The third bullet point can be explored by finding scenarios where losing the location's privacy essentially results in a loss of personal privacy. The process of exploring these issues is as follows:

- Harvest as many tweets from Twitter as possible for analytical use, including support for real-time data acquisition;
- Support (localized) location-based queries through the web application;
- From the retrieved results, perform accumulative analysis, including identifying the frequent topics, finding time patterns occurring at those locations;
- Identify patterns between the location identity and the identities of users inside the region, and
- Explore the consequences of the loss of location identity for users that might have been present in that location.

Observing frequent tweet topics inside a region is an effective way of inferring what the location is used for; however, this can require huge amounts of current and historic data. Indeed, the volume of data required is one of the major barriers in identifying the usage of location. Many consider that the volume of data that is now being created can allay privacy concerns. To explore this issue, we consider a scenario based on the major sporting venue in Melbourne: the Melbourne Cricket Ground, as shown in Fig. 4. Over 100,000 tweets were collected from the MCG. As can be seen, the tweets include a range of hashtags that correspond to sporting events and the location itself, for example, #MCGcrowd

FIG. 4

Identifying Melbourne Cricket Ground usage/events.

and #AFL (Australian Football League). Thus, the identity of use of this location can be identified solely by the tweets that are harvested from that location. This is unsurprising for a location like the MCG, but it is key to understanding location privacy. We can identify what a given location is used for, just by obtaining tweets from that location. We may not have known that this was a sporting location, but from analyzing the data we can establish this.

In relation to less obvious and more disaggregated locations, we consider a scenario based on student accommodations available at the University of Melbourne. Many students, and especially international students, stay in accommodations that are close to the University, for example, UniLodge on Swanston Street. Through harvesting Twitter data from those locations as shown in Fig. 5, it is possible to identify that these are indeed student accommodations. Many of the tweets are made with non-English language settings, for example, Chinese, so it is possible to establish the ethnic background of the individuals that are staying in this accommodation. Obviously, for smaller regions/locations, a reduced amount of tweets is available, but through machine learning algorithms and suitable known (training) data, it is possible to exploit analytical software to determine what the location is used for with increasing degrees of accuracy.

In this regard, case studies based on automatically identifying locations based on the frequencies of tweet content through machine learning approaches were explored. In all of these scenarios, data was collected through querying stored views in CouchDB to count the occurrences of words from particular regions. Detailed analysis in terms of the feasibility of automatically tagging a location's usage and events using machine learning based on other known regions requires creation of associated classifiers.

In supporting this, a range of general classes were used to represent the usage of locations, for example, the class "Sports" covers all locations used for any sports events, regardless of whether the location is a stadium or a fitness center. The work began with a manual task where tweets from locations with known usages were revealed and representative attributes judged manually based on raw

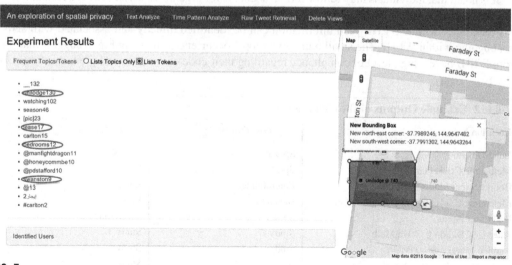

FIG. 5

Increasingly disaggregated location and privacy issues.

term frequencies. Once this training data set was created, it could be compared with the results from the machine learning algorithms. In undertaking this, the Weka software was used. [33]. It is noted that this supervised approach is only one possibility, and unsupervised machine learning can also be considered. Table 2 illustrates some sample comparisons between the expected class and the class assumed by Weka using a K-nearest neighbor algorithm [33] from which the classifier accurately reveals the location usage—despite the absence of formal feature selection processes using criteria such as F-scores and the often small size of the data sets [34].

It should be noted that incorrectly classifying the expected use of a location does not necessarily mean that the classifier is wrong. Rather, it can provide important information revealing some "hidden" usages of a location. For example, one reason for classifying "UniLodge on Swanston Street" as a study area instead of apartments is that most individuals inside the region are students and tend to tweet about their studies. Hence, such instances can also be classified as a study area or indeed as University accommodations. As such, although the model in the experiment might be highly biased due to the absence of in-depth feature selection and the small training set with (presumably) over-generalized classes, the fact that the classifier yields a high degree of correctness in classifying unexpected classes can reveal important information regarding the location identity and use. It can therefore be concluded that using location usage can indeed be predicted *without* contextual knowledge and as such is a serious privacy issue.

It might be considered that the knowledge that a location is used for sports or entertainment is not a major privacy concern; however, extending the system and scenarios can reveal potentially more sensitive location details, for example, identifying police stations or Australian defense locations and the individuals who might work there. Fig. 6 provides an example revealing "bioinformatics research" that is currently ongoing at the Walter and Eliza Hall Institute (WEHI). Events inside the location, such as research projects and the staff working on such projects, can reveal information that may disclose too much information and potentially be revealed to competitors.

It is noted that individuals may follow formal accounts for organizations, such as WEHI and others; however, the issue is that any staff member can tweet using their own account, and by identifying that this took place within WEHI, such information can be identified directly and associated with activities ongoing within WEHI. The small numbers of topic occurrences shown in Fig. 6 suggest that staff from WEHI have a high level of compliance regarding their code of conduct, and prevent information

Table 2 Example Outputs of the Classifiers

Location Name	Expected Output	Actual Output
Etihad Stadium	Sports	Sports
Melbourne Cricket Ground	Sports	Sports
Bourke Street Mall	Entertainment	Entertainment
Melbourne Convention & Exhibition Centre	Business	Entertainment
Rod Laver Arena	Sports	Entertainment
Alice Hoy Building @ UniMelb	Study	Study
Baillieu Library @ UniMelb	Study	Study
UniLodge @ Swanston Street	Apartment	Study
Arrow on Swanston	Apartment	Apartment

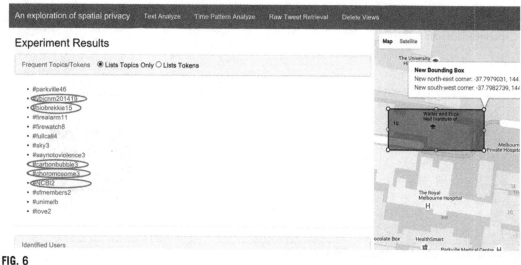

FIG. 6

Revealing potentially confidential events.

leakage by not sending tweets related to their work. However, the fact that the building's usage is identified by analyzing tweets suggested that even small numbers of tweets relevant to the inside events can be critical in identifying the location's usage and location privacy, and potentially result in negative consequences.

The seemingly harmless practice of revealing a nonconfidential location usage, as mentioned previously, may result in negative circumstances, especially if patterns are drawn between the location and the users identified in that region, for example, identifying policemen from a given police station can be used to subsequently track them as illustrated in Fig. 1. Furthermore, occupational and other interests can be inferred from location information, with some representative examples given as follows.

According to the frequent tweet topics from the University of Melbourne Baillieu Libraries shown in Fig. 7, all users identified inside the region can be assumed to be University of Melbourne students working on coursework programs, as the name of the university is revealed on the topics and the terms "assignments" and "finals" negate assumptions that non-Melbourne students are using these facilities.

Furthermore, a more accurate prediction of the identified users' behavior in given locations may be undertaken when analyzing temporal patterns in the data. Fig. 8 shows the amount of tweets made in Aug. 2015 from several study areas at the University of Melbourne, which reveals that the amount of tweets in the second half of the month generally overwhelms the figure in the first half, indicating approaching deadlines for assignments.

Again, this in itself is not a major privacy issue; however, when applied to residential locations, this can become a serious privacy issue. To demonstrate this, we consider the time distribution of tweets from a residential area of a suburb of Melbourne: Fitzroy. As seen in Fig. 9, there is a drop in the amount of tweets at 2 p.m. The discovery suggests that some houses inside the residential area are likely to be empty. The exposure of the resident's possible daily schedule may be disastrous if such information is made known to potential thieves. It is quite possible to look at increasingly disaggregated data, for example, the social media use inside of a given house, but this was not explored for obvious ethical

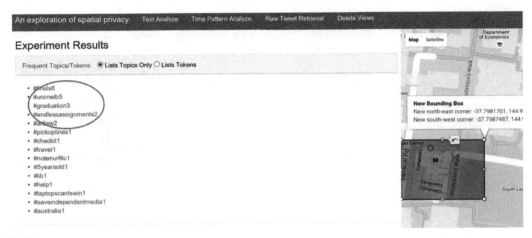

FIG. 7

Identifying user identity from location identity.

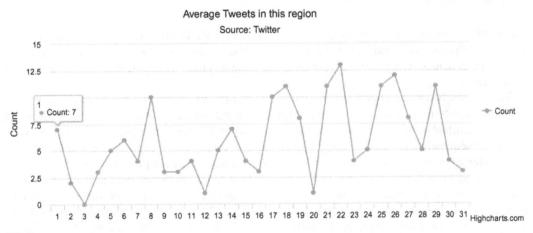

FIG. 8

Tweet patterns across study areas at the University of Melbourne in Aug. 2015.

and security issues. The same capabilities in harvesting and analyzing data can be down to extremely disaggregated levels, for example, the rooms in a house!

In spite of these scenarios showing the severity of consequences of losing location privacy, it can be the case that performing tweet retrieval based on location can be beneficial despite the privacy issues, for example, for pandemics or other national disasters. To explore this issue, an analysis was undertaken in testing the feasibility of using the contents of geotagged tweets as a data source for applications that use such data to provide services. A heavily simplified application whose function was to retrieve tweet texts regarding an input topic within a bound-box was made for the purpose of stimulating the system providing location-based information, and observing whether the text provided

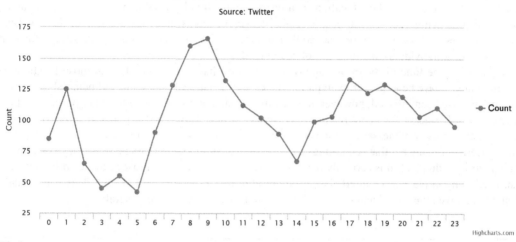

FIG. 9

Amount of tweets on hourly basis from residential areas in Fitzroy.

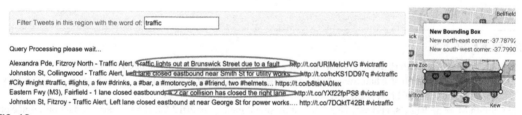

FIG. 10

Potential of positive usage of Tweet data.

information regarding the topic. The result was promising, as most retrieved texts contained detailed descriptions of certain events, which could possibly be useful for others. For example, tweets regarding traffic information from the city entrance of the freeway, detailed reporting of traffic events are shown (Fig. 10). Such observations suggest potential benefits of using geotagged tweets despite the potential privacy issues.

11.6 CONCLUSIONS

Privacy is of increasing concern for many people in the digital, and especially in the social media age. Many individuals use social media as a daily part of their lives. In this chapter we have explored the dangers of erosion of privacy and illustrated how seemingly innocuous information can reveal extensive privacy information related to the use and the activities taking place in that location. We have shown how Big Data infrastructures and technologies can now easily exploit geocoded information to reveal patterns in data that might otherwise have been lost in the noise. The scenarios demonstrated in this chapter have shown how locations can be automatically classified and how individuals can be identified from within those locations. The real danger in this is that once identified, the Big Data technologies now allow users to be tracked thereafter. As shown in Fig. 1, it is a quite straightforward process to track individuals and their use of social media.

Correlating the time of the events and other activities that might take place at those locations at that time might have benefits, for example, in the case of a national pandemic and being able to track who might have been infected; however, it is equally possible to use this data for other purposes which have grades of concern for many regarding personal privacy. Thus, should police be able to identify potential criminals or witnesses of crimes by correlating crime incidents with sources such as Twitter? The concerns of many are that such things are already happening without recall to privacy concerns of the unwitting individual. It is certainly the case that technology has far outpaced the legal frameworks that need to be in place to counterbalance the possibilities of data use and misuse. This is especially challenging given the global nature of the Internet and social media more generally.

ACKNOWLEDGMENTS

The authors are grateful to the National eResearch Collaboration Tools and Resources (NeCTAR) project for the Cloud resources that were used in undertaking this work.

REFERENCES

[1] Davenport TH, Barth P, Bean R. How 'big data' is different. MIT Sloan Manage Rev 2013;54.
[2] Riederer C, Erramilli V, Chaintreau A, Balanchaner K, Rodriguez P. For sale: your data: by: you. Cambridge, MA, USA: ACM; 2011. Hotnets'11.
[3] Smith M, et al. Big Data privacy issues in public social media. In: 2012 6th IEEE international conference on digital ecosystems and technologies (DEST) (2012): N.p., Web; 2015.
[4] Gong Y, Deng F, Sinnott RO. In: Identification of (near) real-time traffic congestion in the cities of Australia through Twitter, understanding the city with urban informatics, CIKM 2015, Melbourne, Australia; 2015.
[5] Zaldumbide JP, Sinnott RO. Identification and verification of real-time health events through social media. In: International conference on data science and data intensive systems, Sydney, Australia; 2015.
[6] Earle PS, Bowden DC, Guy M. Twitter earthquake detection: earthquake monitoring in a social world. Ann Geophys 2012;54(6).
[7] Gubbi J, Buyya R, Marusic S, Palaniswami M. Internet of things (IoT): a vision, architectural elements, and future directions. Future Generation Comput Syst 2013;29(7):1645–60.
[8] Graeff TR, Harmon S. Collecting and using personal data: consumers' awareness and concerns. J Consum Mark 2002;19(4):302–18.
[9] Christofides E, Muise A, Desmarais S. Information disclosure and control on Facebook: are they two sides of the same coin or two different processes? CyberPsychol Behav 2009;12(3):341–5.
[10] Chen L, Wang W, Nagarajan M, Wang S, Sheth AP. Extracting diverse sentiment expressions with target-dependent polarity from Twitter, In: ICWSM; 2012.
[11] Weber RH. Internet of Things—new security and privacy challenges. Comput Law Secur Rev 2010;26(1):23–30.

[12] Smith M, et al. Big Data privacy issues in public social media. In: 2012 6th IEEE international conference on digital ecosystems and technologies (DEST); 2012.

[13] Arndt C. The loss of privacy and identity. Biomet Technol Today 2005;13(8):6–7.

[14] Shin KG, Xiaoen J, Chen Z, Hu X. Privacy protection for users of location-based services. IEEE Wireless Commun 2012;19(1).

[15] Tang M, Wu Q, Guoping Z, Lili H, Huan-Guo Z. A new scheme of LBS privacy protection. In: IEEE 5th International Conference on WiCom'09. In Wireless Communications, Networking and Mobile Computing. 2009. p. 1–6.

[16] de Montjoye YA, Hidalgo CA, Verleysen M, Blondel VD. Unique in the crowd: the privacy bounds of human mobility. Sci Rep 2013;3.

[17] Google Inc., Google+ API Official Document. Google developers. N.p., Web; Oct. 30, 2015.

[18] Facebook Inc., Facebook Graph API Documentation. Facebook developers. N.p., Web; Oct. 30, 2015.

[19] Twitter Inc., Official Twitter API Documentation. Dev.twitter.com. N.p., Web; Oct. 30, 2015.

[20] Instagram.com, Instagram Developer Documentation. Instagram.com. N.p., Web; Oct. 30, 2015.

[21] Flickr.com, Flickr Developer Documentation. flickr.com. N.p., Web; Oct. 30, 2015.

[22] Zhang S. How precise is one degree of longitude or latitude?. Factually. N.p., Web; Oct. 30, 2015.

[23] Ren K, Wang C, Wang Q. Security challenges for the public cloud. IEEE Internet Comput 2012;1:69–73.

[24] Buyya R, Broberg J, Goscinski AM, editors. Cloud computing: principles and paradigms, vol. 87. Hoboken, New Jersey: John Wiley & Sons; 2010.

[25] NeCTAR Climate and Weather Science Laboratory, https://nectar.org.au/labs/climate-and-weather-science-laboratory/ N.p., Web; Oct. 30, 2015.

[26] NeCTAR Humanities Networked Infrastructure, https://nectar.org.au/labs/inspiring-cultural-collaboration/ N.p., Web; Oct. 30, 2015.

[27] NeCTAR Genomics Virtual Laboratory, https://nectar.org.au/labs/taking-the-it-out-of-bioinformatics/ N.p., Web; Oct. 30, 2015.

[28] NeCTAR Endocrine Genomics Virtual Laboratory, https://nectar.org.au/labs/solving-endocrine-disorders-without-borders/ N.p., Web; Oct. 30, 2015.

[29] CouchDB, http://couchdb.apache.org, N.p., Web; Oct. 30, 2015.

[30] PouchDB, http://pouchdb.com, N.p., Web; Oct. 30, 2015.

[31] Open Street Map, http://www.openstreetmap.org, N.p., Web; Oct. 30, 2015.

[32] BusinessDictionary.com, What is privacy? Definition and meaning. N.p., Web; Oct. 30, 2015.

[33] Hall M, Frank E, Holmes G, Pfahringer B, Reutemann P, Witten IH. The WEKA data mining software: an update. ACM SIGKDD Explor Newslett 2009;11(1):10–8.

[34] Ruiz EV. An algorithm for finding nearest neighbours in (approximately) constant average time. Pattern Recogn Lett 1986;4(3):145–57.

SECURITY AND PRIVACY IN BIG DATA

12

L. Ou, Z. Qin, H. Yin, K. Li

12.1 INTRODUCTION

The term "Big Data" refers to the massive amounts of digital information companies and governments collect about us and our surroundings. Human beings now create 2.5 quintillion bytes of data per day. The rate of the data creation has increased so much that 90% of the data in the world today has been created in the last 2 years alone. How to securely store these massive data and how to effectively process them have been more and more important and challenging tasks. An effective method is for institutions to adopt the emerging cloud computing commercial service schema to outsource their massive data sets at remote cloud storage and computing centers. On the other hand, authorized data users can utilize the powerful computation capability of the cloud sever to search and process data. For example, a hospital creates vast data sets of patients' medical records every day, such as EMR (electronic medical records) including X-rays, electrocardiograms, clinical histories, and so on. Facing such a huge amount of data files, hospitals have to resort to third-party data storage and management centers to maintain the massive data sets. Later, authorized physicians can search and obtain individual records through public communication channels.

Generally, Big Data is processed and queried on the cloud computing platform (Fig. 1). Cloud computing, the new term for the long-dreamed of vision of computing as a utility, enables convenient, on-demand network access to a centralized pool of configurable computing resources that can be rapidly deployed with great efficiency and minimal management overhead. The amazing advantages of cloud computing include: on-demand self-service, ubiquitous network access, location-independent resource pooling, rapid resource elasticity, usage-based pricing, transference of risk, etc. Thus, cloud computing could easily benefit its users in avoiding large capital outlays in the deployment and management of both software and hardware. Undoubtedly, cloud computing brings unprecedented paradigm shifting and will be a major part of IT history, especially the Big Data era.

Cloud computing can provide various elastic and scalable IT services in a pay-as-you-go fashion; however, once the massive data sets are outsourced to a remote cloud, the data owners would lose direct control of these data, which raises a major concern of using the cloud—data privacy and security problems. Gartner listed seven security issues in cloud computing and claimed that 85% of large companies refuse to adopt cloud computing just due to data security. For example, the hospital may be reluctant to outsource their data to the cloud because EMRs contain a huge amount of confidential sensitive information that patients are reluctant to publish, such as information about one's lifestyle, medical history, history of drug allergies, etc. To effectively solve the data security problem and promote the development of cloud computing, the Gartner Group thinks that an encryption scheme must be available to protect the outsourced cloud data, which should be encrypted before uploading it to the

Big Data. http://dx.doi.org/10.1016/B978-0-12-805394-2.00012-X

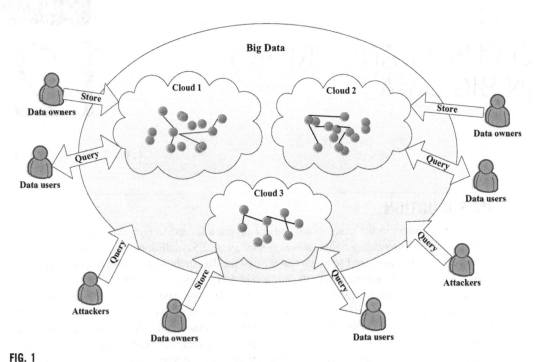

FIG. 1

An overview of Big Data.

cloud. However, data encryption makes cloud data utilization a very challenging problem. In particular, performing a data search is a key challenge because the encrypted data disable the traditional plaintext keyword query. Thus, enabling an encrypted cloud data search service is of paramount importance.

In addition, adversaries can also utilize correlations in Big Data and in background knowledge to steal sensitive information. There are some existing technologies that are designed to prevent adversaries from stealing sensitive information from relational data. But the correlation in Big Data is quite different from the traditional relationship between data stored in relational databases. Correlation in Big Data does not imply causation. Causality means A causes B, where correlation, on the other hand, means that A and B tend to be observed at the same time. These are very, very different things when it comes to Big Data; however, the difference often gets glossed over or ignored, so sensitive information will be exposed and in more danger.

Based on the previous description, in this chapter, we will discuss important security and privacy issues about Big Data from three aspects. One is secure queries performed over encrypted cloud data; the second is security technology related to Big Data; the last is the security and privacy in correlative Big Data. The rest of this chapter is organized as follows. In Section 12.2, we introduce the related topics of secure queries in cloud computing, including system models, security models, and outstanding secure query techniques. In Section 12.3, we introduce other Big Data security, including data watermarking and self-adaptive risk access control. In Section 12.4, we comb the related research about privacy protection on correlated Big Data. This research is divided into two categories, including anonymity and differential privacy. At last, we propose future work in Section 12.5 and conclude this chapter in Section 12.6.

12.2 SECURE QUERIES OVER ENCRYPTED BIG DATA
12.2.1 SYSTEM MODEL

The popular secure query architecture with privacy protection in cloud computing involves three entities: the data owner, data users, and the cloud, as shown in Fig. 2A. The system framework expresses the following application scenario: the data owner decides to employ the cloud storage service to store massive data files, which are encrypted with the guarantee that no actual data contents are leaked to the cloud. On the other hand, to enable an effective keyword query over encrypted data for data utilization, the data owner needs to construct confidential searchable indexes for outsourced data files. Both the encrypted file collection and index are outsourced to the cloud server. An authorized data user can obtain data files of interest by submitting specified keywords to the cloud. The query process includes the following four steps. First, the data user sends query keywords of interest to the data owner via secret communication channels. Second, upon receiving query keywords, the data owner encodes these keywords to generate a query token in the form of ciphertexts and then returns it to the authorized user via the same secure channels. Third, the data user submits a query token to the cloud server to request data files via the public communication channels, such as the Internet. Fourth, upon receiving the query token submitted by the data user, the cloud server is responsible for executing the search algorithm over the secure index and returns the matched set of files to the user as the search result.

A fatal drawback of this architecture is that the data owner must always be online to handle query requests of authorized users. If the data owner is offline, outsourced data cannot be retrieved in time. To improve the availability, an enhanced system architecture is proposed as shown in Fig. 2B.

In Fig. 2B, there is an important difference compared with Fig. 2A: data users can encode keyword(s) to query tokens locally using keys assigned by the data owner through data access control. Queries are performed independently of the state of the data owner. Consequently, the improved system model more rigidly protects user query privacy, eliminates real-time communication overhead, and greatly enhances the availability and scalability of the whole system.

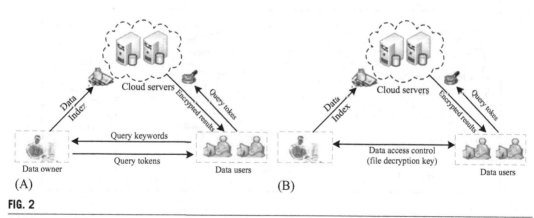

(A)   (B)

FIG. 2

Architecture of the search over encrypted cloud data.

12.2.2 THREAT MODEL AND ATTACK MODEL

In this section, we introduce the threat model and attack model based on the aforementioned secure query model for cloud computing.

(1) Threat Model

Since the massive data set is stored at a remote cloud center, the cloud may not be fully trusted for the following reasons. First, clouds may be vulnerable to corrupt employees who do not follow data privacy policies. Second, cloud computing systems may also be vulnerable to external malicious attacks, and when intrusions happen, cloud customers may not be fully informed about the potential implications on the security of their data. Third, clouds may base services on facilities in some foreign countries where privacy regulations are difficult to enforce. Based on these facts, generally, the cloud server is considered an "honest-but-curious" semitrusted threat model. More specifically, the cloud server acts in an "honest" fashion and correctly follows the designated protocol specification and promises that it always securely stores data and performs computations. However, the cloud server may intentionally analyze contents of data files, or curiously infer the underlying query keyword(s) submitted by the data user. Recently, besides the cloud, researchers have begun to consider some internal adversaries such as a malicious data owner or a compromised data user in the multiowner and multiuser cloud environments, such that the cloud can collude with these internal adversaries to analyze useful information of data files and query keyword(s). Fig. 3 shows the two threat models in cloud computing.

(2) Attack Model

In addition to the threat model, based on what information the cloud server knows, secure query schemes in the cloud environment mainly consider two attack models with different attack capabilities; they are the *Known Ciphertext Model* and *Known Background Model* [1,2]. In the *Known Ciphertext Model*, the cloud is only permitted to access the encrypted data files and the searchable secure indexes. In the *Known Background Model*, as a stronger attack model, the cloud server is supposed to possess more background knowledge than what can be accessed in the *Known Ciphertext Model*. This background knowledge information may include the keywords and related statistical information, correlation relation of different data sets, as well as the correlation

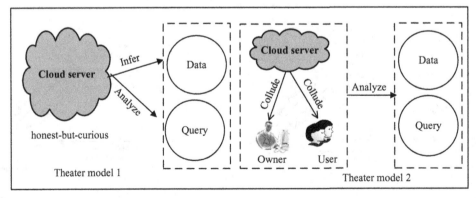

FIG. 3

Threat model.

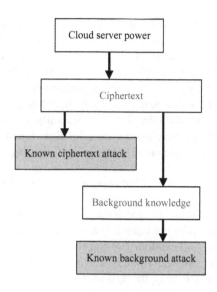

FIG. 4

Attack model.

relationship of given search requests. For example, the cloud server could use the known query token's information combined with previous query results to deduce the plaintext information of certain keywords in the query. Fig. 4 shows the two attack models.

12.2.3 SECURE QUERY SCHEME IN CLOUDS

In fact, as early as 2000, Song et al. set out to research the problem of how to correctly perform a search over an encrypted document via encrypted keywords, and first introduced a practical technique that allows a user to securely perform a search over encrypted documents through specified keywords [3]. In 2006, Curtmola et al. formally named this query technique "searchable encryption (SE)" and presented explicit security requirements and definitions [4]. Meanwhile, they adopted the inverted index data structure [5] (which is widely used in the plaintext information retrieval fields), symmetric encryption schemes [6], and hash table to design a novel searchable encryption scheme named SSE (searchable symmetric encryption). The key goal of an SSE scheme is to allow a server to search over encrypted data on behalf of data users without learning any useful information about the data files or the query contents of data users other than encrypted query results.

The recent rapid development of cloud computing and the sharp increase in organizational, or, enterprise business data, has necessitated that the data outsourcing service model promote further study on secure searches in the cloud computing environment. Researchers have proposed many secure schemes to improve query efficiency, enrich query functionalities, and enhance security. In these secure query schemes, the encrypted searchable indexes are constructed by the data owner, through which an authorized data user can obtain qualified data by submitting encrypted keyword(s) to the cloud.

We will introduce secure query techniques based on the index construction in the symmetric encryption setting in this section. (Note that some public key-based secure query schemes are also proposed by researchers [7], however, which are not suitable for the massive data collection in the cloud environment due to the much more expensive computation overhead of the asymmetric encryption.)

We assume that the data owner owns the file set $F = \{f_1, f_2, ..., f_n\}$ and extracts a set of keywords $W = \{w_1, w_2, ..., w_n\}$ from F. To realize an effective secure query scheme, the data owner constructs an encrypted searchable index for F by invoking an index generation algorithm called **BuildIndex** when taking as input a secret key K. In addition, the file set F should be encrypted for data confidentiality using an algorithm called **Enc** with the other key K'. Generally, the semantically secure symmetric encryption scheme DES or AES is a very good choice for **Enc**. Finally, the encrypted data files and encrypted indexes are stored on a remote cloud center in the following form:

$$\left\{ I = \textbf{BuildIndex}_k \left(F = \{f_1, f_2, ..., f_n\}; W = \{w_1, w_2, ..., w_n\} \right), C = \textbf{Enc}_{k'} \left(f_1, f_2, ..., f_n \right) \right\}$$

When an authorized data user wants to search data files that contain a certain keyword w, he/she invokes the algorithm **Trapdoor** under the same key K used to encrypted the index I to generate a so-called trapdoor (ie, query token) $T = \textbf{Trapdoor}_k(w)$ and submits T to the cloud via public communication channels. With T, the cloud can search the index using an algorithm called **Search** and returns corresponding encrypted data files. Finally, the data user uses the algorithm **Dec** and takes as input the symmetric encryption key K' to decrypt query results. Fig. 5 shows a general model of an index-based searchable encryption scheme in the cloud computing environment.

We formally give the definition of an index-based secure query scheme for cloud computing.

Definition 1 An index-based secure query scheme consists of the following six polynomial time algorithms.

- **Keygen(1^k):** The data owner takes as input a security parameter k and outputs two keys K, K'. The K is used to encrypt and decrypt the data file set and the K' is used to encrypt indexes and to generate query trapdoors.
- **Enc(K, F):** The data owner takes as input the secret key K and a data file set $F = \{f_1, ..., f_n\}$, outputs a sequence of ciphertexts $C = \{c_1, ..., c_n\}$.
- **BuildIndex(K', F, W):** The data owner runs the algorithm and takes as input a key K', a data file set F and a set of keyword W extracted from F, outputs the secure index I.
- **Trapdoor(K', w):** An authorized data user runs the algorithm and takes as input the key K' and a query keyword w, outputs the ciphertext form $T(w)$ of w.

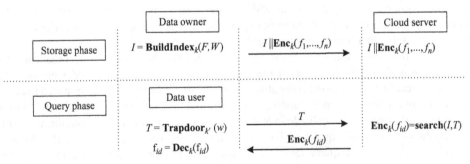

FIG. 5

General model of an index-based searchable encryption scheme in the cloud computing environment.

- **Search**($T(w)$, I): The cloud server runs the algorithm, which performs secure search on I according to the query trapdoor $T(w)$ and outputs the corresponding encrypted data file c that contains w.
- **Dec**(K, c): the data user invokes the algorithm to decrypt query result c returned by the cloud server to get the corresponding plaintext f.

12.2.4 SECURITY DEFINITION OF INDEX-BASED SECURE QUERY TECHNIQUES

The definition of secure query schemes in Section 12.2.3 indicates that the security of outsourced data files itself can be easily achieved due to the semantically secure AES or DES encryption. However, the cloud server may infer actual contents of the data files by attacking searchable indexes, since indexes are often embedded in useful information in data files. So, constructing semantically secure searchable indexes should be the most key security goal for an index-based secure query scheme. How to define the security of indexes? In Ref. [8], Eujin-Goh formally proposed the semantic security against adaptive chosen keyword attack (IND-CKA) security definition, which has been widely adopted in prior secure query schemes.

Definition 2 An index-based search scheme is semantically secure if the constructed searchable index satisfies the following two key security conditions: (1) index indistinguishability (IND) and (2) security under chosen keyword attacks (CKA).

Simply speaking, when given two data files F_1, F_2 and their indexes I_1 and I_2, if the adversary (ie, the cloud server) cannot distinguish which index is for which data file, we say the indexes I_1 and I_2 are IND-CKA secure. In other words, the IND-CKA security definition guarantees that an adversary cannot deduce and obtain any useful plaintext information in data files from the searchable index.

12.2.5 IMPLEMENTATIONS OF INDEX-BASED SECURE QUERY TECHNIQUES

In this section, we will introduce two effective and efficient query techniques over the encrypted data files, which have been widely used in cloud computing environments. One is a single-keyword secure query scheme based on the encrypted inverted index structure, and the other is a multikeyword secure query scheme based on the encrypted vector space model.

An efficient single-keyword secure query scheme

In Ref. [4], Curtmola et al. constructed an efficient single-keyword secure query scheme based on encrypted inverted indexes. In practice, the inverted index is widely used to perform the keyword search in the plaintext retrieval information system due to the simplicity of the construction and the high search efficiency. To the best of our knowledge, almost all modern search engines take advantage of the inverted index technique to design their internal index constructions. Fig. 6 shows a simple inverted

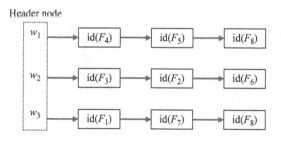

FIG. 6

A simple inverted index structure.

index structure. In this construction, a linked list L_i is used to represent a search index for a keyword item w_i. In each L_i, the header node HN_i stores the specified keyword information w_i and every intermediate node $N_{i,j}$ stores the identifier of a data file that contains w_i. For simplicity, Fig. 6 shows a simple index structure in which there are three keywords w_1, w_2, w_3 and eight data files F_1–F_8.

Obviously, directly storing the inverted indexes to the cloud server in the plaintext form would cause inevitable information leakages because the cloud can see all plaintexts. To avoid gaining information from inverted indexes for any underlying attacker, Curtmola et al. used the symmetric encryption technique to encrypt inverted indexes and made them confidential while maintaining efficient searchable capabilities [4].

Now, we first introduce the proposed index encryption technique and make the indexes demonstrated in Fig. 7 secure, step-by-step, and then illustrate how to perform searches on these encrypted indexes with a simple example.

For ease of understanding, we introduce the implementation details of the index encryption technique by dividing the encryption processes into the following three steps.

(1) Encrypt Nodes Except for the Header Node and the First Node

For a linked list L_i of the distinct keyword w_i, except for the header node HN_i, each node $N_{i,j}$ consists of three fields: the identifier of the data file containing the keyword w_i, a pointer to the next node, and a random key $K_{i,j}$ that is used to encrypt the next node. The pointer field and key field of the last node are set to be null and 0, respectively. Next, except for the first node $N_{i,1}$, each node $N_{i,j}$ is encrypted by the key $K_{i,j-1}$ using a semantically secure symmetric encryption scheme such as AES or DES. Fig. 7 shows the aforementioned encryption processes.

(2) Construct the Header Node and Encrypt the First Node

The header node of each linked list L_i corresponding to the keyword w_i contains two fields: the first field stores a random key $K_{i,0}$ that is used to encrypt the first node $N_{i,1}$, and the second field is a pointer to the first node $N_{i,1}$ in L_i. Thus, the first node $N_{i,1}$ can now be encrypted by the key $K_{i,0}$. Now, except for the header node HN_i, each node in L_i is encrypted with a different key stored at the corresponding previous node.

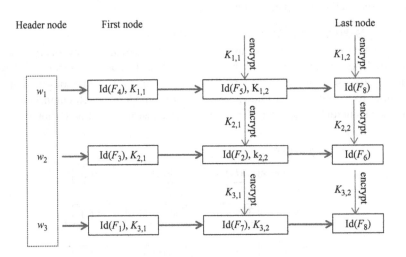

FIG. 7

Intermediate nodes encryption.

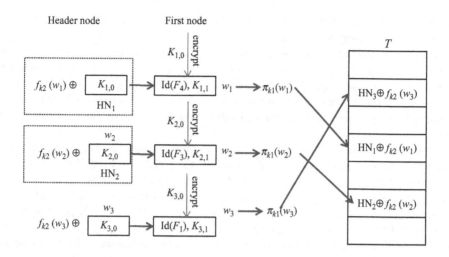

FIG. 8

Head node encryption and look-up table structure.

(3) Encrypt Header Node and Create Encrypted Look-Table

Obviously, the header node still discloses the key information $K_{i,0}$ for L_i, by which the cloud can decrypt all nodes of L_i and make the index very easy to crack. To hide the header node information while keeping searchability, the proposed scheme uses an encrypted look-up table T to store the encrypted header node information. We use $HN_i=(K_{i,0}, addr(N_{i,1}))$ to denote the header node of L_i, where $addr(N_{i,1})$ represents the pointer or address of the first node $N_{i,1}$ in L_i. To make the header node secure, and to protect the key $K_{i,0}$, the scheme uses a pseudorandom function [6] f with the key k_2 to calculate the keyword w_i as $f(k_2, w_i)$ and then encrypt the header node $HN_i=(K_{i,0}, addr(N_{i,1}))$ by computing $f(k_2, w_i)\oplus HN_i$, where $\oplus$ is an exclusive or operation. Next, the scheme generates a look-up table T and uses another pseudorandom function π with the key k_1 to calculate the keyword w_i as $\pi_{k1}(w_i)$ and stores the encrypted header node $f(k_2, w_i)\oplus HN_i$ to the corresponding position $T[\pi(k_1,w_i)]$ in T.

So far, according to these three steps, the linked list L_i of keyword w_i has been totally encrypted. In the next section, we will give a simple example to illustrate how to perform a query on encrypted indexes. Fig. 8 shows a simple example of a head node encryption and look-up table structure.

Last, we provide a secure search example. Suppose that a data user wants to search data files containing the keyword w_2, he/she first encrypts the query keyword w_2 using the keyed hash functions f and π to generate a query trapdoor as $trap=(\pi_{k1}(w_2), f_{k2}(w_2))$ and submits the trap to the cloud server. Upon receiving the trap, the cloud accesses the look-up table T and takes the encrypted value $val=HN_2\oplus f_{k2}(w_2)$ from the position $T[\pi_{k1}(w_2)]$ and then decrypts the header node HN_2 by calculating $val\oplus f_{k2}(w_2)$. Last, the cloud decrypts the whole linked list L_2 starting with the header node HN_2 and outputs the list of data file identifiers in L_2.

An efficient multikeyword secure query scheme

Obviously, the inverted index-based secure query scheme efficiently supports a single-keyword query, which needs to perform multiple rounds of queries to implement a multikeyword conjunction query. In this section, we will introduce an efficient multikeyword query scheme based on the encrypted vector space model. The scheme can effectively perform multikeyword ranked and top-k secure queries over the encrypted cloud data.

The basic idea behind the query scheme is to use an n dimension binary data vector to represent a query index of a data file. In a multikeyword query, the query is also denoted as an n dimension binary vector; meanwhile, the query operation is converted into the inner product computation between the query vector and each file index vector. In this scheme, one can determine which data files are more relevant than others by sorting the inner product values in descending order to implement a multikeyword ranked and top-k query.

We first provide a simple example to illustrate how to create the data file index vector, the query vector, and how to perform a multikeyword ranked query in the plaintext setting. For ease of understanding, we assume that there are two documents D_1 (containing three keywords, w_1, w_3, and w_4) and D_2 (containing three keywords, w_1, w_2, and w_3), which are denoted as $D_1 = \{w_1, w_3, w_4\}$ and $D_2 = \{w_1, w_2, w_3\}$, respectively. To create the n dimensions binary vector indexes for D_1 and D_2, the scheme needs to predefine a keyword dictionary consisting of n keywords, denoted as $W = \{w_1, w_2, w_3, w_4, w_5\}$ (For simplicity, we set $n = 5$). The binary index vector I of the data file D can be created according to the dictionary W as follows: if w_i $(1 \leq i \leq 5)$ in W appears in the data file D, the corresponding ith position is set to be 1; otherwise, the position is set to be 0. Thus, the five-dimension vector indexes of D_1 and D_2 can be denoted as $I_1 = \{1,0,1,1,0\}$ and $I_2 = \{1,1,1,0,0\}$, respectively. Suppose that a data user uses the keywords w_1 and w_2 to request data files, the query is also converted into a five-dimension query vector by adopting the same method, denoted as $Q = \{1,1,0,0,0\}$. Now the query is performed by computing the inner product between the query vector and each data index vector. In this example, $I_1 \cdot Q = 1$ and $I_2 \cdot Q = 2$, which indicates D_2 is more relevant than D_1. If this is a top-1 query, the D_2 should be regarded as the only query result.

We can observe from Fig. 9 that the scheme can achieve relevant ranked queries by comparing the inner product between the index vector and query vector. To implement the secure search over encrypted cloud data, the basic goal is to design an encryption function E to encrypt the file index vector and query vector while still comparing the inner product. We call the encryption function E the innerproduct preserving encryption function (Fig. 10).

In Ref. [9], based on the space vector model, Wong et al. proposed a secure k-nearest neighbor query scheme over an encrypted database and Cao et al. improved this technique and made it suitable for secure queries over encrypted cloud data [10]. In this section, for simplicity, we introduce a simple version of the encryption function E which can preserve the inner product between two encrypted

Document	index vector
$D_1 = \{w_1, w_3, w_4\}$	$I_1 = \{1, 0, 1, 1, 0\}$
$D_2 = \{w_1, w_2, w_3\}$	$I_2 = \{1, 1, 1, 0, 0\}$

Query keywords	query vector
w_1, w_2	$Q = \{1, 1, 0, 0, 0\}$

Inner product
$I_1 \cdot Q = 1$
$I_2 \cdot Q = 2$

FIG. 9

An example of multikeyword query in the plaintext setting.

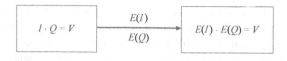

FIG. 10

Secure inner product preserving encryption.

vectors. First, we need to define two encryption functions: E_1 which is used to encrypt the n dimensions index vector I, and E_2 which is used to encrypt the n dimensions query vector Q. The I and Q are represented by column vectors. Given a secret $n \times n$ invertible matrix M as the encryption key, encrypt the index vector I by computing $E_1(I) = M^T \times I$ and encrypt the query vector Q by computing $E_2(Q) = M^{-1} \times Q$. Given an encrypted index $E_1(I)$ and an encrypted query $E_2(Q)$, the search system can get the correct inner product value between I and Q by computing $[E_1(I)]^{-1} \times E_2(Q)$. This is because:

$$\left[E_1(I)\right]^{-1} \times E_2(Q) = I^T MM^{-1} Q = I^T \times Q = I \cdot Q$$

Thus, the search system can correctly perform ranked queries over the encrypted data index according to the inner product. Many security-enhanced versions based on this technique have been widely used in the multikeyword secure query system for cloud computing.

12.3 OTHER BIG DATA SECURITY

Big Data shows promise for enterprises across industries. If there are not the suitable encryption and security solutions for Big Data, Big Data may be in big trouble. Fortunately, there are existing technologies for Big Data security, as follows.

12.3.1 DIGITAL WATERMARKING

Digital watermarking is a technology in which identification information is embedded into the data carrier in ways that cannot be easily noticed, and in which the data usage will not be affected. This technology often protects copyright of multimedia data, and protects databases and text files.

Because of data's randomness and dynamics, methods of watermarking imbedded into databases and text files and multimedia carriers are quite different. And the basic precondition is that there is redundant information in the data, and tolerable precision error. For example, Agrawal et al. embedded watermarking into the least important position of data, randomly based on the tolerance range of error in the numeric data in the database [11,12]. But Sion et al. proposed a schema based on the statistical property of a data set. Watermarking is embedded into a set of attribute data for preventing attackers from destroying watermarking [13,14]. Besides, fingerprint information of databases is embedded into watermarking in order to identify information owners and objects that are distributed [15]. It is beneficial to track leakers. And the public verification of watermarks can be achieved without secret keys through independent component analysis [16]. There are the other relevant works in Refs. [17,18]. If the fragile watermarking is embedded into the tables in databases, the change of data items will be discovered in time [19].

There are many generations of methods of text watermarking, which can be divided into three types. The first type is watermarking based on fine tuning of the document structure, relying on slight differences between the formats of word spacing and line spacing. The second kind is watermarking based on text contents, depending on the modifications of text contents, such as adding white spaces, modifying punctuation, and so on. The third kind is watermarking based on the nature of language, achieving changes by semantic understanding, such as synonym replacement or transformation of sentences, and so on.

Most watermarking described herein considers static data sets; however, the features of Big Data, such as high speed data generation and updating, are not considered sufficiently.

12.3.2 SELF-ADAPTIVE RISK ACCESS CONTROL

In the Big Data scene, security managers may lack sufficient expertise, and they sometimes cannot assign data which can be accessed by users correctly. To counter this, self-adaptive risk access control is proposed. The conception of risk quantification and access quotas are proposed in Jason's report [20]. Subsequently, Cheng et al. proposed an access control solution based on a multilevel security model [21]. Ni et al. proposed another solution based on fuzzy inference, and the amount of information and the security levels of users and information are the main reference parameters for risk quantification. When risk value of the resources that users access is higher than some predetermined threshold, users will not continue accessing. However, in the Big Data application environment, the definition of risk and quantification are more difficult than before.

12.4 PRIVACY ON CORRELATED BIG DATA
12.4.1 CORRELATED DATA IN BIG DATA

The data correlations in Big Data are very complex and quite different from traditional relationships between data stored in relational databases. Some research has been done on data correlations and their privacy problems.

Generally, data correlations are described by social networks graphs. Fig. 11 shows that there is a simple data relationship in the social network. In Fig. 11, nodes represent people or other entities in social networks, and edges represent correlations between them. Adversaries may attack the privacy

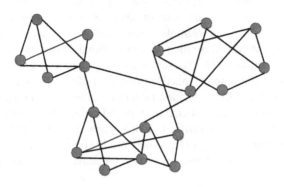

FIG. 11

A simple social networks graph.

of people who have high correlations in social networks by using external information (ie, background knowledge) or the structural similarity between nodes and nodes, or graphs and graphs. For example, adversaries can analyze target individuals' privacy according to the degree of target nodes, attributions of nodes, linking relationships between target individuals, neighborhood structures of target individuals, embedded subgraphs, the features of graphs, and so on [22,23]. Besides, adversaries can also utilize structural information of target individuals to violate their privacy [24].

In fact, adversaries can achieve data correlations easily from social networks, etc. For instance, the structure of the social network may be obtained when adversaries use a web crawler. Therefore, a person's correlations in a social network could be ascertained by analyzing this structure. An adversary may achieve some query results, such as "the number of persons whose hobbies are smoking and drinking," and then the adversary may try to analyze the hobby of one special person based on the high correlated persons with the same hobby [25]. Fig. 12 shows that adversaries attack sensitive information through utilizing data correlation.

Many attributes about correlated data in social networks may be used to analyze the privacy of target individuals. Because correlated data privacy can be leaked more easily, we should pay much more attention to this problem.

However, there may be important, undetected relationships in Big Data. Reshef et al. proposed an approach called the maxim information coefficient to measure a wide range of correlations, both functional and not in large data sets [26]. But the amount of data sets in Big Data is huge, thus data correlations in Big Data are more complex. Besides, adversaries can also utilize the undiscovered data correlations to attack sensitive information. So correlated data privacy in Big Data is an important and growing challenge.

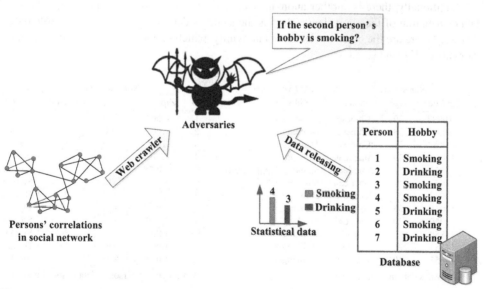

FIG. 12

Sensitive information stolen through utilizing data correlation.

Furthermore, data correlations in Big Data do not mean that data A causes data B. On the other hand, these correlations imply that data A and B may be detected simultaneously. And, these correlations are quite different from the data correlations that existed before Big Data. However, the difference often is neglected, so sensitive information will be more exposed and vulnerable.

Research is ongoing on how to protect sensitive information in Big Data. And the research about data privacy protection focuses on anonymity and differential privacy, primarily.

12.4.2 ANONYMITY

Adversaries can utilize data correlation in Big Data to attack sensitive information. There are some existing technologies to prevent adversaries from stealing sensitive information in relational data. In this section, we will introduce the development of anonymity for data releasing, and data privacy protection for social networks.

(1) Anonymity for Data Releasing

For the structured data in Big Data, the key technologies and basic methods for achieving the anonymity of data releasing are still being developed and improved.

Take k-anonymity, for example. In schemas which are proposed at an early age [27,28] and optimization [29–31], data is processed by tuples generalization and restraint; thus, quasiidentifiers are divided into groups. Quasiidentifiers in every group are converted to be the same, and there are k tuples in every group. So every tuple cannot be identified by other k-1 tuples. Fig. 13 shows the example of k-anonymity.

Then l-diversity anonymity is proposed. The character of this method is that the diversity of sensitive data should be more than l. Implementations of l-diversity contain a scheme based on anatomy and a scheme based on data substitution [32]. Fig. 14 shows the example of l-diversity anonymity.

Additionally, there is another anonymity called t-closeness, which requires that the sensitive data distribution of the equivalence class is the same as data distribution of the whole data table [33]. And there are the other works about anonymity, which include (k, e)-anonymity [34], (X, Y)-anonymity [35], and so on.

No.	Non sensitive			Sensitive
	Zip Code	Age	Nationality	Hobby
1	410082	29	Chinese	Smoking
2	410082	28	Chinese	Drinking
3	410082	21	Chinese	Dancing
4	13068	49	American	Singing
5	13053	37	American	Smoking
6	13053	41	American	Smoking
7	12047	36	Japanese	Drinking
8	12035	35	Japanese	Dancing
9	12050	20	Japanese	Smoking
10	14850	27	Russian	Smoking
11	14853	26	Russian	Drinking
12	14853	40	Russian	Smoking

Person' s data in social networks

Anonymity →

No.	Non sensitive			Sensitive
	Zip Code	Age	Nationality	Hobby
1	4100**	<30	*	Smoking
2	4100**	<30	*	Drinking
3	4100**	<30	*	Dancing
4	130**	>30	*	Singing
5	130**	>30	*	Smoking
6	130**	>30	*	Smoking
7	120**	>20	*	Drinking
8	120**	>20	*	Dancing
9	120**	>20	*	Smoking
10	148**	>20	*	Smoking
11	148**	>20	*	Drinking
12	148**	>20	*	Smoking

3-Anonymous person' s data in social networks

FIG. 13

Example of 3-anonymity, where QI = {ZIP, Age, Nationality}.

No.	Non sensitive			Sensitive
	Zip Code	Age	Nationality	Hobby
1	4100**	<30	*	Smoking
2	4100**	<30	*	Drinking
3	4100**	<30	*	Dancing
4	130**	>30	*	Singing
5	130**	>30	*	Smoking
6	130**	>30	*	Smoking
7	120**	>20	*	Drinking
8	120**	>20	*	Dancing
9	120**	>20	*	Smoking
10	1485*	>20	*	Smoking
11	1485*	>20	*	Drinking
12	1485*	>20	*	Smoking

FIG. 14

Example of 2-diversity anonymity.

The anonymity for data releasing in Big Data is more complex. Adversaries can aquire data from multiple channels, not just the same data publishing source. For example, people have discovered that adversaries can compare their data with public data on IMDB and then identify the account of the object in Netflix. This problem is being researched in more depth [36].

(2) Anonymity for Social Networks

The data produced by social networks is a Big Data source, and contains mass quantities of users' private data. Because of the graph structure features of social networks, anonymity for social networks is quite different from structured data.

The typical requirements for anonymity in social networks are users' identifiers anonymity and attributes anonymity (also called nodes anonymity). When data is released, users' identifiers and attributes information are hidden. Furthermore, relationship anonymity (also called edges anonymity) is the other typical requirement for anonymity in social networks. The relationships between users are hidden when data is published.

Currently, edges anonymity schemes are mostly based on edges deleting and adding. And edges anonymity can be achieved by adding and deleting exchange-edges randomly. In Ref. [37], in the process of anonymity, characteristic values of adjacent matrixes and the second characteristic values of the according Laplace matrixes remain constant. In Ref. [38], nodes are classified according to the degree of nodes. Edges' satisfied requirements are chosen from the nodes of the same degree. The solutions in Refs. [39,40] are similar to those in Ref. [41].

Additionally, it is important to note that the graph structure is partitioned and clustered based on super nodes. Examples include anonymity based on nodes clustering, anonymity based on genetic algorithm, anonymity based on a simulated annealing algorithm, and a schema for filling in the splitted super nodes [40]. In Ref. [42], the concept of k-security is proposed. It achieves anonymity by k isomorphism subgraphs. Anonymization based on super nodes can achieve edges anonymity, but deposed social structured graphs are quite different from the original ones.

However, a major problem of social networks anonymization is that adversaries can use the other public information to infer anonymous users, especially when there are connection relations between users. This creates problems, as follows. First, adversaries utilize weak connections to predict possible connections between users [42]. This is appropriate for networks in which there are sparse user relations. Second, attackers can regain and infer hierarchical relationships in the crowd, according to existing social networks structures [43]. Third, adversaries can analyze the complex social networks, such as Weibo, and infer relations [44]. And last but not least, adversaries can infer the probability of different connection relations based on the restricted random-walk mechanism. Researchers assert that the clustering feature of the social network significantly impacts the accuracy of subrelationship prediction.

12.4.3 DIFFERENTIAL PRIVACY

Differential privacy [45,46] is a powerful tool for providing privacy-preserving noisy query answers over statistical databases. It is also the most popular perturbation for correlated data privacy protection. It guarantees that the distribution of noisy query answers changes very little with the addition or deletion of any tuple.

Definitions of differential privacy

There are two typical definitions of differential privacy, which are classified into unbounded and bounded [47]. The formal definitions of unbounded differential privacy [45] and bounded differential privacy [46] are Definition 3 and Definition 4, respectively.

Definition 3 Let A be a randomized algorithm, S be any set, D_1 and D_2 be any pairs of databases, A will be unbounded ε-differential privacy, if $P(A(D_1) \in S) \leq e^\varepsilon\, P(A(D_2) \in S)$, where D_1 could be achieved from deleting or adding one tuple of D_2.

Definition 4 Let A be a randomized algorithm, S be any set, D_1 and D_2 be any pairs of databases, A will be unbounded ε-differential privacy, if $P(A(D_1) \in S) \leq e^\varepsilon\, P(A(D_2) \in S)$, where D_1 can be obtained from changing the value of exactly one tuple of D_2.

Differential privacy optimization

To improve the precision of inquiry responses, a great deal of research has been done on differential privacy.

Blum et al. proposed a new approach which can respond to an arbitrary "querying class" [48]. The precision of the response relies on the VC dimension of the "querying class." In Ref. [48], an efficient method is described for the querying of responding domains, but precision is worse than that proposed in Refs. [49,50].

In regard to differential privacy for compound queries, Hardt et al. proposed a k-mod method based on linear query sets [51]. This method makes linear queries mapped to the L_1 sphere, and then it is determined how much noise should be added. This method requires uniform sampling from high dimensional convex bodies. In Ref. [52], the cost of the algorithm is searching for the query schema, mainly. This procedure is preceded only once. Once the best schema is determined, its efficiency is the same as Laplace's.

Roth et al. assert that queries will arrive in a chronological sequence in an interactive environment [53]. The condition in which the query will arrive is unknown, but it must be responded to immediately. Hence, the traditional Laplace mechanism is improved. The query response is acquired by computing prior query results using a median approach.

(1) Query Response Optimization Based on the Hierarchy Concept of the Matrix Mechanism

Relevant research about the best response schema for the count query in the related domain is rarely reported. Related researches are gotten down to research since 2010.

Xiao et al. applied the Haar wavelet transformation (WT) to differential privacy [49]. Data is carried out by wavelet transformation before noise is added so that the correctness of the counting query can be improved. At the same time, the applied range is expanded to the attributions of the nouns and the high-dimensional Histogram query. This approach is equivalent to the H query and is the equivalent of a query tree. The summarized data, which is more fine-grained, is on the every layer of this tree, from up to down.

Hay et al. proposed differential privacy based on layered summations and least squares [50]. The query sequence is divided into groups that are satisfied by consistency constraints. And noises are added group by group so that the precision of the query is satisfied and the amount of noise that should be added is reduced.

Li et al. proposed the concept of the matrix mechanism [52], and papers [49,50] have been written on the category of the matrix mechanism. Some relationship between the queries is analyzed, and each query is regarded as a linear combination of basic count operations. Then the queries containing relationships are expressed as the matrixes. The amount of added noise is reduced based on the existing Laplace noise distribution.

These three approaches are all based on the matrix mechanism. And special query questions are improved by them.

(2) The Precision Range of the Linear Query

The range of the precision of the query response that is satisfied by differential privacy is an important research field for researchers. And the most important area for study is the range of the precision of the linear query response.

In the noninteractive mode, Blum et al. proposed differential privacy for releasing synthetic data [48]. This algorithm obeys the error range of $O(n^{2/3})$, where n is the size of the data set, and the error range will expand with the increase in data sets. Dwork et al. improved the algorithm [54,55] proposed in this paper [48]. Gupta et al. proposed a noninteractive query response based on multiplicative weights and agnostic learning [56]. Hardt et al. implemented these algorithms and evaluated them by conducting experiments in Ref. [57]. The experiments' results show that this algorithm is not adjusted to the interactive mode, and, when the number of the query times is many times the size of the data sets, the efficiency of the algorithm is very low.

In the interactive mode, Roth et al. [53] assumed that the query was executed online, and that the query should be responded to before the upcoming query arrived. So that the error range will be: $n^{2/3} (\log k)(\log|X|)^{1/3} / \varepsilon^{1/3}$. Hardt et al. [58] adapted an approach based on additive and multiplicative weights, and the error edge of the query response is reduced to $\left(n^{1/2} (\log k)(\log|X|)^{1/4} \right) / n$. The meaning of the parameters is: under ε-differential privacy protection, n is the size of the data sets, k is the query times, and X is the data domain.

Gupta et al. composited the midvalue algorithm [53] and additive and multiplicative weights [58] in the interactive mode, and summarizes the multiplicative weights [56,57] in the noninteractive mode, as well as defining the iterative database construction (IDC) algorithm abstractly [59]. The IDC algorithm can respond to queries under differential privacy protection, either in the interactive mode or in the noninteractive mode. An assumed data structure is improved iteratively by the IDC algorithm so that this data structure can respond to all the queries. At the same time, the algorithm improves the precision range of the midvalue algorithm and the multiplicative weights algorithm.

Key approaches for differential privacy

(1) Differential Privacy for Histogram

As in the foundation of many data analysis approaches, such as contingency tables and marginals, the histogram query plays an important role in differential privacy protections.

Chawla et al. began to study privacy protections for histogram queries before differential privacy was proposed [60]. Dwork et al. analyzed the essential properties of the histogram query in depth, and pointed out that compared with the existing methods the biggest advantage of differential privacy is that the computation of the sensitiveness is independent of the dimension [46]. With regard to differential privacy for high-dimensional output contingency tables and the covariance matrix analysis, data privacy protection can be created on the premise that noise is added. Dwork et al. provided a complete summary of achieving differential privacy for the histogram query, and pointed out that although the histogram containing k units can be regarded as k independent counting queries, adding or deleting a line of data only effects the counting of the unit corresponding to that line of data, and at most, one count is affected [61]. Therefore, the sensitiveness of a histogram query is 1. This conclusion builds a foundation for applying the differential-private histogram protection to various problems.

(2) The Differential-Private K-Means Clustering

Blum et al. proposed that differential privacy was achieved by adding appropriate noises in the process of K-means clustering, and summarized the sensitiveness of the computing method of the query function and the main steps for achieving the ε-differential private K-means algorithm [62]. In K-means, privacy will be leaked by computing the central point, which is nearest to every sample point. However, for an unknown set, computing the average value only requires that the sum divide by the number. Therefore, as long as the approximate value of the set S_j is released, the set's own information is not needed.

Dwork et al. replenished and improved the algorithm, and analyzed the sensitiveness of the computing method of each query function in the differential-private K-means algorithm in detail, and provided the total sensitiveness of the whole query sequence [61].

The PINQ framework

PINQ (privacy integrated queries) was developed by Dwork et al., and it is a framework for sensitive data privacy protection [63]. The PINQ framework is similar to the LINQ framework. It provides a series of APIs so that developers can develop the differential privacy protection system through using simple and expressive language. This framework includes rich application cases of the differential-private data analysis.

Fig. 15 shows an application example of releasing data by the PINQ framework. In the framework, a privacy budget is set by the owner of the database which needs to be protected. When users query data from the database, some budgets will be consumed. Once the budget is exhausted, users cannot query by the framework. Consider the following database record: "Jerry, male, pneumonia, 28-years old, address: Yuelu Mountain at Changsha of Hunan Province in China." For data users, in the range of the parameter ε, whether Jerry is in the database or not will not affect the query results. The query results can be shared between users freely. Users can also integrate the external information (such as the building owner information, the inhabitant's consuming data and the other data from the other database). Privacy will not be leaked by these operations.

Differential privacy for correlated data publication

To protect correlated data, differential privacy is studied to solve this problem.

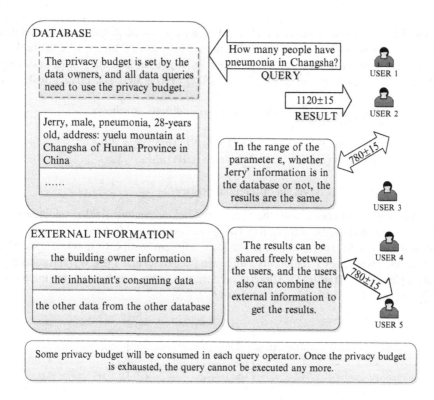

FIG. 15

The PINQ framework.

Chen et al. proposed an approach to protect correlated network data while the data is released. This approach proposes differential privacy by adding an extra correlation parameter. It is a noninteractive method of stopping adversaries from analyzing the presence of a direct link between two people. Meanwhile, research has given us the theorem of the ε-differentially private mechanism under correlations, see Theorem 1 [64].

Theorem 1 *Let A be private mechanism over a database, and k_1 be a correlation parameter which is the database with, besides k_2 is another correlation parameter and $1 \leq k_2 \leq k_1$. So A will be ε-differentially private for all databases with k_2.*

What's more, Zhang et al. researched differential privacy for privacy-preserving data releasing via the Bayesian network and proposed a different solution called *"PRIVBAYES"* to deal with this problem [65]. To depict the correlations of the attribution in a dataset D, a Bayesian network is built. Then noise is added to a set of marginals of D for achieving differential privacy. An approximate data distribution is constructed by utilizing the noisy marginals and the Bayesian network. This data distribution has been published for the sake of research.

Yang et al. studied a perturbation method on correlated data called "Bayesian differential privacy" to deal with the privacy protection of correlated data. The definition of Bayesian differential privacy is as follows [25].

Definition 5 Let $\mathcal{A}$ be an adversary and $\mathcal{M}(x)$ be a randomized perturbation mechanism over a database D, $\mathcal{K}$ be the set of known tuples, $\mathcal{U}$ be the set of unknown tuples, i be the tuple adversaries want to attack, x be an instance of the database D, where an adversary with knowledge $\mathcal{K}$ to attack x_i, that is, $\mathcal{A} = (i, \mathcal{K})$ and $\mathcal{K} \subseteq [n]\backslash\{i\}$, and $\mathcal{M}(x) = \Pr(r \in S|x)$. The privacy leakage of $\mathcal{M}$ is

$$\text{BDPL}_A(\mathcal{M}) := \underset{x_i, x'_i, x_{\mathcal{K}}, t}{\text{SUP}} \log \frac{\Pr(r = t \mid x_i, x_{\mathcal{K}})}{\Pr(r = t \mid x'_i, x_{\mathcal{K}})}, \text{ there are two conditions as follows.}$$

- x is continuous-valued: $\Pr(r \in S \mid x_i, x_{\mathcal{K}}) = \int \Pr(r \in S \mid x) p(x_{\mathcal{U}} \mid x_i, x_{\mathcal{K}}) d_{x_{\mathcal{U}}}$
- x is discrete-valued: $\Pr(r \in S \mid x_i, x_{\mathcal{K}}) = \sum_{x_{\mathcal{U}}} \Pr(r \in S \mid x) \Pr(x_{\mathcal{U}} \mid x_i, x_{\mathcal{K}})$

If $\underset{A}{\sup} \text{BDPL}_A(\mathcal{M}) \le \varepsilon$, M is Bayesian differential privacy.

Then to depict the data correlation, the Gaussian Markov random field is adopted to build the Gaussian Correlation Model. The definition of Gaussian Correlation Model is as follows.

Definition 6 Let $W = (w_{ij})$ $(w_{ij} \ge 0)$ be the weighted adjacent matrix, $G(x, W)$ be a weighted undirected graph, where each vertex x_i represents a tuple i in the dataset and $x_i \in x$, w_{ij} represents the correlation between tuples i and j. And let $\text{DI} = \text{diag}(w_1, w_2, \dots, w_n)$ be the weighted degree matrix of $G(x, W)$ where $w_i = \sum_{j \ne i} w_{ij}$, and L be the Laplacian matrix of $G(x, W)$,

$$L = \text{DI} - W = \begin{pmatrix} w_1 & -w_{12} & \cdots & -w_{1,n} \\ -w_{12} & w_2 & \cdots & -w_{2,n} \\ \vdots & \vdots & \ddots & \vdots \\ -w_{1,n} & -w_{2,n} & \cdots & w_n \end{pmatrix}$$

A Gaussian correlation model $G(x, L)$ is the pair (x, L).

12.5 FUTURE DIRECTIONS

The existing research about security and privacy in Big Data is not perfect. There are some challenges to face. The following section describes the future of the research on this topic.

On the one hand, the secure query schemes which we introduce herein allow cloud users to obtain encrypted files by submitting query keywords of interest to the cloud server. However, there are still many important techniques and functionalities of secure searching worth further study for continuously improving the user query experience and perfecting query functionality, such as keyword fuzzy query, range query, subset query, and query expression relation operation, etc. In addition, recently, researchers have proposed new application requirements dictating that a secure query scheme should provide some mechanisms that allow data users to verify the correctness and completeness of query results returned by the cloud, based on the assumption that the cloud may intentionally omit some qualified query results for saving computation resources and communication overhead. Verifiable secure query schemes will be a research focus in the future.

On the other hand, with the increase of local link density in social network and the clustering coefficient, the link prediction algorithm between correlated data in social networks should be further enhanced. Thus, in the future, anonymity for correlated data in social networks can prevent these kinds of attacks by inferring. The amount of Big Data will be extremely large after years of data collection. The essence of differential privacy is adding noise to protect sensitive information so that the utility of Big Data and the efficiency of the differential privacy will all be affected. Thus additional research is required on how to perform differential privacy appropriately for Big Data.

12.6 CONCLUSIONS

With the growing popularity of cloud computing and sharp increase in data volume, more and more encrypted data is stored on cloud servers, which means the further development of secure query techniques are essential for data utilization in cloud environments. At present, secure query schemes over encrypted data can be classified into two categories: the symmetric-key based solutions and public-key based query schemes. Compared with the symmetric-key, due to the heavy computation cost and inefficiency of public-key cryptosystems, secure query schemes based on public-key setting are not suitable for cloud applications with mass users and mass data, and make those schemes based on symmetric-key preferable in all solutions.

We systemically illustrate the related concepts, models, definitions, and important implementation techniques of secure searching over encrypted cloud data based on symmetric-key setting, including system frameworks, threat models, attack models, etc. We provide the implementation principles and details of secure search techniques over encrypted data by introducing two concrete secure query schemes proposed in Refs. [4] and [10]. Additionally, we point out that if there are not suitable encryption and security solutions for Big Data, Big Data may be in big trouble. And we introduce data watermarking and self-adaptive risk access control in Big Data separately.

What's more, correlated Big Data brings new security and privacy problems, but it is an important solution for these problems by itself. In this chapter, we systematically comb the related key research about correlated data privacy protection from different perspectives such as data releasing, social networks, correlated data publication, and so on. And we group the relevant research into two categories: anonymity and differential privacy, introduced, respectively. Additionally, we look forward to future developments in correlated data privacy in Big Data, as there is very little current research on the topic. Thus, we should pay more attention to studying technical means for preserving the privacy of correlated Big Data. The problem of privacy on correlated Big Data could be solved only through a combination of technical means and relevant policies and regulations.

REFERENCES

[1] Sun W, Wang B, Cao N, Li M, Lou W, Hou YT, et al. Privacy-preserving multi-keyword text search in the cloud supporting similarity based ranking. In: Proceedings of the 8th ACM symposium on information, computer and communications security, Hangzhou, China, May 8–10; 2013.

[2] Wang C, Cao N, Li J, Ren K, Lou W. Secure ranked keyword search over encrypted cloud data. In: Proceedings of the 30th international conference on distributed computing systems, Genoa, Italy, Jun. 21–25; 2010.

[3] Song DX, Wagner D, Perrig A. Practical techniques for searches on encrypted data. IEEE symposium on security & privacy 2002;0044.

[4] Curtmola R, Garay J, Kamara S, Ostrovsky R. Searchable symmetric encryption: improved definitions and efficient constructions. In: Proceeding of the 13th ACM conference on computer and communications security, Alexandria, USA, Oct. 30–Nov. 3; 2006.

[5] Singhal A. Modern information retrieval: a brief overview. Bull IEEE Comput Soc Tech Commttee Data Eng 2001;24(4):35–43.

[6] Bellare M, Rogaway P. Introduction to modern cryptography. Lecture Notes; 2001.

[7] Boneh D, Di Crescenzo G, Ostrovsky R, Persiano G. Public key encryption with keyword search. Adv Cryptol EUROCRYPT 2004;2004(2004):506–22.

[8] Goh EJ. Secure indexes, Stanford University technical report, 2004.

[9] Wong WK, Cheung DW, Kao B, Mamoulis N. Secure kNN computation on encrypted databases. In: Proceedings of the 2009 ACM SIGMOD international conference on management of data, providence, USA, Jun. 29–Jul. 2; 2009.

[10] Cao N, Wang C, Li M, Ren K, Lou W. Privacy-preserving multi-keyword ranked search over encrypted cloud data. In: Proceedings of the 30th IEEE international conference on computer communications, Shanghai, China, Apr. 10–15; 2011.

[11] Agrawal R, Hass PJ, Kiernan J. Watermarking relational data: framework, algorithms and analysis. Int J Very Large Data Bases 2003;12(2):157–69.

[12] Agrawal R, Kieman J. Watermarking relational databases. In: Proceeding of the 28th international conference on very large data bases, Hong Kong, China, Aug. 20–23; 2002.

[13] Sion R, Atallab M, Prabhakar S. On watermarking numeric sets. In: Proceedings of the first inernational workshop on digital watermarking, Seoul, Korea, Nov. 21–22; 2002.

[14] Sion R, Atallah M, Prabhakar S. Right protection for relational data. In: Proceedings of the 2003 ACM SIGMOD international conference on management of data, San Diego, USA, Jun. 10–12; 2003.

[15] Guo F, Wang J, Li D. Fingerprinting relational databases. In: Proceedings of the 2006 ACM symposium on applied computing, Dijion, France, Apr. 23–27; 2006.

[16] Jiang C, Sun X, Yi Y, et al. Study of database public watermarking based on JADE algorithm. J Syst Simul 2006;18(7):1781–5.

[17] Zhang Y, Niu X, Zhao D. A method of protecting relational databases copyright with cloud watermark. Int J Inform Technol 2004;1(1):206–10.

[18] Liu Y, Ma Y, Zhang H, et al. A method for trust management in cloud computing: data coloring by cloud watermarking. Int J Autom Comput 2011;8(3):280–5.

[19] Guo H, Li Y, Liu A, et al. A fragile watermarking scheme for detecting malicious modifications of database relations. Inform Sci 2006;176(10):1350–78.

[20] The MITRE Corporation. Horizontal integration: broader access models for realizing information dominance, http://www.fas.org/irp/agency/dod/jason/classpol.pdf; [2015.9.18].

[21] Cheng PC, Rohatgi P, Keser C, et al. Fuzzy multi-level security: an experiment on quantified risk-adaptive access control. In: Proceedings of the 2007 IEEE symposium on security and privacy, Oakland, USA, May 20–23; 2007.

[22] Zhou B, Pei J, Luk WS. A brief survey on anonymization techniques for privacy preserving publishing of social network data. ACM Sigkdd Explor Newslett 2008;10(2):12–22.

[23] Liu K, Terzi E. Towards identity anonymization on graphs. In: Proceeding of ACM SIGMOD international conference on management of data, Columbia, Canada, Jun. 9–12; 2008.

[24] Backstrom L, Dwork C, Kleinberg J. Wherefore Art Thou R3579X? Anonymized social network, hidden patterns, and structural steganography. In: Proceedings of the 16th international conference on world wide web conference, Banff, Canada, May 8–12; 2007.

[25] Yang B, Sato I, Nakagawa H. Bayesian differential privacy on correlated data. In: Proceedings of the 2015 ACM SIGMOD international conference on management of data, Melbourne, Australia, May 31–Jun. 4; 2015.

[26] Reshef DN, Reshef YA, Finucane HK, et al. Detecting novel associations in large data sets. Science 2011;334(6062):1518–24.

[27] Sweeney L. k-anonymity: a model for protecting privacy. Int J Uncertainty Fuzziness Knowl Based Syst 2002;10(5):557–70.

[28] Sweeney L. k-anonymity: achieving k-anonymity privacy protection using generalization and suppression. Int J Uncertainty Fuzziness Knowl Based Syst 2002;10(5):571–88.

[29] Bayardo RJ, Agrawal R. Data privacy through optimal k-anonymization. In: Proceedings of the 21st international conference on data engineering, Tokyo, Japan, Apr. 5–8; 2005.

[30] LeFevre K, DeWitt DJ, Ramakrishnan R. Incognito: efficient full-domain k-anonymity. In: Proceedings of the 2005 ACM SIGMOD international conference on management of data, Baltimore, USA, Jun. 14–16; 2005.

[31] LeFevre K, DeWitt DJ, Ramakrishnan R. Mondrian multidimensional k-anonymity. In: Proceedings of the 22nd international conference on data engineering, Georgia, USA, Apr. 3–8; 2006.

[32] Machanavajjhala A, Kifer D, Gehrke J, Venkitasubramaniam M. L-diversity: privacy beyong k-anonymity. ACM Trans Knowl Discov Data 2007;1(1):1–52.

[33] Li N, Li T, Venkatasubramanian S. *t*-closeness: privacy beyond k-anonymity and l-diversity. In: Proceedings of the IEEE 23rd international conference on data engineering, Istanbul, Turkey, Apr. 15–20; 2007.

[34] Zeng K. Publicly verifiable remote data integrity. In: Proceedings of the 10th international conference on information and communications security, Birmingham, UK, Oct. 20–22; 2008.

[35] Wang K, Fung B. Anonymizing sequential releases. In: Proceedings of the 21st ACM SIGKDD international conference on knowledge discovery and data mining, Philadelphia, USA, Aug. 20–23; 2006.

[36] Nasayanan A, Shmatikov V. Robust de-anonymization of large sparse datasets. In: Proceedings of the 2008 IEEE symposium on security and privacy, Oakland, USA, May 18–21; 2008.

[37] Ying X, Wu X. Randomizing social networks: a spectrum preserving approach. In: Proceedings of the 8th SIAM international conference on data mining, Atlanta, USA, Apr. 24–26; 2008.

[38] Li N, Das SK. Applications of k-anonymity and l-diversity in publishing online social networks. Security Privacy Soc Netw 2013;53–179.

[39] Zhou L, Chen L, Ozsu MT. K-automorphism: a general framework for privacy preserving network publication. In: Proceedings of the 35th international conference on very large databases, Lyon, France, Aug. 24–27; 2009.

[40] Zhang L, Zhang W. Efficient edge anonymization of large social graph, http://venom.cs.utsa.edu/dmz/techrep/2011/CS-TR-2011-004.pdf; [2015.9.10].

[41] Zhang L, Zhang W. Edge anonymity in social network graphs. In: Proceedings of the 12th international conference on computational science and engineering, Vancouver, Canada, Aug. 29–31; 2009.

[42] Cheng J, Fu AW, Liu J. k-isomorphism: privacy preserving network publication against structural attacks. In: Proceedings of the 2010 ACM SIGMOD international conference on management of data, Indianapolis, USA, Jun. 6–11; 2010.

[43] Clauset A, Moore C, Newman MEJ. Hierarchical structure and the prediction of missing links in networks. Nature 2008;453:98–101.

[44] Yin D, Hong L, Xiong X, Davison BD. Link formation analysis in microblogs. In: Proceedings of the 34th international ACM SIGIR conference on research and development in information retrieval, Beijing, China, Jul. 24–28; 2011.

[45] Dwork C. Differential privacy. ICALP 2006;26(2):1–12.

[46] Dwork C, McSherry F, Nissim K, Smith A. Calibrating noise to sensitivity in private data analysis. In: Proceedings of the 3rd conference on theory of cryptography, New York, USA, Mar. 4–7; 2006.

[47] Kifer D, Machanavajjhala A. No free lunch in data privacy. In: Proceedings of the 2011 ACM SIGMOD international conference on management of data, Athens, Greece, Jun. 12–16; 2011.

[48] Blum A, Ligett K, Roth A. A learning theory approach to non-interactive database privacy, In: Proceedings of the 40th annual ACM symposium on theory of computing, Victoria, Canada, May 17–20.

[49] Xiao X, Wang G, Gehrke J. Differential privacy via wavelet transforms. IEEE Trans Knowl Data Eng 2011;23(8):1200–14.

[50] Hay M, Rastogi V, Miklau G, et al. Boosting the accuracy of differentially private histograms through consistency. J VLDB 2010;3(1–2):1021–32.

[51] Hardt M, Talwar K. On the geometry of differential privacy. In: Proceedings of the 42nd ACM symposium on theory of computing, Cambridge, MA, Jun. 6–8; 2010.

[52] Li C, Hay M, Rastogi V, et al. Optimizing linear counting queries under differential privacy. In: Proceedings of the 29th ACM SIGMOD-SIGACT-SIGART symposium on priciples of database systems, Indianapolis, USA, Jun. 6–11; 2010.

[53] Roth A, Rougharden T. Interactive privacy via the median mechanism. In: Proceedings of the 42nd ACM symposium on theory of computing, Cambridge, MA, Jun. 6–8; 2010.

[54] Dwork C, Naor M, Reingold O, et al. On the complexity of differentially private data release: efficient algorithms and hardness results. In: Proceedings of the 41st annual ACM symposium on theory of computing, Bethesda, USA, May 31–Jun. 2; 2009.

[55] Dwork C, Rothblum GN, Vadhan S. Boosting and differential privacy. In: Proceedings of the 51st annual IEEE symposium on foundations of computer science, Las Vegas, USA, Oct. 24–26; 2010.

[56] Gupta A, Hardt M, Roth A, et al. Privately releasing conjunctions and the statistical query barrier. In: Proceedings of the 43rd annual ACM symposium on theory of computing, San Jose, USA, Jun. 6–8; 2011.

[57] Hardt M, Ligett K, McSheery F. A simple and practical algorithm for differentially private data release, http://www.cs.princeton,edu/~mhardt/pub/mwem.pdf; [2015.08.15].

[58] Hardt M, Rothblum GN. A multiplicative weights mechanism for privacy preserving data analysis. In: Proceedings of the 51st annual IEEE symposium on foundations of computer science, Vegas, USA, Oct. 23–26; 2010.

[59] Gupta A, Roth A, Ullman J. Iterative constructions and private data release. In: Proceedings of the 9th international conference on theory of cryptography, Mar. 19–21, Taormina, Italy; 2012.

[60] Chawla S, Dwork C, McSheery F, et al. On the utility of privacy-preserving histograms. In: Proceedings of the 21st conference on uncertainty in artificial intelligence, Edinburgh, Scotland, Jul. 26–29; 2005.

[61] Dwork C. A firm foundation for private data analysis. Commun ACM 2011;54(1):86–95.

[62] Blum A, Dwork C, McSherry F, et al. Practical privacy: the SuLQ framework. In: Proceedings of the 24th ACM SIGMOD international conference on management of data/principles of database systems, New York, USA, Jun. 13–16; 2005.

[63] McSherry FD. Privacy integrated queries (PINQ), http://research.microsoft.com/en-us/projects/PINQ/; [2015.6.10].

[64] Zhang J, Cormode G, Procopiuc CM, et al. PrivBayes: private data release via Bayesian networks. In: Proceedings of the ACM SIGMOD international conference on management of data, 2014, Snowbird, USA, Jun. 22–27; 2014.

[65] Chen R, Fung BCM, Philip SY, et al. Correlated network data publication via differential privacy. VLDB J 2014;4(23):653–76.

LOCATION INFERRING IN INTERNET OF THINGS AND BIG DATA

13

W. Xi, J. Han, K. Li, Z. Jiang, H. Ding

13.1 INTRODUCTION

Sensing applications are becoming ubiquitous smart applications. Beyond smartphones, tablets and wearable devices, sensing ability will eventually be embedded and integrated in our living spaces. The recent surge in sensing applications is characterized by the distributed collection of data by either self-selected or recruited participants for the purpose of sharing local conditions, increasing global awareness of issues of interest, computing community statistics, and mapping physical and social phenomena.

Most of these applications are location-based services (LBS), which are increasingly important to the user experience. In the Big Data era, the information provided by LBS enables meaningful and reasonable analysis and mining of the collected data. Some of the most common LBS applications include those of local news crews, navigation, locating points of interest, parking assistance, fleet management, emergency team use, asset tracking, enabling location-sensitive buildings, and local advertisements.

To specify the mobile user's location, an intuitive solution depends on the mobile phone system. For example, a current cell phone ID can be used for identifying the base transceiver station (BTS) that the phone is communicating with. Once it is determined, the only thing left is to pinpoint the location of the BTS.

Other solutions use GPS techniques. GPS is much more accurate than BTS-based solutions. Currently, it is very common that devices contain built-in GPS receivers. However, GPS cannot work well in indoor environments. An alternative common method is to use short-range positioning beacons. This is an ideal solution for existing Wi-Fi or Bluetooth technologies and is ideal for indoor LBS applications.

Big Data has spurred the revolution of smart sensing and LBS, which in turn enriches Big Data in terms of data volume and application scale. Every digital process and social media exchange produces Big Data. Besides physical locations, velocity, direction, and acceleration are all involved in Big Data applications.However, applications for Big Data are becoming more selective, because the explosive increase in sensed data will easily overwhelm the computing resources that people currently have. Therefore, sensing should proceed by extracting meaningful value from Big Data, requiring optimal processing power, analysis capabilities and skills.

We are aiming at finding effective ways to estimate locations and sense human behaviors purely by leveraging huge amounts of wireless transmission metadata, including signal strength, transmission successful rates, and so on. The transmission metadata from all clients is collected from Internet of Things (IoT) devices, and we use it to automatically establish the mapping between the spatial location spot and wireless signal strength distribution. When the sensing data obtained from each use reaches

Big Data. http://dx.doi.org/10.1016/B978-0-12-805394-2.00013-1

a certain amount, the features of locations could be extracted through crowdsourcing. All of these elements bode well for the needs of crowdsourcing and Big Data, where little can be assumed about users, and explicit input or other action from users is best avoided.

As a result, we achieve this goal without any explicit human participation using IoT and Big Data technology. We expanded this methodology to estimate the numbers and behavior of people in indoor environments. There are two kinds of sensing approaches based on Big Data: device-based sensing and device-free sensing. Device-based sensing approaches allow users to carry around a mobile phone or other wireless devices, while device-free sensing approaches allow sensing the target without attaching any electronic devices in wireless environments.

We introduce Big Data technology to excavate potential relations between wireless signal variation and the behavior of people, which efficiently reduces training costs, extends the wireless sensing ability, and improves sensing accuracy.

13.2 DEVICE-BASED SENSING USING BIG DATA

13.2.1 INTRODUCTION

A critical challenge of LBS is to find the accurate location of mobile devices. In outdoor environments, GPS-based localization can provide sufficiently high accuracy for every GPS-enabled device [1]. However, in indoor environments, the existing solutions [2–12] are neither pervasive nor interoperable.

Just like the "traffic delay" for each packet transferred in a wired network which may act as an indicator of the logic distance, each packet transferred in a wireless network has a "received signal strength" [2], and can also indicate the distance relationship between APs and clients. Every day TBs of data are silently transferred through wireless infrastructures. Hence, a very large amount of transmission metadata is collected. *Could we discover the location information from these metadata?*

Approaching this problem in a more practical way, we have the question: *"Can we automatically establish the mapping between geo-locations and surrounding Wi-Fi signal fingerprints?"* In the following text, we introduce a Sensor-free crowd sENsing Indoor Localization scheme, SENIL. It could extract the fingerprint map from the mere knowledge of an indoor floor plan and a large number of RSS samples passively collected from the AP-end. In this way, any devices with wireless connections are continuously participating in crowd sensing, while no exclusive APP is required to be installed.

Our solution is based on a key observation that although the location coordinates and wireless fingerprints are so disparate, they are all generated according to the same indoor manifold and, therefore, they share a highly similar intrinsic structure. If we recognize this shared structure embedded in these two disparate data sets, we will directly extract the fingerprints-to-coordinates mapping without indoor space measurement.

13.2.2 APPROACH OVERVIEW

Since RSS can be estimated by both sides, SENIL can be deployed in either the AP-end or client-end. Whenever it is deployed at either end, the core of the system remains the same. We should mention that the positions of Wi-Fi APs are not required to be known in either case. In the rest of the chapter, we assume SENIL is deployed at the AP-end, which means that APs will also work as sniffers to overhear the Wi-Fi traffic and conduct the necessary computations.

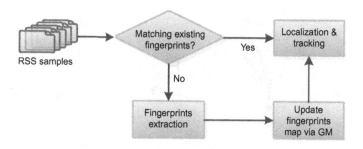

FIG. 1

SENIL System architecture.

Fig. 1 demonstrates our system architecture. When a user enters the building, we assume that the device carried by the user will establish wireless connections. The Wi-Fi APs will record the RSS of the traffic sent from the client device and forward the data to a localization server. The RSS values will be used to build a match with the fingerprint RSS values stored in the fingerprint database, which itself is populated using crowdsourcing techniques. The estimated moving distance, together with the estimated geodesic distance of different fingerprint locations in the map, will be used to further improve the quality of the matching, and thus, the accuracy of the localization.

13.2.3 TRAJECTORIES MATCHING

RSS fingerprints are the most representative RSS point extracted from many samples for a given position, and a fingerprint error will directly affect the mapping and localization accuracy. Besides the strong noise in RSS measurement, there are two main types of errors. The first is the well-known device-based measurement offset, which is mainly caused by the variation of device antenna. Another measurement error, the *directional shadowing problem*, has minor effects on traditional site-surveys, but creates significant interference in crowd-sensing-based direction approaches.

Directional shadowing problem

The human body is a strong electromagnetic energy absorption object, which may cause directional shadowing effects on wireless signals. Therefore, when the same device is placed at different positions near the human body, *eg,* a shirt pocket or back pocket, the RSS measurements will be obviously deviated. This effect has been exploited in previous works [4,13] to achieve Direction-of-Arrival (DoA) detection, however, it may cause significant errors in unsupervised fingerprints-to-floor plan mapping, because there may be multiple parallel RSS trajectories corresponding to the same physical path. Fig. 2 presents an example of directional shadowing from real measurement data. In this situation, the mapping algorithm may wrongfully think that there are parallel paths between the start and end, and it is very likely to cause mapping failure.

Fingerprints extraction

Previous approaches usually adopted cluster-based algorithms to extract fingerprints by merging the nearby RSS samples within a certain threshold. This is a coarse-grained algorithm, and it cannot identify the device offset and directional shadowing. Our solution comes from an intuitive observation: although

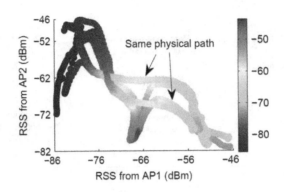

FIG. 2

Four RSS trajectories measured from 3 APs. The gray level denotes the value for 3rd AP: the brighter level denotes higher RSS for the 3rd AP.

the RSS samples are highly deviated for the same physical position if under antenna variation and directional shadowing, the temporal RSS samples transition trends are very similar. If we could correctly identify the matching between these RSS trajectories, the fingerprints could be extracted without the two aforementioned errors.

This intuitive idea could be transformed to an n-partite graph matching problem [14,15], if we see these trajectories as curve-shaped graphs. This can further be done by n-1 times iteratively graph matching between the n-th trajectory and the previously resulting RSS fingerprints graph. Relaxation-based approaches approximate the graph matching elegantly, and the only job is to build the affinity matrix M.

Given two RSS trajectories, G^P and G^Q, each of them contains n^p and n^Q RSS measurements respectively. A possible assignment a is defined as $a=(i,i')$, where $i \in V^P$ and $i' \in V^Q$. Given another possible assignment $b=(j,j')$, the compatibility $m_{a,b} \in M$ is assigned as follows in the current system:

$$M_{(a,b)} = \begin{cases} e^{-\|d_{ij} - d_{i'j'}\|}, & if -\|d_{ij} - d_{i'j'}\| > \epsilon \\ 0, & \text{otherwise} \end{cases} \quad (1)$$

where d_{ij} and $d_{i'j'}$ are the distance between i and j, and their assignment pairs are i' and j', respectively. Since RSS attenuation along distance is nonlinear, in our system the Minkowski distance [16] with value $p=1.7$ is used to define the distance between RSS samples a and b by the following equation:

$$d_{ab} = \left(\sum_{i=1}^{n} |RSS_{ai} - RSS_{bi}|^p \right)^{\frac{1}{p}} \quad (2)$$

where n represents the numbers of all heard APs, and RSS_{ai} for the i-th AP's RSS value of RSS sample a.

In each iteration, the fingerprints extraction is a partial graph matching problem, and it is not tight-integer constrained. We use the spectral matching (SM) algorithm [14] to calculate the optimal column-wise vector X with length $n^P \times n^Q$. X is further reshaped to an *association matrix* $A^{P \times Q}$, where each element $\mathbf{A}_{ij}$ denotes the *matching rate* between $i \in V^P$ and $j \in V^Q$.

When obtaining the association matrix $A^{P \times Q}$, the fingerprints extraction is easy. Due to the representativeness of fingerprints, the task of extracting fingerprints can be easily done by identifying the sampling points which have no correspondence in historical data. Let U_A be the upper triangular matrix of A and D_A for its diagonal matrix, an RSS point i is considered to be an RSS fingerprint **iff**:

$$\sum_i (U_A - D_A) = 0 \tag{3}$$

After identifying the fingerprint points, we need to assign the RSS measurement values for each fingerprint. Due to device variation, the RSS sample points for a single location may present in multiple clusters. We assign the RSS value for the specific fingerprint as the RSS samples which have the overall shortest distance to other RSS samples.

Fingerprints transition graph

The Fingerprints Transition Graph $\mathcal{G}^F = \left(\mathcal{V}^F, \varepsilon^F \right)$ records the spatial connectivity of all fingerprints. Since the vertices set $\mathcal{V}^F$ is the fingerprints set C^F, we only need to determine the edge set E F and the weight of edges $W(\varepsilon^F)$.

Basically, any two nodes i, j $\in \mathcal{V}^F$ have an edge $e_{ij} \in \varepsilon^F$ if they satisfy the following two conditions:

(1) i and j are subsequent RSS fingerprints within the same RSS fingerprints trajectory;
(2) when i and j belong to a different trajectory, the distance d_{ij} is smaller than ϵ and at least one or both is the *start* or *end* of a trajectory.

The weight of edges will be set to the absolute distance between fingerprints in traditional approaches [5–7], however, in SENIL, there is no absolute distance information due to the absence of physical space measurement. Fortunately, the walking duration becomes a distance indicator, and we can assign a virtual distance to the weight of edges. The virtual distance is based on a reasonable assumption: although people may vary their walking speed according to mood or ongoing tasks, they usually maintain a constant speed during a single walking trip. Based on this assumption, we can infer the distance ratio between nearby fingerprints sequences along a trajectory, and eventually obtain a global distance matrix. Our virtual distance assignment algorithm is briefly described as follows:

(1) Find the longest common fingerprints sequence S_c among all RSS trajectories of all users.
(2) Find the most stable user u_s who walks through sequence S_c with minimum time difference, and set the virtual distance $L_v (S_c)$ to the average walking time of sequence S_c by user u_s.
(3) For every trajectory T_i containing sequence S_{lc}, calculate the virtual speed $V_v (T_i)$ according to the virtual distance $L_v (S_c)$, and assign virtual distance for other common fingerprints sequence within T_i.
(4) Calculate the virtual speed for trajectories which pass through the assigned sequences, and calculate virtual distance for those unassigned sequences.
(5) Repeat Step 4 if there is an unassigned fingerprints sequence.
(6) Assign virtual distance for every fingerprint within the same sequence using interpolation.

We design and develop a prototype system of SENIL. The prototype system is deployed in a large $2000\,m^2$ office environment with a circular corridor network as shown in Fig. 3A. We have collected more than 17,000 RSS trajectories across more than 20 different mobile devices. Fig. 3B shows the extracted RSS fingerprint transition graph.

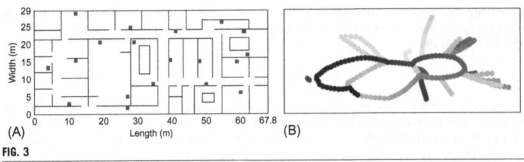

FIG. 3

(A) The 2D floor plan of the deployed area. (B) The RSS transition graph extracted from very large amount of RSS readings.

13.2.4 ESTABLISHING THE MAPPING BETWEEN FLOOR PLAN AND RSS READINGS

Ordinary floor plans are not friendly for crowd-sensing-based approaches, especially when the client-side doesn't provide direction information. By studying the shortest walking distance (SWD) in indoor space, we realize that there is a highly curly 2D manifold embedded in a 2D floor plan polygon [7]. The unfolded version of this manifold will remove the direction information, but preserve the SWD information, which is friendly for crowd-sensing-based approaches.

The technical underpinning of automatically establishing the mapping is based on the topological similarity between the unfolded version of the floor plan, and the fingerprint transition graph, which is a typical graph matching problem. However, challenges exist in many aspects, eg, unacceptable computation cost and low accuracy of large-scale graph matching [14,15], scaling effects, and the unsupervised nature of auto mapping. Here we start from transforming the floor plan, then go through the auto mapping algorithm.

Floor plan in manifold's eyes

The n-dimensional manifold is a topological space that, near each point, resembles n- dimensional Euclidean space, while globally not Euclidean. The indoor floor plan shares the same property. Due to the obstruction of walls, the shortest walking distance (SWD) between two points i and j in the floor plan $\mathbf{P}$ equals the Euclidean distance $d_{eu}(i, j)$ **iff** the points i and j are within the same local isolation with direct line-of-sight distance. When they are not in the same isolation, the SWD would be the geodesic distance $d_{geo}(i, j)$ which detours through various obstructions. In this way, indoor space could be essentially viewed as a 2D-manifold S embedded in a 2D-polygon **P**.

In a manifold space, the Euclidean distance is misleading. The geodesic distance actually reveals the true structure of the manifold. Therefore, we resample the 2D floor plan $\mathbf{P}$ using n points uniformly scatted. An n points graph G^M is then constructed. For every pair of nodes $i, j \in V^M$, there is an edge e_{ij} **iff** the correspondence points i^P, j^P in the floor plan $\mathbf{P}$ are in their mutual neighborhood with *direct line-of-sight* distance, and the weight for the edge is the direct distance that $W(e_{ij}) = d_{eu}(i^P, j^P)$.

Unsupervised mapping

Since the RSS samples are measured along users' walking trajectories, the RSS fingerprints transition graph G^F also shares the same floor plan manifold structure. An intuitive idea of establishing the fingerprint map is to apply a graph matching algorithm directly upon G^F and G^M. However, the accuracy and performance of large-scale graph matching (>50 points) is very poor in unsupervised situations. A lightweight relaxation to the problem is to apply graph matching only on corridor points. Once the corridor points graph is mapped correctly, it is easy to match the room points. Unfortunately, the accuracy and performance of graph matching between such corridor point graphs is still not satisfied.

Fortunately, the highly sparse chain structure of corridor points give us a hint, and we devise a method called "Skeleton-Based Matching" to achieve unsupervised accurate mapping between G^F and G^M, even for very complex indoor environments. The basic idea is that: due to the high sparsity and chained structure of the corridor point graph, we can extract a coarse-grained skeleton graph from it while preserving the identical topological structure. Adopting the G^M algorithm on skeleton graphs will result in high accuracy and performance. Once the main structures of G^F and G^M are matched, the remaining parts will be matched easily.

The algorithm is detailed in following 4 steps, including *skeleton graphs extraction*, *skeleton graphs normalization*, *skeleton graphs matching*, and *fine-grained points matching*.

Skeleton graph extraction

Two substeps are required to extract the skeleton graphs. Identifying the corridor points graph $G^{CF} \in G^F$ and $G^{CM} \in G^M$;2).extracting skeleton graphs G^{SF} and G^{SM} based on the corridor points graph $G^{CF} \in G^F$.

In the first substep, a customized centrality measure $C(V)$ is designed to identify the core corridor network. For a given point $v \in V$, its centrality $C(v)$ is measured as follows:

$$C(v) = \sum_{s \neq v \neq t \in V} \sigma_{st}(v)$$

where $\sigma_{st}(v)$ is the number of the shortest path from s to t via v.

Based on this definition, we design an iterative algorithm to remove the noncentral points effectively. In each round of iteration, the centrality $C(v)$ is measured for every point. If $C(v)$ is smaller than a low-bound τ, then remove the points from the graph. This procedure repeats until no points are removed.

In the second substep, the skeleton graphs V^S is generated by clustering the corridor points graph G^{CF} and G^{CM}. We use spectral clustering (SC) [17] as the clustering algorithm. SC is computationally faster than K-means and it only requires the adjacency matrix, which is exactly suitable in our case because both G^{CF} and G^{CM} are G^{CF} represented only in the adjacency matrix. Fig. 4A and B shows the corridor points of the fingerprint graph.

By clustering on G^{CF} and G^{CM}, we obtain the vertices set of skeleton graph G^{SF} and G^{SM}. The edge set E^{SF} and E^{SM} follow the underlying points, that if two points i, j, belonging to different clusters ca and cb respectively, have an edge, then there is an edge between ca and cb. The weight of edge e_{ab} is defined as the shortest distance between the *central points* of cluster a and b, and the *central point* of a cluster is the point i which has the shortest distances to other points within the cluster. Fig. 4C and D show the extracted skeleton graph of the fingerprint graph and corridor points, respectively.

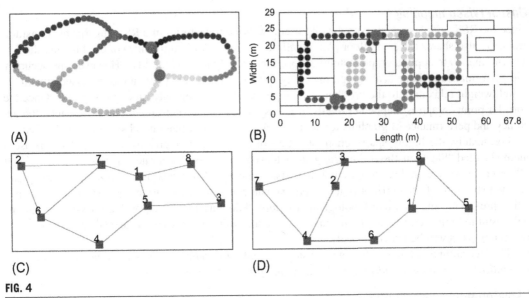

(A)

(B)

(C)

(D)

FIG. 4

Corridor Points and Skeleton Points extraction from fingerprint graph and floorplan graph, respectively. (A) Corridor Points of Fingerprint Graph, (B) Corridor Points of Floor Plan Points, (C) Skeleton Graph of Fingerprint Graph, and (D) Skeleton Graph of Floor Plan Graph.

Graphs normalization

Since the graph matching algorithm assigns the matching score according to pairwise distance, G and G^M must be normalized to the same scale to guarantee an accurate matching result.

The scaling effect can be undone by global normalization of the graph shape. Possible ways include normalization of the bounding box, or normalized Laplace-Beltrami eigenvalues (LBE). The bounding box approach works only for a rigid graph, while LBE is sensitive to deformations. We use the commonly accepted longest geodesic distance L_{lg} as a scale indicator.

Skeletons matching

After the extraction and normalization of skeleton graphs, we now find the best correspondence between G^{SF} and G^{SM}. Let positive symmetrical square matrix M^{SR} and M^{SM} represent their adjacency matrices. We build the affinity matrix $M^{SR \times SM}$ for graph matching as follows:

$$M^{SR \times SM} = e^{\left(1^{SM} \otimes M^{SR} - 1^{SR} \otimes M^{SR}\right)^2}$$

(4)

where $\otimes$ denotes the Kronecker product [18] and 1^{SR} denotes the full-**1** matrix with the same size of G^{SR}. The idea behind Eq. (4) is to enumerate all possible matching candidates and store them in a large adjacency matrix $M^{SR \times SM}$. We use the RRWM algorithm to perform the graph matching, and the Hungarian algorithm is further applied to discretize the χ in order to meet the final integer constraints $\chi \in \{0,1\}^n$ Fig. 5A shows the skeleton graphs matching.

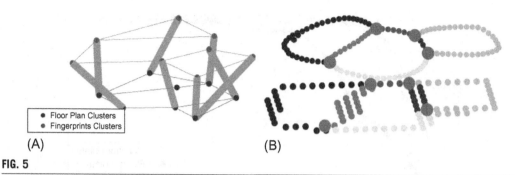

FIG. 5

The Skeleton and corridor points matching, (A) Skeleton Graph Matching and (B) Corridor Points Matching.

Corridor points matching

Although G^{SF} and G^{SM} are matching in the previous step, the corresponding clustering groups in G^{CF} and G^{CM} are not necessarily matched due to the inconsistency of the clustering operation.

In the corridor points graphs, we notice that only a few points connect multiple chain structures, and they may serve as the *bridge points*. Since the topological structures of G^{CF} and G^{CM} are identical, if we could identify the correct correspondences of these *bridge points*, the points within the chain structure will be matched easily. In order to identify the bridge node, we introduce a new metric called "bridge centrality", which is equal to the number of shortest paths from all vertices to all others within nearby clusters that pass through that node, defined as follows:

$$C_{bg}(v) = \sum_{\{(s,t) | v \in c^i, s,t \in NN(c^i), s,t \notin c^i\}} \sigma_{st}(v) \tag{5}$$

where $NN(ci)$ denotes the nearby clusters around ci. The bridge point will be the point with the highest bridge centrality.

After identifying the correspondence of bridge points in G^{CF} and G^{CM}, the chain structures are easily matched according to the start and end bridge points. Fig. 5A shows the corridor points matching.

Rooms points matching

If we remove the corridor points graph G^{CM} from G^M, the room points will naturally form several clusters. Each room points cluster C_R connects to the corridor by a door point, and the rooms matching is also easily done by matching the door points in both G^F and G^M.

However, if there is more than one room connecting to a single door point in the corridor, *eg,* two rooms in opposite sides along the corridor, there may be mismatching. This kind of mismatching can be canceled using the coarse-grained propagation model. Along with the corridor points matching, the coarse-grained position estimation for APs can be done. With the rough location of APs, the rooms mismatching can be easily eliminated by checking the RSS values. The smaller RSS difference means a higher probability of being in the candidate rooms. Fig. 6 shows the accuracy of corridor points matching and room points matching.

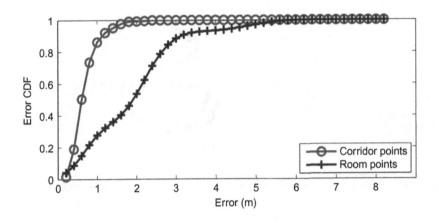

FIG. 6

The matching error of corridor points and room points.

13.2.5 USER LOCALIZATION

SENIL provides a unified localization and tracking service by treating the direct localization request as a tracking request without historical data. Here we mainly focus on the tracking technique in SENIL. In our solution, the users' trajectories are globally determined from the very beginning by transforming the tracking problem to a graph matching problem between the measured RSS samples transition graph G^S and the fingerprint transition graph G^F.

13.2.6 GRAPH MATCHING BASED TRACKING

Graph-matching-based tracking finds the best correspondence between the sequence of RSS samples of tracking requests and extracted fingerprints. This is exactly the same matching process undertaken in Section 13.2.3, except in this section, the tracking is conducted to find the matched points, while in Section 13.2.3, the focus is on collecting RSS fingerprints.

Let $\chi^{n^S + n^F}$ represent the association matrix obtained through spectral matching [14] where n^S and n^F are the numbers of RSS samples and candidate fingerprints sets respectively. Due to the error in RSS measurement and fingerprints map construction, a single RSS sample p_i may correspond to multiple fingerprints in $\chi, e.g.$, an RSS sample may correspond to two fingerprints, one is in a corridor, and another is in a room. Fortunately, the temporal correlation can help eliminate false correspondence by checking the spatial continuity between current and subsequent candidate fingerprints. After eliminating the false correspondence, the globally estimated coordinates sequence will be given by $T_{G^S} = f_{G^F}(G^S)$, where $f: fingerprint \rightarrow G^M$ represents the mapping from fingerprints to the floor plan manifold $G^M y$, and T_{G^S} are the resulting coordinates sequence in G^M.

13.2.7 EVALUATION

We site-survey the testing environment with an approximately 3×3 m grid and implement a RADAR system for comparison with SENIL. Five students walk along a predefined testing trace for 5 rounds. Fig. 7 shows the error CDF of RADAR and SENIL with different lengths of historical data. Based on

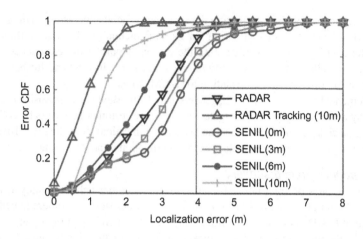

FIG. 7

The localization & tracking error CDF with different amount of RSS fingerprints data. The RADAR scheme is as comparison.

the commonly accepted 3×3 m grid site-survey, RADAR has a less than 3.5 m error in 80% of situations, while SENIL is only a 1 m error larger than RADAR. When in tracking scenarios, every 3 m of increased tracking range brings approximately 0.7 m tracking accuracy improvement. When the tracking range is 10 m, SENIL tracking accuracy is very close to RADAR-based tracking. In practical tracking scenarios, 10 m of tracking range is a very low requirement.

13.3 DEVICE-FREE SENSING USING BIG DATA
13.3.1 CUSTOMER BEHAVIOR IDENTIFICATION

With the explosive development of e-business, making a buck becomes more challenging for brick-and-mortar (B&M) retailers. The availability of online payment, the pervasiveness of smartphones, and the convenience of fast delivery make the future of physical retailing ever more tenuous. According to a report issued last year, Amazon has had tremendous success using collected online data to discover what products users are likely to buy. Moreover, as the study noted, Amazon reported that 30% of sales were due to its recommendation engine [19].

Physical stores and retailers seem destined to be left out in the cold. Fortunately, with recent advanced technologies, retailers have a great opportunity to thrive in the future. In fact, it is possible that traditional retailers could have a better understanding of their customers than eCommerce firms do. Through a combination of Big Data analytics and leading-edge technologies, brick and mortar retailers are promising to stay relevant. Retailers can also benefit from Big Data to unlock the mysteries of customer behavior and understand why, what, and how people buy. Accumulating the data of customer behaviors over a period could help retailers to determine which ads should be introduced, where and how items should be displayed, etc.

As an intuitive solution, retail stores can use videocameras to distinguish whether a customer is male or female, know what he/she buys by identifying the customer's gestures, and analyze why he/she did or did not buy a certain product by interpreting the customer's facial expressions. This solution is attractive. However, privacy concerns raise a barrier for its implementation. To achieve these goals without compromising the user's privacy and disrupting the customer purchasing experience, we propose an RFID-based solution (called CBID) to identify on-site customer behaviors and further deduce products correlations, which can provide rich information for B&M stores.

CBID is implemented by commodity RFID readers and off-the-shelf tags. Supposing each product in the store is attached by a passive tag, the CBID system can identify customer behaviors by collecting and analyzing wireless signal changes of RFID readers and tag communications. Specifically, CBID has three main objectives: discovering popular items, revealing explicit correlations, and disclosing implicit correlations.

Doppler-based popular item discovery

Popular items are the ones of great interest to customers. Customer behavior analysis of sales history can only evaluate the purchase actions taken to indicate the interest of customers in certain items. The unique advantage of CBID is that it can identify other actions, such as picking up an item, as shown in Fig. 8A. Intuitively, the more times an item is picked up, the more attention the item gains. B&M stores can then adjust the display accordingly. In the CBID system, we count the detected pick-up actions of an item as a metric to reflect the amount of customer attention gained by an item, namely *popularity*.

Popular item discovery in CBID can be achieved by detecting and counting the pick-up events by customers. In this part, we propose an accurate and robust discovery algorithm of popular items discovery by detecting variations of a tag's Doppler frequency shift. Doppler reflects the relative velocity between a reader and a tag. When a customer picks up a tagged item, the speed of movement, *ie*, the velocity of the attached tag perpendicular to the reader antenna, can result in frequency shifts.

Adaptive Doppler peaks detection

After an accurate estimation of the Doppler frequency shift, to detect a pick-up action, our system should find the peaks of Doppler frequency values quickly and precisely. Many existing algorithms have been proposed for frequency change detection or peak detection. However, they require the recording of measurement data and then the application of analysis tools. In real deployment of the CBID system, keeping the values of Doppler frequency would be an overloaded task, considering a huge amount of data will be generated by monitoring the movements of thousands of tags in very short time intervals.

Therefore, we design an accurate magnitude threshold-based detection which drops the data not related to the Doppler change as much as possible. A challenge is that such a deterministic threshold does not exist because of two limitations in real deployment. 1) Tag diversity induces diverse noise levels across different tags, and 2) item location diversity also raises different Doppler patterns. For these reasons, we adopt an adaptive CUmulative SUM (CUSUM) algorithm [20] to track possible changes in Doppler values.

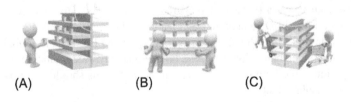

(A)   (B)   (C)

FIG. 8

Three objectives of CBID (A) Discovering popular items, (B) Revealing explicit correlations (C) Disclosing implicit correlations.

Let $d(t)$ denote the Doppler frequency value at time t and its probability density is denoted by p_θ, where θ is the distribution parameter. Assume that a change happens at time T, the probability density of Doppler frequency changes from p_x to p_y. Then we can use a logarithmic ratio to compare these two distributions:

$$l_y = \log \frac{p_y(d(t))}{p_x(d(t))} \qquad (6)$$

The parameter x is easy to obtain from the historical change record. But the parameter y, which is also called a post-change distribution parameter, is unknown. It also varies during the detection process, making it more difficult to predict.

To solve this problem, we define the change time T as:

$$T = \inf\left\{ t \mid \max \sum_{i=k}^{t} l_y(i) \ge h \right\}, 1 \le k \le t, \qquad (7)$$

where h is a predefined value [21]. Given that the post-change distribution is unknown, the time T cannot be directly known from Eq. (7). CBID then recursively applies the CUSUM method proposed in [20] to determine the range of parameter y. Based on the range of y, we can detect changes of the Doppler frequency more accurately.

We verify the feasibility of the aforementioned solution via extensive experiments. We conduct experiments in three different scenarios. Here we only show a small part of the results related to change point detection in Fig. 9. Each of the subfigures 9A–D corresponds to a pick-up experiment. In such an experiment, a volunteer picks up a book from a shelf and puts it back. We record the signal phase and

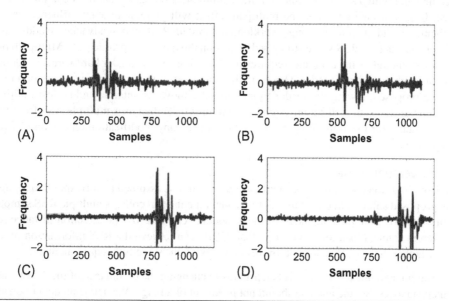

FIG. 9

Change point detection by adaptive CUSUM: The subfigures show the Doppler frequency changes of four continuous pick-up actions. The blue curve shows the estimated Doppler values and the red circles are the change points detected by adaptive CUSUM.

time stamp of every tag packet during this period. The blue curve represents the estimates of Doppler frequency. By examining these estimates using the adaptive CUSUM algorithm, CBID detects a sudden change marked by a red circle in each of the subfigures. Experimental results of four actions indicate that the algorithm works well in different scenarios. As a result, the CUSUM algorithm can success-fully skip perturbations in the signal caused by environmental noise and discover the real change point in the Doppler frequency values.

Location-based explicit correlation discovery

We say items have *explicit correlations* if they are rival or complementary. For example, a customer may compare a bottle of Coca Cola and a bottle of Pepsi. As another example, a customer may pick up a cap and a jacket to decide if they match each other. Sales history analysis may reveal some complementary items, but can hardly determine rival items. The pick-up behaviors of explicit-correlated items are spatially and temporally close, eg, a customer may pick up these items simultaneously (Fig. 8B). The CBID system ap-plies novel passive tag localization methods to reveal such spatial and temporal correlations of moving items.

The main challenge is to connect items that are picked by the same person. However, collected data are unable to report which items belong to whom. For the example of the scenario shown in Fig. 8B, two cus-tomers stand in front of a goods shelf. When three events of item pick-up are detected, our system should further figure out that two pick-up actions belong to the same customer. It is generally the truth that when two items are held by the same person, their positions should be close. Inspired by this, we form the problem of explicit correlation discovery as locating tagged items and deciding which tags are geographically close.

To locate close tags, an intuitive approach is to use the RSS of backscattered RF signals as the position fingerprint. This method has some well-known drawbacks. First, it utilizes the Friis Equation that clarifies that an RSS is inversely proportional to the biquadrate of the distance. The equation can only become valid with a strong assumption: the communication parties should be in an unobstructed free-space. In indoor environments, the multipath effect will yield significant influence on the RSS measurement. Second, it requires a huge workload to build an RSS map in advance. In addition, recent studies show that such an RSS value strongly depends on the multipath profile [22]. Multipath profiling for localization, though being accurate, requires modifications on the reader hardware, *eg*, adopting the technique of synthetic aperture radar. These modifications result in nontrivial customization overhead.

Thus, we propose allowing the reader to intentionally move its antenna and collect multiple RSS samples from the same tag at different antenna locations. CBID then uses multiple RSS from the same tag as a new metric for location. This method does not need any modification on existing RFID hard-ware and protocols.

Antenna movement model

Different from traditional RSS models where one tag location is assumed to correspond to a single RSS value, the proposed solution in CBID moves the reader antenna and collects multiple RSS samples for a tag. We first develop a simple antenna movement model to characterize the direction-distance relation-ship at different antenna locations. Based on that, CBID can retrieve the RSS information of tags and determine whether they are close or not. In this new model, there are two requirements.

- In order to improve the accuracy, it is better to avoid changing the dominance of the direct path when the antenna moves. So, the antenna should not move out of a range. We define an upper bound of this range as $\frac{Y}{5}$, where Y is the vertical distance between the antenna and tag (as shown in Fig. 10).
- Inspired by Jakes Model [23], the signals within half a wavelength are indistinguishable. Therefore the distance of antenna movement (r) has a lower bound $\frac{\lambda}{2}$.

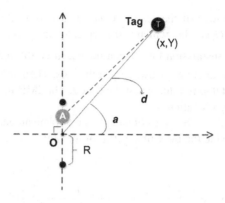

FIG. 10

Illustration of Antenna Movement Model.

In summary, we have $\frac{Y}{5} \le r \le \frac{\lambda}{2}$. To meet these conditions, we prefer to simply move an antenna back and forth in our implementation, termed as shuttle antenna. Fig. 10 illustrates an example of the antenna movement model, where O is the origin location of the antenna, T is a static tag at position (x, Y) with distance d from O, and the direction from O to T is in the angle α. A is the shuttle antenna. The position vector of tag T is:

$$\overrightarrow{OT} = (d \cdot \cos \alpha, d \cdot \sin \alpha) = (x, Y) \tag{8}$$

Suppose that A moves along the vertical axis within a maximum range R. The displacement of A periodically changes with t within the range $(-R, R)$. We take a sine function to simulate this displacement for simplicity. Therefore, the position vector of A can be represented as:

$$\overrightarrow{OA} = (0, R \cdot \sin t) \tag{9}$$

The distance vector from the antenna to tag is $\overrightarrow{AT}$:

$$\overrightarrow{AT} = \overrightarrow{OT} - \overrightarrow{OA} = (x, Y) - (0, R \cdot \sin t) = (x, Y - R \cdot \sin t) \tag{10}$$

Integration of multi-RSS

The Received Signal Strength (RSS) is a measurement of the power of a received radio signal. In RFID systems, RSS is one of the reader outputs, reflecting the power of a received backscattered signal P_{R_x}. RSS can be measured in the unit of dbm and calculated as: $RSS = 10 \lg \left(\frac{P_{R_x}}{1mW} \right)$. According to the Friis Function [24], we can model RSS as:

$$RSS = 10 \log \left(\frac{P_{T_x}}{1mW} T_b G_r^2 G_t^2 \left(\frac{\lambda}{4\pi d} \right)^4 \right) \tag{11}$$

In this part, we propose using a new metric, called Integration of Multi-RSS (IMR), as the fingerprint of a tag's location. By moving the reader antenna, CBID obtains a set of RSS values for a fixed tag (ie, a fixed location) when the antenna moves. The RSS value varies because $\overrightarrow{AT}$ changes. Let $M = \frac{P_{T_x}}{1mW} G_r^2 G_t^2 T_b \left(\frac{\lambda}{4\pi} \right)^4$. According to Eq. (11), at time t, the RSS received from the tag can be represented as:

$$RSS(t) = 10 \lg \left(M \cdot \left(\frac{1}{\sqrt{x^2 + (Y - R\sin t)}} \right)^4 \right) 10 \lg \left(M \cdot \left(\frac{1}{x^2 + (Y - R\sin t)} \right)^2 \right) \tag{12}$$

Let P_{T_x} be the transmit power of the reader, which is set to 32 dbm. G_r is 8 dbi for our reader antenna Laird A9028R30NF. G_t is 2 dbi, which is the typical gain for real dipole-like tag antenna. T_b is $\frac{1}{3}$ [23] here for backscatter transmission loss. Y can be measured through real deployment and in our experiment, we put the shuttle antenna 1 m away from the tags. Then, the only unknown parameters in Eq. (12) are the tag's horizontal axis value x and the time t. The IMR metric is used to reflect t and x, and thereby fingerprint the tag's location.

The CBID reader collects the RSS values of a tag in a complete antenna movement cycle. The multiple RSS values together provide the IMR fingerprint of the tag:

$$
\begin{aligned}
\int_0^{2\pi} RSS(t)\,dt &= \int_0^{2\pi} \left[10\lg\left(M \cdot \left(\frac{1}{x^2 + (Y - R\sin t)} \right)^2 \right) \right] dt \\
&= \int_0^{2\pi} 10\lg M\,dt - \int_0^{2\pi} \left(20\lg\left(x^2 + (Y - R\sin t) \right) \right) dt \\
&= 10\int_0^{2\pi} \lg M\,dt - 20\int_0^{2\pi} \lg\left(x^2 + (Y - R\sin t) \right) dt
\end{aligned}
\tag{13}
$$

Replacing $\sin t$ with θ in Eq. (13), we have

$$
\begin{aligned}
\int RSS(\theta)\,d\theta &= 10\int_0^{2\pi} \lg M\,dt - 20\int_0^{2\pi} \frac{\lg\left(x^2 + (Y - R\sin t) \right) \cdot \cos t\,dt}{\cos t} \\
&= 10\int_0^{2\pi} \lg M\,d\theta - \left(20\int_0^1 \frac{\lg\left(x^2 + (Y - R\theta) \right) d\theta}{\sqrt{1 - \theta^2}} + 20\int_{-1}^1 \frac{\lg\left(x^2 + (Y - R\theta) \right) d\theta}{\sqrt{1 - \theta^2}} \right. \\
&\left. + 20\int_{-1}^0 \frac{\lg\left(x^2 + (Y - R\theta) \right) d\theta}{\sqrt{1 - \theta^2}} \right)
\end{aligned}
\tag{14}
$$

Given different x values, we can achieve the relationship between the tag locations and the proposed fingerprint IMR, which is demonstrated in Fig. 11. We can see that when a tag's vertical distance Y to the antenna is constant, its IMR value is inversely proportional to the tag's horizontal distance x.

The IMR metric is better than those used by traditional RSS methods for tag localization for the following reasons. Let S be the signal vector received from a given tag. S can be considered the sum of a multipath signal MPS and a noise signal N. Thus, we have the expression $S = MPS + N$. Normally, we can assume that the noise signal follows a typical Gaussian distribution with a mathematical expectation of 0. Hence the integral value of N should tend to 0. On the other hand, the multipath effect may cause RSS changes. In some positions and angles the RSS may be strengthened, while in other cases, the RSS may be weakened. In our implementation, we adopt the shuttle antenna pattern and collect a set of RSS values for each tag's position. Multiple sampling of a tag can help the system neutralize the multipath effect. Therefore, IMR-based localization has a better performance than single-RSS based approaches.

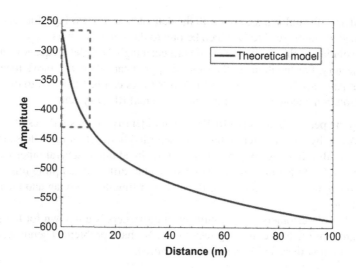

FIG. 11

The IMR values of different tag positions from our theoretical model, given the same vertical distance. The red dotted box marked the practical reader range in 0~10 meters.

Movement pattern-based implicit correlation discovery

We say items have *implicit correlations* if they share similar pick-up, moving, or purchase correlations. The most famous example is the tale of beer and diapers, which says that beer and diaper sales are explicitly correlated because young fathers who are sent to buy diapers would also buy beer for themselves. CBID uses tag trajectory monitoring and clustering to disclose these correlations by detecting and analyzing movement patterns of tags, as shown in Fig. 8C.

Based on Section 13.3.1.1, the CBID system knows which items are picked up by customers. Furthermore, we expect to find out the reasons behind the pickups. For example, a customer who has put onions and tomatoes into the shopping cart may also buy burgers. This correlation can be expressed as $Pre\{Onion, Tomato\} \Rightarrow Pn\{Burger\}$. $Pre\{\}$ represents that a customer picked the item previously, while $Pn\{\}$ represents that the customer is likely to pick the item in the future. Previously picked items may be in hand or in a shopping cart, within a short range in either way. Identifying $Pre\{\}$ and $Pn\{\}$ items can help the system to connect items with implicit correlations.

Problem formulation

When a customer chooses $Pn\{\}$ items and leaves the shopping area with his/her $Pre\{\}$ items, the reader can easily detect the movement of these items. Hence, if only one customer stands in the area, the correlated items are relatively easy to detect. However, real situations are much more complicated. Consider two or more customers $(C_1, C_2, ..., C_n)$ who are shopping in front of a shelf and they all have their desired items. Some of them may have picked some items and left the area almost at the same time. We denote all tags belonging to these customers are *near-context* tags for this area. The near-context tags are actually identified in one area of interest and their time stamps of residence differ slightly within a certain time tolerance. In our experiments, we set the time tolerance as 0.5 second.

Then the problem is formulated as, giving all the data of near-context tags, for each $Pn_i\{\}$ item how to discover the previous items set $Pre_i\{\}$ which belong to the same customer C_i.

One intuitive solution to this problem is to record each tag's Doppler frequency value and monitor its movement trajectory. For the items in the same shopping cart, they will move together and share a similar movement pattern. The traces of all near-context tags can be clustered to different customers. However, such a solution encounters two challenges in a real RFID system.

- Irregular sampling period: In an UHF RFID system, identifying tags will result in a collision-arbitration process, by which different tags are identified in different time slots. This means the sampling time for different tags will not be the same. In addition, several other factors, such as signal attenuation due to tag movement, will also lead to different sampling times for different tags. This problem makes the sample density vary over time for each tag and then ruins the accuracy of clustering.
- Unknown number of customers: As the number of customers is unknown for the system, exhaustive search for the best clustering result is an NP hard problem. Therefore, an effective clustering algorithm with rapid convergence is required.

Segment-based interpolation

To overcome the first challenge, we implement a segment-based interpolation approach which makes all raw data have the same number of samples of different tags. We set the time length of one segment as $T_{seg} = 1s$ and find the minimal time stamp (T_{min}) and maximal time stamp (T_{max}) of all data reported from near-context tags.

Then the whole time period is partitioned into N segments, where $N = [(T_{max} - T_{min})/T_{seg}]$. In each segment, CBID applies the Linear Interpolation method to fit the Doppler curves. The advantage of this method is that we can reduce the interpolated error. In addition, considering each segment of data is indeed one observation, this method will increase the amount of data used for the clustering algorithm presented in the next subsection.

Iterative clustering algorithm with cosine similarity

In this subsection, we present an iterative clustering approach to organize tags in different groups, which utilizes cosine similarity measurements.

To clearly explain the goal of this algorithm, we use one group of experiment data to serve as an example. Fig. 12 shows tags' Doppler frequency data processed by the segment-based interpolation. In this set of experiments, two volunteers emulate a shopping procedure and each of them has a shopping cart. Their trajectories are random. Volunteer A has only one item which is associated with Tag1. The other three items (with Tag2, Tag3, and Tag4, respectively) are all in volunteer B's shopping cart. In order to extract implicit correlations of the items, we have to cluster the four tags.

As described in Section 13.3.1.3, we divide the Doppler data into N segments. Each segment of data is considered a vector. We implement the cosine calculation to measure the similarity between two vector observations within the same time period. Supposing there are M near-context tags. The similarity metric $S_{j,k}{}^i$ for two segments F^i_j, F^i_k can be expressed as:

Segments F^i_j, F^i_k can be expressed as

$$S^i_{j,k} = \frac{F^i_j \cdot F^i_k}{\left\| F^i_j \right\| \left\| F^i_k \right\|}, 1 \le i \le N, 1 \le j, k \le M \tag{15}$$

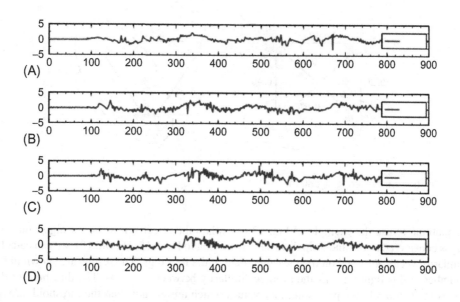

FIG. 12

Doppler data of implicit-correlation experiment: Subfigure (A–D) demonstrate 4 tags' Doppler data after segment-based interpolation. Tag1 belongs to volunteer A and the other 3 belong to volunteer B.

where i denotes the ith segment of Doppler data and j, k are tags' identifiers. The similarity ranges from -1 to 1, where -1 means completely different and 1 means exactly the same.

For each time period I, $\binom{M}{2}$ times of comparisons should be conducted. Considering all the time periods, the size of the result matrix is $\binom{M}{2} \times N$:

$$
\begin{bmatrix}
S_{2,1}^1 & S_{2,1}^2 & \cdots & S_{2,1}^N \\
S_{3,1}^1 & S_{3,1}^2 & \cdots & S_{3,1}^N \\
\vdots & \vdots & \cdots & \vdots \\
S_{M,M-1}^1 & S_{M,M-1}^2 & \cdots & S_{M,M-1}^N
\end{bmatrix}
\tag{16}
$$

The rows of the matrix show all segments' similarity values between two segments of Doppler data. Therefore, the mean value of each row (MS) can reflect the average similarity of the Doppler data under comparison. Then we get the similarity vector:

$$
R^t = MS_{2,1}^t, MS_{3,1}^t, \cdots, MS_{M,M-1}^t
\tag{17}
$$

where t indicates the tth iteration in our clustering algorithm. Giving the vector Rt, we can calculate a similarity threshold $Thre^t$ as

$$
Thre^t = \text{mean}\left(R^t\right) + \alpha \times \text{std}\left(R^t\right)
\tag{18}
$$

where α is a constant value.

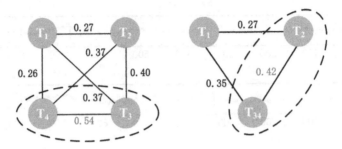

FIG. 13

An example of iterative clustering algorithm.

We continue to use the example of Fig. 12 to explain the effectiveness of our algorithm. At first, each tag is considered as one individual cluster. According to Eqs. (15, 16, and 18), we can calculate the first similarity vector R^1 based on the measured data of the four tags. The results are shown in Fig. 13. Each number in this figure means the average similarity between two tags. The threshold of the first iteration is 0.47, if $\alpha = 1$. We pick similarity values which are greater than the threshold: $MS^1_{3,4}$ in our example and put the two corresponding tags into one cluster. Hence, Tag3 and Tag4 are clustered in the first iteration. The mean similarity R^2 and the threshold $Thre^2$ should be recalculated in the next iteration. When there is no similarity value greater than the threshold, or only one cluster is left in the end, the iterative algorithm is terminated.

13.3.2 HUMAN OBJECT ESTIMATION

Counting people at a certain location is a crucial problem that has been researched within diverse areas and application domains. An estimation of the number of people has extensive applications in customer favor detection, stream of people locations, and quantifications. By collecting these features from a large number of customers, we can reach a conclusion or confirm some experiences about customers purchases, shopping regional design or even people's shopping habits. Currently, technique solutions are based on three main points: mechanical barriers, sensing and imaging. The mechanical barrier-based technology employs specific facilities to construct a one-way gate so that once a person accesses the gate, the facilities will move and count the number. Similarly, the sensing-based method utilizes a break-beam sensor at the entrance of a one-way gate showing that if a person passes through it, the beam will be blocked. Teixeira [25] provides an extensive survey of methods for detecting human presence, count, location, etc. In contrast, the image-based technology uses pattern recognition techniques to identify the number of human beings in the videos.

We propose a system called R#, which employs existing passive Radio Frequency Identification (RFID) tags. According to the reflection, blocking and absorption of images of human beings, we can estimate the number of people by analyzing the Radio Signal Strength (RSS) of the tag population. The R# system has two major advantages. First, R# utilizes off-the-shelf commercial RFID systems, which have been widely deployed in daily life. Secondly, R# is a device-free based solution that does not need to attach any device to human objects, which is suitable for the purpose of collecting information from a large number of people.

However, we also face three key challenges. First, we can extract limited types of information from commodity RFID devices. In addition, tag location and diversity lead to significant differences in the RSS value. Last but not least, it is difficult to model an RF signal pattern.

To solve these challenges, R# employs a predeployed passive RFID system in a supermarket, in which passive tags are attached to items. For a given region, a reader identifies a number (say 20) of passive tags using protocols in EPC C1G2 [26]. In particular, the tags are deployed in a line, as illustrated in Fig. 14. The reader periodically collects the tag IDs and RSS values. For simplicity, we call an RSS sequence collected from such a period an *observation* and each collection from a tag a *sample* in the following sections.

R# works in three phases, data *preprocessing*, *feature extraction*, and *estimation*. In the first phase, R# preprocesses the raw RF signal data collected from the reader for later operations. In the second phase, R# extracts three features from the RSS values to establish a correlation between the number of humans and the backscattered RF signal. Finally, R# employs machine learning techniques for an estimation of the number of people.

Data preprocessing

There are two operations in the preprocess phase, regrouping and interpolation.

Following the specification of EPCglobal Class 1 Generation 2 (EPC C1G2), tags are identified using a slotted ALOHA mechanism. That is, each tag randomly selects a time slot for reporting to the reader query and returning its ID. Hence the RSS values in one observation are 'timeline-based' but not grouped according to the tag ID, and hence cannot be used by the feature extraction scheme of R#. Thus, we regroup the RSS values by tag IDs in each observation.

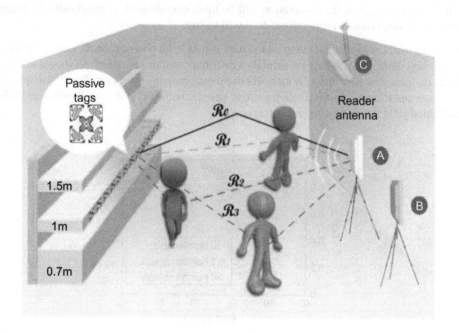

FIG. 14

The multipath propagation of RF signal in R#.

Again due to the slotted ALOHA mechanism, the slot in which a tag replies is randomly and uncontrollably distributed, leading to various numbers of samples from different tags in one observation. In addition, ambient factors, such as the shadowing, interference, and tag location, also influence the backscattered signal, resulting in different sampling periods for these tags. Suppose K is the maximum number of samples collected from a tag within one observation. To avoid the unfairness in the sampling and later processes, for each tag we use a Linear Interpolation method to virtually increase the number of its samples to K.

Feature extraction

In R#, we expect the RF signal to monotonously increase if the number of people is increasing, and decrease if the number of people decreses. To this end, we select three features, entropy, size of dilated area (SDA), and mean squared error (MSE). We present their extraction schemes as follows:

(1) *Entropy.* Given a constant transmission power of the reader (32dBm in our implementation) and fixed location for each tag, the collected RSS values vary within a range, denoted as $[R_{mi}, R_{ma}]$. The human interference may either strengthen or offset the overlapped signal at the reader antenna. Correspondingly, the R_{mi} and R_{ma} may change as well.

(2) *MSE.* Based on the dilated image $f(x, y)$, we introduce another independent feature, the MSE. By compressing $f(x, y)$ using discrete cosine transform (DCT) followed by a decompression, we obtain a recovered image $\hat{f}(x,y)$. We find that the *fidelity* between f and $\hat{f}$ can be used for characterizing the observations. Specifically, the MSE represents the fidelity feature. MSE is normally used to measure information loss. We notice that when there are more humans moving in the area, the image of the observation will be more complicated. Correspondingly, when doing DCT compression, more information will be lost.

We set up a mathematical abstraction on the RSS values in an observation. If we use a random variable to represent them, those values are actually a distribution of this variable. As shown in Fig. 15 and Fig. 16, the distributions with different numbers of moving human objects are distinguishable. Inspired by this, we attempt to apply an information entropy based scheme to reflect the distribution of this variable, and hence yield the first *entropy* feature for R#.

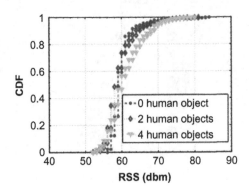

FIG. 15

CDF of RSS.

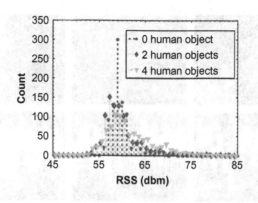

FIG. 16

Distribution of RSS.

According to the information theory, the entropy is a measurement of the uncertainty for a random variable. By monitoring the entropy of different observations, we can measure the degree of their disparity or concentration [27]. To calculate the entropy of an observation, we first establish the empirical distribution for this observation. The RSS range is divided into N bins with an equalized length (BL), where $N = [(R_{ma} - R_{mb}) / BL]$. Let i denote the bin ID, $i < N, x_i$ denote the number of RSS values falling into the ith bin, and $p_i = x_i / \sum_{i=1}^{N} x_i$ denote the probability that x_i RSS values fall into the ith bin. According to entropy theory, the discrete entropy of an observation can be calculated as:

$$E(X) = -\sum_{i=1}^{N} p_i \cdot \log(p_i) \qquad (19)$$

We extract the second feature from the collected RSS values by using a Morphological Image Processing-based Scheme (MIPS). This feature is first discovered from the RSS data visualization. Intuitively, the higher the RSS variance, the larger the area the points could cover. To formalize this observation, we first binary-visualize an observation with the following operations.

To simplify the subsequent processes, we extend the range of $[R_{mi}, R_{ma}]$ to $[R'_{mi}, R'_{ma}]$. Since the RSS resolution of our RFID readers is 0.5 dBM, we normalize each RSS value x with the operation $(x - R'_{mi}) \times 2$. Every x is within $\left[0, (R'_{ma} - R'_{mi}) \times 2\right]$.

We introduce a two-dimensional array $R_{l \times c}$ and initialize its elements as zero. Here l is the length of the observation and c is $(R'_{ma} - R'_{mi}) \times 2$. We then set all elements $R(k, xi)$ to 1, where $1 \le k \le l$, $1 \le i \le c$. Note that there is only one '1' in every column of $R_{l \times c}$. Each element in this array represents a pixel. Let '1' denote a white pixel and '0' denote a black pixel. Then we obtain a binary image. For example, the upper-half parts of Fig. 17A, B, and C show the results of performing the binary visualization operation on the observations with 0, 2, and 4 humans, respectively.

The core operation of MIPS is the morphological dilation, which makes a target in an image 'grow' or 'fatten'. This operation is based on two fundamental morphological operations, *reflection* and *translation*. The reflection of a set A is defined as:

$\hat{A} = \{w \,|\, w = -a, a \in A\}$. The translation from a set A to a point $z = (z_1, z_2)$ is defined as: $(A)z = \{c \,|\, c = a + z, a \in A\}$. To formalize, dilating a set A by using a set B is expressed as: $A \oplus B \left\{z \,|\, \left((\hat{B})_z \cap A\right) \ne \emptyset\right\}$, where B is the *structuring element*, which decides the degree of dilation. Generally, B is a set of '1's with a specific shape, such as a 'line', 'diamond', and the like. When

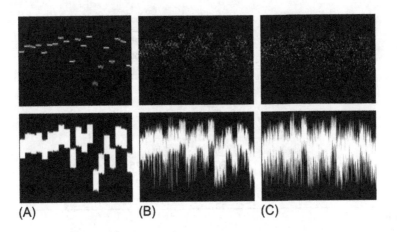

FIG. 17

Binary visualization and dilation results of the observation of 0, 2, 4 human objects. When the number of human objects increases, the size of dilated area is enlarged. (A) 0 human object, (B) 2 human objects, (C) 4 human objects.

conducting a dilation operation, B will translate on the entire image region of A, and examine which position is overlapped with its '1's. The dilation result is a set with all these overlapped positions. The lower parts of Fig. 17A, B, and C demonstrate the dilation results of upper original binary images. We can see that after dilation, white pixels get connected and the area of them is extended. We find that the area of white pixels can well represent the feature of observations. That is, when there are more humans in the surveillance region, the area of white pixels becomes larger in the dilated image (Fig. 18).

After the dilation, we find that the image has many burrs, which are probably derived from some outliers. To eliminate these thin protrusions, we conduct an open operation. The open operation is a combination of dilation and erosion operations. Different from the dilation, erosion can shrink or diminish a target in an image. In the open operation of R#, an erosion is followed by a dilation. An open

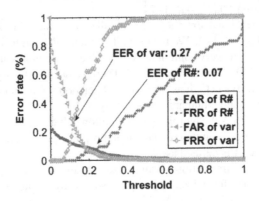

FIG. 18

The error rate of R# vs. the error rate of variance-based method.

operation often makes the edge of an object smooth, fills the gap, or eliminates the burr. Hence, the purpose of performing open operations for R# is to remove the noise and outliers from an observation. We define an erosion on a set A by using a set B as:

$A \ominus B = \{ z | (\hat{B})_z \subseteq A \}$. Hence, the open operation is symbolically expressed as:

$A°B = (A \ominus B) \oplus B$, where B is a structuring element. After the open operation, we calculate the area of white pixels as the second feature.

Considering a $M \times N$ image $f(x, y)$, the forward DCT $T(u, v)$ can be expressed as:

$$T(u,v) = \sum_{u=0}^{M-1}\sum_{v=0}^{N-1} f(x,y)g(x,y,u,v)$$

$$g(x,y,u,v) = a(u)a(v)k(u,v)$$

$$k(u,v) = \cos\left[\left(\frac{(2x+1)u\pi}{2M}\cos\left(\frac{(2y+1)v\pi}{2N}\right)\right)\right]$$

where,

$$a(u)\begin{cases} \sqrt{\dfrac{1}{M}} & \mu = 0 \\ \sqrt{\dfrac{2}{M}} & \mu = 1,2,\cdots,M-1 \end{cases}$$

$$a(v)\begin{cases} \sqrt{\dfrac{1}{N}} & v = 0 \\ \sqrt{\dfrac{2}{N}} & \mu = 1,2,\cdots,N-1 \end{cases}$$

DCT compression is an invertible transformation and can be easily recovered. A brief procedure of DCT compression is as follows: we first divide the original image into 8×8 sub-images. We then use the DCT to represent these subfigures, and discard a part of the coefficients achieved (85% in our implementation). When recovering the image, we run the reverse DCT on the intercepted coefficient matrix. Although the discarded coefficients have little visual influence on the recovered image, they still incur MSE. The incurred MSE between $f(x, y)$ and $\hat{f}(x,y)$ is:

$$MSE = \left(\frac{1}{MN}\sum_{u=0}^{M-1}\sum_{v=0}^{N-1}\left(\hat{f}(x,y) - f(x,y)\right)^2\right)^{1/2}$$

Machine learning-based estimation

We adopt the Naive Bayes method from WEKA as our machine learning classifier. In a real implementation, it is necessary to tune the classifier parameters to optimize the estimation accuracy. To achieve this goal, we organize the aforementioned experiment results into two datasets, one for training and another for testing. We then perform a 10-fold cross-validation on the datasets to determine the key parameters of classification.

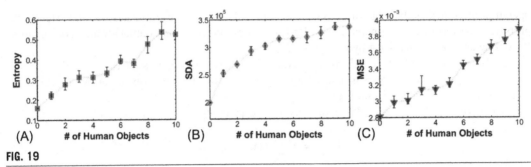

FIG. 19

Three features used by R#. (A) Entropy, (B) SDA, (C) MSE.

Based on this estimation mechanism, we examine the effectiveness of three features. We arrange $0 \sim 10$ volunteers to move arbitrarily in the region and check the trend of features by varying the number of volunteers. The result is reported in Fig. 19A, B, and C. It reveals an interesting insight. Each of the three features shows a good ability to distinguish different numbers of humans in some ranges, *eg*, $0 \sim 4$ people for SDA and $6 \sim 10$ people for MSE. The entropy feature shows an instable variance upon certain numbers of people. Fortunately, the three features exhibit the complementarity with each other, which inspires us to jointly use them in the classifier of R#.

13.4 CONCLUSION

Indoor wireless sensing has spawned numerous applications in a wide range of living, production, commerce, and public services. The increase of mobile and pervasive computing has heightened the need for accurate, robust, and off-the-shelf indoor action recognition schemes. We explore the properties of wireless signals and proposed a robust indoor daily sensing framework using Big Data technology. We can achieve relatively high recognition accuracy for a set of similar daily actions insensitive to location, orientation, speed, and shopping habits.

Considering the advantages and limitations of wireless signals, we will put our effort into exploring how to gain more robust and subtle indoor sensing in future work, and we think vision-based methods and Wi-Fi based methods may be a good complement to each other using crowdsourcing techniques in the age of Big Data.

ACKNOWLEDGEMENTS

This work was supported in part by NSFC under Grant No. 61190112, 61325013, 61572396, and 61402359, and the Fundamental Research Funds for the Central Universities under Grant No. 2015qngz11.

REFERENCES

[1] Hassanieh H, Adib F, Katabi D, Indyk P. Faster gps via the sparse Fourier transform. In: ACM Mobicom'2012; 2012.
[2] Bahl P, Padmanabhan V Radar. An in-building rf-based user location and tracking system. In: IEEE INFOCOM'2000; 2000.

[3] Youssef M, Agrawala A. The Horus location determination system. Wirel Netw 2008;14(3):357–374.

[4] Niculescu D, Nath B. Ad hoc positioning system (aps) using aoa. In: IEEE INFOCOM'2003; 2003.

[5] Chintalapudi KK, Iyer AP, Padmanabhan VN. Indoor localization without the pain. In: ACM Mobicom'2010; 2010.

[6] Rai A, Chintalapudi KK, Padmanabhan VN, Sen R. Zee: zero-effort crowdsourcing for indoor localization. In: ACM Mobicom'2012; 2012.

[7] Yang Z, Wu C, Liu Y. Locating in fingerprint space: wireless indoor localization with little human intervention. In: ACM Mobicom'2012; 2012.

[8] Sen S, Choudhury RR, Nelakuditi S. Spinloc: spin once to know your location. In: ACM HotMobile'2012; 2012.

[9] Sen S, Radunovic B, Choudhury RR, Minka T. You are facing the mona lisa: spot localization using phy layer information. In: ACM Mobisys'2012; 2012.

[10] Wu K, Xiao J, Yi Y, Gao M, Ni LM. FILA: Fine-grained indoor localization. In: IEEE INFOCOM'2012; 2012.

[11] Nandakumar R, Chintalapudi KK, Padmanabhan VN. Centaur: locating devices in an office environment. In: ACM Mobicom'2012; 2012.

[12] Liu H, Gan Y, Yang J, Sidhom S, Wang Y, Chen Y, et. al. Push the limit of wifi based localization for smartphones. In: ACM Mobicom'2012; 2012.

[13] Zhang Z, Zhou X, Zhang W, Zhang Y, Wang G, Zhao B, et. al. I am the antenna: Accurate outdoor ap location using smartphones. In: ACM Mobicom'2011; 2011.

[14] Leordeanu M, Hebert M. A spectral technique for correspondence problems using pairwise constraints. In: IEEE ICCV'2005; 2005.

[15] Cho, M., Lee, J., and Lee, K. (2010) Reweighted random walks for graph matching. Computer Vision–ECCV.

[16] Ichino M, Yaguchi H. Generalized Minkowski metrics for mixed feature-type data analysis. IEEE Trans Syst. Man, Cybern 1994;24(4):698–708.

[17] Von Luxburg U. A tutorial on spectral clustering. Stat Comput 2007;17(4):395–416.

[18] Garsia AM, Remmel J. Shuffles of permutations and the Kronecker product. Graphs and Combinatorics 1985;1(1):217–263.

[19] Matthews C. Future of Retail: How Companies Can Employ Big Data to Create a Better Shopping Experience, http://business.time.com/2012/08/31/future- of-retail-how-companies-can-employ-big-data-to-create-a-better-shopping- experience/; 2012.

[20] Li C, Dai H, Li H. Adaptive Quickest Change Detection with Unknown Parameter. In: Proceedings of IEEE ICASSP; 2009.

[21] Page E. Continuous Inspection Schemes. Biometrika 1954;41(1-2):100–115.

[22] Wang J, Katabi D. Dude, Where's my Card?: RFID Positioning that Works with Multipath and Non-line of Sight. In: Proceedings of ACM SIGCOMM; 2013.

[23] Tse D. Fundamentals of Wireless Communication. Cambridge University Press; 2005.

[24] Dobkin DM. The RF in RFID-Passive UHF RFID in Practice. Elsevier; 2008.

[25] Teixeira T, Dublon G, Savvides A. A Survey of Human-sensing: Methods for Detecting Presence, Count, Location, Track, and Identity. ACM Comput Surv 2010;5.

[26] EPCglobal (2008) Specification for RFID Air Interface EPC: Radio-Frequency Identity Protocols Class-1 Generation-2 UHF RFID Protocol for Communications at 860 MHz-960 MHz.

[27] Zhang J, Qin Z, Ou L, Jiang P, Liu J, Liu A. An Advanced Entropy-based DDOS Detection Scheme. In: Proceedings of 2010 International Conference on Information Networking and Automation (ICINA); 2010.

BIG DATA APPLICATIONS

A FRAMEWORK FOR MINING THAI PUBLIC OPINIONS

14

C. Deerosejanadej, S. Prom-on, T. Achalakul

14.1 INTRODUCTION

Social networks connect human beings. Social networks, in terms of both data and users, have been exponentially growing and connecting our lives in various dimensions. We can connect with people across the planet with the touch of a finger. In every second, hundreds of thousands of messages are shared through social media and websites such as Facebook, Twitter, Foursquare, Pantip, etc. They contain stories about our lives, feelings, experiences and opinions.

Social media networks generate a huge volume of data. They have been used in various types of applications including public health [1], emergency coordination [2], news recommendation [3], and stock market prediction [4]. These social media data are gathered under the catch-all term, "Big Data." However, the data stored is usually in the unstructured format, meaning that it is spontaneously generated and not easily captured and classified. Big Data is only valuable if its content can be utilized. The better the content is used, the better you will be able to take advantage of that data. Understanding the cause behind that trend is crucial to better decision making. This is necessary for the next-generation organizations that utilize intelligence in Big Data.

The major challenge of opinion mining in Thai is in the inherent nature of the language. Unlike English, Thai sentences use neither white space to mark words nor punctuation to mark the end of the sentence. With the lack of research in computational linguistics for the Thai language, these characteristics pose a great challenge in analyzing Thai textual data. In addition, most social media text is written in the form of spoken Thai, which is not included in the existing Thai lexicon. For example, there are some informal words which are used by some people or groups (eg, slang words and local words). Therefore, these characteristics raise difficulty in segmenting Thai sentences based on a dictionary. Another problem is the lack of a system that can automatically extract entities from the text. Without such a system, it is impossible to identify relevant objects within the textual data. Though lots of text mining tools are available in the market, most of them are not applicable to the Thai language due to these two difficulties. Simply speaking, these tools do not understand Thai textual data, especially in the spoken form.

Data and Opinion Mining (DOM) [5] was developed to analyze Thai public opinions on topics of interest. DOM aggregated sentiments and impact positions of authorities in order to facilitate decision making. Though all related sentences of each topic were displayed along with sentiment results, readers usually struggled with reading all relevant opinions in order to seek underlying reasons for supporting their beliefs. Furthermore, the screens of mobile devices usually provides limited space to display

Big Data. http://dx.doi.org/10.1016/B978-0-12-805394-2.00014-3

content. Thus, a summarization system was utilized to compress opinion text in an informative way; that is, a text summary representing majority opinions and also containing less redundant information. To generate the economical and representative summary, Ly et al. [6] selected representative sentences from the generated clusters. They applied two clustering techniques to group sentences, including agglomerative hierarchical clustering and hill-climbing clustering. The hierarchical method began with single-sentence clusters and continuously merged two clusters with the minimum distance in their combination. For the hill-climbing method, the clusters were randomly generated for the first iteration. In subsequent iterations, the algorithm greedily swapped cluster members which minimize an average similarity within clusters (ie, intracluster dissimilarity). Since these two methods suffer from local-optima and computation problems, they could not produce effective opinion clustering of large data in an acceptable timeframe.

Hence, we combine the clustering-based opinion summarization with the original version of DOM in order to provide a representative and economical summary, resulting in stronger evidence. In this work, we present the developments of XDOM (eXtension of DOM), a Big Data analytics engine that is capable of mining Thai public opinions regarding specific issues discussed on social network sites, and its corresponding mobile solution for answering public opinions about events and locations. For the data analytics engine, the opinion summary generation is proposed in this extended version. Software features and design will be discussed in Section 14.2. Section 14.3 explains how the software was implemented using cloud-based technology. Section 14.4 shows the evaluation of the XDOM effectiveness in predicting the sentiment score and in discovering sentence clusters of public opinions. Usages of XDOM for different tasks are presented in Section 14.5. Comparisons of XDOM with respect to others, and future steps in development are discussed in Section 14.6.

14.2 XDOM
14.2.1 DATA SOURCES
We collected data from four different data sources: Twitter, Facebook, Foursquare and Pantip, as described in Table 1.

These social network data were collected in the Bangkok area. Different data sources require the use of different connectors. For Twitter data, we used Search API [7] provided from Twitter Inc. to collect tweets without any keywords. We collected approximately 15 million tweets, or, about 12GB of uncompressed

Table 1 Sources of Social Network Data

Source	Data description
Twitter	Twitter messages, also known as tweets, are short 140-character text messages. Tweets are all public
Facebook	Facebook data can only be retrieved if the privacy is set to public. They are in forms of status posts and Facebook Page posts
Foursquare	Foursquare provides both text comments and review score of a number of places
Pantip	Pantip data are in forms of webboard threads. It is one of the prominent Thailand online social communities

FIG. 1

Twitter activity heat map in Bangkok area.

data. Each tweet contains multiple data fields, including time, username, user followers, retweet, count, location, and the textual comment. The data collected from twitter can be represented as an activity heat map (Fig. 1). For Facebook, we used Graph API [8] developed by Facebook Inc. Unlike Twitter, we can only request and collect data from the Facebook fan page, which consists of posts and comments on specific topics. We collected Facebook data from about 5,000 messages, which is approximately 4 MB per fan page. Graph API provides attributes including time, username, number of Likes, location, and textual comments for each message. For Foursquare, the situation is like Graph API. Foursquare provides some useful APIs, named Venues and Tip search API [9], for developers to gather data. Foursquare provides comments of places. In each month we collected approximately 500 messages, or 0.4 MB per place. Foursquare data includes time, username, like count, location and the textual comment. Our last data source is Pantip.com, one of the prominent Thailand online social communities. We developed a web crawler to gather the data on this website, since they do not provide an API to gather data. The web crawler was designed to have features like Search API. First we simulated the browser by setting the user-agent to be Mozilla, and then assigned the keywords to the search form of web and submitted the request. We found that approximately 300 messages, or about 0.2 MB, were collected for each topic. Each Pantip thread contains time, username, like count and the text comment.

14.2.2 DOM SYSTEM ARCHITECTURE

The original version of DOM is composed of two basic modules: server-side and client-side modules. The architecture design of the DOM framework is shown in Fig. 2. The components of the DOM engine are classified into the server-side, which is a cloud-based cluster. The DOM engine is responsible for collecting, analyzing data and distributing the analyzed data to the client-side. AskDOM components are client-side. The client-side requests the analyzed data, queries, and displays them to end users.

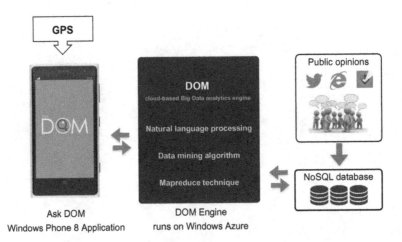

FIG. 2

Conceptual framework of DOM and its corresponding mobile application, AskDOM.

Workflow of our framework is as follows. Public messages are collected from social networks, blogs and forums using DOM's crawler module. All collected messages are stored in MongoDB, a NoSQL database. After that, each message is processed using the basic Natural Language Processing (NLP) technique to parse the text data, categorize its topic, compute its sentimental score, select its representative text in order to form a summary and analyze its influences. DOM also uses the MapReduce technique based on the Apache Hadoop framework to reduce processing time. DOM periodically processed the data to compute their sentimental score as well as to summarize their opinion text. Finally AskDOM, the mobile application, gets the analyzed data, queries, and displays the information to users according to the inquired-upon topics.

In this work, we focus on the usage of XDOM as a Thai public opinion mining framework to track social issues and provide sentiment ratings and information on points of interest (POI) based on public opinions. However, the core functions of the DOM engine were designed to support dynamic data. There are several features that could be added or further developed to provide additional functionality (eg, adding more data sources, supporting other languages). Since DOM is a cloud-based engine, scalability is also available.

Furthermore, DOM can be easily applied in various types of usage, on either the community side or the commercial side. There are case studies in Section 14.5 that show some potential usages of DOM. The current version of DOM consists of five modules, which are MapReduce framework, sentiment analysis, clustering-based summarization framework, influencer analysis, and AskDOM mobile application.

14.2.3 MAPREDUCE FRAMEWORK

Since huge data are involved in this project, MapReduce [10] is used. If the data is processed sequentially, the processing time would be too large for the practical application. The MapReduce technique on the Apache Hadoop framework is therefore the best way to accelerate the analysis speed.

In our research, we apply MapReduce to distribute the computational workload of sentiment analysis and summarization tasks across a flexible number of worker machines. The MapReduce technique separates the mining process of both analysis tasks into two main steps: Map and Reduce, as follows:

For the sentiment analysis, the map function takes the entire text input, breaks it into subsets to be evaluated for their sentiment scores, and distributes them to worker nodes. The reduce function combines the resulting sentiment scores from each small worker node by grouping keywords of specific topics of interest and aggregating the sentiment scores into final results.

For the opinion summarization, for each keyword group, the map function divides sentences into two subgroups according to their polarity sentiments; that is, each keyword group contains three sentence subgroups, including positive, negative and neutral. Then, all subgroups are sent to worker nodes to cluster sentences and select representatives from the generated clusters. The reduce function merges the selected representatives by their keyword groups in order to form a final summary.

14.2.4 SENTIMENT ANALYSIS

In this work we targeted words in which opinions are expressed in each sentence. A simple observation was that these sentences always contain sentiment words (eg, great, good, bad, worst). To simplify the process, if the sentences do not contain any sentiment words, their sentiment values will be neutral (non-opinions). So we designed our framework to classify the sentiment of each sentence based on its sentiment words and the combination of them.

Furthermore, we designed the system to be able to process Thai conditional sentences, which are sentences that describe implications or hypothetical situations and their consequences, for example, the sentence "I like the location of this company but I do not like their staff." The sentiment of "location" is positive but for "staff" it's negative. We found that most conditional sentences contain modifiers and conjunctions (eg, but, and, or).

To classify each message as positive, neutral or negative, we employed a lexicon-based algorithm to measure the sentiment score of each message. We defined five corpora, including positive words, negative words, modifiers, conjunctions, as well as the names of points of interest. Each word in the two sentiment corpora, positive words and negative words, contains sentiment ratings ranging from −5 to 5. The examples of our corpuses are shown in Table 2.

Table 2 The Examples of Sentences in the Corpora

#	Type of Corpus	Word	Value
1	Positive words	เท่ห์ (smart)	3
		ดี (good)	3
		เยี่ยม (best)	4
2	Negative Words	เสื่อมโทรม (decadent)	-3
		แย่ (bad)	-3
		ห่วยแตก (worst)	-4
3	Modifiers	ไม่ (not)	-1
		ค่อนข้าง (likely)	0.5
		ที่สุด (best)	1.5
4	Conjunctions	แต่ (but)	2
		และ (and)	1
		รวมไปถึง (including)	1
5	Names of places	สวนลุมพินี (Lumphini Park)	–
		สยาม (Siam)	–
		จตุจักร (Chatuchak market)	–

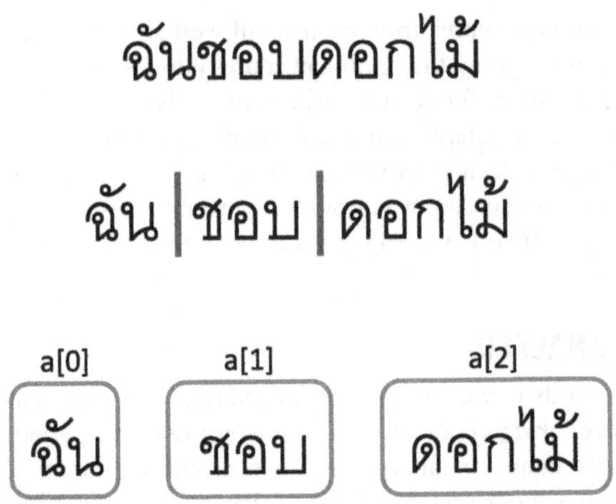

ฉันชอบดอกไม้

ฉัน | ชอบ | ดอกไม้

a[0]   a[1]   a[2]

ฉัน   ชอบ   ดอกไม้

FIG. 3

Example of Thai word tokenization.

    DOM detects and matches words and their sentiment polarity by using these corpora. Since the nature of Thai sentence structure is continuous without any white space breaks between words, we need to tokenize each sentence into a group of words. In this process, we used "LexTo" [11], the open source Thai word tokenizer, to tokenize words in each sentence and then store them as an array using the longest word matching algorithm [12]. An example of this procedure is shown in Fig. 3.

    DOM generates small jobs to detect words of each sentence in parallel. First of all, DOM filters the nonrelated sentences out by matching words with the names of POI corpus. After that, only sentences that relate to specific topics of interest (in this case, points of interest) would remain. DOM then iteratively matches sentiment keywords with remaining corpuses. If there are sentiment words in an array, DOM collect its sentiment score and summarizes it at the end of each sentence. DOM then automatically classifies each sentence into a sentiment group: positive, neutral or negative, depending on its score band (the range of distributed sentiment score). DOM not only determines keywords from sentences, but also determines the context of each sentence. The positions of words, modifiers, conjunctions, and emoticons are also determined in our framework. In some cases these words can be important clues to emphasizing the mood of the sentences. Especially for the modifier keywords, they can invert the sentiment score if their positions are adjacent to the sentiment words as illustrated in Fig. 4.

14.2.5 CLUSTERING-BASED SUMMARIZATION FRAMEWORK

Due to the high impact of textual opinions on decision making, a review summarization system is inevitable, as the system provides a shorter version of informative text apart from overall numerical sentiments. As a result, readers can quickly understand major authors' opinions without losing any key points.

    The opinion summarization framework is able to produce a representative and non-duplicate textual summary. Fig. 5 presents a framework architecture which is composed of three processes—a sentence similarity calculation, a modified genetic algorithm (GA) sentence clustering, and a sentence selection.

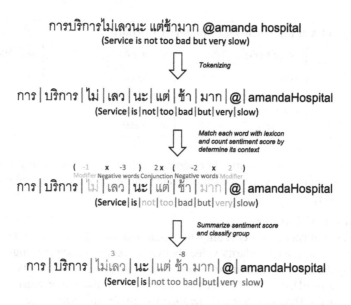

FIG. 4

Example of Thai sentiment analysis.

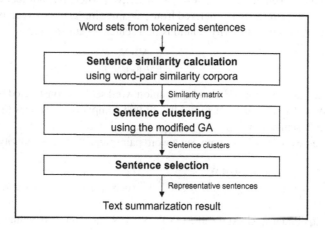

FIG. 5

The architecture of our clustering-based summarization framework.

After completing the sentence analysis task, each sentence is represented with its tokenized words. First, the framework takes these preprocessed sentences to generate a semantic similarity matrix through a sentence similarity calculation process. This matrix reflects semantic similarity relations between sentences. Unlike existing works, we create a semantic similarity corpora in order to identify similarity levels between Thai word pairs. Subsequently, the modified GA assigns sentences into

Table 3 The Examples of the Word-Pair Similarity Corpora

#	Word 1 (r)	Word 2 (s)	Sim_Word(r,s)
1	ดี (good)	เยี่ยม (best)	0.8
2	เก่ง (smart)	ฉลาด (clever)	1.0
3	ดี (good)	หนาว (cold)	0.0
4	ใหญ่ (big)	กว้าง (wide)	0.4

clusters based upon the similarity matrix. In a sentence selection process, a final summary is created by selecting a representative sentence of each generated cluster. The following subsections present the details of each component.

(1) Sentence Similarity Calculation

Since the sentence clustering process aims to assign semantically similar sentences into the same clusters, and vice versa, the similarity values between every sentence pair must be calculated before performing the next process. In this work, we adopt a sentence similarity measure of Li et al. [13] to compute a similarity score between two sentences. Unlike the original method, we create a similarity corpora for Thai language to determine word-pair similarity scores, which range from 0 to 1. The lower values between two comparing words indicate the lower similarity relations. The example of the corpora is shown in Table 3.

According to the preprocessed data of the sentiment analysis in Section 14.2.4, each sentence S_i is represented with its tokenized words, $W_i = \{w_1, w_2, ..., w_n\}$ where n is number of words in sentence S_i. The similarity score, $sim(S_1, S_2)$, is derived from a cosine similarity between two semantic vectors (V_1 and V_2) which represent similarity relations of a sentence pair (S_1 and S_2), denoted as

$$sim(S_1, S_2) = \frac{V_1 \bullet V_2}{\| V_1 \| \bullet \| V_2 \|} \tag{1}$$

To create the semantic vectors (V_1 and V_2), a union word set U is constructed by merging two word sets, $U = W_1 \cup W_2 = \{u_1, u_2, ..., u_q\}$ where q = |U|, of two comparing sentences (S_1 and S_2). After that, each element of two semantic vectors, $V_1 = \{v_{11}, v_{12}, ..., v_{1q}\}$ and $V_2 = \{v_{21}, v_{22}, ..., v_{2q}\}$, is created from the similarity scores, Sim_Word(r,s), between a word pair (r and s) in the similarity corpora, denoted as

$$v_{1i} = \begin{cases} 1, if\ u_i \in W_1 \\ \max_{a \in W_1} sim_{word(u_i, a)}, if\ u_i \notin W_1 \end{cases}, v_{2i} = \begin{cases} 1, if\ u_i \in W_2 \\ \max_{b \in W_2} sim_{word(u_i, b)}, if\ u_i \notin W_2 \end{cases} \tag{2}$$

where $i \in \{1, 2, ..., q\}$ and $u_i \in U$. At the end of this process, the similarity values of all sentence pairs are assembled into the semantic similarity matrix, $M = \{m_{00}, m_{01}, ..., m_{hh}\}$ where h is the number of opinion sentences. For example, a value of element m_{02} in a similarity matrix indicates the similarity score between two sentences, S_0 and S_2.

(2) Sentence Clustering

The objective of our summarization framework is to select underlying text from each cluster. In order to achieve the expectation, the sentence clustering process assists in dividing semantically similar sentences into the same clusters based on the similarity matrix generated in the previous process. In this work, we formulate the sentence clustering problem as an optimization problem which attempts to minimize dissimilarity between sentences in the same clusters. To solve the optimization problem, we apply the genetic algorithm to find near globally optimal results. As the sentence clustering problems contain few good results, the GA suffers from slow convergence. To boost up the algorithm, we utilize the concept of membership degree in data clustering to form an additional solution reassignment operation of our modified GA. In general, a sentence has different degrees of being a member in any cluster. The degree is defined as the similarity level of any sentence to all members in a particular cluster. The higher degrees of sentences in any cluster reflect a higher likelihood that they will be in that cluster. Thus, a sentence should be assigned to the cluster that has the highest degree of belonging. With this clustering characteristic, we reassign all feasible solutions of the modified GA in every generation. By doing this, the algorithm considers only the solutions which satisfy with this clustering characteristic, resulting in faster convergence.

The overall flowchart of the modified GA is shown in Fig. 6. First, the algorithm randomly generates feasible solutions (ie, individuals) and encodes them into the genetic representation. To represent a sentence clustering solution, we use a string of n-digit integers where n is the number of sentences. Each digit presents the cluster index of the corresponding sentence, as illustrated in Fig. 7.

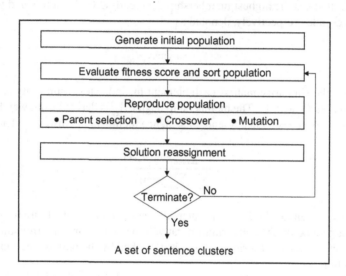

FIG. 6

The flowchart of the modified genetic algorithm.

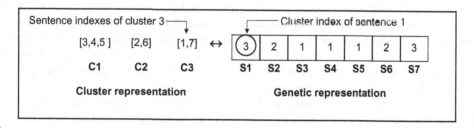

FIG. 7

The example of 7-digit integer representation.

All generated individuals are then formed to a population. After that, a fitness score of each individual is calculated by using the intracluster dissimilarity function in [6]. Then, all individuals are sorted by their fitness scores. The population of the next generation is derived from the best individuals (ie, elitisms) and the reproduced individuals (ie, offspring). To generate each offspring, two individuals from the current population are selected as parents in order to perform a crossover operation. In the crossover operation, the parents exchange their genes based on random probability in order to create new individuals (ie, offspring). Subsequently, the mutation operation is applied only on offspring in which the random values of mutation exceed the predefined values. The mutated offspring are randomly changed in the cluster index at a random point.

After the population of the next generation is generated, each individual F represents a clustering solution, $C = \{c_1, c_2, ..., c_e\}$ where $e = |C|$, of sentences $S = \{S_1, S_2, ..., S_n\}$ where $n = |S|$. To refine the current solution, the individual is then fetched into the solution reassignment process. In this process, the value of each digit of an individual is altered according to a reassignment function $\varphi(S_i)$ which determines new cluster index for sentence S_i. This function will reassign a sentence S_x to the cluster C_y that has the highest membership degree, $d_{xy} \in [0,1]$ where x and y are the sentence index and cluster index respectively, denoted as

$$\varphi(S_x) = \text{argmax}_y d_{xy} \tag{3}$$

According to the similarity matrix, each element m_{ij} indicates a similarity score $\text{sim}(S_i, S_j)$ between two sentences (S_i and S_j). The membership degree d_{xy} is derived from weighted sums of total similarity scores between sentence S_x and all sentence members in cluster C_y, denoted as

$$d_{xy} = \frac{\sum_{a \in C_y} \text{sim}(S_x, a)}{\sum_{i=1}^{k} \sum_{b \in C_i} \text{sim}(S_x, b)} \tag{4}$$

Where $\sum_{i=1}^{k} d_x = 1$ and $x \in \{1, 2, ..., n\}$. Later, all reassigned individuals are formed to the population of the next generation. The algorithm iteratively performs until a termination criteria is met. After termination, the final clustering solution is described by the best-scored individual.

(3) Sentence Selection

Owing to the large number of opinion texts, it becomes difficult for readers to read all relevant text and draw conclusions. Taking the generated clusters from the sentence clustering process, the sentence selection assists in selecting an underlying sentence from each cluster based on a representative score in [6]. The higher scores reflect the sentences that are more similar to other sentences in the same cluster. In this work, the representative sentence of a cluster is defined as the most similar sentence. Thus, for each cluster, we select a sentence which has the highest score as the representative sentence. After all representatives are selected, a list of representatives with their cluster sizes is presented in the final summary. The size of each cluster can indicate its impact on the opinion data; that is, the larger clusters reflect more impact opinions.

The textual summary of this framework provides underlying reasons to support the sentiment analysis. This additional information helps readers make better and stronger decisions, resulting in business success. In other words, the opinion summarization framework is added to increase the reliability of making decisions in a DOM engine.

14.2.6 INFLUENCER ANALYSIS

The rise of social media platforms such as Twitter, with their focus on user-generated content and social networks, has brought about the study of authority and influence over social networks to the forefront of current research. For companies and other public entities, identifying and engaging with influential authors in social media is critical, since any opinions they express can rapidly spread far and wide. For users, when presented with a vast amount of content relevant to a topic of interest, sorting content by the source's authority or influence can also assist in information retrieval. In the social network community, a variety of measures were designed for the measurement of importance or prominence of nodes in a network [14,15]. In the following, we will briefly summarize the centrality measure that we have used to describe possible candidate indicators for the power of influential in message diffusion. For the DOM engine, we have used "Degree centrality" to identify influential users in Twitter's networks.

Degree centrality is the simplest centrality measure, as illustrated in Fig. 8. The degree of a node i denoted by k_i, is the number of edges that are incident with it, or the number of nodes adjacent to it. For networks where the edges between nodes are directional, we have to distinguish between in-degree and out-degree. The out-degree centrality is defined as

$$C_{D_o}(i) = \sum_{j=1}^{n} a_{ij} \tag{5}$$

where a_{ij} is 1 in the binary adjacency matrix A if an edge from node i to j exists, otherwise it is 0. Similarly, the in-degree centrality is defined as

$$C_{D_i}(i) = \sum_{j=1}^{n} a_{ji} \tag{6}$$

where i describes the node i and a_{ji} is 1 if an edge from node j to i exists, otherwise it is 0.

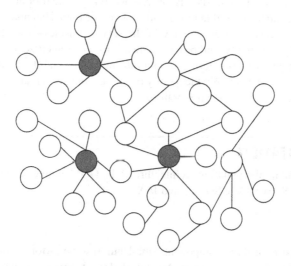

FIG. 8

Simulation of Influencer network graph in the Twitter's networks.

FIG. 9

AskDOM mobile application.

14.2.7 AskDOM: MOBILE APPLICATION

To utilize DOM to its fullest extent, we developed AskDOM (Fig. 9), a mobile solution designed to use DOM to provide a means for the general public to help improve their own communities by providing reviews, feedback, and ratings of service providers automatically analyzed from public opinions on social networks (Twitter, Facebook, Pantip and Foursquare). AskDOM comprises two important modules: (a) a front-end interface with features designed to connect users to service providers such as I-Share (direct feedback), Map (traffic and incident map), Anomaly (abnormal situations reports), and (b) the DOM Engine, the back-end system that periodically gathers and processes social network data, performs public sentiment analysis, discovers underlying textual opinions, determines relationship influencers, and conducts natural language processing for both Thai and English. The integration of both modules will increase the transparency of the service businesses, making the agencies more accountable for their service quality, and provide a means for general citizens to become involved with the improvement of public services in terms of both information availability and general improvement. Such involvement will improve not only the quality of service, but also create a sense of community for general citizens that are part of the social function.

14.3 IMPLEMENTATION

Fig. 10 shows the overall implementation architecture of the DOM engine. The structure has three main components which are Server, Core Service and I/O.

14.3.1 SERVER

The server section consists of three components: the Ubuntu server, MongoDB, and Apache Hadoop. We implemented the DOM engine based on Apache Hadoop MapReduce, which runs on the Ubuntu server. MongoDB, the famous NoSQL database, was also used in this framework. This type of database

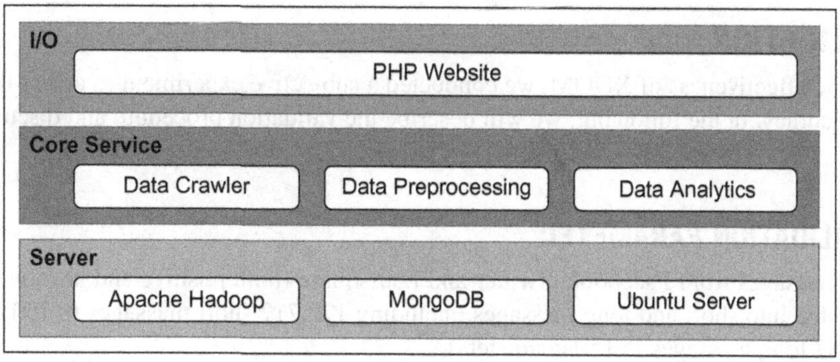

FIG. 10

DOM engine architecture.

often includes highly optimized key value stores intended for simple retrieval and appending operations to improve the performance in terms of latency and throughput.

14.3.2 CORE SERVICE

Core Service, the main part of our framework, consists of three components.

(1) *Data Crawler*: This module automatcially provides a raw data feed from social networks and stores it in the database, MongoDB. Each crawler code is specific for each social network or website.

(2) *Data Preprocessing*: This component prepares raw data for analysis by tokenizing Thai and English words from sentences, removing outliers and reformatting data. Then the cleaned data will be sent to Data Analysis.

(3) *Data Analysis*: There are three data analyzers in this component:

   (3.1) *Sentiment Analysis* evaluates sentiments in Twitter text and finds peoples' moods on a particular topic. For example, how people think about traffic in Bangkok.

   (3.2) *Clustering-based Summarization* organizes Twitter text into clusters and selects representative sentences from each one to form a text summary. The generated summary is presented as supporting evidence for the sentiment analysis results.

   (3.3) *Influencer Analysis* determines people's positions in network, which indicates how influential they are. The influential people are more likely to acquire connections and have more connections.

14.3.3 I/O

I/O, the web-service implemented using PHP, receives the result from Core Service and then sends them to the client-side to display in a JSON format. Since the amount of data in social networks is increasing every second, using the static resources (eg, static server) may not be practical. So we designed DOM to run on the cloud. The cloud provides the ability to add blob storage depending on the size of data. Furthermore, DOM has the ability to scale the number of processers. In other words, DOM can increase or decrease the number of mappers and reducers for running a job.

14.4 VALIDATION

To validate the effectiveness of XDOM, we conducted a subjective experiment to assess the sentiment prediction accuracy. In the following, we will describe the validation procedure and discuss validation results.

14.4.1 VALIDATION PARAMETER

- 184,184 messages from Facebook, Twitter and Foursquare (both positive and negative messages) were divided into short and long messages, including 172,717 short messages (≤150 characters) and 11,467 long messages (>150 characters).
- 12 subjects (6 males and 6 females) participated in the experiment. They were students at the Computer Engineering Department, King Mongkut's University of Technology Thonburi, Thailand.

14.4.2 VALIDATION METHOD

1. For the human end, 184,184 messages were divided into 12 parts, each of which was assigned to each subject. They classified the messages into positive and negative classes.
2. For the DOM engine, 184,184 messages were classified by the engine into positive and negative classes.
3. The results of both human and DOM were compared and analyzed together to assess the system's prediction accuracy.

14.4.3 VALIDATION RESULTS

Tables 4 and 5 show the comparison results of 12 students and the DOM engine. We found that the DOM engine can classify messages and conduct sentiment analysis with an accuracy of over 75%. The

Table 4 Summary of Prediction Accuracy.

Message type	Positive comment accuracy (%)	Negative comment accuracy (%)	Total
Short	79.75	56.33	75.99
Long	86.53	38.95	81.29
Total	80.19	55.57	76.32

Table 5 Detail Analysis of the System Effectiveness.

Msg. Type	TP	FP	TN	FN	Precision	Accuracy (%)
Short	115,643	12,103	15,613	29,358	0.905	75.99
Long	8,830	771	492	1,374	0.919	81.29
Total	124,473	12,874	16,105	30,732	0.906	76.32

accuracy of the DOM engine is in the standard of text classification [16], so the DOM engine is practical for use in social network analysis and can be applied to many dimensions in the real word.

14.5 CASE STUDIES

In addition to the evaluation of the system effectiveness, we tested the XDOM engine further on various case studies that were of interest to the Thai public during the time periods. Each case study aims to explore either a specific social or political issue that people were discussing widely on the Internet, thus it offers a summary of Internet public opinions on that issue.

14.5.1 POLITICAL OPINION: #PRAYFORTHAILAND

Around the end of 2013, citizens of Bangkok were faced with multiple rounds of political protests, and violent acts toward both protesters and officers. Hashtag "#prayforthailand" is one that was frequently used in social media to express the concerns over the situation. Different opinions were expressed regarding this political issue. We used DOM to mine the general public opinions that were expressed in the social network to determine the political climate at that time. We collected tweets around the Bangkok area that contain the hashtag "#PrayForThailand." There were over 100 K tweets collected from 29 November to 7 December 2013. We implemented the Naïve Bayes and Support Vector Machine (SVM) to the DOM engine to classify political opinions into six predefined categories as shown in Table 6. DOM can accurately put tweets into categories with more than 85% accuracy.

14.5.2 BANGKOK TRAFFIC CONGESTION RANKING

Bangkok's traffic is one of the most serious problems that urban citizens have been facing in their daily lives. Knowing such information on which streets the traffic jams often occur would allow citizens to prepare to encounter the problem and allows the government to find a way to solve it.

We used the XDOM engine to track traffic jams keywords, name of streets, and intersections as well as famous places in Bangkok, Thailand that were contained in public tweets, and then rank the streets that were mostly mentioned in tweets about the traffic jam based on 22 K tweets collected from 17 February to 8 March 2014.

Table 6 Summary of Opinions with "#prayforthailand"

Opinions	Percentage
Oppose to the government	29.45
Loyal to the king	20.91
Feeling depressed about the situation	15.61
Oppose to both government and protests	0.82
Oppose to protesters	0.01
Others	33.2

Table 7 Bangkok Traffic Congestion Ranking

Rank	Streets/Intersections	Percentage
1	Ladprao—Paholyothin	19.47
2	Vibhavadi—Rangsit	11.62
3	Petchaburi	7.76
4	Sukhumvit	4.71
5	Ramkumhaeng	4.13
6	Others	52.31

The results as shown in Table 7 are consistent with what Thailand's Department of Highways hotline gathered from phone calls. However, using the XDOM engine is much faster and cheaper.

14.6 SUMMARY AND CONCLUSIONS

We discussed the development, evaluation, and case studies of XDOM, an extension of a Big Data analytics framework for assessing public sentiments and extracting salient opinions of specific social issues. The opinion summarization framework, which is based on a modified genetic algorithm clustering and sentence selection, is combined with the DOM engine. The XDOM is encapsulated as a mobile application known as AskDOM that allows users to interact and find information of places suggested by the sentiment ratings along with their supporting reasons. We have demonstrated both accuracy and generalizability of the engine in the analysis of various topics that are relevant to public interests.

Further improvements are still needed to make the XDOM engine more adaptive and robust. First, the sentiment score associated with each keyword is currently context independent and comes mainly from the manual adjustment by the administrator. A context-dependent keyword-score association study is needed for each of the tasks required. After obtaining these related associations from different contexts, rules can be derived so that the system can work effectively on different tasks. Second, public opinions usually contain a lot of personal messages that are irrelevant to the places under discussion. A filter that is capable of detecting the context of the message is required. Third, the sentence clustering in the summarization framework currently produces a compressed text only for current input sentences. It means that the analyzed data is also required to reprocess when new opinion data is fetched into the framework. Taking the clustering results, they can be treated as training data in supervised learning models. By doing this, the trained models are further used for classifying new incoming text without reprocessing all existing data.

ACKNOWLEDGMENTS

We would like to thank for the financial support of the Faculty of Engineering, King Mongkut's University of Technology Thonburi through the research grant (to SP) and the Office of Higher Education Commission through the National Research University (NRU) grant, fiscal year 2011–2013 (to TA).

REFERENCES

[1] Paul MJ, Dredze M. A Model for Mining Public Health Topics from Twitter. Technical Report, Johns Hopkins University; 2011.

[2] Purohit H, Hampton A, Shalin VL, Sheth AP, Flach J, Bhatt S. What Kind of #Conversation is Twitter? Mining #Psycholinguistic Cues for Emergency Coordination. Comput Hum Behav 2013;29:2438–47.

[3] Phelan O, McCarthy K, Smyth B. Using Twitter to recommend real-time topical news. In: Proceedings of the third ACM conference on Recommender systems, New York City, NY, USA; October 2009. p. 22–5.

[4] Bollen J, Mao H, Zeng X-J. Twitter mood predicts the stock market. J Comput Sci 2011;2:1–8.

[5] Prom-on S, Ranong SN, Jenviriyakul P, Wongkaew T, Saetiew N, Achalakul T. DOM: A big data analytics framework for mining Thai public opinions. In: International Conference on Computer, Control, Informatics and Its Applications, October 21–23; Bandung: IEEE; 2014. p. 1–6.

[6] Zhu L, Gao S, Pan SJ, Li H, Deng D, Shahabi C. Graph-based Informative-sentence Selection for Opinion Summarization. In: IEEE/ACM International Conference on Advances in Social Networks Analysis and Mining (ASONAM 2013), August 25–28; Niagara Falls: IEEE; 2013. p. 408–12.

[7] Twitter Search API, https://dev.twitter.com/rest/public/search.

[8] Facebook Graph API, https://developers.facebook.com/docs/graph-api.

[9] Foursqaure API, https://developer.foursquare.com.

[10] Sathya S, Jose MV. Application of Hadoop MapReduce technique to virtual database system design. In: Emerging Trends in Electrical and Computer Technology (ICETECT), 2011 International Conference. IEEE, 2011.

[11] Lexto, www.sansarn.com/lexto/.

[12] Haruechaiyasak C, Kongthon A. LexToPlus: A Thai Lexeme Tokenization and Normalization Tool. In: The 4th Workshop on South and Southeast Asian NLP (WSSANLP) International Joint Conference on Natural Language Processing, Nagoya, Japan, October 14–18, 2013; 2013.

[13] Li Y, McLean D, Bandar ZA, O'shea JD, Crockett K. Sentence Similarity Based on Semantic Nets and Corpus Statistics. IEEE Trans Knowl Data Eng 2006;18(8):1138–50.

[14] Freemann LC. Centrality in social networks: I. Conceptual clarification. Soc Networks 1979;1:215–39.

[15] Kiss C, Bichler M. Identification of Influencers—Measuring Influence in Customer Networks. Decis Support Syst 2008;46:233–53.

[16] Si J, Mukherjee A, Liu B, Li Q, Li H, Deng X. Exploiting topic based twitter sentiment for stock prediction. In: The 51st Annual Meeting of the Association for Computational Linguistics, Sofia, Bulgaria, August 4–9, 2013; 2013.

A CASE STUDY IN BIG DATA ANALYTICS: EXPLORING TWITTER SENTIMENT ANALYSIS AND THE WEATHER

R.O. Sinnott, H. Duan, Y. Sun

15.1 BACKGROUND

The age of social media is upon us. People tend to use social media tools such as Twitter to broadcast their moods, opinions, and status. It is possible to gage the sentiment of people through Twitter sentiment analysis. The question that is explored in this chapter is whether the weather impacts human emotion. This requires a Big Data processing infrastructure that scales to millions of people and their changing moods over time with extensive disaggregated weather data.

Does the weather affect an individual's emotion? From a biological perspective, different types of weather conditions can potentially increase or decrease chemical responses in the brain, which can influence an individual's sense of happiness. However, there is no definitive scientific result that this is the case for all people, and often weather can impact a person's emotions in less obvious ways. Most physiologists agree that human emotion can be remarkably affected by weather [1].

In this context, John [2] identifies that higher temperatures can elevate an individual's mood, however, this depends on the country. Scandinavian countries, for example, have prolonged cool and dark weather where sun can improve the emotional well-being of an individual. In countries such as Australia, excessive heat can have the opposite effect. Given this, many believe that location plays an important role on the impact of weather on the emotional well-being of individuals. Denissen et al. [3] found that the weather's daily influence has more of an impact on a person's negative mood, rather than helping establish a positive mood. Hsiang et al. [4] found a link between human aggression and higher temperatures.

Understanding a global and systematic evaluation of weather and emotional well-being (sentiment) demands that a Big Data approach is supported. Fortunately, through the global popularity of social media the opportunity exists to explore the correlation between emotion and weather in a much faster, more comprehensive, and less expensive way than other more traditional approaches, conducting large-scale population surveys, for example. Users tend to post tweets broadcasting the emotions, thoughts, ideas, and opinions encountered in their lives. Thus, there is direct or indirect evidence provided by this user-generated content [1].

The task of extracting emotion information from tweets refers to sentiment analysis, which is defined as automatically determining the valence (positive and negative dimension) of a piece of text [5]. Researchers tend to simply use presence or absence of sentiment terms in sentences to determine the valence [1]. Furthermore, there are many frameworks that have been proposed for sentiment analysis, however, little benchmarking has been done on which is most accurate.

Through Big Data and the application of machine-learning techniques, it is possible to explore whether the correlation between emotion and weather exists, and ultimately, quantify it. There are many forms of social media data. In this chapter, we focus on Twitter due to its openly accessible APIs and the geospatial query capabilities.

The rest of this chapter is structured as follows. We first introduce the system architecture and associated cloud-based Big Data processing software stack. Following this, we introduce the approach taken for machine learning and sentiment analysis with justification for features selection and models adopted based on their accuracy. Following this, we introduce the methodology for correlation analysis and visualization and interpretation of results. Finally we present our key findings related to the correlation between sentiment and weather.

15.2 BIG DATA SYSTEM COMPONENTS

In this section, we introduce the system architecture and associated software stack that is used for Big Data analytics on the cloud.

15.2.1 SYSTEM BACK-END ARCHITECTURE

The back-end architecture is realized through Python (version 2.7) and the noSQL database CouchDB. Python 2.7 is used to compile programs for fetching and filtering Twitter and weather data, for sentiment analysis and integrating data collection based on views. In contrast, CouchDB is responsible for data storage, view creation, and the return view result to the website.

As shown in Fig. 1, the system includes two external sources of data and one internal source. The Twitter streaming API provides a targeted location's raw tweets, which are content-filtered and sentiment-analyzed before being stored in the CouchDB. We focus explicitly on those tweets including geo-location information. During this work, we collected over 700,000 tweets from eight Australian cities and over 33,000 tweets from 174 suburbs in Melbourne. A list of cities and suburbs follows:

1. Name of eight cities:

Name of cities			
Melbourne	Canberra	Brisbane	Sydney
Perth	Adelaide	Hobart	Darwin

2. Name of 174 Melbourne suburbs:
   We explored 174 suburbs in Melbourne. The shopping mall and coast suburbs explored were:
   - Shopping Malls
     HighPoint Shopping Centre, Emporium, Chadstone Shopping Centre, Essendon DFO, and South Wharf DFO.
   - Cxoast suburbs
     Altona, Altona Meadows, Seaholme, Williamstown, Port Melbourne, Newport, Albert Park, St. Kilda West, St, Kilda, Elwood, Brighton, and Middle Park.

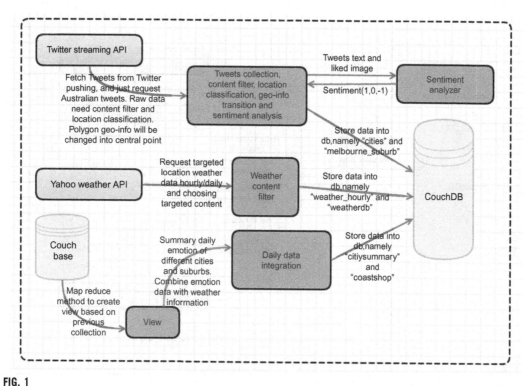

FIG. 1

System back-end architecture.

In terms of weather data, daily and hourly weather data was obtained from the Yahoo weather API for these eight cities. Based on the weather and tweets collection, we utilized cloud-based MapReduce methods to create the views of the data. These views are used for web site requests and to provide data to daily integration programs. We have two scheduled integration programs (for city and suburb levels) that are used for calculating the summary of emotions and their relationship with daily weather.

15.2.2 SYSTEM FRONT-END ARCHITECTURE

The web service architecture support capabilities to present data. The core technologies implemented include HTML5, CSS3, JavaScript, AJAX, Google Maps API (based on JQuery), eChart API, and Bootstrap for the responsive web design. The main presentation of information utilizes eChart and Google API, which support asynchronous communication with the server.

As we can see from Fig. 2, some functions of the web-based front end require data directly from CouchDB. These data are created in the back end using MapReduce methods to generate views in CouchDB.

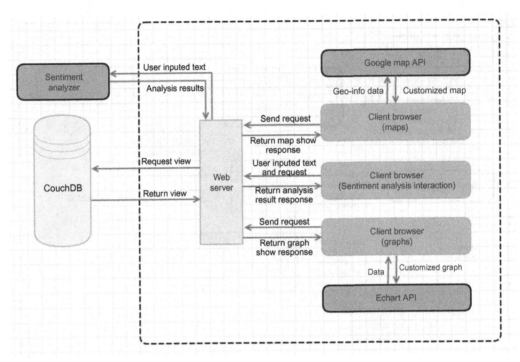

FIG. 2

System front-end architecture.

15.2.3 SOFTWARE STACK

Fig. 3 presents the software stack that was adopted in this work.

To support sentiment analysis, various approaches were explored: toolkits such as the Natural Language Toolkit (NLTK), open CV, Pattern, and SK Learn packages NLTK support preprocessing of tweet text contents, and also offer the Naïve Bayes supervisor to implement frequency of terms analysis. Open CV is used for analysis of images associated with Twitter profiles. Pattern is a mature tweet sentiment analysis tool that is based on parts of speech (POS), which are used for computational linguistics analysis. Each of these tools is used to generate features for sentiment analysis. SK learning is subsequently used to apply these features to different machine-learning models and finally return the analyzed results.

15.3 MACHINE-LEARNING METHODOLOGY

There are many ways to support machine learning and analysis of data. In this chapter, we used the Naïve Bayes machine-learning technique as our baseline approach. After that we utilize deep supervised machine-learning techniques, including random forest (RF) [6], support vector machine (SVM) [7], and logistic regression (LR) [8], which are applied to classify the emotion (sentiment) of tweets.

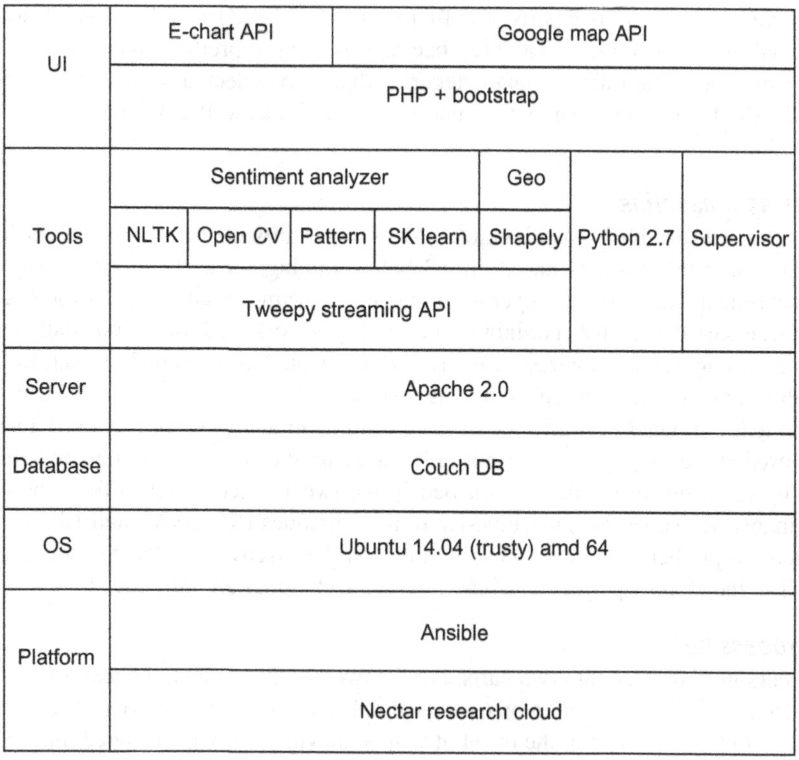

UI	E-chart API	Google map API					
	PHP + bootstrap						
Tools	Sentiment analyzer				Geo	Python 2.7	Supervisor
	NLTK	Open CV	Pattern	SK learn	Shapely		
	Tweepy streaming API						
Server	Apache 2.0						
Database	Couch DB						
OS	Ubuntu 14.04 (trusty) amd 64						
Platform	Ansible						
	Nectar research cloud						

FIG. 3

Software stack in the system.

For correlation analysis, an unsupervised machine learning (density-based spatial clustering of applications with noise (DBSCAN) cluster algorithm [9]) and time series are implemented to explore the relation between weather and tweets clusters and their emotions.

15.3.1 TWEETS SENTIMENT ANALYSIS

Text-based sentiment analysis is a well-studied area. Go et al. (2009) [10] point out that an accuracy of 82.9% can be achieved with SVM and a simple unigram model. They also mention several important attributes that differentiate twitter messages from other text-based resources. First, the length of a twitter message is restricted to 140 characters. This means that multiple-sentence-based sentiment analysis is not suitable. In addition, twitter users tend to use slang and abbreviations to express their opinions. There are already developed tools for supporting this task, for exapmle, the Pattern module of Python, which focuses on word level sentiment classification. For this project, due to the limited length of tweets, the word becomes more significant to the sentiment of a sentence. In addition, it also includes slang such as: "lol," which is commonplace in Twitter.

This section is divided into five parts. The first is mainly related to our baseline of tweet sentiment analysis. Second, we focus on how data preprocessing is used to produce machine-learning features. The next part illustrates the training data categories that were selected. Finally, we demonstrate the classifiers (RF, SVM, and LR) and how their parameters are set as well as their corresponding learning curves.

Naïve Bayes as a baseline

The most direct way to establish a user's emotion in tweets is through the textual content. Traditionally, terms-frequency statistics features based on a labeled training set is the simplest way to predict a tweet's text sentiment. Naïve Bayes supervised machine learning usually is used for this purpose. To this end, it is necessary to establish a training data set. In this work, 80% of our manually labeled tweets were used as a training set, and the rest of the tweets are treated as the actual test set. Regrettably, the accuracy of this approach was limited, achieving just 54%.

In order to achieve better performance of tweet sentiment analysis, we proposed a novel solution whereby we predict the tweet's emotion not only based on the tweet's text content sentiment analysis, but also by referring to the picture attached in the tweets. According to those two dimensions, better performance for supervised machine-learning techniques (RF, SVM, and LR) was supported. The dimensions of prediction on a tweet's emotion will be discussed in the Section 15.3.1.4. In the Section 15.3.1.8, the aforementioned machine-learning techniques are introduced.

Tweet preprocessing

Tweet preprocessing is divided into two parts. For the tweet's text content, the text needs to be filtered, for example, to remove Unicode for emojis, external links, and special strings ('#' and '@'). Second, if there is picture or photo attached to the tweet, it will be downloaded via its source link.

Training set

The main training set contained 2613 tweets (data available at: http://115.146.86.188:5984/_utils/database.html?traindata), which are labeled manually. It includes 395 negative tweets, 1079 neutral tweets, and 1139 positive tweets. Examples of these tweets are presented in Table 1.

Feature engineering

There are three kinds of features. The first one is the twitter sentiment score, which includes the Pattern Sentiment Parser and sentiment word-frequency classification. The second category is based on the color of images and the last one explores an analysis of the images, for exapmle, for smile detection.

Table 1 Example of Labeled Tweets

Sentiment	Example
Negative	@Ducky_Tape ugh sorry — I'm on MEL-AUH-AMS in a month
Neutral	The MDA game framework can be applied outside of game design.
Positive	Glazing today. Think we're gonna need a bigger kiln!!

Twitter sentiment score feature

There are four features in this part (Pattern Sentiment Parser [11], the number of positive words divided by the length of sentence, the number of negative words divided by the length and sentiment word-frequency classification). The second and third features are used to take the length of a sentence and the ratio of positive and negative words into consideration. They are also based on the Pattern Sentiment Parser. The last one is based on the labeled data.

The first feature can be illustrated as shown in Fig. 4. The main process of the Parser method is to get a POS tagged Unicode string. The POS is a method to remove the ambiguous content of an English sentence. Actually, Pattern tags the word according to the Brill's rule's based tagger v1.14 and Penn TreebankII tag set. In order to increase the accuracy of tagging, Pattern generates its own lexical references as a dictionary. For example, except for Eric Brill's tag dictionary (1992), the en-lexion.txt has introduced Twitter POS annotated data provided by Carnegie Mellon University (2011). Some of the support references have been trained under the Brown Corpus and Penn Treebank. Thus, the part-of-speech tagging for tweets is much more accurate through the Pattern Parser method.

Based on the result of the Parser process, the Sentiment method calculates the degree of sentiment according to its own sentimental lexical resource. This dictionary assigns to each synset of Wordnet 3.0 and collects about 2900 adjectives with sentiment polarity. Thus, this process of sentiment extracts the adjectives from the previous results and then establishes the score from the lexical resources. Finally, the score of sentiment is given as a figure from −1 to 1.

Color degree feature

Currently, people tend to post photos without words in social media. This cannot be used for sentiment analysis using the measures herein. This work requires two parts (color degree and smile detection) to handle this challenge. According to the report of Feng et al. [12], colors have a relationship with a range of emotions. Among them, the color with the most significant relationship with emotion is black, which is associated with sadness, anger, and fear, and hence expresses negative emotion. In this project, color degree is calculated as $\mathrm{sum}(\mathrm{red}+\mathrm{blue}+\mathrm{green})/(3*\mathrm{graphsize})$. When the graph is black, this value can be near to zero. As a result, it can be used to evaluate the degree of blackness.

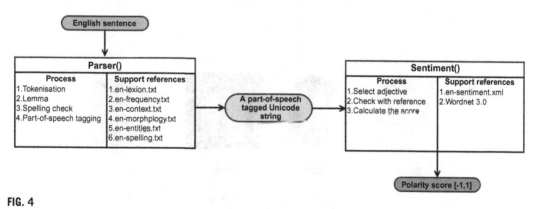

FIG. 4

The process of sentiment analysis in pattern module.

Smile detection feature

For smile detection, Haar feature-based cascade classifiers proposed by Viola and Jones [13] have been applied. This algorithm includes four stages as shown in Fig. 5.

The cascade function is the core part of this algorithm. It is trained with a considerable amount of right and wrong pictures. In the OpenCV package, there are pretrained classifiers for faces and smiles that are stored as XML files. In this project, the "haarcascade_frontalface_default.xml" is used to detect faces and "haarcascade_smile.xml" is applied to detect smiles. To increase the accuracy, a smile can only be detected when it is within a face.

As Fig. 6 shows, a smile detected, a face detected, other photo, and no photo are converted to the values 2, 1, 0, and −1 respectively as feature values. In the case where multiple smiles are detected, this is also equal to 2. If someone posts a neutral tweet (based on their text) but with a photo including a smile, it would be recognized overall as a positive tweet.

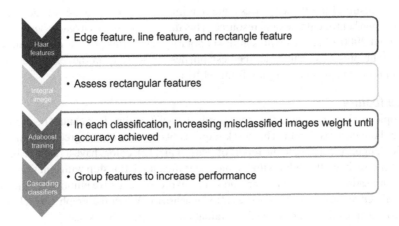

FIG. 5

Haar cascade algorithm steps.

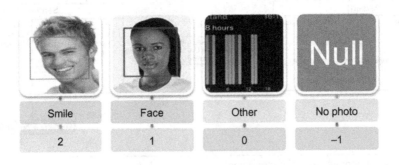

FIG. 6

Smile and face detection to smile feature value.

Classifier models

A range of machine-learning techniques (SVM, RF, LR, and ensemble stacking [14]) have been explored in this chapter. This section includes an evaluation of the system robustness through the learning curve and reliability in indicating sentiment through Precision, Recall, and F1-scores [15].

In addition, the parameters for each model have been optimized with a grid search method. The grid search in this project is used to examine all the combinations of proposed parameters for each estimator. The grid search is based on fivefold crossvalidation and evaluation metrics for Precision. Due to this exhaustive search, there are too many combinations of results.

To evaluate whether current classifiers are reliable, the learning curve graph is drawn. The horizontal axis corresponds to the number of samples (from 10%, 20% ... to a 100% training set) and the vertical axis corresponds to the accuracy score. The score is the mean accuracy for threefold crossvalidation of that part of the dataset. A smaller value implies that fewer instances are misclassified. The difference between cross-validation scores and training scores is used to determine whether the model is robust enough. If the gap of these two scores is large, it means the model may overfit the training set. Otherwise, it means the training error and test error are similar, and hence, the model is robust.

Support vector machine

As Hsu et al. [16] demonstrate, SVM is a non-probabilistic classifier, which uses hyper-plane with the maximum margin for vectors (support vectors) to divide data into different categories. It can be quite robust for the training data due to the maximum margin. The formula of SVM is:

$$\frac{1}{2}w^{\mathrm{T}}w + C\sum_{i=1}^{l}\xi_i$$

$$\text{Subject to } y_i\left(w^{\mathrm{T}}\varnothing(x_i)+b\right) \geq 1-\xi_i, \ \xi_i \geq 0 \tag{1}$$

Here x_i stands for an instance with attributes, y_i represents corresponding label, and l is the total number of instances. The x_i is mapped to a higher dimension by the function $\varnothing$. The hyper-plane in this dimension divides the data based on the maximum distance. The C is the penalty for error-classified points. In this chapter, there are two kernels: linear and radial basis function kernels. Their formulas are:

$$\text{Linear: } K\left(x_i, x_j\right) = x_i^{\mathrm{T}} x_j \tag{2}$$

$$\text{Radial basis function: } K\left(x_i, x_j\right) = \exp\left(-\gamma \left\| x_i - x_j \right\|^2\right), \gamma > 0 \tag{3}$$

To make a robust SVM model, it is essential to optimize the parameters setting. Table 2 shows how the following parameters were tested. When the kernel is linear and the "C" penalty is equal to 1, it produces the highest precision (0.703).

Table 2 SVM Parameters for Grid Search		
Kernel	C	Gamma
Radial basis function (RBF)	1, 10, 100, 1000	1e-3, 1e-4
Linear	1, 10, 100, 1000	

There are two learning curve graphs. One uses the default parameters. The other applies the optimized parameters. As we can see from Figs. 7 and 8, after being optimized, the difference between the training score and the cross-validation reduces and the final score increases from 0.62 to 0.66.

Random forest

RF is an ensemble learning technique which implements a large number of decision trees based on different samples and different feature combinations. The final prediction depends on the majority of predictions from the trees mentioned herein. Generally, it combines Breiman's "bagging" and random feature selection [17]. As the number of trees increase, the accuracy increases. However, the speed gets slower. In most cases, 100 trees are sufficient. In this work, the number of trees is slightly more than that (110 trees). The formula for RF tree is:

$$\hat{f} = \frac{1}{B}\sum_{b=1}^{B}\hat{f}_b(x')$$

(4)

Here $\hat{f}$ stands for the final tree prediction; "B" is the total number of trees; "b" represents the current tree and x' is the training sample.

The experiment parameters for RF are as follows. The *max_depth* stands for the maximum depth of the tree. When it is "None," it would stop only when all leaves are pure or less than the number of minimum sample splits. The *max_features* is the number of features of the optimized tree division. The *min_samples_leaf* is the least number of samples for a leaf. There are two main criteria to divide a tree. One is Gini impurity. The other is Information gain. They are represented as "gini" and entropy, respectively, in Table 3.

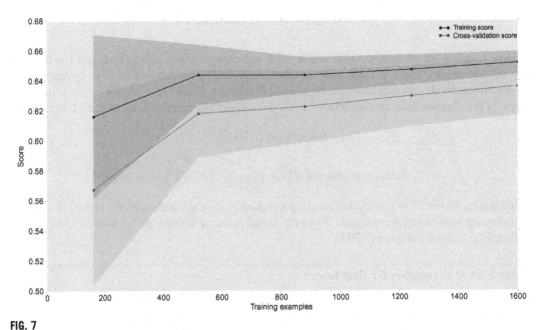

FIG. 7

Default SVM parameter setting learning curve.

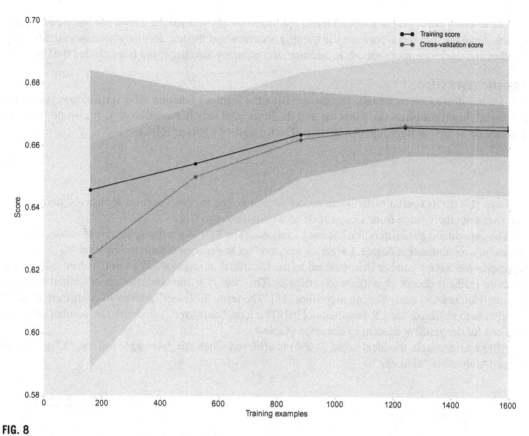

FIG. 8

Optimized SVM parameter setting learning curve.

Table 3 RF Parameters for Grid Search

Max_depth	Max_features	Min_samples_split	Min_samples_leaf	Criterion
3, none	1, 3, 6	1, 3, 10	1, 3, 10	Gini, entropy

Their formulas are as follows:

$$\text{Gini: } I_G(f) = \sum_{i=1}^{m} f_i(1 - f_i) \tag{5}$$

$$\text{Information gain: } I_E(f) = -\sum_{i=1}^{m} f_i \log_2 f_i \tag{6}$$

Here f_i is the probability of being correctly classified. In this case, the highest score 0.689 is achieved with the following parameters ($min\_samples\_leaf = 10$, $min\_samples\_split = 10$, $criterion = \text{gini}$, $max\_features = 3$, $max\_depth = 3$).

The learning curve graphs for default and optimized parameters RF are shown in Figs. 9 and 10. It is apparent that the difference between the training accuracy and the test accuracy becomes significantly smaller, and therefore, more robust. In addition, the accuracy also improves from around 0.65 to 0.68.

Logistic regression

LR is a transformation of a linear regression using the sigmoid function. The vertical axis stands for the probability for a given classification and the horizontal axis is the value of x. It assumes that the distribution of $y|x$ is Bernoulli distribution. The formula of LR is as follows:

$$F(x) = \frac{1}{1 + e^{-(\beta_0 + \beta_1 x)}} \tag{7}$$

Here $\beta_0 + \beta_1 x$ is similar to the linear model $y = ax + b$. The logistic function applies a sigmoid function to restrict the y value from a large scale to within the range 0–1.

The experiment parameters for LR are as follows. The "C" is similar to the SVM model. It is an inverse of a regularization degree. Larger values stand for lower regularization. The term "fit_intercept" represents a constant number that is added to the LR decision function. The term "solver" allows for different gradient decent algorithms to set the β_i. The "lbfgs" is the abbreviation of limited-memory Royden-Fletcher-Goldfarb-Shanno algorithm [18]. The term "liblinear" applies to coordinate descent algorithms to optimize the LR parameters [19]. The term "max_iter" stands for the number of times required for the gradient descent to converge (Table 4).

After a grid search, the ideal score (0.686) is achieved when "fit_intercept" is True, "C" equals to 1.0 and "solver" is "liblinear."

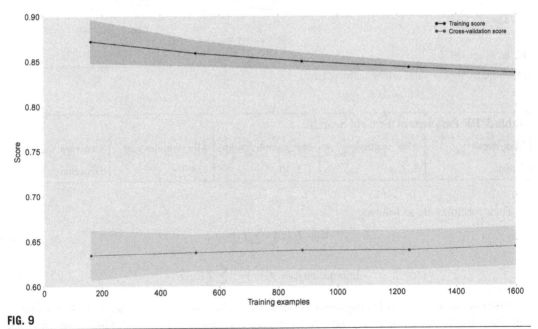

FIG. 9

Default RF parameter setting learning curve.

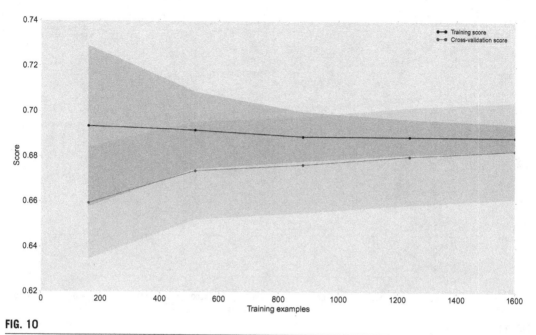

FIG. 10

Optimized RF parameter setting learning curve.

Table 4 LR Parameters for Grid Search			
C	Fit_intercept	Solver	Max_iter
1.0, 1e5	True, false	lbfgs, liblinear	100, 200

The learning curve graphs for default and optimized parameters of LR are shown in Figs. 11 and 12. As seen, the difference between training accuracy and test accuracy gradually reduces, however, the accuracy shows no improvement.

Stacking

From the preceding results, it is difficult to choose which algorithm is better for this topic because their scores are similar to each other. As a result, a stacking ensemble method is applied to achieve a more accurate prediction. This is based on a weighting system used for prediction of the final result. If all classifier predictions are different from each other, the prediction is dependent on the SVM classifier, due to its robustness and accuracy. After application of this method, overall performance is improved, as shown in Table 5.

The resultant learning curve (see Fig. 13) is more robust than the single model and the accuracy achieved is around 0.8. This means that less misclassification occurs and that the model is not over/under-fit based on the training data set.

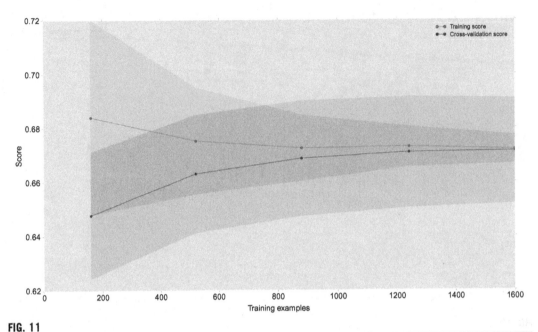

FIG. 11

Default LR parameter setting learning curve.

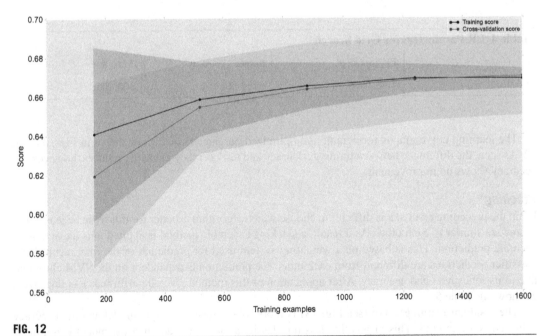

FIG. 12

Optimized LR parameter setting learning curve.

Table 5 Comparison for Overall Performance

Method	Precision	Recall	F1-score
SVM	0.79	0.78	0.77
LR	0.77	0.76	0.75
RF	0.74	0.73	0.73
Stack	0.8	0.8	0.79

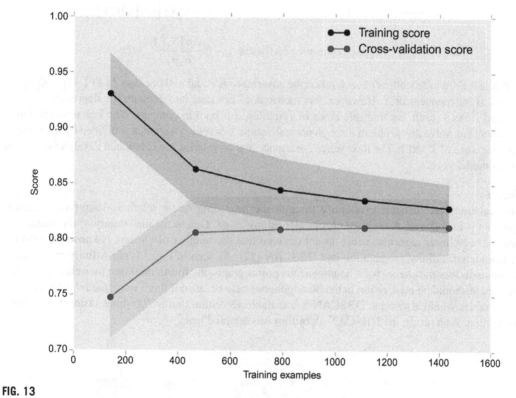

FIG. 13

Stacking method with three optimized learning algorithms.

15.3.2 WEATHER AND EMOTION CORRELATION ANALYSIS

In this section, two approaches are introduced to determine the correlation between weather and emotion. One is based on a time series, whilst the other is based on a cluster algorithm. For the time series, the covariance is used to evaluate whether two variables are independent and the Pearson correlation coefficient is introduced to evaluate the degree of relation [20]. For the clustering algorithm, a comparison using the DBSCAN cluster method is chosen and its corresponding evaluation metrics are shown.

Time series

Time series analysis can evaluate whether two variables are correlated over time. It takes the order of events into consideration rather than only evaluating two variables [21]. The formula for time series is:

$$Y_t = \beta_0 + \beta X_t + u_t \tag{8}$$

Here Y_t, X_t are the variables Y and X value at time t, u_t is a constant number similar to β_0 but it takes time into consideration.

There are two metrics used to evaluate the correlation degree: the covariance and the Pearson correlation coefficient. Their formulas are given as:

$$\text{Covariance: } \sigma(X,Y) = E\big[(X - E[X])(Y - E[Y])\big] = E[XY] - E[X]E[Y] \tag{9}$$

$$\text{Pearson correlation coefficient: } \rho_{X,Y} = \frac{\text{cov}(X,Y)}{\sigma_X \sigma_Y} \tag{10}$$

If X and Y are independent of each other, the covariance is equal to 0 because $E[XY] - E[X]E[Y] = 0$ when X is independent of Y. However, this metric does not take into account the degree of variance of X and Y. As a result, for multiple kinds of variables, it is hard to compare. The Pearson correlation coefficient can solve this problem through normalization, whereby covariance is divided by the product of the variance of X and Y. The time series covariance and correlation are calculated through the Python Pandas model [21].

Cluster

Some relations are difficult to identify through the preceding linear relation. Therefore, a cluster algorithm is introduced. A range of cluster algorithms exists. Due to the uncertainty of the number of clusters, two cluster algorithms that do not demand that the number of clusters is known in advance are considered: affinity propagation and DBSCAN [22]. As seen in Fig. 14, the Affinity propagation algorithm divides the cluster for a homogeneous points graph (the fourth one) into four clusters. In this work, there should be no division in the homogeneous case because if there were, the relation between two variables would also exist. DBSCAN is a scalable algorithm that is 200 times faster than affinity propagation. As a result, the DBSCAN algorithm was adopted here.

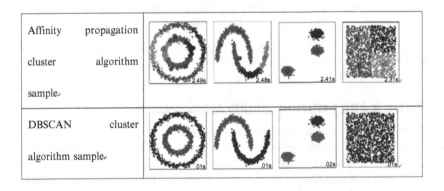

FIG. 14

Cluster algorithms comparison [12].

DBSCAN definition

DBSCAN can cluster points as a cluster if they are close to (nearby) each other and recognize outlier points if the point is far away from the most nearby point [23].

Manifold algorithm

There are a considerable number of possibilities for the correlation between weather and emotion: high/cold temperatures and positive/negative emotion, rain/wind and positive/negative emotion. To support this, we produce two 2D similarity planes to detect whether there exists a correlation between two general categories (weather phenomenon and sentiment). The Isomap method calculates the distance between points through the shortest path algorithm (Dijkstra's algorithm [24]) rather than the Euclidean distance. There are three stages in supporting this method. First, it conducts a nearest neighbor search. Following this, the Dijkstra's algorithm is implemented to find the nearest path for the identified points. Last, it uses partial eigenvalue decomposition to reduce the dimension to the request dimension [25].

Cluster evaluation metrics

Two metrics are introduced to evaluate the clustering results: the Silhouette coefficient (SC) [26] and Adjusted Rand index (ARI) [27]. Their formulas are as follows:

$$SC = \frac{(b-a)}{\max(a,b)} \tag{11}$$

$$ARI = \frac{(RI - \text{expected}(RI))}{(\max(RI) - \text{expected}(RI))} \tag{12}$$

The SC is used to evaluate whether points are clustered well and separated well. Here the "b" represents the average nearest cluster distance for every sample and "a" stands for the mean cluster centroid distance. If two clusters are near each other, this value would be near to 0. If they overlap, the value would be nearer to −1 [26].

The Adjusted Rand score is introduced to determine whether two cluster results are similar to each other. In the formula, the "RI" stands for the rand index, which calculates a similarity between two cluster results by taking all points identified within the same cluster. This value is equal to 0 when points are assigned into clusters randomly and it equals to 1 when the two cluster results are same [27]. This metric is used to evaluate whether dimension-reduced similarity cluster results are similar to one other.

15.4 SYSTEM IMPLEMENTATION

In this section, the Big Data processing and analysis functions implemented in the system are introduced. The web front end consists of three main parts: a home page, a sentiment page and a weather page. Their content and functions are described here.

15.4.1 HOME PAGE

Fig. 15 shows the function used to present and analyze tweets. The sentiment analyzer program analyses tweets as they are harvested before they are stored into CouchDB. Additionally, the tweets' geo-location has been marked in the map. Second, historical weather information and summarized emotion situations of eight cities has been provided for users to search according to the cities' name and specific dates.

FIG. 15

Home page in the web site.

15.4.2 SENTIMENT PAGES

The sentiment pages consist of a features description page, a models description page and a test your-self page. The previous pages are used to introduce the features and models utilized in the sentiment analysis process. Fig. 16 illustrates an interaction page provided for users to interact with the sentiment analyzer program. After the user types the text of interest, the system will return and display the analysis results for each model and a final result.

15.4.3 WEATHER PAGES

The weather pages implement the front-end data visualization in the system. This allows exploring the correlation between emotion and weather from the whole city down to individual suburb levels. Fig. 17

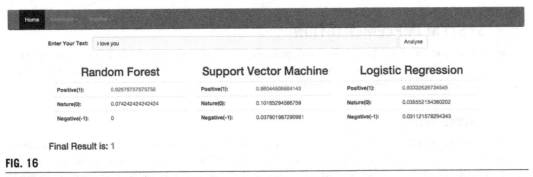

FIG. 16

Interaction functions in web site.

FIG. 17

Heat map for Melbourne suburbs.

shows a heat map illustrating the tweet distribution across Melbourne. Users can further view the tweet distribution based on temporal aspects, for exapmle, a given date.

Fig. 18 shows a more detailed scenario of Twitter sentiment across the Melbourne suburbs. Here the map in the middle displays the suburbs under consideration. The coastal suburbs area and shopping mall locations can also be highlighted and marked in the map. Thus, it is hypothesized that in extremely hot weather many people go to malls where it is cooler. The system allows exploration of such phenomenon. Additionally, users can visualize the distribution of emotions in different areas compared to the whole of Melbourne, factoring in the temperature and other phenomenon (Fig. 19, left). Further functions include allowing users to choose the data to be included in the graphs. For example, users can adjust the average emotion graph to show only negative emotions and adjust the period of time of interest (Fig. 19, right).

It is worth mentioning that in order to objectively present the trend of emotion change, the first curve graph in Fig. 19 is generated via calculating daily the ratio of percentage of positive/negative sentiment in shopping mall/coastal areas against the percentage of positive and negative sentiment for the whole Melbourne area.

Fig. 20 shows the data for different Australian cities. As seen, three graphs are used to present the data (the average emotion, the temperature and the corresponding tweets numbers). Customization functions are offered to control the content and display of the graphs. Users can also access different cities' data via the navigation buttons on the graphs.

Finally, the weather condition of the web front end presents the positive and negative tweets percentages as well as the total tweets number based on different weather conditions (clear, cloudy, rainy, sunny, and windy). Fig. 21 shows the percentage of emotions displayed through a pie graph. Additionally, the bar graph is used to present the total number of tweets. Fig. 21 has been generated via calculating the average of daily positive emotion percentages based on specific weather conditions

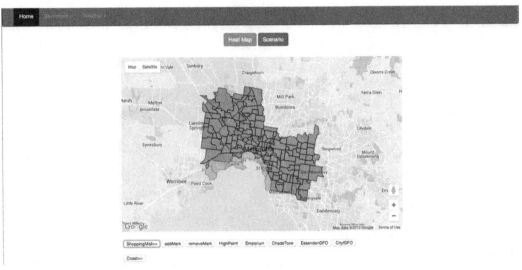

FIG. 18

Map for Melbourne suburbs.

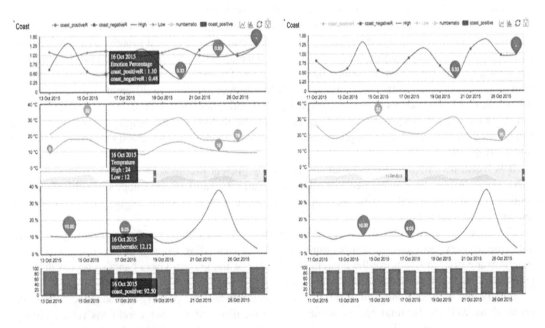

FIG. 19

Original graphs for coast suburbs *(left)* and customized graphs *(right)*.

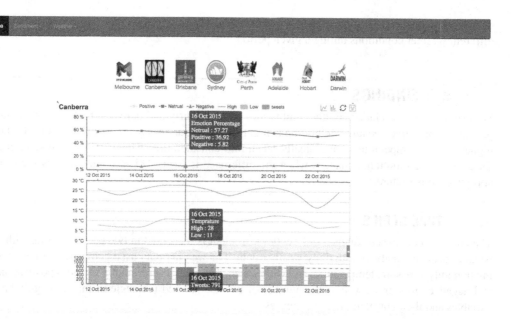

FIG. 20

Web pages for eight Australian cities.

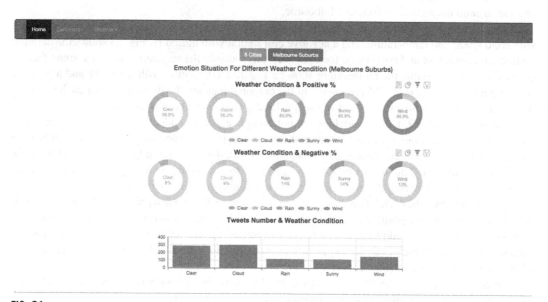

FIG. 21

Web page for presenting data for specific weather conditions.

during a given period. The data in the bar graph in Fig. 21 shows the average number of daily tweets in different weather conditions during a given period.

15.5 KEY FINDINGS

We explored the correlation weather and twitter data at hourly and daily intervals. Hourly data is especially informative because Melbourne can get through four seasons in one day. For daily data, the highest/lowest temperatures are typically taken into consideration. This is still useful since it allows for establishing emotional changes when the difference is large. This section explores the results of applying infrastructure.

15.5.1 TIME SERIES

The correlation between weather and Twitter sentiment is presented in two parts: analysis with hourly weather data and analysis with daily weather data. The weather data used comprises variables including humidity, pressure, temperature, and wind speed. The twitter information includes positive, neutral, and negative emotion as well as the number of tweets. The red rectangle in Fig. 22 highlights these variables and their correlation scatter figures.

15.5.2 ANALYSIS WITH HOURLY WEATHER DATA

This section contains three scenarios. The first scenario is the overall Melbourne analysis. The second scenario is twitter information from air-conditioned shopping malls. The last one is based on Twitter analysis around the coastal regions of Melbourne.

As seen from Fig. 22, the red rectangle shows tweet numbers expressing a positive correlation with wind speed and temperature, and a negative correlation with humidity. Fig. 23 shows the detailed correlation coefficient and covariance for each variable. Outside the rectangle, there are some further correlations. For example, the temperature shows a negative correlation with humidity and a positive correlation with wind speed. The red curves in the diagonal area are the distribution for each variable. As we can see from those curves, most of them exhibit a Gaussian-like distribution.

As seen from Fig. 23, twitter variables are not completely independent because covariance is not equal to zero. Furthermore, the tweet numbers show a strong positive correlation with temperature with around a 0.45 correlation coefficient and a negative correlation with humidity with around a −0.58 correlation coefficient. This means people tend to tweet less when the humidity is high or when the temperature is low. However, the emotion shows a marginal correlation with weather attributes.

Fig. 24 shows that the correlation coefficient in shopping malls for each pair is similar to the overall area figure. However, the positive percentage becomes a little more positively correlated with humidity than the overall graph. In addition, the number of tweets is less related to weather attributes than the overall figure, even though both are negatively correlated with humidity, but positively correlated to other weather phenomenon (Fig. 25).

Twitter data of people tweeting in nearby coastal regions shows less correlation with weather attributes, with all emotion attributes' correlation coefficients near to zero.

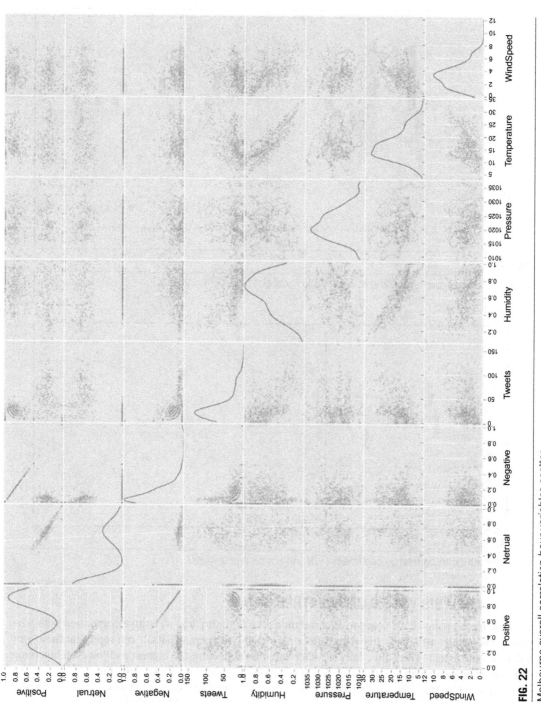

FIG. 22

Melbourne overall correlation hour variables scatter.

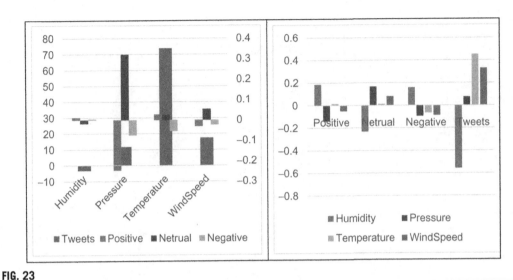

FIG. 23

Melbourne overall covariance *(left)* and correlation *(right)*.

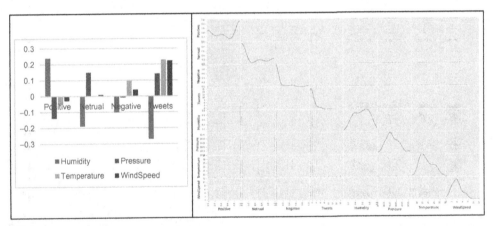

FIG. 24

Shop area attributes correlation coefficient *(left)* and scatter graph *(right)*.

15.5.3 ANALYSIS WITH DAILY WEATHER DATA

As seen, temperature shows a negative correlation with humidity and a positive correlation with wind speed. The results also obey this observation. As a result, temperature itself can represent these variables to some extent. Therefore, daily weather variables reflecting the highest and lowest temperature differences in one day are aligned with Twitter sentiment analysis as shown from Fig. 26.

As seen in Fig. 26, Twitter and temperature variables are not independent of one other. However, the correlation coefficient (0.35) is not as significant as the overall correlation. Although the correlation is low, the

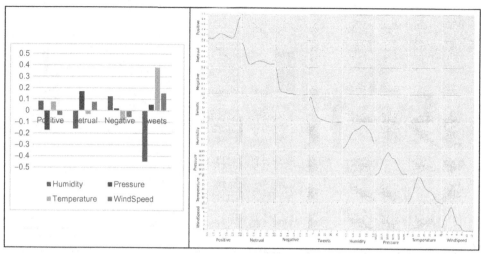

FIG. 25

Coast area attributes correlation *(left)* and scatter graph *(right)*.

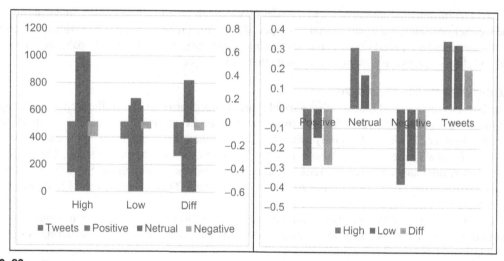

FIG. 26

Melbourne overall covariance *(left)* and correlation *(right)*.

correlation figure still shows that people tend to post more positive and negative tweets when the temperature is low, and they tend to post more tweets when the temperature is high or the difference is significant.

Fig. 27 shows the correlation in coastal and air-conditioned shopping areas. Surprisingly, the difference between the highest and lowest temperatures and the percentage of negative tweeters in coastal areas exhibit a strong negative correlation. One reason for this might be that when the difference becomes large, coastal areas tend to have unpredictable weather patterns.

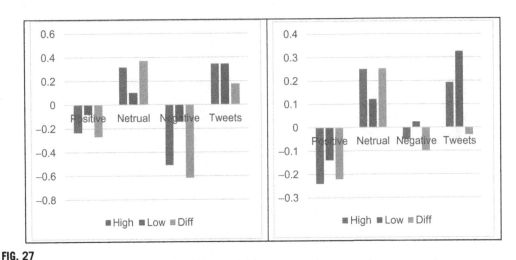

FIG. 27

Coast *(left)* and shop *(right)* area correlation.

15.5.4 DBSCAN CLUSTER ALGORITHM

The weather information considered here includes humidity, air pressure, temperature, and wind speed. The weather condition is also introduced to support dimensional reduction. The dimensional reduction results are aimed at general observations for the integrated data. For each variable pair, the top three high SC cluster results are presented to evaluate their correlation.

Dimensional reduction analysis

Four Twitter variables and four weather variables are reduced into two 2D similarity planes through the manifold algorithm Isomap. As seen from Table 6, the SC for these two cases is quite different, the Weather 2D plane SC is only around 0.32. This means this cluster is not separated well. However for the Twitter plane, whilst it achieves a high SC, it only has one cluster. This implies the cluster result cannot be used to predict weather relationships. Although the SC is 0.76, a single cluster is still a good result. As for the ARI, it is near to zero. This means it is hard to distinguish one category from another.

Weather variables within weather conditions were also explored. The weather conditions are categorized into five variables: clear, sunny, rain, wind, and cloud. The result of this clustering is shown in Table 7.

As seen from Table 7, the SC for these two cases is not high — both are under 0.4. This means the clusters are not separated well. As for the ARI, it is near to zero. This means it is still hard to

Table 6 Weather and Twitter Cluster Result			
Cluster Results	**Cluster Number**	**SC**	**ARI**
Weather 2D plane	6	0.3257532551	0.0501659952
Twitter 2D plane	1	0.7642227912	0.0501659952

Table 7 Weather with Condition and Twitter Cluster Result

Cluster Results	Cluster Number	SC	ARI
Weather 2D plane	5	0.211608929	0.009202134
Twitter 2D plane	8	0.376280428	0.009202134

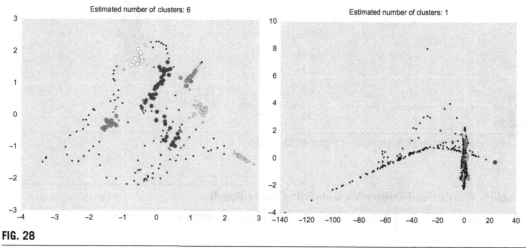

FIG. 28

Weather *(left)* and twitter *(right)* cluster graph.

predict one category with another. Fig. 28 shows the clustering results. As seen, the dimension reduction results are not ideal. The reason is that any manifold algorithm leads to information loss. There may be some important information that is dropped during that process. The following figure shows the clustering of results. The black points are outliers and the grey/lighter points are points within a given cluster (Fig. 29).

Pair variable analysis

Next, each weather and Twitter variable is paired to build cluster figures. There are considerable combination possibilities. This report presents three cluster results with high SCs while the number of clusters is greater than 1.

As seen from above Table 8 and Fig. 30, Twitter emotion indeed correlates with temperature and humidity because the clusters are separated well and can be used to predict one another. For example, as the graph in the middle shows, if humidity is high, the positive percentage of tweets tends to be large because there are high-density red points on the upper-right corner of this graph. This reflects the prediction from the time series distribution given.

15.5.5 STRAIGHTFORWARD WEATHER IMPACT ON EMOTION

In this section, findings of correlations between emotion and weather based on the graphs provided, and the Big Data processing infrastructure will be discussed.

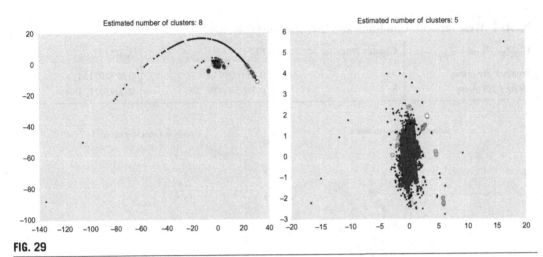

FIG. 29

Weather with condition *(left)* and twitter *(right)* cluster graph.

Table 8 Weather and Twitter Variable Pair Cluster Result

Weather Variable	Twitter Variable	Number of Cluster	SC
Temperature	Neutral %	3	0.58998
Humidity	Positive %	2	0.52402
Temperature	Positive %	3	0.48529

Higher temperature makes people happier in Melbourne coast

As seen from Fig. 31, people who live in coastal suburbs are the most affected by highest temperatures. There is a trend showing that when the temperature increases, the percentage of positive tweets increases. When the highest temperature reduces, the percentage of positive tweets follows a similar trend.

People prefer windy days in Melbourne

Fig. 32 shows the highest factor affecting the percentage of positive and negative sentiment is the wind. It is also noted that 85% of people exhibit a positive emotion in rainy weather, while only 15% of people exhibit a negative emotion. Furthermore, it can be observed that people tend to post tweets in clear weather conditions.

15.6 SUMMARY AND CONCLUSIONS

In summary, with Big Data and machine-learning techniques, the possibilities to explore the correlation between weather and emotion is increasingly easy.

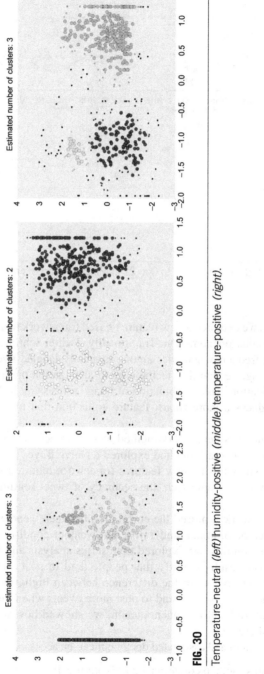

FIG. 30

Temperature-neutral *(left)* humidity-positive *(middle)* temperature-positive *(right)*.

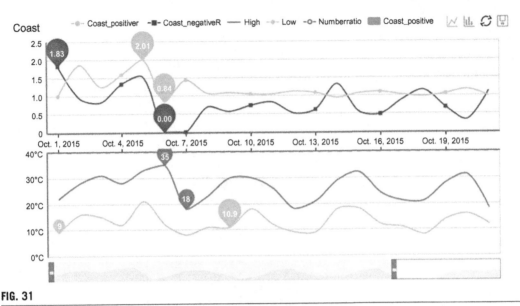

FIG. 31

Emotion and weather data from Oct. 1 to Oct. 21 in Melbourne coast area.

In this chapter, we explored a new features-based framework to analyze Twitter sentiment, including a range of weather phenomenon. Traditionally, Twitter sentiment analysis relies on a sentiment lexicon and term-frequency statistics among manually labeled tweets. We extended this approach by introducing image recognition technology to analyze the pictures attached in tweets to help in sentiment classification. The combination of image processing techniques and text sentiment analysis features produces a more robust feature collection that underpins the accuracy of sentiment classification.

A sentiment analysis benchmark method was introduced to evaluate the effectiveness of these new features. The benchmark method explored a Naïve Bayes Classifier based on word-frequency features. The classifier for the new features framework required stacking between SVM, RF, and LR models. Through this approach, the accuracy of tweet sentiment analysis has improved from 54% to 80%.

Ultimately this work explored the correlation between weather and sentiment. To explore this we analyzed different emotions under different weather conditions to obtain correlations and observation. Building on this, we explored time series analysis and DBSCAN clustering to quantify the correlation. The results identify that people tend to post more positive and negative tweets when the temperature is low or the difference between highest degree and lowest degree in one day is small. In addition, people tend to post more tweets when there is low humidity or high temperatures. To explore localized phenomenon, we showed how higher temperatures make people happier in coastal areas.

The software system and associated document can be accessed from:

Source code: https://github.com/evanslight/Exploring-Twitter-Sentiment-Analysis-and-the-Weather.
System Function Introduction Video Link: https://youtu.be/jzTMADmY4tY.

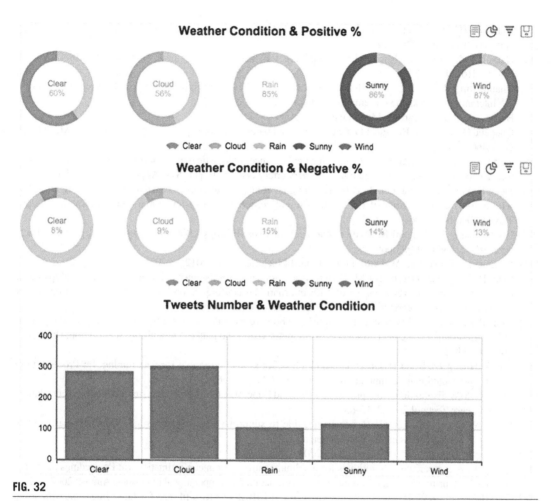

FIG. 32

Emotion data for different weather condition from Oct. 1 to Oct. 26.

ACKNOWLEDGMENTS

We would like to thank the National eResearch Collaboration Tools and Resources (NeCTAR) Research Cloud for the resources that were used in this work. We would like to express our best regards and appreciation to our friend Scott Shi for advice and support on the front-end system.

REFERENCES

[1] Li J, Wang X, Hovy E. What a nasty day: exploring mood-weather relationship from twitter. In: Proceedings of the 23rd ACM international conference on information and knowledge management, ACM, November; 2014. p. 1309–18.

[2] John MG. Can weather affect your mood? http://psychcentral.com/blog/archives/2014/08/29/can-weather-affect-your-mood/; 2015.

[3] Denissen JJA, Butalid L, Penke L, Van Aken MAG. The effects of weather on daily mood: a multilevel approach. Emotion 2008;8:662–7.

[4] Hsiang SM, Burke M, Miguel E. Quantifying the influence of climate on human conflict. Science 2013;341(6151):1235367.

[5] Chaumartin FR. UPAR7: a knowledge-based system for headline sentiment tagging. In: Proceedings of the 4th international workshop on semantic evaluations; 2007. p. 422–5.

[6] Breiman L. Random forests. Mach Learn 2001;45(1):5–32.

[7] Chapelle O, Vapnik V, Bousqnct O. Choosing kernel parameters for support vector machines[J]. Mach Learn 2001;46(1):131–60.

[8] Kurt I, Ture M, Turhan Kurum A. Comparing performances of logistic regression, classification and regression tree, and neural networks for predicting coronary artery disease. Expert Syst Appl 2008;34:366–74.

[9] Duan L, Xiong D, Lee J, Guo F, Duan L, Xiong D, et al. A local density based spatial clustering algorithm with noise. In: Proceedings of IEEE international conference on systems, man, and cybernetics, Taipei, Taiwan, October; 2006.

[10] Go A, Huang L, Bhayani R. Twitter sentiment analysis. Entropy 2009;17. http://www-nlp.stanford.edu/courses/cs224n/2009/fp/3.pdf.

[11] De Smedt T, Daelemans W. Pattern for python. J Mach Learn Res 2012;13:2031–5.

[12] Feng H, Lesot MJ, Detyniecki M. Using association rules to discover color-emotion relationships based on social tagging. In: Proceedings of 14th international conference on knowledge-based and intelligent information and engineering systems; New York: Springer; 2010. p. 544–53.

[13] Viola P, Jones M. Rapid object detection using a boosted cascade of simple features. In: Proceedings of the 2001 IEEE computer society conference on computer vision and pattern recognition. Washington, DC: IEEE; 2001. p. 511–8.

[14] Gao Y, Huang JZ, Rong H, Gu D. Learning classifier system ensemble for data mining. In: Proceeding of genetic and evolutionary computation conference; 2005. p. 63–6.

[15] Powers DMW. Evaluation: from precision, recall and F-measure to informedness, markedness and correlation. J Mach Learn Technol 2011;2:37–63.

[16] Hsu CW, Chang CC, Lin CJ. A practical guide to support vector classification. Taipei: Department of Computer Science, National Taiwan University; 2003.

[17] Breiman L. Random forests. Mach Learn 2001;45(1):5–32.

[18] Malouf R. A comparison of algorithms for maximum entropy parameter estimation. In: Proceedings of the 6th conference on natural language learning: vol. 2. Association for computational linguistics, August; 2002. p. 1–7.

[19] Fan RE, Chang KW, Hsieh CJ, Wang XR, Lin CJ. LIBLINEAR: a library for large linear classification. J Mach Learn Res 2008;9:1871–4.

[20] Shumway RH. Applied statistical time series analysis. Englewood Cliffs: Prentice Hall; 1988 Jan.

[21] Pandas.pydata.org. Computational tools — pandas 0.17.1 documentation, http://pandas.pydata.org/pandas-docs/stable/computation.html; 2015.

[22] Scikit-learn.org. Comparing different clustering algorithms on toy datasets — scikit-learn 0.17 documentation. http://scikit-learn.org/stable/auto_examples/cluster/plot_cluster_comparison.html; 2015.

[23] Baralis E, Cerquitelli T, Chiusano S, Grimaudo L, Xiao X, Baralis E, et al. Analysis of twitter data using a multiple-level clustering strategy. In: Model and data engineering. Heidelberg: Springer; 2013. p. 13–24.

[24] Dijkstra E. A note on two problems in connexion with graphs. Numer Math 1959;1(1):269–71.

[25] Tenenbaum JB, De Silva V, Langford JC. A global geometric framework for nonlinear dimensionality reduction. Science 2000;290(5500):2319–23.

[26] Scikit-learn.org. Silhouette coefficient, http://scikit-learn.org/stable/modules/generated/sklearn.metrics.silhouette_score.html; 2015.

[27] Scikit-learn.org, Adjusted rand score, http://scikit-learn.org/stable/modules/generated/sklearn.metrics.adjusted_rand_score.html; 2015.

DYNAMIC UNCERTAINTY-BASED ANALYTICS FOR CACHING PERFORMANCE IMPROVEMENTS IN MOBILE BROADBAND WIRELESS NETWORKS

16

S. Dutta, A. Narang

16.1 INTRODUCTION

The rapid evolution of wireless network-based services has been augmented by significant developments in network technologies, cheaper infrastructure, and diversified business strategies. As such, interactive multimedia technology and its applications have recently received a great deal of attention from the industry, as well as from researchers. The promise of viewing movies, holding conferences, browsing online bookstores, online shopping and many other activities from the confines of one's home is quite lucrative. The advent of mobile devices and smartphones such as iPhones, iPads and others, has provided users with a wealth of applications and services anywhere, anytime. Development of such interactive multimedia systems incurs a diverse set of technical difficulties, many of which are intractable in isolation. A complete architectural framework that efficiently tackles the problems continues to be a significant obstacle. Wireless analytics would enable catering to a broad range of ubiquitous services such as advertising recommendations, location-based services, and other use-case scenarios, some of which are presented in Fig. 1.

One of the key emerging applications is video-on-demand (VoD), wherein a user may request movie clips, trailers, video songs, etc., on his/her wireless device. Such services combine the quality of TV while enabling the same interactions as that of a DVD. Advancements in information retrieval, networking, and digital signal processing have augured the need for such services for end users. Streaming of a requested video involves a *latency*, or *wait period* for the users while the video is fetched. Naïve approaches involving dedicated video streams or sessions per user for reducing the latency are not viable given the enormous infrastructure requirements. On the other end of the spectrum, batch mode viewing and resource sharing among users calls for far less engagement of the providers, but leads to a delayed response.

Several solutions, such as the split-and-merge protocol [1], co-operative caching [2] using Vickrey-Clarke-Groves (VCG) auctions, the segment-based buffer management approach [3], and MPEG-4 fine grained scalable (FGS) video with post-encoding rate control [4], among others, have been proposed for improving hit rates while lowering storage costs. However, these methods are limited in that their transmission characteristics are inadequate for bandwidth-intensive applications or

Big Data. http://dx.doi.org/10.1016/B978-0-12-805394-2.00016-7

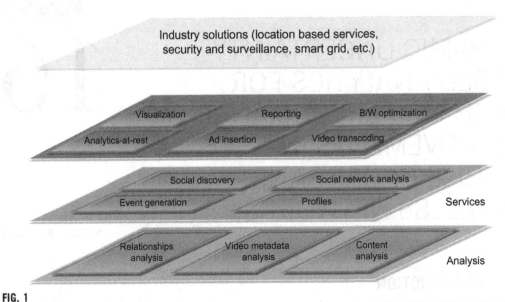

FIG. 1

Applications of wireless network analytics.

for large numbers of simultaneous users. Although GigE and DWDM hardware technologies (from Motorola) cater to scalable VoD along with push-pull policies for peer-to-peer VoD systems [5], limited work exists in the theoretical formulation of the quality-of-experience (QoE) optimization problem, and leveraging insights from user patterns and fine-grain user profiles [6] to improve cache performance.

In this chapter, we discuss the state-of-the-art method for how predictive analytics can be leveraged to improve the QoE from both theoretical and experimental perspectives. The users' movement and access patterns exhibit dynamic temporal uncertainty — where uncertainty changes as more information is revealed after every action. In these scenarios, using short-term predictions (leveraging analytics) about the behavior of the system, the information about future time steps is refined as we get close to them. The QoE optimization problem is thus formulated as an online resource allocation problem that lies at the intersection of Markov predictive control (MPC) (incorporates predictions) and Markov decision processes (MDP) (model state and action space).

This chapter discusses a recently proposed VoD framework employing an intelligent caching mechanism based on user behavior predictions, enabling low latency as well as scalability. We impress the need for Big Data architecture and paradigms to tackle the massive amount of data involved. We further present an outline for the theoretical formulation of the QoE optimization problem and a framework that uses a k-lookahead scheme for higher cache performance. This leads to an efficient VoD system that ensures a better QoE of the users. We also present the novel analytics-driven video caching algorithm, intelligent network caching algorithm (INCA), that leverages prediction of the location of users and request patterns using historical data and performs lookahead-based prefetch and replacement. This helps in avoiding backhaul congestion as well as in reducing the access latency for end users with low prefetch costs.

16.1.1 BIG DATA CONCERNS

Given the proliferation of mobile devices and the popularity of associated multimedia services, traditional approaches further suffer from the *data deluge* problem. Typically, the call data records (CDRs) or the event data records (EDRs), including the subscriber information, caller-callee information, temporal data, and other factors, can be in the order of 300 GB per day to cater to over 50 million subscribers. This is further aggravated in the VoD scenario with user-profile information (eg, age, language, etc.), movie preferences, list of watched videos, among others. For performing predictive analysis in the VoD framework, one needs to process the massive CDR data as well as the deep packet inspection (DPI) data to gather information on videos watched and URLs accessed.

Given these constraints, scalable Big Data architectures such as Hadoop (with Pig/Spark) and efficient data stores such as Hbase along with fast SQL query engines like PrestoDB are vital to efficiently process such massive data. In addition to handling massive data, this problem requires execution of the following computationally expensive kernels:

- *Social network analysis*: community detection algorithms for recommendations.
- *Segmentation using CRM and movie-watched information*: clustering algorithms such as Gaussian mixture models.
- *Association rule mining*: extracting meaningful patterns and rules (along with confidence and support) using user spatio-temporal data.
- *Collaborative filtering analysis using a hybrid approach*: providing video/genre recommendations to users using ratings and usage data as well as the metadata of the movies and user-profile information.
- *Rank aggregation or ranking algorithm*: combining a video preference list of the users to form a single list that fits in the cache at the basestation.

In fact, when the proposed VoD framework is deployed at higher levels of the wireless network architecture, such as the RAN or SGSN level, it results in even more processing requirements for both compute and data handling.

16.1.2 KEY FOCUS AREAS

In a nutshell, the salient areas of focus of this chapter are as follows:

- We provide an extensive discussion on the existing wireless network architecture, and existing works on VoD services.
- We present the complete architectural structure for an end-to-end efficient scalable VoD framework, simultaneously providing user personalization, reduced latency and operational costs.
- We describe the recently proposed video caching algorithm, INCA [7,8] combining predictive analytics and caching models. It leverages user location and request pattern mining (from historical data) and performs k-lookahead schemes for cache prefetch and replacement. This leads to higher cache hits and a better QoE for the users. This further helps in avoiding backhaul congestion as well as incurring low prefetch costs.

- We also provide a theoretical formulation of the QoE optimization problem, and provide a performance bound for our algorithm.
- We demonstrate experimental results to demonstrate that with a small increase (less than 10%) in prefetch bandwidth, INCA achieves a 15–20% QoE improvement and around 12–18% improvement in the number of satisfied users over well-known caching strategies.

16.2 BACKGROUND
16.2.1 CELLULAR NETWORK AND VoD

For a cellular network, the base stations (BS), along with the radio network controllers (RNC), are equipped with IT capabilities, and thus edge analytics would enable us to track real-time user context to enhance service delivery and improve overall QoE for the end users. In this context, we define:

Edge This refers to the basestations (BS), or the (distributed) wireless system comprising the BS, to which a user connects. The edge is restricted in its storage capacity and computational capability. The primary role of the edge lies in performing fast online or incremental analytics. In the remainder of the chapter we use the terms "edge" and "BS" interchangeably.

Core This refers to the central backbone components of the network comprising RNC, SGSN, and GGSN, and is considered to be endowed with practically infinite storage and computation resources for performing rigorous batch mode or offline analytics.

The edge takes part in the real-time handling of users (device hand-off, etc.) and other analytical decisions. The core, bestowed with greater storage and computing power, usually works in an offline fashion, receives online user tracking from the basestations, updates the historical database correspondingly, and executes a rigorous frequent-pattern-mining, association-rule-mining algorithm to generate the frequent rules and behaviors on a per-user basis. These rules are later queried by the edges for subsequent online processing (eg, ranking and prefetching). It also handles housing, log generation, and updating the databases and performing queries. Thus, an efficient system evolves as a result of interplay between the online and offline computations.

The combination of frequent pattern mining, prediction, and aggregation of the results forms the basis of the INCA algorithm and provides a novel approach to efficiently tackle the expanse of such network-based services. The proposed system can cater not only to the VoD domain, but also other wireless network-based applications such as advertisement insertion, location-based services, etc., thereby making it a general framework for a broad range of scenarios requiring network intelligence and analytics at the heart.

A typical VoD scenario involves a user request to the basestation. If the requested video is available, it is directly streamed. Otherwise, the basestation initiates a request to the core. The video is then fed to the basestation from where it is provided to the users. Fig. 2 depicts a simple VoD request scenario.

Interactive VoD services can be broadly classified into the following categories [9,10]:

1. broadcast (no VoD),
2. pay-per-view,
3. quasi VoD,
4. near VoD, and
5. true Video-on-Demand (T-VoD).

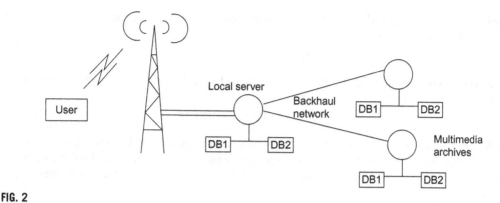

FIG. 2

A simple wireless VoD request processing.

In this chapter, we aim to propose a novel framework for delivering T-VoD by efficiently prepopulating the cache of the basestations with the most probable user request videos, thereby increasing the hit ratio and reducing user latency.

16.2.2 MARKOV PROCESSES

MDPs are applicable in fields characterized by uncertain state transitions and a necessity for sequential decision making, such as robot control, manufacturing, traffic signal control and others. MDPs satisfy the Markov property, defining that the state transitions are conditionally independent of actions and states encountered before the current decision step. An agent can therefore rely on a policy that directly maps states to actions for determining the next action. After execution of an action, the system is assumed to stay in the new state until the next action, ie, the system, has no autonomous behavior.

At each step the system is in one of these possible finite sets of states: $S = s_1, s_2, ..., s_N$. In each state, $s \in S$ there exists a finite set of actions, A_s, that the agent can perform $\left(A_s = \{a_1, a_2, ..., a_{Mx}\} \right)$. The system evolves according to the system model, $\Sigma : P(s'|s, a)$, where $P(s'|s, a)$ is the probability of transitioning from state s to state s' after action a is performed. The performance function is given by r, where $R(x, a, x', w)$ is the reward obtained with the transition from state s to state s' under action a and state of nature, $w \in W$. The fundamental problem of the MDP is to find a function that specifies the action $\pi(s_t)$ that needs to be chosen at state s and time t. The goal is to choose π in such a way that maximizes the expected reward under some cumulative function. Mathematically:

$$\sum_{(t=0)}^{\infty} \gamma^t R_{(a_t)}\left(s_t, s_{(t+1)} \right) \text{ for } a_t = \pi\left(s_t \right) \text{ and } 0 \leq \gamma < 1$$

Here, γ is typically close to one and is known as the *discount factor*.

The MDP can be solved using dynamic programming. Suppose we know the state transition function P and the reward function R, and we wish to calculate the policy that maximizes the expected discounted reward. The standard family of algorithms to calculate this optimal policy requires storage of two arrays indexed by state value V, which contains real values, and policy π which contains actions. At the end of the algorithm, π will contain the solution and $V(s)$ will contain the discounted sum of the rewards to be earned (on average) by following that solution from state s. The algorithm has the following two kinds of steps, which are repeated in some order for all the states until no further changes take place. They are defined recursively as follows:

$$\pi(s) = \max_{a} \left\{ \sum_{s'} P_a(s,s') \cdot \left(R_a(s,s') + \gamma V(s') \right) \right\}$$

In the preceding equation, a stands for the action taken to change the state of the machine from s to s'. Next, the $V(s)$ is computed as:

$$V(s) = \sum_{s'} P_a(s,s') \cdot \left(R_a(s,s') + \gamma V(s') \right)$$

Fig. 3 demonstrates a simple MDPs with three event states and two actions. INCA leverages a predictive analytics framework to compute reasonable accuracy on the predicted state of nature for k steps into the future. A typical sequence of events, when the online algorithm is in state, s_t, at the start of time step t, is as follows:

(1) the active disturbances set W is chosen arbitrarily by nature (as an adversary) and it is revealed to the online algorithm with certain accuracy;
(2) the online algorithm takes some action a and moves to state $\sigma(s, a)$ and obtains a reward $R(s, a, w)$; and
(3) time is incremented to $t \leftarrow t+1$.

In this context, an offline algorithm with the total reward *OFF* has prescient information regarding the disturbance profile. The regret of the online algorithm equals the maximum value of $(OFF - ON)$, and the competitive ratio equals the maximum value of (OFF/ON), over all choice of the disturbance parameters, where *ON* is the total reward obtained by the online algorithm. Further, the average regret is defined as $((OFF - ON)/T)$ over a time horizon T.

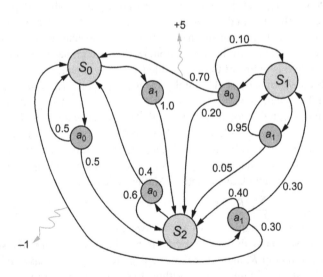

FIG. 3

A simple Markov decision process with three event states and two actions. The large nodes (colored green) are the states while the smaller nodes (colored red) are the actions. With the edges, the values less than one denote the transition probability from one state to the other by taking the action. The machine is at state S_1 at the initial stage. The integer values (+5, −1) denote the rewards of reaching S_0 by taking different actions. The edges with no integer values have zero as rewards for performing the corresponding action S_2.

16.3 **RELATED WORK**

Numerous approaches in the past have been studied for efficient video caching that cover a variety of techniques including collapsing of multiple related cache entries, collaborative caching, distributed caching over femto-cells, and the segment-based buffer management approach.

Shen and Akella [11] introduced a video-centric proxy cache called iProxy. iProxy [11] uses information-bound references to collapse multiple related cache entries into a single one, improving hit-rates while lowering storage costs. iProxy incorporates a novel dynamic linear rate adaptation scheme to ensure high stream quality in the face of channel diversity and device heterogeneity. Our framework can leverage these techniques (with minor modifications) to improve cache performance and lower storage costs. Zhang et al. [12] introduced a price-based cache replacement algorithm for a single cache server. For the case of multiple cache servers, the authors present a server selection algorithm. Tan et al. [13] introduced a smart caching design to replicate video contents in multiple access points which improves the quality of experience by reducing the delay of video streaming.

For collaborative clustering, He et al. [14] decomposed the problem of caching video into two subproblems, namely:

(a) content selection problem and
(b) server selection problem.

They then developed a system capacity reservation strategy to solve the content placement problem. For the source selection problem, the authors proposed an adaptive traffic aware algorithm known as LinkShare. Borst et al. [15] designed a distributed hierarchical cache clustering algorithm to maximize the traffic volume served by caches while minimizing the total bandwidth cost. However, the algorithm performs well only when the request pattern across all the nodes is uniform.

Prior works on efficient video caching can be categorized into one of the following four approaches:

(a) independent caching,
(b) collaborative caching,
(c) segment-based buffer management, and
(d) adaptive video caching.

Some of the important works in the area of independent caching are [11–13,16].

Collaborative caching paradigms among cache servers that are deployed by different wireless service providers (WSPs) has also been studied in [2] to consider benefits and address the challenges related to both incentives and truthfulness of selfish WSPs. Dai et al. [2] proposes a collaborative mechanism that aims to maximize social welfare in the context of VCG auctions (used in game theory). The incentives designed for WSPs encourage them to spontaneously and truthfully cooperate for trading their resources in a self-enforcing manner. The simulation results show that the performance of streaming systems can be substantially improved by maximizing the social welfare in these auctions, in which bandwidth units are used to serve more valuable demands.

The segment-based buffer management approach [3] for multimedia streams groups blocks of media stream into variable-sized segments. The cache admission and replacement policies are then performed on a per-segment basis. Segment-based caching leads to an increase in the byte-hit ratio (total traffic reduction) as well as a reduction in the number of requests that require a delayed start, and is especially useful for limited cache sizes and when the set of hot media objects changes over time. We use segment-based caching in our VoD framework. Wu et al. [3] demonstrated the effectiveness of the variable-sized distance sensitive segment caching schemes for large media objects. This is a recursive scheme where a media file is divided into multiple equal sized blocks. Multiple blocks are then grouped into a segment by a proxy server. The cache admission and replacement policy for the proxy server attaches different values of priority to different segments. The size of a segment is sensitive to its distance from the beginning of the media. The smaller the distance, the smaller the size. In general, the size of the segment $i+1$ is twice the size of the segment i. The purpose of doubling the size for the consecutive segments is to let the cache manager discard a big chunk of cached media objects, especially if a viewer decides to stop viewing the video. However, the scheme may not be much more effective for videos of smaller sizes.

An adaptive video caching framework that enables low-cost and fine-grained adaptation has been proposed [4] which employs MPEG-4 FGS video with post-encoding rate control. This framework is designed to be both network-aware and media-adaptive. Zhang et al. [12] presents a lookahead video delivery scheme for stored video delivery in multi-cell networks that simultaneously improves the streaming experience as well as reduces the basestation power consumption. It exploits the knowledge of future wireless rates that users can anticipate facing. We leverage the behavior of user mobility and video access to deliver higher cache performance using lookahead-driven prefetch and replacement policies.

Further, uncertainty handling is critical in mobile and video caching scenarios. Robust planning under uncertainty has been studied in the past in multiple contexts, including renewable energy such as solar and wind, financial markets, and others. Over the last couple of decades, MPC has become an important technology for finding control policies for complex, dynamic systems as found in the process industry and other domains. MPC is based on models that describe the behavior of the systems which could consist of differences or differential equations or MDPs. Regan and Boutilier [17] presents a method for computing approximate robust solutions to imprecise-reward MDPs in the context of online reward elicitation. It presents the non-dominated region vertex algorithm, deriving from insights in partially observable MDPs which generates approximate sets of nondominated policies with provable error bounds. This can be leveraged to efficiently approximate minimax regret using existing constraint generation methods. Regan and Boutilier [17] also shows how online optimization of the non-dominated set, as reward knowledge is refined, allows regret to quickly decrease to zero with only a small fraction of all non-dominated policies.

Incorporation of short-term predictions under dynamic temporal uncertainty for renewable integration in intelligent energy systems has been studied in [3]. It provides online randomized and deterministic algorithms to handle time-varying uncertainty in future rewards for nonstationary MDPs for energy resource allocation; and also presents theoretical upper and lower bounds that hold for a finite horizon. In the deterministic case, discounting future rewards can be used as a strategy to maximize the total (undiscounted) reward. This chapter discusses INCA, which presents the first theoretical model of the QoE optimization problem for video caching under dynamic temporal uncertainty and compares the results of our lookahead-driven caching with the algorithm presented in [18]. Negenborn et al. [19] proposes a learning-based extension for reducing the online computational cost of the MPC algorithm, using reinforcement learning to learn expectations of performance online. The approach allows for system models to gradually change over time, reduces computations over conventional MPC, and improves decision quality by making decisions over an infinite horizon.

16.4 VoD ARCHITECTURE

This section presents the detailed architectural design of the recently proposed VoD framework and the interactions among the various subsystems therein [7,8]. The framework works by predicting the impending actions of the current and future users (from historical data) within the ambit of each basestation, and utilizes them to improve the startup latency, or QoE, as well as reduce the video delivery cost for the service providers.

The logical working of the system is modularized into two related components, *the edge* and *the core*. The handoff of a user into the ambit of a basestation (BS), or a video request by an existing user, generates an event record at the BS. The set of such events are forwarded to the core and logged to be used as historical data for mining predictive rules for users. These events may also be used by the edge for rule updating in realtime. The core uses rigorous predictive algorithms such as associative rule mining to generate intelligence regarding user behavior for optimizing the QoE of the users for video, network constraints, and other requirements of the providers. The overall components at play for such scenarios are summarized in Fig. 4.

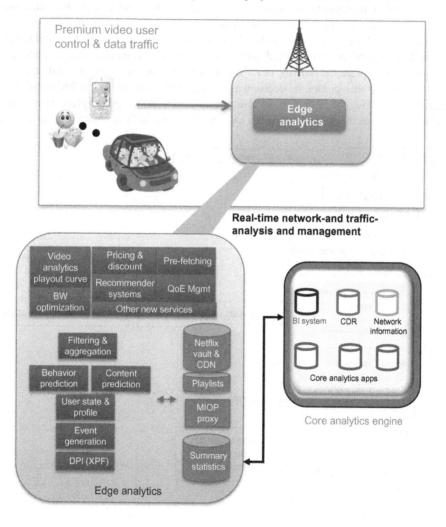

FIG. 4

Core and edge components.

16.5 OVERVIEW

Given a basestation, B and time, t, we would like to predict and prefetch the probable videos to be requested at time $t+1$ along with videos that could be used multiple times in future time slots (referred to as a lookahead scheme). Using historical data and by considering the current location and direction of movement of the users, we initially predict the users that might be connected to B at $t+1$.

Given this set of probable users, the edge is fed the complete set of video watching patterns and rules of the users by the core. Video usage pattern rules of these users are provided to the edge by the core. Along with possible user-generated view-lists, user usage pattern rules are generated based on historical data using association rule mining techniques. Further, collaborative filtering is applied to also obtain other probable requests based on similar interests of different users, along with the other currently most-watched ones or videos relating to real-time occurring events, eg, budgeting, sports, etc. This procedure further strengthens the prediction confidence of user video requests based on other users sharing the same taste and behavior [20].

Based on the complete set of rules for all such users, the support and confidence of each rule, and the view lists of the users, a preferred ordering or ranking of the different videos is computed in an online fashion. This ranked corpus then guides the decision as to which videos should be prefetched or evicted from the edge cache. Without loss of generality, we assume that users usually request videos from their preferred viewlist. Fig. 5 represents the components and a top-level information flow within the framework.

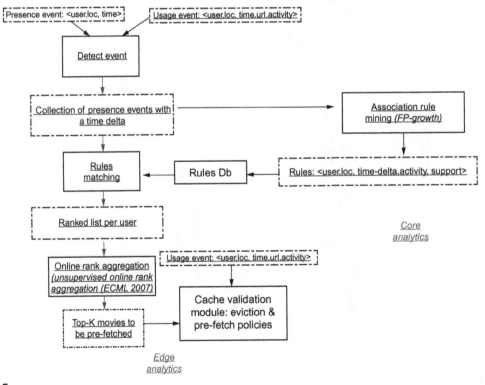

FIG. 5

Interaction between the components.

16.6 **DATA GENERATION**

A layered approach is adopted, wherein the lower layers in the stack are responsible for simple analytics providing a compact synopsis for sophisticated operations at higher layers. When a user connects to a basestation, the MIOP subscriber activation agent processes the control traffic and generates PDP context (de)activation records or EDRs. A presence event is generated upon the entry of a user into a basestation region, while a usage event corresponds to the activities of a user, such as video request, URL lookup, etc. All communications are uniquely identified by the IP address and the MSISDN of the user mobile device. The extensible packet filter (XPF) along with DPI intercepts the raw IP packets and constructs a semantically richer protocol object on the y containing TCP/IP header, images, JavaScripts, etc. It also decompressed protocol objects when required. These objects then feed into a stream layer as a sequence of events and are logged for constituting the historical data. This application layer can then be provided to the third-party applications as a complete protocol. Fig. 6 summarizes the process.

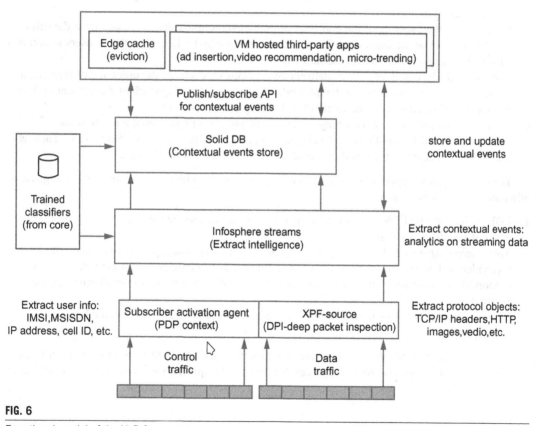

FIG. 6

Functional model of the VoD framework.

16.7 EDGE AND CORE COMPONENTS

In this section we provide the complete modularization of the VoD framework, working of the core and edge components, and their interactions based on the models as discussed in the previous sections. It can be observed that the prototype is quite simple and requires no major engineering on the part of the service providers, given the currently used infrastructures across the globe. This renders our proposed end-to-end VoD system effective as well as practically viable.

The broad performance components of the edge are:

1. *Event generation*: the *EDR*s (presence and usage events) are generated and passed on to the XPF (packet extraction) and stream layer for initial processing. It is then communicated to the core for persistence in the data records to be treated as historical data.
2. *Association rule checking*: the generated events are checked against the rules obtained from the core, and online learning or rule updating of the current rules are performed. The core is also queried for the rules pertaining to prospective users and their probable request videos.
3. *Activity inference*: the probability of a video being requested is computed from the support and confidence of the rules obtained from the core. Collaborative filtering is used to make the predictive analysis robust.
4. *Rank aggregation*: scoring of the entire set of predicted request videos obtained from the rules and the view list of the users is performed based on score and relative priority of users to obtain a ranking for the probability of request activity.
5. *Content analysis*: based on content delivery of previous sessions for the users, the resume point of the to-be-prefetched video can be inferred. This involves keeping track of the amount of data previously delivered and can be easily done by simple byte counting.
6. *Caching optimizations*: video caching, eviction and placement based on the result of the ranking of the videos and lookahead scheme is employed. Video delivery optimizations such as smoothing can also be performed on the set of videos identified for prefetch.

The core provides support and assists the entire system with its high computation and storage capability and performs the following:

1. EDR collection: the EDRs collected by the edge are shipped to the core during off-peak hours, where it is collected and stored.
2. Rule mining: *Apriori* and *FP-tree* techniques are applied to extract specific rules associated with user video watching patterns from the EDRs collected over a long period of time. Rules having support above a threshold are filtered out as relevant and are indexed by user identity, location and time.
3. *Query reporting*: the rules mined from the historical data are reported back to the basestations when queried.

The complete architectural design, the components, and the data flow among them to provide a highly efficient end-to-end system for true VoD applications enhancing the end-user experience.

16.8 INCA CACHING ALGORITHM

Based on the VoD framework described previously, we now introduce the working principles of the INCA. An EDR is generated when a user enters a basestation (*Presence Event*) and/or performs an activity (*Usage Event*). A *Presence Event*, when a user enters a basestation, consists of three fields <*UserID, LocID, TimeStamp*>, with the time slots within a day discretized. For example, the event <*ABC123, B0, MORN*> denotes a user with ID *ABC123* connected to basestation *B0* at the time-slot *Morning*.

A *Usage Event*, such as a video request, involves the addition of another tuple, EventActivity. Each tuple may have further sub-tuples, eg, Activity may be subdivided into sub-tuples TypeOfActivity, Genre, etc. to classify different kinds of activities such as video, audio, or just web page browsing and Genre to accurately capture the genre of the specific activity.

In reality, EDRs have several other fields in addition to the ones mentioned herein. For extracting meaningful information out of these EDRs, it is essential to remove the unnecessary fields and store the resulting transactions at the edge. The processed set of transactions (after duplicate and unnecessary field removal) are periodically sent to the core from the BS. The FP-growth algorithm [21] is employed for association rule mining, and rules having support above a threshold are filtered out as relevant and are indexed by user identity, location and time. A day is divided into several time slots, such as early morning, late-afternoon, early evening, etc., of appropriate duration (roughly three hours has been used for experimental analysis in this chapter). During event generation, the TimeStamp in each EDR can be mapped to one of these time slots.

The idea here is to prefetch, in the current timeslot, the videos that have a high possibility of being requested in the next time slot. At the start of a particular timeslot at a given basestation, the rules database is queried for a list of users and videos/movies (genres) that exist in the next timeslot for that particular basestation. It is important to mention here that each user has a small preference list of movies, which is assumed to be created by the user explicitly.

For prefetching using lookahead, $k=1$, INCA first predicts (in the current timeslot), the videos that have a high possibility of being requested per user in the next time slot. The prediction is based on rules (extracted at the core) stored at the edge, and the FP-growth algorithm [21] for the association rule mining procedure. Collaborative filtering techniques are also used to incorporate possible video requests from other users with similar behavior. Interestingly, the current location of direction of travel of connected and nearby users are used to predict the users that would connect to a basestation in the next time slot. For higher values of lookahead, $k > 1$, time slots beyond the next one are also considered and video requests are predicted per user. Rules not pertaining to the time slots or to users not within the basestation are filtered out.

The predicted videos (for the next time slot) are ranked using rank aggregation algorithms such as [22] under the constraint of total number (or percent) of available cache slots that can be evicted for prefetching. The relative priority of the users (eg, premium or normal) as well as priority of videos (decreasing with the increase in future time slots) are considered during rank aggregation. A small bandwidth, from the current time slot, is then dedicated for prefetching the selected videos. We later show that only a small percentage of the current bandwidth is required for high performance (in terms of cache hits), thereby making the framework extremely scalable.

When a user requests a video it is first looked up in the basestation cache. In the case of cache miss, the video is fetched from the core, and the analytics-driven cache replacement policy is followed. In this replacement policy, with each entry of the cache, we maintain three metrics:

- p-score that refers to a usage metric from history, such as least recently used (LRU) or least frequently used (LFU);
- f-score that refers to its usage frequency predicted in the future for k time slots; and
- pop-score that refers to global popularity of the movie.

During replacement, the set of movies which are on the skyline (with the lowest scores criteria) across the three metrics are selected, and randomly, one of these cache lines is replaced. For skyline computation, we use the online algorithm for d-dimensional skyline computation, as given by Kossmann et al. [23].

It is interesting to note that individual components of the proposed architecture can be customized with different state-of-the-art techniques to suit various needs of the application at hand, making the framework extremely robust. The complete end-to-end architecture is presented in Fig. 7.

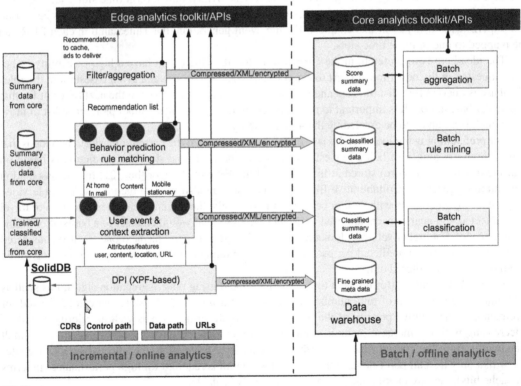

FIG. 7

Overall architecture and flow diagram of the VoD system.

16.9 QoE ESTIMATION

To evaluate the effectiveness of INCA, QoE (the delay experienced by a user after the request has been placed) is computed and used as the primary measure for comparison.

For INCA we have:

$$\text{QoE (per user in seconds)} = \text{INCA miss ratio} * \#\text{requests} * \text{frame size} * \#\text{frames} / (\text{backhaul bandwidth} - \text{prefetch bandwidth})$$

The prefetch bandwidth (B_p) can be expressed as:

$$B_p = \text{Backhaul bandwidth} * (\text{total prefetch per day} / \text{Max.prefetch per day})$$

where

$$\text{max.prefetch per day} = \text{max.prefetch in a time slot} * \#$$
$$\text{time slots in a day} * \#\text{simultaneous users a base station can support}$$

Similarly, for first-in-first-out (FIFO), LRU and LFU schemes with no prefetch, the QoE is:

$$\text{QoE (per user in seconds)} = \text{miss ratio} * \#\text{requests} * \text{frame size} * \#\text{frames} / \text{backhaul bandwidth}.$$

We later exhibit performance of the system with varying parameters such as bandwidth availability, number of simultaneous users, etc. The model is also compatible with partial object caching, involving frame storage, to handle high-definition videos at limited backhaul bandwidth. The number of frames to be fetched depends on the frame rate of the video, the bandwidth, and the cache size.

Therefore, the reduction in delay due to INCA over other approaches is given by the:

$$\text{Improvement in QoE (per user in seconds)} = \text{QoE (due to LRU)} - \text{QoE (due to INCA)}$$

16.10 THEORETICAL FRAMEWORK

At time slot t, let $v(u, t)$ be the video requested by user u and $x(v(u, t))$ ($x(v)$ in short) be an indicator variable which is 1 if $v(u, t)$ is present in the cache, $C(z)$, otherwise 0. The state of the MDP is defined by $v(u, t)$ and $C(z)$. Let, $n(u, t)$ be the number of times a user u requests videos in time slot t. The wait time for user u is denoted as $w(u, t)$ and equals $(1 - x(v)) * |v|/B_{av}$, where $|v|$ denotes the size of the part of the video prefetched, and B_{av} is available bandwidth.

Let $d(v, t)$ denote the prefetch data transfer in time slot t, and it equals $(1 - y(v)) * |v|$, where $y(v, t)$ is 1 if the video v was prefetched, else 0. The actions in the MDP consist of prefetch actions denoted by $y(v, t)$ as well as fetch actions taken when a particular video requested by a user is not in the cache. The prefetch actions are controlled by the system to improve hit rate, while the fetch actions are forced onto the system due to user video request. Further, let $G(u, t)$ denote the utility gained by user u in time slot t: it is a function of the wait time incurred by the user, $w(u, t)$, in that slot.

For a prefetch action, the reward associated is 0, while when a user u requests a video, the reward gained is $G(u, t)$. $G(u, t)$, which could be positive or negative, depending on if the requested video is in the cache or not and how much wait time $w(u, t)$ is experienced by that user. The QoE optimization problem can be formulated as a maximization of the sum of the difference in the utility across the users, and the cost of prefetch data transfer across all prefetches, ie,

$$\max_{y(v,t)} \sum_{t=1}^{T} \left\{ \sum_{u \in U} G(u,t) - \sum_{v \in V} y(v,t) * d(v,t) \right\}$$

$$\text{subject to}: \forall t \in T : \sum_{u} |v(u,t)| \leq C_{\max}$$

$$\forall t \in T, \forall u \in U : n(u,t) = 0,1$$

Our online algorithm, INCA, leverages the short-term predictions from the joint edge and core analytics and performs actions $y(v, t)$ using k-step lookahead. For such delayed MDP, under the assumption of no uncertainty in rewards for $L+1$ steps in future, Garg et al. [18] provides an online algorithm that chooses the future path with best discounted future reward, and proves bounds on average regret as $\Theta(\log L / (L - \rho + 1))$ and a competitive ratio as $(1 + \Theta(\log L / (L - \rho + 1)))$.

Hence, such a bound also applies to our proposed algorithm. However, in practice, these short-term predictions are not accurate. In the next section, we study the behavior of INCA experimentally with varying numbers of lookahead steps, k.

To evaluate the effectiveness of INCA, QoE, the delay experienced by a user after the request has been placed, is computed and compared with other caching policies. For INCA, QoE (per user) in seconds is given by:

$$\text{QoE} = \sum_{t=1}^{T} \sum_{u \in U} w(u,t)$$

Here, $B_{av} = B_{\max} - B_p$, and prefetch bandwidth (B_p) is given by:

$$B_p = \frac{B_{\max} * \text{total prefetch per day}}{\text{Max. prefetch per day}}$$

And Max prefetch per day = Max. prefetch per time slot * #time slots per day * Max. #simultaneous users.

Our model considers partial object caching, involving frame storage, to handle high- definition videos at a limited backhaul bandwidth. The number of frames to be fetched depends on the frame rate of the video, the bandwidth and the cache size.

16.11 EXPERIMENTS AND RESULTS

This section presents the experimental results of the studied VoD framework with the INCA algorithm, based on real data from the web video data set. This data set had a total of 10,000 videos corresponding to the search results for the top 25 queries at three popular video content providers. We use realistic data from the web video data set 4. For mobility pattern of users, we model our setup to represent real-life query logs of a large Fortune 500 Telecom organization obtained from http://vireo.cs.cityu.edu.hk/webvideo.

We compare the performance of the INCA algorithm based on cache hits under varying parameters. The QoE of users (as defined earlier) present at a basestation provides the performance benchmark of our proposed VoD system. Additionally, we define the satisfied users metric to model "*premium membership*" users to whom enhanced multimedia services need to be guaranteed.

Some applications would routinely flush the cache contents at the end of each day, while others might flush it dynamically by monitoring the activity (frequency of requests to the cache) in an effort to improve the hit rate. However, frequent flushing of the cache in the context of the INCA approach would lead to consumption of the costly network bandwidth, which is required for prefetching the cache with videos relevant to the current time slot. In some situations, if the cache is relatively large compared to the volume of requests it receives, it takes a while for the cache to warm up, and therefore frequent flushing is prohibitive in this case. In the current setting, we count the number of cache hits (or misses) at the end of each day.

In the experiments, we empirically set the pre-fetch amount to 30% and assume a limited bandwidth of 10 Mbps, to model a realistic cellular network setting. Our setup measures the cache hit (or miss) ratio per day. Each unit/entry of cache is assumed to accommodate part of a single video.

16.11.1 CACHE HITS WITH N_U, N_C, N_M AND K

To demonstrate the effectiveness of the approaches, we measure the cache hit rates of INCA, and compare the results with those obtained by FIFO, LRU, LFU and greedy dual size (GDS)-frequency [24] by varying:

(i) the cache size (N_C),
(ii) the number of users connected to a basestation (N_U),
(iii) the number of videos present (N_M), and
(iv) the amount of lookahead (**k**).

Variation of cache hits with N_C

We study the gain of the cache hit ratio of INCA over other policies with variation in the cache size (N_C). N_U and N_M are set to 200 and 10 K respectively. Each unit of cache is considered to store 250 video fragments. Fig. 8A shows the cache hit gain of INCA (with lookahead, $k=2$) over FIFO, LRU, LFU and GDS. At a 1500 cache size (6 units), the hit gain ranges from 26% (over FIFO) to 13% (over GDS). The gain increases with an increase in cache size and stabilizes at around 1000 cache entries. As cache size increases, more relevant entries are prefetched into the cache by INCA, giving it a higher gain over other policies.

Variation of cache hits with N_U

The behavior of the cache hit gain percentage of INCA (with $k=2$) over FIFO, LRU, LFU and GDS with variation in the number of users (N_U) is presented in Fig. 8B. The cache size is fixed at 1000 entries. At 1600 users, the hit gain varies from 9.9% (over GDS) to 14% (over FIFO). The decrease in the gain with an increase in the number of users is expected due to the fixed cache size across increasing users (increased video requests). But this decrease is not large, owing to the adaptability of INCA for increasing users by analyzing their access and movement patterns and incorporating these insights in prefetch and replacement decisions.

Variation of cache hits with N_M

The variation in cache hit gains of INCA (with $k=2$) over other cache polices with an increase in the number of videos present (N_M) is depicted in Fig. 8C with 200 users. At 6400 movies, the hit gain of

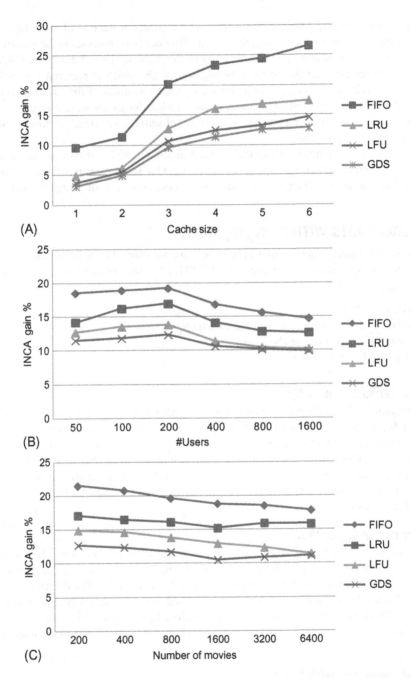

FIG. 8

(A) Cache hit gain of INCA with variation in N_c. (B) Cache hit gain of INCA with variation in N_U. (C) Cache hit gain of INCA with variation in N_M.

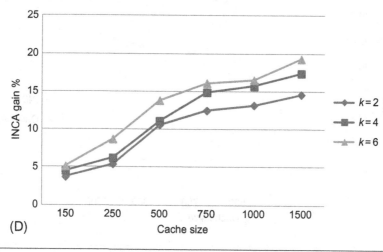

FIG. 8, CONT'D

(D)

(D) Cache hit gain of INCA with variation in k.

INCA ranges from 11% (over GDS) to 16% (over FIFO). We also observe a slight reduction in gains with an increase in the number of videos. Again, this decrease is not large, owing to the discriminative ability of our algorithm to make good online decisions for both prefetch and replacement, even with larger numbers of videos.

Variation of cache hits with k

The impact of lookahead, k, on the performance of INCA versus GDS (best performing amongst other cache policies) is illustrated in Fig. 8D. As the lookahead is increased to 6, the overall hit gain improvement in INCA is around 15% at a cache size of 1000, and increases to about 20% for higher cache sizes. This criticality of lookahead for the cache performance of INCA corroborates with theoretical bounds (with a perfect L-lookahead assumption) on the competitive ratio and regret mentioned previously.

INCA versus online algorithm

Fig. 9 presents the comparison between INCA and the online algorithm [18] which has proven regret bounds. INCA closely follows the online algorithm [18] even though it is, on average, 11% lesser. This is due to the fact that INCA has reasonable accuracy in short-term predictions (using the k lookahead strategy) while [18] assumes perfect accuracy of short-term predictions.

16.11.2 QoE IMPACT WITH PREFETCH BANDWIDTH

We next study the QoE of the users (as defined earlier) by varying the current bandwidth available for prefetching videos (for next time slots).

The variation in aggregate QoE improvement across users with respect to GDS (best performing amongst other caching policies) with varying prefetch bandwidth requirement is presented in Fig. 10. Here, we set lookahead, $k=2$ for INCA, and curves with varying cache sizes have been plotted.

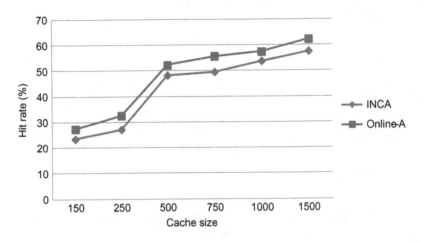

FIG. 9

INCA vs. online algorithm.

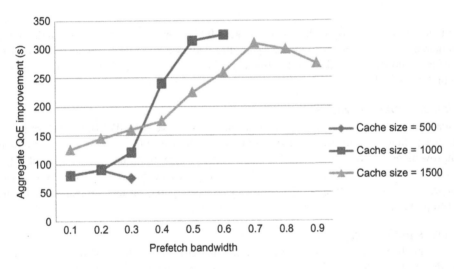

FIG. 10

QoE Improvement with prefetch bandwidth.

We assume 100 users (N_U), the average number of requests per time slot to be 310 and $N_M = 10$ K. We also consider 300 movies to present in the preference list of each user.

Fig. 10 demonstrates improvement in QoE in INCA with an increase in the prefetch bandwidth. With only 0.7 Mbps prefetch bandwidth and a cache size of 1000, the improvement in QoE is around 300 s, which is a 15% gain over the start-up latency in GDS. As compared to other cache policies, INCA has an even higher aggregate QoE gain of around 20%. Further, an increase in cache size beyond 1000 does not significantly improve the QoE gain. In fact, with higher cache size and prefetch bandwidth, the QoE slightly decreases due to high latency incurred for activity requests within the current time slot leading to an overall QoE degradation.

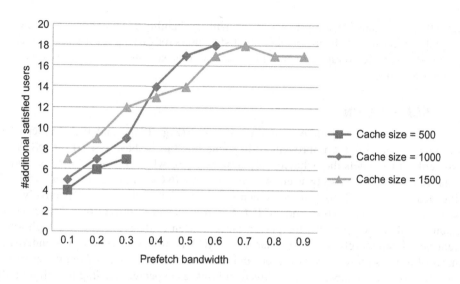

FIG. 11
User satisfaction with prefetch bandwidth.

16.11.3 USER SATISFACTION WITH PREFETCH BANDWIDTH

Service providers often offer "*premium services*" at additional cost. Such premium users need to be supplied with enhanced performance and extremely low latency. To this extent, this is defined as the *satisfied users metric. A user is said to be satisfied if all his requests are cache hits at basestations, thereby exhibiting practically 0 fetch latency*. Such guarantees on high viewing experiences would enable higher revenue generation for the providers. The number of satisfied users can be approximated by:

$$\# satisfied\ users = \# requests\ with\ a\ hit\ (RH)\ /\ average\ movie\ requests\ per\ user,$$

where RH = (gain% of INCA * #requests)/100.

For performance analysis based on QoE, we use similar parameter settings. Fig. 11 demonstrates around 18 additional satisfied users for INCA ($k=2$) over GDS per time slot, by using a small prefetch bandwidth of 0.7 Mbps. This corresponds to a 12% improvement over GDS, while improvement over other caching policies is up to 18%. These experiments demonstrate that the prefetch requirement of INCA is less than 10% of the available bandwidth, to deliver strong improvements in QoE and number of satisfied users. Interestingly, the prefetch requirement of INCA is a meager 7% of the available bandwidth.

16.12 SYNTHETIC DATASET

We explore the scalability performance of our proposed VoD framework with randomly generated synthetic video request data. We capture the robustness of INCA with respect to the LRU caching technique by varying the randomness. A user is considered to request videos outside her preference list with a certain probability. Keeping in view the unorganized and haphazard nature of user behavior, we try to model the user requests by introducing a certain percentage of *randomness* while generating user requests at a basestation. We consider a data randomness D_R of 50% and 70%, wherein a user requests a video outside the preference list with probability D_R. As before, we measure the improvement in cache hits, QoE, and number of satisfied users for varying cache sizes. We set $N_U = 100$ and $N_M = 20,000$, with the average number of requests per time slot and user preference list size set to 310 and 300 respectively.

16.12.1 INCA HIT GAIN

We vary the cache size (Fig. 12A), number of users (Fig. 12B), and the number of videos (Fig. 12C) while studying the improvement in cache hits (at the basestation) for INCA over the LRU protocol. This models the behavior of a new user (for whom historical data is unavailable) or unusual request of an existing user. We observe that INCA significantly outperforms LRU, obtaining nearly 15% and 10% improvements for $D_R = 50\%$ and 70% respectively. With an increase in cache size, the performance of INCA improves and stabilizes for a cache size of 750. As the number of users increases, the performance is seen to decrease due to a high number of video requests. Interestingly, the performance of INCA is observed to be nearly independent of the number of movies present. With higher randomness of video requests from the users (outside the preference list), the number of cache hits decreases, as expected, leading to a slight reduction in the performance of INCA.

16.12.2 QoE PERFORMANCE

INCA exhibits enhanced QoE of users (over LRU) for varying cache sizes and a prefetch bandwidth with different D_R values. Fig. 13A and B exhibit that with an increase in cache size, the QoE improves.

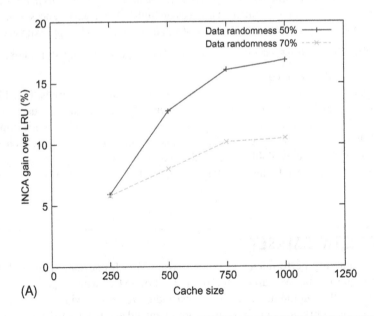

(A)

FIG. 12

(A) INCA gain over LRU with cache size (N_C).

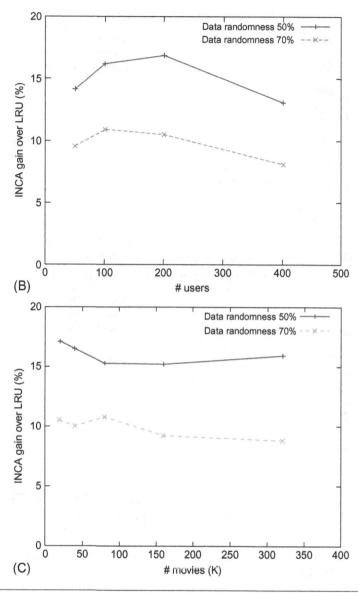

FIG. 12, CONT'D

(B) INCA gain over LRU with # of users (N_U). (C) INCA gain over LRU with # of videos (N_M).

INCA obtains around 300 and 150 s enhanced QoE as compared to LRU with a cache size of 1000 for $D_R = 50\%$ and 70% respectively. With an initial increase in the prefetch bandwidth available, INCA significantly outperforms LRU in QoE. However, as before, the QoE slightly decreases with a further increase in prefetch bandwidth, due to increased latency for current time slot operations. Similar trends are observed for the different D_R values.

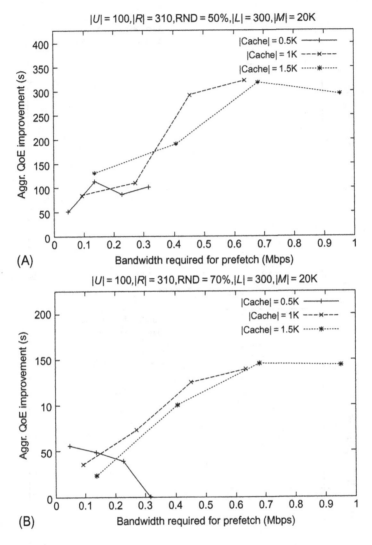

FIG. 13

(A) QoE of INCA with prefetch b/w and varying cache size for D_R=50%. (B) QoE of INCA with prefetch b/w and varying cache size for D_R=70%.

16.12.3 SATISFIED USERS

Fig. 14A and B depict that with an increase in the available prefetch bandwidth, the number of satisfied users in INCA is higher than that for LRU. We observe more than 14 additional satisfied users for INCA (with varying D_R), which stabilizes at around 0.7 Mbps bandwidth. Additionally, the number of satisfied users in INCA increases with an increase in cache size, and is seen to stabilize at N_C=1000.

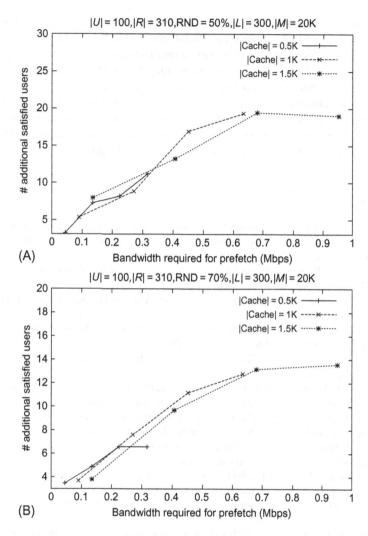

FIG. 14

Satisfied users with prefetch b/w and N_c for $D_R = 50$ (A) and 70% (B).

16.13 CONCLUSIONS AND FUTURE DIRECTIONS

We discussed a novel framework for efficient VoD services for multimedia applications. Leveraging predictive rule extraction coupled with collaborative filtering for its k-lookahead scheme, INCA performs prefetching and replacement and obtains higher performance. We also provided the theoretical formulation for QoE that is at the intersection of MPC and MDP. Using empirical results, we demonstrate superior performance of our framework with enhanced cache hits, QoE, and the number of satisfied users as compared to well-known approaches. It provides a robust VoD architecture encompassing and optimizing multiple infrastructural factors such as bandwidth, cache size, etc., as well as demonstrating scalability for modern large-scale applications. Intelligent caching based on user behavior prediction enables the prefetch of probable videos using only a small amount of the current available bandwidth, leads to enhanced quality of experience for the users. Empirical results as shown herein showcase the improved performance of our framework under various real-time scenarios.

Future research direction involves computation of bounds for regret and competitive ratio considering imprecise rewards in the lookahead scheme. Further extension for 4G connectivity provides the scope for further improvements. Performance comparison with other frequent/association rule mining algorithms might provide valuable insights into the working of the algorithm.

REFERENCES

[1] Liao W, Li V. The split and merge protocol for interactive video-on-demand. IEEE Multim 1997;4(4):51–62.
[2] Dai J, Liu F, Li B, Liu J. Collaborative caching for video streaming among selfish wireless service providers. In: Proceedings of Globecom; 2011. p. 1–5.
[3] Wu KL, Yu PS, Wolf JL. Segment-based proxy caching of multimedia streams. In: Proceedings of WWW; 2001. p. 36–44.
[4] Liu J, Chu X, Xu J. Proxy cache management for fine-grained scalable video streaming. In: Proceedings of INFOCOM; 2004. p. 1490–500.
[5] Suh K, Diot C, Kurose J, Massoulie L, Neumann C, Towsley D, et al. Push-to-peer video-on-demand system: design and evaluation. IEEE J Commun 2007;25(9):1706–16.
[6] Kumar P, Ranganath S, Huang WM. Framework for real time behavior interpretation from traffic video. IEEE Intel Transp Syst 2005;6(1):43–53.
[7] Dutta S, Narang A, Bhattacherjee S, Das A, Krishnaswamy D. Predictive caching framework for mobile wireless networks. In: IEEE international conference on mobile data management; 2015.
[8] Dutta S, Bhattacherjee S, Narang A. Mining wireless intelligence using unsupervised edge and core analytics. In: Proceedings of workshop on smarter planet and big data analytics; 2015.
[9] Little TDC, Venkatesh D. Prospects for interactive video-on-demand. Boston: Multimedia Communications Laboratory, Boston University; 1994. Technical report.
[10] Gelman AD, Kobrinski H, Smoot LS, Weinstein SB, Fortier M, Lemay D. A store and forward architecture for video-on-demand service. In: Proceedings of ICC; 1991. p. 27.3.1–5.
[11] Shen S, Akella A. An information-aware qoe-centric mobile video cache. In: Proceedings of Mobicom; 2013. p. 401–12.
[12] Zhang Q, Xiang Z, Zhu W, Gao L. Cost-based cache replacement and server selection for multimedia proxy across wireless internet. IEEE Trans Multim 2004;6(4):587–98.
[13] Tan E, Guo L, Chen S, Zhang X. SCAP: smart caching in wireless access points to improve p2p streaming. In: Proceedings of ICDCS; 2007. p. 61.
[14] He J, Zhang H, Zhao B, Rangarajan S. A collaborative framework for in-network video caching in mobile networks. In: CoRR, abs/1404.1108; 2014.
[15] Borst SC, Gupta V, Walid A. Distributed caching algorithms for content distribution network. In: Proceedings of INFOCOM; 2010. p. 1478–86.
[16] Xie F, Hua KA, Jiang N, Ho YH. Study of patching-based and caching-based video-on-demand in multi-hop wimax mesh networks. Wirel Commun Mob Comput 2011;11(3):357–70.
[17] Regan K, Boutilier C. Robust online optimization of reward-uncertain mdps. In: Proceedings of IJCAI; 2011. p. 2165–71.

[18] Garg VK, Jayram T, Narayanaswamy B. Online optimization with dynamic temporal uncertainty: incorporating short term predictions for renewable integration in intelligent energy systems. In: Proceedings of AAAI; 2013. p. 36–44.

[19] Negenborn R, Schutter B, Wiering M, Hellendoorn H. Learning-based model predictive control for Markov decision processes. In: Proceedings of IFAC world congress; 2005. p. 354–9.

[20] Terveen L, Hil W. Beyond recommender systems: helping people help each other. New York: Addison-Wesley; 2001. pp. 6–26.

[21] Han J, Pei J, Yin Y, Mao R. Mining frequent patterns without candidate generation: a frequent-pattern tree approach. Data Min Knowl Disc 2004;8(1):53–87.

[22] Klementiev A, Roth D, Small K. An unsupervised learning algorithm for rank aggregation. In: Proceedings of ECML; 2007. p. 616–23.

[23] Kossmann D, Ramsak F, Rost S. Shooting stars in the sky: an online algorithm for skyline queries. In: Proceedings of VLDB; 2002. p. 275–86.

[24] Cao P, Irani S. Cost aware www proxy caching algorithms. In: Proceedings of USITS; 1997. p. 193–206.

BIG DATA ANALYTICS ON A SMART GRID: MINING PMU DATA FOR EVENT AND ANOMALY DETECTION

17

S. Wallace, X. Zhao, D. Nguyen, K.-T. Lu

17.1 INTRODUCTION

Tomorrow's Smart Grid will help revolutionize the efficiency of power transmission while also providing improvements in security, robustness, and support for heterogeneous power sources such as wind and solar. The phasor measurement unit (PMU) provides a core piece of technology that measures critical system state variables in a time-coherent fashion across a geographically dispersed area.

PMUs are typically placed at power substations where they generally measure voltage and current phasors (magnitude and phase-angle) for each of the three phases (A, B, and C) as well as frequency and rate of change of frequency. In contrast to legacy systems, PMUs record measurements at high frequency (typically 10–60 Hz [1]) and time stamp each measurement using the global positioning system (GPS). Together, high measurement and precise GPS timestamps create so-called "synchrophasors" or time-synchronized phasors that allow the state of a wide area monitoring system to be observed with high fidelity. Between 2009 and 2014, the number of deployed PMUs within the United States has significantly increased, from ~200 PMUs in 2009 [2] to more than 1700 in 2014 [3].

Data from individual PMUs is routed to a phasor data concentrator (PDC) that aggregates and time-aligns the data before passing it on to downstream application consumers. As PMUs and PDCs have become more widely adopted, PDCs have expanded to provide additional data processing and storage functions [4].

Although the comprehensive coverage and high sampling rate of PMUs provide new resources for improving grid operation and control, the data generated by these devices also presents real computational and storage challenges [5]. A typical PMU can measure 16 phasors with a 32-bit magnitude and 32-bit phase-angle. Secondary values such as frequency and rate of change of frequency are also stored as 32-bit values. These, along with 8 bytes for the timestamp and 2 bytes for a PMU operating status flag represent a minimal archival signal set for each device. Recording 60 samples per second, this leads to 5,184,000 samples per day, or ~721 MB of data per PMU, per day. However, often there is value in keeping much more data. For example, the Bonneville Power Administration (BPA), who supplies our dataset, has an installed PMU base in the Pacific Northwest of the United States containing roughly 44 PMUs at the time our dataset was collected (2012–14). This dataset requires roughly 1 TB of storage per month of data acquired. Scaling this to the national level then would require more storage by roughly a factor of 40 to incorporate data from all 1700 PMUs.

Big Data. http://dx.doi.org/10.1016/B978-0-12-805394-2.00017-9

Traditional approaches for data processing and evaluation are pushed well beyond their feasible limits given the size of the dataset described herein. In this chapter, we describe how cloud computing and methods borrowed from data analytics and machine learning can help transform Smart Grid data into usable knowledge.

17.2 SMART GRID WITH PMUs AND PDCs

Data aggregated by a PDC is sent to downstream consumers in a format defined by IEEE Std. C37.118.2 [1]. The specification indicates two message types that are critical for data analysis: the configuration frame and the data frame.

A configuration frame specifies the number of PMU measurements that are aggregated by the PDC along with the name of the PMU station and the name and type of each signal measured by the station.

A data frame contains the measurements themselves, which have been time-aligned across all stations. Records are fixed-length with no delimiters, and measurements appear in an order prescribed by the configuration frame. Thus, the data frame (with the exception of a short header) can be viewed as a matrix of binary data in which PMU signals span the columns and time spans the rows.

Since this format is readily machine readable, it can also serve as an archival file format. Indeed, the Bonneville Power Administration currently stores archival PMU data as a binary file consisting of: (1) brief metadata including the file specification version; (2) the "active" configuration frame and (3) a data frame typically spanning 60 s of data. This format has the benefit of being entirely self-contained (since a configuration frame is stored along with the data frame); easily portable (1 min of data from roughly 40 PMUs requires about 30 MB of storage) and easily indexed as the flow of time presents a natural mechanism to partition data (eg, by month) using only the filesystem for organization.

17.3 IMPROVING TRADITIONAL WORKFLOW

A traditional workflow involving the archival PMU/PDC data may unfold along the following lines:

1. A researcher is notified of an interesting phenomenon at some point in recent history.
2. The researcher obtains archival data for a span of several minutes based on the approximate time of the phenomena.
3. The researcher plots or otherwise analyzes the signal streams over the retrieved timespan to isolate the time and signal locations at which the phenomena are most readily observed.
4. The researcher finally creates plots and performs an analysis over a very specific time range and narrow set of PMU signals as appropriate for the task at hand.

While this workflow is entirely reasonable, it likely leaves the bulk of the data unanalyzed. We view this as a good opportunity to leverage the methods of Big Data analytics and machine learning to turn the latent information in this archived data into useful knowledge.

Specifically, we see the following opportunities:

- characterizing normal operation,
- identifying unusual phenomena, and
- identifying known events.

These operations can all be performed on the historic archive of PMU data using Hadoop/Spark. Typically this would be done at the data center housing that content. Once normal operation has been appropriately characterized, and identification has been performed on the historic data, identification of unusual phenomena and known events can proceed on the incoming (live) PMU data stream in real time with minimal hardware requirements.

17.4 CHARACTERIZING NORMAL OPERATION

The vast majority of the time, the grid operates within a relatively narrow range of conditions. Many parameters are specified by regulating agencies, and deviation outside of normal conditions may require reporting. As a result, existing infrastructure is well tailored to monitoring for such events. However, smaller deviations in operating conditions that fall below the threshold for reporting are also potentially of interest, both to researchers and operating teams alike. Thus, the first step in identifying such deviations is to characterize normal operation.

A baseline approach for characterizing normal operation is to collect signal statistics across all PMUs. In our work, we began measuring "voltage deviation," a metric described in [6] and useful for identifying faults (eg, caused by lightning strikes or falling trees).

Voltage deviation is defined as follows:

$$\Delta V = \frac{\sqrt{(\Delta V_a^2 + \Delta V_b^2 + \Delta V_c^2)}}{3}$$

where $\Delta V_a = (ss_a - V_a) / ss_a$ and V_a represents the voltage of phase A at the point of interest, while ss_a represents the steady state voltage of phase A. Thus, voltage deviation represents the three-phase momentary drift away from steady state values.

Examining normal operation across 800 min spread across 11 months of BPA's 2012–13 data yields the histogram shown in Figs. 1 and 2.[1] In Fig. 1, we have plotted only bins where the deviation is less than or equal to 0.018 kV. As expected, we see the bulk of the probability mass with very low deviations, and the likelihood of a higher deviation from steady state drops off rapidly from its peak around 0.0007 kV. Plotting the remainder of the observed distribution (ie, $\Delta V >= 0.018\text{kV}$), one would expect a long tail with a continued slow decay toward zero.

Surprisingly, the distribution shows a secondary spike near 0.12 kV with a noisy decay profile as illustrated in Fig. 2. Note that the y-axis has been scaled for clarity.

By comparing each PMU's contribution toward the global distribution illustrated herein, we can identify sites that exhibit *long-term* anomalous behavior. In this case, there is one site contributing to the unusual spike observed above $\Delta V = 0.10\text{kV}$. Removing this site's contribution from the global histogram results in no observable differences in the shape for values $\Delta V \le 0.018$ and a tail that decays more rapidly and smoothly for values of $\Delta V \ge 0.018$. Further analysis revealed that the unusual tail resulted from data within a few months' time at the beginning of the data set's coverage period, signaling a potentially defective or misconfigured device.

---

[1] For computational efficiency, we used a single steady state value for each voltage signal. This was determined by first taking the median value from each minute (and each signal) in our sample, and then the median of those values. While this is computationally expedient, it does lead to higher deviations than if the steady state were calculated with higher locality.

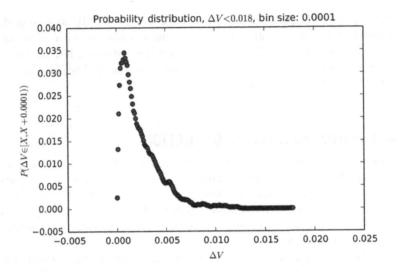

FIG. 1

Voltage deviation below 0.018 kV.

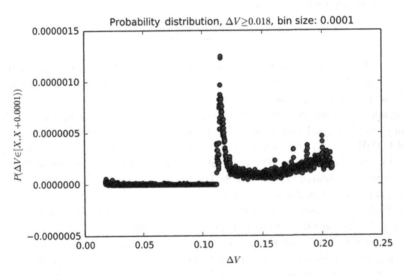

FIG. 2

Voltage deviation above 0.018 kV.

17.5 IDENTIFYING UNUSUAL PHENOMENA

Outlier, or anomaly detection, aims to identify unusual examples, in our case, of grid performance. A host of methods exist for this task, some of which are reviewed in Section 17.7. In this chapter, we examine how even the simplest approach, based on the observed probability distribution for normal data, can also be used to find individual moments in time where the data stream is extremely unusual.

Taking the histogram described and illustrated in Section 17.4, we can create a cumulative probability distribution that represents the likelihood that a signal experiences a voltage deviation at or below a given threshold. This operation processes a set of 770 signals from a single day in 16.9 min when performed on our small Spark cluster (4 nodes, 5 GB RAM per node). Once the distribution function has been produced, new data captured from the grid or archived data streamed from disk can be scanned in time, linear, with respect to the number of signals being inspected. Given a distribution function represented as a 1 million element list, we can issue more than 1 million queries per second on commodity hardware using a single core through direct hashing with Python. For our dataset, a 1 million element distribution function has a resolution of 1 V or less. This performance profile well exceeds the requirements for real-time operation.

Fig. 3 shows an unusual voltage signature; the corresponding voltage deviation is illustrated in Fig. 4. Note that the scale on the left y-axis of Fig. 4 shows the deviation from steady state while the scale on the right y-axis shows the expected likelihood of the observed deviation based on the histogram data collected previously.[2] Although this time period has not been marked by BPA as a line event, the signature is typical of a LL fault, and could represent a fault observed from a distance (perhaps off of BPA's network). Note that the voltage deviations are low likelihood and the point of maximum deviation has an expected likelihood of less than 7E-7.

This outlier detection approach can be viewed abstractly as a process of first predicting the next signal value, and then comparing the observed true value to the prediction. A high discrepancy may suggest an event worthy of investigation. The process is illustrated in Fig. 5.

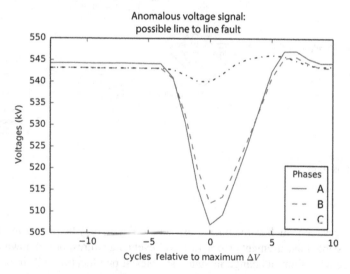

FIG. 3

An unusual voltage deviation during "normal" operation.

[2]The histogram used to compute the probabilities in Fig. 4 has been cleaned of data from the problematic PMU and thus shows the characteristic slowly decaying tail, as opposed to the extreme outliers illustrated in Fig. 2.

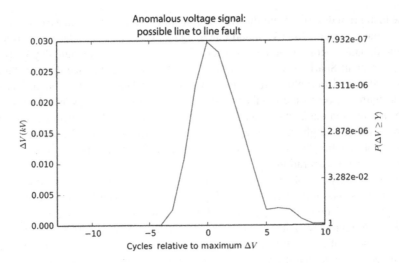

FIG. 4

Voltage deviation.

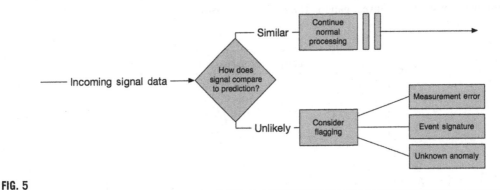

FIG. 5

Detecting unusual phenomena.

An unlikely observation, such as the ones illustrated in Fig. 3, may be further investigated to determine if they are possible measurement errors, (known) event signatures, or unknown anomalies. Since the grid is a connected system, a change in state variables at one location will impact state variables at other locations. A drop in voltage, as one that occurs with a fault, can be observed across a wide geographical area, although with attenuation based on the electrical distance between sites. A measurement error, then, can be identified as an anomaly that is detected by a single PMU or on a single data stream. Other anomalies (known events or otherwise) will be identified because they create outliers at multiple locations. In the following section, we describe how to further characterize an anomaly observed at multiple sites.

17.6 **IDENTIFYING KNOWN EVENTS**

In contrast to anomaly detection that aims to identify unusual activity using only information about typical (or normal) operational conditions, classification aims to distinguish one type of known event from another. Between 2013 and 2015, we worked with a domain expert to develop a set of hand-coded rules that distinguish between several types of "line faults" that frequently occur on a transmission system: single line to ground (SLG), line to line (LL), and three phase faults (3P) [6,7]. Concurrently, we developed a set of classifiers using machine learning to identify these same fault types. A full comparison of the approaches can be found in [7]. In this chapter, we focus on one specific classifier and discuss performance on both the training and testing data.

We began with a set of events obtained from the Bonneville Power Administration covering an 11 month span between 2012 and 2013. The event dataset includes the time and location of all known line events that occurred on transmission lines that were instrumented with a PMU on at least one end of the line. BPA verified the accuracy of this list and was able to further verify the specific type of event in the majority of cases (60 faults total).

A typical fault is illustrated in Fig. 6. During the event, one or more voltage phases sags and then typically recovers back to steady state voltage within ~0.1 s (6 cycles at 60 Hz). Training examples are selected by finding the moment in time where the voltage sags furthest below its steady state value, and then drawing samples from all PMUs (and all voltage phases) at that moment in time. In Fig. 6, this moment occurs at $x = 0$ cycles (since the x-axis has been labeled relative to the maximum deviation cycle). Thus, this classification process views the data as individual instances, and does not leverage the time-series nature of the data. Note that while we take fault samples at the moment in time where the sag is most extreme, the voltage's actual deviation from steady state is very much a function of the distance between the PMU making the measurement and the location of the fault itself [8]. Since we

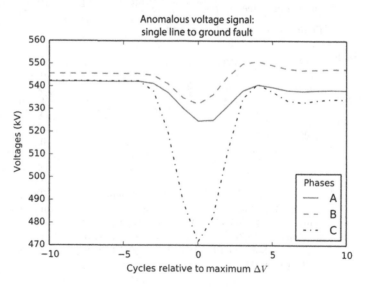

FIG. 6

Typical single line to ground fault.

take training examples from each PMU for each fault, the actual voltage sags used for training cover a large range of deviations and a fault may be effectively "unobservable" from a PMU that is located far enough from the origin.

Our training set consists of 57 of the 60 faults described herein along with additional samples of normal operation. Three of the original 60 faults were unusable for training because our feature extraction algorithms were unable to process those events (eg, because a specific PMU signal was unavailable at that moment in time). For each fault, we sampled voltage from all available PMUs. In total, this method yields 4533 data points, of which 4135 are SLG faults, 348 are LL faults, and 50 are 3P faults. To this set, we add 17,662 data points sampled from roughly 800 min of normal operation over the one-year period. We randomly selected half (8831) of these normal samples to use for training. In all, this represents 12,966 training samples of both normal operation and fault condition.

Fig. 7 shows the performance of the decision tree that is inferred using the training data described herein. The figure shows two matrices: the matrix on the left indicates Boolean fault-detection performance while the matrix on the right indicates refined classification into the three fault types (SLG, LL, and 3P) and the "Normal" class. Each cell contains two values. The value at the top represents the prediction *at the PMU* nearest to the fault (there are 57 of these, one for each fault in the training set). The value at the bottom of each cell represents the predicted class for all measurements that occur at PMUs further from the fault. Note that for "Normal" data, there is no notion of a fault location, and thus the top value in the rows labeled "Normal" is always zero.

The table following the matrices illustrates performance characteristics on the training data. For most measurements, we include the measurement at the fault location and across the grid as a whole (on the left and right side of the slash, respectively). In the table, site redundancy indicates the number of

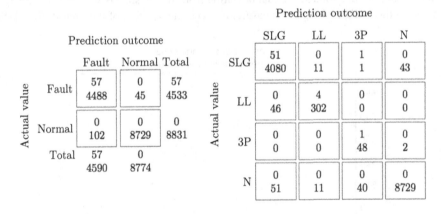

	Boolean classification		Type-specific classification		Site redundancy
Accuracy	100%/98.9%	Accuracy	98.2%/98.4%		84/49
Precision	100%/97.8%	Precision	83.3%/81.6%		
Recall	100%/99.0%	Recall	99.4%/93.8%		
Specificity	98.8%				

FIG. 7

Training set performance.

PMU signals (ie, the number of voltage signals) that detect each fault where the value on the left of the slash is the median redundancy and the number on the right represents the fifth percentile redundancy. For these results, a fifth percentile redundancy of 49 indicates that 95% of the faults are detected by 49 different voltage measurements in the dataset (where one voltage measurement includes all three phases: A, B, and C). Note that each PMU often makes multiple voltage measurements for different substation buses, and at times, for individual transmission lines as well. So for our dataset, this number tends to be larger than the number of actual PMUs.

Fig. 8 illustrates the performance of the same decision tree on a test set that was unseen during training. Test data here was obtained using the same procedure outlined in [7]. That is, test instances are obtained for faults from the moment prior to the largest voltage deviation (cycle −1 in Fig. 6). This approach yields the same number of test instances as training instances and in some sense is a more challenging test than randomly partitioning the training and testing set because this method guarantees that test instances will have an equal or smaller deviation from steady state as compared to training instances. For simplicity of comparison, we show the performance *relative* to the training set. Note that *at the fault location*, there are *no changes* to the classification results. As we consider PMUs further afield, however, we acquire more errors than with the training set.

Fig. 9 illustrates the performance of the decision tree when applied to the data in the vicinity of the anomaly from Figs. 3 and 4. Viewed by itself, the classifier does a good job of identifying the main voltage signature (the drop below steady state that occurs between cycles −2 and 5) as a probable LL fault. However, it makes a poor prediction at cycle 5, where the voltage has almost returned to steady state values. Here, the classifier predicts a 3P. Note that if we combine the predictions with the likelihood information in Fig. 4, it is easy to constrain the event predictor to only those signals that are relatively unlikely to occur in normal operation. For example, if we set the likelihood threshold at 1E-6,

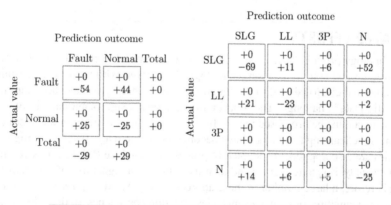

Boolean classification

	Fault	Normal	Total
Fault	+0/−54	+0/+44	+0/+0
Normal	+0/+25	+0/−25	+0/+0
Total	+0/−29	+0/+29	

Prediction outcome (type-specific)

	SLG	LL	3P	N
SLG	+0/−69	+0/+11	+0/+6	+0/+52
LL	+0/+21	+0/−23	+0/+0	+0/+2
3P	+0/+0	+0/+0	+0/+0	+0/+0
N	+0/+14	+0/+6	+0/+5	+0/−25

Boolean classification		Type-specific classification		Site redundancy
Accuracy	+0.0%/−0.6%	Accuracy	+0.0%/−0.8%	−3/+0
Precision	+0.0%/−0.6%	Precision	+0.0%/−4.1%	
Recall	+0.0%/−1.2%	Recall	+0.0%/−2.7%	
Specificity	−0.2%			

FIG. 8

Test set performance (change relative to training performance).

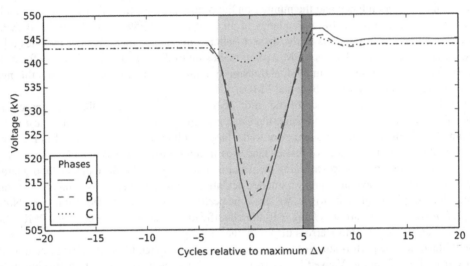

FIG. 9

Classifier applied in vicinity of anomalous "normal" data: light shaded region (cycles -3-5) LtL fault; dark shaded region (cycles 5-6) 3P fault.

then only the predictions at $x=-1 \dots 1$ will be created. Not coincidently, this is when the classifier also gives the best predications.

17.7 RELATED EFFORTS

Smart grid technology provides great potential to build more reliable electrical grid systems by utilizing advanced digital and communication technologies. However, with the worldwide initiative of upgrading the traditional electrical grid to the Smart Grid, new challenges have been introduced, among which is the "Big Data" challenge. The Smart Grid generates a significant amount of data on a daily basis, and these data must be processed in an efficient way in order to monitor the operational status of the grid. As machine learning techniques have become the de facto approaches for Big Data analytics, these techniques are also applied and adapted to process and analyze PMU data. A common objective of the PMU data analysis is to recognize and identify patterns, or signatures of events that occur on the Smart Grid. Therefore, a large number of these approaches are based on *pattern recognition* [9].

For identifying signatures of known events, classification approaches, or detection trees, are proven to be most effective. For instance, in [10], a classification method is proposed for tracing the locations where faults occur on a power grid. This method is based on the pattern classification technology and linear discrimination principle. Two features of the PMU data are used in the classification: nodal voltage, and negative sequence voltage. For localizing a fault, irrelevant data elements are identified and filtered out using linear discriminant analysis. Similar classification technologies can also be used to identify other signatures of events in power systems, such as voltage collapse [11] and disturbances [12]. Diao et al. [11] develop and train a decision tree using PMU data to assess voltage stability. The decision tree is threshold based, and it can be used to evaluate both static and dynamic post-contingency power system security. A J48 decision tree is used in [7] for classifying different types of line faults using a set of novel features derived from voltage deviations of PMU data, and this approach greatly improves the accuracy of detecting line faults from a distance, compared with an approach based on an expert's hand-built classification rules. In Ray et al. [12] build support vector machines (SVMs) and decision tree classifiers based on a set of optimal features selected using a genetic algorithm, for the purpose of detecting disturbances on the power grid. SVM-based classifiers can also be used to identify fault locations [13], and predict post-fault transient stability [14].

For anomaly detection, machine learning techniques are often applied for detecting security threats, such as data injections or intrusions, instead of detecting bad data measurements. The latter is usually addressed by developing PMU placement algorithms that allow measurement redundancy [15,16]. In [17], various machine learning methods are evaluated to differentiate cyber-attacks from disturbances. These methods include OneR, Naive Bayes, SVM, JRipper, and Adaboost. Among these approaches, the results show that applying both JRipper and Adaboost over a three-class space (attack, natural disturbance, and no event) is the most effective approach with the highest accuracy. Pan et al. [18] propose a hybrid intrusion system based on common path mining. This approach aggregates both synchrophasor measurement data and audit logs. In addition, SVMs have also been used in detection data cyberattacks. For instance, Landford et al. [19] proposes a SVM based approach for detecting PMU data spoofs by learning correlations of data collected by PMUs which are electrically close to each other.

Due to the time sensitivity of event and anomaly detection on the Smart Grid, a major challenge of applying machine learning techniques to perform these tasks is the efficiency of these approaches. This is especially important for online detection of events. Two different types of approaches have been used to address this challenge. Dimensionality reduction [20] is a commonly used approach to improve learning efficiency by reducing the complexity of the data while preserving the most variance of the original data. A significant amount of efforts have been made in this direction. For instance, Xie et al. [21] propose a dimensionality reduction method based on principal component analysis for online PMU data processing. It has been shown that this method can efficiently detect events at an early stage. In [22], a similar technique is used to reduce the dimensionality of synchrophasor data by extracting correlations of the data, and presenting it with their principal components. Another type of approach for improving the efficiency of PMU data processing is to adopt advanced high-performance computing and cloud computing techniques, such as Hadoop [23], and the data cloud [24].

Although a variety of machine learning techniques have been proposed to analyze PMU data for event classification and anomaly detection, very few have been applied to real PMU data collected from a large-scale wide area measurement system (WAMS). Gomez et al. [14] apply a SVM based algorithm to a model of practical power system. However, the number of PMUs considered is restricted to 15. Most other approaches are based on simulations. The work presented in this chapter, in contrast, is based on mining real PMU data collected from BPA's transmission grid.

17.8 CONCLUSION AND FUTURE DIRECTIONS

We presented our experience in mining PMU data collected from BPA's WAMS, for the purpose of detecting line events, and anomalies. This work aims for improving the traditional workflow of analyzing archival PMU data to identify events. Specifically, we first characterize the PMU data collected during the period when the grid is under normal operational status. Based on the statistical results obtained in this step, we can easily identify outliers by examining the likelihood of the measurement indicated by the probability distribution of the normal data. Besides anomaly detection, we have also developed a classification method using machine learning techniques for identifying known events, namely SLG, LL, and 3P. The experimental results on our dataset show that our classification method can achieve high accuracy in detecting these events, even when the PMU site is far away from the fault location.

Work is ongoing in several directions. First, we are examining other learning algorithms for event classification. To this end, instead of using an existing classification algorithm, we are building our own decision tree by leveraging other machine learning techniques, such as SVMs. Second, we are also applying unsupervised clustering techniques to PMU data. Different from the classification approach in which sufficient labeled data are needed for training purposes, clustering approaches do not require substantial labeled data. This approach can potentially identify unknown events and signatures similar to anomaly detection, but with the added benefit of identifying potential relationships between anomalies. Third, we are repurposing these machine learning techniques to solve different problems in the power grid domain, eg, data cleansing and spoofed signal detection. Finally, building on our understanding of the Smart Grid, we are investigating novel interaction models and resource management approaches to support energy-efficient data centers powered by the Smart Grid.

ACKNOWLEDGMENTS

The authors would like to thank the Department of Energy/Bonneville Power Administration for their generous support through the Technology Innovation Program (TIP #319) and for providing the PMU data used in this study.

REFERENCES

[1] IEEE. IEEE standard for synchrophasor data transfer for power systems. In: IEEE Std C37.118.2-2011 (revision of IEEE Std C37.118-2005), December 2011; 2011. p. 1–53.

[2] North American Electric Reliability Corporation. Real-time application of synchrophasors for improving reliability; 2014. http://www.nerc.com/docs/oc/rapirtf/RAPIR%20final%20101710.pdf, 2014 [accessed 09.08.15].

[3] Americans for a Clean Energy Grid. Synchrophasors; 2014. http://cleanenergytransmission.org/wp-content/uploads/2014/08/Synchrophasors.pdf [accessed 09.08.15].

[4] IEEE guide for phasor data concentrator requirements for power system protection, control, and monitoring. In: IEEE Std C37.244–2013, May 2013; 2013. p. 1–65.

[5] Hu Y, Novosel D. Challenges in implementing a large-scale pmu system. In: International conference on power system technology, October 2006; 2006. p. 1–7.

[6] Liang X, Wallace S, Zhao X. A technique for detecting wide-area single-line-to-ground faults. In: Proceedings of the 2nd IEEE conference on technologies for sustainability (SusTech 2014), ser. SusTech 2014; Washington, DC: IEEE; 2014. p. 1–4.

[7] Nguyen D, Barella R, Wallace S, Zhao X, Liang X. Smart grid line event classification using supervised learning over pmu data streams. In: Proceedings of the 6th IEEE international green and sustainable computing conference; 2015.

[8] Barella R, Nguyen D, Winter R, Lu K-T, Wallace S, Zhao X, et al. A sensitivity study of pmu-based fault detection on smart grid. In: Proceedings of the 4th international conference on smart cities and green ICT systems (SMARTGREENS); 2015. p. 1–8.

[9] Al Karim M, Chenine M, Zhu K, Nordstrom L. Synchrophasor-based data mining for power system fault analysis. In: 3rd IEEE PES international conference and exhibition on innovative smart grid technologies (ISGT Europe 2012); Washington, DC: IEEE; 2012. p. 1–8.

[10] Zhang YG, Wang ZP, Zhang JF, Ma J. Fault localization in electrical power systems: a pattern recognition approach. Int J Electr Power Energy Syst 2011;33(3):791–8.

[11] Diao R, Sun K, Vittal V, O'Keefe R, Richardson M, Bhatt N, et al. Decision tree-based online voltage security assessment using PMU measurements. IEEE Trans Power Syst 2009;24(2):832–9.

[12] Ray PK, Mohanty SR, Kishor N, Cataĩao JP. Optimal feature and decision tree-based classification of power quality disturbances in distributed generation systems. IEEE Trans Sustain Energy 2014;5(1):200–8.

[13] Salat R, Osowski S. Accurate fault location in the power transmission line using support vector machine approach. IEEE Trans Power Syst 2004;19(2):979–86.

[14] Gomez FR, Rajapakse AD, Annakkage UD, Fernando IT. Support vector machine-based algorithm for post-fault transient stability status prediction using synchronized measurements. IEEE Trans Power Syst 2011;26(3):1474–83.

[15] Chen J, Abur A. Placement of pmus to enable bad data detection in state estimation. IEEE Trans Power Syst 2006;21(4):1608–15.

[16] Tarali A, Abur A. Bad data detection in two-stage state estimation using Phasor measurements. In: Proceedings of the 3rd IEEE PES international conference and exhibition on innovative smart grid technologies (ISGT Europe). Washington, DC: IEEE; 2012. p. 1–8.

[17] Borges Hink RC, Beaver JM, Buckner M, Morris T, Adhikari U, Pan S, et al. Machine learning for power system disturbance and cyber-attack discrimination. In: Proceedings of the 7th international symposium on resilient control systems (ISRCS). Washington, DC: IEEE; 2014. p. 1–8.

[18] Pan S, Morris T, Adhikari U. Developing a hybrid intrusion detection system using data mining for power systems. IEEE Trans Smart Grid 2015;6(6):3104–13.

[19] Landford J, Meier R, Barella R, Zhao X, Cotilla-Sanchez E, Bass R, et al. Fast sequence component analysis for attack detection in synchrophasor networks. In: Proceedings of the 5th international conference on smart cities and green ICT systems (SmartGreens 2016), Rome, Italy, 2016.

[20] van der Maaten LJ, Postma EO, van den Herik HJ. Dimensionality reduction: a comparative review. J Mach Learn Res 2009;10(1–41):66–71.

[21] Xie L, Chen Y, Kumar PR. Dimensionality reduction of synchrophasor data for early event detection: linearized analysis. IEEE Trans Power Syst 2014;29(6):2784–94.

[22] Dahal N, King RL, Madani V. Online dimension reduction of synchrophasor data. In: IEEE PES transmission and distribution conference and exposition (T&D); Washington, DC: IEEE; 2012. p. 1–7.

[23] Trachian P. Machine learning and windowed subsecond event detection on PMU data via Hadoop and the openPDC. In: Proceedings of the IEEE power and energy society general meeting; 2010. p. 1–5.

[24] Rusitschka S, Eger K, Gerdes C. Smart grid data cloud: a model for utilizing cloud computing in the smart grid domain. In: Proceedings of the first IEEE international conference on smart grid communications (SmartGridComm), October 2010; 2010. p. 483–8.

eScience and Big Data Workflows in Clouds: A Taxonomy and Survey

18

A.C. Zhou, B. He, S. Ibrahim

18.1 INTRODUCTION

The development of computer science and technology widens our view to the world. As a result, the amount of data observed from the world to be stored and processed has become larger. Analysis of such large-scale data with traditional technologies is usually time-consuming and requires a large-scale system infrastructure, and therefore can hinder the development of scientific discoveries and theories. eScience offers scientists the scope to store, interpret, analyze and distribute their data to other research groups with state-of-the-art computing technologies. eScience plays a significant role in every aspect of scientific research, starting from the initial theory-based research through simulations, systematic testing and verification, to the organized collecting, processing and interpretation of scientific data. Recently, cloud computing has become a popular computing infrastructure for eScience. In this chapter, we review the status of cloud-based eScience applications and present a taxonomy specifically designed for eScience in the cloud.

eScience is an important type of Big Data application. eScience is also considered the "big-data science", which includes broad scientific research areas, from the areas that are close to our everyday life (eg, biological study), areas concerning the planet that we live on (eg, environmental science), to areas related to outer space (eg, astronomy studies to find the origins of our universe). Although the term 'eScience' has only been used for about a decade, the study of eScience problems started much earlier. In the early days, scientists were not able to efficiently study the value of scientific data due to the lack of technologies and tools to capture, organize and analyze the data. Technological advances such as new computing infrastructures and software protocols have brought great opportunities for eScience projects in various fields [1–4]. For example, grid computing has greatly advanced the development of eScience. Many eScience applications are becoming data-driven. For example, the development of the modern telescope has given us the Large Synoptic Survey Telescope (LSST) [5], which obtains 30 trillion bytes of image data from the sky every day. Currently, almost all major eScience projects are hosted in the grid or cluster environments [6]. With aggregated computational power and storage capacity, grids are able to host the vast amount of data generated by eScience applications and to efficiently conduct data analysis. This has enabled researchers to collaboratively work with other professionals around the world and to handle data enormously larger in size than before.

In the past few years, the emergence of cloud computing has brought the development of eScience to a new stage. Cloud computing has the advantages of scalability, high capacity and easy accessibility compared to grids. Recently, many eScience projects from various research areas have been shifting from grids to cloud platforms [7–9]. It breaks the barrier of doing eScience without a self-owned large-scale computing infrastructure. In this chapter, we review the current status of scientific

Big Data. http://dx.doi.org/10.1016/B978-0-12-805394-2.00018-0

applications in the cloud, and propose a taxonomy to clearly classify the related projects, according to the infrastructure, ownership, application, processing tools, storage, security, service models and collaboration aspects. We find that, for scientific applications in the cloud, resource provisioning is a major concern for the monetary cost and performance optimizations of the applications. In this chapter, we briefly introduce our initial efforts on the resource provisioning problems of scientific workflows in the cloud.

Both eScience and cloud computing are rapidly developing and becoming more mature. It is time to examine the efforts related to scientific computing in the cloud. This chapter focuses especially on eScience projects in the cloud. Due to the pay-as-you-go service model of the cloud, monetary cost and performance are two important concerns for eScience applications in the cloud. In this chapter, we introduce our existing studies on cloud resource provisioning to optimize the cost and performance for eScience in the cloud. We compare the advantages and weaknesses against eScience in the grid to discuss the obstacles and opportunities of eScience services in the cloud.

The rest of this chapter is structured as follows. Section 18.2 introduces the background of eScience history and grid-based and cloud-based eScience. Section 18.3 gives the taxonomy and reviews the current status of eScience in the cloud. Section 18.4 introduces some of our efforts on optimizing the resource provisioning problems of scientific applications in the cloud. Last, we discuss the open problems for scientific computing on the cloud in Section 18.5 and summarize this chapter in Section 18.6.

18.2 BACKGROUND

In this section, we briefly discuss the history of scientific computing development, particularly for eScience. Next, we focus our review on grid-based scientific computing, and introduce cloud computing.

18.2.1 HISTORY

Computer infrastructures have long been adopted to host scientific data sets and computations. eScience is a new science paradigm that uses distributed computing infrastructures for computation, simulation and analysis. In addition, scientists can make use of high-speed networks to access huge distributed and shared data collected by sensors or stored in databases. Computing infrastructures allow scientists around the world to share knowledge and resources, and to build close scientific collaborations.

The term *eScience* was first introduced in 1999[10]. During the development of eScience, it has gone through roughly three stages. Table 1 shows the major development stages that scientific computing has gone through. We review the history in the following dimensions.

Table 1 Development Stages of the Scientific Computing			
Stage	**Data Generated**	**Research Period**	**Infor. Tech.**
Manual	By hand	Ad-hoc	Paper and pencil
(Semi-) Automated	With the help of machinery	Short-term	Computer assisted
Large-scale Sensing	From satellites and sensors around the world	Real-time	Cluster and grid

Dimension 1: the evolution of science. We observed that technology (particularly information technology) is one of the main driving factors in pushing science forward. From the perspective of experimental methods, eScience first used *manual* measurements: meaning the measurements were taken by hand, not using machinery or electronics to fulfill the function. Then with the development of technology, machinery such as computers and metering instruments were used to help in the measurements, but with manual operations still involved. This stage is called the *semi-automated* stage. After this stage, machinery took a greater part in the measurements and eScience evolved to the *automated* stage where machines took almost all the work, with a minimal amount of human involvement required. Technologies such as high-performance computers, sensor networks, and various types of experimental software make the eScience measurements evolve to the *large-scale sensing* stage [11].

Take the research in Meteorology for example, in the early stage (classified to the manual stage), researchers used thermometers, barometers and hygrometers to measure the temperature, air pressure and water vapor, and write down the records. In the nineteenth century (classified as the semi-automated stage), breakthroughs occurred in meteorology after observing the development of networks. The data collected in local meteorological observatories are transmitted through networks and then are gathered by different spatial scales to study the various meteorological phenomena. Since the twentieth century (classified as the automated stage), with the adoption of radar, lasers, remote sensors and satellites into meteorological research, collecting data in a large area is no longer a challenging problem, and special instruments, together with the automation of computers, can automatically fulfill the measuring tasks. At the end of the twentieth century (classified as the large-scale sensing stage), large-scale observation experiments are performed. The experiments relied on satellites, meteorological rockets, meteorological observatories on the ground around the world, automatic meteorological stations, airplanes, ships, buoy stations and constant level balloons. These instruments were combined to form a complete observing system to automatically measure the meteorological variables worldwide.

Dimension 2: the length of the research period. eScience has gone through an *ad-hoc* stage, when research was done just for a specific problem or task, and not for other general purposes. Later, in the *short-term plan* stage, researchers made plans in priori for their problems about what to do in what time, so that a project of a short term could be kept on schedule. In the *real-time* stage, the research is subject to real-time constraints, such as the experimental data being collected in real-time, wherein the system needs to give out results in real-time. This evolution of research periods also requires the experimental methods to be more efficient and support high technology.

Dimension 3: technology. eScience has gone through the *paper and pencil* stage, when no machinery was involved in our research and human work with paper and pencil was the only tool for science. When computers appeared, eScience was able to move to the *computer-assisted* stage when computers played a great role in helping with complex calculations and solving logical problems. With the scientific problems getting more complicated and traditional computers not sufficient for the computing power required, *cluster and grid* computing are coming to scientists' attention and helping them solve many data-intensive or compute-intensive problems within a reasonable time, which is not possible on traditional computers.

We summarize our findings in the three dimensions. Initially, scientists only dealt with specific problems using manual methods such as doing theoretical calculations using paper and pencil in the early days. As problems are getting more complicated, more planning is needed for the research, and semi-automated and automated methods are also required for research during this time. Computers are used, and when the problem scale gets larger, new technologies such as clusters and grids are applied for solving the problems faster. New challenges from science have risen. We have witnessed these recent challenges, including the large-scale of scientific data (Big Data) and the requirements of real-time processing.

18.2.2 GRID-BASED eSCIENCE

Current major eScience projects are mostly hosted in the grid or high-performance computing (HPC) cluster environments. With aggregated computational power and storage capacity, grids have been considered an ideal candidate for scientific computing for decades. There are many labs around the world working on grid-based projects, such as GridPP in the UK, XSEDE in the US, CNGrid in China, France Grilles in France, D-Grid in Germany and Kidney-Grid in Australia. In the following, we present some details about the grid infrastructure in the UK, USA and China.

In the UK, particle physicists and computer scientists have been collaboratively working on the GridPP project, aiming at providing distributed computing resources across the UK for particle physicists working on the Large Hadron Collider experiments at CERN [6]. These organizations include all of the UK universities and institutions that are working as members of this project. At the end of 2011, the project has contributed a large number of resources (29,000 CPUs and 25 Petabytes of storage) to the worldwide grid infrastructure.

The Grid Infrastructure Group (GIG) along with eleven resource provider sites in the United States have initiated an eScience grid computing project called TeraGrid. In 2007, TeraGrid provided more than 250 Teraops of computation resources, more than 30 Petabytes of data storage resources, and over 100 databases of different disciplines for many researchers. The resources had grown to 2 Petaflops of computing capability and over 60 Petabytes of storage in late 2009. In 2011, after the termination of the TeraGrid project, the National Science Foundation (NSF) funded another high-performance project named XSEDE (Extreme Science and Engineering Discovery Environment) as a follow-up to TeraGrid.

The China National Grid (CNGrid) has quickly grown to serve more than 1,400 users, including both research institutes and commercial companies, providing more than 380 Teraflops of computation resources and more than 2 Petabytes of shared data storage resources. Since 2009, this project has built three Petaflop-level supercomputers, in which Tianhe-1 was ranked the fastest supercomputer in the top 500 supercomputers in 2010 [12].

Besides nationwide initiatives, volunteer computing projects have taken place to build grid platforms with the public donation of computing resources. For example, SETI@home [13] is such a volunteer computing project employing the BOINC software platform to search for extra-terrestrial signals with the spare capacity on home and office computers.

The strength of grid computing has attracted many scientific applications.

- First, since governments are very concerned about the research on grid and frontier scientific research, most of the grid-based projects are funded by national funding. Resourceful funding offers good chances to boost eScience in the grid.
- Second, sharing the vast computational and storage resources from grids becomes possible.
- Third, the tools and software developed on the grid can benefit more research groups besides the developers themselves. This strength can save a lot of development time for the projects developed on the grids.

While the grid is the dominant infrastructure for eScience, it faces a number of limitations. First, due to the limitation of its structure, the grid is not able to provide the elasticity required by most scientific projects which are pursuing cost efficiency. Second, it is not easy to get access to grid resources for everyone because a program getting access to grid resources needs to be authorized on the project's behalf, and resources would then be distributed to this project as a whole. Since grids are mostly nationwide initiatives, getting the authorization is very hard for most small-scale projects. Third, while the grid offers access to many heterogeneous resources, many applications need very specific and consistent environments.

18.2.3 CLOUD COMPUTING

According to the definition of the National Institute of Science and Technology (NIST), cloud computing is

> The delivery of computing as a service rather than a product, whereby shared resources, software, and information are provided to computers and other devices as a utility (like the electricity grid) over a network (typically the Internet) [14].

Cloud computing became popular in the early 2000's. Officially launched in 2006, Amazon Web Service (AWS) was the first utility computing platform to provide computation resources as services to external customers. Many other cloud service providers, including Microsoft Azure, Google Cloud Platform and Rackspace, have come into the market since then. Open-source systems and research projects are developed to facilitate use of the cloud. For example, Eucalyptus allows deploying AWS-compatible private and hybrid cloud computing environments. The OpenNebula toolkit is designed for building private and hybrid clouds with different cloud models and flexibility from Eucalyptus.

Cloud computing shares many similarities with, and differences from grid computing. In the year 2008, Foster et al. [15] has compared clouds and grids mainly from a technological perspective. Compared to the grid, the cloud has better scalability and elasticity.

- When developing applications on the grid infrastructure, it is not easy to scale up or down according to the change of data scale. In the cloud, with the use of virtualization, clients can scale up or down as they need and pay only for the resources they used.
- Virtualization techniques also increase the computation efficiency as multiple applications can be run on the same server, and increase application availability since virtualization allows quick recovery from unplanned outages with no interruption in service and improves responsiveness using automated resource provisioning, monitoring and maintenance.
- The cloud has easier accessibility compared to the grid. Users can access commercial cloud resources through a log-in and use the resources as they need them as long as they can pay with a credit card. In this case, even small-scale scientific projects can also have the chance to use powerful clusters or supercomputers on their computer-intensive or data-intensive projects.

Scalable data analytics for Big Data applications in the cloud has become a hot topic. Due to the large volumes of input data, many data analytics tasks usually take a long time to finish the data processing. However, in many Big Data applications such as weather analytics, the input data must be analysed in a cost- and time-effective way to discover the value of the data. The easy accessibility and good scalability of the cloud make it a perfect match for serving scalable (big) data analytics applications. More and more eScience applications are beginning to shift from grid to cloud platforms [16,17]. For example, the Berkeley Water Centre is undertaking a series of eScience projects collaborating with Microsoft [7–9]. They utilized the Windows Azure cloud to enable rapid scientific data browsing for availability and applicability and enable environmental science via data synthesis from multiple sources. Their BWC Data Server project is developing an advanced data synthesis server. Computer scientists and environmental scientists are collaborating to build new tools and approaches to benefit regional and global scale data analysis efforts [7,8].

18.3 TAXONOMY AND REVIEW OF eSCIENCE SERVICES IN THE CLOUD

There have been various cloud computing techniques for eScience. We need a taxonomy to reflect the interplay between eScience and cloud computing. The taxonomy in this section gives a clear classification of cloud computing techniques used in eScience services from several perspectives, including the computation *infrastructure* for eScience applications, the *ownership* of cloud infrastructures, the eScience *application* types, the *processing tools* used for eScience applications, the *storage* model, the *security* insurance method, *service models* of the cloud and the *collaboration* goal between different research groups. Fig. 1 summarizes our taxonomy. Some are mainly from eScience's perspective, and some are mainly from cloud computing's perspective.

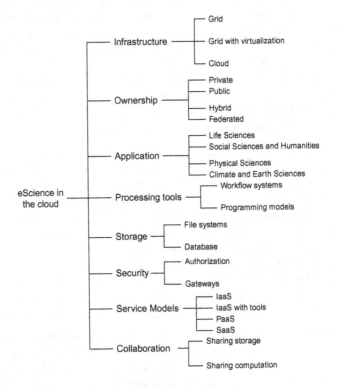

FIG. 1

Taxonomy of eScience in the Cloud.

18.3.1 INFRASTRUCTURE

The infrastructure of the cloud provides access to computing and storage resources for eScience applications in an on-demand fashion. The cloud shares some similarities with the grid while at the same time is modified to overcome the limitations of the grid. Roughly, we can classify the infrastructure into three kinds: the grid, the grid with virtualization (ie, a hybrid approach), and the cloud.

One characteristic of the grid is that it assigns resources to users in the unit of organizations, and each individual organization holds full control of the resources assigned to it. However, such a coarse-grained resource assignment is not efficient. There are efforts in the grid to use virtualization to address the deficiency issue. The nimbus scientific cloud is one such effort that provides a virtual workspace for dynamic and secure deployment in the grid. Virtualization hides from users the underlying infrastructures which are usually heterogeneous hardware and software resources, and provides the users with fine-grained resource management capabilities.

As for cloud infrastructures, several national cloud initiatives have also been announced to provide on-demand resources for governmental purposes [18], such as the US Cloud Storefront [19], the UK G-Cloud [20], and the Japanese Kasumigaseki [21] cloud initiatives. Many industry players have also dived into the cloud business, and provide users with seemingly infinite public cloud resources. With the popularity of the cloud, many eScience applications have been deployed in the general public cloud infrastructures such as Amazon EC2, Windows Azure to benefit from its high performance, scalability and easy-access [7–9,22–24].

There have been a number of studies comparing the performance of the cloud with other infrastructures. The NG-TEPHRA [24] project performed a volcanic ash dispersion simulation on both the grid and the cloud, using the East Cluster at Monash University and the Amazon EC2 computing resources, separately. Experiments show efficient results on both platforms, and the EC2 results have shown very small differences in their standard deviation, indicating the consistent QoS of the cloud. Cloudbursting [9] implemented its satellite image processing application with three different versions: an all-cloud design on Windows Azure, a version that runs in-house on Windows HPC clusters, and a hybrid cloud-bursting version that utilizes both in-house and cloud resources. The hybrid version achieves the best of the previous two versions, namely the development environment of a local machine and the scalability of the cloud. Their experimental results showed that the application is benefiting from the hybrid design, both on execution time and cost.

From the existing studies, we find that the performance comparison between the cloud and HPC is application dependent. Due to the scheduling and communication overhead, the applications involving large and frequent data transfers over multiple computation nodes usually perform worse on the cloud than on HPC clusters which are equipped with a high-bandwidth network. In contrast, the advantage of the cloud is its high scalability. Users can easily and quickly scale up and down their applications as needed, without wasting too much money. Applications such as Cloudbursting [9] can benefit from this characteristic of the cloud.

18.3.2 OWNERSHIP

The ownership of cloud infrastructures can be classified as the following types: private, public, hybrid and federated. They have different levels of security and ownership scope.

Private clouds are infrastructures operated only by a single organization for internal use. The security level of private clouds is the highest among the four types. eScience applications which have high security requirements or possess highly sensitive data can be deployed on private clouds. OpenNebula is the first open-source software supporting private-cloud deployment and is widely used by industry and research users [25].

On the contrary, public clouds are more open, with their application, storage and other resources available to the public on the pay-as-you-go basis.

A federated cloud, also known as a community cloud, is a logical combination of two or more clouds from private, public, or even federated clouds. In this combination, two or more clouds often have similar goals in security, compliance and jurisdiction. Many countries have built federated clouds to support the research and education purposes of their own countries. The EGI Federated Cloud Task Force [26] is a federation of academic private clouds to provide services for the scientific community. It has been used by a wide areas of eScience applications, including Gaia (a global space astrometry mission [27]) and the Catania Science Gateway Framework (CSGF) [28].

A hybrid cloud utilizes cloud resources from both private and public clouds. The benefit of hybrid clouds is off-loading. While the workload is bursting and the private cloud can no longer support users' requirements, users can then request resources from the public cloud to sustain performance and scalability.

18.3.3 APPLICATION

Cloud computing techniques have been applied to various eScience applications. We have surveyed a lot of eScience papers and summarized them in the following four categories based on their areas of expertise: Life sciences [4,29], Physical sciences [30,31], Climate and Earth sciences [7,23] as well as Social sciences and Humanities [32,33].

We note that those application categories can overlap with each other. There is no absolute boundary between categories. Still, different categories have their own requirements on the cloud. The first three categories, ie, life sciences, physical sciences and climate and earth sciences, are focusing more on extending their works to large-scale datasets and thus require the cloud platform to deal with large-scale data analysis efficiently. The fourth category, ie, social science and humanities, is focusing more on collaboration, and thus requires the cloud platform to be easy for sharing.

Another observation is that the development of eScience projects is *ad-hoc*. Some applications are developed on Amazon EC2 cloud [34], some on Windows Azure [9] while some others on both cloud platforms to verify their design [35].

However, it is not clearly explained why certain cloud platforms should be chosen over others in those projects. For example, MFA [34] is a Life Science project developed with the cloud services provided by Amazon. Its aim is to investigate whether utilizing the MapReduce framework is beneficial for performing simulation tasks in the area of Systems Biology. The experiments on a 64-node Amazon MapReduce cluster and a single-node implementation have shown up to a 14times performance gain, with a total cost of on-demand resources of $11. MODIS-Azure [7] is a Climate and Earth science application deployed on Windows Azure to process large-scale satellite data. The system is implemented with the Azure blob storage for data repositories and Azure queue services for task scheduling. However, neither of the two projects has technically explained their choice of cloud platforms. To compare the performance on different cloud platforms, a Physical science project, Inversion [35], was deployed on both Amazon EC2 and Windows Azure with symmetry structures.

All these examples indicate that it can be a challenging problem to choose cloud platforms for eScience applications. Due to the current *ad-hoc* implementation in specific cloud providers, the lessons learned during the implementation of one project may not be applicable to other projects or other cloud providers.

18.3.4 PROCESSING TOOLS

From the perspective of processing tools, we have witnessed the deployment of classic workflow systems in the cloud, new cloud-oriented programming models such as MapReduce and DryadLINQ, and hybrids of such newly proposed tools and models.

Scientific workflows have been proposed and developed to assist scientists in tracking the evolution of their data and results. Many scientific applications use workflow systems to enable the composition and execution of complex analysis on distributed resources [36]. 'Montage' is the example of a widely-used workflow for making large-scale, science-grade images for astronomical research [31]. Workflow management systems (WMSes) such as Pegasus [37] and Kepler [38] are developed to manage and schedule the execution of scientific workflows. WMSes rely on tools such as Directed Acyclic Graph Manager (DAGMan) [39] and Condor [40] to manage the resource acquisition from the cloud and schedule the tasks of scientific workflows to cloud resources for execution. The application owners have to separately deploy and configure all the required software such as Pegasus and Condor on the cloud platforms to make their applications run. Such re-implementation and redesign work requires effort from the application owners and should be avoided. Recently, container techniques, such as Docker [41], have been emerging to address this issue.

Emerging cloud-oriented programming models hold great promise for the development of cloud computing. MapReduce is a framework proposed by Google in 2004 [42] for processing highly distributable problems using a large number of computers. This makes this framework especially suitable for eScience application users who may not be experts in parallel programming. We have observed the emergence of eScience applications adopting MapReduce framework for data-intensive scientific analyses [3].

Due to the large data size of many eScience applications, new data processing models, such as in-situ [43] and in-transit processing [44], have been proposed to reduce the overhead of data processing. An eScience workflow typically includes two parts, namely the simulation part which simulates the scientific applications to generate raw data and the analysis part which analyses the raw data to generate findings. The in-situ processing model co-locates the simulation and analysis parts on the same machine to eliminate data movement cost, while in the in-transit processing model, the simulation output data are staged to the analysis node directly through interconnect to avoid touching the storage system.

18.3.5 STORAGE

Data is centric to eScience applications. With the development of science, the hypothesis to data has evolved from the empirical description stage, theoretical modelling stage, and computational simulation stage to the fourth paradigm today, the data-intensive scientific discovery stage. Due to the vast data size, knowledge on the storage format of scientific data in the cloud is very important. Facing the massive data sets, there are two major ways for data storage: data can be stored as files in file systems or in databases.

Many distributed file systems have been proposed to provide efficient and reliable access to large-scale data using clusters of commodity hardware [45,46]. For example, distributed and reliable file systems such as the Hadoop Distributed File System (HDFS) are the primary storage system used by Hadoop applications which utilize the MapReduce model for large dataset processing. OpenStack Swift [47] is a distributed storage system for large-scale unstructured data. It currently serves the largest object storage clouds, such as Rackspace Cloud Files and IBM Softlayer Cloud. To efficiently organize and store the massive scientific datasets, scientific data formats such as NetCDF [48] and HDF5 [49] have been widely used to achieve high I/O bandwidth from parallel file systems. The scalable and highly efficient distributed file system models together with the scientific data formats provide a promising data storage approach for data-intensive eScience applications.

Databases for eScience have been emerging for a number of advantages in query processing capability, relatively mature techniques, and data integrity. HBase, a Hadoop project modelled on Bigtable, has been applied to many eScience applications such as bioinformatics domains [50]. Some array-based databases such as SciDB [51] have also been proposed to satisfy the special requirements of array-based eScience applications. SciDB is a scientific database system built from the ground up that has been applied to many scientific application areas, including astronomy, earth remote sensing and environmental studies [52].

Although the data size of most eScience applications is enormous, we have observed that many of the eScience data are statically stored. For example, the SciHmm [53] project is making optimizations on time and money for the phylogenetic analysis problem. The data involved in this application are genetic data, which do not require frequent updates and can be viewed as statically stored. Similarly, the bioinformatics data in the CloudBLAST [4] project and the astronomy data in the Montage Example [30], although they may be updated from time to time, are seldom modified once obtained. Existing blob-based or distributed storage like Amazon S3 can be an ideal storage system for eScience.

18.3.6 SECURITY

Security is a big issue in regard to eScience applications, especially for those with sensitive data. On one hand, scientists need to make sure that the sensitive data is secured from malicious attacks. On the other hand, they also need to share data between scientific groups (possibly from different nations) working on the same project. Thus, how to find a balance point between the two aims is a challenging problem. Currently, the security level in the cloud is relatively immature compared to the grid computing platform. One common way to make sure of security in the cloud is through logging in. Many eScience applications deployed on the cloud have designed their own way of authentication and authorization to further ensure security. Such as in [54], the Group Authorization Manager is used to grant access permission based on a user-defined access control policy. The emerging Open authorization (OAuth2.0) protocol is used to support authorization for users to share datasets or computing resources. In [55], the Gold security infrastructure is utilized to deal with the authentication and authorization of users to keep sensitive data secure. Data owners could specify their security preferences for the security infrastructure to control role- and task-based access.

Unlike in grid computing, where the authentication and authorization mechanisms are mainly based on the public key infrastructure (PKI) protocol [56], many cloud vendors support multiple security protocols such as OAuth2.0. The eScience gateway is a commonly adopted approach to reinforce security mechanisms.

18.3.7 SERVICE MODELS

There are different levels of computing services offered by the cloud (ie, IaaS, IaaS with tools, PaaS and SaaS). The IaaS model is the most basic cloud service model, where cloud providers only offer physical infrastructures such as virtual machines and raw storage to users. Amazon EC2 is such an example [23,24,57]. To enable the execution of scientific applications in IaaS clouds, a number of domain-specific supporting software and tools need to be installed. In order to save scientists' effort of installation, platforms providing IaaS level services but with additional tools and software, have been proposed. Nimbus [31] and Eucalyptus are examples of this kind. In the PaaS model, cloud providers offer a computing platform typically equipped with operating system, programming language execution environments and databases. Users of the PaaS cloud can simply develop their applications on the platform without the effort and cost of buying and managing the underlying hardware and software layers. Typical examples of this type include Windows Azure, and Google's App Engine. In the SaaS model, cloud providers provide a computing platform installed with application software. Cloud providers are in charge of the software maintenance and support. One example is Altair SaaS [58], which provides high-performance computing (HPC) workload management and scheduling services for applications such as scientific simulations.

Due to the pay-as-you-go pricing feature of cloud services, monetary cost is an important consideration of eScience in the cloud. MFA [34] reported a 14-times speedup for their metabolic flux analysis on Amazon cloud with an $11 cost, which includes the EC2 cost, EMR cost and S3 storage cost. SciHmm [53] aims to reduce the monetary cost for scientists via deciding the most adequate scientific analysis method for the scientists a priori. It reported the cost for the parallel execution of SciHmm on the Amazon EC2 cloud and showed that it is acceptable for most scientists (US $47.79). Due to the large scale of data and long-running jobs, eScience applications have to carefully manage the cloud resources used to optimize their monetary cost. However, this resource management problem is not trivial and requires both domain expertise and knowledge on cloud computing. A lot of ongoing studies have concentrated on the monetary cost optimizations for scientific workflows [30,59–62]. In Section 18.4, we present our experiences on cloud resource provisioning problems to optimize the monetary cost and performance of eScience in the cloud.

18.3.8 COLLABORATION

Another important usage of the cloud for eScience applications is collaboration. Collaboration between the groups includes two different focuses: sharing storage and/or sharing computation. Sharing storage is the sharing mechanism of scientific data and analysis results between different research groups working on the same project. Sharing computation is to share the idle computing resources of one group to the others such that the resource utilization rate of all the collaborating groups can be highly improved. Collaboration between these groups is very important to the success of the projects. With the development of the Internet and the popularity of social networks, some previous studies have leveraged cloud computing techniques and social network APIs to provide a collaboration platform for eScience researchers [63,64].

The Life science project CloudDRN [65] moves medical research data to the cloud to enable secure collaboration and sharing of distributed data sets. It relies on authentication and authorization to ensure security. Also, many applications in Social Science and Humanities have shown increasing collaboration. The SoCC [63] project leverages social network platform for the sharing of resources in scientific communities. They provide a PaaS social cloud framework for users to share resources and support creating virtual organizations and virtual clusters for collaborating users. The SCC [64] project is also leveraging social network and cloud computing to enable data sharing between social network users.

18.4 RESOURCE PROVISIONING FOR eSCIENCE WORKFLOWS IN CLOUDS

From our survey on existing scientific applications, we find that resource provisioning is an important problem for scientific applications in the cloud. In this section, we present our existing studies on this direction. We can easily classify the resource provisioning problems using our taxonomy. We study the problems in public IaaS clouds for scientific workflows. Workflows in physical sciences (eg, Montage and Ligo) and biological sciences (eg, Epigenomics) are studied. The Pegasus workflow management system is used to run the scientific workflows in the cloud. Distributed file systems are used to store the large-scale scientific data and workflow tasks that share cloud computation resources for monetary cost optimization.

18.4.1 MOTIVATION

Scientists often use scientific workflows to analyse and understand scientific data. Scientific workflows involve complex computational processes, often requiring accessing a large amount of data. Montage workflow [66] is an example in astronomical study for generating sky mosaics in the scale of hundreds of GBs. CyberShake [67] is a data-intensive workflow for characterizing earthquake hazards. CyberShake workflows are composed of more than 800,000 tasks and have input data larger than 200TBs. Another example is the Epigenomics workflow [67], which is a biological application that studies the set of epigenetic modifications on human cells. All these example workflows involve managing and processing very large data sets, such as the sky image data and human genetic data.

Due to the pay-as-you-go characteristic of the cloud, many real-world scientific workflows are currently deployed and executed in IaaS clouds [68]. Although the scalability and elasticity of the cloud have brought great opportunities for the workflows, many research problems also arise. Resource provisioning is one important problem for the monetary cost and performance optimizations of scientific workflows in IaaS clouds. Since cloud providers usually offer multiple instance types with different prices and computational capabilities, we need to carefully decide the types of instances that each task of a workflow executes on to optimize the performance and monetary cost. However, making the resource provisioning decisions is non-trivial, involving the complexities from cloud, workflows, and users.

The resource provisioning for workflows in IaaS clouds is a complex problem, from the following three aspects.

Diverse cloud offerings. The IaaS clouds usually offer a large number of instance types. For example, Amazon EC2 provides more than 20 types of instances (only counting the latest generation) for the users [69]. Different types of instances usually have diversified capabilities and prices. For example, Amazon EC2 offers storage optimized instances to provide very high random I/O performance for I/O-intensive applications. If we consider multiple clouds, the situation is even worse since the cloud providers usually adopt different cloud offerings. For example, Amazon EC2 adopts an hourly pricing scheme, while Google Compute Engine charges users by the minute.

The dynamics in cloud performance and prices make the problem even more complex. Most existing resource provisioning approaches for scientific workflows in IaaS clouds [61,70,71] assume that the execution time of each task in the workflow is static on a given VM type. However, this assumption does not hold in the cloud. The cloud environment is, by design, a shared infrastructure. The performance of cloud resources, such as I/O and network, is dynamic due to interferences between users [72]. We have observed remarkable dynamics in the I/O and network performances from Amazon EC2 [73]. Fig. 2 shows the quantiles of the normalized execution time of the Montage workflows in different scales running on Amazon EC2 for 100 times each. The execution time of the three workflows varies significantly. The variances are mainly from the interferences from disk and network I/O. In fact, scientific workflows may process input data of a large size. Due to the significant performance variance of scientific workflows in IaaS clouds, the deterministic notions of performance/cost constraints are not suitable, and a more rigorous notion is required.

On the other hand, the cloud is an economic market, and has dynamic prices [74]. Amazon EC2 offers spot instances, whose prices are determined by market demand and supply. Most existing optimization approaches for scientific workflows in IaaS clouds [61,75] adopt static notions of performance and cost, which are not suitable for performance and cost optimizations in the dynamic cloud environment. Effective optimization techniques and more rigorous QoS notions are needed to capture the cloud dynamics.

Complex workflow structures and characteristics. Workflows can have very different and complex structures. For example, Fig. 3 shows the DAG structure of Ligo, Montage and Epigenomics workflows. We can easily observe from the figure that the structure of Montage is the most complicated in the three workflows while Ligo and Epigenomics workflows have higher parallelism compared to Montage. Within a single workflow, the characteristics of tasks also vary. For example, in the Montage workflow, some tasks are computation-intensive (ie, most of the task execution time is spent on CPU computations) and some are I/O-intensive (ie, most of the task execution time is spent on I/O operations). There are also different application scenarios of workflows. For example, the workflows can be continuously submitted to the cloud and the optimizations are made for each workflow individually [75,76]. Users can also group the workflows with similar structures but different input parameters as an ensemble, and submit QoS and optimization requirements for the entire ensemble. We need an effective system that is capable of simplifying the optimizations of different kinds of tasks and workflows. We should also consider how to make use of the different workflow structures for cost and performance optimizations.

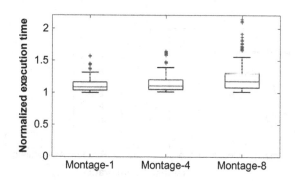

FIG. 2

Execution time variances of running Montage workflows on Amazon EC2.

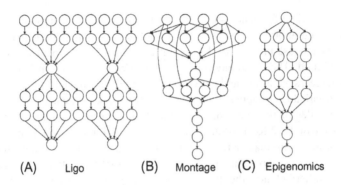

FIG. 3

Workflow structure of Ligo, Montage and Epigenomics.

Various user requirements. Scientists submit their workflow applications to the IaaS clouds usually with some predefined optimization objectives and QoS requirements. For example, one may desire to finish a workflow execution with a minimum monetary cost before a predefined deadline while another one may desire to execute a workflow as fast as possible with a given budget. Users may also define skyline optimization objectives, eg, minimizing both the monetary cost and the execution time of workflows. The users' requirements are also evolving. For example, a user may want to minimize the execution time of a workflow on a cloud $C1$ with a predefined budget. In the other scenario, she may consider running the workflow on multiple clouds other than $C1$. At this point, the optimal solution depends on the offerings of the multiple clouds and the network performance across clouds. Existing optimization algorithms are specifically designed for certain optimization problems and are usually not extensible or flexible to various evolving user requirements. Different resource provisioning schemes result in significant monetary cost and performance variations. Fig. 4 shows the normalized average cost of running the Montage workflow with deadline constraint using different instance configurations

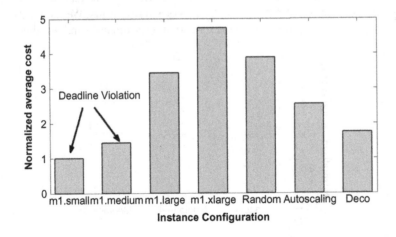

FIG. 4

Average cost of running Montage workflows under different instance configurations on Amazon EC2.

on Amazon EC2. We consider seven scenarios: the workflow is executed on a single instance type only (m1.small, m1.medium, m1.large and m1.xlarge), on randomly chosen instance types, and using the instance configurations decided by Autoscaling [75] and by a optimization engine proposed in this chapter (denoted as Deco). Although the configurations m1.small and m1.medium obtain low average cost, they cannot satisfy the performance constraint of the workflow. Among the configurations satisfying the deadline constraint, Deco achieves the lowest monetary cost. The cost of Deco is only 40% of the cost of the most expensive configuration (ie, m1.xlarge).

18.4.2 OUR SOLUTION

To address these challenges, we design a flexible and effective optimization system to simplify the optimization of monetary cost and performance for scientific workflows in IaaS clouds. Fig. 5 shows our overall design. Specifically, we propose a probabilistic scheduling system called *Dyna* [73] to minimize the cost of workflows while satisfying the probabilistic performance guarantees of individual workflows predefined by the user. We also abstract the common monetary cost and performance optimizations of workflows as transformation operations, and propose a transformation-based optimization framework named *ToF* [59] for the monetary cost and performance optimizations of workflows. Finally, we propose a declarative optimization engine named *Deco* [77], which can automatically generate resource provisioning plans for various workflow optimization problems, considering the cloud performance dynamics. We introduce the details of the three projects in the following subsections.

Effective monetary cost optimizations for workflows in IaaS clouds

Cloud dynamics, including the price and performance dynamics, can greatly affect the resource provisioning result of workflows in IaaS clouds. In this project, we consider a typical scenario of providing software-as-a-service for workflows in the IaaS clouds. We denote this model as workflow-as-a-service (WaaS). We propose a dynamics-aware optimization framework called Dyna, to improve the effectiveness of monetary cost optimizations for WaaS providers. Compared with existing scheduling algorithms

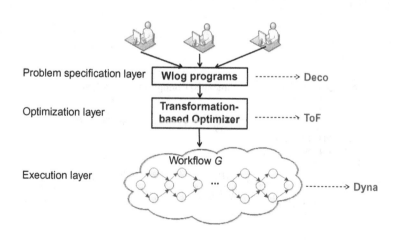

FIG. 5

Overall Design.

or systems [75], Dyna is specifically designed to capture the cloud performance and price dynamics. The main components of Dyna are illustrated in Fig. 6.

When a user has specified the probabilistic deadline requirement for a workflow, WaaS providers schedule the workflow by choosing the cost-effective instance types for each task in the workflow. The overall functionality of the Dyna optimizations is to determine the suitable instance configuration for each task of a workflow so that the monetary cost is minimized while the probabilistic performance requirement is satisfied. We formulate the optimization process as a search problem, and develop a two-step approach to find the solution efficiently. The instance configurations of the two steps are illustrated in Fig. 6. We first adopt an A^*-based instance configuration approach to select the on-demand instance type for each task of the workflow, in order to minimize the monetary cost while satisfying the probabilistic deadline guarantee. Second, starting from the on-demand instance configuration, we adopt the hybrid instance configuration refinement to consider using a hybrid of both on-demand and spot instances for executing tasks in order to further reduce costs. After the two optimization steps, the tasks of the workflow are scheduled to execute on the cloud according to their hybrid instance configuration. At runtime, we maintain a pool of spot instances and on-demand instances, organized in lists according to different instance types. Instance acquisition/release operations are performed in an auto-scaling manner. For the instances that do not have any tasks and are approaching multiples of full instance hours, we release them and remove them from the pool. We schedule tasks to instances in the earliest-deadline-first manner. When a task with the deadline residual of 'zero' requests an instance and the task is not consolidated to an existing instance in the pool, we acquire a new instance from the cloud provider, and add it into the pool. In our experiment, for example, Amazon EC2 poses the capacity limitation of 200 instances. If this cap is met, we cannot acquire new instances until some instances are released.

The reason that we divide the search process into two steps is to reduce the solution space. For example, consider searching the instance configuration for a single task, where there are n on-demand types and m spot instance types. If we consider spot and on-demand instances together, the number of configurations to be searched is $\binom{n}{1} \times \binom{m}{1}$ while in our divide-and-conquer approach, the complexity is reduced to $\binom{n}{1} + \binom{m}{1}$. In each search step, we design efficient techniques to further improve the

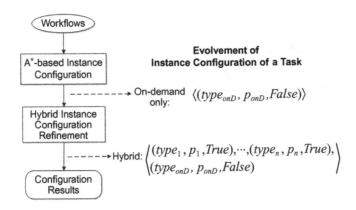

FIG. 6

Overview of the Dyna system.

optimization effectiveness and efficiency. In the first step, we only consider on-demand instances and utilize the pruning capability of the $A\star$ search to improve the optimization efficiency. In the second step, we consider the hybrid of spot and on-demand instances as the refinement of the instance configuration obtained from the first step. We give the following example to illustrate the feasibility of the two-step optimization.

EXAMPLE 1

Consider the instance configuration for a single task. In the A*-based instance configuration step, the on-demand instance configuration found for the task is $\langle(0,0.1,False)\rangle$. *In the refinement step, the on-demand instance configuration is refined to* $\langle(0,0.01,Ture),(0,0.1,False)\rangle$. *Assume the expected execution time of the task on type 0 instance is 1 hour and the spot price is lower than $0.01 (equals to $0.006) for 50% of the time. The expected monetary cost of executing the task under the on-demand instance configuration is $0.1 and under the hybrid instance configuration is only $0.053 ($0.006 \times 50\% + $0.1 \times 50\%). Thus, it is feasible to reduce the expected monetary cost by instance configuration refinement in the second step.*

Evaluation results. We compare Dyna with the state-of-the-art algorithm [75] (denoted as Static) on three different workflow applications shown in Fig. 3 and find that Dyna saves monetary costs over Static by 15{73% when the probabilistic deadline requirement is 96%. Although the average execution time of Dyna is longer than Static, it can guarantee the probabilistic deadline requirements under all settings.

Transformation-based optimizations for workflows in IaaS clouds

Due to the diversified cloud offerings and complex workflow structures and characteristics, resource provisioning for scientific workflows in IaaS clouds is a complicated optimization problem. To address the complexity issues, we propose a transformation-based optimization framework called ToF to simplify workflow optimizations effectively. In ToF, we abstract the common operations in the monetary cost and performance optimizations of scientific workflows as *transformations* and design a cost model to guide the selection of transformations effectively.

We have developed six basic transformation operations, namely *Merge*, *Split*, *Promote*, *Demote*, *Move* and *Co-scheduling*. These basic transformations are simple and lightweight. Moreover, they can capture the current cloud features considered in this chapter. They are the most common operations and widely applicable to workflow structures. For example, the operations of all the comparison algorithms used in the experiments can be represented using those transformations. However, we do not claim they form a complete set. Users can extend more transformation operations into the transformation set. Adding a transformation operation requires the modifications, including adding the cost model, and transformation implementation on the instance DAG.

Based on their capabilities in reducing monetary costs, we categorize the transformation operations into two kinds, namely *main* schemes and *auxiliary* schemes. A main scheme can reduce the monetary cost while an auxiliary scheme simply transforms the workflows so that the transformed workflow is suitable for main schemes to reduce costs. By definition, Merge and Demote are main schemes, and the other four operations are auxiliary schemes. Table 2 summarizes the definition and categorization for the six operations.

Some examples of transformation are illustrated in Fig. 7. We illustrate the transformation operations with an instance-time chart, where the x axis represents time and y axis represents the instance. An instance-time chart is similar to a Gantt chart, with the box width as the execution time and with dependencies between boxes. The height of the boxes stand for prices of instances. During the transformation, we maintain the structural dependency among tasks even after transformations.

Table 2 Details of the Six Transformation Operations. The Formulation $V_i(t_0,t_1)$ Stands for an Instance of Type i and the Task on this Instance Starts at t_0 While Ends at t_1.

Name	Category	Description	Formulation
Merge	Main	Merge multiple tasks to the same instance to fully utilize partial hours.	$\mathcal{M}(V_i(t_0,t_1),V_i(t_2,t_3)) \to V_i(t_0,t_3)$
Demote	Main	Assign a task to a cheaper instance type.	$\mathcal{D}(V_i(t_0,t_1)) \to V_j(t_2,t_3)$, where $i > j$
Move	Auxiliary	Delay a task to execute later.	$\mathcal{V}(V_i(t_0,t_1)) \to V_i(t_2,t_3)$, where $t_3 = t_2 + (t_1 - t_0)$
Promote	Auxiliary	Assign a task to a better instance type.	$\mathcal{P}(V_i(t_0,t_1)) \to V_j(t_2,t_3)$, where $i < j$
Split	Auxiliary	Stop a running task at some checkpoint and restart it later.	$\mathcal{S}(V_i(t_0,t_1)) \to V_{i1}(t_0,t_2),V_{i2}(t_3,t_4)$
Co-scheduling	Auxiliary	Assign two or more tasks to the same instance for execution.	$\mathcal{C}(V_i(t_0,t_1),V_i(t_2,t_3)) \to V_i(\min(t_0,t_2),\max(t_1,t_3))$

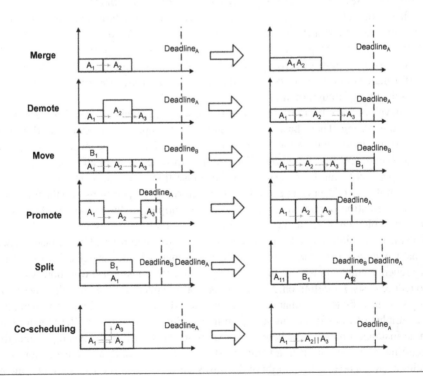

FIG. 7

Use cases of the six transformation operations shown in the instance-time chart.

We develop simple yet effective cost models to estimate the cost and the time changes for applying one transformation operation on the instance DAG. Since an auxiliary scheme does not directly reduce the cost, we estimate the potential cost saving of the main schemes after applying the auxiliary scheme. As for the time estimation, the changes of execution time need to be propagated to all the tasks with dependencies on the vertices affected by the transformation operation. This article estimates the worst case for the change of execution time, since worst-case analysis usually can have simplified estimation processes. For details on cost models, readers can refer to the paper [73].

In one optimization iteration, we first estimate the (potential) cost reduction of each operation which satisfies the deadline constraint, using the cost models. Second, we select and perform the operation with the most cost reduction. All selected transformations form the optimization sequence.

Fig. 8 shows an example of a simple structured workflow with three tasks. The deadline of the workflow is 120 minutes and the execution time of Tasks 0, 1 and 2 on the assigned instance types are 30, 30 and 40 minutes respectively. In the first iteration, we first check the operations in main schemes and find that no one can reduce cost. We then check the operations in auxiliary schemes and select the Move operation to perform as it can introduce the most cost reduction. In the next iteration, Merge from the main schemes is selected and performed, after which no operation can further reduce the cost of the workflow. After applying the Move and Merge operations, the charging hours of executing this workflow is reduced from three to two.

Evaluation results. We demonstrated the accuracy of our cost model estimation and compared ToF with the state-of-the-art algorithm [75] on the Montage and Ligo workflows. ToF outperforms the state-of-the-art algorithm by 30% for monetary cost optimization, and by 21% for the execution time optimization. Please refer to our previous work [59] for experimental details.

A declarative optimization engine for workflows in IaaS clouds

WMSes [78–80] are often used by scientists to execute and manage scientific workflows. Those workflow management systems often have dependent software tools such as Condor and DAGMan [39], and require specific skills to implement the specific optimization algorithms in the cloud. All those software packages are interplayed with the resource provisioning problem in the cloud. It is desirable to abstract these complexities from users and shorten the development cycle. In this chapter, we develop a declarative resource provisioning engine named Deco and integrate it into a popular WMS named Pegasus for executing scientific workflows in IaaS clouds. Fig. 9 presents a system overview of Deco and its integration in the Pegasus WMS.

In order to schedule the workflows in the cloud, users can alternatively choose from several traditional schedulers provided by Pegasus and our proposed Deco. For example, Pegasus provides a Random scheduler by default, which randomly selects the instance to execute for each task in the

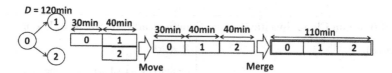

FIG. 8

Example of applying transformation operations on a three node structured workflow.

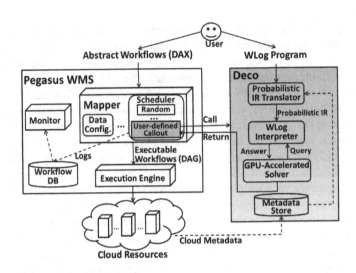

FIG. 9

System overview of Deco with integration in Pegasus.

workflow. With Deco, we model the resource provisioning problem as a constrained optimization problem. Users can specify various optimization goals and constraints with WLog programs. WLog is a declarative language extended from ProLog, with special extensions for scientific workflows and the dynamic clouds. Table 3 gives several examples of such extensions and explains their functionality.

Deco allows users to use probabilistic notions to specify their optimization requirements in the dynamic clouds. We model the dynamic cloud performance with probabilistic distributions, which is transparent to users. Deco automatically translates a WLog program submitted by users to a probabilistic intermediate representation (IR) and interprets it using the WLog interpreter. We traverse the solution space to find a good solution for the optimization problem. For each searched solution, we evaluate it with the probabilistic IR, which requires a lot of computation [81]. To effectively and efficiently search for a good solution in a reasonable time, we implement a GPU-accelerated parallel solver to leverage the massive parallelism of the GPU. After the optimization process, Deco returns the found resource provisioning plan (indicating the selected execution site for each task in the workflow) to Pegasus for generating the executable workflow.

Evaluation results. We use Deco to solve three different workflow optimization problems. Specifically, we formulate a workflow scheduling problem (single workflow and single cloud), a workflow ensemble optimization problem (multiple workflows and single cloud) and a workflow migration

Table 3 Workflow and Cloud Specific Built-in Functions and Keywords in WLog.

Function/Keyword	Remark
goal	Optimization goal defined by the user.
cons	Problem constraint defined by the user.
var	Problem variable to be optimized.

problem (multiple workflow and multiple clouds). These use cases have covered a large part of re-source provisioning problems for scientific workflows. Our experimental results show that Deco is able to obtain better optimization results than heuristic based methods in all use cases. Specifically, Deco can achieve more effective performance/cost optimizations than the state-of-the-art approaches, with the monetary cost reduction by 30-50%. The optimization overhead of Deco takes 4.3-63.17 ms per task for a workflow with 20–1000 tasks.

18.5 OPEN PROBLEMS

Previous sections have reviewed the status and the observations in building eScience applications and systems in the cloud. Despite the fruitful results along this research direction, we clearly see that there are still many open problems to be addressed in order to fully unleash the power of cloud computing for eScience. We present the open problems for developing the next-generation eScience applications and systems in the cloud. Those open problems are rooted at the interplay between eScience requirements and cloud computing features.

Data Lock-In: There is no standardization between different cloud platforms, such as different clouds used for different data storage formats. For example, data stored in Amazon S3 cannot be easily used by the jobs running on the Windows Azure platform due to different APIs, data storage techniques such as encryption techniques and security protocols. On the other hand, due to the fact that eScience projects usually involve a large amount of data for scientific research, such as the genome sequence data and seismographic data, data transfer costs between different cloud platforms is substantial. It requires further research on reducing the network data transfer in terms of both performance and monetary cost.

Performance Unpredictability: Some eScience applications have rather rigid performance require-ments. Performance unpredictability is a critical problem for running those applications in the cloud, due to the interference among concurrent applications running in the same cloud. This problem is particularly severe for disk I/O and network traffic, especially for data-intensive eScience applications. The other factor of performance unpredictability is VM failures or unreliability. In [8], the authors is-sued a total of 10,032 VM unique instance start events on the Windows Azure cloud and only 8,568 in-stances started once during their lifetimes while the others had encountered various unknown problems during their run and were restarted by the Azure infrastructure many times.

Data Confidentiality and Auditability: Current commercial clouds are essentially open to the public and are consequently exposing themselves to more attacks. For eScience applications, the data involved could be relevant to the homeland security of a country, such as the geographical data of the country, or even the security of human beings, such as the human genome data. So protecting this sensitive data from unauthorized or even malicious access is an important ongoing research topic.

Lacking of eScience Common System Infrastructure: As we discussed in the previous section, the ef-forts of implementing eScience projects on the cloud are quite ad-hoc. For example, the Montage work-flow, an astronomy toolkit, is commonly used to discuss the pros and cons of using cloud computing for scientific applications [30,31] and such physical science systems built in the cloud are specifically designed to better fit the cloud for scientific workflow applications. Thus, such developmental experi-ences may not be useful to scientific applications in other areas. In order to save the development cycle and better exploit the experiences of current systems, we need a holistic platform which various re-search fields can build their systems on that offers opportunities for application-specific optimizations.

Resource Management on Future Clouds: With the presence of new cloud service models and new technologies, the resource management problem is becoming more important and complex for future clouds. The high-speed Internet connection makes hybrid cloud resources available as if they are physically located close to the users. However, to enable such cost-efficient and low-latency services to users, we need to design a fine-grained and extensive resource management system providing different ways of measuring and allocating resources. As the cloud gets popular, cloud autonomics is on its way. As a result, automated resource management systems are also required to ease the users from tedious system configurations, monitoring and management.

18.6 SUMMARY

Scientific computing is an emerging and promising application in the Big Data era. Recently, we have witnessed many scientific applications that have been developed and executed on the cloud infrastructure, due to its elasticity and scalability. In this chapter, we developed a taxonomy and conducted a review of the current status of eScience applications in the cloud. Due to the pay-as-you-go pricing feature of the cloud, we find that resource provisioning is an important problem for scientific applications in the cloud. We presented our experiences on improving the effectiveness of monetary cost and performance optimizations for scientific workflows in IaaS clouds. Finally, we proposed the open problems in this area and call for more support from the cloud community and more investment and efforts from other communities.

REFERENCES

[1] Antoniu G, Costan A, Da Mota B, Thirion B, Tudoran R. A-brain: using the cloud to understand the impact of genetic variability on the brain. ERCIM News 2012;2012(89).

[2] Hu DH, Wang Y, Wang C-L. Betterlife 2.0: large-scale social intelligence reasoning on cloud. In: CLOUDCOM '10; 2010. p. 529–36.

[3] Ekanayake J, Pallickara S, Fox G. MapReduce for data intensive scientific analyses. In: ESCIENCE '08; 2008. p. 277–84.

[4] Matsunaga A, Tsugawa M, Fortes J. Cloudblast: combining MapReduce and virtualization on distributed resources for bioinformatics applications. In: ESCIENCE '08; 2008. p. 222–9.

[5] The Large Synoptic Survey Telescope (LSST). http://www.lsst.org/ [accessed April 2016].

[6] Zurek RW, Martin LJ. GridPP: development of the UK computing grid for particle physics. J Phys G Nucl Part Phys 2006;32:1–20.

[7] Li J, Humphrey M, Agarwal DA, Jackson KR, Van Ingen C, Ryu Y. eScience in the cloud: a MODIS satellite data re-projection and reduction pipeline in the windows azure platform. In: IPDPS'10; 2010. p. 1–10.

[8] Li J, Humphrey M, Cheah Y-W, Ryu Y, Agarwal DA, Jackson KR, et al. Fault tolerance and scaling in e-science cloud applications: observations from the continuing development of modisazure. In: eScience'10; 2010. p. 246–53.

[9] Humphrey M, Hill Z, Van Ingen C, Jackson KR, Ryu Y. A case study of satellite image processing on windows azure. In: eScience'11; 2011. p. 126–33.

[10] Bohle S. What is e-science and how should it be managed? 2013. http://www.scilogs.com/scientificandmedicallibraries/what-is-e-science-and-how-should-it-be-managed/.

[11] US Naval Research Laboratory, Monterey, CA. http://www.nrlmry.navy.mil/sec7532.htm [accessed April 2016].

[12] Top 500 Supercomputer. http://www.top500.org/lists/2010/11/; 2010.

[13] University of California. http://setiathome.berkeley.edu/; 2012.

[14] Peter M, Timothy G. The NIST definition of cloud computing. Gaithersburg: National Institute of Standards and Technology; 2009.

[15] Foster I, Zhao Y, Raicu I, Lu S. Cloud computing and grid computing 360-degree compared. In: GCE08; 2008.

[16] Church PC, Goscinski AM. A survey of cloud-based service computing solutions for mammalian genomics. IEEE Trans Serv Comput Oct 2014;7(4):726–40.

[17] Zhao Y, Li Y, Raicu I, Lu S, Lin C, Zhang Y, et al. A service framework for scientific workflow management in the cloud. IEEE Trans Serv Comput 2014;8(6):1.

[18] Lee CA. A perspective on scientific cloud computing. In: HPDC '10; 2010. p. 451–9.

[19] The US Cloud Storefront. http://www.gsa.gov/portal/content/103758; 2009.

[20] The UK G-Cloud. http://johnsuffolk.typepad.com/john-suffolk-government-cio/2009/06/government-cloud.html; 2009.

[21] The Kasumigaseki Cloud Concept. http://www.cloudbook.net/japancloudgov; 2011.

[22] Subramanian V, Wang L, Lee E-J, Chen P. Rapid processing of synthetic seismograms using windows azure cloud. In: Proceedings of the 2010 IEEE second international conference on cloud computing technology and science, CLOUDCOM '10; 2010. p. 193–200.

[23] Evangelinos C, Hill CN. Cloud computing for parallel scientific HPC applications: feasibility of running coupled atmosphere — ocean climate models on Amazon's EC2. In: Cloud computing and its applications; 2008.

[24] Nunez S, Bethwaite B, Brenes J, Barrantes G, Castro J, Malavassi E, et al. Ng-tephra: A massively parallel, nimrod/g-enabled volcanic simulation in the grid and the cloud. In: ESCIENCE '10; 2010. p. 129–36.

[25] OpenNebula. http://opennebula.org/users:users [accessed April 2016].

[26] EGI Federated Cloud Task Force. https://www.egi.eu/infrastructure/cloud/ [accessed April 2016].

[27] GAIA-Space. http://sci.esa.int/gaia/ [accessed April 2016].

[28] Catania Science Gateway. http://www.catania-science-gateways.it/ [accessed April 2016].

[29] Newman A, Li Y-F, Hunter J. Scalable semantics — the silver lining of cloud computing. In: ESCIENCE '08; 2008. p. 111–8.

[30] Deelman E, Singh G, Livny M, Berriman B, Good J. The cost of doing science on the cloud: the montage example. In: SC '08; 2008. p. 50:1–12.

[31] Hoffa C, Mehta G, Freeman T, Deelman E, Keahey K, Berriman B, et al. On the use of cloud computing for scientific workflows. In: ESCIENCE '08; 2008. p. 640–5.

[32] Curry R, Kiddle C, Markatchev N, Simmonds R, Tan T, Arlitt M, et al. Facebook meets the virtualized enterprise. In: EDOC '08; 2008. p. 286–92.

[33] Markatchev N, Curry R, Kiddle C, Mirtchovski A, Simmonds R, Tan T. A cloud-based interactive application service. In: E-SCIENCE '09; 2009. p. 102–9.

[34] Dalman T, Doernemann T, Ernst Juhnke MW, Smith M, Wiechert W, Noh K, et al. Metabolic flux analysis in the cloud. In: ESCIENCE '10; 2010. p. 57–64.

[35] Craig Mudge J, Chandrasekhar P, Heinson GS, Thiel S. Evolving inversion methods in geophysics with cloud computing — a case study of an escience collaboration. In: eScience; 2011. p. 119–25.

[36] Deelman E, Gannon D, Shields M, Taylor I. Workflows and e-science: an overview of workflow system features and capabilities. Futur Gener Comput Syst 2008; http://dx.doi.org/10.1016/j.future.2008.06.012.

[37] Vockler J-S, Juve G, Deelman E, Rynge M, Berriman B. Experiences using cloud computing for a scientific workflow application. In: ScienceCloud '11; 2011. p. 15–24.

[38] Wang J, Altintas I. Early cloud experiences with the Kepler scientific workflow system. Proc Comput Sci 2012;9:1630–4.

[39] Condor Team. DAGman: a directed acyclic graph manager, http://www.cs.wisc.edu/condor/dagman/; 2005.

[40] Litzkow M, Livny M, Mutka M. Condor — a hunter of idle workstations. In: ICDCS, June; 1988.

[41] Docker. An open platform for distributed applications for developers and sysadmins, https://www.docker.com/ [accessed April 2016].

[42] Dean J, Ghemawat S. Mapreduce: simplified data processing on large clusters. Commun ACM 2008;51(1):107–13.

[43] Wang Y, Agrawal G, Bicer T, Jiang W, Wang Y, Agrawal G, et al. Smart: a MapReduce-like framework for in-situ scientific analytics. In: Proceedings of the international conference for high performance computing, networking, storage and analysis, SC '15, New York, NY, USA; 2015. p. 51:1–12.

[44] Bennett JC, Abbasi H, Bremer P-T, Grout R, Gyulassy A, Jin T, et al. Combining in-situ and in-transit processing to enable extreme-scale scientific analysis. In: Proceedings of the international conference on high performance computing, networking, storage and analysis, SC '12; Los Alamitos, CA: IEEE Computer Society Press; 2012. p. 49:1–9.

[45] Ghemawat S, Gobioff H, Leung S-T. The Google file system. In: SOSP '03; 2003. p. 29–43.

[46] Shvachko K, Kuang H, Radia S, Chansle R. The hadoop distributed file system. In: MSST '10; 2010. p. 1–10.

[47] OpenStack Swift. https://swiftstack.com/openstack-swift/architecture/ [accessed April 2016].

[48] NetCDF. http://www.unidata.ucar.edu/software/netcdf [accessed April 2016].

[49] The HDF5 Format. http://www.hdfgroup.org/HDF5 [accessed April 2016].

[50] Taylor R. An overview of the Hadoop/MapReduce/HBase framework and its current applications in bioinformatics. BMC Bioinf 2010;11(Suppl. 12):1.

[51] Brown PG. Overview of SciDB: large scale array storage, processing and analysis. In: SIGMOD '10; 2010. p. 963–8.

[52] SciDB Use Case. http://www.paradigm4.com/life-sciences/ [accessed April 2016].

[53] Ocana KACS, De Oliveira D, Dias J, Ogasawara E, Mattoso M. Optimizing phylogenetic analysis using SciHmm cloud-based scientific workflow. In: IEEE 7th international conference on eScience; 2011. p. 62–9.

[54] Wu W, Zhang H, Li ZA, Mao Y. Creating a cloud-based life science gateway. In: IEEE 7th international conference on eScience; 2011. p. 55–61.

[55] Watson P, Lord P, Gibson F, Periorellis P, Pitsilis G. Cloud computing for e-science with carmen. In: 2nd Iberian grid infrastructure conference; 2008. p. 3–14.

[56] Alfieri R, Cecchini R, Ciaschini V, Spataro F. From gridmap-file to voms: managing authorization in a grid environment. Futur Gener Comput Syst 2005;21:549–58.

[57] Nagavaram A, Agrawal G, Freitas MA, Telu KH, Mehta G, Mayani RG, et al. A cloud-based dynamic workflow for mass spectrometry data analysis. In: IEEE 7th international conference on eScience; 2011. p. 47–54.

[58] Altair SaaS. http://www.altair.com/cloud/ [accessed April 2016].

[59] Zhou AC, He B. Transformation-based monetary cost optimizations for workflows in the cloud. IEEE Trans Cloud Comput 2014;2(1):85–98.

[60] Chi Zhou A, He B. Simplified resource provisioning for workflows in IaaS clouds. In: EEE CloudCom; 2014. p. 650–5.

[61] Malawski M, Juve G, Deelman E, Nabrzyski J. Cost- and deadline-constrained provisioning for scientific workflow ensembles in IaaS clouds. In: SC '12; 2012. p. 22:1–11.

[62] Kondo D, Javadi B, Malecot P, Cappello F, Anderson DP. Cost-benefit analysis of cloud computing versus desktop grids. In: IPDPS '09; 2009. p. 1–12.

[63] Thaufeeg AM, Bubendorfer K, Chard K. Collaborative research in a social cloud. In: ESCIENCE '11; 2011. p. 224–31.

[64] Chard K, Bubendorfer K, Caton S, Rana O. Social cloud computing: a vision for socially motivated resource sharing. IEEE Trans Serv Comput 2012;5(4):551–63.

[65] Marty H, Jacob S, Kee Kim I, Kahn Michael G, Jessica B, Michae A. Clouddrn: a lightweight, end-to-end system for sharing distributed research data in the cloud. In: ESCIENCE '13; 2013.

[66] Montage Workflow. http://montage.ipac.caltech.edu/docs/download2.html [accessed 07.14].

[67] Juve G, Chervenak A, Deelman E, Bharathi S, Mehta G, Vahi K. Characterizing and profiling scientific workflows. Future Gener Comput Syst 2013;29(3):682–92.

[68] Amazon Case Studies. http://aws.amazon.com/solutions/case-studies/ [07.14].

[69] Amazon EC2 Instance Types. http://aws.amazon.com/ec2/instance-types/ [07.14].

[70] Fard HM, Prodan R, Fahringer T. A truthful dynamic workflow scheduling mechanism for commercial multicloud environments. IEEE Trans Parallel Distrib Syst 2013;24(6):1203–12.

[71] Deng K, Song J, Ren K, Iosup A. Exploring portfolio scheduling for long-term execution of scientific workloads in IaaS clouds. In: Proceedings of the international conference on high performance computing, networking, storage and analysis, SC '13; New York, NY: ACM; 2013. p. 55:1–12.

[72] Schad J, Dittrich J, Quianfie-Ruiz J-A. Runtime measurements in the cloud: observing, analyzing, and reducing variance. Proc VLDB Endow 2010;3(1–2):460–71.

[73] Zhou AC, He B, Liu C. Monetary cost optimizations for hosting workflow-as-a-Service in IaaS clouds. IEEE Trans Cloud Comput 2015; http://dx.doi.org/10.1109/TCC.2015.2404807.

[74] Wang H, Jing Q, Chen R, He B, Qian Z, Zhou L. Distributed systems meet economics: pricing in the cloud. In: Proceedings of the 2Nd USENIX conference on hot topics in cloud computing, HotCloud'10, Berkeley, CA, USA; 2010.

[75] Mao M, Humphrey M. Auto-scaling to minimize cost and meet application deadlines in cloud workflows. In: Proceedings of 2011 international conference for high performance computing, networking, storage and analysis, SC '11, New York, NY, USA; 2011. p. 49:1–12.

[76] Calheiros RN, Buyya R. Meeting deadlines of scientific workflows in public clouds with tasks replication. IEEE Trans Parallel Distrib Syst July 2014;25(7):1787–96.

[77] Chi Zhou A, He B, Cheng X, Tong Lau C. A declarative optimization engine for resource provisioning of scientific workflows in IaaS clouds. In: Proceedings of the 24th international symposium on high-performance parallel and distributed computing, HPDC '15; New York, NY: ACM; 2015. p. 223–34.

[78] Deelman E, Singh G, Mei-Hui S, Blythe J, Gil Y, Kesselman C, et al. Pegasus: a framework for mapping complex scientific workflows onto distributed systems. Sci Program 2005;13(3):219–37.

[79] Ludascher B, Altintas I, Berkley C, Higgins D, Jaeger E, Jones M, et al. Scientific workflow management and the Kepler system: research articles. Concur Comput Pract Exper 2006;18(10):1039–65.

[80] Tang W, Wilkening J, Desai N, Gerlach W, Wilke A, Meyer F. A scalable data analysis platform for metagenomics. In: The proceedings of the 2013 IEEE international conference on Big Data, BigData, 2013; 2013.

[81] De Raedt L, Kimmig A, Toivonen H. Problog: a probabilistic prolog and its application in link discovery. In: Proceedings of the 20th international joint conference on artificial intelligence, IJCAI'07; San Francisco, CA: Morgan Kaufmann; 2007. p. 2468–73.

Index

Note: Page numbers followed by b indicates boxes, f indicates figures, and t indicates tables.

Printed in the United States
By Bookmasters